A Body of Divinity

A Body of Divinity
or
The Sum and Substance
of the Christian Religion

Catechistically Propounded and Explained,
by Way of Question and Answer.
Methodically and Familiarly Handled,
for the Use of Families.
To which are adjoined a Tract, entitled,
IMMANUEL: or The Mystery of the
Incarnation of the Son of God.

By the most Reverend
JAMES USSHER,

Archbishop of Armagh

Edited by Michael Nevarr

Solid Ground Christian Books
Birmingham, Alabama USA

...uncovering buried treasure...

Solid Ground Christian Books
715 Oak Grove Road
Birmingham, AL 35209
205-443-0311
sgcb@charter.net
www.solid-ground-books.com

A BODY OF DIVINITY
The Sum and Substance of the Christian Religion
was first published in 1648.
This *Solid Ground Classic Reprint*, in which spelling, grammar,
and formatting changes have been made is a
2007 copyright by Solid Ground Christian Books.

Special thanks to Providence Bible Fellowship
PO Box 1515
Herndon, Virginia 20172
(703) 935-4845
www.providencebiblefellowship.org

Archbishop James Ussher (1581-1656)

Solid Ground Classic Reprints

First printing of paperback edition July 2007

Cover work by Borgo Design, Tuscaloosa, AL
Contact them at borgogirl@bellsouth.net

ISBN: 1-59925-118-3

TABLE OF CONTENTS.

The Eleventh Commandment	ix
A New Introduction	xi
To The Christian Reader	xiv
The Heads of The Body of Divinity	1
The Principles of Christian Religion	409
A Brief Method of The Doctrine of Christian Religion	419
Immanuel	431
Advices to Young Ministers at Their Ordination	453
Table	457

THE HEADS OF THE BODY OF DIVINITY, DIVIDED INTO TWO AND FIFTY HEADS.

1. Of Christian Religion, and the grounds thereof; Gods Word contained in the Scriptures. (1 Pet. 1:19, 21; 2 Tim. 3:15, 16, 17)   1

2. Of God and his Attributes, Perfection, Wisdom, and Omnipotence. (1 Tim. 1:17; Psalm. 147:5)   23

3. Of Gods Goodness and Justice, and the Persons of the Trinity. (Exod. 34:6, 7; 1 John 5:7)   52

4. Of Gods Kingdom, and the Creation of all things. (1 Chron. 29:11, 12; Psalm. 145:10, 11, 12; Acts 17:24)   77

5. Of the Creation of man in particular, and the Image of God according to which he was made. (Gen 1:26; 27)   89

6. Of Gods Providence, and continual government of his creatures. (Psalm 130:19 & 66:7)   95

7. Of the good Angels that stood, and the evil Angels that forsook their first integrity. (Jude verse 6; Rev. 12:7)   102

8. Of the Law of nature, or the Covenant of works made with man at his Creation, and the event thereof in the fall of our first Parents. (Gal. 3:10; Gen. 2:17; Eccl. 7:31)   109

9. Of Original and Actual sin, where unto all mankind by the fall is become subject. (Rom. 5:12, 14)   125

10. Of Gods curse, and all the penalties due unto sin; whereunto man is become subject as long as he continues in his natural state. (Gal. 3:10; Duet. 28:45) *137*

11. Of the Covenant of Grace, and the Mediator thereof, Jesus Christ our Lord; his two distinct natures in one Person, together with his Conception and Nativity. (Mat. 1:21, 22, 23; Gal. 4:4, 5) *139*

12. Of the state of Humiliation and Exaltation of our Savior, his office of Mediation, and calling thereunto. (Phil. 2:7, 8, 9; Heb. 5:4, 5) *142*

13. Of his Priestly office, and the two parts thereof, Satisfaction, and Intercession. (Rom. 8:34; Heb. 10:12) *154*

14. Of his Prophetical and Kingly Office (Luke 4:18, 29; Isa. 9:6, 7) *157*

15. Of the calling of men to partake of the grace of Christ both outward and inward; & of the Catholic Church thus called out of the world, with the members and properties thereof (Heb. 3:1; 2 Tim. 1:9, Heb. 12:23) *166*

16. Of the mutual Donation, whereby the Father gives Christ to us, and us unto Christ: And the Mystical Union, whereby we are knit together by the Band of God's quickening Spirit; with the Communion of Saints arising from thence, whereby God for his Son's sake, is pleased of Enemies to make us Friends. (Cant. 2. 16. John 17. 21, 22, 23, 24) *169*

17. Of justification; and therein of justifying faith and forgiveness of sins. (Rom. 3:24, 25, 26; and 4:6, 7) *172*

18. Of Adoption; whereby in Christ we are not only advanced into the state of friends, but also of sons and heirs : and therein of the spirit of Adoption and Hope. (Rom. 8:15, 16, 17, 23, 24, 25) *179*

19. Of Sanctification; whereby the power of sin is mortified in us, and the image of God renewed : and therein of love. (Eph. 1:4; Col 3:9, 10, 12, 14) *180*

20. Of the direction given unto us for our Sanctification, contained in the Ten Commandments; with rules of expounding the same, and the distinction of the Tables thereof. (Mat. 22. 37, 38, 39, 40) *185*

21. The first Commandment, of the choice of the true God; and the entertaining him in all our thoughts. (Exod. 20:2, 3) *191*

22. The Second Commandment; of the solemn worship that is to be performed unto God : and therein of Images and Ceremonies. (Exod. 20:5, 6) *199*

23. The third; of the glorifying of God aright in the actions of our common life: and therein of swearing and blaspheming. (Exod. 20:7) *212*

24. The fourth; of the certain time set apart for Gods Service : and therein of the Sabbath and Lords Day. (Exod. 20:8, 9, 10, 11) *218*

25. The fifth; of the duties we owe one unto another; in regard of our particular relation unto such as are our Superiors, Inferiors, and Equals. (Exod. 20:12)   229

26. The sixth; of the preservation of the safety of men's persons : and therein of peace and meekness. (Exod. 20:13)   242

27. The seventh; of the reservation of chastity : and therein of temperance and marriage. (Exod. 20:14)   249

28. The eight; of the preservation of our own and our neighbors goods : & therein of the maintaining of justice in our dealing one with another. (Exod. 20:15)   257

29. The ninth, of there preservation of our own and our neighbors good name, and the maintaining of truth in our testimony, and dealings. (Exod. 20:16)   277

30. The tenth, of the contentedness, and the first motions of concupiscence which do anyway cross that love we owe to our neighbor. Whereto for conclusion may be added to the use of the Law. (Exod. 20)   291

31. Of Repentance. (Acts 26:10; 2 Cor. 7:10, 11)   299

32. Of the spiritual warfare, and Christian armor. (Jer. 31:18, 19; Eph. 6:10, 11, 12)   301

33. Of resistance of the temptations of the Devil. (1 Pet. 5:8, 9)   302

34. Of resisting the temptations of the world, both in prospering and adversity: and here of patient bearing of the Crosse. (Gal. 6:14; Rom. 8:35, 36, 37)   303

35. Of the resisting the temptations of the flesh. (Gal 6:14; Col. 3:5, 6)   304

36. Of new obedience and good works, and necessity thereof. (Lev. 1:74, 75; Tit. 2:11, 12, 13, 14)   305

37. Of prayer in general; and the Lords Prayer in particular, with the Preamble thereof. (Mat. 6:6, 7)   309

38. Of the three first Petitions which concern Gods glory. (Mat. 6:9, 10)   322

39. Of the three latter, which concern our necessities. (Mat. 6:. 11-13)   330

40. Of the conclusion of the Lords Prayer; wherewith is to be handled the point of praise and thanksgiving. (Mat. 5:13)   341

41. Of Fasting. (Mat. 5:16, 17, 18)   345

42. Of mutual edifying one another, and liberality towards the poor. (Eph. 4:28, 29; Heb. 13:16)   354

43. Of Ministers, and Ministry of the Gospel; and therein of preaching and hearing the Word. (Rom. 10:14, 15; Eph. 4:11, 12, 13)   356

44. Of the Appendants of the Word : Sacraments, which are the seals of the promises; and Ecclesiastical censures, which are the seals of the threatenings of the Gospel. (Rom. 4:11; Mat. 18:15, 16, 17)   364

45. Of the ministry of the Old Testament, before the coming of Christ; with the Word, Types, and Sacraments thereof. (Heb. 9:1, 9, 10; 1 Cor. 10:1, 2, 3, 4)   370

46. Of the ministry of the New Testament, and comparing the Word and Sacraments thereof with the Old. (John 1:17; Heb. 12:27, 28)   370

47. Of Baptism. (Mat. 28, 19; 1 Pet. 3:21)   372

48. Of the Lords Supper (1 Cor. 11:23, 24)   381

49. Of the diverse states of the Church in prosperity & under persecution, integrity and corruption, and the reading thereof by schisms and heresies. (1 Tim. 4:12, 13; 2 Thes. 2:3, 4)   390

50. Of death, and the particular Judgment following. (Heb. 9:27)   403

51. Of the general Judgment : and therein of the Judge Christ Jesus his coming in glory; and the parties to be judged, both quick and dead, with the resurrection of the one, and the change of the other. (1 Thes. 4:15, 16, 17; 1 Cor. 15:51, 52)   404

52. Of the last sentence and execution thereof; of the torments of the damned, and joys of the blessed. (Mat. 25:34, 35)   407

THE ELEVENTH COMMANDMENT.

"The Rev Sam Rutherford was Presbyterian minister of the parish of Anwoth between 1627 and 1638, there are many stories told regarding the life of this most intelligent and pious man. In one of these tales archbishop Ussher, who had heard many stories concerning Mr. Rutherford and his religious devotion, was returning through Galloway to his home in Ireland. One of these stories related how the minister often spent the entire night in prayer, especially before the Sabbath. This interested the archbishop greatly and he resolved to observe the ministers' ritual in person. This, however, would not be an easy thing for and Episcopalian bishop to accomplish during this period of distrust and religious intolerance.

At length the archbishop, unsure of what his welcome may be, came to the conclusion that the only solution was to visit Anwoth in disguise. It was thus, dressed as a pauper, that he presented himself at Bush o' Bield, around dusk on a Saturday and requested lodgings for the night. Mr. Rutherford immediately consented and brought the poor man into the kitchen where he might be fed. Mrs. Rutherford, according to her custom on a Saturday evening, was examining the servants on their religious knowledge in order that they may be suitably prepared for the Sabbath. During the course of the examination Mrs. Rutherford asked the stranger if he could tell her how many commandments there were? When the pauper confidently answered that there were eleven commandments in the bible the Goodwife was shocked and dismayed. Thinking him very ignorant she lamented his condition to the servants saying that any six year old child of the parish could, when asked the question, tell an elder that there were ten commandments. Mrs. Rutherford silently resolved to embarrass their visitor with no more questions and, at length, he was amply fed and shown to a room in the garret.

This location, directly above Mr. Rutherford's' chamber, was ideal for the archbishops' purpose; here he would be able to observe the ministers' devotions without detection. However, he was to be disappointed, after a short time he heard the minister make himself ready for bed then all was silent. The bishop did not retire himself but sat listening for a long time, still hoping to hear Mr. Rutherford at prayer. At length he concluded that he was out of luck and, being wide-awake himself, resolved to take a short walk down the wooded path (that, to this day, is still called "Rutherford's Walk") and view the ministers' church.

Once there the bishop decided to dispel his disappointment by taking the opportunity to offer up a prayer himself, and there, in the middle of the night, he poured out his heart with abandon. So involved was the bishop in his prayers that he didn't hear Mr. Rutherford, who commonly arose about three o' clock in the morning, enter the church with intent to observe his own devotions. On discovering the bishop so deeply involved Mr. Rutherford stood waiting at the church door until he had concluded his prayers; upon which he knocked gently at the door to make his presence known.

Mr. Rutherford took the bishop by the hand, saying, "Sir I am persuaded you can be none other than archbishop Ussher; and you must certainly preach for me today, being now the Sabbath morning." The bishop confessed who he was; and after telling Mr. Rutherford what induced him to take such a step, said he would preach for him on condition that he would not disclose his identity to the parishioners. Mr. Rutherford agreed and proceeded to furnish the bishop with a suit of his own clothes.

Later that morning, but before the household awoke, the bishop and Mr. Rutherford left the house separately but returned together, with bishop Ussher being introduced as a strange minister passing by who had promised to preach for them. On calling the pauper to his breakfast Mrs. Rutherford discovered that he had departed the house before any of the family were out of bed.

After their domestic worship and breakfast the family went out to the kirk; and the bishop chose for his text, John xiii. Verse 34. "A new commandment I give unto thee; that ye love one another." In the course of his sermon, the bishop observed that this might be reckoned to be the *eleventh* commandment. This was not lost upon Mrs. Rutherford who, remembering the answer she had received the night before from the stranger, was greatly astonished and struck with the strange coincidence. Looking up to the pulpit, she still could not believe that the visiting minister and the vagabond from the previous night were indeed one and the same person.

After the public service the archbishop and Mr. Rutherford spent the rest of the day in convivial conversation; and on Monday morning the former went away in the clothing that he had arrived in. Their deception remained, for a very long time, a secret between the two men."[1]

While we may not agree with every point of doctrine archbishop Ussher teaches within the following pages[2], we do stand together with John Downame and Samuel Rutherford having both a deep respect for and an eager desire to hear from this man who faithfully served our Lord Jesus Christ throughout his life.   -MFN

---

[1] Taken from *Anecdotes Religious and Moral* by Rev. Charles Buck, 1843, available as a re-print through Solid Ground Christian Books
[2] sacramentalism, infant baptism etc.

A NEW INTRODUCTION.

James Ussher was one of the most influential theologians of the early Protestant world, and his *Body of Divinity* (1645) was Puritanism's earliest and most important volume of systematic theology. Ussher was born into a well-connected and highly-respected Dublin family in January 1581. His early education was supervised by two Scottish refugees, James Fullerton and James Hamilton, whose emphatic Calvinism had caused them to be driven from their native church. They exercised immense influence on their student, and, when Ussher entered Trinity College, Dublin, in 1593, one year after its opening, they were among the college's teaching staff. The atmosphere of the college was vigorously theological, with a strong bias towards Puritanism, and Fellows educated their students within the parameters of Reformed orthodoxy. Ussher made rapid progress. He gained his B.A. in 1598, his M.A. in 1601, and in 1603 was appointed Chancellor of St. Patrick's Cathedral. In 1607 he graduated with a B.D. and was appointed Professor of Divinity. In 1613 he was awarded his D.D. and was appointed Vice-Chancellor. But Ussher's influence transcended the narrow limits of college life. In 1621 he was appointed Bishop of Meath, and four years later, only days before the death of King James, Ussher was appointed Archbishop of Armagh.

Ussher's installation as primate of the Irish church was the climax of a meteoric career, and a position he maintained until his death in March 1656. It was as Archbishop of Armagh that Ussher became recognized as the doyen of the puritan movement. Today, Ussher is best-known for his interest in the chronology of Scripture, a reputation consolidated by the inclusion of his dates in the margins of numerous editions of the Authorized Version. This reputation, though it certainly reflects one part of his scholarly interests, was gained posthumously. Ussher's publications on chronological subjects occupied only the latter years of his life, which the aging Archbishop spent in scholarly seclusion in England. *The Annales Veteris et Novi Testamenti* appeared in 1650; its English translation, *The Annals of the World*, and his definitive chronology, the *Chronologica Sacra*, were published after his death. In his own lifetime, Ussher's reputation was based on his status as one of the leading theologians of the Protestant world, a status reflected in his commitment to a generic Reformed theology and to a pan-Protestant irenicism. This reputation was justified by Ussher's substantial theological contribution. In 1615, while still a professor, Ussher oversaw the composition of the Irish Articles, the confession of faith of the Church of Ireland which clearly reflected the puritan ethos that had been disseminated by the college's first tutors. As the first confession of faith to identify the Antichrist as the Pope, and the first to be obviously structured around a system of covenant theology, the Irish Articles became a major influence on the development of Protestant scholasticism in the later seventeenth century. But Ussher's emphasis on irenicism was also well known. Preachers from across the theological spectrum--from Presbyterians to Baptists--hailed the Archbishop with delight. Ussher also exchanged ideas and books with scholars across the Roman Catholic world. Despite his vigorous opposition to the Roman Catholic Church, Ussher remained on good personal terms with numerous Catholic scholars.

In the last fifteen years there has been a remarkable recovery of interest in Ussher's life and ideas. Of course, Ussher has always been highly regarded in his own college. In the middle of the nineteenth century, it was two Trinity academics who put together the 17 volumes of his Whole Works (1847-1864). At the beginning of this century, the college's prize-winning new library building was given his name. It is hardly surprising, therefore, that Trinity also hosts the most important contemporary Ussher project, which is compiling the substantial corpus of Ussher's correspondence. Dr

Elizabethanne Boran, who leads the project, also hosts an Ussher website, which includes a comprehensive bibliography of literature related to her subject. At the University of Nottingham, in England, Professor Alan Ford is building on his many years of Ussher scholarship by preparing an intellectual biography, which is due to be published by Oxford University Press. But interest in Ussher has also revived outside the academic world, and particularly among evangelicals. The *Annals of the World* has been re-set into modern English and presented with updated textual apparatus in an impressive new edition. Similarly, the present author published *The Irish Puritans: James Ussher and the Reformation of the Church* (2003), a brief history of the religious cultures of Ussher's Ireland which includes a rare reprinting of the Irish Articles. Interest in Ussher has revived in the church and in the academy, and in both contexts, the republication of the *Body of Divinity* will be central to the ongoing re-consideration of his importance.

Nevertheless, some readers of the *Body of Divinity* will be surprised to learn that the book was not included in the 17 volumes of the Whole Works. There are a number of interesting reasons for this omission. Ussher himself never claimed to be the author of the text, and when the volume appeared in 1645, it did so under his name but without his permission. This pirated edition has been the source of controversy ever since. Its unofficial status makes it difficult to date, or to properly assess. It appears that Ussher had prepared the text for private use as a kind of scrapbook of theological ideas. Richard Parr, Ussher's earliest biographer and confidante, claimed that the Body of Divinity 'was not intended ... to be published, being only some Collections of his, out of several modern Authors, for his own private use, when he was a young man', but this comment significantly underplays the novelty of the text. John Downame, who edited and introduced the text in 1645, claimed that it represented a collation of ideas from Ussher's reading 'above thirty years' earlier, in the mid-1610s, around the same period that the Irish Articles were being composed. Downame also indicated that these ideas, 'collected long since out of sundry Authors', had been 'reduced ... to one common method'--a significant step forward in puritan divinity. But Ussher appears to have been keen to play down his puritan links. By the mid-1640s, when the *Body of Divinity* appeared, Ussher found himself in the middle of the English civil war, and his commitment to support the king made him wary of appearing too close to more radical Puritans on the side of Parliament. He wrote to Downame to downplay the significance of the *Body of Divinity*-- he argued that it was no more than 'a kind of common place book' --but Downame's claim that the manuscript can be dated to the mid-1610s confirms other evidence that links the text to Ussher's early theological development. Perhaps it is significant that those closest to him to him believed that it represented Ussher's opinions. After Ussher's death, Parr defended its statements and identified them with the Archbishop's continuing convictions. The *Body of Divinity* therefore demonstrates Ussher's redaction of important themes in early puritan thought, and shows that this collation and organization represents a significant advance in the development of the Protestant dogmatic tradition. The structure and organization of the Body of Divinity undermine any claim that it was merely a careless scrapbook of theological maxims. Ussher may have drawn the ideas from sources throughout his wide reading, but he gathered them together into a coherent whole that has all the concurrence and integrity of a truly systematic theology.

The coherence and integrity of the *Body of Divinity* has been linked by a number of scholars to the most important theological statements of the seventeenth century. In his *Lectures on Evangelical Theology* (1890), the Princeton theologian A. A. Hodge argued that the *Body of Divinity* had more to do in forming the [Westminster] Catechism and Confession of Faith than any other book in the world; because it is well known that this book, which he compiled as a young man, was in circulation in this Assembly among the individuals composing it. And if this is true, you could easily see how much of suggestion there is in it which was afterward carried into the Catechism--the Larger Catechism especially--of that Assembly.

And, if that is the case, then Ussher's influence stretches far beyond the boundaries of Anglicanism or Presbyterianism, for the Westminster Confession also provided the framework for subsequent confessions of faith by Congregationalists (the Savoy Confession, 1658) and Baptists (the Second London Confession, 1677 and 1689). The *Body of Divinity* is therefore one of the foundational texts in the construction of pan-Reformed orthodoxy.

Ussher's world was very different to our own, but the struggle to articulate the truth was as difficult then as it is now. Ussher's balancing of scholasticism and irenicism provides a model of theological engagement that has much to teach Christians today. In the seventeenth century, as much as the in twenty-first, Christian people had to remember the apostolic injunction to 'speak the truth in love'. Ussher shows that irenicism can go hand-in-hand with scholasticism. If the *Body of Divinity* shows us nothing else, it shows us that we too can combine unwavering commitment to maintaining the complex balance of truth and love. *Moladh go deo leis.*

Dr. Crawford Gribben
Lecturer in Renaissance Literature and Culture
English and American Studies
University of Manchester, UK

November 2005

TO THE CHRISTIAN READER.

Christian Reader, I do here present and commend unto thee a Book of great worth and singular use, which was written and finished about 60 years since: The Author whereof is well known to be so universally eminent in all Learning, and of that deep Knowledge and Judgment in Sacred Divinity, that he transcends all Eulogies and Praises which I can give him. I commend it unto thee (Christian Reader) under a twofold Notion. The first respects the Subject Matter of this whole Work, which is of greatest Excellency; as being The Sum and Substance of Christian Religion; upon which, as a most sure Foundation, we build our Faith, ground all our Hopes, from which we reap and retain all our Joy and Comfort in the Assurance of our Salvation. Which as at all times it is most profitable to be read, studied, and known, so now (if ever) most necessary in these our Days, wherein Men never more neglected these Fundamental Principles, as being but common and ordinary Truths, and spend their whole Time, Study, and Discourse about Discipline, Ceremonies, and Circumstantial Points; and herein also not contenting themselves with those common Rules, and that clear Light which shines in the Word; they are only led by their own Fantasies, daily creating unto themselves diversities of new Opinions; and so falling into Heats, they break the Bond of Love, and fall off from the Communion of Saints, as though it were no Article of their Creed; and being in love with their own new Tenets, as being the conception and birth of their own Brains, they contend for them more than for any Fundamental Truths; and not only so, but also hate, malign, and most bitterly and uncharitably censure all those that differ from them in their Opinions, though never so conscientious and religious, as though they professed not the same Faith; yea, served not the same God, nor believed in the same Christ, but remain still Aliens from the Common-wealth of Israel, and in comparison of themselves no better than Papists, or at the best but carnal Gospellers. The second Notion under which I commend it, respects the Work it self, or the manner of the Author's handling it, which is done so soundly and solidly, so judiciously and exactly, so methodically and orderly, and with that familiar plainness, perspicuity and clearness, that it gives place to no other in this kind, either Ancient or Modern, either in our own, or any other Language which ever yet came to my view; in which regard I may say of it, as it is said of the Virtuous Woman; Many have done excellently, but this our Author exceeds them all. I will add no more in the deserved Praises of this Work, but leave it (Christian Reader) to thy self to peruse and judge of it; commending thee to the Word of God's Grace, and the good guidance of his Holy Spirit, who is able to build thee up in a fruitful Knowledge, to lead thee into all Truth, to direct and support thee in the Ways of Godliness, and to give thee an everlasting Inheritance amongst the Blessed.

Yours in the Lord Jesus Christ,

John Downame.

A LARGE EXPLICATION OF THE BODY OF CHRISTIAN RELIGION.

1 TIM. 4. 15. Meditate upon these things; give thy self wholly to them, that thy profiting may appear to all.

[1ST HEAD.]

What is that which all Men especially desire?
Eternal Life and Happiness.

How do Men look to obtain Happiness?
By Religion: Which is a thing so proper to Man, that it does distinguish him more from Beasts than very Reason, that is made his form. For very Beasts have some sparkles or resemblance of Reason, but none of Religion.

Is Religion so generally to be found in all Men?
Yes: For the very Heathens condemned them to Death that denied all Religion: And there are no People so barbarous, but they will have some form of Religion to acknowledge a God; as all India, East and West, showeth.

May a Man be saved by any Religion?
No; but only by the true, as appeareth by John 17. 3. This is Life Eternal to know thee, and, whom thou hast sent, Jesus Christ: And, he that knoweth not the Son, knoweth not the Father.

Which are the chief false Religions that are now in the World?
Heathenism (humanism), Turkism (Islam), Judaism, and Papism (Roman Catholicism).

What do you observe out of this diversity of Religions in the World?
The Misery of Man, when God leaveth him without his Word. An Example whereof may be seen in the idolaters, 1 Kings 18. 28. 2 Kings 17. 25. and Rom. 1. 22, 23. and some making a Stick or a Straw, other some a Red Cloth for their God, as the Lappians.

Seeing then there are so many Religions in the World, and every one looketh to obtain Happiness by his own Religion: Of what Religion are you?
I am a Christian.

What is Christian Religion?
It is the acknowledgment of the only true God, and of Jesus Christ whom he hath sent.

How do you prove that?
By that saying of our Savior Christ, John 17. 3. This is Life Eternal (which is the Reward of Christian Religion) that they may know thee to be the only true God, and Jesus Christ whom thou hast sent. Where he meaneth not a bare contemplative Knowledge, but a thankful acknowledging, which comprehendeth all Christian Duties, consisting in Faith and Obedience. For he that being void of the fear of God, (which is the beginning and chief point of Knowledge, Prov. 1. 7.) abideth not in God, but sinneth, hath not seen God, nor known him, 1 John 3. 6.

What do you call that Doctrine which showeth the way unto everlasting Life and Happiness?
It is commonly termed Theology or Divinity: and the familiar declaration of the Principles thereof (for the use especially of the ignorant) is called Catechizing, Heb. 5. 12, 13, 14. & 6. 1, 2.

What is Catechizing?
A teaching by Voice and Repetition of the Grounds of Christian Religion, Gal. 6. 6. Acts 18. 25, 26. 1 Cor. 14. 19.

Where should it be used, and by whom?
Both at home by the Master of the House, and in the Church likewise by the Minister.

Why at home?
Because Houses are the Nurseries of the Church.

Show some Reasons and Arguments to prove the necessity of Catechizing and Instructing in Religion.
First, God accounteth of Abraham for his care in this Duty, Gen. 18. 19.

Second, He commandeth all Parents to perform this Duty to their Children, Deut. 6. 6, 7. Ephes. 6. 4.

Third, All Children are made blind in the knowledge of God and of Religion by Adam's fall; and consequently they must be enlightened and informed by teaching, if they will not die so; which Solomon therefore commandeth, Prov. 22. 6. and our Savior Christ biddeth Children be respected, Mark 10. 14, 15, 19.

Fourth, The Examples of the Godly for this Duty, in bringing their Children with themselves to Holy Exercises. So Hannah brought up Samuel to the Tabernacle, 1 Sam. 1. 24. and Mary Jesus to the Temple when he was twelve years old, Luk. 2. 42. by which we perform the effect of Consecrating our Children to God, Exod. 13.

Fifth, Common Equity should move Parents to this Duty. For as their Children receive from them Original Sin, by which they are made so blind in God's Matters: It is equity they should labor to remove that blindness, by teaching them after God's Word.

Sixth, God promiseth as the greatest blessing to Men, that their Children should speak of him under the Gospel, Joel 2. 28. Acts 2.

But is it not some disgrace and baseness, that Men of years and place should be catechized?
If Men will be Christians, which is their greatest honor, they must hold it no disgrace to learn Christ. Noble Theophilus held it none, who was thus catechized, as Luke showeth, Chap. 1. 4. likewise Apollos, Acts 18. 26.

To come then to the Declaration of Christian Religion: Tell me, Wherein does the Happiness of Man consist?
Not * in himself, nor in any other Created Thing; but only † in God his Creator, who alone being infinite, is able to fill the Heart of Man. (* Eccles. 1. 2, 3. † Psal. 37. 4. and 37. 25.)

How may we come to enjoy God?
By being joined unto him, and so partaking of his Goodness. For Happiness is to be found by * acquaintance and fellowship with him, who is the Fountain of Blessedness: Man † so knowing him, or rather being known of him, that he ‖ may serve him, and be

* accepted of him; † honor him, and be honored by him. (* Job 22. 21. † John 17. 3. Gal. 4. 9. ‖ Eccles. 12. 13. * 2 Cor. 5. 9. † 1 Sam. 2. 30.)

By what Means come we to the Knowledge of God?
By such Means as he hath revealed himself. For God dwelleth in the Light that no Man can come unto; whom no Man hath seen nor can see, (1 Tim. 6. 16.) except he show himself unto us. Not that he is hidden in the Darkness, (for he dwelleth in the Light) but that the dullness of our Sight, and blindness of our Hearts, cannot reach unto that Light, except he declare himself unto us: Like as the Sun is not seen but by his own Light, so God is not known but by such Means as he hath manifested himself.

By what Means hath God Revealed himself?
By his Divine * Works, and by his Holy † Word. As the Prophet David plentifully and distinctly expresseth in the Nineteenth Psalm , The Heavens declare the Glory of God, and the Firmament showeth his Handiwork; and so continueth unto the Seventh Verse, touching his Works: And from thence to the end of the Psalm concerning his Word. The Law of the Lord is perfect, converting the Soul; the Testimony of the Lord is sure, making wise the simple. (* Rom. 1. 20. † Job 22. 22. John 6. 68.)

What gather you of this?
That all curious searching to know of God, more than he hath showed of himself, is both vain and hurtful to the Searchers; especially seeing by his Works and Word he hath declared as much as is profitable for Men to know for his Glory and their Eternal Felicity. Therefore Moses saith, Deut. 29, 29. The secret things belong unto the Lord our God; but those things which are revealed, belong unto us, and to our Children for ever.

What are the Divine Works whereby God hath showed himself?
The Creation and Preservation of the World and all things therein. So the Apostle to the Romans saith; That which may be known of God, is made manifest within them; for God hath made it manifest unto them: For the invisible things of God, while they are understood in his Works by the Creation of the World, are seen, even his Eternal Power and Godhead, Rom. 1. 19, 20. Also Preaching amongst the Gross Idolatrous Lystrians, Acts 14. 17. he saith, That God hath not left himself without Testimony, bestowing his Benefits, giving Rain and Fruitful Seasons from Heaven, filling our Hearts with Food and Gladness. And Preaching among the Learned, and yet no less Superstitious Athenians, he cites and canonizes the Testimony of the Poets, to show that God is not far from every one of us: For in him we live, and move, and have our being, Acts 17. 27, 28. For whosoever have not been willfully Blind among the Heathen Poets and Philosophers which professed Wisdom, have learned by Contemplation of the Creatures of the World, that God is the Maker and Preserver of the same.

What use is there of the Knowledge obtained by the Works of God?
There is a double use. The one, to make Men void of Excuse; as the Apostle teacheth, Rom. 1. 20. and so it is sufficient unto Condemnation. The other, is to further unto Salvation; and that by preparing and inducing Men to seek God, if happily by groping they may find him, (as the Apostle showeth, Acts 17. 27.) whereby they are made more apt to acknowledge him when he is perfectly revealed in his Word. Or after they have known God out of his Word, by contemplation of his infinite Power, Wisdom, and Goodness, most gloriously shining in his Works, to stir them up continually to reverence his Majesty, to honor and obey him, to repose their trust and confidence in him. And so the Children of God do use this Knowledge of God gathered out of his Divine Works; as appeareth in many places of the Scriptures, and especially of the Psalms, which are appointed for the exercise of the whole Church, Psal. 8. Psal. 19. Psal. 95. Psal. 104. Psal. 136, &c.

Are not the Works of God sufficient to give knowledge of the only True God, and the way unto Everlasting Happiness?
They may leave us without excuse, and so are sufficient unto condemnation; but are not able to make us wise unto Salvation. Because of things which are necessary unto Salvation, some they teach but imperfectly, others not at all; as the distinction of the Persons in the Godhead, the fall of Man from God, and the way to repair the same.

Where then is the saving Knowledge of God to be had perfectly?
In his Holy Word. For God, according to the riches of his Grace, hath been abundant towards us in all Wisdom and Understanding, and hath opened unto us the Mystery of his Will, according to his good pleasure, which he hath purposed in himself, as the Apostle teacheth, Ephes. 1. 7, 8, 9.

What course did God hold in the delivery of his Word unto Men?
In the beginning of the World he delivered his Word by Revelation, and continued the knowledge thereof by Tradition, while the number of his true Worshippers were small: But after he chose a great and populous Nation, in which he would be honored and served, he caused the same to be committed to writing for all Ages to the end of the World. For about the space of two thousand five hundred years from the Creation, the People of God had no written Word to direct them. Thence, for the space of three thousand one hundred years, unto this present time, the Word of God was committed unto them in writing: yet so, that in half that time God's Will was also revealed without writing extraordinarily, and the Holy Books written one after another, according to the necessity of the times; but in this last half, the whole Canon of the Scriptures being fully finished, we and all Men, unto the World's end, are left to have our full instruction from the same, without expecting extraordinary Revelations, as in times past.

Were these Revelations in times past delivered all in the same manner?
No. For (as the Apostle noteth, Heb. 1. 1) at sundry times, and in divers manners, God spake in times past unto the Fathers by the Prophets. The divers kinds are set down in Numb. 12. 6. and 1 Sam. 28. 6. and may be reduced to these two general heads; Oracles and Visions.

What call your Oracles?
Those Revelations that God as it were by his own Mouth delivered to his Servants: and that ordinarily by Urim and Thummim, or by Prophets extraordinarily called.

What do you understand by Visions?
Those Revelations whereby God signified his Will by certain Images and Representations of things offered unto Men: as may be seen in the Visions of Daniel, Ezekiel, Jeremy, &c.

How are these Visions presented unto Men?
Sometime to Men Waking, sometime to Men Sleeping; sometime to the Mind, sometime to the Eyes. To the imagination of Men sleeping were offered Divine Dreams: in expounding whereof we read that Joseph and Daniel excelled. But now they, together with all other extraordinary Revelations, are ceased.

Where then is the Word of God now certainly to be learned?
Only out of the Book of God, contained in the Holy Scriptures; which are the only certain Testimonies unto the Church of the Word of God. John 5. 39. 2 Tim. 3. 15.

First Head

Why may not Men want the Scriptures now, as they did at the first from the Creation until the time of Moses, for the space of 2513 years?
First, Because then God immediately by his Voice and Prophets sent from him, taught the Church his Truth: which now are ceased, Heb. 1. 1, 2.

Second, Tradition might then be of sufficient certainty by reason of the long life of God's faithful Witnesses. For Methuselah lived with Adam, the first Man, 243 years, and continued unto the Flood. Shem lived at once with Methuselah 98 years, and flourished above 500 years after the Flood. Isaac lived 50 years with Shem, and died about 10 years before the descent of Israel into Egypt. So that from Adam's death unto that time, three Men might by tradition preserve the purity of Religion. But after the coming of Israel out of Egypt, Man's Age was so shortened, that in the days of Moses, (the first Penman of the Scriptures) it was brought to 70 or 80 years; as appears by Psal. 90. 10.

Third, God saw his true Religion greatly forgotten in Egypt, (Israel then falling into Idolatry, Ezek. 20. 8.) and having brought Israel his People from thence did not only restore, but also increased it; adding thereunto many more particulars concerning his Service; which were needful for Men's Memories to be written.

Fourth, God having gathered his Church to a more solemn Company than before; it was his pleasure then to begin the writing of his Will. And therefore first with his own Finger he wrote the Ten Commandments in two Tables of Stone; and then commanded Moses to write the other words which he had heard from him in the Mount, Exod. 34. 27, 28.

Fifth, Thus God provided that the Churches of all Ages and Times might have a certain rule to know whether they embraced sound Doctrine or no; and that none should be so bold as to coin any new Religion to serve him with, but that which he had delivered in writing.

What is Scripture then?
The Word of God written by Men inspired by the Holy Ghost, for the perfect Building and Salvation of the Church: or, Holy Books written by the Inspiration of God to make us wise unto Salvation. 2 Tim. 3. 15, 16. 2 Pet. 1. 21. John. 20. 31.

If the Scriptures be written by Men which are subject unto Infirmities; How can it be accounted the Word of God?
Because it proceeded not from the Will or Mind of Man, but Holy Men set apart by God for that Work, spake and writ as they were moved by the Holy Ghost. Therefore God alone is to be accounted the Author thereof, who inspired the Hearts of those Holy Men, whom he chose to be his Secretaries; who are to be held only the Instrumental Causes thereof. (2 Pet. 1. 20, 21.)

When Jeremy brought the Word of God to the Jews, they said it was not the Word of the Lord, but he spake as Baruc the Son of Neriah provoked him, Jeremiah 43. 2. and so some perhaps in these Days are so ungodly as to take the Jews Part against Jeremy and all his Fellows. How may it appear therefore, that this Book which you call the Book of God, and the Holy Scripture, is the Word of God indeed, and not Men's Policies?
By the constant Testimony of Men in all Ages, from them that first knew these Penmen of the Holy Ghost with their Writings, until our Time: And Reasons taken out of the Works themselves, agreeable to the Quality of the Writers. Both which kinds of Arguments the Holy Scriptures have as much, and far more than any other Writings. Wherefore as it were extreme Impudence to deny the Works of Homer, Plato, Virgil, Tully, Livy, Galen, and such like, which the Consent of all Ages have received and delivered unto us; which also by the Tongue, Phrase, Matter, and all other

Circumstances agreeable, are confirmed to be the Works of the same Authors whose they are testified to be: So it were more than Brutish Madness to doubt of the certain Truth and Authority of the Holy Scriptures, which no less, but much more than any other Writings, for their Authors, are testified and confirmed to be the Sacred Word of the Ever-living God. Not only testified (I say) by the uniform Witness of Men in all Ages, but also confirmed by such Reasons taken out of the Writings themselves, as do sufficiently argue the Spirit of God to be the Author of them. For we may learn out of the Testimonies themselves, (as David did, Psal. 119. 152.) that God hath established them for ever.

Let me hear some of those Reasons which prove that God is the Author of the Holy Scriptures.
First, The true Godliness and Holiness, wherewith the Writers of the Scriptures shined as Lamps in their Times, and far surpassed all Men of other Religions: Which showeth the Work of God's Spirit in them; and how unlike it is that such Men should obtrude into the Church their own Inventions instead of God's Word.

Second, The Simplicity, Integrity and Sincerity of these Writers, in Matters that concern themselves, and those that belong unto them: Doing nothing by Partiality, (1 Tim. 5. 21.) neither sparing their Friends nor themselves. So Moses, for Example, in his Writings, spareth not to report the Reproach of his own Tribe, Gen. 34. 30. and 49. 5, 7. nor the Incest of his Parents, of which he himself was Conceived, Exod. 6. 20. nor the Idolatry of his Brother Aaron, Exod 32. nor the wicked Murmuring of his Sister Miriam, Numb. 12. 1. nor his own declining of his Vocation by God to deliver the Children of Israel out of Egypt, Exod. 4. 13, 14. nor his Murmuring against God, and Impatience, Numb. 11. 11, 12, 13, 14. nor his want of Faith, after so many wonderful Confirmations, Numb. 20. 15. and 27. 14. Deut. 32. 51. And though he were in highest Authority, and had a Promise of the People to believe whatsoever he said, (Exod. 19 8. and 20. 19. and 24. 3.) he assigneth no place for his own Sons to aspire, either to the Kingdom, or to the High Priesthood; but leaveth them in the mean degree of common Levites. All which things declare most manifestly, that he was void of all Earthly and Carnal Affections in his Writings, as was meet for the Penman and Scribe of God. Whereunto also may be added, that he writeth of himself, Numb. 12. 3. that he was the meekest of all the Men that were upon the face of the Earth: Which no wise Man would in such sort report of himself, if he were left to his own Direction.

Third, The Quality and Condition of the Penmen of these Holy Writings: some of whom were never trained up in the School of Man, and yet in their Writings show that depth of Wisdom, that the most Learned Philosophers come not nigh unto; some also were before professed Enemies to that Truth, whereof afterwards they were Writers. Amos was no Prophet, but an Herdsman, and a gatherer of Wild Figs, Amos 7. 14. Matthew a Publican, employed only in the gathering of Toll, Mat. 9. 9. Peter, James, and John Fishermen, whose liberty of Speech, when the Chief Priests and Elders of Jerusalem beheld, and understood that they were unlettered and ignorant Men, it is recorded, Acts 4. 12. that they marveled, and took knowledge of them, that they had been with Jesus. Paul from a bloody Persecutor converted to be a Preacher and Writer of the Gospel, showed by that sudden Alteration, that he was moved by a Command from Heaven to defend that Doctrine which before he so earnestly Impugned.

Fourth, The Matter of the Holy Scripture being altogether of Heavenly Doctrine, and favoring nothing of an Earthly or Worldly Affection, but every where Renouncing and Condemning the same, declareth the God of Heaven to be the only Inspirer of it.

Fifth, The Doctrine of the Scripture is such as could never breed in the Brains of Man, Three Persons in one God; God to become Man; the Resurrection, and such like, Man's Wit could never hatch: Or if it had conceived them, could never hope that any Man could believe them.

Sixth, The sweet Concord between these Writings, and the perfect Coherence of all things contained in them; notwithstanding the Diversity of Persons by whom, Places where, Times when, and Matters whereof they have written. For there is a most Holy and Heavenly Consent and Agreement of all Parts thereof together, though written in so sundry Ages, by so sundry Men, in so distant Places. One of them does not gainsay another, as Men's Writings do: and our Savior Christ confirmeth them all, Luke 24. 44.

Seventh, A Continuance of wonderful Prophecies, foretelling Things to come so long before, marked with their Circumstances; not doubtful, like the Oracles of the Heathen, or Merlin's Prophecies, but such as expressed the Things and Persons by their Names: Which had all, just in their Times their certain Performance. And therefore unto what may we attribute them, but to the Inspiration of God? Vide Calvin's Instit. lib. 1. c. 8. Thus was the Messiah promised to Adam 4000 Years before he was Born, Gen. 3. 15. and to Abraham 1917 Year before the accomplishment, Gen. 12. 3. The deliverance of the Israelites from Egypt, to the same Abraham 400 Years before, Gen. 15. 13, 14. The Prophecies of Jacob, Gen. 49 concerning the twelve Tribes, were not fulfilled till after the Death of Moses; and that of the continuance of the Tribe and Kingdom of Judah held until the coming of Christ. In the first Book of Kings, Chap. 13. 2, 3. there is delivered a Prophecy concerning Josiah by Name, 331 Years; and in Isaiah 45. 1. concerning Cyrus, 100 Years before either of them were Born. Daniel's Prophecies, and that especially of the 70 Weeks, in the Ninth Chap. are wonderful. So likewise are those of the Rejection of the Jews, the Calling of the Gentiles, the Kingdom of Antichrist, &c. which now we see fulfilled.

Eighth, The great Majesty, full of Heavenly Wisdom and Authority, such as is meet to proceed from the Glory of God, shining in all the Holy Scriptures: Yes, oftentimes under great simplicity of Words, and plainness and easiness of Stile; which nevertheless more affecteth the Hearts of the Hearers, than all the painted eloquence and lofty stile of Rhetoricians and Orators, and argueth the Holy Ghost to be the Author of them, 1 Cor. 1. 17. 21, 24. and 2. 15.

Ninth, In speaking of Matters of the highest nature, they go not about to persuade Men by Reasons, as Philosophers and Orators; but absolutely require credit to be given to them, because the Lord hath spoken it. They promise Eternal Joy to the Obedient, and threaten Eternal Woe to the Disobedient: they prescribe Laws for the Thoughts, to which no Man can pierce: they require Sacrifice, but they prefer Obedience; they enjoin Fasting, but it is also from sin; they command Circumcision, but 'tis of the Heart; they forbid Lusting, Coveting, &c. which is not to be found in any Laws but in his that searcheth the Heart.

Tenth, The end and scope of the Scriptures, is for the Advancement of God's Glory, and the Salvation of Man's Soul. For they entreat either of the noble Acts of God and of Christ, or the Salvation of Mankind. And therefore by comparing this with the former Reason, we may frame this Argument: If the Author of the Scriptures were not God, it must be some Creature; If he were a Creature, he was either Good or Bad; If a Bad Creature, why forbids he evil so rigorously, and commands good so expressly, and makes his mark to aim at nothing but God's Glory and our good? If he were a Good Creature, why does he challenge to himself that which is proper to God only. As to make Laws for the Heart, to punish and reward eternally, &c. If it were no Creature, Good nor Bad, it must needs be God.

Eleventh, The admirable Power and Force that is in them to convert and alter Men's Minds, and to incline their Hearts from Vice to Virtue, (Psal. 19. 7, 8. Psal. 119. 111. Heb. 4. 12. Acts 13. 12.) though they be quite contrary to Men's Affections.

Twelfth, The Scriptures, as experience showeth, have the Power of God in them, to humble a Man when they are preached, and to cast him down to Hell, and afterward to restore and raise him up again, Heb. 4. 12. 1 Cor. 14. 25.

Thirteenth, The Writers of the Holy Scriptures are the most ancient of all others. Moses is more ancient than the Gods of the Heathen, who lived not long before the Wars of Troy, about the time of the Judges: and the Youngest Prophets of the Old Testament match the most ancient Philosophers and Historians of the Heathen.

Fourteenth, The deadly hatred that the Devil and all wicked Men carry against the Scriptures, to cast them away and destroy them, and the little love that most Men do bear unto them, prove them to be of God. For if they were of Flesh and Blood, then Flesh and Blood would love them, read them, practice them, and every way regard them more than it does. For the World loveth his own, as our Savior Christ saith, John 15. 19. but we (being but carnal and earthly) favor not the things that be of God, as the Apostle Paul saith, 1 Cor. 2. 14. And until the Lord open our Hearts, and we be born again of God's Spirit, and become as new born Babes, we have no desire unto them, 1 Pet. 2. 2.

Fifteenth, The marvelous preservation of the Scriptures. Though none in time be so ancient, nor none so much oppugned; yet God hath still by his Providence preserved them, and every part of them.

Show now how the Holy Scriptures have the consonant testimony of Men of all times since they were written, that they are the most Holy Word of God.
First, Joshua the Servant of Moses, the first Scribe of God, (to whom God spake in the presence and hearing of Six Hundred Thousand Men, besides Women and Children) who was an Eye Witness of many Wonders by which the Ministry of Moses was confirmed, testifieth his Writings to be the undoubted Word of God. The same do the Prophets which continued the History of the Church in the time of the Judges, both of Moses and Joshua.

Likewise all the Prophets who successively recorded the Holy Story and Prophecy by Divine Revelation, from Samuel unto the Captivity; and from the Captivity to the Building again of the Temple and of the City, and sometimes after; receiving the same Books of Heavenly Doctrine from the former Age, delivered them to their Posterity: And Malachi, the last of the Prophets, closeth up the Old Testament with a Charge and Exhortation from the Lord, to remember the Law of Moses delivered in Horeb, and to use the same as a School-Master to direct them unto Christ, until he came in Person himself, Mal. 4. 4.

Finally, From that time the Church of the Jews, until the coming of Christ in the Flesh, embraced all the former Writings of the Prophets as the Book of God. Christ himself appealeth unto them as a sufficient Testimony of him, John 5. 39. The Apostles and Evangelists prove the Writings of the New Testament by them: And the Catholic Church of Christ, from the Apostles Time unto this Day, hath acknowledged all the said Writings, both of the Old and New Testament, to the undoubted Word of God.

Thus have we the Testimony both of the Old Church of the Jews, God's peculiar People and First-born, to whom the Oracles of God were committed, (Acts 7. 38. Hos. 8. 12. Rom. 3. 2. and 9. 4.) and the New of Christians: Together with the general account which all the Godly at all times have made of the Scriptures, when they have crossed their Natures and Courses, as accounting it in their Souls to be of God; and the special Testimony of Martyrs, who have sealed the certainty of the same, by shedding their Blood for them. Hereunto also may be added the Testimony of those which are out of the Church; Heathens, out of whom many ancient Testimonies are cited to this purpose by Josephus contra Appion. Turks, Jews, (who to this Day acknowledge all the Books of the Old Testament) and Heretics, who labor to shroud themselves under them, &c.

Are there not some Divine Testimonies which may likewise be added to these?
Yes. First, The known Miracles (which the Devil was never able to do) that did so often follow the Writers and Teachers of the Scriptures. Secondly, The manifold Punishments and Destruction of those that have reviled and persecuted the same.

Are these Motives of themselves sufficient to work saving Faith, and persuade us fully to rest in God's Word?
No. Besides all these, it is required, that we have the Spirit of God, as well to open our Eyes to see the Light, as to seal up fully unto our Hearts that Truth which we see with our Eyes. For the same Holy Spirit that inspired the Scriptures, inclineth the Hearts of God's Children to believe what is revealed in them, and inwardly assureth them, above all Reasons and Arguments, that these are the Scriptures of God. (1 Cor. 2. 10. and 14. 37. Ephes. 1. 13.). Therefore the Lord by the Prophet Isaiah, promiseth to join his Spirit with his Word, and that it shall remain with his Children for ever, Isa. 59. 21. The same promiseth our Savior Christ unto his Disciples concerning the Comforter, which he would send to lead them into all Truth, to teach them all things, and to put them in mind of all things which he had said unto them, John 14. 26. and 15. 26. and 16. 23. The Lord, by the Prophet Jeremiah, also promiseth to give his Law into their Minds, and to write it in the Hearts of his People, Jer. 31. 33. And St. John saith to the Faithful, that by the anointing of the Holy Spirit which is on them, they know all things, 1 John 2. 20.

This Testimony of God's Spirit in the Hearts of his Faithful, as it is proper to the Word of God, so is it greater than any Human Persuasions grounded upon Reason or Witnesses of Men; unto which it is unmeet that the Word of God should be subject, as Papists hold, when they teach that the Scriptures receive their Authority from the Church. For by thus hanging the Credit and Authority of the Scriptures on the Churches Sentence, they make the Churches Word of greater Credit than the Word of God. Whereas the Scriptures of God cannot be judged or sentenced by any: And God only is a worthy Witness of himself, in his Word, and by his Spirit; which give mutual Testimony one of the other, and work that assurance of Faith in his Children, that no Human Demonstrations can make, nor any Persuasions or Enforcements of the World can remove.

Show some farther Reasons, that the Authority of the Scriptures does not depend upon the Church.
First, To believe the Scripture, is a Work of Faith; but the Church cannot infuse Faith. Second, Any Authority that the Church hath, it must prove it by the Scripture; therefore the Scripture dependeth not upon the Church. Third, If an Infidel should ask the Church, How they are sure that Christ Died for them? if they should answer, Because themselves say so, it would be ridiculous, &c.

What Books are the Holy Scriptures; and by whom were they Written?
First, The Books of the Old Testament, in number Nine and Thirty, (which the Jews, according to the number of their Letters, brought to Two and Twenty) written by Moses and the Prophets; who delivered the same to the Church of the Jews, Rom. 3. 2. Secondly, The Books of the New Testament, in number Seven and Twenty; written by the Apostles and Evangelists, who delivered them to the Church of the Gentiles, Rom. 1. 16. Rev. 1. 11.

What Language were the Books of the Old Testament written in?
In Hebrew; which was the first Tongue of the World, and the most orderly Speech, in comparison of which all other Languages may be condemned of barbarous confusion: But chosen specially, because it was the Language at that time best known unto the Church (teaching that all of them should understand the Scriptures.) Only some few Portions by the later Prophets were left written in the Chaldean Tongue, (understood by God's People after their carrying away into Babylon:) namely, the 11th verse of the 10th Chapter of Jeremy; six Chapters in Daniel (from the 4th verse of the 2nd Chapter, to the end of the 7th Chapter) and three in Ezra, (the fourth, fifth, and sixth.)

Had the Hebrew Text Vowels or Points from the beginning, as now it hath?
Our Savior saith, Mat. 5. 18. that not one Jot or Prick of the Law shall perish. Whereby it should appear, that the Law and the Prophets (for of both he speaketh immediately before) had Vowels and Pricks. God also by Moses commanded the Law to be written upon two great Stones at the entrance of the People into the Land of Promise, that all Strangers might read and know what Religion the Children of Israel professed: And he Commanded that it should be written well, and plainly, or clearly, Deut. 27. 8. which could not be performed, except it were written with the Vowel Points. Whereunto also belong all those places of Scripture, which testify of the clearness and certainty of the Scripture, which could not at all be, if it lacked Vowels.

What are the Books of the Old Testament?
The Books of Moses (otherwise called the Law) and the Prophets. For so are they oftentimes divided in the New Testament; as Mat. 5. 17. and 7. 12. and 22. 40. Luke 16. 29. and 24. 27. John 1. 45. Acts 13. 15. and 24. 14. and 26. 22. and 28. 23. Where it is to be understood, that the Law is taken for the whole Doctrine of God delivered by Moses, which containeth not only the Law, but also Promises of Mercy in Christ, as he himself testifieth, John 5. 46. If ye did believe Moses you would also believe me; for Moses wrote of me. And whereas our Savior Christ, Luke 24. 44. unto the Law and the Prophets addeth the Psalms, which are a part of the Prophets, it is because they were most familiar to the Godly, and generally known of the People by the daily Exercise of them, the former Division notwithstanding being perfect.

Which are the Books of Moses?
Five in number; which are called Genesis, Exodus, Leviticus, Numbers, Deuteronomy.

How are the Books of the Prophets distinguished?
Into Historical and Doctrinal; the former whereof contain the Explication of the Law by Practice principally, the latter by Doctrine chiefly.

How many Historical Books be there?
Twelve in number, viz. the Book of Joshua, the Book of Judges, the Book of Ruth, the two Books of Samuel, the two Books of Kings, the two Books of Chronicles, the Book of Ezra, the Book of Nehemiah, and the Book of Esther.

First Head

How are the Doctrinal Books distinguished?
Into Poetical and Prosaical. Which distinction is thought of many to be observed by our Savior Christ, Luke 24. 44. where he under the name of Psalms comprehendeth all those Books that are written in the Holy Poetical Style.

Which are the Poetical Books?
Such as are written in Meter or Poesy; containing principally Sage and Holy Sentences, (whence also they may be called Sentential) and they are five in number, viz. the Book of Job, the Psalms; and Solomon's three Books, the Proverbs, Ecclesiastes, and the Canticles.

Which are the Prosaical Books?
Such as are for the most part written in Prose, and foretell things to come, (whence also more specially they are termed Prophetical or Vaticinal.) Of which kind are sixteen Writers in number; four whereof are called the Greater Prophets, viz. Isaiah, Jeremiah, (to whose Prophecy is annexed his Book of Lamentations, though written in Meter) Ezekiel and Daniel; and twelve are called Smaller Prophets, viz. Hosea, Joel, Amos, Obadiah, Jonah, Micah, Nahum, Habakkuk, Zephaniah, Haggai, Zechariah, Malachi. Which twelve of old were reckoned for one Book; and therefore Acts 7. 42. Stephen citing a place out of Amos 5. 25. useth this form; As it is written in the Book of the Prophets.

Be there no other Canonical Books of the Scripture of the Old Testament besides these that you have named?
No; for those other Books which Papists would obtrude unto us for Canonical, are Apocryphal, that is to say, such as are to lie hid, when there is proof to be made of Religion.

How prove you that those Apocryphal Books are no part of the Canonical Scriptures?
First, They are not written first in Hebrew, the Language of the Church before Christ, which all the Books of the Old Testament are originally written in.

Second, They were never received into the Canon of Scripture by the Church of the Jews before Christ, (to whom alone in those times the Oracles of God were committed. Rom. 3. 2.) nor read and expounded in their Synagogues. See Josephus contra Appion. lib. 1. & Eusebius lib. 3. 10.

Third, The Jews were so careful to keep Scriptures entire, as they kept the number of the Verses and Letters; within which is none of the Apocrypha.

Fourth, The Scripture of the Old Testament was written by Prophets, (Luke 24. 27. 2 Pet. 1. 19.) But Malachi was the last Prophet, after whom all the Apocrypha was written.

Fifth, They are not authorized by Christ and his Apostles, who do give testimony unto the Scriptures.

Sixthly, By the most Ancient Fathers and Councils of the Primitive Churches after the Apostles, both Greek and Latin, they have not been admitted for trial of Truth, though they have been read for instruction of Manners. As may appear by Euseb. lib. 6. cap. 18. (out of Origin) the Council of Laodicea, Can. 59. (which is also confirmed by the sixth General Council of Constantinople, Can. 2.) and many other Testimonies of the Ancient Fathers.

Seventhly, There is no such constant Truth in them, as in the Canonical Scriptures. For every Book of them hath Falsehoods in Doctrine or History.

Show some of those Errors in the particular Books.

In the Book of Tobit, the Angel maketh a lie, saying, That he is Azariah the Son of Ananias, Tob. 5. 12. which is far from the Spirit of God, and the Nature of Good Angels that cannot Sin. There is also the Unchaste Devil Asmodeus; the seven Angels which present the Prayers of the Saints, Tob. 12. 15. and the Magical Toys of the Fish's Heart, Liver, and Gall, for driving away of Devils, and restoring of Sight; not savoring of the Spirit of God.

Judith in her Prayer commendeth the Fact of Simeon, Gen. 34. which the Holy Ghost condemneth, Gen. 49. 5. and prayeth God to prosper her feigned Tales and Lies, Jud. 9. 13.

Baruc saith, He wrote this Book in Babylon, Chap. 1. v. 1. whereas it appeareth by Jeremiah 43. 6. that he was with Jeremiah at Jerusalem, and went not from him. Likewise he writeth for Offerings and Vessels, after the Temple was burned. And in the 6th Chapter, v. 3. Jeremiah writeth, that the continuance of the Jews in Babylon shall be for seven Generations, whereas the Canonical Jeremiah prophecieth but of 70 years, Cap. 29. 10. For ten years cannot make a Generation, neither is it ever so taken in the Canonical Scriptures.

The Story of Susanna maketh Daniel a Young Child in the days of Astyages, and to become famous among the People by the Judgment of Susanna. Whereas Daniel himself writeth otherwise of his carriage into Babylon in the days of Jehoiakim under Nebuchadnezzar, and of the means by which he was known first to be a Prophet; Dan. 1. and 2.

The Story of Bell and the Dragon speaketh of Habakkuk the Prophet in the days of Cyrus; who prophesied before the Captivity of Babylon, which was 70 years before Cyrus.

The first Book of Maccabees, writing a History of things said and done, does not much interlace his own Judgment; and therefore does err the less: yet is his Narration contrary to the second Book of Maccabees in many places, and to Josephus in some things. For Example; The first Book of Maccabees saith, That Antiochus died at Babylon in his Bed, being grieved in Mind for Tidings brought unto him out of Persia, 1 Mac. 6. vers. 8, and 16. But in the first Chapter of the second Book of Maccabees, v. 15, 16. it is said, That he was cut in pieces in the Temple of Nanea: and in the ninth Chapter of the same Book, That he died of a grievous Disease of his Bowels in a strange Country in the Mountains, 2 Mac. 9. 28.

The second Book of Maccabees is far worse. For the Abridger of Jason's Chronicle, who set it forth, does not only confound and falsify many Stories, (as it is easy to be proved out of the first Book of Maccabees, Josephus and others) but also whilst he giveth his Sentence of divers Facts, does more betray the weakness of his judgment. As he commendeth Razis for killing himself, 2 Maccab. 14. 42. and Judas for offering Sacrifice for the Dead, that were polluted with Idolatry, 2 Mac. 12. 45. whereas it is to be thought rather, that the Sacrifice was offered to pacify the Wrath of God for them that were alive, that they should not be wrapped in the Curse of the Wicked, as in the Story of Achan, Josh. 7. Yet he is the more to be born withal, because he confesseth his insufficiency: (2 Mat. 15. 38.) which agreeth not with the Spirit of God.

The Additions unto Esther are fabulous, convinced of many Untruths by the Canonical Book: As namely, 1. In the Apocryphal Esther; Mordecai is said to dream in the second year of Ahashuerus, (chap. 11. 2.) but in the Canonical, the seventh year, (Esther 2. 16.) and Bellarmine making the Dream in the seventh year, and the Conspiracy in the second, maketh five years difference, and is contrary to the 11 chap. 2. The True saith, that Mordecai had no Reward, (Esther 6. 3.) the False saith he had, (chap. 12. 5.) 3.

The True calleth Haman an Agagite, (Esther 3. 1.) that is, an Amalekite: the False calleth him a Macedonian, (chap. 16. 10.) Also the Author of those Additions describeth the countenance of the King to be full of Cruelty and Wrath, (chap. 15. 7.) yet he maketh Esther to say, it was glorious like an Angel of God, and full of Grace, (ver. 13, 14.) either lying himself, or charging Esther with impudent lying and flattering.

The Book of Wisdom is so far off from being any Book of the Old Testament, that it is affirmed by divers Ancient Writers, that it was made by Philo the Jew, which lived since Christ, as St. Jerome witnesseth in his Preface to the Proverbs. Howsoever the Author would fain seem to be Solomon, (chap. 9. 8.) See his cruel Sentence against Bastards in the end of the third Chapter.

Jesus the Son of Sirach showeth the frailty of Man in divers places of Ecclesiasticus; and namely, chap. 46. 20. where he acknowledgeth that Samuel indeed, and not a wicked Spirit in the shape of Samuel, was raised by the Witch of Endor, 1 Sam. 28. Also chap. 48. 10. he understandeth the Prophecy of Malachi, of the Personal coming of Elias, which our Savior Christ does manifestly refer unto John the Baptist, Mat. 11. 14.

The Third Book of Esdras is full of impudent Lies and Fables, convinced by the Book of Ezra, Nehemiah. Haggai and Esther. For Example; Ezra saith, That all the Vessels of Gold and Silver which Cyrus delivered Sheshbazzar, were by Sheshbazzar carried from Babylon to Jerusalem, Ezra 1. 11. This Esdras saith, they were only numbered by Cyrus, not sent, but afterwards Darius delivered them to Zerubbabel, and by him they were brought to Jerusalem, 1 Esdras 4. 44. 55.

The Fourth Book of Esdras is now rejected of the Papists themselves, as it was of Hierom; containing also many Falsities, Dreams and Fables, Chap. 6. 49, 50. and 13. 43, 44, &c. and 14. 21, 22, &c.

Thus much for the Books of the Old Testament. In what Language were the Books of the New Testament written?
In Greek, because it was the most common Language, best known then to Jews and Gentiles; teaching, that all Kingdoms should have the Scriptures in a Language which they understand.

How are the Books of the New Testament distinguished?
They are of Things revealed.

1) Before the writing of them: Which are either
    a) Historical: Five in number, containing the History of
        i) Christ; the 4 Gospels;
            (1) Matthew
            (2) Mark
            (3) Luke
            (4) John
        ii) according to His Apostles: viz. the Acts.
    b) Doctrinal: 21 Epistles of
        i) Paul to the
            (1) Romans
            (2) Corinthians, 1&2
            (3) Galatians
            (4) Ephesians
            (5) Philippians

         (6) Colossians
         (7) Thessalonians, 1&2
         (8) Timothy, 1&2
         (9) Titus
         (10) Philemon
         (11) Hebrews.
    ii) James
    iii) Peter, 1&2
    iv) John, 1, 2 &3
    v)   Jude

2) After the Writing of them; as the Apocalypse, or Revelation of St. John, which is the Prophetical Book of the New Testament.

Is it agreed that all these Books, and they alone, are the Holy Scriptures of the New Testament?
Yes: Howsoever in Ancient Time they have not been all received with like consent. Yet they have the Testimony of all Ages; and there is nothing in any of them repugnant to the rest of the Canonical Scriptures.

Were there never any Books of Canonical Scripture lost?
No, Heaven and Earth shall perish, before one Jot or Tittle of them shall perish.

What say you to the Books of Gad and Nathan, (2 Chron. 9. 29.) of Ahijah and Iddo, (2 Chron. 9. 29.) and Paul's Epistle to the Laodiceans, Col. 4. 16?
These Books often mentioned in the Old Testament, were not Canonical Scripture, but Civil Chronicles, wherein the Matters of the Common-Wealth were more largely written; as the Chronicles of the Medes and Persians, Esther 10. 2. And the Epistle mentioned Col. 4. was rather of the Laodiceans to Paul, than of Paul to the Laodiceans.

What are the Properties of the Holy Scriptures?
First, They are perfectly Holy in themselves and by themselves: whereas all other Writings are profane, further than they draw some holiness from them; which is never such but that their Holiness is imperfect.

Secondly, The Authority of these Holy Writings, inspired of God, is highest in the Church, as the Authority of God; whereunto no Learning or Decrees of Angels or Men, under whatever name or color it be commended, may be accounted equal, (Gal. 1. 8, 9. 2 Thess. 2. 2.) neither can they be judged or sentenced by any.

Thirdly, The Books of Holy Scripture are so sufficient for the knowledge of Christian Religion, that they do most plentifully contain all Doctrine necessary to Salvation. They being perfectly profitable to instruct to Salvation in themselves; and all other imperfectly profitable thereunto, further than they draw from them. Whence it followeth that we need no unwritten Verities, no Traditions or Inventions of Men, no Canons of Councils, no Sentences of Fathers, much less Decrees of Popes, for to supply any supposed defect of the Written Word, or for to give us a more perfect direction in the Worship of God, and the Way of Life, than is already expressed in the Canonical Scriptures, Mat. 23. 8. John 5. 39. Mat. 15. 9. Finally, These Holy Scriptures are the Rule, the Line, the Square, and Light, whereby to examine and try all Judgments and Sayings of Men and Angels, John 12. 48. Gal. 1. 9. All Traditions, Revelations, Decrees of Councils, Opinions of Doctors, &c. are to be embraced so far forth as they may be proved out of the Divine Scriptures, and not otherwise. So that from them only all Doctrine concerning our Salvation must be drawn and derived: That only is to be taken for Truth, in Matters appertaining to Christian Religion, which is agreeable unto them; and whatsoever disagreeth from them is to be refused.

How do you prove that the Scripture is such a Rule?
Since God hath appointed the Holy Scriptures, which bear witness of Christ; (John 5. 39.) to be written for our Learning: (Rom. 15. 4.) He will have no other Doctrine pertaining to Eternal Life to be received, but that which is consonant unto them, and hath the ground thereof in them. Therefore unto them only is the Church directed for the saving Knowledge of God, Isa. 8. 20. Luke 16. 29, 31. Insomuch that all Prophecies, Revelations, and Miracles are to be judged by their consent with the Law of God written by Moses; to which nothing is to be added, nor any thing to be taken away from it, (Deut. 12. 32. and 13. 1. 2.) Yea, Christ himself appealeth to the trial of those things which Moses did write of him, (John 5. 46.) being none other in any respect, but even the same whom Moses in the Law and the Prophets (which were the Interpreters and Commentators upon the Law Written by Moses) did write of, (John 1. 45.) And his Apostles preaching the Gospel among all Nations, taught nothing beside that which Moses and the Prophets had spoken to be fulfilled in Christ, as Paul testifieth, Acts 26. 22. seeing as he taught, all the rest of the Apostles did teach.

Where do you find that the Scriptures are able to instruct us perfectly unto Salvation?
The Apostle Paul, in 2 Tim. 3. 15. does expressly affirm it; and the Reasons which may be gathered out of the two Verses following do plainly prove it.

What are these Reasons?
1. God being Author of these Books, they must needs be perfect, as he himself is. Who being for his Wisdom able, and for his Love to his Church willing to set down such a Rule as may guide them to Eternal Life, hath not failed herein. 2. They are profitable to teach all True Doctrine, and to confute the False; to correct all Disorder private and public, and to inform Men in the way of Righteousness. 3. The Man of God, that is, the Preacher and Minister of the Word, is thereby made complete and perfect, sufficiently furnished unto every good Work or Duty of the Ministry.

How does this last Reason hold?
Most strongly. For the People being to learn of the Minister, what to believe and what to do; and more being required of him that must be the Eye and Mouth of all the rest: If he may be perfectly instructed by the Scriptures, they are much more able to give every common Man sufficient instruction. Again, seeing the Minister is bound to disclose the whole Counsel of God to his People, (Acts 20. 27. he being thereto fully furnished out of the Treasury of the Word of God; it followeth, that by him out of the Scriptures they may also be abundantly taught to Salvation.

What further proof have you of the Sufficiency of the Scriptures?
The five Books of Moses, which was the first Holy Scripture delivered to the Church, was sufficient for the instruction of the People of that Time, in all that God required at their hands. As appeareth by that they were forbidden to add any thing unto it, or to take any thing from it, but to do that only which was prescribed by the Law, (Deut. 12. 32.) The Prince and the People are commanded to be directed thereby altogether, and not to depart from it, either to the right hand or to the left, (Deut. 17.) How much more the Law and the Prophets (which did more at large set forth the Doctrine delivered by Moses, both in Precepts and Promises, in Practice and Example, was sufficient for the time that succeeded until John the Baptist? Mat. 11. 12. Luke 16. 16.

What more can you allege for this purpose?

1. Psal. 19. 7. David saith, The Law of the Lord is perfect, converting the Soul. And Psal. 119. 96. I have seen an end of all Perfection: but thy Commandment is exceeding large.

2. Luke 16. 29. Abraham in the Parabolical Story testifieth, that Moses and the Prophets were sufficient to keep Men from Damnation.

3. John 5. 39. Our Savior Christ affirmeth of the Scriptures of the Old Testament, that they were Witnesses of him, in whom our Salvation is perfect.

4. Acts 17. 11. The Bereans are commended for examining the Doctrine of the Apostles by the Scriptures of the Old Testament.

5. Acts 26. 22. Paul taught nothing but that which Moses and the Prophets had written of Christ to be fulfilled.

6. 1 John 1. 1, 2, 3. John saith, That what they had heard and seen, that they livered.

7. Gal. 1. 8, 9. Paul wisheth, That if an Angel from Heaven came and taught any other Doctrine, we should hold him accursed.

8. Rev. 22. 18, 19. There is a Curse pronounced against him that addeth any thing, or taketh away any thing from Scripture.

9. 1 Cor. 4. 6. Paul saith, That no Man must presume above that which is written.

10. John 20. 31. St. John saith, That these things are written that we might believe that Jesus is the Christ, the Son of God, and that believing we might have life through his Name. Where he speaketh not only of his Gospel, but being the survivor of the rest of the Apostles, of all their Writings, Seeing then that Faith by those things that are written, and eternal Salvation by Faith, may be attained; it ought to be no Controversy amongst Christians, that the whole Scriptures of the Old and New Testament does most richly and abundantly contain all that is necessary for a Christian Man to believe and to do for Eternal Salvation.

Object. 1. Yet our Adversaries quarrel against this most rich and plentiful Treasure of the Holy Scriptures; alleging that we receive many things by tradition which are not in Scripture, and yet we believe them: As Mary's perpetual Virginity, and the Baptism of Infants.

We make not Mary's perpetual Virginity any Matter of Religion, but a likely Opinion so far as it can be maintained, that it were an unseemly and unfitting thing for a sinful Man to use to the Act of Generation, that Vessel which was chosen and consecrated by the Holy Ghost to so high an use, as was the bringing forth of the Savior of the World: it hath warrant from the Apostle's Charge, Phil. 4. 8. of doing whatsoever is honest, whatsoever is of good report, whatsoever is praise-worthy, &c. As for Baptism of Infants, it is sufficiently warranted by Reasons of Scripture, though not by Example.[1]

---

[1] On both of these points we would strongly yet respectfully disagree with Ussher. We do not believe the Scriptures allow for the opinion of the perpetual virginity of Mary (Matthew 1:25, 13:55; John 7:5). Nor do we agree that Infant Baptism is sufficiently warranted by reasons of Scripture, but rather that such a practice is inconsistent with it.

Object. 2. They Object that it is by Tradition, and not by Scripture, that we know such and such Books to be Scripture.

Though new Beginners do first learn it from the Faithful; yet afterwards they know it upon grounds of Scripture. As an ignorant Man may be told of the King's Coin: but it is not that telling, but the King's Stamp that maketh it current and good Coin.

Object. 3. It is Objected, That it was by Tradition, and not by Scripture, that Stephen knew Moses to be 40 years old when he left Pharaoh, Acts 7. 23. That Luke knew a great part of the Genealogy of Christ, Luk. 3. That Jude knew Satan's striving for Moses Body, Jude v. 9. and the Prophecy of Enoch, vers. 14. That Paul knew Jannes and Jambres, 2 Tim. 3. 8. and the saying of Christ, That it is more blessed to give than to receive, Acts 20. 35.

Such particular Histories or Speeches might be received from hand to hand: but no different Doctrine from that which was written.

Object. 4. The Apostles testimony is objected, 1 Cor. 15. 3. and 2 Thess. 2. 15. Hold the Traditions which you have been taught, whether by Word or our Epistle.

He meaneth the Doctrine he delivered unto them, which is nothing different from that which is contained in the Scriptures.

The Scriptures you say are a Rule and a Line: But are they not (as the Church of Rome imagineth) like a Rule of Lead which may be bowed every way at Men's pleasures?

They are as a Rule of Steel that is firm and changeth not, (Mat. 5 18. Psal. 19. 9.) For seeing they are sufficient to make us wise unto Salvation, (as is before proved); it followeth of necessity, that there is a most certain Rule of Truth for instruction, both of Faith and Works, to be learned out of them, by ordinary means of Reading, Prayer, Study, the Gifts of Tongues, and other Sciences; to which God promiseth the assistance of his Grace, (John 5. 39. James 1. 5.) And this Sword of the Spirit, which is the Word of God written, as the Example of Christ our General Captain showeth, Mat. 4.) is delivered unto us by the Holy Ghost, both to defend our Faith, and to overcome all our Spiritual Enemies, which are the Devil and his Instruments, false Prophets, Heretics, Schismatics, and such like, (Ephes. 6. 12.) Therefore the Holy Scriptures are not as a Nose of Wax, or a Leaden Rule, (as some Papists have blasphemed) that they be so writhed every way by impudent Heretics, but that their folly and madness (as the Apostle saith, 2 Tim. 3. 9.) may be made manifest to all Men.

Are the Scriptures then plain and easy to be understood?

There are some hard things in the Scriptures that have proper relation to the time in which the Scripture was written and uttered, or which are Prophecies of things to be fulfilled hereafter; which if we never understand, we shall be never the worse for the attaining of everlasting Salvation. There are other things in Scripture belonging unto the saving Knowledge of God: All which are dark and difficult unto those whose eyes the God of this World hath blinded, (2 Cor. 4. 4. 2 Pet. 3. 5. John 8. 43.) But unto such as are by Grace enlightened, and made willing to understand, (Psal. 119. 18.) howsoever some things remain obscure (2 Pet. 3. 16.) to exercise their diligence, yet the fundamental Doctrines of Faith, and Precepts of Life, are all plain and perspicuous. For all Doctrine necessary to be known unto Eternal Salvation, is set forth in the Scriptures most clearly and plainly, even to the capacity and understanding of the simple and unlearned: so far is it that the Scriptures should be dangerous to be read of the Lay-folks, as Papists hold.

How prove you this which you have said?

1. Deut. 30. 10, 11, &c. Moses taketh Heaven and Earth to witness, that in the Law which he had written, he hath set forth Life and Death, and that they can make no excuse of difficult of obscurity. This Commandment which I command thee this day, is not hidden from thee, neither is it far off, &c. which Paul also, Rom. 10. 16. applieth to the Gospel.

2. Psalm 19. 8. The Prophet David testifieth, That the Law of the Lord is perfect, converting the Soul; the Testimonies of the Lord are true, giving Wisdom to the Simple: And Psal. 119. 105. Thy Word is a Lamp (or Candle) unto my Feet, and a Light unto my Path.

3. Prov. 1. 4. It giveth subtlety to the simple, to the young Man knowledge and discretion: And Prov. 8. 9. All the words of Wisdom are plain to him that will understand.

4. Isa. 45. 19. The Lord saith, I have not spoken in secret, in a dark place of the Earth; I have not said in vain to the Seed of Jacob, Seek me.

5. 2 Cor. 4. 3. Paul saith; If our Gospel be hid, it is hid to them that are lost, &c.

6. 2 Pet. 1. 19. St. Peter commendeth Christians for taking heed to the Word of the Prophets, as unto a Light that shineth in a dark place, &c.

7. The Scripture is our Father's Letter unto us, and his last Will to show us what Inheritance he leaveth us. But Friends write Letters, and Fathers their Wills, plain.

8. It were to accuse God of Cruelty, or desire of Man's Destruction, to say that he should make the means of their Salvation hurtful unto them.

9. Women and Children have read the Scriptures. In 2 Tim. 3. 15. St. Paul affirmeth Timothy was nourished up in the Scriptures from his Infancy: Namely, by his Grandmother Lois, and his Mother Eunice; whom the same Apostle commendeth, chap. 1. 5. If little Children are capable of the Scriptures by the small understanding they have, and less judgment: there is none so gross (which hath the understanding of a Man) but may profit by it, coming in the fear of God, and invocation of his Name.

But here the Papists have many things to object against you, to prove that the Scriptures are dark and hard to be understood: And,

Object. 1. First, That the Matters contained in them are Divine, High, and beyond man's Reason; as the Trinity, the Creation of nothing, &c.
These Matters indeed are above Human Reason: and therefore are we to bring Faith to believe them, not human Reason to comprehend them. But they are delivered in Scripture in as plain terms as such Matter can be.

Object. 2. Peter saith, That some things in Paul's Epistles are hard, and wrested by unlearned and unstable Men, (2 Pet. 3. 16.)
First, He saith not that all Paul's Epistles are hard, but something in them; which we grant. Secondly, They are the wicked and unsettled in knowledge that wrest them, as Gluttons and Drunkards abuse Meat and Drink.

Object. 3. If the Scriptures were not dark, what need so many Commentaries upon them? And why are they so full of Parables and Allegories as they are?
The whole Doctrine of Salvation is to be found so plain, that it needeth no Commentary. And Commentaries are for other Places that are dark; and also to make more large use of Scripture than a new beginner can make of himself; which we see necessary in all Human Arts and Sciences. Further, though the Speech of Scripture seem hard at first, yet by custom it becometh easy: as Reading does to Children.

Object. 4. The Godly Eunuch saith, he could not understand the Scripture without an Interpreter, Acts 8. 31.
Though he understood not some dark places, yet that hindered him not from reading plainer places.

Object. 5. The multitude of Learned Men that fall into Heresies, which they labor to confirm by Scripture, proveth that the Scripture is dark.
It is their naughty hearts that come not with an humble and godly Affection that maketh them do so.

Object. 6. But we see by experience that there are many that daily read the Scriptures, and yet understand not the thousandth part of them.
They read them not with Care and Conscience, with Prayer and Study; but like the Women that are always learning, and never come to the knowledge of the Truth, 2 Tim. 3. 7.

Object. 7. If the Scriptures be so plain and perspicuous; what need is there then of an Interpreter?
First, To unfold obscure places, (Acts 8. 31.) Secondly, To inculcate and apply plain Texts, (2 Pet. 1. 12, 13. 1 Cor. 14. 3.)

Why did God leave some places obscure in the Scriptures?
First, That we might know that the understanding of God's Word is the Gift of God; and therefore might beg it of him by continual Prayer. Second, Lest we should flatter our own wits too much, if all things could presently be understood by us. Third, That the Word, for the high and heavenly Mysteries contained therein, might be accounted of; which for the plainness possibly might be less esteemed. Fourth, That profane Dogs might be driven away from these Holy Mysteries; which are Pearls prized highly by the Elect alone, (Mat. 13. 45.) but would be trodden under-foot by Swine, (Mat. 7. 6.) Fifth, That we might be stirred up to a more diligent search of the same. Sixth, That we might esteem more of the Ministry, which God hath placed in the Church, that by the means thereof we might profit in the knowledge of these Mysteries.

What assurance may be had of the right understanding the Holy Scriptures?
For the words, it is to be had out of the Original Text, or Translations of the same: for the sense or meaning, only out of the Scriptures themselves, (Nehem. 8. 8.) which by places plain and evident, do express whatsoever is obscure and hard touching Matters necessary to eternal Salvation.

Why must the interpretation of words be had out of the original Languages?
Because in them only the Scriptures are, for the Letter, to be held authentic. And as the Water is most pure in the Fountain or Spring thereof: so the right understanding of the words of the Holy Scriptures is most certain in the Original Tongues of Hebrew and Greek, in which they were first written and delivered to the Church, out of which Languages they must be truly translated for the understanding of them that have not the knowledge of those Tongues.

What gather you from hence?
That all Translations are to be judged, examined, and reformed according to the Text of the Ancient Hebrew and Original Chaldee, in which the Old Testament was penned, and the Greek Text, in which the New Testament was written. And consequently that the vulgar Latin Translation, approved by the Tridentine Council for the only Authentic Text, is no further to be received of true Christians, than it agreeth with the Original of the Hebrew and Greek Text.

But what say you of the Greek Translation of the Old Testament, commonly called the Septuagint, approved by the Apostles themselves?
The same that we say of other Translations. For although the Apostles used that Translation, which was commonly received and read among the Gentiles and Jews that dwelt amongst them, where it differed not in sense from the true Hebrew: yet where it differed from it, they left it; as by many Examples may be confirmed, (*Vide Hieronym. Prolog. in Mat.*).

How can the certain understanding of the Scriptures be taken out of the Original Tongues; considering the difference of Reading, which is in divers Copies both of Hebrew and Greek; as also the difficulty of some Words and Phrases upon which the best Translators cannot agree?
Although in the Hebrew Copies there hath been observed by the Masorites some very few differences of Words, by similitude of Letters and Points; and by the Learned in the Greek Tongue there are like diversities of Reading noted in the Greek Text of the New Testament, which came by fault of Writers: yet in most by circumstance of the place, and conference of other places, the true reading may be discerned. And albeit in all it cannot, nor the Translator in all places determine the true Interpretation; yet this diversity or difficulty can make no difference or uncertainty in the sum and substance of Christian Religion; because the Ten Commandments, and the principal Texts of Scripture on which the Articles of our Faith are grounded, the Sacraments instituted, the Form of Prayer taught, (which contain the sum or substance of Christian Religion) are without all such diversity of Reading, or difficulty of Translating so plainly set down, and so precisely translated by consent of all Learned Men in the Tongues, that no Man can make any doubt of them, or pick any quarrel against them.

Why must the true sense or meaning of the Scriptures be learned out of the Scriptures themselves?
Because the Spirit of God alone is the certain Interpreter of his Word, written by his Spirit. For no Man knoweth the Things pertaining to God, but the Spirit of God, 1 Cor. 2. 11. And no Prophecy of Scripture is of Man's own Interpretation: For Prophecy was not brought by the Will of Man, but the Holy Men of God spake as they were led by the Holy Ghost, 2 Pet. 1. 20, 21. The Interpretation therefore must be by the same Spirit by which the Scripture was written: of which Spirit we have no certainty upon any Man's Credit, but only so far forth as his Saying may be confirmed by the Holy Scripture.

What gather you from hence?
That no Interpretation of Holy Fathers, Popes, Councils, Custom or Practice of the Church, either contrary to the manifest words of the Scripture, or containing Matters which cannot necessarily be proved out of the Scriptures, are to be received as an undoubted Truth.

How then is Scripture to be interpreted by Scripture?
According to the Analogy of Faith, (Rom. 12. 6.) and the scope and circumstances of the present place; and conference of other plain and evident places, by which all such as are obscure and hard to be understood, ought to be interpreted. For there is no

First Head

Matter necessary to eternal Life, which is not plainly and sufficiently set forth in many places of Scripture: by which other places that are abused by the Devil or his Ministers, may be interpreted. As our Savior Christ giveth us Example, Mat. 4. 6, 7. when the Devil abused the Text of Scripture, Psal. 91. 11. declaring that this place must be so understood as it may agree with that most evident and express Commandment written in Deut. 6. 16. Thou shalt not tempt the Lord thy God.

What are the special Uses of the Scriptures rightly understood?
Two. First, To teach Doctrine, by laying out the Truth, and confuting Errors. Second, To exhort out of it, by stirring us to good, and turning us back from evil. Whereunto belong those four Uses mentioned by the Apostle in 2 Tim. 3. 16. two whereof are Theoretical, pertaining to the information of our Judgment in matters of Doctrine; viz. First, Teaching of Truth: Secondly, Reproving or Convincing of Errors. Two are practical, pertaining to the direction of our Life and Actions; viz. First, Reformation or Correction of Vice: under which is comprehended Admonition. Secondly, Instruction, or Direction to good Life: under which is comprehended Exhortation and Consolation, which is a special Instruction to Patience in Adversities; (Rom. 15. 4.)

What Persons are meet to Read or Hear the Scriptures?
The Holy Scriptures are reverently and profitably to be read and heard of all sorts and degrees of Men and Women: and therefore to be truly translated out of the Original Tongues into the Language of every Nation which desireth to know them. For the Lay people as well as the Learned must read the Scriptures, or hear them read, both privately and openly, so as they may receive profit by them: and consequently in a Tongue they understand, (1 Cor. 14.)

How do you prove that the Scriptures ought to be read and heard of all sorts of People?
First, Deut. 31. 11, 12. Moses commandeth the Book of the Law to be read unto all the Children of Israel, Men, Women, Children, and Strangers that dwelt amongst them; that they might thereby learn to fear the Lord their God, and diligently to observe all the words of the Law.

Second, Joshua 8. 35. There was not a word of all that Moses commanded which Joshua read not before all the Congregation of Israel, with the Women and the little Ones, and the Strangers that were conversant among them. So like wise did Josiah, (2 Kings 23. 2. and 2 Chron. 34. 30) and Ezra. (Nehem. 8. 2, 3.)

Third, Psal. 1. 2. David showeth this to be the property of a Godly Man, and pronounceth him to be happy, whose delight is in the Law of the Lord, and studieth therein day and night.

Fourth, Mat. 22. 29. Our Savior teacheth, that ignorance of Scriptures is the Mother of Error; not the Mother of Devotion, as Papists have affirmed.
Fifth, John 5. 39. Christ commandeth all Men that seek eternal Life in him, to search the Scriptures. Search the Scriptures, for in them ye think to have eternal Life, &c.

Sixth, Acts 17. 11. The Bereans are commended for searching the Scriptures.
Seventh, 2 Tim. 3. 15. The Apostle Paul approved in Timothy, that he had learned the Holy Scriptures from a young Child.

Eighth, 2 Pet. 1. 19. The Apostle Peter commendeth the Faithful for taking heed to the Scripture of the Prophets.

Ninth, Rev. 1. 3. Blessed is he that readeth, and they that hear the Word of this Prophecy.

Tenth, Col. 3. 16. Let the Word of Christ dwell in you richly in all Wisdom.

Eleventh, Rom. 15. 4. Whatsoever things were written aforetime, were written for our Learning, that we through patience and comfort of the Scriptures might have hope. If the Scriptures be written for our Learning, they are necessarily to be read by us.

Twelfth, Rom. 7. 7. Paul saith, He knew not sin but by the Law. But the knowledge of sin is necessary for all that will repent and be saved; therefore also is the knowledge of the Law necessary.

Thirteenth, Luke saith, That he wrote the Gospel to Theophilus, that he might know the certainty of those things, which before he was catechized in, Luke 1. 4. But every one ought to labor to be most certain of their Salvation, &c.

Divers things are opposed by the Adversaries against the necessity of the Scriptures, and the reading of them by all sorts: as first, That there were many Believers among the Gentiles in the time of the Old Testament, who yet wanted the Scripture, (which was kept in Jury) as Job and his Friends.
Those, if any such were after the Law, (for Job was before) were bound to have the Scripture when it was delivered by God: And the Eunuch had it and read it, Acts 8. 28.

Object. 2. The Book of the Law was lost for many years; as appeareth by 2 King. 22. 1. and yet the Church was then: Therefore it may want it.
The loss of that Book does argue rather the carelessness of the Priests in not keeping it, and the sins of the People, in that God for a time deprived them of it.

Object. 3. The Church of Christians many years after Christ wanted the Scripture of the New Testament, and contented themselves with bare teaching.
First, Though the Church for certain years then had not the New, yet they had the Old. Second, There passed not many years before the Gospels and the Epistles of the Apostles were written: And in the mean time their Heavenly Doctrine, inspired from God, sufficed till they wrote.

Object. 4. There are many poor Country men, as Plough men and Shepherds, which never learned to read; which yet are saved, though they never read Scripture.
They ought to have learned to read: And being not able to read, yet they might hear the Scriptures read by others.

Object. 5. If all ought to read Scripture, then should they understand Hebrew and Greek, wherein Scripture was written.
It were happy if they could understand the Hebrew and Greek; but howsoever, they may read Translations.

Will it not follow hereof, that Preaching and Expounding of the Scriptures may be neglected as unnecessary?
No. For God hath appointed not only Reading, but also Preaching of his Word; especially to apply it to the use of all sorts of Men to their eternal Salvation, Rom. 10. 13, &c. So were the Prophets Interpreters of the Law, (as is before showed.) The Scribes and Pharisees taught in the Chair of Moses, Mat. 23. 2. The Eunuch could not understand the Prophecy of Isaiah without an Interpreter, Acts 8. 31. The Ministry of the Word therefore is necessary, as the ordinary means unto Salvation, 1 Tim. 4. 16. and the People by reading and hearing of the Scriptures are better prepared to receive profit by Preaching, not discharged from hearing the Preacher.

Second Head

What is the sum of all that hath been delivered hitherto?
That we should labor for a due knowledge of the True God, that we may know what we worship, and worship what we know, (1 Chron. 28. 9. Joh. 4. 22. and 17. 3.) That this knowledge of God is to be had partly by his Works, namely, so much as may serve to convince Man, and make him inexcusable, (Rom. 1. 19, 20. Acts 14. 15.) but most sufficiently by his Word contained in the Holy Scriptures, which therefore are called his Testimonies, (Psalm 119. 14.) because they testify of God (John 5. 39.) what he is, and how he will be served of us. Lastly, That forasmuch as all that is written in the Word of God, is written for our instruction and learning, (Rom. 15. 4.) therefore we (being prepared by true Prayer, sanctified with Faith, and seasoned with the Spirit of Sobriety and Humility) may safely learn so much as is revealed in the Scriptures for our profiting in the knowledge of God.

[2ND HEAD.]

What is the first Point of Religion that we are taught in the Scriptures?
That there is a God.

Why do you make this the first Point?
Because the Scripture saith, He that cometh to God, must believe that he is, Heb. 11. 6.

Have any called this into question at any time?
Yea, so saith the Prophet David: but he showeth also that it was by wicked, proud, and foolish Men, whose lives were nothing else but abomination and corruption, (Psal. 10. 4. and 14. 1.)

What pretence of Reason might they have for this wicked imagination?
Because no Man ever saw God yet: By which foolish Argument they might deny also that there is any Wind, or that Man hath a Soul. For no Man yet ever saw them.

But how come you to persuade your self that there is such a God?
Beside infinite Testimonies of the Scriptures, as Gen. 1. 1. Psal. 19. 1, &c. the common consent of all Nations approveth this Truth, who rather worship any God or Gods, than none at all. And though Man by Nature does desire to be exalted, and in respect of himself despiseth all other Creatures, as Wood and Stone: yet when a piece of Wood is framed out like a Man, and set in the Temple, and Man conceiveth an Opinion that it is a God, he falleth down and worshippeth it, (Isa. 44. 15, 17.)

How then cometh it to pass that the Wicked say there is no God? (Psal. 14. 1.)
First, Though upon a sudden passion they may seem to say so, as the Devil labors to tempt them; yet their very Conscience after does check them. Secondly, They deny rather God's Providence, than his Being; as appeareth by Psal. 10. 4, 11.

What other Reasons have you to prove that there is a God?
God's Works of Creation and Providence both ordinary and extraordinary.

1. For first, the glorious frame of the World, the Heavens, and the Earth, and the Sea, and all that is in them, must needs argue that their Maker was God, (Rom. 1. 19, 20. Acts 14. 17. Zech. 12. 1.) it being evident that the World could not be made by the Creatures that are in it, neither could it make it self. As when a Man comes into a strange Country, and sees fair and sumptuous Buildings, and finds no Body there but Birds or Beasts; he will not imagine that either Birds or Beasts reared those Buildings, but he presently conceives that some Man either are or have been there.

2. The Creation of the Soul of Men, endued with Reason and Conscience, does specially prove the same, Zech. 12. 1.

3. The preserving of things created, together with the wonderful and orderly Government of the World, Day and Night, Summer and Winter, &c. manifestly convince the same. For Example: Bread is no better in it self than Earth; yet Man is preserved by Bread, and if he eat Earth, he dieth. The reason whereof must be attributed to the Blessing of God, giving to the one force and power to nourish more than to the other.

4. By the Order of Causes, even the Heathen Men have found out that there must be a God; seeing that of every Effect there must be a Cause, until we come to the first Cause, which is the Universal Cause of the Being of all Things, and is caused of none.

5. If we shall observe in God's Works an infinite Multitude, a wonderful Variety, (Psal. 104. 24.) as amongst so many millions of Men, never an one like another in the compass of the Face; a most constant order, a seemly agreement, and an endless continuance or pleasant intercourse of things coming and going, and what exceeding Majesty is in them, we must needs attribute these things to a God.

6. The Consciences of Wicked Men after sin are perplexed with fear of being punished by some supreme Judge, who disliketh and detesteth dishonest things, and exerciseth Judgment upon the Mind: Which maketh the most ungodly Miscreants refuse to acknowledge and tremble at him, &c. (Rom. 2. 15. Isa. 33. 14. and 57. 20, 21. and 66. 24. Psal. 14. 5. and 53. 5.) For a Man that commits any Sin, as Murder, Fornication, Adultery, Blasphemy, &c. albeit he conceal the Matter never so close that no Man living know of it; yet oftentimes he hath a griping in his Conscience, and feels the very flashing of Hellfire: Which is a strong reason to show that there is a God, before whose Judgment Seat he must answer for this Facts

7. There is a Devil that suggesteth Temptations against God into the Minds of Men, and sometimes also really possesseth their Bodies. Which is a sufficient Argument to prove that there is a God.

8. The death of the Wicked, with God's apparent Judgments upon them, (besides the terror of their Conscience (and the dreadful punishment executed even in this World upon many Atheists that have labored to deny it, prove that there is a God. This is David's Argument, Psal. 9. 16. and 58. 10, 11.

9. The same appeareth by the rewards of the Godly; and the merciful preservation of those that trust in God, above and against natural means.

10. By the wonderful Miracles which God hath wrought for his Church.

11. By the foretelling of things to come so many thousand years before they were accomplished.

12. By the divers Revelations he hath made of himself to Men: As to Adam, Noah, Moses, &c.

This ground being now laid, that there is a God: What does Christian Religion teach us concerning him?
It informeth us, first, Concerning his Nature; secondly, Concerning his Kingdom. And that respectively, as they have relation one to the other, (Acts 8. 12. and 28. 23.)

Second Head

What is to be known concerning his Nature?
First, What his Essence is; and secondly, To whom or what Persons it does belong. In the first he is considered in his Unity; in the second, in Trinity. The former whereof in the Hebrew Tongue is noted by the singular name of Jehovah, betokening the simplicity of Essence: The latter by the plural term of Elohim, importing a distinction of Persons in the Godhead.

Can we understand what the Essence of God is?
Very imperfectly. For all Nature is not able to teach us what God is in himself, neither can Man in Nature comprehend him, Job 36. 26. 1 Tim. 6. 16.

Why is not all Nature able to teach us what God is?
Because no Work is able perfectly to express the Worker thereof. But all Nature is a thing wrought by God; therefore it cannot perfectly teach us what God is.

How prove you that Man cannot comprehend him?
1. The less cannot comprehend the greater. But every Man is less than God; therefore no Man can comprehend God. 2. We cannot know the Things created; much less can we know the Creator. As for Example; We know that there are Angels, and that every Man hath a Soul; but what manner of things they are we know not. 3. The Scripture saith, The Judgments of God are past finding out, Rom. 11. 33. therefore much more is God himself past finding out. And the Joys of Heaven are unspeakable: Much more therefore is God himself unspeakable.

How then can he be known of us, being Incomprehensible?
Though his Substance be past finding out of Man or Angels, yet may he be known by his Properties and Actions, (Amos 4 13.) and we may conceive of him by his Name, (Exod. 33. 19. and 34. 5, 6. Psal. 145. 1, 2, &c.) expressing what an one he is to us; though we are not able to know him according to the excellency of his Glorious Nature, only known unto himself, (Judg. 13. 18.) therefore he said to Moses, Exod. 33. 20. My Face, that is the Glory of my Majesty, (he does not say, thou might not, or thou shalt not, but) thou canst not see; for there shall no Man see me, and live. But thou shalt see my back parts, (ver. 23.) that is, some small measure of my Glory, so far as thou art able to comprehend it. And even as Princes have their Secrets, whereunto all their Subjects are not made privy, neither is it lawful for them to search into them; and yet do they so far forth publish their Commandments as is profitable for them to know: So the Prince of all Princes hath his Secrets, unto which we are not privy, and into which we may not search; yet he hath so far revealed himself unto us (by his Works and Word) as is necessary and profitable for us to know, Deut. 29. 29.

What does the Scripture teach us concerning the Name of God?
Exod. 3. 13. Moses asketh this question of God; Behold, when I shall come unto the Children of Israel, and shall say unto them, The God of your Fathers hath sent me unto you: If they say unto me, What is his Name? What shall I say unto them? Whereunto God returneth this Answer in the next verse: I AM THAT I AM: Thus shalt thou say unto the Children of Israel, I AM hath sent me unto you.

What learn you out of Moses his Question?
First, That we be careful to be instructed in all things concerning our Calling, thereby to be able to answer all Doubts that may be moved. Secondly, That asking any thing concerning God, as of his Name or Nature, we must ask it of himself; who because now he speaketh not but by his Ministers, Interpreters of the Scriptures, (2 Cor. 5. 20. Hos. 12. 10.) we must have our recourse unto them.

What learn you out of God's Answer?
That the proper Name of God is, I am that I am; or (as the Hebrew soundeth) I will be what I will be; the Hebrews using the future time for the present, as that which noteth a continuance.

What is meant by these words?
Hereby is set forth the manner of the Being or Essence of God, far otherwise than the proper Names of Men; which declare either nothing of their Nature and Being, or else not the whole and full thereof.

Is there nothing of God to be known besides his Name?
Nothing as touching his Being, falling under our weak and shallow capacity.

What Names of God in the Scripture are derived from these words?
Two; the Name of Jehovah, and the Name Jah: Both which being drawn from this description of God, do set forth his Essence and Being. Teaching us, that his Eternal and Almighty Being (which no Creature is able to conceive) dependeth of no other Cause, but standeth of himself.

How is God only said to Be, seeing the Creatures have their Being also?
God is said only to Be, because he only is of himself: All other things have their Being of him, so that in comparison nothing had a Being but God. Therefore the Prophet saith, Isa 40. 17. that all Nations before him are nothing, yea, to him less than nothing: And if Men be nothing, for whom the World was made, how much more are all other Creatures in Heaven and Earth nothing before him, and to him less than nothing?

Can you from hence define what God is?
He must have the Art and Logic of God himself, that must give a perfect definition of God: But he may in such sort be described, as he may be discerned from all false Gods and all Creatures whatsoever.

Why can there no perfect definition of God be given?
Forasmuch as God is in himself Eternal, Infinite, and Incomprehensible, the first Cause of all Causes and Effects, there can no definition be given of him. Seeing every Definition is an Explication of the Nature of the Thing defined, by words expressing the material and formal cause thereof. But of the first Cause there can be no Causes; therefore no words to express them. For these over-reaching terms of Thing, Being, Somewhat, Nature, &c. which seem to contain the word God, as well as all other things created by him, do not express any material cause of God: Neither do they contain these words God and Creature, as the general does his Specials or Kinds, but are spoken of them equivocally; so that the term only, and not the definition of the term, does agree to them. For in the Kinds or specials of one general, there is no priority of Nature, as is between the Cause and Effect.

Neither is this word Cause affirmed of God, but as a term of the Art of Logic. And if Substance be that which upholdeth Accidents, as Aristotle teacheth, neither may God be called a Substance, for that in him are no Accidents. But if Substance be taken generally for a Being, it may be said that God is a Substance; yet none otherwise than as he is a Being, Thing, Nature, &c. And if there be no material Cause, there can be no formal Cause of God. For although we read in the Scripture the form of God, Phil. 2. 6. yet the form is not there taken for any Cause of God; but either for that which God indeed is, or for that Glory which of right belongeth unto him. For in speaking of God, whom no words of Man are able to express, the Holy Ghost oftentimes condescending to the weakness of our Understanding, useth such terms, as being known to Men do signify something that is like to that, which God indeed is of himself; that we may understand so much as is expedient for us to know of him.

Whence may the Description of God be taken?
From the things whereby he does manifest himself (called in Scripture his Name, Psal. 145. 1, 2, 3, &c.) among which the chief principal are his Attributes or Properties.

What are the Properties or Attributes of God?
They are essential Faculties of God, according to the diverse manner of his working, 1 Pet. 3. 12. 1 John 4. 16. Psal. 145.

Are they communicable with the Creatures?
No. Yet of some of them there are some shadows and glimpses in Men and Angels, (as Wisdom, Holiness, Justice, Mercy, &c.) other some are so peculiar to the Divine Essence, that the like of them are not to be found in the Creatures, as Simpleness, Infiniteness, Eternity, &c.

How may these Properties be considered?
They may be considered either in themselves as they are Essential, or in their Works or Effects, which are all perfect, either as they be Absolute, or as they be Actual. Absolute in himself, by which he is able to show them more than ever he will, (as he is able to do more than ever he will do, Mat. 3. 9. God is able of Stones to raise Children unto Abraham.) Actual, is that which he showeth in the Creation and Government of the World, (as Psal. 135. 7. All things that he will, he does, &c.) Again, something we may conceive of his Essence affirmatively, knowing that all Perfections which we apprehend must be ascribed unto God, and that after a more excellent manner than can be apprehended: As that he is in himself, by himself, and of himself; that he is One, True, Good and Holy. But much more by denial, or by removing all Imperfections whatsoever: As of Composition, by the titles of Simple, Spiritual and Incorporeal; of all circumscription of Time, by the title of Eternal; of all bounds of Place, by that of Infinite; of all possibility of Motion, by those titles of Unchangeable, Incorruptible, and such like.

What Description can you make of God by these Properties?
God is a Spirit Eternal. Or more fully: God is a Spiritual Substance, having his Being of himself, infinitely Great and Good, John 4. 24. and 8. 58. Exod. 3. 14. and 34. 6, 7. Psal. 145. 3, 8, 9.

What learn you hence?
To acknowledge both my Being and Well-being from him, and from him alone, Acts 17. 28. 1 Cor. 10. 30. Ephes. 2. 10.

What mean you when you say, That God is a Substance?
God is such a Thing as hath a being in himself, of himself, and which giveth a being to all other things.

What mean you by that addition of himself?
It hath a secret opposition to all Creatures which have a Being, but not of themselves: Whereas God alone is he, in whom we live, and move, and have our Being, Acts 17. 28. which proveth that he alone hath his Being of himself.

How many things conceive you of God, when you say that he is a Spirit?
Six things. First, That he is a Living Substance. Secondly, That he is Incorruptible. Thirdly, That he is Incorporeal; without Body, Flesh, Blood, or Bones. For a Spirit hath no such Matter, Luke 24. 39. Fourthly, That he is Invisible, i.e. he hath not been seen

with any mortal eye, neither can any Man possibly see him. Fifthly, That he is Intangible, not felt. Sixthly, That he is Indivisible, i.e. he cannot be divided.

How prove you that God is Invisible, and not to be seen with carnal Eyes?
That no Man hath seen God, is plainly set down, 1 John 4. 12. That no Man can see God, is as plainly proved, Ex. 33. 20. 1 Tim. 6. 16. and beside Scripture, the same is also manifest by Reason. For we cannot see our own Souls, which are ten thousand times a more gross substance than God: much less can we see God, which is a most pure and spiritual Substance.

Object. 1. We read, Gen. 18. 1. that God appeared to Abraham: And, Deut. 5. 24. that he showed himself to the Israelites.
God gave them indeed some outward sights, whereby they might be certain of his Presence; and therefore it is said that the Lord appeared unto them, but his Substance or Essence they saw not. For to know God perfectly, is proper to God only, John 6. 46.

Object. We read, Gen. 1. 26. that Man was made according to the Image of God. It would seem therefore that God is Corporeal and Visible, as Man is.
The Image of God consisteth not in the Shape and Figure of the Body, but in the Mind and Integrity of Nature, or (as the Scripture saith) in Wisdom, Righteousness and Holiness, Col. 3. 10. Ephes. 4. 24.

Object. Why then does the Scripture attribute unto him Hands, Feet, &c?
The Scripture so speaketh of him as we are able to conceive: And therefore in these and such-like Speeches, humbleth it self to our Capacity, attributing Members unto God to signify the like Actions in him.

To what use serveth this Doctrine, That God is a Spirit?
It teacheth us, first, To worship him in Spirit and in Truth, John 4. 23, 24. Secondly, To drive away all fond Imaginations and gross Conceits of God out of our Hearts, and all Pictures and Similitudes of God out of our Sights: That we frame not any Image of him in our Minds, as ignorant Folks do, who think him to be an Old Man sitting in Heaven, &c. For seeing that God was never seen, whereunto shall he be resembled? Moses urged this Point hard and often to the Israelites; saying, Deut. 4. 12. Ye heard the Voice, but saw no Similitude. And addeth, vers. 15. Take ye therefore good heed unto yourselves: (He saith not only, Take heed; but, Take good heed: and, Therefore take good heed): For (saith he again) ye saw no manner of Similitude on the day that the Lord spake unto you in Horeb, out of the midst of the Fire. Then he cometh in the next four Verses to the thing that they must therefore take heed of: That ye corrupt not yourselves, and make you a graven Image, the Similitude of any Figure, the Likeness of Male or Female, &c. See also Rom. 1. 23.

How may the Attributes or Properties of God be distinguished?
Some do concern the Perfection of his Essence, some his Life; which in God be one and the same thing, distinguished only for our Capacity.

What call you the Perfection of God's Essence?
His absolute Constitution, by which he is wholly complete within himself; and consequently needeth nothing without himself, but alone sufficeth himself, having all things from himself and in himself. Or thus: Perfection is an essential property in God, whereby whatsoever is in God is perfect, Gen. 17. 1. Psal. 16. 2. and 50. 12. Rom. 11. 35, 36.

What ariseth from hence?
All Felicity and Happiness: All endless Bliss and Glory.

Second Head

What is the Felicity of God?
It is the Property of God, whereby he hath all fullness of delight and contentment in himself.

What learn you from the Perfection of God?
That he is to seek his own Glory, and not the Glory of any, in all that he willeth or willeth not, does or leaveth undone.

What gather you thereof?
They are confuted that think God is moved to Will or Nill things in respect of the Creatures; as Men that seeing a miserable Man are moved to pity: whereas God of himself, and in himself, is moved to save or reject, (we speak here of Reprobation, not of Condemnation) to receive some, and to cast away others.

What else?
That all which he does is perfect, howsoever he deal with us.

Wherein does the Perfection of God's Essence principally consist?
In Simpleness, (or Singleness) and Infiniteness.

Why are these two counted the principal Properties of God?
Because they are not only incommunicable themselves, whereas those which concern the Life of God have some resemblance in the Creature) but also make all other Properties of God incommunicable.

What is Simpleness or Singleness in God?
It is an essential Property in God, whereby every thing that is in God is God himself. Therefore without parts, mixture or composition, Invisible, Impassible, all Essence: Whence he is not called only Holy, but Holiness; not only Just, but Justice, &c. Exod. 33. 19, 20.

What gather you from hence?
First, That God hath no Qualities nor Adjuncts in him, as the Creatures have: But such as are attributed unto him for our Capacity, when it is his Nature this is such, 1 John 1. 5. John 5. 26. with John 14. 6. Secondly, That God's Essence or Substance cannot be augmented or diminished, that his Nature and Will cannot be changed; but he remaineth constant, without shadow of change, and will be always such as he hath been from all eternity, Numb. 23. 19. James 1. 17. Psal. 33. 11. Isa. 46. 10.

By what light of Reason may it be proved, that God is thus unchangeable?
Whatsoever is changed, must needs be changed either to the worse or to the better, or into a state equal with the former. But God cannot be changed from the better to the worse; for so he should become of perfect imperfect, And to exchange from the worse to the better, it is impossible also: For then he should have been imperfect before. Lastly, If he should alter from an equal condition to an equal, so that he should forego some good which before he had, and assume some other which before he had not; both before and after this change he should be imperfect, being destitute of some part of that good which appertained unto him, which to affirm is high blasphemy.

But divers things are objected against that immutability of God's Nature and Will: As, first, that in the Mystery of the Incarnation, God was made Man, which before he was not.
That was done, not by any conversion or change of the Divinity, but by the assumption of the Humanity.

Object. 2. If God cannot change his Mind; why is it said he repented that he made Man?
The Repentance attributed so often to God in the Scriptures, signifieth no mutation in God's Nature; but in his Actions immutably decreed from all Eternity. And the Scripture in this speaketh after our manner, that we may better understand what is the Nature of God against sin.

Declare how that is.
When we are grieved with any thing, we do then repent us that ever we did that thing for which we are grieved: And so is God said to repent him that ever he made Man, with whom he was angry; to show that he was sincere and highly displeased with the evil ways of Mankind.

Did not God then change his Mind when he drowned the World?
No. But then he did execute that which from everlasting he had decreed.

Object. 3. It is said, Exod. 32. 14. The Lord changed his Mind from the evil which he threatened to his People.
That is still after the manner of Men. For Man, because he is but Man, cannot speak unto God but as a Man. And therefore God speaks again unto Man like a Man, because else Man should not understand what God is, nor what is his Will.

Show me one Example hereof in the Scripture.
When Moses prayed for the Israelites, he used many Reasons to persuade the Lord, (but especially to confirm his own hope): At the last he said thus; Turn from thy fierce Wrath, and change thy Mind from this evil towards thy People. Thus did Moses speak to God, and if he had spoken to a mortal Man he could have said no more nor no less; for Man's Speech is according to his Capacity, and both are limited, and beyond himself he cannot go. Therefore when he showeth what the Lord did, he saith, he changed his Mind: Which was as much as he could conceive of God concerning that Matter. Thus we speak, as well as we can, yet in a broken and imperfect speech to God; as little Children speak to their Nurses: And Almighty God speaks in a broken and imperfect Language to us again for our weakness and understandings sake, as the Nurse does to the Child. For if the Nurse should speak so perfectly to the Child, as she could to one of greater capacity, the Child would not understand her: So if God should speak unto us as he could, and according to his own Nature, we were never able to understand him, nor conceive his meaning.

Object. 4. The Promises and Threatenings of God are not always fulfilled; therefore it seemeth that sometimes he changeth his Mind.
His Promises are made with a condition of Faith and Obedience, Deut. 28. 13. and his Threatenings with an exception of Conversion and Repentance, Psal. 7. 12.

What use may we make of this Doctrine of the Simpleness and Immutability of God's Nature?
First, It ministreth comfort unto the Faithful, for strength of their weak Faith: Whilst they consider that the Mercy and Clemency of God is in all perfection, and without change unto them. For this is the Foundation of our Hope and Comfort in this Life, That he does not now love and now hate; but whom he loveth, to the end he loveth them, John 13. 1.

Secondly, It giveth matter of terror unto the wicked, whilst they consider his Wrath and Severity against them to be in most full measure; the one and the other being God himself. It may also make us fear to offend him, because all his Threatenings are unchangeable except we repent.

What is Infiniteness?
It is an essential property of God, whereby all things in his Essence are signified to be without Measure and Quantity: And consequently, that the Substance of God, his Power and his Wisdom, and whatsoever is in him, is incomprehensible, Psal. 139. 7. 1 Kings 8. 27. Rom. 11. 33.

Wherein does the Infiniteness of God's Essence especially consist?
In Immensity or exceeding Greatness, and Eternity or Everlastingness.

What is his Immensity or exceeding Greatness?
It is an essential Property in God, whereby he containeth all things, and is contained of nothing, that either is or may be imagined: And consequently is free from increasing or decreasing, and all comprehension of place; being present every-where, both within and without the World, and filling all places wholly at all times with his presence. For he is in all places, in Heaven and in Earth, and the Sea and Hell, and all at one time; neither can he be contained in any compass of place, (as is a Man or Angel, or any other Creature) but he is in all places, and filleth all places at once, and is beyond all compass of place that we can imagine, 1 Kings 8. 27. Psal. 139. 7. and 145. 3. Isa. 66. 1. and 40. 12. Jer. 23. 24.

Is God every-where bodily?
No. For he hath no Body.

Is God every-where in speculation only?
No. For he worketh in every thing which he beholdeth.

How then is he every-where?
He is every-where essentially. For his Essence is not contained in any place, because he is incomprehensible.

Does he not remove himself from place to place?
He filleth Heaven and Earth, and all places, therefore he can neither depart from any Place, nor be absent from any place.

Is he not half in one half of the World, and half in the other half of the World?
No. But as the whole Soul is wholly in every part of the Body, so God is whole and wholly in every part of the World.

Object. 1. If God be every-where essentially, then he is in the most filthy Sink and Puddle.
1. It is no abasing of the Glory of his Majesty, to say that he is there: No more than it is to the Sun, whose Beams and Light are there; or to a Physician to be amongst those that are sick. 2. All the Creatures of God in themselves are exceeding good: And when he is in the most filthy Sink in the World, he is not in a more filthy place than ourselves, whether we be sick or sound. 3. They are his Workmanship; and it is no abasement of the Workmaster to be amongst his Works.

Object. 2. If God be every-where; why is it said he dwelleth in the Heavens? Psal. 2. 4.
Because his Glory and Majesty, which is every-where alike, shineth most perspicuously and visibly in Heaven.

Object. 3. It is said, Numb. 14. 42. he is not amongst the wicked.
He is not amongst them with his grace and favor, to protect and defend them: but otherwise by his Power and Providence he is amongst them, to bridle their raging

Affections, to plague their furious Obstinacy, and to dispose of their desperate Attempts to his own Glory and the good of his People.

Object. 4. *If God be every-where at the same instant of time, how is he said to be sometimes nearer, further off? Isa. 55. 6.*
God is said to be near unto us, when by his Word or any other Means he offereth us grace and favor; and when he heareth and granteth our Prayers, as Moses saith, Deut. 4. 7. What Nation is there so great, who hath God so nigh unto them, as the Lord God is in all things that we call upon him for?

Object. 5. *If God be in Hell, then all Goodness is there: for he is all Goodness; and so consequently there is no want of joy in the Damned.*
The Damned in Hell feel no part of his Goodness, that is, of his Mercy and loving Favor, but of his Power and Justice. So that God is in Hell, by his Power, and in his Wrath.

To what purpose and use serveth this Doctrine of Immensity, or infinite Greatness of God?
The consideration thereof should put us in mind, that nothing which is vile and base should be offered unto God in the worship of him. Secondly, It serveth to drive all gross and idolatrous conceits of God out of our Minds: And to detect and betray the impiety and blasphemy of those Persons, who either by making of Pictures (as they thought) of God, or by maintaining of them being made, or by suffering them to stand still (especially after it be known) have thereby denied God to be incomprehensible. For these Pictures and Resemblances of God which ignorant Men have forged in their own Brain, do tell us and say, That God may be comprehended and contained within a place, yea, in a small place, or in any place, as a Man or other Creature: which is most high Blasphemy against the Majesty of Almighty God.

What is his Eternity?
It is an Essential Property in God, whereby his Essence is exempted from all measure of time, and therefore is the first and the last, without either beginning or end of days, 1 Tim. 1. 17. Isa. 41. 4. and 44. 6. Psal. 90. 2. Rev. 1. 8, 11.

In what respect is God called Eternal in the Scriptures?
1. That he hath been from all Eternity without beginning, is now, and shall be for all eternity without end. 2. That all times are present with him continually; and so nothing former nor latter, nothing past or to come. 3. That he is the Author of Everlastingness unto others. Because he hath promised to give his Children of his eternal Goodness, and to have a continual care of them through all Eternity: And will have a Kingdom in Angels and Men, whereof shall be no end.

Is it necessary that we should know this?
Yea: That we may here stay ourselves with the certain hope of eternal life grounded upon his Eternity.

How may that hope be grounded upon his Eternity?
Very well. For God being Eternal, he can for ever preserve us: And seeing he hath promised, he will for ever preserve us, Psal. 48. 14. and 103. 17. Hereby likewise are we strengthened, not only in the immortality of our Soul, but also in the immortality of our Bodies after the Resurrection: considering that by his Everlastingness he giveth continual Being to such of his Creatures as he is pleased to give a perpetual continuance unto.

Second Head

Why else is God said to be eternal?
That so he might be discerned from all other things created. For nothing is like unto God; as the Scripture testify, Isa. 40. 18. Psal. 113. 5.

How is God said to be alone everlasting; seeing Angels and Souls of Men shall be also everlasting?
1. In regard of the time to come they are everlasting, but not in regard of the time past. For though they shall continue always, yet they had their beginning, which cannot be said of God; who therefore is called Alpha and Omega, Rev. 1. 8.

2. Their continuance is, such as it is, not absolute and by it self, but proceeding from the Power of God, who is able (if so he pleased) to give unto them an end as well as a beginning. In which respect God is said only to have immortality, 1 Tim. 6. 16.

Is it necessary we hold God to be Eternal, that so he may be discerned from all things created?
Yea, and we hold it in that respect for two causes. First, Because certain Heretics have thought either all the Creatures, or some of the Creatures at least, to be derived from the very Nature and Essence of God by propagation, as Children from their Mother's Womb. Secondly, That all Idolatrous Cogitations of God may be excluded out of our Minds.

What is the Life of God?
It is an Essential Property of God, whereby the Divine Nature is in perpetual action, living and moving in it self. Hereof is that Speech in the Scripture so often used; The Lord liveth. Hereof likewise is that form of Asseveration or Oath, used so often both by God, Numb. 14. 21. Rom. 14. 11. and by Man, 1 Sam. 19. 6. Jer. 4. 2. As the Lord liveth. And hereof it is, that the Lord so ordinarily in the Scriptures hath the Name of the Living God, Psalm 42. 2. Jer. 10. 10. Heb. 3. 12. and 10. 31. 1 Tim. 6. 17.

Why is God called a Living God?
For Four Causes. First, because he only hath life in himself, and of himself; and all other Creatures have Life from him, Psal. 36. 9. 1 Tim. 6. 16, 17. John. 5. 26. with 14. 19. Second, because he is the only giver of Life unto Man, Gen. 2. 7. Acts 17. 28. John 1. 4. Third, because he is the God especially, not of the Dead, but of the Living, Mat. 22. 32. for all live unto him. Fourth, to distinguish him thereby from all the false Gods of the Heathen, which have no life in them, Psal. 115. 5, 6. Isa. 41. 23. Acts 14. 15.

What may be known as touching the Life of God?
As all Life is active in itself, so the chief Life (such as is in the highest degree to be attributed unto God) is operative in three Faculties and Operations, viz. in Understanding, Power, and Will.

What then be the Attributes, whereby this Life of God is signified?
His All-sufficiency, and his Holy Will: The former whereof comprehendeth his Omniscience or All-knowing Wisdom, and his Omnipotence or Almighty Power, Job 9. 4, 19. and 12. 13. Psal. 147. 5. Isa. 40. 26, 27, 28. Prov. 8. 14. Jer. 10. 12. and 32. 19. Dan. 2. 20.

What is the Knowledge or Wisdom of God?
It is an Essential Property of God, whereby he does distinctly and perfectly know himself, and of and by himself all other things that are, were, shall be, or can be: understanding all things aright, together with the reason of them, Mat. 11. 27. Heb. 4. 13. Job 12. 13. Psalm 139. 11. John 21. 17. 1 Tim. 1. 17.

How many things do you conceive of God by this Attribute?
Four things. 1. That he knoweth all things. 2. That he can be deceived in nothing. 3. That he hath most wisely disposed and ordered all things; insomuch that he cannot justly be reproved in any of them. 4. That he keepeth not his Wisdom to himself, but bestoweth it upon his Creatures: So that whatsoever Wisdom they have, they have it from God.

After what sort does God understand things?
Not by certain Notions abstracted from the things themselves, but by his own Essence: nor successively, (remembering one thing after another) or by discourse of Reason, but by one and the same eternal and immutable Act of Understanding, he conceiveth at once all things, whether they have been or not.

How great is this Wisdom of God?
It is Infinite, even as God is Infinite, Psal. 147. 5. Isa. 40. 28.

What are the Branches thereof, when it is referred to God's Actions?
Fore knowledge and Counsel, Acts 2. 23.

What is the Fore-knowledge of God?
That by which he most assuredly fore-sees all things that are to come, Acts 2. 23. 1 Pet. 1. 2. Though this be not properly spoken of God, but by reason of Men to whom things are past or to come.

Is this Fore-knowledge of God the cause why things are done?
No; but his Will.

What is the Counsel of God?
That by which he does most rightly perceive the best reason of all things that are or can be, Job 12. 12, 13. Prov. 8. 14. Ephes. 1. 9.

For the clearer knowledge of this Wisdom of God, what is there further to be considered?
For the better understanding of this Attribute, we must consider that the Wisdom of God is twofold. First, It is absolute: and we do so term it, because by it God can, and does simply and absolutely know all things from all Eternity, Heb. 4. 13. Psal. 94. 11. Secondly, It is special; whereby he does not only know his Elect Children as he knoweth all things else, but also he does acknowledge them for his own; and does discern them from others, and love them before others. 2 Tim. 2. 19.

Of which do the Scriptures properly speak, when they attribute Wisdom to God?
They speak then of his Absolute Knowledge, whereby he does not only know always and most perfectly himself, and the whole order of his Mind; but also understandeth and knoweth all his Works, and the works of all his Creatures, past, present, and to come, with all the Causes and Circumstances of all.

How do the Scriptures speak of this absolute Knowledge?
The Scriptures speak of it two ways: Either of the Knowledge it self, or else of the things known. And so they show first, what and what manner of thing it is; and secondly, what things are known of God.

Second Head

Now tell me what Knowledge is in God, and what Wisdom does best agree to his Divine Nature.
The best way to find out that, is first to consider what Wisdom and Knowledge does not agree with his Nature and Essence: For his Knowledge and Wisdom are infinitely greater than any we can affirm to be in God.

How shall we find what Knowledge is not agreeing with his Divine Nature?
This is the best way. We must consider and set before us all the kinds of Knowledge, and all the ways and means whereby any Knowledge is to be attained unto amongst Men and Angels: Then shall we see that the Wisdom and Knowledge of God are far more excellent every way, than the most excellent that can be found or thought upon amongst Men and Angels.

Declare then by what ways and means we know a thing.
By two ways or means we do know all that we do know. One way is by our Senses, viz. by Hearing, Seeing, Feeling, Smelling and Tasting; another way is by our Understanding.

Whether does God know any thing by Senses or no?
He cannot. Because he is not as Man, but is a Spirit, and bodiless; and therefore hath no Senses.

Why then do the Scriptures speak of the Eyes, Ears, &c. of God?
Although the Scriptures do attribute Eyes to God, whereby he beholdeth all things, and Ears, whereby he heareth all things, &c. yet indeed he hath none of all these; but these be figurative Speeches used for our capacity and understanding, signifying that nothing is hidden from the Lord.

Whether then does God know things by Understanding, or no?
Yes; but not as we do.

Why, what manner of Knowledge is that which we have by our Understanding.
It is either an Opinion, or a Belief, or a skill and learning.

What is an Opinion?
An Opinion is no certain and evident knowledge of a thing, but is still doubtful what to affirm or deny: And therefore such a Knowledge is not in God, for he knoweth certainly.

What manner of thing is Belief or Faith?
It is a certain, but not an evident Knowledge. For look what we believe only, that we do not see nor know by the Light of natural Understanding: Therefore it is no evident Knowledge, but it is a certain and true Knowledge, because he is most true which revealed it unto us. For Faith or Belief is a most certain Knowledge grounded upon the report of another.

Whether does this kind of knowing things agree with the Nature of God or no?
No. For God knoweth all things in himself and of himself; but not by the report of another.

What say you to Skill and Learning, that is both a certain and evident Knowledge of things: Does not that agree with the Nature of God?
Such Knowledge does not agree with his Nature.

Why so?
Because it cometh by Knowledge that went before, and is gotten by reasoning and debating of things, by defining and dividing, and by searching out the causes of things: But in God is

neither before, nor after, first nor last; and God hath no knowledge after such a sort. Again, our Knowledge which way soever it be considered, whether it be a habit in us, or an action in us, is imperfect: For we know not all things, and these things which we do know we know not all at once, but one thing after another, and yet still but in part.

Declare then in a word how God does know all things?
God does most perfectly know and understand all things at one instant, without any conceit of Mind altering this way or that way.

All our Knowledge is a thing distinguished from our Mind and Understanding: Is it so in God?
No. For the Knowledge or Wisdom of God is a most simple and perfect Essence, yea, it is his very Essence and Substance; and God is all Knowledge, all Wisdom, and all Understanding, infinitely more than all Men and Angels can conceive.

Does God know and understand every thing particularly?
Yea: He knoweth the natures and properties of every particular thing.

How prove you that?
By the Scripture, and by Reason. For the Scripture saith, That God saw every thing that he made that it was Good: This is not spoken generally of all, but especially of every one Creature. Again, Reason makes it manifest by three Examples in the Scriptures, Gen. 1. First, Adam gave to every living thing a proper Name, Gen. 2. 20. according to its proper Nature; whereby it appeareth that Adam had a distinct and particular knowledge of every thing: how much more then had God this special Knowledge of every particular thing, who gave to Adam whatsoever Wisdom and Knowledge he had?

Secondly, Solomon's Wisdom and Knowledge was so great that he was able to dispute, and did thereby dispute of the nature of all Trees, Plants, Fishes, Fowl, Worms, Beasts, and all natural things, as one that was most skillful in them: How much more then does God know all things and their natures particularly, who gave such Wisdom to Solomon? 1 Kings. 4. 33.

Thirdly, Our Savior Christ saith of the Father, That all our Hairs be numbered by him; and that a Sparrow falleth not to the ground without the Will of our Heavenly Father. If not without his Will, then not without his Knowledge. Mat. 10. 29, 30.

Whether does God know all the motions of our Wills and our Thoughts?
Yea; God does certainly know the Motions of the Will, and the Thoughts of the Heart in all Men, and the issue of them all. Which is manifest by these places of Scripture following, Gen. 6. 5. Psal. 94. 11. Prov. 21. 1. Jer. 17. 9, 10. Hereof it is that we cite him to be the Witness of our Hearts when we swear by him.

Whether hath God the knowledge of all Evils or no?
God knoweth all Evils and Sins, which lie lurking in all Men's Hearts. And this is manifest by these places of Scripture following, Gen. 6. 5. Job 11. 11. Psal. 90. 8, 9.

What if he did not know all these Evils?
It is impossible but he must know them, for two causes. First, If he did not, his Knowledge would be imperfect. Secondly, If he did not know them, he could not be a Just Judge, neither could he reward every one according to his Works and Thoughts: Which to affirm were Ungodly and Blasphemous.

Object. That which is nothing cannot be known; but Sin and Evil is nothing, (for it is nothing else but a taking away, and failing of good, and it is a mere corruption) and therefore Sin and Evil cannot be known of God.

We know what is Evil, and we know Evil Things, and we do discern them from Good Things: But we know Evil only by his contrary, that is Good. As we know Nothing by Something, Darkness by Light, Death by Life, Sickness by Health, Vice by Virtue. Thus by the knowledge of Good, Evil is known unto us; and therefore seeing God (who is the chief Good) does by himself know all Good things, he must of necessity also know and understand all the Evil that is contrary thereunto.

Whether may God know those things which are not?

God knoweth the things which are not; and he does also truly know the things which shall never come to pass.

What Reason can you yield for this?

The Reason is; because he knoweth all things by his Essence: Therefore he knoweth all things which are subject to his Divine Essence and Power; and therefore also are possible, but shall never come to pass.

But does he know them eternally, or in time?

He knoweth them all eternally: That is, for ever and ever, he knew, and does know them; as the Scripture does testify, Ephes. 1. 4. 2 Tim. 2. 19.

Can you make this manifest by an earthly comparison?

Yea. A Builder by virtue of his Art does conceive in his Mind the form of a House, which House he will never build: how much more can God do the same? For God can make more Worlds; and he knoweth that he can, and yet he does it not.

Again; although there were never an Eagle in the City, yet we can conceive in our minds what an Eagle is: much more does God know all things which are not in act, and which never shall be.

Object. This is something which you say: But your last similitude of the Eagle does not hold. For therefore we keep the knowledge of an Eagle in our minds, though all be gone, because the similitude of the Eagle which was sometimes in the City, does still remain in our minds and understandings. But what similitude can there be in the Mind of God, of those things which are not, which never were, and which never shall be?

Yes; the very Essence and Similitude of God, is a Similitude of all those things that may be if he will, which he must needs know; for he does most perfectly know himself. And thus if we consider his Power, or Almighty Essence, all things should be done which he can do and does know.

Then whether is his Knowledge and Power the cause of all things, which are, which have been, and which shall be?

The only foreknowledge of God alone which the Grecians call Theoretical Knowledge; that is, a Knowledge beholding all things, is not the cause of things; but his foreknowledge with his Will, which the Grecians call Practical Knowledge, that is, a Working Knowledge, that is the cause of things.

Whether may the Knowledge or Wisdom of God fail or be deceived at any time, or no?

The knowledge of God is most certain, and cannot any way be deceived. For all things are known of God as they are; and all things are as they are known of God: And therefore his Knowledge cannot any way be deceived, Heb. 4. 13.

Object. But things do often change and alter: And therefore they are not always as they are known.

Although things be changed, and altered, yet God does know thereof: and although they change and alter, yet his Knowledge does never alter nor change, neither is it uncertain.

Whether may the Knowledge which God hath, be increased, diminished, or altered?

No; it cannot, it is always the same, firm and constant, and can by no means be increased, diminished, nor altered. For he neither forgets any thing, nor is ignorant of any thing, neither is any thing new unto him. For the Scripture saith, all things are always manifest in his sight. St. James saith, (1. 17.) with God is no change, nor shadow of change. Therefore his Knowledge is always one and the same. Solomon saith, Many devices are in a Man's Heart, but the Lord's Counsel shall stand, Prov. 19. 21.

But if his Knowledge be always one and the same, why does the Scripture say, That the Lord will forget our sins, and blot them out of his remembrance, and remember them no more?

These and such-like phrases of Speech are not to be understood of the simple Knowledge of God, as though he should know them no more; but of his Judicial Knowledge unto Punishment. For although he does know and remember our sins always most perfectly; yet he will not know them, nor remember them to bring them into Judgment, and so to punish us for them when we do truly repent: That is, they shall be no more judged or punished, or laid to our charge, if we be in Christ, than if he had quite and clean forgotten them, and never did remember them. And these Speeches serve to arm us against the despair and doubting of our Salvation, being truly in Christ.

Where is the Wisdom of God specially of us to be considered?

The Wisdom of God shineth unto us most clearly in his Works of Creation and Preservation of the World: and not only in his Works, but also in his Gospel, whereby he calleth and gathers his Church out of the World, to be saved by his Son our Mediator Jesus Christ, Eccles. 3. 11. Psal. 104. 24. 1 Cor. 1. 21.

Was this Saving Wisdom of God known to the Philosophers and natural wise Men of the World?

No; it was not, but only to the Children of God, Mat. 11. 25.

Is the Wisdom of God to be perfectly conceived of us?

No; neither is it communicated to any Creature, neither can be. For it is unconceivable, as the very Essence of God himself is unconceivable and unspeakable as it is: And his Wisdom (as we have heard before) is his very Essence, that is, his very Godhead or God himself; and that it is unconceivable, the Scriptures do testify, Psal. 147. 5. Rom. 11. 33.

What Use may we make of this Doctrine?

The Uses. First, By this Doctrine of God's unspeakable Knowledge and Wisdom, the True God is discerned from all False Gods, and from all things made. For that is no God which hath not this Divine Knowledge and Wisdom, which the Scriptures do attribute to God.

Second, Seeing our God is such a God as knoweth all things that are done, said, or thought, and sees into the most hidden corners and thoughts of our Hearts: We must study and learn thereby to drive all hypocrisy and dissembling from us, and learn to open our Hearts to God of our own accord, and to beseech him in his own Son's Name, to cleanse us from our secret Faults.

Third, It must make us to walk always before the Lord according to his Will revealed in his Word, with great fear and reverence, as Men always in his sight and knowledge.

Fourth, It serveth to confirm our Faith and Trust in the Providence of God. For although we know not what to do, nor how to do, nor what shift to make in dangers and necessities, yet God does; and he hath knowledge enough for us, though we be ignorant; and his Wisdom shall succor our foolishness, if we do truly and faithfully serve him, Psal. 103. 13, 14.

Fifth, This should be our Consolation against the fear of Hell and despair, and should uphold in us the certainty of our Salvation: Because this Knowledge and Wisdom of God, joined with his Will to save us, is firm and constant; and he knowing all his Elect, will not lose one of them that are in Christ his Son, John 17. 12. 2 Tim. 2. 19. John 10. 27, 28, 29.

What is the Omnipotence or the Almighty Power of God?
It is an Essential Property in God, whereby he is able to effect all things; being of Power sufficient to do whatsoever he willeth or can will, Gen. 35. 11. Deut. 10. 17. Nehem. 1. 5. Job 8. 3. and 9. 4. and 11. 7. and 42. 2. Psal. 115. 3. Dan. 4. 35. Mat. 19 26. Luk. 1. 37.

Are there any things which God cannot will or do?
Yea; three kinds of things. 1. Such things as are contrary to his Nature: As to destroy himself, and not to beget his Son from Eternity.

2. Those things whose action argueth impotency, and are a sign of weakness, as to lie, Tit. 1. 2. to deny himself, 2 Tim. 2. 13. to allow wickedness, Hab. 1. 13. to be forgetful, to do the works of a created Nature, &c. For the disability of such things confirms, not weakens God's Omnipotence.

3. Such things as imply contradiction. For God cannot make a Truth false; or that which is, when it is not to be; or a Man to be a Man and a Stone at one and the same time; or Christ's Body to be a true Body and yet to be in all places or divers places at once, and to be without circumscription and occupying of a place, which is the Essential Property of a Body. For one of these being true, the other must be false; and God, who is the Truth it self, cannot work that which is false and untrue. So that God's Omnipotence must always teach us that he is glorious, and true, and perfect, and not the contrary.

In what respects then is God said to be Almighty?
Because, First, he is able to perform whatsoever he will, or is not contrary to his Nature, Psal. 135. 6. Isa. 40. 28. Second, he can do all things without any labor, and most easily, Psalm 33. 9. and 148. 5. Third, he can do them either with means, or without means, or contrary to means, as pleases him. Fourth, there is no Power which can resist him. Fifth, all Power is so in God only, that no Creature is able to do any thing, but as he does continually receive Power from God to do it, Acts 17. 28. Isa. 40. 29. and 45. 24. Dan. 2. 20, 23. 1 Chron. 29. 12. John 19. 11. Rom. 16. 25. 2 Tim. 4. 17. So that there is no Power but what is from God.

What mean you when you say, All Power is in God? It should seem by that speech, that there are more Powers in God than one?
That we may rightly understand what Power is in God; it were very requisite that we did first consider how many ways this word Power is taken in the Scriptures.

Declare then how or in what sense it is taken in the Scriptures.
In the Scripture this word Power is taken two ways, or in two senses; sometimes for Authority, which is grounded upon Law, by which Authority one may do this or that if he

be able to do it; sometimes it is taken for might and strength, or ability to do a thing if one hath Authority to do it. And these are distinguished by two words amongst the Grecians and the Latins. For when the Grecians speak of Power, that signifieth Authority and Right, Mat. 28. 18. then it is called ἐξουσία: When they take Power for Strength, then it is termed by them δύναμις. Amongst the Latins being taken the first way, it is called Potestas: being taken the second way, that is, for Might or Strength, it is called Potentia; and in English we call them both Power.

It seemeth by your speech, that they are not only distinguished, but that they may also be separated the one from the other.
It is true, for so they are. As for Example, A King may have great force and strength, and by his great Power he may be able to overthrow and destroy a whole Country or Kingdom over which he hath no Authority. Again, some King hath Power, that is, Authority over his Rebels, and yet hath not Power, that is, strength enough to subdue them: So some perhaps have might and strength enough to govern and rule another Man's Wife, another Man's Children, or another Man's Servant, over which he hath no Power, that is Authority. And again, Fathers have Authority over their own Children; all Husbands over their own Wives; and all Masters over their own Servants: And yet all have not Power, that is, strength and ability to rule them.

I perceive by this which you have said, that in Creatures these two may be separated one from the other, and many times are: But what are they in God?
In God they are not divided, but distinguished. For he hath all Power, that is, all Authority over all things; and he hath all Power, that is, all strength, force, might and ability to do all things with all things at his good pleasure: and this Power is not given him, but he hath it in himself, and of himself, most perfectly, absolutely, and eternally.

But of what Power do we speak when we say, that God is Almighty? Whether do you mean his Right and Authority, or his Strength and Ability, or both?
Both are in God essentially: But when the Scripture speaketh of God's Omnipotence, it meaneth (and so do we) his Strength and Ability, whereby he is able to do whatsoever he will, not excluding his right.

If all Power and Might be in God; tell me how manifold is this Power which is attributed to God in the Scriptures?
To speak simply, the Power of God is but only one, and a must simple and single thing, which is his Essence and Substance: Yet for divers respects it is said to be manifold; and it may be considered two ways.

1. As it worketh always, and can work in God himself: For God in himself does always understand, will, love, &c. 2. As it worketh out of God himself, in the Creatures: As when he created all things, and does now work in governing all things, and can work if it please him, infinite things: And of this working of God's power, do the Scriptures properly speak when they call God Almighty.

How many ways may God's Power be considered, as it worketh in himself?
Two ways: First, As it is common to all the three Persons in the Trinity, that is, a Power whereby God the Father, the Son, and the Holy Ghost does understand himself, love himself, and work in himself: And these Actions do not differ from the Essence of God, for that in God there is nothing which is not his Substance. Secondly, The other working in God himself, is that by which the Father does beget eternally a Son of his own Nature and Substance equal to himself: And this Power of begetting the Son of God is proper only to the Father, and not to the Son and Holy Ghost.

Second Head

How many ways do you consider the Power of God working out of himself?
That Power which hath relation or respect to things created is twofold: The first is a Power absolute, whereby he is able to do whatsoever he will; the other is a power actual, whereby he does indeed whatsoever he will.

Where does the Scripture speak of the absolute Power of God, by which he can do more than he does if he would?
Of such a Power speaketh our Savior Christ, I could pray to my Father, and he could give me more than twelve Legions of Angels; but he would not ask it, Mat. 26. 53. Phil. 3. 21.

How does the Scripture speak of God's Actual Power?
Of this Power the Prophets and Apostles make mention, when they join his Power and his Promises together; that is, when they say he is not only able to perform, but does and will perform indeed whatsoever he hath promised. And of this Power Paul does speak when he saith, that God will have mercy upon whom he will: And everywhere in the Scriptures we read, that God hath done what he would, given to whom he would, Psal. 135. 6.

How great is this working or mighty Power of God?
It must needs be high and very great; for it is infinite, and hath no end.

Declare how it is infinite.
It is Infinite two ways, or in two respects. First, In it self, and of it self it is Infinite. Secondly, As it is extended to the Creatures, which may be called the Object of God's Power, it is also Infinite.

Why do you say it is infinite of it self, or of its own Nature?
Because the Power of God is nothing else but his Divine Essence; and the Essence of God is of his own Nature, by it self, and of it self Infinite.

Show how God's Power is Infinite as it is extended to the Creatures.
Because the Power of God does extend it self to Infinite things, therefore we say that it is Infinite.

Declare how that is.
I mean the things which God can perform or bring to pass by his Power are Infinite, and therefore his Power is Infinite. For God never made so many, nor so great things, but he could have made more, and greater if he would. As for Example; He adorned the Firmament with an innumerable company of Stars, and yet he could have decked it with more. And to speak in a word, God can always perform infinite things more than he does, if he will: And therefore both in it self, and out of it self, it is Infinite.

Whether can this Omnipotence of God be communicated to any Creature?
No, it cannot. For to be truly and essentially Omnipotent, is proper to God only, and Omnipotence is God's Essence: And therefore whosoever is God is Omnipotent, and whosoever is Omnipotent must needs be God, whose Power is a chief Power Infinite: And the Power of any Creature is not infinite, but finite: And so consequently no Creature can be Omnipotent, except he would say that a Creature, or a thing created, can be both a Creature and a God, or a Creator too; which is both absurd and blasphemous.

If God can do all things, whether can he Sin or no? As to lie and to be unfaithful in his Promises, &c.
God cannot Sin, and yet for all that he is Omnipotent: For to Sin is no part or point of Omnipotence, but of Impotency: To Sin is nothing else but to leave the right and perfect

Way, or to fall from a right and perfect Action: Which showeth want of Power to uphold himself that does so. Which Power is not wanting in God, for he is Omnipotent; and being Omnipotent, he cannot go from Strength to Weakness, and from Perfection to Imperfection, &c. and therefore he cannot Sin.

By what Scripture can you prove this that you say?
The Apostle Paul is of that mind, 2 Tim. 2. 13. If we believe not, yet abideth he faithful, he cannot deny himself. He does not say he will not deny himself, but he cannot deny himself; and his reason is, because (as he saith himself) God is faithful, not only in his Will, but also by his Nature: And therefore since God is faithful by Nature, he cannot but stand to his Promises which he made according to the good pleasure of his Will; and by Nature he is Omnipotent, therefore he cannot be Impotent: By Nature he is Good, and the chief Good, therefore he cannot become Evil, nor do Evil.

But whether can God be moved, or be subject to Passions or Sufferings, or no?
He cannot. For the Power whereof we speak, when we say that God is Omnipotent, is altogether Active and not Passive; neither can any Passive Power be in God. And to this effect speaketh St. Augustine, when he saith, *Dicitur Deus Omnipotens faciendo quod vult, non patiendo quod non vult*; that is, God is called Omnipotent in doing what he will, not in suffering what he will not.

Object. Some say that God can sin, but he will not; and that he can be subject to Passions, but he will not; and that he can do whatsoever can be imagined or thought, but he will not; what say you to those?
Of them I say nothing: but their Opinion is both foolish and ungodly. For God cannot do any thing which disagreeth from his Nature, and therefore he cannot sin, &c. Rom. 9. 14. Not because his Will is against it, but because it is against his Nature and natural Goodness, 1 John 1. 5. Deut. 32. 4. therefore do the Scriptures deny any iniquity to be in God: And St. Augustine saith to that effect; *Deus iniusta facere non potest, quia ipse est summa iustitia*; that is, God cannot do unjust things, because he is most just, and Righteousness it self.

Object. But yet for all this, God does in some sort will Sin: For he does not permit it against his Will: And besides that he commanded some things which were sins; as Abraham to kill his innocent Son, and Shimei to curse David; did he not?
So far forth as God does command, or will, or work any thing, that thing is not sin in God: For he both willeth and worketh in great Wisdom, and according to his most holy Will: And therefore no action can be sin in God, but every action in God is most holy and good: And so saith the Scripture, Psal. 145. 17.

To what use serveth the Doctrine of God's Omnipotence?
It serveth, 1. To sustain and strengthen our Faith, touching the certainty of our Salvation. Because God hath promised eternal Life to the Faithful: And he can do and he will do what he hath promised.

2. To teach us that we should not despair of any thing that God does promise, either in respect of our own weakness, or in respect of the apparent weakness of the things that God hath sanctified for our good. For whatsoever God as a Father hath promised, that same as Almighty, he can and will see performed, Jos. 23. 14. Numb. 23. 19. This did strengthen Abraham's Faith greatly, for Paul saith thus of him; He did not doubt of the Promise of God through unbelief, but was strengthened in the Faith, and gave glory to God, being fully assured, that he which had promised was also able to do it, Rom 4. 20, 21.

3. To stir us up to pray, and to call for those things which God hath promised, without any doubting. For in our Prayers we ought always to have before eyes the Promises of God, and the Almightiness of God. The Leper was persuaded only of Christ's Power, he knew not his Will; and therefore he said: Lord, if thou wilt, thou canst make me clean: And he was made clean, Mat. 8. 2. How much more shall we obtain those things which we ask, if we be persuaded of his Power, and doubt not of his Promises.

4. It serveth both for a Spur to do well, considering that God is Able to save; and a Bridle to restrain from evil, seeing he hath Power to destroy. Fear not them, saith our Savior, that can kill the Body, &c.

5. It serveth in prosperity to continue us in our Duties, that we abuse not God's Blessings: Because as he gave them, so he is able to take them away again, as Job acknowledgeth, Job 1. 21.

6. To make us undergo the Cross with patience and cheerfulness, and to hope for help in the midst of adversity and death; because he which hath promised to hear and help us, is able also to deliver us out of all our troubles, Psal. 50. 15. John 10. 29. Dan. 3. 17, 18. and 4. 32.

7. To keep us from despairing of any Man's Salvation, although he seem to be rejected of God; and to make us walk in Faith and Fear: Because God is able to raise him up that is down, and to cast us down that stand. And so Paul does reason from God's Omnipotence, about the Rejection and Election of the Jews and Gentiles, Rom. 11. 23, 25.

8. It serveth to confirm all the Articles of our Christian Faith; the sum whereof is contained in the Creed.

Thus much concerning the All-sufficiency of God. What is his Will?
It is an Essential Property of God, whereby of himself, and with one Act, he does most holily will all things, approving or disapproving whatsoever he knoweth, Rom. 9. 18. James 4. 15. Ephes. 1. 5.

What learn you of this?
First, That nothing cometh to pass by mere Hap or Chance but as God in his eternal Knowledge and just Will hath decreed before should come to pass. Secondly, That whatsoever cometh to pass, though we know not the Causes thereof, and that it be contrary to our Wills, yet we should bear it patiently, and therein submit our Wills to the good Will and Pleasure of God.

How is the Will of God distinguished?
Into his secret or hidden, and his revealed or manifest Will. The former is known to himself: by which he willeth divers things, of which Man neither does know nor is to ask a reason of. And of this the Scripture speaketh thus; If the Will of God be so, 1 Pet. 3. 17. The latter, is the guide of Man in all his Actions: containing God's Commandments, wherein is set down what we ought to do, or leave undone; as also his Promises, which we ought to believe, Deut. 29. 29.

Is not the Secret Will of God contrary to his Revealed Will?
No, in no wise. It differeth in some respect, but it is not another Will, much less contrary.

How differeth it?
The Secret Will of God considereth especially the end; the Revealed Will the things that are referred to the end. And the Secret Will of God is the event of all things: Where the

Revealed Will is of those things only which are propounded in the Word; as to believe in Christ, and to be sanctified, &c. John 14. 1. 1 Thess. 4. 3.

It may seem that the Revealed Will of God is sometimes contrary to it self: as when God forbiddeth Murder and Theft; yet God commandeth Abraham to kill his Son, and the Israelites to take the Goods of the Egyptians.
Here is no contrariety: Because God in giving a Law to Man, giveth none to himself, but that he may command otherwise. Therefore the Law hath this exception; that it is always just, unless God command otherwise.

But it seemeth that the Secret Will of God is often contrary to the Revealed Will: seeing by the former many evil things are committed, and by the other all evil is forbidden.
In as much as by the Providence of God evil things come to pass, it is for some good of God's Glory, or good of the Church, or both: In which only respect they by the Providence of God are suffered to be done.

How then does God will that which is good, and that which is evil?
He willeth all good so far as it is good; either by his effectual good pleasure, or by his revealed approbation: And that which is evil, in as much as it is evil, by disallowing and forsaking it. And yet he voluntarily does permit evil, because it is good, that there should be evil, Acts 14. 16. Psal. 81. 12.

Is there any profit of this Knowledge of God's Will?
Yea; great profit for us to know what God will have us to do; and what he will do with us, and for us, is a thing wherein standeth our Salvation. Therefore   Page 112 (45) we are willed by the Apostle to inquire diligently after the same, Rom. 12. 2.

But the same Apostle, Rom. 11. 34. before saith, Who hath known the Mind of the Lord, or who was his Counselor? That is to say, none. Therefore it seemeth that the Will of God cannot be known; and consequently, that it may not be sought after.
Indeed by that we learn not to search into the secret Counsels of God, which he never revealed in his Word, neither hath promised to reveal in this World; but after the revealed Will of God, which he hath vouchsafed to make known in his Word, we may and ought to inquire of God. As for the Will and Counsel which he hath kept to himself, we may admire and adore it with Paul and David: But that we may not search after it, is manifestly proved by these places following, Acts 1. 7. Exod. 33. 18, 19, 20. Job 21. 22.

Whether can God's secret Will be known, or no?
If he does reveal it, it may.

How does God reveal his Secret Will?
Two ways. Sometimes by his Spirit: As when he showed his Prophets many of his Judgments that were to come. Sometime by the thing it self which he willeth, or by the effects of his Will: As when a thing does fall out which was before unknown. As for Example; A Man does not know before it come, whether he shall be sick or not, or of what Disease, or when, or how long: But when all these things are come to pass, then it is manifest what was God's Will before concerning the Matter.

Show we what is our Duty in respect of this Secret Will of God.
Our Duty is twofold: First, We must not curiously search after the knowledge of it, but worship and reverence it. Secondly, Before it be made manifest by the Effects, we must generally rest quietly in the same.

Second Head

Show me how by an Example.
Thus a Christian must resolve with himself; Whatsoever the Lord will do with me, whether I live or die, whether he make me rich or poor, &c. I rest content with his good Will and Pleasure.

What must we do when his Will is revealed unto us?
Then much more must we rest in it, and be thankful for it: As Job was, who said, The Lord hath given and taken, even as it pleases the Lord, &c. Job 1. 21.

What call you the Revealed Will of God?
The Revealed Will of God is twofold: The one is that which is properly revealed in the Law, that is, what God requireth to be done of us; and therefore it is called the Law: And after this we must inquire. The other is in the Gospel, which showeth God's Will towards us, and what he hath decreed of us in his eternal Counsel as touching our Salvation.

God indeed by his Law hath made it known what his Will is, that of us must be done and fulfilled: But hath he revealed in his Word what is his Will and Pleasure towards us?
Yea, he hath so: And that is proved by these places of Scripture following, Ephes. 1. 5. Mat. 3. 17. Joh. 5. 39. and 6. 40. and after this knowledge of this Will of God we must diligently inquire.

But whether may this Will of God be known of us, or no?
Yes, it may. For as it is revealed in the Scripture, so it is also confirmed and sealed before our eyes in the Sacraments, and the daily Benefits which we receive from the Lord.

And is this sufficient to persuade us to believe his Will?
No. For except the Lord does persuade us by his Holy Spirit, we shall neither believe it nor know it; as appeareth by these places of Scripture, 1 Cor. 2. 16. Mat. 11. 25. But if we have the Spirit of God, there is no need to go up into Heaven, or to go beyond the Sea to know it, because the Word is near unto us, in our Hearts, as Paul saith, Rom. 10. 6, 7, 8. For touching the Matter of our Salvation, the Will of God is so clearly laid open in the preaching of the Gospel, that it needs not to be more clear.

If at any time we cannot know nor understand this Will of God, as touching our Salvation, in whom is the fault?
The fault is in ourselves: And the Reason is, because we are carnal and natural, and destitute of the Spirit of Christ. For Paul saith, The carnal and natural Man cannot perceive the things of God. But if the Spirit of Christ does come and open our Understanding, and correct our Affections, we can no longer doubt of his Will. And therefore the Apostle immediately after addeth, and saith, But we have the Mind of Christ, 1 Cor. 2. 16.

Whether is this Will of God made known to every one of God's Children particularly, or no?
Yes; it is. For Paul, having the Spirit of Christ, saith, That this Will of God was manifested unto him, Gal. 2. 20. Christ loved me, and gave himself for me. And to the Corinthians he saith, But God hath revealed them (i.e. the Joys of Heaven) to us by his Spirit, 1 Cor 2. 10.

How does this prove that we can have this Knowledge?
Very well. For if all the Elect are led by the same Spirit that Paul had, it will also persuade them of this Will of God, as well as Paul.

But how prove you that they have the same Spirit?
That the same Spirit is given to all the Elect, I prove it out of the Prophet Isaiah, who saith thus, My Word and my Spirit shall not depart from thy Mouth, nor from thy seed for ever, Isa. 59. 21. Which is such a Blessing, as no Blessing can be desired in this World greater, more excellent, or more heavenly. For when we are once armed with the knowledge of this Will of God, we shall pass though Fire and Water without any danger; (Isaiah 43. 2.) we shall overcome the World and Death, and triumph over our Enemies, as Paul did, Rom. 8. 38, 39.

Whether are there more Wills in God than one or no?
The will of God in some respects is but one, and in some respects it is manifold.

How is it but one?
For the better determining of this Point, we must first consider how many significations there be of this word, Will, in God.

1. It signifieth the Faculty or Ability of willing in God; and so it is God himself, and the very Essence of God: And so his Will is but one. 2. It signifieth the Act it self of Willing; and if it be so taken, it is all but one: For God does that in one, and that eternal Act will whatsoever he will. 3. It signifieth the free Decree of his Will, concerning either the doing or the suffering of any thing to be done. If we take it in this sense, the Will of God is still but one, and that eternal and immutable.

May we call the Decree of God's Will, the Will of God?
Yea, very well. As the Testament of one that is deceased is called the last Will of the Testator; because it is the firm and last Decree of the Testator's Will and Mind, concerning the disposing of his Goods. And the Scriptures do make the Will of God, and the Counsel or Decree of his Will, to be all one: As appeareth in these places following, Isa. 46. 10. Acts 4. 27. Joh. 6. 40.

How is the Will of God manifold?
There be two respects chiefly for which the Will of God is said to be manifold, or more than one. First, For the divers kinds of things which God does will: And hereof it is, that it is called sometime the Will of God concerning us, and sometime the Will of God done by us. The first is his favor and love towards us in Christ Jesus, in which he willeth and decreeth that we shall be saved through his Son: Of this Christ speaketh, John 6. 40. The other which he will have done of us, is that which is expressed in his word: And that is to believe in Christ, and to walk in his Laws. Of which David saith thus, Teach me to do thy Will, because thou art my God, Psal. 143. 10 and Paul saith, Rom. 2. 18. Thou knowest his Will, that is, his Law.

Which is the other respect for which God is said to have many Wills?
The Will of God is said to be manifold and divers: For that those things which he willeth, he does seem to will them after divers sorts, and not after one and the same manner. First, After one manner he does will good things; and after another manner he does will evil things.

Show how that is?
He willeth good things properly and absolutely by themselves, and for themselves; he willeth evil things for another end, Rom. 12. 2. and that is for good too: And the first is called the Good Will of God, and acceptable to himself; the latter is called the Permissive Will of God, or a voluntary permission in God, because he is not compelled or constrained against his Will, to will them. Again, sometime he willeth simply and absolutely, sometimes he seemeth to will conditionally: And some things he revealeth

at one time, some at another; and some things he does for which he giveth a Reason, and the Reasons of some things are secret to himself only and for ever.

When then belike you grant that in God there be many Wills?
No, I deny that. For although in those aforesaid respects the Will of God is said to be manifold for our understanding, yet for all that, indeed and in truth the Will of God is but one only, and that most constant, eternal, and perpetual. As for Example; He willed some things in the Old Testament, he hath willed other things in the New Testament, yet one and the same Will in God decreed both. Again, his Will was, that some things in the Old Testament should last for a time, that is, to the coming of Christ: or, as the Apostle saith, to the time of Reformation, Heb. 9. 10. but he willeth that the things of the New Testament shall last to the end of the World: And yet one Will in God decreed both these from everlasting. Again, although God seemeth to us to will some things absolutely and simply, and some things conditionally; yet in truth, to speak properly, all things whatsoever God willeth, he willeth absolutely that simply. And whereas he is said to will some things conditionally, that is to be referred to the manifestation of his Will. For there is not in God any Conditional Will, but only that which openeth his Will in this or that, or on this or that Condition: For a Condition in God is against the nature of his eternal Kingdom and Knowledge.

Object. God commandeth many things to be done which are not done: so that there is a Will declared in his Word, and there is another in him forbidding or hindering that which he commandeth in his Law; and therefore there are in God many Wills.
The things which God commandeth are of two sorts, some are absolutely commanded without any condition expressed or concealed; as that Moses should cause all things about the Tabernacle to be made according to the Pattern given him in the Mount. Other some things are commanded and set down with condition; as when Christ said, Mark 10. 17, 19. If thou wilt inherit eternal Life, keep the Commandments. And the Law saith, Do this and this, if thou wilt live. And these are propounded conditionally to all, as well the Elect as the Reprobate. God his absolute Will is always one and the same.

And are they propounded to both after one sort?
No, not so. For although they be given to the Elect with Condition, yet the Will of God to them is absolute. For God's Will simply is, that all his Elect shall be saved, if not always, yet at the last; and because of their own strength they cannot do the Commandments of God, therefore God does give them strength by his Spirit; and because by this strength they cannot do God's Will perfectly, therefore it is fulfilled for them by Christ, which is made theirs by Faith, and in whom God does accept their broken and imperfect Obedience, as if it were whole and perfect. But as for the Wicked and Reprobates it is not so with them. For although God does give them a Law to obey, and does promise them Life if they do obey it: Yet his Will to them is not so absolute, that they shall keep it; neither shall they obtain the Promises either in themselves or in Christ.

Does not God mock and delude the Reprobate, when he willeth them in his Law to do this and that, which yet is not his Will to be done?
No, he does not delude them. For although he does not show what he will absolutely have done of them, which is properly his Will indeed; yet by his Law he does teach what is their Duty, and the Duty of all Men: Adding moreover, that whosoever shall neglect and fail in this their Duty, he sinneth grievously against God, and is guilty of Death.

Can you make this plain by some Instance or Example, or any Parable in the Scripture?
Yea, it is manifest in the Parable of the King's Supper, and the bidden Guests. They which were first bidden and came not, were not deluded by the King; because he signified unto them what he liked, and what was their Duty; but yet he did not command that they should be compelled to come in, as the two sorts which were bidden afterwards. Where we see that the King's Will was not alike in bidding the first, as it was in the second: For in calling the latter sort, his Will was absolute that they should come indeed, and so caused, that they did come; but to the first he only signified what he liked if they had done it.

How do you apply this to the Matter in Question?
I apply it thus. As it cannot be said that the first bidden Guests were mocked by the King, although his will was not so absolute for their coming, as it was in calling and commanding the second sort of Guests: So it cannot be said that God does delude and mock the Reprobate in giving them a Law to obey, although it be not his absolute Will that they should come and obey the Law. For it is sufficient to leave them without excuse, that they know what is acceptable to God, and what is their Duty to God; who hath absolute Authority and Power over them, and over all.

Object. God commandeth Pharaoh to let Israel go, and yet his Will was to the contrary: Therefore there were two contrary Wills in God, one revealed, the other concealed.
It followeth not. For the Will of God was one only, and most constant, and that was that Israel should not be sent away by Pharaoh, and so that was fulfilled. As for the Commandment given to Pharaoh, it was a Doctrine to teach Pharaoh what he must have done if he would avoid so many Plagues, and showed him his Duty, and what was just and right to be done: but it was no testimony of the absolute Will of God.

Whether does God will Evil or Sin, or no?
Before we answer to this Question, we must consider of three things. 1. How many ways Sin may be considered. 2. How many things are to be considered in Sin. 3. How many ways one may be said to will a thing.

Go to then; show first how many ways Sin is to be considered.
Sin is to be considered three ways. 1. As it is of it self Sin, and striving against the Law of God. 2. As it is a punishment of Sin that went before: For God does oftentimes punish one Sin with another. 3. As it is the cause of more Sin following, Rom. 1. 26. for one Sin does beget another, as one Devil calleth seven Devils, 2 Thess. 2. 11.

Now declare how many things you do consider in Sin.
In every Sin there are three things. The Action: And that is either Inward or Outward. The Action which we call Inward is threefold: Either of the Mind, as evil Thoughts; or of the Heart, as evil Affections and Desires; or of the will, as an evil choice, or consent to Sin. The Actions which we call Outward, are the Actions or Work of the Senses fighting against the Law of God.

The second thing in every Sin, is the deformity or corruption of the Action; that is, when the Action does decline from the Rule of God's Law: And this properly is Sin, or the form of Sin.

The third thing in every Sin, is the Offence or Guiltiness thereof, whereby the Party offending is bound to undergo Punishment. This Guiltiness and Obligation whereby we are bound to undergo the Penalty of Sin, hath its Foundation in Sin it self; but it ariseth from the Justice of God, Rom. 6. 23. who in his Justice rewardeth Sin with Death, as Justice indeed giveth to every one his due.

Now come you to your third Point, and show how many ways one is said to will a thing.
We are said to will a thing two ways; either properly, for it self; or improperly, for another end.

What mean you by a proper willing of a thing?
We do will a thing properly for it self, or for its own sake, when the thing which we will or desire is of its own nature to be wished and desired: As for the Body, Health, Food, Apparel, and such like; or for the Soul, Faith, Repentance, Patience, &c. We do will a thing improperly, when the thing which we will is not of it self to be wished, but yet we will have it for some good that may come thereof: As for Example, We will the cutting off some Member of the Body, not because of it self it is to be wished, but for the health of the Body which does follow that cutting.

What difference is there between these two Wills?
There is great difference. For those things which we will properly, we love and approve them, we incline unto them, and we delight in them, but that which is known of it self to be evil, our Will is not carried unto that with love and liking, but does decline from it. And whereas a Man willeth a Member of his Body to he cut off, we may rather call it a Permission than a Willing, and yet a willing Permission.

You have showed how many ways Sin is to be considered, how many things are to be considered in every Sin, and how we are said to will a thing. Now let me hear what you say to the Matter in Question; that is, Whether God does will Sin, or no?
Before I answer directly to your Question, I think it is not amiss to show what every one must carefully take heed of in answering to this Question: For in answering there is danger.

Let me hear what Dangers must be avoided in answering.
There are two: And every one must avoid them, and sail between them as between two dangerous Rocks.

The first is this; We must take heed lest we make God the Author of Sin by affirming that he willeth Sin, as the Libertines do, and as Adam did, Gen: 3. 12. for that were the next way, not only to put off our Sins from ourselves, and lay them upon God, but also to cast off all Conscience of Sin, and all Fear of God; than which nothing can be more blasphemous against God, and pernicious to ourselves.

What is the second thing to be avoided?
The other is this: We must take heed that we affirm not any evil to be in the World which God knoweth not of, or whether God will or no: For that were to deny God's Omnipotence, and All-knowledge.

These are two dangerous Rocks and Heresies indeed: But now I expect a direct Answer to the Question.
That cannot be at once, but by going from Point to Point according to our former distinction of Sin, and Willing.

Very well then; declare first of all, what things God does properly Will, which of themselves are to be willed.
God does first and chiefly will himself; that is, his own Glory and Majesty, as the end for which all things are: And this he is said to will properly; that is, he loveth it, advanceth it, and delighteth in it. And to this purpose serve all those Scriptures which commanded us to sanctify his Name, and to adore his Glory, as in Isa. 48. 11. Prov. 16. 4. Rom. 11. 36. 1 Cor. 10. 32. 2.

Besides himself, he does properly will all other things which he made, and which he does himself, insomuch as he does approve them, and love them, as appeareth by these places following; God saw all that he made, and it was good, (Gen. 1. 31.) and therefore gave a Commandment, that one should preserve another, by multiplying and increasing. Again, it is said, Whatsoever the Lord will, that he does, (Psal 135. 6.) therefore whatsoever he does, that he wills: And although he hateth Evil, yet he does properly will and love that Good which cometh of Evil; that is, his own Glory, and the Salvation of his People.

Whether does God will Punishments or no?
Yea, his Will is the first and efficient cause of all Punishment: Which is proved by this Reason and Argument. Every good thing is of God; every Punishment being a Work of Justice is a good thing; therefore every Punishment is of God, and he does will it.

What say you to the words in Ezekiel 18. 23, 32. I will not the death of a Sinner?
That place is to be understood only of the Elect. For properly indeed God does not will their Death, and therefore to keep them from Death, meaning eternal Death, he giveth them Repentance.

Whether does God will Sin as it is a punishment of Sin that went before?
Yes, he does: And it is usual with God to punish one Sin with another. As for Example; The hardening of Pharaoh's Heart was a sin in Pharaoh, and God brought it upon him, not as sin, but as a punishment of his former sins.

You say that in every Sin is an Action or Deed, which is either Inward, or Outward, whether does God will that or no?
So far forth as it is an Action only, God does will it: But not the corruption and deformity of the Action. For in him we live, move, and have our being. Acts 17. 28.

But whether does God will Sin properly, as it is a transgression of the Law, and a corruption in the Action, or no?
No, he does not, neither can he; for it is against his Nature. And to this effect serve these places of Scripture following, Psal. 5. 5. Heb. 1. 9. 1 Joh. 1. 5. and Reason does confirm it many ways. For look what God does will properly, he loveth and alloweth it: But God hateth and damneth Sin, as the Scriptures witness; and therefore he does not will it properly, Zech. 8. 17. Again, he hath sent his Son to take away the sins of the World, and to destroy the Works of the Devil; therefore he does not will them. Lastly, If God should properly will Sin, then he must be the Author of Sin: But he is not the Author of Sin: For the Scriptures do never attribute sin unto God, but unto the Devil and unto Men, Rom. 9. 14. 1 John 2. 16.

But although God does not properly will Sin, yet he does willingly permit Sin; does he not?
Yes. But for the better understanding how God does permit Sin, we must consider how many ways, or in how many senses one is said to permit a thing: and that is three ways.

To permit, is sometime of two good things to grant that which is less good, although it were against our will. As for Example; A Man would bring up his Son in Learning, rather than in Warfare, or in any other Occupation; but because his Son hath more mind to an Occupation than to Learning, and does crave of his Father to go to some Occupation, or to be a Soldier rather than a Doctor, his Father does grant him his desire, but he had rather have him to be a Scholar; and this is a kind of a Permission and Suffering: But this Permission ought rather to be called a Will indeed; for that which is less good (yet because it is good) he does will it, and approve it, and it is a true Object of his Will: And it may be called a Permission in respect of that Will which had rather have had the greater good.

And is thus God said to permit Sin in this sense?
No, by no means. For Sin (as it is Sin) hath no show of good in it, which may be compared with a greater good.

Which is your second way of permitting?
Sometimes to permit, is to grant one Evil to go unpunished, that many and more grievous Evils thereby may be prevented; as many times Princes and Magistrates are wont to do: And so some do think that God hath granted some Sin to be done without danger or threatening of punishment, lest more and more heinous mischief should ensue.

And are not you of this mind?
No, God forbid I should. For the Apostle's Rule is both general and true, We must not do Evil that Good may come thereof, left we be damned justly: therefore no Man may by the Law of God admit any sin to avoid another, Rom. 3. 8.

What is your third way of permitting?
To permit, does sometime signify not to hinder and stop Evil when he may: and so God is said to permit Sin, because he could by his Grace hinder and prevent sins that none should be committed; and yet he does willingly permit us in our Nature to Sin. That God does thus permit Sin it is evident by these places of Scripture, Psal. 81. 11, 12. Acts 14. 16. That he does permit them willingly, and not constrained thereunto, these places do show, Rom. 9. 19. Isa. 46. 10.

For what cause does not God hinder Sin, but permit it?
Not without cause; but that he may use our Sins (which is his infinite Goodness and Wisdom) to his own Glory: For hereby his Justice in punishing of Sin, and his Mercy in pardoning of Sin, is made manifest and known, to the great Glory of God, and Praise of his Name.

Whether does God alter his Will at any time, or no?
For the better understanding of this Question, we must consider two things. First, How many ways our Will is changeable. Secondly, The Causes that move us to change our Wills.

Very well: Declare the first, How many ways our Wills are changeable?
The will of Man is changeable two ways: First, When we begin to will a thing which we did not will before. Secondly, When we leave to will that which we willed before.

Now show what are the causes thereof: And first, Why a Man does will that which he willed not before.
The causes of these are two. First, Our Ignorance: Because we know that to be good afterward which we knew not before to be good, and then we will that which we could not before; for ignoti nulla cupido, of that which is unknown there is no desire. The second cause ariseth from the alteration of Nature: As if that which was hurtful to us at one time, became profitable to us at another time; then we will have that at one time, which we would not at another: As for Example, In Summer our Will is inclined to cold places, but in Winter our Will is altered, and does affect and desire the warm.

Whether is there any such cause in God to make him change his Will, or not?
No; neither of these Causes can be in God. Not the first, for he does most perfectly know all things from all eternity: Not the second, for there is nothing in God for which any thing may be found to be profitable or hurtful, he is always the same, having need

of nothing; and therefore he cannot will any thing that is new to him, and consequently his Will is not changeable.

But what say you to the second way of changing our Will; that is, of leaving to will that which before we had determined: whereof cometh that?
For this there may be yielded two Reasons. 1. We do change our Wills of our own accord; because the latter thing does seem to us to be better than the former. 2. Being constrained, or against our minds, we do oftentimes change our Wills; because our first Counsel was hindered by some cross event, that it could not have its due effect.

Whether are any of these two Causes in God, that for those he should change his Will?
No; God does neither of his own accord, nor yet by constraint, change his Will: but his Decrees are, and ever have been, and always shall be fulfilled, and none shall hinder the Will of God; for it does always remain one and the same. And this Doctrine is most strongly guarded and fenced with these Places of Scripture; Numb. 23. 19. Mal. 3. 6. Isa. 46. 10. Rom. 11. 29.

Paul saith, 1 Tim. 2. 4. It is the Will of God that all Men should be saved, and come to the Knowledge of the Truth; and yet all are not saved: therefore God's Will is mutable?
If this Place be understood of God's Revealed Will, then the Sense is this: that God does call all Men by the preaching of his Word, to the Knowledge of his Truth, and to Eternal Salvation, if they will believe in Christ. But if it be understood of the Secret Will of God, the Sense may be threefold. First, All Men, that is, of all sorts and degrees, he will have some. Secondly, So many as are saved, all are saved by the Will of God. Thirdly, Therefore, God willeth that all shall be saved; that is, all the Elect. For in the Scriptures this Word All is put sometimes for the Elect, without the Reprobate, as Rom. 5. 18. 1 Cor. 15. 22.

[3RD HEAD.]

What is there comprehended under the Holiness of God's Will?
Holiness is a general Attribute of God, in regard of all the special Properties of his Nature, in respect whereof he most justly loveth, liketh, and preferreth himself above all. Unto which most Holy Will must be referred both Affections, (to speak according unto Man) as Love and Hatred; with their Attendants, (Goodness, Bounty, Grace and Mercy, on the one side; Displeasure, Anger, Grief, and Fury, on the other): and also the ordering of those Affections, by Justice, Patience, Long-suffering, Equity, Gentleness, and readiness to Forgive. Isa. 6. 3. Psal. 145. 17.

What Instructions do you draw from the Holiness of God?
1. That as every one cometh nearer unto him in Holiness, so they are best liked and loved of him: and consequently it should breed a Love in our Hearts of Holiness, and Hatred of the contrary. 2. That this ought to kill in us all evil Thoughts and Opinions which can rise of God in our Hearts; seeing that in him, that is Holiness it self, there can be no Iniquity.

Wherein does the Holiness of God specially appear?
In his Goodness and Justice; Exod. 20. 5, 6. and 34. 6, 7. Nahum 1. 2, 3. Jer. 32. 18, 19.

Third Head

What is God's Goodness?
It is an Essential Property in God, whereby he is infinitely Good, and of himself; and likewise beneficial to all his Creatures, Psal. 145. 7. Mark 10. 18. James 1. 17. Mat. 5. 45. Psal. 34. 8, 9, 10.

How many ways then is the goodness of God to be considered?
Two ways. Either as he is in his own Nature, of himself simply Good, and Goodness it self; (i. so Perfect, and every way so absolute, as nothing can be added unto him): or else as he is good to others. Both ways God is in himself a Good God: but especially for his Goodness towards us, he is called a Good God, as a Prince is called a Good Prince.

Show how that is.
A Prince may be a good Man, if he hurt no Man, and liveth Honestly, &c. But he is not called a Good Prince, except he be good to his Subjects; that is, if he be not mild, gentle, liberal, just, a defender of the Godly, a punisher of the Wicked; so that the Good may lead a quiet and peaceable Life in all Honesty and Goodness, (1 Tim. 2. 2.) So the Scriptures call God a Good God, because he is not only Good in himself, yea, and Goodness it self, but also because he is Good to others; that is, Mild, Gracious, Merciful; his Nature is not cruel, savage, nor bloody towards, but most mild, pleasant, sweet, and such as may allure all Men to trust in him, to love him, to call upon him, and to worship him, Psalm 16. 11. and 34. 8, 9.

Is nothing Good but God?
Nothing of it self, and perfectly, (Mat. 19. 17.) howbeit by him, and from him, do come good things, (Gen. 1. ult.) which have not their goodness of themselves. For whatsoever goodness is in the Creatures, it is of God the Creator: and they are so far forth good, as they are made good by God, and are made partakers of his goodness, 1 Cor. 4. 7. James 1. 17. Again, that goodness which is in the things created, whether it be natural or supernatural, is imperfect and finite, but the goodness of God is most perfect and infinite; and therefore only God is truly good, and goodness it self; yea, he is Summum Bonum, that chief Good of all to be desired.

Is the Goodness of God extended unto all Creatures?
Yea, it is so: and as this is known by daily Experience, so it is witnessed by these Scriptures following, Psal. 119. 64. and 145. 15. Mat. 5. 45.

Hath God showed his Goodness to all alike?
No: for the things created are of two sorts; either Invisible, or Visible. Invisible, as Angels; unto whom the Lord hath given more excellent Gifts than to the other.

And was his Goodness parted equally amongst them?
No: for some he suffered to fall into Sin, for which they were thrust down from Heaven to Hell, 2 Pet. 2. 4. others he hath preserved by his Grace, that they should not fall away from him.

Is his Goodness alike to his Visible Creatures?
No: for of them some are endued with Reason, as Mankind, some are void of Reason; and therefore is Man called a Lord over the rest of the Creatures.

Is the Goodness of God alike to Reasonable Creatures?
No: for of them God in his Mercy hath chosen some to eternal Life, whom he hath purposed to call effectually in his time, that they may be justified and glorified by Christ: others he hath in his justice left to their sins without any effectual calling, to perish for ever.

What testimony of Scripture have you, that God's Goodness is far greater to the Elect, than to the Reprobate?

It appeareth by the words of our Savior Christ, Mat. 13. 11. and of the Prophet Asaph, Psal. 73. 1. yet God is good, that is, singularly good, to Israel, even to the pure in heart: but God makes his Elect only to be pure in heart, Psal. 51. 10.

Does the Goodness of God towards all Men turn to the good of all Men?

No: for in the Reprobate God's Goodness is turned into Evil, and serveth to their Destruction, 2 Cor. 2. 15, 16. and that is through their own fault: for they do condemn and altogether abuse the Goodness of God; and for all his Goodness bestowed upon them continually, they never trust him, nor trust in him, Rom. 2. 4. Psal. 106. 13.

How may we use the Goodness of God to our Good, and to our Salvation?

If we have the Goodness of God in a true and worthy estimation; if we use it with fear and reverence, and thereby learn to repent us of our sins; and to repose all our trust and confidence in the Lord for his goodness; then shall all things, yea, even our sins, work for our good, Rom. 8. 28.

What Use must we make of God's Goodness?

1. It teacheth us that we have and do serve a true God: for he is no true God, that is not so good as our God is. 2. We learn hereby, that by this Goodness of his, he useth all things well. 3. If our God be so good, we should be ashamed to offend him. As it is intolerable to hurt an Infant, that is innocent and harmless; so it is most intolerable to require the Lord's Goodness with Evil. 4. If God be so good, and Goodness it self; we must trust him, and trust in him. For we will repose trust in a good Man: and shall we not much more in our good God? 5. It teacheth us never to lay the Fault upon God for any thing, nor to complain of God's dealing. For he is always perfectly good; and all that he does is perfectly good, whatsoever Men judge of it. 6. Seeing God is good to us, we ought to be good one towards another.

To what end is it, that the Goodness of God is not to all alike?

First, it serveth to the adorning and beautifying of God's Church, 1 Tim. 2. 9. 2 Tim. 2. 20. Second, it serveth to the maintenance of mutual Love and Society amongst Men. For if the Goodness of God were to all alike, then one could not help another: and to this end serves the variety of Gifts, 1 Cor. 12. 20. Ephes. 4. 7, 12. Third, it maketh to the greater manifesting of the Glory of the Goodness of God. For if all had alike, we would condemn his Goodness, thinking that he were bound to be good to us: of Necessity. Fourth, from the Consideration of God's special Goodness towards us his Elect by Christ to Salvation, we must arise to the study of Good Works, whereby God's Goodness may be glorified, Tit. 3. 3, 4, 5, 6, 7, 8.

What are the special Branches of the Goodness of God?

His Graciousness, his Love, and Mercy, Tit. 3. 3, 4, 5.

What is the Graciousness of God?

It is an Essential Property, whereby he is of himself most gracious and amiable; and freely declareth his Favor unto his Creatures above their desert, Psal. 145. 8, 15, 16. Rom. 11. 6. Tit. 2. 11.

Is he only gracious?

Only in and of himself: for that whatsoever is gracious and amiable, it is from him.

What learn you from this?
That we ought to love and reverence God above all. For seeing gracious and amiable Men do win love and reverence from others, in whose Eyes they appear gracious and amiable; who is able more to win this at our Hands than God, who is the Fountain of all Graciousness and Amiableness?

For the better understanding of this Attribute, show how this Word Grace is used in the Scriptures.
It is used in three special Significations: Sometimes it is put for Comeliness, Stature, Meekness, or Mildness, (Luke 2. 52.) Sometimes for free Favor, whereby one embraceth another, pardoning former Injuries, and receiving the Party offending into Favor again, (Gen. 6. 8.) Sometimes it is taken for all kind of Gifts and Graces, which of his free Favor are bestowed, whether temporal or eternal, Ephes. 4. 7.

Whether is there Grace in God, according to the first Signification of Grace, or no?
Yea: for God is of his own Nature most gracious, and Grace it self. Which Grace was in Christ Jesus from his Infancy, (as he was Man) and did every Day more and more Increase, Luke 2. 52. Psalm 45. 2. And amongst all things that were created, there was nothing endued with such Grace as was the Human Nature of Christ; and that was by the fullness of the Godhead, which dwelt bodily in him, Colos. 2. 9.

Whether is Grace properly attributed to God in the second Sense, or no?
Yea, most properly. For God does justify us, that is, he does account us for just, through his Son Jesus Christ; and that of his free Grace and Favor, without any desert of our parts, or any thing in us, Rom. 3. 20, 24. and 4. 16.

What are the Causes of this Grace or Favor of God?
The Efficient Cause is his Goodness and Free Will: The Final Cause thereof, is the Salvation of his chosen Children, and the Glory of himself, and of his Son Christ Jesus.

What are the Effects of God's Grace to us-ward?
In general; the Grace of God (whereof there is no Cause in us, but only his own Goodness and Will) is the first Cause, the middle Cause, and the last Cause, and the only Cause of all that belongs to our Salvation, Rom. 9. 11. And particularly, it is the Cause of our Election, of our Redemption, of the sending of Christ into the World, of our Calling, of the preaching of the Gospel, Ephes. 1. 4. John 3. 16. Rom. 5. 8. It was the Cause why the Apostles were called to the preaching of the Gospel, Gal. 1. 15, 16. Ephes. 3. 8, 9. It is the Cause of our Faith, of Forgiveness of our Sins, of our whole Justification, of our Regeneration, of our Renovation, of our Love to God and our Neighbor, of the Holy Ghost in us; of our good Works, of our Obedience, of our Perseverance, of the Fear of God, of Eternal Life, of Life it self, 2 Tim. 1. 9. Phil. 2. 13. Rom. 12. 6. 1 Cor. 12. 9. Rom. 3. 24. Tit. 3. 5. 1 Joh. 4. 9. Ezek. 36. 27. Jer. 32. 40. And in a word, the beginning, the continuance, and the accomplishment of our whole Salvation does depend wholly upon the Grace and Favor of God: and what good thing soever we have, or have had, or may have, belonging either to this Life or the Life to come, is to be attributed wholly to the Grace and Favor of God.

What is the Love of God?
It is an Essential Property in God, whereby he loveth himself above all, and others for himself, 1 John 4. 16. Rom. 5. 8. John 3. 16. Tit. 3. 4. Mal. 1. 2, 3.

What learn you from hence?
That we should love him dearly, and other things for him.

That we may the better know what the Love of God is, declare first, What Love is in ourselves.
It is a Passion, of the Mind, whereby we are so affected towards the Party whom we Love; that we are rather his than our own, forgetting ourselves to do him good whom we so Love.

And is Love such a thing in God?
No: the true Love of God is not such as our Love is.

What difference is there?
There is great difference two ways. First, In time: for Love was in God before it was in us, or in any thing created; for he loved himself, and us also, before the World was, Joh. 17. 23. Secondly, They differ in Nature and Quality: for that Love which is in God is most perfect and pure, without Passion; but in us it is imperfect, and matched with Passions, with impure Affections and Grief of the Mind.

After what manner does the Scripture express the Love of God?
In the Scriptures God does compare himself to a Father and to a Mother loving their Children; to a Hen gathering her Chickens together under her Wings; to a good Shepherd seeking up his Sheep, and to divers other things.

And wherefore serve these Comparisons?
They are for our Profit two ways. First, To show us that God's Love towards us is most vehement and sincere. Secondly, To make us bold in coming to him, and calling upon him. So for this Love Christ Jesus calleth us by all the Names of Love: as his Servants, his Kinsmen, his Friends, his Spouse, his Brethren, and by many Names more: to show, that he loveth us with all Loves, the Father's Love, the Mother's Love, the Master's Love, the Husband's Love, the Brother's Love, &c. and if all Loves were put together, yet his Love exceedeth them all: for all could not do so much for us as he alone hath done.

If Love does not signify any Affection or Passion in God, as it does in us: What then does it signify?
In God it signifieth three things most perfect. First, The eternal good Will of God towards some Body: for the Love of God (suppose towards the Elect) is his ever lasting good Will, or his Purpose and Determination to show them Mercy, to do them Good, and to Save them, as in Rom. 9. 11, 13. Secondly, The Effects themselves of this Love or good Will; whether they be temporal concerning this Life, or eternal concerning the Life to come, as in 1 John 3. 1. Thirdly, The Pleasure and Delight which he taketh in that which he loveth: and so it is taken in Psal. 45. 7.

What things does God love besides himself?
Besides himself, God loveth all things else whatsoever he made: But he loveth not Sin and Iniquity; for he never made it, as S. John saith, 1 John. 2. 16. Again, he loveth his Son, being manifested in the Flesh; and he loveth his chosen Children for his Son's Sake, with whom he is well pleased, Mat. 3. 17.

Object. 1. The Scripture saith, That God does hate all that work Iniquity: How then can God both hate and love one and the same Man?
In every wicked Man we must consider two things. First, His Nature. Secondly, His Sin. His Nature is the Work of God, and that he loveth: But his Iniquity is not of God, and that he hateth.

Object. God does afflict his Children; therefore he does not love them.
Whom he loveth he correcteth, (Prov. 3. 12.) and therefore he correcteth them because he loveth them; even as a Goldsmith trieth his Gold in the Fire, because he loveth it.

Whether does God love all alike, or no?
No: He preferreth Mankind before all his other Creatures; for which cause God is called Philanthropos, that is, a Lover of Men. And this appeareth by three Effects of his Love.

First, He made him according to his own Image; that is, in Righteousness and true Holiness, Gen. 1. 26. Ephes. 4. 24. Secondly, He made him Lord over all his Creatures, Psal. 8. 5, 6. Thirdly, He gave his own Son to Death for his Ransom.

Does God love all Men alike?
No: For he loveth his Elect better than the Reprobate. For the Elect he calleth effectually by his Spirit in their Hearts; when he calleth others but by the outward Voice of the Gospel, &c.

Again, amongst the Elect themselves, some are actually Wicked, and not yet reconciled nor called, as was Paul before his Conversion. But the rest are called and already made Holy by Faith in Christ, as Paul was after his Conversion. And of these, he loveth the latter sort with a greater measure of Love than the former, as the Scripture testifieth in Prov. 8. 17.

What manner of Love does God bear to his Elect?
It hath three adjuncts or properties. First, It is free without desert. Secondly, It is great without comparison. Thirdly, It is constant without any end.

How is the Love of God said to be free?
It is free two ways, First, because nothing caused God to love us, but his own Goodness and Grace: And therefore St. John saith, that his Love was before ours, 1 John 4. 10. Secondly, It is free, because God in loving us, did not regard any thing that belonged to his own Commodity: For, as David saith, Psal. 16. 2. he hath no need of our Goods; but only to our own Salvation he loved us.

Wherein does the Greatness of God's Love appear to his Elect?
It appeareth two ways. 1. By the means which God used to save us by, that is, the Death of his Son: And so St. John setteth forth his Love, John 3. 16. 1 John 3. 16. when he saith οὕτω, that is, So, (as if he should say, so vehemently, so ardently, so earnestly, so wonderfully) did he love us, that for our Salvation he spared not his own only Begotten Son, but gave him to the Death of the Cross for our Salvation.

What else does set forth the greatness of God's Love unto us?
The consideration of our own selves. For he did not only give his only Son to Death for us, but it was for us being his Enemies. And this Circumstance is used by the Apostle to express the same, Rom. 5. 7, 8.

Where find you it written, that God's Love is constant and perpetual?
That is manifestly showed in these Scriptures following, Hos. 11. 9. Joh. 13. 1. Rom. 11. 29. For as God is unchangeable in his Essence and Nature; so is he unchangeable in his Love, which is his Essence and Nature: And therefore is God called Love in the Scriptures, 1 John 4. 8.

What use must we make of God's Love?
First, It filleth our Hearts with Gladness, when we understand that our God is so loving, and Love it self: And what is this but the beginning of eternal Life? If eternal Life consist in the true Knowledge of God, as our Savior Christ saith, John 17. 3.

Secondly, Out of the Knowledge of this Love, as out of a Fountain, springeth the Love of God and our Neighbor. For St. John saith, He that loveth not, knoweth not God, for God is Love, 1 John 4. 8.

Thirdly, When we consider that God loveth all his Creatures which he made, it should teach us not to abuse any of the Creatures, to serve our Lust and beastly Affections. For God will punish them which abuse his Beloved; as he punished the rich Glutton which abused the Creatures of God, Luke 16.

Fourthly, We are taught to love all the Creatures, even the basest of all, seeing that God loveth them, and for the Love he beareth to us he made them: and we must (if we love them for God's Sake) use them sparingly, moderately, and equally or justly. To this end we are commanded to let our Cattle rest upon the Sabbath Day, as well as ourselves: to this end we are forbidden to kill the Dam upon her Nest; and to this end we are forbidden to muzzle the Mouth of the Ox which treadeth out the Corn, Deut. 25. 4. 1 Cor. 9. 9.

Fifthly, We are taught from hence to love Mankind better than all other Creatures, because God does so: and therefore we must not spare any thing that we have, that may make for the safety of his Body, and the Salvation of his Soul. And for this Cause, we are commanded to love our Enemies, and to do them good; because our good God does so.

Sixthly, From God's Love, we learn to prefer the Godly Brethren, and those that Profess sincerely the same Religion that we Profess, before other Men; because God's Love is greater to the Elect, than to the Reprobate: and this does the Apostle teach us, Gal. 6. 10.

Seventhly, Whereas God's Love is freely bestowed upon us, this teacheth us to be humble, and to attribute no part of our Salvation to ourselves, but only to the free Love of God.

Eighthly, From hence ariseth the certainty of our Salvation. For if God's Love was so free and great when we were his Enemies; much more will it be so, and constant also to us, being reconciled to God by Jesus Christ, Rom. 5. 10.

What is the Mercy of God?
It is his Mind and Will, always most ready to Succor him that is in Misery. Or, an Essential Property in God, whereby he is merely ready of himself to help his Creatures in their Miseries, Isa. 30. 18. Lam. 3. 22. Exod. 33. 19.

Why add you this Word merely?
To put a difference between the Mercy of God, and the Mercy that is in Men: for their Mercy is not without some Passion, Compassion, or Fellowfeeling of the Miseries of others: but the Mercy of God is most Perfect and Effectual, ready to help at all Needs of himself.

But, seeing Mercy is a Grief and Sorrow of the Mind, conceived at another's Miseries; how can it be properly attributed to God, in whom are no Passions nor Grief's?
Indeed in us Mercy may be such a thing; but not in God. Mercy was first in God, and from him was derived to us: (and therefore God is called the Father of Mercies, (2 Cor.

1. 3.) and when it came to us, it was matched with many Infirmities and Passions. But it is improperly attributed to God from ourselves; as though it were first in us.

Declare then briefly what things of Perfection are signified by this Word [Mercy] in God.
By the Name of [Mercy] two things are signified in God Properly. First, the Mind and Will ready to help and succor. Secondly, The help it self, and succor or pity that is then showed.

Where in the Scripture is Mercy the first way?
Those Places of Scripture are so to be understood, wherein God does call himself Merciful, and saith, that he is of much Mercy; that is, he is of such a Nature as is most ready to free us from our Evils.

Where is it taken in the other Sense for the Effects of Mercy?
In Rom. 9. 15. where it is said, God will have mercy on whom he will have mercy; that is, he will call whom he will call, he will justify whom he will, he will pardon whom he will, and will deliver and save from all their Miseries and Evils whom he will: and these be the Effects of God's Mercies. Again, in Exod. 20. 6. it is so taken.

From whence springeth this Mercy of God?
The Essence and Being of God is most simple without any mixture or composition; and therefore in him there are not divers Qualities and Virtues as there be in us, whereof one dependeth upon another, or one differs from another; but for our capacity and understanding, the Scripture speaketh of God as though it were so, that so we may the better perceive what manner of God, and how good our God is.

Well then; seeing the Scriptures do speak so for our Understanding, let us hear whereof this Mercy cometh.
The Cause is not in us, but only in God himself, and Mercy in God does spring out of his free Love towards us.

Why do you say out of the free Love of God? Are there more Loves in God than one?
There are two kinds of Love in God: one is wherewith the Father loveth the Son, and the Son the Father, and which the Holy Ghost beareth towards both the Father and the Son: and this Love I call the Natural Love of God, so that the one cannot but love the other. But the Love wherewith he loveth us is voluntary, not being constrained thereunto, and therefore is called the free Love of God: and thereof it cometh to pass, that Mercy is also wholly free, that is, without Reward or Hope of Recompense, and excludeth all Merit.

How prove you that the Mercy of God ariseth out of his Love?
That the Love of God is the cause of his Mercy, it is manifest in the Scriptures, 1 Tim. 1. 2. Paul saluteth Timothy in this order, Grace, Mercy and Peace from God the Father, and from the Lord Jesus Christ: to show that that Peace which the World cannot give, the Mercy of God is the cause of it; and the cause of his Mercy is his Grace, and his Grace is nothing else but his free Favor and Love towards us. The same order does Paul observe in Titus 3. 4, 5. where he saith; When the goodness and love of God our Savior appeared; not by the Works of Righteousness, which he had done, but according to his Mercy he saved me. First, He sets down the Goodness of God as the cause of his Love. Secondly, His Love as the cause of his Mercy. And thirdly, His Mercy as the cause of our Salvation; and our Salvation as the effect of all. And therefore there is nothing in us, which may move the Lord to show Mercy upon us, but only because he is Goodness it self by Nature. And to this does the Psalmist bear

Witness, Psal. 100. 5. saying, that the Lord is good, his Mercy is everlasting, and his Truth is from Generation to Generation.

Towards whom is the Mercy of God extended or showed?
For the opening of this Point, we are to consider that the Mercy of God is two fold. First, General. Secondly, Special. God as a God does show Mercy generally upon all his Creatures being in Misery; and chiefly to Men, whether they be Just or Unjust: and so does Succor them, either immediately by himself, or else mediately by Creatures, as by Angels or Men, by the Heavens, by the Elements, and by other living Creatures (Psal. 104. and 147.). And this general Mercy of God is not extended to the Eternal Salvation of all, but is only temporary, and for a while. Of this read Luke 6. 36.

What say you of the Special Mercy of God?
That I call the Special Mercy of God, which God as a most free God hath showed to whom he would, and denied to whom he would. And this pertaineth only to the Elect, and those which fear him, Psal. 103. 11. for he showeth mercy upon them to their eternal Salvation, and that most constantly, while he does effectually call them unto himself, while he does freely and truly pardon their sins, and justify them in the Blood of the Lamb Jesus Christ; while he does sanctify them with his Grace, and does glorify them in eternal Life: And of this Special Mercy we may read in Ephes. 2. 4, 5, 6.

How great is the Mercy of God?
It is so great that it cannot be expressed, nor conceived of us: And that is proved by Psal. 57. 10. and 108. 4.

How long does the Mercy of God continue towards us?
Although the Mercy of God be great and infinite in Christ, yet for that Mercy which pardoneth our sins, and calleth us to Faith and Repentance by the Gospel, there is no place after death, but only while we live in this World: which is warranted by these places ensuing, Gal. 6. 10. Let us do good whilst we have time: To show that a time will come when we shall not be able to do good.

Rev. 2. 10. Be faithful unto Death, and I will give thee a Crown of Life: to show, that the time which is given unto Death, is a time of Repentance, and of exercising of Faith, and of Works: But after Death there is no time, but to receive either an immortal Crown, if we have been faithful; or everlasting Shame, if we have been unfaithful. Besides these, see Rev. 14. 13. Mark 9. 44, 45. Isa. ult. 24. Luk. 16. 24, 25, 26. Mat. 25. 11, 12. Joh. 9. 4.

What Uses may we make of God's Mercy?
First, It serveth to humble us: For the greater Mercy is in God, the greater Misery is in us. Secondly, We must attribute our whole Salvation unto his Mercy. Thirdly, We must flee to God in all our troubles, with most sure confidence. Fourthly, We must not abuse it to the liberty of the flesh in sin, although we might find Mercy with God after Death: For the Mercy of God pertaineth especially to those that fear him, Psal. 103. 11. Fifthly, The meditation of God's Mercy towards us, should make us to Love God, Psal. 116. 1. Luke. 7. 47. Fear God, Psal. 130. 4. Praise God, Psal. 86. 12, 13. and 103. 2, 3, 4. Sixthly, It must make us merciful one to another, Luke 6. 36. Mat. 18. 32, 33.

What is the Justice of God?
It is an Essential Property in God, whereby he is infinitely just in himself, of himself, for, from, by himself alone, and none other, Psal. 11. 7.

Third Head

What is the Rule of this Justice?
His own free Will, and nothing else. For whatsoever he willeth is just: And because he willeth it, therefore it is just; not because it is just, therefore he willeth it, Ephes. 1. 11. Psal. 115. 3. Mat. 20. 15. which also may be applied to other Properties of God.

Explain this more particularly.
I say, that God does not always a thing because it is just, but therefore any thing is just that is just, because God will have it so: And yet his Will is joined with high Wisdom. As for Example; Abraham did judge it a most just and righteous thing to kill his Innocent Son; not by the Law, for that did forbid him, but only because he did understand it was the special Will of God: and he knew that the Will of God was not only just, but also the Rule of all Righteousness.

That we may the better understand this Attribute, declare unto me how many manner of ways one may be Just or Righteous.
Three manner of ways: Either by Nature, or by Grace, or by perfect Obedience.

How many ways may one be Just by Nature?
Two ways. First, By himself, and of himself, in his own Essence and Being. Thus we say, that in respect of this Essential Righteousness, there is none just but God only; as Christ said, None is good but God only, Luk. 18. 19. Secondly, By the benefit of another, to be either made Righteous, or born Just. And in respect of this natural gift of Righteousness we say, that in the beginning Adam was made just; because he was created just, and in his whole Nature was righteous and good. But this Righteousness was derived from God.

Whom do you call Just by Grace?
All the Elect, which are redeemed by the death of Christ; and that in two respects. First, Because the Righteousness of Christ is imputed unto them, and so by grace and favor in Christ their Head, they are just before God. Secondly, Because of grace and favor they are regenerated by the Holy Ghost; by the virtue of whose inherent Righteousness and Holiness, they are made Holy and Just; and whatsoever they do by it, is accepted for just for Christ's sake.

Whom do you call Just and Righteous, by yielding perfect obedience to God and his Law?
No Man in this World after the fall of Adam (Christ only excepted) ever was or can be just after that manner.

What say you of Christ, how was he Just?
Our Lord and Savior Jesus Christ is most perfectly Just and Righteous every manner of way.

First, As he is God, he is in his own Essence, of himself, and by himself, most just, even as the Father is; and eternal Righteousness it self. Secondly, As he was Man, he was just by Nature; because he was conceived without Sin, and so was born Just and Righteous. Thirdly, By virtue of his Union with his Divine Nature, which is eternal Righteousness it self, he is most just. Fourthly, By receiving the Gifts of the Holy Ghost without measure, he is most just, Psal. 45. 7. John 3. 34. Fifthly, He did most perfectly obey the Law of God, and kept it most absolutely: Therefore that way also he is most Righteous and Just.

What conclude you upon all this?
That forasmuch as God only is in his own Essence and Nature, by himself and of himself, eternal Justice and Righteousness; therefore this Attribute of Justice or Righteousness does most properly agree to God.

In how many things is God just?
In three, First, In his Will. Secondly, In his Word. Thirdly, In his Works.

What mean you when you say, that God is just in his Will?
That whatsoever he willeth is just, his Will (as hath been declared) being the Rule of Justice.

What mean you, when you say, that God is just in his Word?
That whatsoever he speaketh, is just.

What are the parts of God's Word?
Four. First, The History: Which is all true. Secondly, The Precepts and the Laws: Which are perfect. Thirdly, Promises and Threatenings: Which are accomplished. Fourthly, Hymns and Songs: Which are pure, holy, and undefiled.

In what respect is God just in his Word?
First, He speaketh as he thinketh. Secondly, He does both as he speaketh and thinketh. Thirdly, There is no part of his Word contrary to another. Fourthly, He loveth those that speak the Truth, and hateth those that are Liars.

What are the Works of God?
1. His eternal Decree; whereby he hath most justly decreed all things, and the Circumstances of all things, from all Eternity. 2. The just execution thereof in time.

What Justice does God show herein?
Both his Disposing and Rewarding Justice.

What is God's Disposing Justice?
That by which he, as a most free Lord, ordereth all things in his Actions rightly, Psal. 145. 17.

In what Actions does that appear?
First, He hath most justly and perfectly created all things of nothing. Secondly, He hath most wisely, justly, and righteously disposed all things being created.

What is God's Rewarding Justice?
That whereby he rendereth to his Creatures according to their Works.

Wherein does that appear?
First, He does behold, approve, and reward all good in whomsoever. Secondly, He does behold, detest, and punish all evil in whomsoever. To which Justice both his Anger and his Hatred are to be referred.

What must we understand by Anger in God?
Not any Passion, Perturbation, or Trouble of the Mind, as it is in us: But this word Anger, when it is attributed to God in the Scripture, signifieth three things. First, a most certain and just Decree in God, to punish and avenge such Injuries as are offered to himself, and to his Church: And so it is understood, John 3. 36. Rom. 1. 18. Secondly, the threatening of these Punishments and Revenges: As in Psal. 6. 1. Hos. 11. 9. Thirdly, the Punishments themselves, which God does execute upon ungodly Men: And these

are the Effects of God's Anger, or of his Decree to punish them. So it is taken in Rom. 2. 5. Mat. 3. 7. Ephes. 5. 6.

What Use may we make of this Attribute?
First, It teacheth us that Anger of it self is not simply Evil: But then it is Good, when it is such as the Scripture attributeth to God, and commendeth to Men; when it saith, Be angry and sin not, Ephes. 4. 26. Secondly, God's Anger serveth to raise us up from security. Thirdly, We must not be slothful when we see the signs of God's Wrath coming, but use ordinary means to prevent it.

What is that Hatred that is attributed to God?
Not any passion or grief of the Mind as it is in us: But in the Scriptures these three things are signified thereby.

First, His denial of Good Will, and Mercy, to eternal Salvation: As Rom. 9. 13. I have hated Esau; that is, I have rejected him, and have not vouchsafed him that favor and grace which I have showed upon Jacob. And we also are said to hate those things which we neglect, and upon which we will bestow no benefit nor credit, but do put them behind other things: And therefore it is said, If any Man come unto me, and hate not his Father and Mother, and Wife and Children, &c. he cannot be my Disciple. That is, he that does not put all these things behind me, and neglect them for me: So that the love which he beareth to them, must seem to be hatred, in comparison of that love which he must show to me, (Luke 14. 26. with Mat. 10. 37.) And in this sense it is properly attributed to God.

Secondly, The Decree of God's Will to punish Sin, and the just punishment it self; which he hath decreed, as in Psal. 5. 6. and Job 30 21. Thou turnest thy self cruelly against me, and art an enemy unto me with the strength of thine hand: that is, thou dost so sore chastise me, as if thou didst hate me. And in this sense also it is properly attributed to God: For it is a part of his Justice to take punishment of Sinners.

Thirdly, God's Displeasure: For those things which we hate do displease us. And in this sense also it is properly attributed to God: For it is the property of a most just Judge to disallow and detest Evil, as well as to allow and like that which is Good.

By what Reasons may this be confirmed?
1. It is the property of him that loveth, to hate and detest that which is contrary to himself, and that which he loveth. For love cannot be without its contrary of hatred: And therefore as the love of good things does properly agree to God; so does also the hatred of evil things as they are evil things. 2. It is manifest by David, that it is no less virtue to hate the Evil, than it is to love the Good. And this hatred of sin (as it is a virtue and perfect hatred) cannot be in us but by the Grace of God: For every good Gift is from above, &c. (Jam. 1. 17.) and there can be no good thing in us, but it is first in God after a more perfect manner than it is in us.

What are we to learn thereby?
First, That it is a great virtue, and acceptable to God, to hate Wickedness, and wicked Men themselves; not as they are Men, but as they are wicked; and as David did, Psal. 139. 21, 22. And we are no less bound to hate the Enemies of God, as they are his Enemies, than to love God, and those that love him. And if we do so, then we must also flee their company, and have no friendship or fellowship with them.

Secondly, That we must distinguish betwixt Men's Persons and their Sins and not to hate the Persons of Men, because they are the good Creatures of God: But their sins we must hate every day more and more, 2 Thess. 3. 6, 14, 15.

Having spoken of the Essence and the Essential Properties of God; tell me now whether there be many Gods, or one only?
There is only one God, and no more.

How may this Unity of the Godhead be proved?
By express Testimonies of God's Word; by Reasons grounded thereon, and by Nature it self, guiding all things to one Principle.

What express Testimonies of God's Word have you for this?
Deut. 6. 4. Hear, O Israel, the Lord our God is one Lord. So in 1 Sam. 2. 2. Psal. 18. 31. Isa. 44. 6. and 46. 9. Mark 12. 29, 32. 1 Cor. 8. 4, 6.

What Reasons have you to prove that there is but one God?
First, We are charged to give unto God all our Heart, all our Strength, and all our Soul, Deut. 6. 4, 5. Mark 12. 29, 30. If one must have all, there is none left for any other. Secondly, God is the chiefest Good, Psal. 144. 15. the first Cause, and the high Governor of all things, Acts 17. 28. Psal. 19. 1. but there can be but one such. Thirdly, The Light of Reason showeth that there can be no more but one that is Infinite, Independent, and Almighty: If God be Infinite and Omnipotent that does all things, there can be but one; for all the rest must be idle.

How does Nature guide all things to one Principle?
The whole course of the World tendeth to one end, and to one unity, which is God.

How can that be, when there be so many sundry things of divers kinds and conditions, and one contrary to another?
That is true indeed, but yet they all together serve one God.

Is that possible? Can you give an Instance hereof in some familiar Resemblance?
Yea, very well. In a Field there are many Battles, divers Standards, sundry Liveries, and yet all turn Head with one sway at once: By which we know that there is one General of the Field which commands them all.

What makes this to confirm your Assertion, that there is but one God over so many divers and contrary things in the World?
Yes; for even so in the World we see divers things, not one like another: for some are noble, some base; some hot, some cold; some wild, some tame; yet all serve to the Glory of God their Maker, and the benefit of Man, and the accomplishment of the whole World.

And what gather you by all this?
That there is but one God, which commandeth them all, like the General of a Field.

If one God be the Author of all; why are there so many Poisons, and noisome Beasts?
First, They were not created noisome and hurtful at the first: But the sin of Adam brought the Curse upon the Creatures, Gen. 3. 17, 18. Secondly, Although God hath cursed the Creatures for Man's sin; yet in his Mercy he does so dispose and order them, that they are profitable for us: For Poisons, we use them for Physic; and the Skins of wild Beasts serve against the Cold, &c. Thirdly, The most hurtful things that

are, might benefit us, if we knew how to use them: And whereas they annoy us, it is not of their own Nature so much as of our Ignorance.

And what do you conclude by all this?
That they have not two beginnings, one good and another bad, as some would imagine: But one Author thereof, which is God himself, always most good and gracious.

If there be but one only God, how is it that many in Scripture are called Gods? (1 Cor. 8. 5.) as Moses is called Pharaoh's God, Exod. 7. 1. and Magistrates are called Gods, Psal. 82. 6. as Idols, and the Belly, Phil. 3. 19. yea, and the Devil himself is called the God of this World, 2 Cor. 4. 4.
The name Elohim or God is sometimes improperly given to other things, either as they participate of God his communicable Attributes, (as in the two first Instances or as they are abusively set up by Man in the place of God, (as in the other). But properly it signifieth him, who is by Nature God, and hath his Being not from any thing but himself; and all other things are from him. And in this sense, unto us there is but one God and Lord, 1 Cor. 8. 6. unto whom therefore the Name Jehovah is in Scripture incommunicably appropriated.

Why then are Magistrates called Gods?
For Four Causes. First, To teach us that such must be chosen to bear rule which excel others in Godliness, like Gods among Men. Secondly, To encourage them in their Offices, and to teach them that they should not fear the Faces of Men; like Gods, which fear nothing. Thirdly, To show how God does honor them, and how they must honor God again. For when they remember how God hath invested them with his own Name, it should make them ashamed to serve the Devil, or the World, or their own Affections; and move them to execute judgment justly, as if God himself were there. Fourthly, To teach us to obey them, as we would obey God himself; for he which condemneth them, condemneth God himself, Rom. 13. 2. and we must not dishonor those whom God does honor.

Why are Idols called Gods?
Not because they are so indeed, but because Idolaters have such an opinion of them.

Why is the Belly called a God?
Because some make more thereof than of God and his Worship. For all that they can do and get, is little enough for their Bellies; and when they should serve God, they serve their Bellies and beastly Appetites.

And why is the Devil called the God of this World?
Because of the great Power and Sovereignty which is given him over the Wicked, whom God hath not chosen out of this World.

There being but one simple and undivided Godhead; to whom does this Divine Nature belong? Is it to be attributed to one, or to many Persons?
We must acknowledge and adore three distinct Persons, subsisting in the Unity of the Godhead.

But do you not believe the Godhead to be divided, whilst you believe that in one God there are three Persons?
No: Not divided into divers Essences, but distinguished into divers Persons. For God cannot be divided into several Natures, nor into several Parts: And therefore must the Persons, which subsist in that one Essence, be only distinct, and not separate one from another: As in the Example of the Sun, the Beams and the Light.

What are those Resemblances that are commonly brought, to shadow out unto us the Mystery of the Trinity?

First, The Sun begetteth his own Beams, and from thence proceedeth Light: and yet is none of them before another, otherwise than in consideration of Order and Relation; that is to say, that the Beams are begotten of the Body of the Sun, and the Light proceedeth from both. Secondly, From one flame of Fire proceed both Light and Heat, and yet but one Fire. Thirdly, In Waters there is the Well-head, the Spring boiling out of it, and the Stream flowing from them both; and all these are but one Water: And so there are three Persons in one Godhead, yet but one God. Fourthly, In Man, the Understanding cometh from the Soul, and the Will from both.

May it be collected by natural Reason, that there is a Trinity of Persons in the Unity of the Godhead?

No: For it is the highest Mystery of Divinity; and the knowledge thereof is more proper to Christians. For the Turks and Jews do confess one Godhead; but no distinction of Persons in the same.

How come we then by the Knowledge of this Mystery?

God hath revealed it in the Holy Scripture unto the Faithful.

What have we to learn of this?

1. That they are deceived who think this Mystery is not sufficiently delivered in the Scripture, but dependeth upon the Tradition of the Church. 2. That since this is a wonderful Mystery which the Angels do adore; we should not dare to speak any thing in it farther than we have warrant out of God's Word: yea, we must tie ourselves almost to the very words of the Scripture, lest in searching we exceed and go too far, and so be overwhelmed with the Glory.

How does it appear in Holy Scripture, that the three Persons are of that Divine Nature?

1. By the Divine Names that it giveth to them; as Jehovah, &c. 2. By ascribing Divine Attributes unto them; As Eternity, Almightiness, &c. 3. By attributing Divine Works unto them; As Creation, Sustentation, and Governing of all things. 4. By appointing Divine Worship to be given unto them.

What special proofs of the Trinity have you out of the Old Testament?

First, The Father is said by his Word to have made the Worlds, the Holy host working and maintaining them, and as it were sitting upon them, as the Hen does on the Eggs she hatches, Gen. 1. 2, 3. Second, Gen. 1. 26. The Trinity speaketh in the Plural Number: Let us make Man in our Image after our Likeness. Third, Gen. 19. 24. Jehovah is said to rain upon Sodom from Jehovah out of Heaven; that is, the Son from the Father, or to the Holy Ghost from both. Fourth, 2 Sam. 23. 2. The Spirit of Jehovah (or the Lord) spake by me, and his Word by my tongue: Here is Jehovah (the Father) with his Word (or Son) and Spirit. Fifth, Prov. 30. 4. What is his Name, and what is his Son's Name, if thou canst tell? Sixth, Isa. 6. 3. The Angels in respect of the three Persons do cry three times, Holy, Holy, Holy. Seventh, Isa. 42. 1. Behold my Servant whom I uphold, mine Elect in whom my Soul delighteth: I have put my Spirit upon him. Eighth, Hag. 2. 5. The Father with the Word and his Spirit make a Covenant.

What are the Proofs out of the New Testament?

1. As all other Doctrines, so this is there more clear; as first, Mat. 3. 16, 17. at the Baptism of Christ, the Father from Heaven witnesseth of the Son; the Holy Ghost appearing in the likeness of a Dove. John Baptist saw the Son in his assumed Nature going out of the Water: There is one Person. He saw the Holy Ghost descending like a

Third Head

Dove upon him: There is another Person. And he heard a Voice from Heaven saying, This is my beloved Son: There is a third Person. 2. Mat. 17. 5. At the Transfiguration, the Father in like manner speaketh of his Son. 3. Mat. 28. 19. We are baptized into the Name of the Father, the Son, and the Holy Ghost. 4. John 14. 16, 26. and 15. 26. and 16. 13, 14, 15. The Father and Son promise to send the Holy Ghost. 5. Luke 1. 35. The Holy Ghost shall come upon thee, and the Power of the Highest shall overshadow thee: Therefore that Holy Thing which shall be born of thee, shall be called the Son of God. 6. Acts 2. 33. Therefore being by the right Hand of God exalted, and having received of the Father the promise of the Holy Ghost; He hath shed forth this which you now see and hear. 7. 2 Cor. 13. 14. The Grace of the Lord Jesus Christ, and the Love of God; and the Communion of the Holy Ghost be with you all. 8. Gal. 4. 6. God hath sent forth the Spirit of his Son into your hearts. 9. Tit. 3. 4, 5, 6. God saved us by the washing of the New Birth, and renewing of the Holy Ghost, which he shed on us abundantly through Jesus Christ our Savior.

What clear Proof have you that these three are but one God; and so that there is a Trinity in Unity?
1 John 5. 7. It is expressly said, there are three that bear record in Heaven, the Father, the Word, and the Holy Ghost; and these three are one.

What learn you of that the Apostle saith they are three?
We learn that the word Trinity, although it he not expressly set down in the Word, yet it hath certain ground from thence.

What learn you of that, that they are said to be three Witnesses?
The singular Fruit that is in the Trinity of the Persons, in one Unity of the Godhead: Whereby great assurance is brought unto us of all things that God speaketh in promise or threat; seeing it is all confirmed by three Witnesses, against whom no exception lieth.

What are they said here to witness?
That God hath given eternal Life unto us, and that this Life is in that his Son, 1 John 5. 11.

How are these, being three, said to be but one?
They are one in Substance, Being, or Essence: But three Persons distinct in Subsistence, Acts 20. 28. 1 Cor. 12. 4, 5. Deut. 6. 4. Mar. 12. 32. 1 Cor. 8. 4, 5, 6. John 14. 16. and 15. 26. and 17. 1.

If three Persons among Men be propounded, whereof every one is a Man; can it be said these three are but one Man?
No: But we must not measure God's Matters by the measure of Reason; much less this which of all others is a Mystery of Mysteries.

For the better understanding of this Mystery, declare unto me what a Person is in general, and then what a Person in the Trinity is.
In general; a Person is one particular Thing, Indivisible, Incommunicable, Living, Reasonable, subsisting in it self, not having part of another.

Show me the reason of the particular Branches of this Definition.
I say that a Person is, first, one particular Thing: Because no general Notion is a Person. Secondly, indivisible: Because a Person may not be divided into many Persons; although he may be divided into many parts. Thirdly, incommunicable: Because, though one may communicate his Nature with one, he cannot communicate his Person-ship with another. Fourthly, living and Reasonable: Because no dead or unreasonable thing can be a Person. Fifthly, subsisting in it self: To exclude the

humanity of Christ from being a Person. Sixthly, not having part of another: To exclude the Soul of Man separated from the Body, from being a Person.

What is a Person in the Trinity?
It is whole God, not simply or absolutely considered, but by way of some personal Properties. It is a manner of being in the Godhead, or a distinct Subsistence (not a Quality, as some have wickedly imagined: For no Quality can cleave to the Godhead) having the whole Godhead in it, John 11. 22. and 14. 9, 16. and 15. 1. and 17. 21. Col. 2. 3, 9.

In what respect are they called Persons?
Because they have proper things to distinguish them.

How is this distinction made?
It is not in nature, but in relation and order.

Declare then the order of the Persons of the blessed Trinity?
The first in order is the Father: Then those that come from the Father; the Son who is the second, and the Holy Ghost who is the third Person in the Trinity.

How are these three distinguished by Order and Relation?
The Father is of himself alone, and of no other: The Son is of the Father alone begotten: The Holy Ghost is of the Father and the Son proceeding. And the Father is called the Father in respect of the Son, the Son in respect of the Father, the Holy Ghost in respect that he proceedeth from the Father and the Son: But the one is not the other; as the Fountain is not the Stream, nor the Stream the Fountain, but are so called one in respect of another, and yet all but one Water.

What then is the Father?
The first Person in the Trinity, who hath his Being and Foundation of Personal Subsistence from none other; and hath by Communication of his Essence eternally begotten his only Son of himself, John 5. 27. and 14. 11. and 20. 17. Psal. 2. 7. Heb. 1. 3.

How is it proved that the Father is God?
By express Testimonies of the Scriptures, and by reason drawn from the same.

What are those express Testimonies?
John 17. 3. This is Life Everlasting to know thee to be the only God, Rom. 1. 7. Grace and Peace from God the Father, Ephes. 1. 3. Blessed be God the Father of our Lord Jesus Christ, &c.

What are the Reasons drawn from the Word of God?
That we are bidden to Pray to him, Mat. 6. 6, 9. that he revealeth the Mysteries, Mat. 11. 25, 27. suffereth his Sun to shine, &c. Mat. 5. 45.

How is it showed that he begat his Son of himself?
In that he is called the Brightness of his Glory, and the engraven Form of his Person, Heb. 1. 3. And in that this Generation being from Eternity, there was no Creature of whom he might beget him.

In what respects is he called the Father?
First, in respect of his natural Son Jesus Christ, begotten of his own Nature and Substance, Mat. 11. 27. John 1. 14. 1 John 4. 14. whence he is called the Father of our Lord Jesus Christ, Ephes. 1. 3. Secondly, In respect of his Adopted Sons, whom he hath chosen to be the Heirs of Heaven, through the Mediation of his Natural Son Jesus

Christ, Ephes. 3. 14. John 1. 12. Rom. 8. 14, 15. Mat. 6. 9. For as he is by Nature the Father of Christ, so is he by Grace to us that believe our Father also.

What learn you hence?
To honor and obey him as a Father; and to be followers of God as dear Children, Mal. 1. 6. 1 Pet. 1. 14. Ephes. 5. 1.

What other Names are given in the Scripture to the first Person?
The Father spake most commonly in the Old Testament, (for in these last times he hath spoken by his Son); and he is called by these Names.

Jehovah; that is, I am that I am, without beginning or ending, Isa. 42. 8. Exod. 3. 14. Rev. 1. 4, 8. Elohim; that is, Mighty and Strong. Adonai; that is, Judge, or in whose Judgment we rest. Lord of Hosts; because he hath Angels, and Men, and all Creatures at Command to fight for him, 1 Kings 19. 14. The God of Jacob or of Israel; because he made a Promise to Abraham, that he would be his God, and the God of his Seed, and the Israelites were the Seed of Abraham, Acts 3. 13.

Of the other Persons of the Trinity in general. Essentia Filii est à seipsa; & hac ratione dici potest αὐτό θεος. Essentia tamen Filii non est à seipso; ideoque non potest hac ratione dici αὐτό θεος. Persona enim eius genita est à Patre accipiendo ab eo essentiam ingenitam.

Hitherto of the Father: Do the other Persons that are of the Father, receive their Essence or Godhead from him?
They do. For howsoever in this they agree with the Father, that the Essence which is in them, is of it self uncreated and unbegotten: Yet herein lieth the distinction, that the Father hath his Essence in himself originally, and from none other; the Son and the Holy Ghost have the self-same uncreated and unbegotten Essence in themselves, as well as the Father, (otherwise they should have had no true Godhead) but not from themselves.

If these Persons that come from the Father have a beginning; how can they be eternal?
They have no beginning of time or continuance; but of order of subsistence and off-spring, and that from all Eternity.

Are you able to set down the manner of this Eternal Off-spring?
We find it not revealed touching the manner: And therefore our Ignorance herein is better than all their Curiosity, that have enterprised arrogantly the search hereof. For if our own Generation and Frame in our Mother's Womb be above our capacity, Psal. 139. 14, 15. it is no marvel if the Mystery of the eternal Generation of the Son of God cannot be comprehended. And if the Wind, which is but a Creature, be so hard to know, that Man knoweth not from whence it cometh and whither it goeth, John 3. 8. it is no marvel if the proceeding of the Holy Ghost be unsearchable.

Thus much in general touching the Persons which come from the Father. Now in special, What is the Son?
The second Person of the Trinity, having the Foundation of personal Subsistence from the Father alone; of whom by Communication of his Essence, he is begotten from all Eternity, John 5. 26. Psal. 2. 7. Prov. 8. 22, &c. Prov. 30. 4.

What Names are given unto him in this respect?
First, The only Begotten Son of God, John 1. 14. and 3. 18. because he is only begotten of the Nature and Substance of the Father. Secondly, First Begotten, Heb. 1. 6. Rom. 8. 29. not as though the Father begat any after; but because he begat none

before. Thirdly, The Image and Brightness of the Father's Glory, Heb. 1. 3. because the Glory of the Father is expressed in his Son.

But why is he called the Word? 1 John 5. 7. and John 1. 1.
He is called a Word, or Speech, (for so does Logos more properly signify): Because, First, As Speech is the birth of the Mind; so is the Son of the Father. Secondly, As a Man revealeth the meaning of the Heart by the Word of his Mouth; so God revealeth his Will by his Son, John 1. 18. Heb. 1. 2. Thirdly, He is so often spoken of and promised in the Scriptures; and is in a manner the whole Subject of the Scriptures, John 1. 45.

How prove you that the Son is God?
He is in the Scriptures expressly called God, and Jehovah: And likewise the Essential Properties, the Works and Actions of God are given to him, Isa. 9. 6. and 25. 9. Zech. 2. 10, 11. Prov. 8. 22. John 1. 1. and 20. 28. Rom. 9. 5. Phil. 1. 6. Heb. 1. 8, 10. 1. John 5. 20.

How do you prove it by his Works?
His Works were such as none could do but God: For,

1. He made the World: which none could do but God, Heb. 1. 2.
2. He forgave Sins: which none can do but God, Mat. 9. 2.
3. He giveth the Holy Ghost: which none can do but God, John 15. 16.
4. He maintaineth his Church: which he could not do if he were not God, Ephes. 4. 11, 12.

Can you prove the Son to be God, by comparing the Old and New Testaments?
Yes. For what the Old Testament speaks of Jehovah, which is God, that the New Testament applieth to Christ. As, First, David saith, Jehovah went up on high, and led Captivity captive, Psal. 68. 18. Paul applieth it to Christ, Ephes. 4. 8. Secondly, The Psalmist saith, Jehovah was tempted, Psal. 95. 9. which Paul applieth to Christ, 1 Cor. 10. 9. Thirdly, Isaiah saith, Jehovah is the first and the last, Isa. 41. 4. that is also applied to Christ, Rev. 1. 8. and 21. 6. and 22. 13. Fourthly, Isaiah saith, Jehovah will not give his Glory to any other than to himself, Isa. 42. 8. But it is given to Christ, Heb. 1. 6. Therefore Christ is Jehovah.

For the better understanding of the generation of the Son; show me the divers manners of begetting.
There be two manners of begetting: The one is carnal and outward, and this is subject to corruption, alteration, and time. The other is spiritual and inward: as was the begetting of the Son of God; in whose Generation there is neither corruption, alteration, nor time.

Declare then after what manner this Spiritual Generation of the Son of God was: and yet in sobriety, according to the Scriptures.
For the better finding out of this Mystery, we must consider in God two things. First, That in God there is an understanding, Psal. 139. 2. Secondly, We must consider how this Understanding is occupied in God.

Declare after what manner it is in God.
This Understanding is his very Being, and is everlastingly, and most perfectly occupied in God.

Whereupon does God's Understanding Work?
Upon nothing but it self; and that I prove by Reason. For God being Infinite and all in all, it cannot meet with any thing but himself.

Third Head

What Work does this Understanding in God effect?
It does understand and conceive it self. For as in a Glass a Man does conceive and beget a perfect Image of his own Face: So God in beholding and minding of himself, does in himself beget a most perfect and most lively Image of himself; which is that in the Trinity which we call the Son of God.

Where do you find that the Son is called the Perfect Image of God?
Heb. 1. 3. He is called the Brightness of his Glory, and the Engraven Form of his Person, which is all one.

What mean you by Engraven Image?
That as Wax upon a Seal hath the Engraven Form of the Seal: So the Son of God, which his Father had begotten of his own Understanding, is the very Form of his Father's Understanding; so that when the one is seen, the other is seen also.

When then he is Understanding it self, for so is his Father.
Yea, he is so; and he saith so of himself, I have Counsel and Wisdom, I am Understanding, Prov. 8. 14.

But where find you that he was begotten?
He saith so himself, in the Name of Wisdom, in these Words; When there was no depths, then was I begotten; before the Mountains and Hills were settled was I begotten, Prov. 8. 24, 25.

Yea, he was made the Son of God when he was born of the Virgin Mary; was he not?
He was indeed then the Son of God, but he was not then made the Son of God.

When then was he made the Son of God?
He was never made in time; for he was begotten of the substance of his Father from all Eternity, without beginning or ending.

How prove you that the Son of God was not made, but begotten eternally of the substance of his Father?
I prove it, first, by Scripture: For he saith no less himself; I was set up from everlasting, from the beginning, and before the Earth, Prov. 8. 23. and therefore he prayed that he might be glorified of his Father with the Glory which he had with him before the World was, John 17. 5. Secondly, I prove it by Reason. For God's Understanding is everlasting: therefore the second Person which it begetteth, is so too. For the Father in his Understanding did not conceive any thing less than himself, nor greater than himself, but equal to himself.

Although the Son of God be from everlasting, yet he is not all one with the Father; is he?
Yes, that he is: And yet not joined with his Father in Heaven as two Judges that sit together on a Bench; or as the Seal and the Wax, as some do grossly imagine; but they are both one without parting (John 10. 30.) or mingling:

Whereupon I conclude, that whatsoever the Father is, the Son is the same: And so consequently that they be Co-eternal, Co-equal, and Co-essential.

Men by reason do conceive and beget Reason: What difference is there between the conceiving of Understanding in Men, and the conceiving of Understanding in God?
There is great difference For, first, this conceiving in Men proceedeth of Sense or outward Imagination, which is an outward thing for Reason to work upon, as Wood is to

Fire: But God the Father of himself begetteth and conceiveth himself, and still in himself; as John saith, The only begotten Son which is in the Bosom of the Father, John 1. 18. Secondly, In Men, the thing which is understood, and the Understanding it self is not all one: But in God it is all one.

What reason have you for this?
The reason is, because only God is altogether Life, and his Life is altogether Understanding, and his Understanding is the highest degree of Life: And therefore he hath his conceiving and begetting most inward of all.

What mean you when you say most inward of all?
I mean that the Father conceiveth of himself, and in himself; and his conceiving is a begetting, and his begetting abideth still in himself; because his Understanding can no where meet with any thing, but that which he himself is: and that is the second Subsistence in the Trinity, which we call the Everlasting Son of God.

Now let me hear what the Holy Ghost is, and how he proceedeth from the Father and the Son.
For the understanding of this Matter, we must consider two things. First, That in the Essence of God, besides his Understanding, there is a Will, Isa. 46. 10. Secondly, What are the Properties of his Will in God.

What are the Properties of God's Word?
First, It applieth his Power when, where, and how he thinks good; according to his own Mind. Secondly, It worketh everlastingly upon it self, as his understanding does.

What gather you by this?
That because it hath no other thing to work upon but it self, it does delight it self in the infinite good which it knoweth in it self; for the action of the Will is delight and liking.

And what of that?
That delight which God or his Will hath in his own Infinite Goodness, does bring forth a third Person or Subsistence in God; which we call the Holy Ghost.

What is that same third Subsistence in God?
The mutual kindness and lovingness of the Father and the Son.

What mean you by this mutual lovingness and kindness?
The Father taketh joy and delight in the Son, or his own Image conceived by his Understanding; and the Son likewise rejoiceth in his Father, as he saith himself, Prov. 8. 30. and the reason thereof is this: The Action of the Will, when it is fulfilled, is love and liking.

What resemblance can you show thereof in something that is commonly used amongst us?
When a Man looketh in a Glass, if he smile, his Image smileth too; and if he taketh delight in it, he taketh the same delight in him: for they are both one.

If they be all one, how can they then be three?
The Face is one, the Image of the Face in a Glass is another, and the smiling of them both together is a third; and yet all are in one Face, and all are of one Face, and all are but one Face.

And is it so in God?
Yea, for even so the Understanding, which is in God, is one; the Reflection or Image of his Understanding which he beholdeth in himself as in a Glass, is a second; and the love and liking of them both together, by reason of the Will fulfilled, is a third: And yet all are but of one God, all are in one God, and all are but one God.

Which of these three is first?
There is neither first nor last, going afore or coming after, in the Essence of God: But all these as they are everlasting, so they are all at once and at one instant: Even as in a Glass the Face and the Image of the Face, when they smile, they smile together, and not one before nor after another.

What is the conclusion of all?
As we have the Son of the Father by his everlasting Will in working by his Understanding; so also we have the Holy Ghost of the love of them both by the joint working of the Understanding and Will together. Whereupon we conclude three distinct Persons Subsistences (which we call the Father, the Son, and the Holy Ghost) in one Spiritual, yet unspeakable Substance, which is very God himself.

But what if some will be yet more curious to know how the Son of God should be begotten, and how the Holy Ghost should proceed from the Father and the Son: How may we satisfy them?
Well enough. For if any will be too curious about this Point, we may answer them thus. Let them show us how themselves are bred and begotten, and then let them ask us how the Son of God is begotten: And let them tell us the Nature of the Spirit that beateth in their Pulses, and then let them be inquisitive at our Hands for the proceeding of the Holy Ghost.

And what if they cannot give us a reason for the manner of their own Being, may they not be inquisitive for the manner of God's Being?
No. For if they must be constrained to be ignorant in so common matters which they daily see and feel in themselves; let them give us leave to be ignorant, not only in this, but in many things more, which are such as no Eye hath seen, nor Ear hath heard, nor Wit of Man can conceive.

Let us now hear out of the Scriptures what the Holy Ghost is?
He is the third Person of the Trinity by Communication of Essence, eternally proceeding from the Father and from the Son.

Are you able to prove out of the Scriptures that the Holy Ghost is God?
Yes. Because the Name, Properties and Actions of God are therein given to him, as to the Father and to the Son.

Let us hear some of those Proofs.
First, Gen. 1. 2. the Work of the Creation is attributed to the Spirit of God. Secondly, Isa. 61. 1. the Spirit of the Lord God is said to be upon Christ, because the Lord anointed him, &c. Thirdly, 1 Cor. 3. 16. and 2 Cor. 6. 16. Paul calleth us God's Temples; because the Holy Ghost dwelleth in us. St. Augustine in his 66 Epistle to Maximinus, saith it is a clear Argument of his Godhead, if we were commanded to make him a Temple but of Timber and Stone, because that Worship is due to God only: Therefore now we must much more think that he is God, because we are not commanded to make him a Temple, but to be a Temple for him ourselves.

What other Reason have you out of the Scriptures?
Fourthly, Peter reproving Ananias for lying to the Holy Ghost, said, that he lied not to Men, but to God, Acts 5. 3, 4.

Have you any more Reasons from the Scripture?
Yea, two more: One from St. Paul, and another from St. Paul and Isaiah together.

What is your Reason from St. Paul?
Fifthly, when he showeth how many sundry Gifts are given to Men, he saith, that one and the self-same Spirit is the distributor of them all: Therefore he is God; for none can distribute those Gifts which Paul here speaketh of, but God, 1 Cor. 12. 6, 11.

What is your Reason from Isaiah and St. Paul together?
Sixthly, Isaiah saith in Chap. 6. 8, 9. I heard the Lord speaking: Which place Paul expounded of the Holy Ghost, Acts 28. 25.

But how can you prove out of the Scriptures, that the Holy Ghost is God, proceeding from the Father and the Son?
First, John 15. 26. When the Comforter is come, whom I will send unto you from the Father, even the Spirit of Truth, which proceedeth from the Father, he shall testify of me. That he proceedeth from the Father, is here expressly affirmed: That he proceedeth from the Son, is by necessary consequence implied, because the Son is said to send him; at John 14. 26. the Father is said to send him in the Son's Name. By which sending, the Order of the Persons of the Trinity is evidently designed. Because the Son is of the Father, and the Father is not of the Son; therefore we find in Scripture that the Father sendeth his Son, but never that the Son sendeth his Father. In like manner because the Holy Ghost proceedeth from the Father, and from the Son; we find that both the Father and the Son do send the Holy Ghost, but never that the Holy Ghost does send either the Father or Son.

Secondly, John 16. 15. The Son saith of the Holy Ghost; All things that the Father hath are mine; therefore, said I, that he shall take of mine, and shall show it unto you. All things that the Father hath, the Son receiveth from him, as coming from him; and so whatsoever the Holy Ghost hath, he hath it not of himself, vers. 13. but from the Son, and so from the Father; as a Person proceeding as well from the one as from the other.

Thirdly, Gal. 4. 6. God hath sent forth the Spirit of his Son into your Hearts. As the Holy Ghost is called the Spirit of the Father, (Isa. 48. 16. The Lord and his Spirit hath sent me); so is he here also called the Spirit of the Son; and Rom. 8. 9. the Spirit of God, and the Spirit of Christ. Now, if the Spirit of Man, in whom there is no perfection, be all one with Man, much more the Spirit of the Father is all one with the Father, and the Spirit of the Son is all one with the Son; and so the Holy Ghost with the Father and the Son, is the same in Deity, Dignity, Eternity, Operation, and Will.

Why is the third Person called the Spirit?
Not only because he is a Spiritual, (that is) an immaterial and pure Essence, (for so likewise is the Father a Spirit, and the Son as well as he): But first, In regard of his Person; because he is inspired, and, as it were, breathed both from the Father and the Son, proceeding from them both. Secondly, In regard of the Creatures; because the Father and the Son do work by the Spirit: Who is as it were the Breath of Grace, which the Father and the Son breatheth out upon the Saints, blowing freely where it listeth, and working Spiritually for manner, means, and matter, where it pleases, John 20. 22. Psal. 33. 6. John. 3. 8. Acts 2. 2, 3, 4. 1 Cor. 2. 12, 13.

Third Head

Why is he called the Holy Spirit?
Not only because of his Essential Holiness as God; for so the Father and the Son are also infinitely Holy as he: But because he is the Author and Worker of all Holiness in Men, and the Sanctifier of God's Children.

Why, does not the Father and the Son sanctify also?
Yes verily: But they do it by him: and because he does immediately sanctify, therefore he hath the Title of Holy.

What other Titles are given unto him in the Word of God?
First, The Good Spirit: Because he is the Fountain of Goodness, Psalm 143. 10. Secondly, The Spirit of God: Because he is God, 1 Sam. 11. 6. Thirdly, The Finger of God: Because God worketh by him as a Man by his Hand, Luke 11. 20. Fourthly, The Spirit of Adoption: Because he assureth our Hearts that we be the Adopted Sons of God, Rom. 8. 15. Gal. 4. 6. Fifthly, The Spirit of Love, Power, Sobriety, Wisdom, &c. because it worketh all these things in us, 2 Tim. 1. 6, 7. Isa. 11. 2. Sixthly, The Comforter: Because he strengtheneth the weak Hearts of his Saints, John 14. 1, 16, 26.

What are the Special Comforts which the Children of God receive from the Holy Ghost?
He is in their Hearts the Pledge of Christ's Presence, John 14. 16, 17, 18, 26. the Witness of their Adoption, Rom. 8. 15, 16. the Guide of their Life, Job. 16. 13. the Comforter of their Soul, John 14. 26. and 15. 26. the Seal of their Redemption, Ephes. 1. 13. and 4. 30. and the first Fruits of their Salvation, Rom. 8. 23.

But how are you assured that you have the Spirit?
Because it hath convinced my Judgment, John 16. 8. converted my Soul, Acts 26. 18. Isa. 61. 1. and having mixed the Word with my Faith, Heb. 4. 2. it is become as Life to quicken me, John 6. 63. as Water to cleanse me, Ezek. 36. 25. as Oil to cheer me, Heb. 1. 9. as Fire to melt and refine me, Mat. 3. 11.

And how may you keep the Spirit now you have it?
By nourishing the good motions and means of it, 1 Thess. 5. 17, 18, 19. being fearful to grieve, quench, resist, or molest it, Ephes. 4. 30. 1 Thess. 5. 19. Acts 7. 51. and careful to be led by it, and show forth the Fruits of it, Rom. 8. 1, 14. Gal. 5. 18, 22.

Thus much of the three Persons severally. What now remaineth more to be spoken of the Mystery of the Trinity?
To set down briefly, what are the things common wherein the three Persons agree: and what are the things proper to each of them, whereby they are distinguished one from another.

What are the things wherein the three Persons do communicate?
They are considered in regard of themselves or of the Creatures.

What are they in regard of themselves?
They agree one with another in Nature, Being, Life, Time, Dignity, Glory, or any thing pertaining to the Divine Essence: For in all these they are one and the same; and consequently, Co-essential, Co-equal, and Co-eternal.

What mean you, when you say they be Co-essential?
That they be all the self-same Substance or Being; having one individual Essence or Deity common to them all, and the self-same in them all.

What mean you, when you say they be Co-equal?
That as they agree in Deity, so they agree in Dignity: Being of one State, Condition, and Degree, and the one having as great excellency and majesty every way as the other. Therefore their Honor and Worship is equal and alike; and one of them is not greater nor more glorious than another, John 5. 18. Rev. 5. 12, 13.

What mean you, when you say that they be Co-eternal?
That one was not before another in time; but that one hath been of as long continuance as another, and all of them have been and shall be for ever, (as being all of one selfsame everlasting continuance.)

How prove you this?
John 1. 1. In the beginning was the Word, &c. and at that time the three Persons speak, Gen. 1. 26. Let us make Man, &c. Heb. 13. 8. Jesus Christ yesterday, to day, and the same for ever.

How can there be this equality betwixt the three Persons of the Trinity, seeing the Father is the first, the Son the second, the Holy Ghost the third?
Because every one of them is perfect God; who is Infinite, Eternal, and Incomprehensible.

Have they all three one Will likewise?
They have: And therefore they will all one and the same thing without any crossing, contradiction, or varying in themselves; as the Son himself saith, John 8. 29. I do always those things that please him, viz. the Father.

Is there nothing else to be said of the Communion of the three Persons betwixt themselves?
Yes. That first one is in another, and possesseth one another: the Father remaining with the Son, the Son with the Father, the Holy Ghost in and with them both, Prov. 8. 22. John 1. 1. and 14. 10, 20. Secondly, they have glory one of another, from all eternity, John 17. 5. Thirdly, they delight one in another, and infinitely rejoice in one another's fellowship: The Son being the delight of the Father, the Father of the Son, and the Holy Ghost of both, Prov. 8. 30.

What things have they common in regard of the Creatures?
All outward Actions; as to decree, to create, to order, govern, and direct, to redeem, to sanctify; are equally common to the three Persons of the Trinity. For as they are all one in Nature and Will, so must they be also one in Operation, all of them working one and the same thing together, Gen. 1. 26. John. 5. 17, 19.

What are the things proper to each of them?
They likewise are partly in regard of themselves, and partly of the Creatures, whereby the distinction of them is conceived; partly in relation and order of subsistence betwixt themselves, and partly in order and manner of working in the Creatures.

What things are proper to each of them in regard of themselves?
First, In manner and order of Being: the Father is the first Person, having his Being from himself alone, and is the Fountain of Being to the other Persons; the Son is the second, having his Being from the Father alone, (and in that respect is called the Light, the Wisdom, the Word, and the Image of the Father); the Holy Ghost is the third, having his Being from them both; and in that respect is called the Spirit of God, of the Father, and of Christ.

Secondly, In their Inward Actions and Properties: The Father alone begetteth, (and so in relation to the second Person is called the Father; the Son is of the Father alone begotten; the Holy Ghost does proceed both from the Father and the Son.

What is proper to each of them in regard of the Creatures?
First, The Original of the Action is ascribed to the Father, John 5. 17, 19. the Wisdom, and manner of working, to the Son, John 1. 3. Heb. 1. 2. the Efficacy of Operation to the Holy Ghost, Gen. 1. 2. 1 Cor. 12. 11.

Secondly, The Father worketh all things of himself, in the Son, by the Holy Ghost: The Son worketh from the Father, by the Holy Ghost; the Holy Ghost worketh from the Father and the Son.

[4TH HEAD.]

Having spoken of the first part of Divinity, which is the Nature of God; it followeth that we speak of his Kingdom, which is the second.

What is the Kingdom of God?
His Universal Dominion over all Creatures, whereby he dispenseth all things externally according to his own Wisdom, Will and Power. Or, an everlasting Kingdom, appointed and ruled by the Counsel of his own Will, Luke 1. 33. Isa. 9. 7. Dan. 2. 44. Isa. 40. 13, 14. Psal. 99. 1. and 115. 3. Rom. 11. 34, 35, 36. Ephes. 1. 11. Isa. 44. 24.

Wherewith does he Reign and Rule?
Principally by his own powerful Spirit, which none can resist.

What end does he propound to himself in his Kingdom?
His own Glory, Rom. 11. 36. Psal. 97. 6. Isa. 48. 11. Ephes. 1. 12, 14.

What is that about which his Kingdom is occupied?
All things, Visible and Invisible.

When shall it end?
Never; either in this World, or in the World to come, Psal. 145. 13.

What manner of Kingdom is it?
A Righteous Kingdom, Psal 45. 6, 7. and 97. 2.

What Instructions are you to gather out of the Doctrine of the Kingdom of God?
They are expressed in Psal. 99. in the beginning whereof the Prophet speaketh in this manner.

1. The Lord reigneth: Which teacheth us that God alone hath, and exerciseth sovereign and absolute Empire over all; and that he admitteth no Fellow Governor with him. 2. Let the People tremble: Showing that all Nations and sorts of People should tremble; forasmuch as he alone is able to save and to destroy. For if Men tremble under the Regiment and Kingly Rule of Men: How much more ought they to tremble under the powerful Kingdom of God, which hath more power over them than they have over their Subjects.

This trembling, does it stand only in fear?
No: But in reverence also; that that which we comprehend not in this Kingdom with our Reason, we reverence and adore.

What learn you thereby?
1. That we submit ourselves to his Kingdom erected amongst us. 2. That we presume to know nothing but that he teacheth us; to will nothing but what he biddeth us; to love, hate, fear, and affect nothing but what he requireth.

What does follow in this 99 Psalm?
Vers. 1, 2. He sitteth between the Cherubim, let the Earth he moved: The Lord is great in Zion, and he is high above all the People. Whence we learn, that although all the world roar and fret, yet we should not fear, because the Lord is greater, Psal. 97. 1, 3. They shall praise thy great and fearful Name, for it is Holy: Which showeth that God ought to be magnified, because he is great and fearful, and yet holy, and Holiness it self. Psal. 99. 4. The King's strength also loveth Judgment? Thou dost establish Equity; Thou executest Judgment and Righteousness in Jacob. Whereby we learn this comfort from God's reigning, that when we are wronged and oppressed by tyranny of Men, we may have our recourse to the just and righteous Judgment of God, which is the Righteous Judge of the World, (Eccl. 5. 7, 8.) Psal. 99. 5. Exalt ye the Lord our God, &c. out of the Might, and Majesty, and Holiness of the Lord, we should learn to extol him with praise, Psal. 145. 11, 12.

Seeing God is without beginning: What did he in that infinite space which was e're the World was made; it being unbeseeming the Majesty of God to be idle and unoccupied all that time?
It Behooveth us to think that he did things agreeable to his Divine Nature: But we should be evil occupied in the search of them further than himself hath made them known. Which made an ancient Father to give this Answer to a curious Inquirer of God's doings before he made the World: That he was making Hell for those that should trouble themselves with such vain and idle questions, August. lib. 1. Confess. Chap. 12.

What is that he hath revealed unto us concerning what he did before the beginning of the World?
Besides the inward Works of the three Persons of the Blessed Trinity, (whereof we have spoken) and the mutual delight which they took one in another, (Prov. 8. 30.) and Glory which they gave one to another, (John 17. 5.) this external Act of his is revealed unto us in the Scriptures, that he hath in himself decreed all things, together with all the Circumstances of all things which have or shall be done from the beginning of the World unto the end thereof.

The Decree, determining all things from all eternity; and the execution thereof, fulfilling the same in time. For as from eternity he decreed, so in time and everlastingly he accomplisheth all things unto the full execution of that his Decree, 1 Cor. 2. 16. Ephes. 1. 11. Acts 4. 28. Psal. 99. 4. and 135. 6. So that the first is an eternal, the second a temporal Work of God.

What is the Decree?
It is that Act, whereby God from all eternity, according to his free Will, did by his unchangeable Counsel and Purpose, fore appoint and certainly determine of all things; together with their Causes, their Effects, their Circumstances and Manner of Being, to the Manifestation of his own Glory, Psal. 99. 4. Mat. 10. 29. Rom. 9 20, 21. and 11. 36. Prov. 16. 4. Ephes. 1. 4, 11. Acts 2. 23. Jer. 1. 5, 15.

Fourth Head

What gather you of this; that God's Decree is defined by his most perfect Will?
First, That the things which he decreeth are most perfectly good. Secondly That we must not subject his Decree to our shallow and base capacity, or measure it by our Reason, considering that the Will of God, from whence the Decree cometh, is unsearchable.

What are the Parts or Kinds of God's Decree?
That which God hath decreed concerning all his Creatures generally, for the declaration of his Power, Wisdom, and Goodness in their creation and preservation: And that which he hath decreed specially, touching the Good or Evil of the chief or reasonable Creatures, Angels and Men, to declare the Glory of his Grace and Justice.

What note you in the former?
That God, according to his good pleasure, hath most certainly decreed every (both) Thing and Action, whether past, present, or to come; and not only the Things and Actions themselves, but also all their Circumstances of Place and Time, Means, Manner, and End; so that they shall not come to pass in any other place or time than he hath ordained; and then and there they shall come to pass necessarily, Psal. 99. 4. Acts 27. 20, 21, 22, 23, 24, 25, 26, 27, 31, 32, 33, 34.

Does this necessity take away freedom of Will in Election, or the nature and property of second Causes?
No: But only brings them into a certain order, that is, directeth them to the determined end. Whereupon the Effects and Events of things are contingent or necessary, as the nature of the second Cause is. So Christ according to his Father's Decree died necessarily, Acts 17. 3. but yet willingly; and if we respect the temperature of Christ's Body, he might have prolonged his life; and therefore in this respect may be said to have died contingently.

What consider you in the special Decree, which concerneth the Good or Evil of the principal Creatures?
The fore-appointment of their everlasting Estate, and of the means tending thereunto; called Predestination.

What is Predestination?
It is the Special Decree of God, whereby he hath from everlasting freely, and for his own Glory, fore-ordained all reasonable Creatures to a certain and everlasting state of Glory in Heaven, or Shame in Hell.

What Creatures come within this Decree?
Both Angels, 1 Tim. 5. 21. Mat. 25. 41. and Men, 1 Thess. 5. 9. Rom. 9. 13, 22, 23. 1 Pet. 2. 8. Ephes. 1. 5. John 17. 12, 22. Exod. 33. 14.

What is the cause of this Decree?
Only the mere will and free pleasure of God to dispose of his own Work as he will, Rom. 9. 21. Isa. 64. 8.

What manner of Decree is this?
It is a deep and unsearchable, an eternal and immutable Decree, Rom. 11. 33. Ephes. 1. 4.

Is this Decree certain and unchangeable?
Yea, it must needs be so: Because it is grounded on the eternal and unchangeable Will of God: And therefore there is a certain number of the Elect and Reprobate known only to God, which cannot possibly be increased or diminished, John 13. 18. 2 Tim. 2. 19.

How then does Moses wish himself to be blotted out of the Book of Life, Exod. 32. 32.?
He speaketh conditionally, if it were possible; to declare his Love to God's Glory, and his People, as Paul does, Rom. 9. 3.

But if God's Decree cannot be altered; then we may be secure, and not care how we live.
No more than we may neglect and forsake our Meat and Drink, because the term of our Life is fore-appointed: The end and the means are joined together of God, and cannot be separated by any Man.

What are the Parts of Predestination?
Election and Reprobation, 1 Thess. 5. 9. Rom. 9. 13, 22, 23.

What is Election?
It is the everlasting Predestination or Fore-appointing of certain Angels and Men unto everlasting Life and Blessedness, for the praise of his glorious Grace and Goodness, 1 Tim. 5. 21. John 15. 16. Rom. 9. 22, 23. Ephes. 1. 4, 5, 6, 9.

Is there no Cause, Reason, or Inducement of Election, in the Elected themselves?
None at all. It is wholly of free Grace, without respect of any goodness that God foresaw in us, 2 Tim. 1. 9. Rom. 9. 16. Phil. 2. 13. Ephes. 1. 9. For otherwise Man should have whereof he might glory in and of himself, as having discerned himself from others: And God should not be the cause of all Good, nor should his Counsel be incomprehensible.

Is not Christ the Cause of our Election?
No; not of God's decreeing of it, (for that he did of his own free Will): but of the execution of it; that is, our Salvation is for and through Christ.

What Tokens have we of our Election?
A true Faith, and a godly Life.

What Use are we to make of our Election?
First, It is our great comfort, that our Salvation standeth by God's eternal Decree, that cannot be changed; and not in ourselves, that daily might lose it. Secondly, It showeth God's infinite Mercy, that before we were, or had done Good or Evil, he elected us, rather than others as good as we. Thirdly, It should make us love God all our life to our utmost, for his Love to us. Fourthly, It is a help against all Temptations of Satan, or our doubting Nature; and also against all Afflictions and Contempt of the World, Rom. 8. 38, 39. Fifthly; It serveth to humble us, that we had nothing of ourselves for our Salvation, but it freely came from God.

What is Reprobation?
It is the eternal Predestination or Fore-appointment of certain Angels and Men unto everlasting dishonor and destruction: God of his own Free-will determining to pass them by, refuse, or cast them off, and for sin to condemn and punish them with eternal Death, Prov. 16. 4. Exod. 9. 16. Rom. 9. 17, 22. 2 Tim. 2. 20. Mat. 25. 41.

Is not Sin the cause of Reprobation?
No: For then all Men should be reprobate, when God foresaw that all would be Sinners. But Sin is the cause of the execution of Reprobation; the damnation whereunto the Wicked are adjudged, being for their own sin.

Fourth Head

Is there no cause then of Reprobation in the Reprobate?
None at all, in that they rather than others are passed by of God; that is wholly from the unsearchable depth of God's own free-will and good pleasure.

But is not God unjust, in reprobating some Men, and electing others, when all were alike?
No; for he was bound to none: And to show his freedom and power over his Creatures, he disposeth of them as he will for his Glory: As the Potter is not unjust in making of the same Clay sundry Vessels, some to honor, and some to dishonor.

Does Predestination only come within the compass of God's Decree; and not the Means also of accomplishing the same?
Yes: The Means also comes within this Decree: As the Creation, and the fall of the reasonable Creatures.

If God hath decreed the Works of the Wicked: Must not he of force be the Author of Sin and Evil?
God is not the Cause of Sin and Evil, which he forbiddeth and condemneth, but Satan and Man: Yet God in his secret Will hath justly decreed the Evil Works of the Wicked (for if it had not so pleased him, they had never been at all) for most Holy Ends, both of his Glory and their Punishment: As may be seen in the Jews crucifying of Christ, Acts 2. 23. and Joseph's selling into Egypt, Gen. 45. 7. and 50. 20. For the thing that in it self, by reason of God's prohibiting of it, is sin; in respect of God's decreeing of it for a holy end, comes in the place of a good thing: As being some occasion and way to manifest the Glory of God in his Justice and Mercy. For there is nothing sin as God decreeth it, or commandeth it: Neither is there any thing of it self absolutely evil, (1 Pet. 3. 17.) but because God hath forbidden it, therefore it is evil, and only to them unto whom God hath forbidden it: As Abraham killing of Isaac, being commanded of God, was to be obeyed, and sin it were to have disobeyed it: Which otherwise, by reason of God's Commandment forbidding to kill, was a sin. For God forbiddeth not things because they are of themselves, and first Evil; but therefore are they to Man Evil, because God hath forbidden them. For all sin is a transgression of a Law; and God does in Heaven and in Earth whatsoever pleases him; neither is there any greater than he to command him.

So much of the Decree or Purpose of God; What is the execution of it?
It is an Action of God, effectually working all things in their time according to his Decree, Ephes. 1. 11. Acts 4. 28.

What are the Parts of the Execution?
Creation and Providence, Psal. 33. 6, 7, 9, 10, 11. and 146. 6, 7. Jer. 10. 12.

What is Creation?
It is the execution of God's Decree, whereby of nothing he made all things very good, Gen. 1. 1, 7. Heb. 11. 3.

How many things in general are you to know concerning the Creation?
The Causes and the Adjuncts. In the former whereof we are to consider the Author or efficient Cause, the Matter, the Form or Manner, and the End. In the latter, the Goodness of the Creatures, and the Time of the Creation.

Who is the Author of this wonderful Work?
God alone.

How does that appear?
Not only by the plain and manifold Testimonies of Holy Scripture, but also by Light of Reason well directed. For Reason teacheth, That there must needs be a first Cause of all things, from whence they proceed, not only as they are this or that, but simply as they are: That all Perfections which are in other things by participation, should be in it essentially, and that the same must be of infinite Wisdom, in that all things are made and ordered unto so good purposes as they are: None of which things can agree to any but to God alone. Whence it is that the Apostle Paul, Acts 14. 15. and 17. 24. does point out God to the Heathen by his Work above other.

Is not Creation then an Article of Faith above Reason?
Yes; in regard of the time and manner of it: As likewise in respect of a full and saving assent unto it with comfort.

Is the Father alone to be held the Creator of all things?
No: But together with him the Son also and the Holy Ghost. For so St. John testifieth, that by Christ the eternal Word and Wisdom of God, all things were made, and without him was made nothing, John 1. 3. In like manner St. Paul teacheth that by him all things were created in Heaven and Earth, both things Visible and Invisible, whether they be Thrones, or Dominions, or Principalities, or Powers, by him and for him they were all created, Col. 1. 16. Moses also declareth, that the Spirit of the Lord moved upon the Waters; sustaining and holding up, and as it were brooding (for that Metaphor he useth) the unformed Matter, to bring forth the most comely and beautiful forms of all things, Gen. 1. 2.

Did not the Angels create some Creatures at the beginning? Or cannot Man or the Devils now create Creatures?
No; Creation is a Work which God only is able to do: And therefore whatsoever the Devil or Jugglers, like the Sorcerers of Egypt, seem to do, it is nothing but a delusion of the Senses: As the Devil himself confesseth, Mat. 4. and the Sorcerers, Exod. 8.

But was there not something before the Creation, as the first Matter of all things, or Time, or the space in which this World was made?
No: For then there should be something eternal as well as God.

Whereof then were all things made?
Of nothing, that is, of no Matter which was before the Creation.

How does that appear?
Because they are said to have been made in the beginning, Gen. 1. 1. that is, when before there was not any thing but God the Creator; and before which there was no measure of Time by Men or Angels.

How and in what manner did God create all things?
By no Means or Instruments, (which he needeth not, as Man does) but by his powerful Word, that is, by his only Will; calling those things that are not, as though they were, Heb. 11. 3. Rom. 4. 17. Psal 148. 5.

Was that Word by which he made all things, Christ his Son?
All things indeed that were made, were made by the Son, the second Person of the Trinity, John 1. 3. Col. 1. 16. Heb. 1. 2. yet that Word mentioned in the first of Genesis, (when it is written, that the Lord said, Let there be Light, &c.) was God's Command, which then had beginning: Whereas the Son was from all eternity.

Fourth Head

To what end were all things created?
For God's Glory, Prov. 16. 4.

How does the Glory of God appear in them?
First, His eternal Power and Godhead is seen, in raising all things out of nothing by his Word alone, Isa. 40. 11. Rom. 1. 20. Jer. 10. 12. and 51. 15. Secondly, His infinite Wisdom is made known by them, Psal. 104. 24. Jer. 10. 12. and 51. 15. Thirdly, His Goodness unto all his Creatures is hereby manifested, which is very excellently set out by the Prophet in Psal. 104. Fourthly, His infinite Authority does appear by them.

What Uses then are we to make of the Creation?
First, We are thereby taught to discern the True God, from all Heathen and Idol Gods in the World, Isa. 45. 7. Jer. 10. 11, 12. For nothing in Heaven and Earth can give a Being unto a Creature but God. Secondly, We are to weigh them and learn their Properties, Eccles. 7. 25. Thirdly, We should learn to give God glory for them, Rev. 4. 11. Psal 92. 5. (where it is made one end of the Sabbath) Psal. 104. throughout. Fourthly, We are to gather comfort to ourselves from hence: That resting upon this Faithful Creator, our hope needs not fail us, so long as either Heaven or Earth have any help for us, 1 Pet. 4. 19. Isa. 37. 16, 17. and 40. 28, 31.

What does the Scriptures teach us concerning the Goodness of the Creatures?
That God made them all in such excellency of Perfection, for their Being, Working, Order and Use, that himself did fully approve of them, and so establish them, Gen. 1. 31. which established Order is that which is called Nature.

In how many things does the Goodness of the Creatures consist?
In three. First, In the perfection of their Nature. Secondly, In their Properties and Qualities, whereby they are able to do those things for which they were created. Thirdly, In their Uses unto Man.

How manifold is that Good which Men receive by them?
Threefold, First, Profitable Good. Secondly, Pleasant Good. Thirdly, Honest and Christian Good.

How were all things made Good; when we see there be divers kinds of Serpents and noisome or hurtful Beasts?
That they are hurtful, it cometh not by the Nature of their Creation; in regard whereof they at the first should only have served for the good of Man.

What do you note in the Time of their Creation?
The beginning and the continuance thereof.

Might not the World have been before all Time, even from Eternity?
No. For Absolute Eternity belongeth only to God: Neither could any thing that is subject to Time be after an infinite succession of other things.

What say you then to Aristotle, accounted of so many the Prince of Philosophers; who laboreth to prove that the World is eternal?
Where he seemeth to have found out a point of Wisdom which he had learned of none other that was before him, he therein betrayeth his greatest folly. For his chiefest Reason, being grounded upon the eternity of the first Mover, is of no force to prove his most absurd Position: Seeing God as he is Almighty, and always able to do what he will; so he is most free, and not bound to do all that he can, but what, when, and how it pleased him. But seeing Aristotle was enforced by Reason to acknowledge God to be

the first Mover, even against his Will, (for it seemeth that he endeavored as much as he could to quench the Light of Divine Knowledge shining in his face; or obstinately to close his eyes against the same); and yet not only spoileth God of the glory of his Creation, but also assigneth him to no higher Office than is the moving of the Spheres, whereunto he bindeth him more like to a Servant than a Lord: The Judgment of God uttered by St. Paul, Rom. 1. 21. is most notoriously showed upon him; in that he knowing God did not glorify him, nor give him thanks; but became vain in his Disputations, and his foolish Heart was darkened: While he professed Wisdom he was made a Fool, approving Idolatry, and that wickedness which the Apostle there showeth to be a just punishment of Idolatry, and Nature it self abhorreth, (Arist. Polit. l. 7. c. 16. & l. 2. c. 8.)

How long is it since God did create the World?
Four thousand Years before the Birth of our Savior Christ: And so about 5614 years before this time.

Why is the Order of the Years of the World so carefully set down in the Scripture?
1. To convince all Heathen, that either thought the World was without beginning, or that it began millions of Years before it did. 2. To give light to all Sacred Histories of the Bible. 3. To show the Time of the fulfilling of the Prophecies which God foretold.

But why was not the World made sooner?
Saving the hidden Wisdom, and free Pleasure of the Maker: Therein appeareth the free Power of God, to make or not to make; and his absolute sufficiency within himself, as having no need of any external Being, only creating that he might communicate and manifest his Goodness.

How long was God creating the World?
Six Days and six Nights.

Why was he Creating so long, seeing he could have perfected all the Creatures at once and in a moment?
First, To show the variety, distinction, and excellency of his several Creatures. Secondly, To teach us the better to understand their Workmanship; even as a Man which will teach a Child in the frame of a Letter, will first teach him one Line of the Letter, and not the whole Letter together. Thirdly, To admonish us, that we are bound to bestow more time in discerning and knowing them than we do. Fourthly, That we might also by his Example finish our Work in six days. Fifthly, That we might observe, that many of the Creatures were made before those which are ordinarily their Causes; and thereby learn that the Lord is not bound to any Creature, or to any Means. Thus the Sun was not Created before the fourth day: And yet days (which now are caused by the rising of the Sun) were before that. So Trees and Plants were created the third day: But the Sun, Moon, and Stars (by which they are now nourished and made to grow) were not created till after the third day.

Hitherto of the Creation in general: What are the particular Creatures?
The World, and all things therein, Acts 17. 24. or, the Heavens, and the Earth, and all the Host of them, Gen. 2. 1.

How many Heavens are mentioned in the Scriptures?
Three. The first is the Air wherein we breathe, the Birds do fly, and the Snow, Rain, Frost, Hail, and Thunder are begotten, Mat. 6. 26. Gen. 7. 11. The second is the Sky, where in the Sun, the Moon, and the Stars are placed, Gen. 1. 14, 15. Deut. 17. 3. The

third, that wherein the Angels, and the Souls of the Saints from hence departed are now, 2 Cor. 12. 2. Mat. 18. 10. Mark. 12. 25.

What understand you by the Earth?
The lowest part of the World; containing the Globe of the Land and the Waters.

What mean you by the Host of them?
All the Creatures which the Lord made to have their beginning and being in them, Psal. 103. 20, 21. and 148. 2, &c. Deut. 17. 3. Joel 2. 10, 11.

How are the Creatures distinguished?
Into Visible and Invisible, Col. 1. 16.

What are the things Invisible?
The third Heaven, and the Angels placed therein.

Why is there no more express mention in the first of Genesis of the Creation of these, especially being Creatures in Glory so far passing others?
1. They are not expressly mentioned, because Moses setteth forth the things that are Visible, and therefore does not only pass them by, but also Minerals, and other things enclosed within the Bowels of the Earth. 2. Some respect also might be had of the weakness and infancy of the Church at that time. God did first teach them more plain and sensible things, and as they grew in Knowledge, he afterwards revealed other things unto them. But that they were (in one of the six days) created, it is most evident by Psal. 103. 20. and 148. 2, 5. Col. 1. 16.

In which of the six days were they created?
Though it be not so plainly revealed in Scripture, yet it may be gathered by Gen. 1. 1. (where under the term of Heavens those glorious Creatures may be also comprehended) and Job 38. 6, 7. that they were created the first day.

Of what Nature are the Angels?
They are Substances wholly Spiritual, (not in parts, as Man is), and in respect of this simple Essence, in the scripture they are called Spirits.

How many things conceive you of the Angels, when you say that they are Spirits?
Six. 1. That they are living Substances. 2. That they are Incorruptible. 3. That they are Incorporeal. 4. That they are Indivisible. 5. That they are Intangible. 6. That they are Invisible.

Have they any Matter?
They have their Spiritual Matter, (as Man's Soul hath); but not any Earthly or Corporeal Matter.

They are not then Fantasies, as some do wickedly imagine.
No: But they are Subsistence and Being. For some are said to have fallen; others to appear unto Men.

How many of them were created at the beginning?
They were all created at once; and that in an innumerable multitude.

How did God create them?
He made them all at the first very good and glorious Spirits, yet mutable, Gen. 1. 31. Job 4. 18.

With what other Properties are the Angels especially endued?
With greater Wisdom, Power, Swiftness, and Industry than any Man.

Where is the Creation of things Visible especially taught?
In the first and second Chapters of Genesis, where Moses declareth at large, how God in the beginning created the World, and all things therein contained, every one in their several nature and kinds.

What does Moses note of these Creatures generally?
Three things. First, That they are all said to be good: Which stoppeth the mouths of all those that speak against them. Secondly, That their Names are given them. Thirdly, That their Uses and Ends are noted.

In what order did God create them?
First, The dwelling Places were first framed, then the Creatures to dwell in them. And provision was made for the Inhabitants of the Earth before they were made: As Grass for the Beasts, and Light for all living and moving Creatures, and all for Man. Secondly, God proceedeth from the things that be more imperfect, to those that are more perfect, until he come to the most perfect. As from the Trees, Corn, Herbs, &c. which have but one Life, that is, whereby they increase and are vegetative, unto the Beasts which have both an increasing and feeling, or sensitive Life; as Fishes, Fowls, Beasts, &c. and from them to Man, which hath besides them a reasonable Soul.

What learn you from the first?
Not to be carking for the things of this Life, not to surfeit with the cares thereof: Seeing God provided for the necessity and comfort of the very Beasts, e're he would bring them into the World.

What from the Second?
That we should therein follow the example of the Lord, to go from good to better, until we come to be perfect.

What are the visible Creatures in particular?
Two. First, The rude Mass or Matter of the World made the first Night; wherein all things were confounded and mingled one in another. Secondly, The beautiful Frame thereof, which were made the rest of the six Days and Nights.

What are the parts of that rude Mass?
Heaven and Earth (for so the Matter whereof all the bodily Creatures were made, seemeth by a Trope, Gen. 1. 1. to be signified) as it were the Center and Circumference. For as the Arch-builders first shadow out in a Plot the Building they intend; and as the Painters draw certain gross Lineaments of that Picture, which they will after set forth and fill up with Orient Colors: So the Lord our God in this stately Building, and cunning Painting of the Frame of the World, hath before the most beautiful Frame set out as it were a Shadow and a common Draught thereof.

It seems the rudeness was in the Earth only, containing the Water and the dry Land; because the Prophet saith, that the Earth was void, and without Shape.
It is true that Moses giveth this to the Earth, rather than the Mass of the Heavens; because the confusion and rudeness was greater there than in the Mass of the Heavens; for the Water and dry Land being mingled together, there was no Form or Figure of them.

It being without Form and Void, how was it kept?
By the Holy Ghost, which (as a Bird sitting over her Eggs) kept and preserved it, Gen 1. 2.

Fourth Head

What are the things which were made of this rude Mass?
The beautiful Frame and Fashion of the World, with the Furniture thereof.

What do you consider in the Frame and Fashion of the World?
Two things. First, The Elements, which are the most simple Bodies, by the uneven mixture whereof all Bodies are compounded. Secondly, The Bodies themselves that are compounded of them.

How many Elements are there?
There are commonly counted four. 1. First, The Fire: Which some think to be comprehended under the term of Light, Gen. 1. 3, 4. because that is a quality of the Fire. 2. The second is the Air: Which some would have signified by the Spirit or Wind of God moving upon the Waters, vers. 2. Others, by the Firmament, vers. 6, 7. set between the Clouds and Earth to distinguish between Water and Water; and to give Breath of Life to all things that breathe. 3. Thirdly, The Waters, (vers. 2.) severed from the Mass called the Earth, (vers. 9, 10).4. Fourthly, The Earth, (vers. 2.) called the dry Land, (vers. 9, 10.) which remaineth, all other being sent of God to their proper places.

What are the mixed or compounded Bodies?
Such as are made of the four Elements unequally mingled together.

How many kinds be there of them?
Four. Things that have, 1. A Being without Life. 2. A Being and Life, without Sense. 3. A Being, Life and Sense, without Reason. 4. A Being, Life, Sense, and Reason; (as, Man.)

What is common to the three last kinds?
That together with Life, there is power and virtue given unto them to bring forth the like unto themselves for the continuance of their Kind. Which Blessing of Multiplication is principally in the two last sorts of Creatures, (that have the Life of Sense, beside the Life of Increase): And therefore the Lord is brought in to speak to them in the second Person, Gen. 1. 22, 28. which he did not to the Grass, Corn, and Trees, which are Creatures of the Second Kind.

What learn you from hence?
That the chief and special cause of the continuance of every kind of Creatures to the Worlds end, is this Will and Word of God, without the which, they, or sundry of them, would have perished ere this, by so many means as are to consume them.

Declare now in order the several Works of the six days: And show first, what was done the first day.
The rude Mass or Matter of Heaven and Earth, being made of nothing the first night of the World, (as hath been declared); God did afterward create the Light, and called it Day, Gen. 1. 3, 4, 5.

What note you hereof?
The wonderful Work of God, not only in making something of nothing, but bringing Light out of Darkness, 2 Cor. 4. 6. which is contrary: And distinguishing betwixt Day and Night, before either Sun or Moon were created.

What was the Work of the Second Day?
The Firmament was created, to divide the waters above from the Waters below.

What was done the third Day?
The third Night (as it seemeth) God caused the Waters to retire into their Vessels, and severed them from the dry Land; calling the one Seas, the other Earth. Then in the third Day, which followed that Night, he clad the Earth with Grass for the use of Beasts only, Corn and Trees for the use of Man.

What shape is the Water and the Earth of?
They both together make a round Globe.

Whether is the Water or the Earth bigger?
The Waters.

Why then do they not overwhelm the Earth?
They are restrained and kept in by the mighty Power of God.

How many sorts of Waters be there?
Two: Salt waters, as the Sea; and fresh Waters, as Floods, Springs, Lakes, &c.

What are the Parts of the Earth?
First, Hills Secondly, Valleys and Plains.

How many benefits do you receive by the Earth in general?
Four. First, We are made of the Earth. Secondly, We dwell on the Earth. Thirdly, It giveth Fruits and Nourishment to all living Creatures. Fourthly, It is our Bed after Death.

What benefit receive you by the Hills?
They are a shadow against Storms and Heat: They be fit for grazing of Cattle; they are fit places to set Beacons on, to show that the Enemy is at hand, &c.

What benefits receive you by the Valleys and Plains?
1. They receive Water, to water the Earth. 2. They are most fit places ring forth all kind of Fruit, and Herbs, and Grass.

How cometh it to pass that God first maketh the Grass, Corn, and Trees; e're he made the heavenly Bodies of the Sun, Moon, and Stars, from whose influence the growth of these proceedeth?
To correct our error, which tie the increase of these so to the influence of the Heavenly Bodies, even to the worshipping of them; therein forgetting the Lord, who thereby showeth, that all hangeth upon him, and not on them; forasmuch as he made them when the Heavenly Bodies were not.

What do you gather from hence?
That the Fruitfulness of the Earth standeth not so much in the labor of the Husbandman, as in the power which God hath given to the Earth to bring forth Fruit.

Thus much of the Works of the third Day; what was made the fourth Day?
Lights: Which are as it were certain Vessels wherein the Lord did gather the Light, which before was scattered in the whole Body of the Heavens.

How are these Lights distinguished?
Although they be all great in themselves, to the end they might give Light to the Dark Earth, that is far removed from them: yet are they distinguished into:

1) Great,
   a) Sun.
   b) Moon.
2) Small:
   a) The Stars.

Why does Moses call the Sun and Moon the greatest Lights; when there are Stars that exceed the Moon by many degrees?
First, Because they are greatest in their use and virtue that they exercise upon the Terrestrial Bodies. Secondly, Because they seem so to us: It being the purpose of the Holy Ghost by Moses to apply himself to the capacity of the unlearned.

What is the use of them?
First, To separate the Day from the Night. Secondly, To be Signs of Seasons, and Days and Years. Thirdly, To send forth their Influences upon the whole Earth, and to give Light to the Inhabitants thereof.

How are the Signs of Times and Seasons?
First, By distinguishing the Times; Spring, Summer, Autumn, Winter; by their work and natural effect upon the earthly Creatures. Secondly, By distinguishing the Night from the Day, the Day from the Month, the Month from the Year.

Have they not Operation also in the extraordinary Events of singular Things and Persons, for their Good and Evil estate?
No verily: There is no such use taught of them in the Scriptures.

What Creatures were made the fifth Day?
Fishes and Birds.

What were the Fishes made of?
Of all four Elements: But more (it seemeth) of the Water than other living things, Gen. 1. 20.

What were the Birds made of?
Of all four Elements: Ye have more of the Air, (Gen. 2. 19.) and therefore that they are so light, and that their delight is in the Air, it is so much the more marvelous.

[5TH HEAD.]

What did God make in the sixth and last Day of Creation?
It is probable that he made in the,

1) Night thereof, the Beasts of the Earth.
   a) going: Tame, or home Beasts.
   b) creeping: Wild, or Field Beasts.

2) Day, Man in both Sexes; that is, both Man and Woman. The History of whose Creation is set down, Gen. 1. 26, 27. in the discourse of the Six-days Work: and repeated in c. [2.] v. 7. and more at large, after the Narration of the Lord's Rest in the seventh Day, vers. 18, 19, 20, &c.

Why was Man made last of all the Creatures?
1. Because he was the most excellent of all the Works of God in this inferior World. 2. Because he was the end of all unreasonable Creatures: And therefore that he might glorify God for all the Creatures that he saw the World was furnished with for his sake. 3. Because God would have him first provided for, e're he brought him into the World; that so he might have this World, of which God had made him Prince, as it were, his Palace, furnished with all things convenient. And if he had care of him before he was; how much more now he is?

What note you thereof?
That Man hath not to boast of his Antiquity; all the Creatures being made before him, even to the vilest Worm.

What is to be observed in his Creation?
That here, for the excellency of the Work, God is brought in as it were deliberating with himself, the Father with the Son and the Holy Ghost, and they with him: The whole Trinity entering into a solemn Counsel to make Man after their Image, (Gen. 1. 26.) which is not said of any other Creature. For whereas the other Creatures were made suddenly; Man was (as we shall see) not so, but with some space of time. Hitherto also belongeth, that the Holy Ghost standeth longer upon his Creation than upon the rest.

What learn you from thence.?
That we should mark so much the more the Wisdom and Power of God in the Creation of him: And likewise imitate God, in using most diligence about those things which are most excellent.

What Parts does he consist?
Of two Parts: Of a Body and a Soul, Gen. 2. 7. Job 10. 11, 12.

Whereof was his Body made?
Of the very Dust of the Earth, Gen. 2. 7. In which respect the work of God, in making him, is set forth by a Similitude of the Potter, which of the Clay maketh his Pots. And the name of Adam is from hence in the Hebrew given unto Man, to put him in mind not to be proud, nor to desire to be like God: which God foresaw he would do, through Satan's Temptation.

What learn you from hence?
That seeing it pleased God to make Man's Body more principally of the basest Element; thereby he may take occasion of being lowly and humble in his now sight: According as the Scripture it self directeth us to this Instruction, Gen. 18. 27.

What else learn you?
The absolute Authority that God hath over Man; as the Potter hath over his Pots, and much more, Rom. 9. 21.

How was the Soul made?
His Soul was made a Spiritual Substance, which God breathed into that frame of the Earth to give it a Life: whereby Man became a living Soul, (Gen. 2. 7. Mal. 2. 15.)

Why is it called the Breath of God?
Because God made it immediately: Not of any earthly Matter (as he did the Body) nor of any of the Elements, (as he did the other Creatures) but of a Spiritual Matter. Whereby it signified the difference of the Soul of Man, which was made a Spiritual and Divine, or everlasting Substance, from the Soul or Life of Beasts, which cometh of the

same Matter whereof their Bodies are made, and therefore dieth with them. Whereas the Soul of Man cometh by God's Creation from without, (in which respect God is said to be the Father of our Spirits, Heb. 12. 9.) and does not rise as the Souls of Beasts do, of the temper of the Elements, but is created of God, free from composition, that it might be immortal, and free from the corruption, decay, and death that all other Creatures are subject unto. And therefore as it had Life in it self when it was joined to the Body, so it retaineth Life when it is separated from the Body, and liveth for ever.

What other Proofs have you of the Immortality of the Soul, besides the Divine Nature thereof?
First, Eccles. 12. 7. It is said that at death, The Dust shall return to the Earth, as it was, and the Spirit unto God who gave it. Second, our Savior Christ, Luke 23. 46. and his Servant Stephen, Acts 7. 59. at their death commend their Souls unto God. Third, Luke 23. 43. The Thief's Soul after separation from the Body is received into Paradise. Fourth, Mat. 10. 28. The Soul cannot be killed by them that kill the Body. Fifth, Psal. 49, 14, 15. Mat. 22. 32. Rev. 6. 9. and 7. 9. Sixth, the guiltiness of the Conscience, and fear of Punishment for Sin, proveth the same. Seventh, otherwise all the comfort of God's Children were utterly dashed. For if in this Life only we have hope in Christ, we are of all Men most miserable, 1 Cor. 15. 19.

Why is it said, that God breathed in his Face or Nostrils, (Gen. 2. 7.) more than in any other part?
1. To put Man in Mind of his frailty; whose Breath is in his Nostrils, Isa. 2. 22.
2. Because the Soul showeth her Faculties most plainly in the Countenance, both for outward Senses and inward Affections.

But is the Head the Seat of the Soul?
It is thought that in regard of the Essence of it, all of it is over all and every part of the Body, as Fire is in hot Iron. But howsoever the Faculties thereof appear in the several parts of the Body; yet the Heart is to be accounted the special Seat of the Soul: Not only in regard of Life, being the first part of Man that liveth, and the last that dieth; but for Affections also and Knowledge. As appeareth by 1 Kings 3. 9, 12. Mat. 15. 18, 19. Rom. 2. 15. and 10. 10. 1 Pet. 3. 4.

Is there many, or one Soul in Man?
There is but one: Having those Faculties in it of Vegetation and Sense, that are called Souls in Plants and Beasts.

What reason have you for this saying?
1. Otherwise there should be divers essential forms in Man. 2. God breathed but one breathing: Though it be called the breathing of Lives, Gen. 2. 7. for the divers Lives and Faculties. 3. In all Scripture there is mention but of one Soul in Man, Mat. 26. 38. Acts 7. 59.

When may the Soul be truly said to come, or be in the Body of a Child?
When in all essential Parts it is a perfect Body; as Adam's was, when God gave him his Soul.

What are the Faculties of the Soul?
The Understanding, under which is the Memory (though it be rather one of the inward Senses, than one of the principal Faculties of the Soul) and the Conscience. The Will, under which are the Affections. So there be five special Faculties.

What is meant by the Image of God, after which Man was made? Gen. 1. 26, 27.
Not any bodily shape, (as though God had a Body like Man) but the divine state wherein his Soul was created.

How many ways is the Image of God taken in Scripture?
Either for Christ; as Col. 1. 15. Heb. 1. 3. John 12. 45. and 14. 9. or for the Glory of Man's lively Personage, as Gen. 9. 6. or for his Authority over the Woman, as 1 Cor. 11. 7. or for the Perfection of his Nature, endued with Reason and Will, rightly disposed in Holiness and Righteousness, Wisdom and Truth; and accordingly framing all Motions and Actions, both inward and outward, Col. 3. 9, 10. Ephes. 4. 24.

How is it then here to be taken?
It may be taken either strictly and properly, or more largely and generally.

What is the strictest and most proper Acceptation of it?
When it is taken for that integrity of Nature, which was lost by Adam's Fall, and is contrary to Original Sin.

Wherein standeth that integrity of Nature?
In the Holy Perfection of Virtues, appearing in the five Faculties: As

1. In the Understanding; true Wisdom, and heavenly Knowledge of God's Will and Works.
2. In Memory; all holy remembrance of things we ought.
3. In Will; all cheerfulness to obey God's Command.
4. All moderation and sanctity of Affections.
5. All integrity of Conscience.

Is any part of God's Image in the Body?
No: But as Original Sin in our corrupt estate, so in the state of integrity these Virtues shine and are executed by the Body.

But is not Man the Image of God, in respect of the essential Faculties of his Soul, his Mind and Will, and in the Immortality thereof?
Not in this strict and proper Acceptation of God's Image, whereof now we speak. For the Essential Faculties of the Soul are not lost by Adam's Fall: And the Immortality remaineth still.

What is the larger Acceptation of God's Image?
When it is taken for that dignity and excellency, given unto Man in his Creation; which is partly inward, and partly outward.

Wherein do his inward Excellencies consist?
Both in his Substance, and in his Qualities.

Wherein standeth the excellency of his Substance?
In that he only, of all the Creatures of the visible World, hath a reasonable and immortal Soul given unto him, (as hath been declared); and in respect of this Spiritual Nature, resembleth God, who is a Spirit.

What is the excellency of Man consisting in Qualities?
Knowledge and Wisdom in the Understanding, (Psal. 51. 6. Col. 3. 10.) Righteousness and Holiness in the free Will, (Ephes. 4. 24. 1 Pet. 1. 15, 16.) and herein, as hath been showed, did Man especially resemble his Maker.

Wherein standeth the excellency of the Understanding?
In knowledge of all Duties, either concerning God, his Neighbor, or himself. Unto which Knowledge may be referred Wisdom, to use Knowledge to discern when, where, and how every thing should be done: Conscience to accuse or excuse, as his doings should

be good or evil: Memory to retain; Providence to foresee what is good, to do it; what is evil, to avoid it: Reason, to discuss of the lawfulness or unlawfulness of every particular Action of a Man's own self.

Wherein standeth the excellency of Man's Will?
In Holiness (as hath been said) and Righteousness, or Uprightness of Desires and Actions. Holiness comprehending all the Virtues of the first; and Justice of Righteousness containing all the Virtues of the second Table; imprinted in the Soul of Man at his Creation.

What were the outward Gifts wherein Man's excellency did consist?
1. God gave him a Body answerable to his Soul; endued with Beauty, Strength, Immortality, and all Gifts serving to Happiness, 1 Cor. 11. 7.

2. God set such a Grace and Majesty in the Person, specially in the Face of Man, as all the Creatures could not look upon without fear and trembling: As appeareth when they all came before Man to receive their Names.

3. God gave him dominion and rule over all Creatures of the World, which were made to serve him; being by this excellent Creation made and adopted to be as it were the Son and Heir of God, who is the absolute Lord over all, Psal. 8. 6, 7. Gen. 1. 26, 28. of which Dominion the Authority to name them was a sign, Gen. 2. 19, 20.

What are the Ends and Uses of the making of Man according to God's Image?
1. That God, who is in himself invisible and incomprehensible, might in some measure be known of Man: As a Picture or Image showeth the Person whom it representeth. 2. To move Man to love God, that hath so gloriously made him like himself. 3. That Men between themselves might love one another, as like does like.

How many of Mankind did God create at first?
First, Only one Man, Adam, Gen. 2. 7. Second, Out of him, and for him, one Woman, Eve, Gen. 2. 21, 22. Mal. 2. 15. so made he them Male and Female, Gen. 1. 27. and 5. 2.

How does God say, Gen. 2. 18. It is not good for Man to be alone? Did he make any thing that was not good?
God forbid. By Good is not meant that which is set against Sin or Vice: But in saying, It is not good for Man to be alone, he meaneth that it is not so convenient and comfortable.

What learn you from hence?
1. How foully they have been deceived, that upon the words of the Apostle, 1 Cor. 7. 1. It is not good for Man to touch a Woman, have gathered, that Marriage is little better than Whoredom: Considering, that as here, so there, by good is meant only that which is convenient and commodious. 2. That Man is naturally desirous of the society of Women: And therefore that Monkeries, Nunneries, and Hermitages are unnatural, and consequently ungodly.

What is meant by these words in the same place, Gen. 2. 18. [as before him?]
That she should be like unto him, and of the same form for the perfection of Nature, and Gifts inward and outward.

What is the end why she was made?
To be a help unto Man.

Wherein?
First, In the things of this Life: By continual society, (1 Pet. 3. 7.) And for Generation, Gen. 1. 28. Secondly, In the things of the Life to come; as they which are Heirs together of the Grace of Life, (1 Pet. 3. 7.) And now a fourth use is added, to be a Remedy against Sin, which was not from the beginning, 1 Cor. 7. 2, 9.

What reason is brought to prove that God was to make a Woman an help unto Man?
Either he must have a Help or Companion from some of these Creatures that are already made; or else I must make him a Helper and Companion. But amongst all the Creatures there is none fit; therefore I must create one. The first Proposition being evident; the second is proved by God's own Testimony, and Adam's experience; who having given Names to all the Creatures, truly, and according to their Natures, found none fit for his company, Gen. 2. 20.

What learn you from thence, that the Lord would have Adam see whether there were an Helper amongst the other Creatures, which he knew well to be unfit?
To teach us, that e're we enter into Marriage, we should have a feeling of our own Infirmity, and need of a Wife; whereby that benefit may become more sweet, and we more thankful unto God. Which if it be true in a Man, it ought to be much more in a Woman, which is weaker, and much more insufficient than he.

What else?
That it is a perverse thing to love any Creature so well as Mankind: against those Men that make more of their Horses and Hounds than of their Wives; and against those Women which make more of a Monkey, or of a Parrot, or of a Spaniel, than of their Husbands.

What note you of that, that when Adam was asleep, his Wife was made?
That the Lord is the Giver of the Wife without our care: And that besides our Prayers to God for one, the care is to be laid upon the Lord, and upon our Parents, which are to us as God was to Adam, to direct us therein, Prov. 19. 14.

Why was not Eve made of the Earth, as Adam was; but of a Rib of her Husband?
1. To admonish her of her subjection and humility. As the Apostle teacheth; The Man was not of the Woman, but the Woman of the Man, 1 Cor. 11. 8. Which subjection also appeareth in this, that Adam gave her the Name. 2. To put them in mind of the near conjunction that should be between the Man and his Wife, in love and affection.

Wherefore does God bring the Woman to Adam?
To note, that how fit soever a Woman be, yet she should not be received to Wife until God giveth her: And when he giveth her by the Ordinance he hath appointed, that then he should receive her.

Whereof dependeth this; That a Man shall leave Father and Mother, and cleave to his Wife? Gen. 2. 24.
Of this, that she was Flesh of his Flesh, and Bone of his Bone; and that God did give her unto Man, and he accepted her.

[6TH HEAD.]

The Creation, which is the former part of the execution of God's Decree, being ended; what is the other?
Providence.

How may it appear that there is a Providence?
Partly by the Word of God, Mat. 10. 30. Prov. 16. 33. and partly by Reason.

What Reasons have you to prove that there is a Providence?
1. The agreement of things which are most contrary in the World, and which would consume one another if they were not hindered by the Providence of God.

2. The subjection of many Men and Women unto one Person, both in Commonwealths and Families.

3. The means of our preservation and nourishment. For Meat, Drink, and Clothing, being void of Heat and Life, could not preserve the Life of Man, and continue heat in him, unless there were a special Providence of God to give virtue unto them.

4. Those Beasts that are hurtful unto Man, though they increase more, and no Man kill them, yet are fewer than those that are profitable unto Man.

5. The feeding of the young Ravens in the Nest, when the Dam forsaketh them.

6. The hatching of the Ostriches Egg.

7. The Lord hath so disposed of the wild Beasts, that they go abroad in the night time to seek their Prey; and lie in their Dens in the day time, that Men may go abroad to their work, Psal. 104. 22, 23.

8. God does preserve his Church from the Devil and the Wicked; so that though they be stronger than it, yet they cannot hurt it.

Object. 1. But it seemeth that the inequality holden in the government of Men should prove, that all things are not governed by the Lord, for the worst are richest oftentimes, and the best poor.
His Government in all things whatsoever is good: For he is no less good in his Government than his Creation.

Object. 2. If God do guide all things, we should have no Serpents and other noisome and hurtful things; no war, no sickness.
They are the instruments and means of the execution of God's Justice and Vengeance upon Men that offend against him: in which respect the Prophet saith, There is no evil in the City, which the Lord hath not done, Amos 3. 6.

Object. 3. How cometh it to pass then, if these be Instruments of Vengeance for sin, that they fall upon the Good, and rather upon them than upon the Wicked?
The most godly having the remnant of sin that dwelleth in their mortal Bodies, deserve everlasting condemnation; and therefore in this Life are subject to any of the plagues of God. As for that they are more sharply handled oftentimes than the Wicked, it is to make trial of their patience, and to make show of the Graces he hath bestowed upon them, which he will have known: And that it may be assured that there is a judgment of

the World to come, 2 Thess. 1. wherein every one shall receive according to his doing in this Life, either Good or Evil.

Having showed that there is a Providence; declare now what it is?
It is a temporary Action of God, whereby he moveth and directeth all things after the counsel of his own Will to their proper ends. Or thus; It is the second part of the execution of God's Decree, whereby he hath a continual care over all his Creatures, once made; sustaining and governing them, with all that belongeth unto them, and effectually disposing of them all to good ends, Ephes. 1. 11. Rom. 11. 36. Zech. 4. 10. Prov. 15. 3. Jer. 23. 23. Psal. 139. 2. and 119. 91.

Why say you it is an Action?
To distinguish it from the Attributes of God.

Why say you that it is Temporary?
To distinguish it from the eternal Decree of God.

Why say you [whereby he moveth and directeth all things?]
1. To show first, that God is not idle in Heaven, as Epicures do dream. 2. That nothing can come to pass without the Providence of God.

Why say you [after the Counsel?]
To show that God does nothing unadvisedly and rashly: But useth, first, His Knowledge, whereby he perfectly understandeth all things. Secondly, His Wisdom, whereby he does dispose all things being known.

Why say you [of his own Will?]
To show, first, that God is not compelled to do any thing, but whatsoever he does, he does it voluntarily, without compulsion. Secondly, That the Lord in the dispensation and government of all things does not follow the advice and counsel of any other; neither regardeth any thing without himself.

Why say you [to their proper ends?]
To show that the Lord does not only govern things generally, but every thing particularly, together with their Properties, Qualities, Actions, Motions, and Inclinations.

Is God's Providence then extended unto all his Creatures?
Yea; unto all Persons, Things, Actions, Qualities, and Circumstances, how usual soever they seem to be: God exercising his Providence about all things in general, and every thing in particular; for not one Sparrow (whereof two are sold for a Farthing) falleth without the Providence of our Heavenly Father; not so much as a Hair off our Head, Mat. 10. 29, 30. no, (it may truly be said) not the Bristle of a Swine falleth without the Providence of God.

But it seemeth a thing unworthy of God's great and infinite Majesty to deal and have a hand in small Matters; as for a King to look to the small Matters of his Household.
No more than it is a disgrace to the Sun that shineth in the foulest places.

How is that then to be understood that the Apostle saith, 1 Cor. 9. 9. [Hath God care for Oxen?]
It is spoken only by way of comparison, having regard to the great care he hath of Men. For in respect he commanded that they should not muzzle the Mouth of the Ox that did

tread out the Corn; by the care he hath of Oxen, he would show that his care is much more for Men, especially for the Ministers of his Gospel.

What other things be there, from which some do exclude the Providence of God?
Things done by, 1. Necessity. 2. Art. 3. Nature. 4. Fortune and Luck. 5. Casualty and Chance. 6. Destiny. 7. Free Will.

How manifold is necessity?
Twofold. 1. Absolute Necessity, the contrary whereof cannot be.
2. Necessity with condition; which is such, as put down the Cause, the Effect followeth; but take away the Cause, the Effect ceaseth.

How prove you that God hath a Government in things that come by Chance and Casualty?
Prov. 16. 33. The Lots are cast in the Bosom; yet the issue of them and their event hang upon the Lord.

Is there not then any Fortune or Chance of things in the World?
Not in respect of God, (by whose appointment the very Hairs of our Heads are governed and numbered) but in respect of Man, that knoweth not future things, the Scripture useth such words to show the suddenness and uncertainty of a thing, Exod. 21. 13. with Deut. 19. 4, 5. Eccles. 9. 11. Luke 10. 31.

Do the Creatures, ever since the first six days, continue of themselves; being only governed of God?
No. The Creation is after a manner still continued, in that all things are sustained by the same Power, whereby they were made. For God is not like a Builder, that is the cause only of the Making, and not of the Being of his Building: But he is such a Cause of Being to all Creatures, as the Sun is of Light unto the Day; so that without his continual working, all would return to nothing.

What Proof have you of this continual working of God?
Our Savior saith, John 5. 17. My Father worketh until this time, and I al so work: Meaning in continuance and preservation of all Creatures. For in him we live, and move, and have our Being, Acts 17. 28. And the Apostle testifieth, Heb. 1. 2, 3. That our Savior Christ, by whom the World was made, heareth up all things, and upholdeth them in their Being, with the Word of his Power, or his mighty Word. Thus Moses teacheth how the Lord establisheth the continuance and preservation of all the Creatures in the World, both living, and void of Life, Gen. 1. So does the Prophet also in Psal. 104. and 119. 91.

How does God sustain all Creatures?
Partly, by the continuation of particulars: Either for the whole time of this World, as Heaven and Heavenly Bodies, Earth and other Elements, &c. 2 Pet. 3. 4. or for the time of Life allotted, as all Living Creatures, Psal. 36. 6. Psal. 104. 27, &c. Partly, by propagation of Kind: Whereby Creatures, even of shortest continuance, do successively abide unto the end of the World, Gen. 7. 3. and 8. 21, 22.

Thus God sustaineth and preserveth all that he hath made: How does he govern them, and dispose of them?
God ordereth all his Creatures according to his pleasure, Dan. 4. 34, 35. guiding and employing them, and their Natures, to those several ends and uses, whereby they may best serve unto his Glory, (Psal. 119. 91.) and the good of themselves and their fellow

Creatures, especially of Man, (Psal. 8.) But he hath one general manner of Government belonging to all; and another special, which is proper to the principal Creatures.

How does God work in all Creatures generally?
First, He does move and stir up that Power which he hath given the Creature unto working. Secondly, He does assist, direct, and help it in working of that which is good. Thirdly, He does work together, and give Being unto that which is wrought.

What are the principal Creatures you speak of?
The reasonable Creatures, Angels and Men: Which were created like unto God, in a high estate of Holiness and Happiness, Psal. 8. 4, 5. and 103. 20. and 104. 4. Luke 2. 13. Mat. 25. 31.

How cometh it to pass, that there is a particular kind of Government for the reasonable Creatures, above others?
Because that they are Creatures of another Nature than the rest: Being not only acted and moved in one course, as the other are, but having a Power of understanding what does concern them, and of moving themselves accordingly.

What Government does follow hereupon?
That which is by teaching, and answerable fulfilling of that which is taught.

How by teaching?
By instructing, commanding, praising, forbidding, promising, threatening, and permitting.

How by fulfilling?
Especially by Blessing and Cursing.

What is the manner of God's Providence?
It is sometimes Ordinary, other times Extraordinary.

What is the Ordinary course of God's working in his Providence?
When he bringeth things to pass by usual means, and that course which he hath settled in Nature, Isa. 55. 10.

What is Extraordinary?
When he bringeth things to pass, either without means, or by means of themselves too weak; or beside the course of such Means, and course of Nature, which Works are usually called Miracles.

May we indifferently expect God's extraordinary working, as we may his ordinary?
No: where ordinary Means may be had, we cannot look for an extraordinary Work.

What do they that run unto the immediate and extraordinary Providence of God, without necessary occasion?
They do tempt God.

How many ways is God tempted?
Two. First, By Distrust. Secondly, By Presumption.

When is God tempted by Distrust?
When Men think that God either cannot, or will not fulfill his Promises.

When is God tempted with Presumption?
When Men depend upon the immediate Providence of God, without any Warrant of the Word so to do.

How many sorts of Men do thus tempt God?
First, They that do wastefully mis-spend their Goods. Secondly, They that having received Gifts of Mind, and Strength of Body, do not use them in some lawful Calling for the maintenance of them, but do live idly. Thirdly, They that make an Occupation of Dicing and Carding, and such like. Fourthly, They that thrust themselves upon unnecessary Dangers. Fifthly, They which take pains for the maintenance of their Bodies in this Life, but have no care of those things which belong to the Salvation of their Souls in the Life to come.

What are the means by which God does use to exercise his Providence?
Two: The first Passive; the second Active.

What call you passive Means?
Those, which, although the Lord does use them, yet have no knowledge nor understanding to move or direct themselves, but are wholly moved and directed by God.

What call you Active Means?
Those which although God useth, yet have Reason, Knowledge, and Understanding in themselves how to move or direct themselves: Such as are Men and Angels, whether they be good or Evil.

Does God work after the same manner by the Wicked, that be does by the Godly?
No. For God worketh by the Wicked, but not in them: As for the Godly, he worketh not only by them, but also in them. Whereby it cometh to pass, that the Work of the Godly is acceptable unto God: But the Work of the Wicked is not acceptable, although they do the same thing which God does.

How can it be showed out of the Scriptures, that God hath a Hand whereby he governeth even the Transgressor against his Holy Will?
Gen. 45. 8. It is expressly said, that God did send Joseph before into Egypt, and that his Brethren did not send him. Wherein God is said to have had a further and a stronger hand in his sending into Egypt, than his Brethren: And therefore it is manifest, that God did that well which the Patriarchs did sinfully, Gen. 50. 20.

1. Exod. 7. 3. God hardened Pharaoh's Heart.

2. 2 Sam. 16. 10. It is said, that God had commanded Shimei to curse David.

3. 2 Sam. 24. 1. God moved David to number the People.

4. 2. Chron. 10. 15. It is said, that it was of God, that Rehoboam harkened not to the People.

5. 1 Kings 22. 19, 20, 23. It is said, that the Devil was hidden of God, sitting in the Seat of his Righteous Judgment, to be a lying Spirit in the Mouths of the false Prophets.

6. Isa. 19. 14. God mingled among them the Spirit of Error.

7. Isa. 42. 24. Who gave Jacob for a spoil? And Israel to the Robbers? Did not the Lord.

8. Isa. 63. 17. Why hast thou made us to err out of thy way, and hardened our Heart from thy fear?

9. Rom. 1. 26. God gave them up to vile Affections.

10. 2 Thess. 2. 11. God sent them strong Delusions, &c.

11. And to be content with one more testimony among many: Let us consider how the most vile and horrible Act that ever was done upon the Face of the Earth, the Lord God is said to have wrought most holily. For as Judas, the Jews, and Pilate, are all said to have given Christ to Death: So the Father and Christ are said to have done the same, and that in the same words; though the manner and purpose are diverse, Acts 2. 23. and 4. 28. Rom. 8. 32.

Did not God then suffer such things to be done?
He suffereth indeed. Yet this is not an idle permission, as some imagine; but joined with a very Doing or Work of God; as in the crucifying of Christ, it is said that they did nothing, but that which the Hand of God had determined before, Acts 2. 23. and 3. 18. and 4. 28. For God is not only a bare Permitter of the evil Work, but a powerful Governor of it to his Glory, and an Affecter also of it, so far as it hath any good in it.

But does not this draw God to some strain of Sin, from which he is most free, as being that which he punisheth?
In no wise. For that which is Evil hath some respect of Goodness with God. First, As it were a mere Action; God being the Author of every Action, Acts 17. 28. But the Devil and our Concupiscence, of the Evil in it. As he that rideth upon a lame Horse, causeth him to stir, but is not the cause of his halting.

Secondly, As it is the Punishment of Sin. For Punishment is accounted a moral Good, in that it is the part of a Just Judge to punish Sin. And thus God willeth the sin of the Wicked for their Punishment; without sin in himself, Rom. 1. 26.

Thirdly, As it is a Chastisement, a Trial of one's Faith, as Martyrdom; or Propitiation for Sin; as the Death and Passion of Christ, Acts 2. 23. and 4. 27, 28. where although the giving of Christ to the Death of the Cross be attributed in the same words to God and Christ, to Judas, Pilate, and the Jews: Yet diversly, and in several respects, they are declared to meet in one and the same Action; whereby there appeareth no less difference between God and Christ's Purpose, and theirs, than between Light and Darkness.

Declare how God can have a band in these things, and yet be free from Sin.
He is a cunning Workman, which with an ill Tool will work cunningly. And as a most excellent Apothecary maketh a Medicine of the mixture of Poison in it, which is not yet Poisonous, but rather Medicinal; so the Lord in guiding and managing the Poison of Sin, draweth Treacle from the sins of Men, as it were Poison, in such sort as they turn to his Glory and Good of his Church: And cannot be charged with Sin, no more than the Apothecary with Poisoning, in so ordering the Poison, as it does the contrary, by his skill, unto that which by nature it would do. And as in Painting, the black Color giveth grace to other beautiful Colors, in making them show better: So it is in this Work of God, in which the sin and untruth of Men, (as by a black and dark Color) causeth the Truth and Righteousness of God (as the white) to be more commended, and to appear better.

But how are these Actions of the Wicked discerned from the Work of God in them?
First, By the Cause from whence the Action cometh. For Joseph's Brethren of Envy sent him into Egypt, but God in Mercy. Shimei cursed David of Malice; but God of Justice against David's Murder and Adultery. Rehoboam out of the unadvisedness of his Heart refused the request of his People; but God by his wise Counsel did so dispose of it. The Devil from Hate to Ahab was a lying Spirit in the Mouth of all his Prophets; but God in Justice against his Idolatry. Pilate of Ambition and Fear, the Jews of malicious Envy and Ignorance, Judas of Covetousness; but God of Love gave Christ, and Christ himself in Obedience to his Father: And therefore that Action, as it was from God and Christ, was most Just and Righteous; as from the other, most Wretched and Abominable.

Secondly, By the End whither they tend. For Joseph's Brethren sent him, to the end he should not come to the honor he foretold out of his Dream: But God sent him to provide for his Church, and to fulfill that which was foretold. Shimei cursed, to drive David to despair: But God directed him for exercise of David's Patience. The Devil lied in the false Prophets, to ruin Ahab: But God justly to punish him for his Idolatry. Rehoboam, to satisfy the desire of his young beardless Counselors: But God to perform the Word that he had spoken by his Prophet. Pilate to please the People, and to keep his credit with Caesar: Judas for obtaining of the Money he desired; and the Jews, that our Savior Christ should not reign over them: But God and Christ to save his People.

But were it not better to say, That these things were done by God's Permission, rather than by his Providence and Government; thereby to avoid an absurdity in Divinity, that God is the Author of Evil?
It is most truly said, that God is not the Author of Sin, whereof he is the Revenger; and also that it is done by God's Permission: But it is not an idle Permission, separated from the Providence and Government of God; and therefore a distinction of God's Permission, separated from his Government of Sin, is not good: Especially considering, that the distinction of such a Permission does not defend the Justice of God, for the which it was devised.

How may that appear?
If he permit sin, he does it against or with his Will. If he do it against his Will, then is he not Almighty; as one that cannot let that he would not have done. If with his will; how can his Justice be defended, if there were not some good thing, for which he does willingly permit it? For if a Captain should willingly suffer his Soldiers to be murdered when he might hinder the slaughter of them; although he put no hand to the Murder, he is not therefore excusable and free from the Blood of his Soldiers.

What else can be alleged against the Permission, that is separated from the Government of the Providence?
For that by this means God should be spoiled of the greatest part of the Government of the World: Seeing the greatest part and most of the World are wicked, all whose Actions are (as they themselves are) wicked.

Is there yet any other matter against this distinction?
If in that God does permit sin, he should have no hand in guiding and governing it; then he should have no hand in guiding and governing of good things: For as it is said, that he permitteth sin, so it is also said, that he permitteth the good, Heb. 6. 3.

What Use is to be made of the Doctrine of God's Providence?
First, As in the Creation, so in the Continuation, Preservation, and Government of all things, the Power, Wisdom, and Goodness of the only True God is set forth. And

therefore in all things he is to be glorified, (Rom. 11. 36.) yea, even in the sins of Men, for the Good things he draweth forth from their Evil.

Secondly, The consideration of this, that nothing can come to pass without the Providence of God, should move us to fear God, and make us afraid to commit any sin; far otherwise than the Wicked conclude: Who upon that, that it is taught that all things come to pass by the Providence of God, according to that he hath decreed, (Eccles. 3. 11, 14.) would conclude, that then a Man may give himself liberty to do any thing, considering that it must needs be executed that God hath decreed.

Thirdly, We must banish all slavish fear out of our hearts; knowing that nothing can come to pass without the Providence of God.

Fourthly, This should breed thankfulness to God in prosperity, and in all things that come unto us according to our desire. Whatsoever Blessing we receive, we must acknowledge it to come from God, and give him the praise and glory, (Rom. 11. 36.) not sacrifice to our own Nets, (Hab. 1. 16.) or stay our minds in the Instruments thereof, without looking up to him by whose special Providence and Government we obtain our desires.

Fifthly, This should cause humility under the Hand of God, when things come otherwise than we desire.

Sixthly, In Adversity we should patiently suffer whatsoever affliction the Lord layeth upon us. For this consideration hath wrought patience in God's Servants; It is the Lord, let him do what pleases him, 1 Sam. 3. 18.

Seventhly, We must mark and observe the Providence of God in former times; that thereby we may gather Arguments of his Goodness unto us in the time to come.

[7TH HEAD.]

Having thus spoken generally of the Providence of God: We are now to descend unto the special consideration of that which does concern the principal Creatures; upon whom God hath declared the glory of his Mercy and Justice. And first to begin with Angels: Show how they are upheld in their Being.
They are all sustained by the Power of God, so that they shall never die, or return to nothing, Luke 20. 36.

How does God dispose of them?
First, Concerning their everlasting Condition: They had a Law given them in their Creation, which the Elect observe, and are established in their Perfection; but the Reprobate sinning against it, have lost their first Estate, and are reserved unto further Judgment. For all being by God created good at the first, (Gen. 1. 31.) some continued in humility and obedience, according to that dignity in which they were created: Others continued not in the truth, (Job. 8. 44.) and so kept not their beginning or excellency, (Jude, v. 6.) in which they were created of God, (by whom nothing could be made but Good) but transgressed and fell from it, by their sin and wickedness becoming Devils.

Secondly, For their Employment: God useth them all, both Good and Evil Angels, as his Servants and Ministers, for the accomplishment of his Will and Work, Job 1. 6.

Seventh Head

How are the Good Angels called in Scripture?
1. Elohim, or Gods; for their Excellency and Power, Psal. 8. 5. compared with Heb. 2. 7. Psal. 97. 7. with Heb. 1. 6.
2. Sons of God, Job 1. 6.
3. Angels of Light, 2. Cor. 11. 14.
4. Elect Angels, 1 Tim. 5. 21.
5. Heavenly Soldiers, Luke 2. 13.
6. Men of God; for their Office.
7. Principalities, and Powers, and Dominions.
8. Seraphim, and a flame of Fire; for their swift Zeal to do God's Will.
9. Cherubim, from the form of young Men, wherein they appeared.

Have they any proper Names?
Some, for our capacity have Names given unto them; as Gabriel, &c.

How many are there of them?
They be innumerable, Heb. 12. 22. Dan. 7. 10. Psal. 68. 17.

Are there divers degrees of Angels?
Yes; for some are Principalities, and Powers, and Dominions, and Thrones, Col. 1. 16. Which showeth not so much a difference in Nature, as a diverse employment in Office. But what those degrees are, it is not observed out of Scripture, and therefore to us is unknown.

With what Properties are these Angels especially endued?
They are endued with Wisdom, Holiness, Willingness to put in execution the Will of God, Power, Swiftness, Industry, Glory, &c. far above any Man.

What measure of Knowledge have they?
Very great, in comparison of Man; both by creation, and otherwise.

How many sorts be there of their Knowledge?
Three. First, Natural, which God endued them with at their creation, far above any Man, as their Nature is more Heavenly. Secondly, Experimental, which they do mark and observe far more carefully than Man, in God's Government of the World, and out of all Creatures, Ephes. 3. 10. Luke 15. 10. Thirdly, Divine, of which God informeth them, according to the several Matters that he sendeth them about: And hereby they know things to come, as Dan. 9. the Angel telleth before to Daniel the time of Christ's death: and Mat. 1. God telleth the Angel Joseph's thoughts.

Do not Angels of themselves know the thoughts of Men?
No: For that is God's Property only, 1 Kings 8. 39. 2 Chron. 6. 30. But in some Messages, (as that in the first of Matthew) God is pleased to manifest it unto them.

Have they not knowledge then of all things done here upon Earth?
No: For all things are only known to God alone, Heb. 4. 13. yet they know the Matters of those Men and Places where God appointeth them a Message: As Cornelius his Alms, Acts 10. 4. and the uncomeliness of Women in the Congregation where they are, 1 Cor. 11. 10.

Can the Good Angels fall at any time?
No: God hath confirmed them in their well-being, that they might never fall by sin from their first blessed Estate, Mat. 18. 10.

Whence cometh this?
Not from their own Nature, (which was subject to mutability) but from God's Mercy. For seeing those Angels are Elect of God, 1 Tim. 5. 21. it followeth of necessity that they are kept and upholden only by his Grace and Mercy, whereupon his Election is grounded.

Now for the employment of these Angels; what are you to note therein?
Their Apparitions, and the Offices which they perform.

In how many sorts have Angels appeared?
In as divers as it pleased God to send them; but especially in two; namely, in Visions or true Bodies.

What mean you by Visions?
Their appearing in some extraordinary sort to the Mind and inward Senses: either in the Night by Dreams, as to Joseph, Mat. 2. 13. or in the Day by some strange Shows, as they did to the Prophets, Zech. 2. 3.

How manifold was their Apparition in Body?
In the true Bodies, either of Men or of other Creatures.

What Examples have you of their Apparition in the Bodies of Men?
Gen. 19. 1. Two Angels (beside Christ) appeared to Abraham. So did two likewise to the Apostles, Acts 1. 10. and Gabriel to the Virgin Mary, Luke 1. 26.

Were these the Bodies of living Men, who had Souls; or Bodies created upon occasion?
They were Bodies extraordinarily created upon that occasion by God, having no Souls but the Angels to give them motion; and after were dissolved by God to nothing, having neither Birth nor Burial.

Did they move from place to place in these Bodies?
Yes: And did many other Actions proper to Man. The Angels appearing to Abraham did truly eat and drink, though without need: The Angels did truly speak, and touch Lot, pulling him. But these Actions were done by them in an extraordinary speediness and manner; more than any Man can do.

Have Angels ever appeared in the Bodies of other Creatures?
Yes: For therefore they are called Cherubim; of Creatures that have Wings; Satan spoke in the Body of a Serpent to Eve: And so to the Heathen in sundry other Creatures.

With what feeling did the Godly find the Apparition of Angels?
Many times with great fear and terror, (as may be seen in Dan. 7. 28. and 10. 7, 8, 9, 16, 17.) which was caused by the small glimpse of Glory that God vouchsafed to them, which Man for his sin could not bear.

What learn you by that?
To know our misery and corruption; and that in comparison of God's appearing, we should be ready to turn to Dust.

How many are the Offices the Good Angels perform?
Twofold: First, In respect of God. Secondly, In respect of the Creatures.

Seventh Head

How many are their Duties concerning God?
Three: 1. They do continually praise and glorify God in Heaven. 2. They do always wait upon the Lord their God in Heaven, to expect what he would have them do. 3. They knowing his Will, do put it in execution.

How manifold are their Duties concerning the Creatures?
Twofold: either general, in respect of all the Creatures; or special, in respect of Man.

What is the general Duty?
That they are the Instruments and Ministers of God for the Administration and Government of the whole World.

What are the Offices which they perform towards Man?
They are either in this Life, or in the Life to come.

How manifold are the Offices which they perform towards Man in this Life?
Twofold: Either such as respect the Godly, the procuring of whose Good is their special Calling, (Heb. 1. 14. Mat. 4. 11. Psal. 104. 4.) or such as respect the Wicked.

How many Good Angels hath every one attending upon him in this Life? hath he one only, or hath he many?
That is as the Glory of God and the necessity of the Saints requireth, sometimes there do many attend upon one, and sometimes one upon many.

What are the good Offices which the Angels perform towards the Godly in this Life?
They are used as Instruments; 1. To bestow good things upon them. 2. To keep them from Evil.

How manifold are those good things, which by the Ministry of the Angels are bestowed upon the Godly?
They are partly concerning the Body, partly the Soul.

What are the Good things that concern the Body?
First, the are used as Instruments to bestow things needful for the Preservation of it: And to bring necessary Helps to Men in their Distress; as to Elias and Hagar. Second, they are appointed of God to be as a Guard and Garrison unto his Children, to comfort and defend them walking in their lawful Callings, Psal. 34. 7. & 91. 11. Third, they give an happy Success to them in the good things they go about, Gen. 24. 7, 40. Fourth, they are appointed as Watchmen over the Saints; that by their Presence they might keep their Bodies in Shamefacedness, Holiness and Purity, 1 Cor. 11. 10.

What are the good things of the Soul, which the Lord does bestow upon the Saints by the Ministry of the Good Angels?
First, t the Will of God to them; and to inform them in things which he would have done, Acts 10. 5. Second, to stir up good Motions in their Hearts. Third, to comfort them in Sorrow: As Christ was comforted being distressed in Soul, Luke 22. 43. and Paul, Acts 27. 23, 24. Fourth, to rejoice at the Conversion of the Saints, Luke 15. 10.

How manifold are the Evil things from which the Good Angels do keep the Godly?
They likewise do partly concern the Body, partly the Soul.

What are the Evils of the Body?
They are either without, or within us.

From what Evils without us are we preserved by the Ministry of the Angels?
1. From those Dangers that one Man bringeth upon another. 2. From those that they are subject unto, by reason of wild Beasts. 3. From those Evils whereunto we are subject by reason of other Creatures without Life. 4. They do not only preserve the Bodies of the Saints; but also all things that are theirs; as their Goods, Wife, Children, and Families.

What are the Evils within us, from which the Angels do keep us?
First, Sickness. Secondly, Famine. Thirdly, Death.

What are the Evils of the Soul, from which the Angels do keep us?
From Sins, and that two ways. 1. By their continual Presence. 2. By their Power.

What are the Actions which the Good Angels perform towards Wicked Men in this Life?
1. They restrain and hinder them from many wicked things which they would bring to pass. 2. They execute Judgments upon the Wicked, and punish them for their sins committed, 2 Kings 19. 35. Gen. 19. 11.

What are the Offices which the Good Angels are to perform towards Man after this Life?
First, They carry the Souls of the Godly, being separated from the Body, with comfort into Heaven, (as Lazarus, Luke 16. 22.) and thrust the Wicked into Hell. Secondly, They wait upon Christ at the Day of Judgment, to gather all the Faithful unto him, and to separate the Wicked from among them, (Mat. 13. 41. & 24. 31.) and to rejoice at the Sentence which he shall give.

Are we not to worship the Blessed Angels for the good Offices which they perform towards Man, and to pray unto them?
Not in any Case: For, tey themselves refuse it, Rev. 19. 10. & 22. 9. Secondly, they are but God's Messengers, and our fellow Brethren. Thirdly, God is only to be worshipped, Judges 13. 16. Mat. 4. 10. Col. 2. 18.

Thus much concerning the Good Angels: What are you to know concerning the Evil Ones?
First, Their Sin or Fall. Secondly, The evil Offices they perform.

How many things are we to consider in their Fall?
Two: 1. The Manner. 2. The Backsliding it self.

What must be considered in the manner?
Four things. 1. They were created, though Good, yet mutable; so as they might fall. 2. Being created mutable, they were tried, whether they would fall or not. 3. Being tried, they were forsaken of God, and left to themselves. 4. Being left to themselves, they committed all Sin even with Greediness.

How many things must be considered in the Fall it self?
Three. 1. From whence they fell. 2. Whereunto they fell. 3. The Punishment God laid upon them for their Fall.

From whence fell they?
First, From their Innocence, and Estate which God had set them in, Job 4. 18. John 8. 44. 2 Pet. 2. 4. Jude v. 6. Secondly, From God; and thereby from Fullness of Joy, and Perfection of Happiness.

Seventh Head

Whereunto fell they?
God suffered them voluntarily and maliciously, without any outward Temptation, to fall into that unpardonable Sin of Apostasy; and into the most grievous Sins that could be committed.

What was the principal Sin that the Angels committed?
Howsoever some think it was Pride, abusing the place of Isa. 14. 13, 14. which is meant of the King of Babylon; others Envy towards Man, out of Wisdom 2. 24. others Lying, out of John 8. 44. yet it comprehended all these and more too; being an utter falling away from God, and that holy standing God placed them in, especially to minister for Man's good.

How cometh it to pass that the Fall of Angels is without hope of Restitution; since Man is recovered after his Fall?
The Devil committed the Sin against the Holy Ghost, (Mat. 12. 31. 1 John. 5. 16.) sinning willfully and maliciously; which is proved by his continual dealing against God: And therefore he shall never be restored.

Were there many Angels that did thus fall?
Yes: As appeareth by Rev. 12. 7. & Luke 8. 30. where a Legion possessed one Man.

What Punishments were laid upon the Angels for their fall?
First, The fearful Corruption of their Nature from their first Integrity, and loss of God's Image; so that they can never repent. Secondly, The casting of them out from the Glory of Heaven; and the want of the comfortable Presence of God for evermore. 2 Pet. 2. 4. Thirdly, A Grief and Vexation at the Prosperity of the Saints. Fourthly, A Limitation of their Power, that they cannot do what hurt they would. Fifthly, Horror and Fear of the Judgment of the Great Day; whereunto they are reserved in everlasting Chains under Darkness, 2 Pet. 2. 4. Jude v. 6. Sixthly, A more heavy Torment after the Day of Judgment in Hell Fire; where they are to feel the infinite Wrath of God, World without end, Mat. 8. 29. Luke 8. 31. Mat. 25. 41. Rev. 20. 10.

Can the Devil work Miracles, and tell things to come?
No: But God only, Mat. 4. 3. Isa. 41. 23.

What Power have they to hurt Man?
They have no more Power than is under Nature, (for above Nature they cannot work); and yet they can do nothing by that Power, but what GOD appointeth; not so much as the entering into Hogs, Mat. 8. 31.

How are they effected towards Man?
Very maliciously: As their several Names given them do declare.

What are those Names?
First, Satan, because they mortally hate Men. Secondly, Devil: Because they slanderously accuse them to God and Man, Job 1. 11. & 2. 5. Rev. 12. 10. Thirdly, The Old Serpent: For their subtle Temptation. Fourthly, The Great Dragon: For their destroying of Man, Rev. 12. 9.

How many of them do attend upon every Man?
Sometimes many upon one, and one upon many.

What are the Evil Offices they perform against Man?
Some are common to the Godly with the Wicked; others are proper to the Wicked alone.

Have they a like Power over the Godly and the Wicked?
No. For though God permitteth them often to try and exercise the Godly, (2 Sam. 24. 1. compared with 1 Chron. 21. 1. Ephes. 6. 12.) both in Body and Mind, (as Satan afflicted Job both outwardly with grievous Sores, and inwardly with Dreams and Visions; and sometimes buffeted Paul, 2 Cor. 12. 7. sometimes hindered him from his Journeys, 1 Thess. 2. 18.) yet he limiteth them, and turneth their malice to the good of his Children, Luke 22. 31.

How manifold are the evil Offices which they perform in common against the Godly and the Wicked?
Two-fold: Either such as respect the Body, and the things belonging thereunto; or such as respect the Soul.

How do they hurt the Body, or the things belonging to the Body?
They are permitted by God for Man's Sin; First, To hurt the Creatures that should serve for our Comfort; as the Air, Seas, Trees, &c. Rev. 7. 2, 3. Secondly, To abuse the Bodies both of Men and Beasts, for the effecting of their wicked Purposes. Thirdly, To delude the Senses; making Men to believe things to be such as they are not. As the Devil did by Jannes and Jambres in Egypt, and by the Witch of Endor. Fourthly, To inflict Sickness and Evils upon the Bodies of Men, and to torment and pain them; as in Job and the Egyptians. Fifthly, To strike some dumb. Sixthly, To enter into, and really to possess the Bodies of Men, using them in most fearful sort, as Mat. 8. 16. & 12. 28. Seventhly, To inflict Death upon the Bodies both of Men and Beasts.

How do they hurt the Soul?
First, By depriving some of the use of their Reason; by Frenzy and Madness. Secondly, By troubling and tormenting some with Grief and Vexation of Soul. Thirdly, By abusing some with Passions and Melancholy Fits, as Saul, 1 Sam. 16. 14. Fourthly, By seducing others, 1 Kings 22. 21, 22. 2 Cor. 4. 4. Fifthly, By manifold and fearful Temptations to Sin and Wickedness. Sixthly, By prevailing in some Temptations. Seventhly, By accusing before God those with whom they have so prevailed. Eighthly, By hindering Men from doing good things.

What are the Offices of Evil Angels, that respect the Wicked alone?
First, To Rule and Reign in them without hindrance, and to finish his Work in them. Secondly, To murder and destroy them in this World, and in the World to come, to torment Soul and Body in Hell for ever.

What Use are we to make of this Doctrine concerning the Evil Angels?
First, To tremble at the Lord's Severity towards them, 2 Pet. 2. 4. and to be thankful for his Bounty and Mercies towards ourselves, Psal. 8. 1, 4, 5. Ephes. 1. 3, 4. Secondly, To remember that if God spared not those Spiritual Creatures sinning against him; neither will he spare us rebelling against his Majesty, 2 Pet. 2. 4. Thirdly, To fear to offend God, that hath such Messengers to send at his Command. Fourthly, To learn to arm ourselves with the Shield of Faith and Fear of God; since we have such great Enemies to fight against, Ephes. 6. 11. 1 Pet. 5. 9. Fifthly, To be comforted, that though the Devil be powerful and most malicious against us, yet Christ hath broken his Head, Gen. 3. 15. and at last will tread Satan under our feet, Rom. 16. 20.

Eighth Head

[8TH HEAD.]

Thus much of the Providence that concerneth Angels: Show now how God does deal with Man.
As with that Creature in whom, above all other, he intendeth to set forth the Glory of his Wisdom, Power, Justice, and Mercy, Prov. 8. 31. Psal. 8. 3, &c. and therefore the Scriptures do most plentifully declare the dealing of God with Man, both in the time of this World, and for ever hereafter.

How is Man upheld in his Being?
Two Ways. First, As all other bodily Creatures: Partly by Maintenance of every Man's Life here on Earth, for the time allotted by God himself, Acts 17. 28. Psal. 36. 6. Partly, by Propagation of Kind, unto the end of the World, through the Blessing of Procreation, Gen. 1. 28. Eccles. 1. 4.

Secondly, As Angels after a sort; God so providing, that though the Body of Man returneth to the Earth from whence it was taken, yet the Soul perisheth not, but returneth to God that gave it, (Eccles. 12. 7.) yea, that the same Body also, and every part thereof, is preserved in the Grave, and shall be joined entire to the Soul at the last Day, so to continue for ever, Job 16. 26, 27.

How manifold is the State wherein Man is to be considered?
Three fold. First, The State of Innocence; commonly had and lost of all Mankind, both Elect and Reprobate, without difference, Eccles. 7. 29.

Secondly, The State of Corruption and Misery; seizing on all Men naturally, but abiding without Recovery only on the Reprobate, Rom. 3. 23.

Thirdly, The State of Redemption; proper to the Elect, 1 Pet. 2. 9. Psal. 130. 8. All which do make way unto that final and everlasting Estate of Honor or Dishonor, fore-appointed unto all Men; beginning at the end of this Life, perfected at the Day of Judgment, and continuing for ever in the World to come. And thus touching this part of God's Providence, the Scriptures do teach us, both the Benefits of God bestowed upon Man before his Fall; and likewise his Justice and Mercy towards him after his Fall. His Justice upon the Reprobate, who are left without hope of Restitution, and reserved together with the Devils unto everlasting Punishment, Mat. 25. 41. Rev. 20. 10, 15. His Mercy upon the Elect, who notwithstanding their Fall are restored again by Grace, Gen. 3. 15.

Is it not likely, that all the visible World, together with Men, is fallen with hope of Restitution by Mercy?
Yes. For it standeth well with the Justice of God, that seeing the Visible World was made for the use of Man, (Gen. 2.) that with the Fall of Man it should be punished, (Gen. 3. 17, 18.) and with his raising up again be restored, Rom. 8. 20, 21, 22.

What is that special Order of Government which God useth towards Mankind in this World, and in the World to come?
In this World he ordereth them according to the Tenor of a Two-fold Covenant; in the World to come, according to the Sentence of a Two-fold Judgment.

What understand you by a Covenant?
An Agreement which it pleases Almighty God to enter into with Man, concerning his everlasting Condition.

What are the Parts of this Agreement?
Two: The one is the Covenant that God maketh with us; the other is the Covenant that we make with God. The Sum of the former is, that he will be our God: Of the latter, that we will be his People, Jer. 31. 33.

What gather you from the former?
The Sir name of God, as it is in divers Places of Scripture, and namely, Exod. 3. 15. where it is said, The Lord God of your Fathers, the God of Abraham, the God of Isaac, and the God of Jacob, hath sent me unto you; this is my Name for ever, and this is my Memorial unto all Generations. From whence we may observe the singular Glory and Privilege of God's People, in that God is content to take his Sir name of them, Heb. 11. 16.

Why is this Sir name added?
For that it is a fearful thing, to think of the proper Name of God alone, unless this be added to it; whereby he declareth his Love and Kindness to us.

What gather you from the latter?
That Man standeth bound by these Covenants of Agreement, to perform that Duty which God requireth at his hands.

How many such Covenants be there?
Two. First, The Law, or Covenant of Works. Secondly, The Free Promise, or Covenant of Grace; which from the coming of Christ is called the Gospel, Rom. 10. 5, 6. Gal. 3. 11, 12.

Which of them was first?
The Law. For it was given to Adam in his Integrity; when the Promise of Grace was hidden in God.

How so, since it is said that the Law was not before Moses?
That is to be understood of the Law, as it was written by Moses, and engraved in Tables of Stone by the Finger of God: Otherwise the same Law (for the substance thereof) was imprinted in the beginning in the Hearts of our first Parents; and therefore it is called the Law of Nature, Rom. 2. 14.

How was this Law given unto Adam in the beginning?
It was chiefly written in his Heart at his Creation, and partly also uttered to his Ear in Paradise. For unto him was given both to know Good, and also to be inclined thereunto, with Ability to perform it. There was something likewise outwardly revealed, as his Duty to God, in the Sanctification of the Sabbath; to his Neighbor, in Institution of the Marriage; and to himself, in his daily working about the Garden.

How does it appear that the Substance of the Moral Law was written in the Hearts of Adam and Eve?
First, By the effect of it in them both; who immediately after their Fall, were forced by the only Guilt of Conscience (not yet otherwise charged) to hide themselves from God's Presence, Gen. 3. 8. Secondly, By the remainders thereof in all Mankind; who even without the Law, are by the Light of Nature a Law unto themselves, Gen. 4. 6. Rom. 2. 14, 15.

How hath the Moral Law been delivered since the Fall?
The Sum thereof was comprised in ten Words, (Exod. 34 28. Deut. 4. 13.) commonly called the Decalogue or Ten Commandments; solemnly published and engraved in Table of Stone by God himself, (Deut. 4. 14. & 10. 4.) Afterwards the same was more fully delivered in the Books of Holy Scripture, and so committed to the Church for all Ages,

as the Royal Law for Direction of our Obedience to God our King, (James [2.] 8.) and for the Discovery of Sin, and the Punishment due thereto, Deut. 27. 26. Rom. 1. 31. & 3. 20.

What then does the Law now require of us?
All such Duties as were required of Adam in his Innocence, (Levit. 18. 5.) and all such as are required since by reason of his Fall, (Deut. 17. 26.) binding us to eternal Death for our least defect therein.

Declare now out of that which hath been said, what the Covenant of Works is?
It is a Conditional Covenant between God and Man, whereby on the one side God commandeth the Perfection of Godliness and Righteousness, and promiseth that he will be our God, if we keep all his Commandments; and on the other side, Man bindeth himself to perform entire and perfect Obedience to God's Law, by that Strength wherewith God hath endued him by the Nature of his first Creation.

What was done in this Covenant on God's part?
There was his Law, backed with Promises and Threatenings; and unto them were added outward Seals.

What was the Sum of this Law?
Do this, and thou shalt live: If thou dost it not, thou shalt die the Death.

What is meant by, Do this?
Keep all my Commandments in Thought, Word, and Deed.

What is meant by Life, promised to those that should keep all the Commandments?
The Reward of Blessedness and Everlasting Life, Levit. 18. 5. Luk. 10. 28.

What is meant by Death threatened to those that should transgress?
In this World the Curse of God, and Death, with manifold Miseries both of Body and Soul: And (where this Curse is not taken away) Everlasting Death both of Body and Soul in the World to come, Deut. 27. 26. & 29. 19, 20. & 32. 22. Levit. 26. Deut. 28.

What were the outward Seals added hereunto?
The two Trees, planted by God for that purpose in the midst of the Garden, Gen. 2. 9. & 3. 3. that Adam before and in the sight of them might resort to some special place to serve God in, and might by the Sight of them be put in mind of those things whereof they were Signs and Seals.

What did the Tree of Life serve for?
It sealed up Happiness, Life, and Glory unto Man, upon condition of Obedience: That by tasting thereof (which no doubt, according to the manner of Sacramental Signs, was a Tree of marvelous Comfort and Restoring) he might be assured he should live in Paradise for ever, if he stood obedient unto God's Commandments, Gen. 2. 9. Prov. 3. 18. Rev. 2. 7.

Was this Tree able to give Everlasting Life to Man? Or otherwise, why did God after the Fall shut Man from it?
It was no more able to give Everlasting Life, than the bodily eating of any other Sacrament: But Adam having by Sin lost that which was signified hereby, God would have him debarred from the use of the Sacrament.

What did the Tree of Knowledge of Good and Evil serve for?
Both for Trial of Obedience, and also for a warning of their Mutability, and of what would follow upon Sin; so sealing Death and Damnation in case of Disobedience. Not

as though the Tree was able to give any Knowledge: But that by tasting of it contrary to God's Command, they should have experimental Knowledge of Evil in themselves, which before they had of Good only; and by woeful Experience should learn, what difference there was between knowing and serving God in their Integrity, and being ignorant of him by their Sin, Gen. 2. 17.

What was done in this Covenant on Man's part?
Man did promise by that Power which he had received, to keep the whole Law; binding himself over to Punishment in case he did not obey.

In what State is Man to be considered, under this Covenant?
In a Two-fold State. 1. Of Innocence. 2. Of Corruption and Misery.

What things are you to note in the Innocent Estate of Man?
First, The Place where he was seated. Secondly, The happy and glorious Estate he there enjoyed both in Soul and Body.

Where did God place Man when he created him?
In a most glorious, pleasant and comfortable Garden; which is called Paradise, or the Garden of Eden from the Pleasantness, Gen. 2. 8.

What does the Scripture teach concerning it?
The Place where it was, and the Commodities thereof.

Where, and in what part of the World was it?
In Asia near the meeting of Euphrates and Tigris, those two famous Rivers.

What Commodities had it?
All the principal Creatures of God did adorn it: And therefore it is said to be, more extraordinary than the rest of the Wild, planted by God. There are set down also the precious Stones thereof, under the Sardonyx; pure Metals, under the Gold; precious Woods under the Bdellium; and so all other living Things and growing Creatures; that it might be, as it were, a Shop furnished for Man; to see in, and learn by it God's Wisdom, Power and Majesty.

Does this place now continue?
The Place remaineth; but the Beauty and Commodities be partly by the Flood, partly by Man's Sin (for which the whole Earth is cursed) almost abolished; though (as may be observed out of good Authors) it is a very fruitful Place still.

What Happiness did Man enjoy thus placed in Paradise?
It was partly Inward, partly Outward.

Wherein did the Inward appear?
First, In his wonderful Knowledge, whereby he made use of all the Creatures of God, as the greatest Philosopher that ever was. Secondly, In that Holy and Heavenly Image of God, of which Adam had the Use and Comfort before his Fall: It shining in him without Tincture or Blemish, and he thereby being without all Sin, or Punishment of Sin. Thirdly, In the full Fruition and Assurance of the favorable and blissful Presence of his Creator, [Mat. 5. 8. Psal. 17. 15.] and his Heavenly Company and Conference with God, without all Fear, as a Subject with his Prince, (Gen. 3. 8.).Fourthly, In his joyful serving God; together with absolute Contentment in himself, (Gen. 2. 25.).

Wherein did the Outward appear?
First, In having so comely, perfect and glorious a Body, in which there was no Infirmity, Pain, nor Shame, though naked, (Gen. 2. 25.). Secondly, In his Dominion over all the Creatures, that submitted themselves, and did Service unto him: To whom also as their Lord, he gave their Original Names, Gen. 2. 19, 20. Thirdly, In the comfortable State and Sense, not of Paradise alone, but of all the World round about him; having neither Storm, Winter, nor Extremity in any Creature.

What Employment had Man in this Estate?
A Two fold Employment: The first Outward, to till and dress the Garden, Gen. 2. 15. the other Spiritual, to worship and serve God his Creator, and to procure his own Everlasting Blessedness; whereto he was fitted with Freedom of Will and Ability for perfect Obedience unto God, according to the Tenor of the Covenant of Works.

What use are we to make of the knowledge of Man's Happiness before his Fall?
First, To admire and praise the great Goodness and Favor of God in so dealing with Man, a Clod of the Earth. Secondly, To bewail the Loss of that happy Estate, with blaming ourselves for our Sin in Adam. Thirdly, To learn how grievous a thing Sin is in God's Sight, that procured Man this doleful Change. Fourthly, To labor and gasp to be Heirs of the Heavenly Paradise purchased for the Elect by Christ; by which we shall eat of the Tree of Life, Rev. 2. 7.

Thus far of the State of Innocence: What is the State of Corruption and Misery?
The fearful Condition whereunto in Adam all Mankind fell, (Eccles. 7. 29.) by transgressing and violating that Covenant of Works which God made with him at the beginning. For Man continued not in his Integrity, but presently transgressed that Holy Law which was given unto him; willingly revolting from God's Command, through Satan's Temptation, into many sins by eating the forbidden Fruit: And so by the Disobedience of one, sin reigned unto Death, and Death went over all, Rom. 5. 12, 18.

What are we then to consider herein?
First, Adam's Fall. Secondly, The wretched Estate he threw all his Posterity into.

In what place of Scripture is the History of Adam's Fall handled?
In the third Chapter of Genesis: The six former Verses whereof, setteth out the Transgression of our first Parents, (which was the Original of all other Transgressions) the rest of the Chapter declareth at large the things that following immediately upon this Transgression.

How was the way made unto this Fall of Man?
By God's Permission, Satan's Temptation, Man's Carelessness and Infirmity in yielding thereunto.

What Action had God in this Business?
He permitted the Fall of Man; not by instilling into him any Evil, (James 1. 13. 1 John 2. 16.) or taking from him any Ability unto Good; but, first, suffering Satan to assail him, (2 Sam. 24. 1. with 1 Chron. 21. 1.) Secondly, Leaving Man to the Liberty and Mutability of his own Will; and not hindering his Fall by supply of further Grace, (2 Chron. 32. 31.)

Was God then no cause of the Fall of our first Parents?
None at all: But as hath been said, having created them Holy he left them to themselves to fall if they would, or stand if they would, in respect of their Ability: As a Staff put on an end right, does fall without the furtherance of the Man that setteth it right. Yet came it not to pass by the bare Permission of God alone, but also by his

Permissive Decree; thereby to make way for the Manifestation of his Power, Justice and Mercy. For being able to bring Good out of Evil, as Light out of Darkness; he ordereth, in his great Wisdom, the Fall of Man to the setting out of the Glory, both of his Mercy in those that shall be saved in Christ, and of his Justice in those that shall perish for their Sins, (Rom. 11. 32.) yet without wrong to any; being not bound to his Creature, to uphold by his Grace from falling, Rom. 11. 35.

What hand had Satan in procuring the Fall of Man?
Being himself fallen, upon a proud, envious, and murderous Mind, he deceived our first Parents by tempting them to sin; to the end he might bring them into the like estate with himself. And as in this respect he is said to have been a Murderer from the beginning, John 8. 44. so does he ever since seek to do what hurt he can to Mankind; moving them still to sin against God, and laboring to bring them to Damnation.

What do you observe herein?
His Envy of God's Glory and Man's Happiness; together with his Hatred and Malice against Mankind, whom (as a Murderer does his Enemy) he hateth and laboreth to destroy.

What gather you from this Attempt of his against our first Parents in the State of Innocence?
That Satan is most busy to assail them in whom the Image of God in Knowledge and Holiness does appear; not laboring much about those which either lie in Ignorance, or have no Conscience of walking according to Knowledge, as those that are his already.

What Instrument did Satan use in tempting Man?
He used the Serpent as an Instrument to deceive the Woman, and the Woman for an Instrument to tempt the Man, Gen. 3. 1. 2 Cor. 11. 3. 1 Tim. 2. 14.

Why did he use those outward Instruments, and not rather tempt their Fancy and Affection inwardly?
It seemeth that in their Integrity he could not have that advantage against them, in those things whereunto they were made subject by their Fall.

Why did he choose rather to speak by a Serpent, than by any other Beast?
Because it was the fittest that God permitted him, and wisest of all the Beasts of the Earth; especially possessed by him to deceive Man, (Gen. 3. 1.) It was of all other Beasts the subtlest and fittest to creep into the Garden unseen of Adam, (who was to keep the Beasts out of it) and to remain there without being espied of him, and creep out again when he had done his Feat.

If there were Craft before the Fall; then it seemeth there was Sin?
Craft in Beasts is not Sin: Although the Word here used signifieth a nimbleness and Slyness to turn and wind it self any way; in which respect it seemeth the Devil chose this Beast before any other.

What learn you from hence?
That the Devil, to work his Mischief, is exceedingly cunning to make his Choice of his Instruments, according to the kind of Evil he will follicite unto, Mat. 7. 15. 2 Cor. 11. 13, 14. 1 Tim. 2. 14.

But we do not see that he cometh any more in the Body of Serpents?
He may; and in the Body of any other Beast which the Lord will permit him to come in. Howbeit our case in this is more dangerous than that of our first Parents. For now he

useth commonly for Instruments Men like unto us, and familiar with us: Which he could not do before the Fall, Ephes, 6. 12. Rev. 2. 10.

Why did Satan assail the Woman rather than Man?
Because she was the weaker Vessel; which is his continual Practice, where the Hedge is low there to go over, (Luke 5. 30. Mark 2. 16. Mat. 9. 11. 2 Tim. 3. 6.) and might afterwards be a fitter means to deceive and draw on her Husband.

What are we to consider in his tempting of the Woman?
First, The time which he chose to set upon her. Secondly, The manner of the Temptation.

What note you of the Time?
First, That it was immediately, or not long after the placing of them in that happy Estate: Which teacheth how malicious the Wicked One is, who if he could let, would not suffer us to enjoy any Comfort, either of this Life, or of that to come, so much as one poor Day.

Secondly, That he came unto her when she was some space removed from her Husband: That he that should have helped her from and against his Wiles, might not be present to hear their Conference. Whence we learn, that the Absence of Wives from their Husbands, who should be a Strength unto them, is dangerous: Especially that we absent not ourselves from the means of Spiritual Strength, the hearing of the Word, the receiving of the Sacraments, and Prayer.

Thirdly, That she was near to the Tree of Knowledge at the time he set on her: Which showeth his Watchfulness in taking Advantage of all Opportunities that might further his Temptations.

What was the manner of the Temptation?
First, He subtlety addressed himself to the Woman; and entered into Conference with her. Secondly, He made her doubt whether the Word of God was true or not. Thirdly he offered her an Object. Fourthly, He used all the means he could to make her forsake God and yield unto him: pretending greater Love and Care of Man's well-doing than was in God, and bearing them in hand that they should be like unto God himself if they did eat of the forbidden Fruit, Gen. 3. 5.

What was the Devil's Speech to the Woman?
It was even so, that God hath said, Ye shall not eat of all the Fruit in the Garden, Gen. 3. 1.

What do you note in this?
That it is likely, there had been some Communication before between the Serpent and the Woman, that Satan had asked why they did not eat of the forbidden Fruit, seeing it was so goodly and pleasant to behold; and that the Woman had answered that they were forbidden: Whereupon he inferreth this, that Moses setteth down; wherein we may observe,

First, The Devil's Sophistry, who at the first does not flatly contrary God's Command; but to bring her to doubting and Conference with him, asketh this Question, Whether God had forbidden to eat of all the Trees in the Garden?

Secondly, The wicked Spirits malicious, and subtle Suggestion: In that passing by the great Bountifulness of the Lord in the grant of the free Use of all the Fruits in the Garden, he seeks to quarrel with the Lord's Liberality.

Thirdly, We learn from hence to take heed left for want of some one thing which God withholdeth from us, which we gladly would have, we be not unthankful to the Lord for his great Kindness and Liberality; and enter further into a Dislike of him for that one Want, than into the Love and liking of him for his innumerable Benefits we enjoy: Especially it being for out good that he withholdeth it, and that being not good which we desire.

What did follow upon this Question of Satan?
The Woman answering thereunto, not as God had spoken, that surely they should die if they did eat of the forbidden Fruit, but by a Term of doubting, lest ye die; Satan by this Conference and Doubting taketh advantage, and assureth them that they should not die, but have their Eyes open and receive Knowledge.

What observe you in this Reply of the Devil?
First, His Craft, in applying himself to the Woman: Whom he seeing to be in doubt of the Punishment, contents himself with it, and abstaineth from a precise Denial, whither he would willingly draw her: Because he deemed that the Woman would not come so far, and that in a flat Denial he should have been betrayed; which notwithstanding in the latter end of this Sentence does by Implication flatly do. Whence we learn, that the Devil proceedeth by degrees, and will not at the first move to the grossest: As in Idolatry he laboreth to draw Man first to be present, after to kneel only with the Knee, keeping his Conscience to himself; lastly, to the greatest Worship. In Whoredom, first to look, then to dally, &c. and therefore we must resist the Evil in the beginning.

Secondly, That he is a Calumniator or Caviler; whereof he hath his Name Diabolus, Devil, and an Interpreter of all things to the worst. And it is no marvel, though he deprave the best Actions of good Men, seeing he dealeth so with God; surmising that GOD had forbidden to eat of the Fruit, lest they should know as much as he.

Thirdly, That knowing how desirous the Nature of Man (especially they of best Spirits) is of Knowledge, he promiseth unto them a great Increase thereof: Whereas we ought to remember that which Moses saith, That the Secrets of the Lord are to himself, and that the things that he hath revealed are to us and to our Children, Deut. 29. 29.

Hitherto of Satan's Temptation, the cause of the Fall without Man. What were the Causes arising from our first Parents themselves?
Not any of God's Creation, but their Carelessness to keep themselves entire to God's Command. For though they were created Good, yet being left by God to the Mutability of their own Will, they voluntarily inclined and yielded unto that Evil, whereunto they were tempted: And so from one degree unto another were brought unto plain Rebellion, Gen. 3. 6. Eccles. 7. 29.

What was their first and main Sin?
In general it was Disobedience: The Degrees whereof were, first Infidelity, then Pride, and lastly the disavowing of Subjection by eating the forbidden Fruit; which they imagined to be the means whereby they should attain to a higher degree of Blessedness, but proved to be the Sin that procured their Fall, Gen. 2. 16, 17. & 3. 6, 7.

Did not Adam confer with Satan, and take the Fruit from the Tree?
No: He received it from his Wife, and by her was deceived, and she by Satan, Gen. 3. 4, 17. 1 Tim. 2. 14.

Satan indeed was the outward Cause of Eve's Fall: But what are the Causes arising from her self?
They are either outward things of the Body, or the inward Affections of the Mind moved by them.

Eighth Head

What are the Outward things of the Body?
They are the Abuse of the Tongue, of the Ears, of the Eyes, and of the Taste. For in that she entertained Conference with the Devil, the Tongue and Ears; in that it is said that the Fruit was delectable to look on, the Eyes; and in that it was said it was good to eat, the Taste is made to be an Instrument of this Sin.

What learn you from hence?
That which the Apostle warneth, Rom. 6. 13. that we beware, that we make not the Parts of our Bodies Weapons of Iniquity. For if without a circumspect use of them they were Instruments of Evil before there was any Corruption, or any Inclination at all to sin; how much more dangerous will they be now after the Corruption, unless they be well looked unto?

What do you observe in Eve's Conference with the Devil?
First, Her folly to enter into any Conference with Satan. For the might have been amazed that a Beast should speak unto her in a Man's Voice: But her Carelessness and Curiosity moved her to it. Secondly, Her Boldness in daring to venture on such an Adversary without her Husband's Help or Advice. Thirdly, Her Wretchedness in daring once to call in Question the Truth of God's Command, or to Dispute thereof, and then to doubt of it.

What Instructions gather you from her entertaining Conference with Satan?
That it is dangerous to talk with the Devil, so much as to bid him to depart. If the Lord, to try us, should suffer him to tempt us visibly as he did Eve, unless we have a special calling of God thereunto. 1. Because he is too subtle for us, we being simple in regard of him. 2. Because he is so desperately malicious, that he will give place to no good thing we can allege to make him leave off his malicious purpose.

What shall we then do?
We must turn ourselves unto God, and desire him to command him away, at whose only Commandment he must depart.

Is there any thing blame-worthy in Eve's Answer to the Question of the Serpent?
Notwithstanding that so far she answered truly, that God had forbidden them to eat of the Fruit of that Tree, and telleth also the Punishment truly that would follow thereof: Yet began she to slip in the Delivery, both of the Charge and of the Punishment. For where she saith they were forbidden to touch it, it is more than the Lord did make mention of: And she thereby seemeth to insinuate some Rigor of the Lord, forbidding even the touch of the Fruit. And where the Lord had most certainly pronounced, that they should die if they did eat of the forbidden Fruit; she speaketh doubtfully of it, as if they should not certainly die.

What learn you from this latter Observation?
That albeit Men are oft persuaded they sin, yet that they are not persuaded of the Justice of God against it; whereby the door is opened to sin. Which is to make God an Idol, in spoiling him of his Justice; as if he were so all Mercy, as he had forgotten to be just, when as he is as well Justice as Mercy, as infinite in the one as in the other; which correcteth sharply the sins of such as he will save.

What learn you of the Abuse of the Tongue in this Conference?
That as the Tongue is a singular Blessing of God, whereby Man excelleth all the Creatures upon Earth: So the abuse of it is most dangerous, because it setteth on fire the whole course of Nature, and it is set on fire of Hell, Jam. 3. 6.

What observe you of that it is said, That Eve saw the Fruit was delectable to look on?
Her lustful and wicked Eye; in suffering her Mind to be allured to look on the Beauty of the Fruit, with a purpose to affect the eating of it.

How is it said, that she saw it was good to eat, when she had never tasted of it?
She knew by the beautiful Color it was so. For if we are able, in this Darkness we are fallen into, to discern commonly by the sight of the Fruit, whether it be good; and the skillful in Physic by the Color only of the Herb, to tell whether it be hot or cold, sweet or sour: How much more were Adam and Eve, who had the Perfection of the Knowledge of those things, more than ever Solomon himself?

What learn you by the Abuse of these Outward Senses?
That they are, as it were, Windows whereby Sin entered into the Heart, when there was no sin; and therefore will much more now, the Heart being corrupted.

What Instructions gather you from thence?
First, That we must shut them against all Evil, and unlawful Use of their Objects, and open them to the Use of good things: Make a Covenant with   Page 185 (118) them, as Job did with his Eyes, Job 31. 1. by a strong and painful Resistance of the Evil that cometh by the Abuse of them, as it were cut them off, and throw them away, as our Savior giveth Counsel, Mat. 5. 29, 30.

Secondly, That as the Senses are more noble, as the Hearing and Sight, called the Senses of Learning; so there should be a stronger watch set upon them: those being the Senses that Adam and Eve were especially deceived by.

What observe you of that it is said, She saw that it was desirable for Knowledge?
That was only her Error, which she having begun to sip of by Communication with the Devil, did after drink a full draught of, by beholding the Beauty of the Fruit, and receiving the delicate Taste thereof. And withal, observe how we can heap Reason true and false to move us to follow our Pleasure.

What learn you from thence?
That the Heart inclining to Error, does draw the Senses to an unlawful Use of them: And that the Abuse of the Senses does strengthen the Heart in Error.

What gather you hereof?
That before the Heart was corrupted, there was no abuse of these outward Senses: But that being corrupt, the Abuse of them does settle the Heart deeper in Error:

What was the Effect of all these Outward and Inward Means?
First, Eve yielded to Satan, and put his Will in Execution, in eating of the Fruit that was forbidden. Secondly, She gave it also to Adam to eat.

What force hath the Word [also] here used by the Holy Ghost?
Thereby, as a special Word of Amplification, the Sin is aggravated against her: To show her Naughtiness, not only in committing the sin her self, but also in alluring her Husband to do as she done.

What learn you from thence?
1. The Nature of Sinners to draw others to the Condemnation they are in (as Satan Eve, and Eve her Husband) even those that are nearest them; whose Good they should procure. 2. That we should take heed of that the Apostle warneth us, not to be partakers of other Men's sins; as if we had not enough of our own to answer for: Which

especially belongeth unto those in Charge, 1 Tim. 5. 22. 3. How dangerous an Instrument is an evil and deceived Wife; which the Lord commandeth Men should beware to make Choice of: And if the Man which is strong, much more the Woman.

What learn you of that, Adam eat forthwith?
First, That which hath been before noted, that the Devil by one of us tempteth more dangerously than in his own Person: So that Satan knew he could not so easily have deceived Adam by himself, as by Eve. Secondly, For that in excess of Love he yielded; it teacheth Husbands to love their Wives, but it must be in the Lord, as the Wives must do their Husbands.

How does it agree with the Goodness, or with the very Justice of God, to punish Mankind so fearfully for eating of a little Fruit?
Very well. For first, the Heinousness of an Offence is not to be measured by the thing that is done, but by the worthiness of the Person against whom it is committed. Secondly, How much more the Commandment our first Parents brake was easy to be kept, (as to abstain from one only Fruit in so great Variety and Plenty) so much more grievous was their Sin in breaking it. Thirdly, Though God tried their Obedience in that Fruit especially, yet were there many other most grievous sins, which in desiring and doing of this they did commit: Insomuch that we may observe therein the grounds of the Breach in a manner of every one of the Ten Commandments. For the Transgression was horrible, and the Breach of the whole Law of God; yea, an Apostasy, whereby they withdrew themselves from under the Power of God, nay rejected and denied him: And not so little an Offence as most Men think it to be.

What Breaches of the first Commandment may be observed in this Transgression?
First, Infidelity: Whereby they doubted of God's Love towards them, and of the Truth of his Word. Secondly, Contempt of God: In disregarding his Threatenings, and crediting the Word of Satan, God's Enemy and theirs. Thirdly, Heinous Ingratitude and Unthankfulness against God for all his Benefits? In that they would not be beholding unto him for that excellent Condition of their Creation (in respect whereof they ought unto him all Fealty) but would needs be his equal. Fourthly, Curiosity in affecting greater Wisdom than GOD had endued them withal by Virtue of their Creation, and a greater measure of Knowledge than he thought fit to reveal unto them. Fifthly, Intolerable Pride and Ambition: In desiring not only to be better than GOD made them, but also to be equal in Knowledge to God himself: And aspiring to the highest Estate due to their Creator.

How did our first Parents break the second Commandment?
Eve, by embracing the Word of the Devil, and preferring it before the Word of GOD: Adam, by hearkening to the Voice of his Wife, rather than to the Voice of the Almighty, Gen. 3. 17.

What were the Breach of the third?
First, Presumption in venturing to dispute of God's Truth, and to enter into Communication with God's Enemy, or a Beast who appeared unto them, touching the Word of God; with whom no such Conference ought to have been entertained. Secondly, Reproachful Blasphemy: By subscribing to the Sayings of the Devil, in which he charged God with lying, and envying their good estate. Thirdly, Superstitious Conceit of the Fruit of the Tree; imagining it to have that Virtue which God never put into it: As if by the eating thereof, such Knowledge might be gotten as Satan persuaded. Fourthly, Want of that Zeal in Adam for the Glory of God, which he ought to have showed against his Wife, when he understood she had transgressed God's Commandment.

How was the fourth Commandment broken?
In that the Sabbath was made a Time to confer with Satan in Matters tending to the high Dishonor of God: If it be true that on that Day Man fell into this Transgression, as some not improbably have conjectured. For at the Conclusion of the Sixth Day, all things remained yet very good, Gen. 1. 31. and God blessed the seventh Day, Gen. 2. 3. Now it is very likely that Satan would take the first advantage that possibly he could entrap them, before they were strengthened by longer Experience, and by partaking of the Sacrament of the Tree of Life, (whereof it appeareth, by Gen. 3. 22. that they had not yet eaten): And so from the very beginning of Man, became a Man slayer, John 8. 44.

Show briefly the grounds of the Breach of the Commandments of the second Table, in the Transgression of our first Parents.
The fifth was broken, Eve giving too little to her Husband, in attempting a Matter of so great Weight without his Privity: And Adam giving too much to his Wife, in obeying her Voice rather than the Commandment of God, and for pleasing of her, not caring to displease God, Gen. 3. 17.

The sixth. By this Act they threw themselves and all their Posterity into Condemnation and Death, both of Body and Soul.

The seventh. Though nothing direct against this Commandment: Yet herein appeared the Root of those evil Affections which are here condemned; as not bridling the Lust and wandering Desire of the Eye; as also the inordinate appetite of the Taste, (Gen. 3. 6.) in lusting for and eating that only Fruit which God forbad, not being satisfied with all the other Fruits in the Garden.

The eighth. First, Laying hands upon that which was none of their own, but by a special Reservation kept from them. Secondly, Discontent with their present Estate, and covetous Desire of that which they had not.

The ninth. Judging otherwise than the Truth was of the Virtue of the Tree, (Gen. 3. 6.) and receiving a false Accusation against God himself.

The tenth. By entertaining in their Minds Satan's Suggestions, and evil Concupiscence appearing in the first Motions leading to the forenamed sins.

Thus much of our first Parents sin, and the Causes thereof; now let us come to the Effects of the same. Show therefore what followed in them immediately upon this Transgression.
Three Fruits were most manifest: Namely, Guiltiness of Conscience, Shame of Face, and Fear of God's Presence.

Did any Punishment follow upon this Sin?
Sin, Guiltiness, and Punishment, do naturally follow one upon another: otherwise the Threatening, that at what time soever they did transgress God's Commandment they should certainly die, should not have taken effect.

Declare how that Threatening took effect.
They were dead in sin, which is more fearful than the Death of the Body, as that which is a Separation from the Favor of God. For there came upon them the Decay of God's glorious Image in all the Faculties of their Soul, and also a Corruption of the Powers of their Body from being so fit Instruments to serve the Soul as God made them: And this in them is signified by Nakedness, Gen. 3. 7. and in their Children called Original Sin. Then there issued from thence a stream of Actual Sins in the whole Course of their

Life: Which appeared in Adam even upon his Fall, by his flying from God's Presence, and affirming that it was his Nakedness that made him fly, his excusing of his Sin, and laying it on the Woman, &c. By Sin an entry being made for Death. Rom. 5. 12. they became subject to the separating of the Soul from the Body, which is Bodily Death; and of both from God, which is Spiritual Death: Signified by expelling them out of Paradise, and debarring them of the Sacramental Tree of Life. Gen. 3. 22. &c. And thus, by the just Sentence of God, being for their sin delivered into the Power both of Corporal and of Eternal Death, they were already entered upon Death and Hell: To which they should have proceeded, until it had been accomplished both in Body and Soul in Hell with the Devil and his Angels for ever, if the Lord had not looked upon them in the Blessed Seed.

For the fuller understanding of the things that immediately followed the Transgression of our first Parents: Let us consider more particularly what is recorded in the third Chapter of Genesis. And first show what is meant by that in the seventh Verse , that their Eyes were opened, and that they saw themselves naked. Were they not naked before? And having the Eye sharper than after the Fall, must they not needs see they were naked?

It is true, howbeit their Nakedness before the Fall was comely, yea more comely than the comliest Apparel we can put on: Being clad with the Robe of Innocence, from the top of the Head unto the sole of the Foot; wherefore by Nakedness he meaneth a shameful Nakedness both of Soul and Body; as the Scripture speaketh of elsewhere, Rev. 3. 17, 18. Exod. 32. 25.

What gather you from hence?
That the Loathsomness of Sin is hidden from our Eyes, until it be committed, and then it flusheth in the faces of our Consciences, and appeareth in its proper Colors.

Was that well done that they sewed Fig-tree Leaves to hide their Nakedness?
In some respect: Forasmuch as they sought not remedy for their Nakedness inward, it was not well: But that they were ashamed to behold their own Nakedness of the Body, it was well. For in this corrupt and sinful estate there is left this Honesty and Shamefacedness, that neither we can abide to look on our own Nakedness and shameful Parts, much less upon the shameful parts of others; although it be of those that are nearest joined unto us.

What gather you from thence?
First, That those that can delight in the beholding, either of their own Nakedness, or the Nakedness of any other, have lost even that Honesty, that the sinful Nature of Man naturally retaineth. Secondly, That such as for Customs-sake have covered their Nakedness with Clothes, and do notwithstanding with filthy Words, as it were, lay themselves naked, are yet more wretched, and more deeply poisoned with the Poison of the unclean Spirit, and have drunk more deeply of his Cup.

Seeing our Nakedness cometh by sin, and is a Fruit thereof; it may seem that little Infants have no sin, because they are not ashamed?
So indeed do the Pelagian Heretics reason: But they consider not, that the want of that feeling is for the want of the Use of Reason, and because they do not discern between being naked and clothed.

What followeth?
That at the noise of the Lord in a Wind, they fled from the Presence of God, and hid themselves where the Trees were most thick.

What gather you from hence?

First, That the Guilt of an evil Conscience striketh horror into a Man, and therefore it is said, that Terrors terrify him round about and cast him down, following him at the heels; and leave him not till they have brought him before the terrible King, Job 18. 11, 14. Thereof it is, that the Feast of a good Conscience is so extolled, as to be a continual Feast, Prov. 15. 15.

Secondly, The Fruit of Sin coming from the Fear, which is to fly from God as from an Enemy. Whereof it is that the Apostle affirmeth, that having Peace of Conscience, we have access and approach to God, Rom. 5. 2.

Thirdly, Their Blindness, which esteemed that the Shadow or Thickness of Trees would hide them from the Face of God: Whereas if we go up into Heaven, he is there; if into the Deep, he is there also, (Psal. 139. 7. to 13.) he being not so hidden in the Trees, but that a Man might find him out.

What followeth?

That God asketh where he is, which knew well where he was.

What learn you from thence?

First, That we would never leave off running from God, until we come to the Depth of Hell, if God did not seek us and follow us, to fetch us as the good Shepherd the lost Sheep, Isa. 65. 1. Luke 15. 4. Secondly, That the means of calling us home, is by the Word of his Mouth.

What followeth?

That. Adam being asked, assigneth for Causes, things that were not the Causes, as namely, the Voice of the Lord, his Fear, and his Nakedness: Which were not the true Causes; considering that he had heard the Voice of God and was naked when he fled not; dissembling that which his Heart knew to be the true Cause, viz. his sin.

What learn you from thence?

That it is the property of a Man unregenerate to hide and cloak sin: And therefore, that the more we hide and cloak our sins when we are dealt with for them, the more we approve ourselves the Children of the Old Man, the cursed Adam, Job 31. 33.

What followeth?

The Lord asketh how it should come, that he felt his Nakedness as a Punishment; and whether he had eaten of the forbidden Fruit.

What note you from thence?

That before that our sins be known in such sort, as the Denial of them is in vain and without Color, we will not confess our sins.

What learn you out of Adam's second Answer unto God?

That the Man unregenerate dealt with for his sins, goeth from Evil to worse. For the sin that he hid before, now he cannot hide it, he excuseth, and for excusing it he accuseth the Lord: As those do, which when they hear the Doctrine of Predestination and Providence, thereupon would make God party in their sins.

What learn you further?

That howsoever Adam alleged it for an Excuse, because he did it by persuasion of another, yet God holdeth him guilty, yea dealeth with him as with the Principal, because his Gifts were greater than his Wife's.

Eighth Head

What learn you from the Answer of Eve to the Lord's Question; why she did so?
The same which before; that the unregenerate Man does go about to excuse the sin he cannot deny. For she casteth her sin upon the Serpent, and said that which was true; but kept back the Confession of her Concupiscence, without which the Serpent could not have hurt her.

How cometh it to pass that the Old Serpent, the Author of all, is not called to be examined?
Because that the Lord would show no Mercy unto him: wherefore he only pronounceth Judgment against him.

What learn you from thence?
That it is a Mercy of God, when we have sinned, to be called to account; and to be examined, either by the Father of the Household, or by the Magistrate, or by the Governor of the Church; and a Token of God's fearful Judgment, when we are suffered to rest in our Sins, without being drawn to question for them.

What observe you in the Sentence against the Serpent?
That the first part contained in the 14 vers. is against the Instrument of the Devil; and that the other part, contained in the 15 vers. is against the Devil.

What learn you of this proceeding to Sentence?
That after the Cause well known, Judgment should not be slacked.

Why does God use a Speech to the Serpent that understandeth it not?
It is for Man's sake, and not for the Beasts sake.

Why for Man's sake?
To show his Love to Mankind, by his displeasure against any thing that shall give any help to do hurt unto him. In which respect, he commandeth that the Ox that killeth a Man should be slain, and that the flesh thereof should not be eaten, (Exod. 21. 28.) like a * kind Father that cannot abide the Sight of the Knife that hath maimed or killed his Child, but breaketh it in pieces. * *Chrysostom Homil. 17. in Gen.*

What manner of Curse is this, when there is nothing laid upon the Serpent, but that he was appointed at the beginning, before he became the Devil's Instrument to tempt Eve?
It is true, that he crept upon his Belly before, and eat Dust before, as appeareth in the Prophet, Isa. 65. 25. But his meaning is, that he shall creep with more Pain, and lurk in his hole for fear, and eat the Dust with less Delight and more Necessity.

What learn you from thence?
Not to suffer ourselves to be Instruments of Evil to any in the least sort, if we will escape the Curse of God. For if God did punish a poor Worm, which had no Reason or Will to choose or refuse Sin; how much less will he spare us which have both?

What is the Sentence against the Devil?
The Ordinance of God, that there shall be always Enmity between the Devil and his Seed on the one side, and the Woman and her Seed on the other; together with the effect of this Enmity.

What do you understand by the Seed of the Devil, seeing there is no Generation of the Devils, for that there is no Male nor Female among them, neither have they Bodies to engender?
The Seed of the Devil are all both wicked Men and Angels, which are corrupt as he is, and carry his Image. In which respect the Wicked are called the Children of the Devil, and every where the Sons of Belial, (Job 8. 44. 1 John. 3. 8. Acts 13. 10.)

What learn you from thence?
That the War of Mankind with the Devil is a lawful War proclaimed of God, which is also perpetual and without any Truce: And therefore that here it is wherein we must show our Choler, our Hate, our Valor, our Strength; not faintly and in show only, but in Truth. Whereas we being continually assaulted with our Enemy, leave our Fight with him to fight against our Brethren, yea against our own Souls; he continually, and without ceasing, fighting with us, and not against his own, as the blasphemous Pharisees said, Mat. 12. 24.

What is the Sentence against the Woman?
First, In the Pain of Conception and bearing Child. Secondly, In the Pain of bringing forth: Wherein is contained the Pain of nursing and bringing them up. Thirdly, In a desire to her Husband. Fourthly, In her Subjection to her Husband.

Was she not before desirous and subject to her Husband?
Yes, but her desire was not so great through Conscience of her Infirmity; nor her Subjection so painful, and the Yoke thereof so heavy.

What is the Sentence against Adam?
First, His Sin is put in the Sentence, and then his Punishment.

What was his Sin?
One, that he obeyed his Wife, whom he should have commanded; then, that he disobeyed God, whom he ought to have obeyed: The first being proper to him, the other common to his Wife with him.

What was the Punishment?
A Punishment, which although it be more heavy upon Adam, yet it is also common to the Woman: Namely, the Curse of the Earth for his sake; from whence came Barrenness by Thistles and Thorns, &c. whereof, first, the Effect should be Sorrow and Grief of Mind. Secondly, Labor to the sweat of his Brows, to draw necessary Food from it, and that as long as he lived. Lastly, The Expulsion out of Paradise, to live with the Beasts of the Earth, and to eat of the Herb which they did eat of.

What learn you from thence?
That all Men, from him that sitteth on the Throne, to him that draweth Water, are bound to painful Labor, either of the Body or of the Mind; what Wealth or Patrimony soever is left them, although they had wherewith otherwise plentifully to live.

What observe you else?
I observe further out of this Verse, and out of the two next, that in the midst of God's Anger he remembreth Mercy. For it is a Benefit to Adam that he may live of the sweat of his Brows; to Eve, that she should bring forth, and not be in continual Travel: unto them both, that he taught them Wisdom to make Leather Coats. Hab. 3. 2.

Ninth Head

What learn you from that it was said, God made them Coats?
That in every profitable Invention for the Life of Man, God is to be acknowledged the Author of it, and have the Honor of it, and not the Wit of Man that invented it: As is the manner of Men in such Cases to sacrifice to their own Nets, Hab. 1. 16.

When there were better means of Clothing, why did they wear Leather?
It seemeth that thereby they should draw themselves the rather to Repentance and Humiliation by that course clothing.

What learn you from hence?
That howsoever our Condition and State of Calling affords us better Array; yet we learn even in the best of our Clothes to be humbled by them, as those which are given us to cover our shame, and carry always the Mark and Badge of our Sins: Especially when these, which were even after the Fall the goodliest Creatures that ever lived, learned that Lesson by them.

What followeth?
A sharp Taunt that the Lord giveth Adam, vers. 22. further to humble him; as if he should say, Now Adam dost thou not see and feel how greatly thou art deceived in thinking to be like God in eating of the forbidden Fruit?

What learn you from it?
That by the things we think to be most esteemed, contrary to the Will of God, we are most subject to Derision: And that it must not be a plain and common Speech, but a labored Speech that must bring us to Repentance.

Why does God banish him out of Paradise, lest he should live if he should eat of the Tree of Life; seeing there is no corporal thing able to give Life to any that sin hath killed?
It is true, that the eating of the Fruit of the Tree of Life would not have recovered him: But the Lord therefore would have him banished from it, lest he should fall into a vain Confidence thereof, to the end to make him seek for Grace.

Wherefore are the Angels set with a glittering Sword to keep them from the Tree of Life?
To increase their Care to seek unto Christ, being banished from it, without hope of coming so much as to the sign of Life.

What learn you from hence?
The necessary use of keeping obstinate Sinners from the Sacraments, and other holy things in the Church.

[9TH HEAD.]

Thus much of the miserable and unhappy Condition which our first Parents brought upon themselves. Did this Estate determine in their Persons, or was it derived from them to all their Posterity?
It was. For their Sin in eating the forbidden Fruit, was the Sin of all Men; and we therein became Sinners, and guilty of eternal Condemnation. So that they, by this first Transgression, did not only lose for themselves the Image and Favor of God, but withal deprived their Posterity of that blessed Estate, (Rom. 3. 23.) and plunged them into the contrary, (Rom. 5. 12.) bringing Damnation upon themselves and us all.

Wherefore this cursed Estate of Mankind is called in the Scriptures the Image of Adam, Gen. 5. 3. the Old Man, Eph. 4. 22. the Flesh, Gen. 6. 3. John 3. 6. &c. And the Apostle teacheth expressly, Rom. 5. 12. that by one Man Sin entered into the World, and Death by Sin; and so Death went over all Men, for as much as all Men have sinned.

How does the Apostle here call this the sin of one Man; seeing both Adam and Eve sinned, which are two, and that Eve sinned before Adam?
In the Name of Adam was comprehended the Man and the Woman; for by Marriage two are made one; and Moses calleth both the Man and the Woman Adam, Gen. 5. 2. and last of all, the Apostle useth a Word here signifying both Man and Woman.

What reason is there that all their Posterity should take part with them both in their Fall, and in the woeful effect thereof? It seemeth not to stand with the Justice of God to punish us for the sin that we never did.
Our first Parents were by God's Appointment to stand or fall in that Trial; not as singular Persons only, but also as the Head and Root of all Mankind; representing the Persons of all that should descend from them by Natural Generation. And therefore for the understanding of the ground of our Participation with Adam's Fall, two things must be considered.

First, That Adam was not a private Man in this Business, but sustained the Person of all Mankind, as he who had received Strength for himself and all his Posterity, and so lost the same for all. For Adam received the Promise of Life for himself and us, with this condition, if he had stood: But seeing he stood not, he lost the Promise of Life both from himself and from us. And as his Felicity should have been ours, if he had stood in it; so was his Transgression and Misery ours. So that as in the second Covenant, the Righteousness of the second Adam (CHRIST JESUS the Mediator) is reckoned to those that are begotten of him by spiritual Regeneration, (even those that believe in his Name) although they never did it: So in the Covenant, the sin of the first Adam (who herein sustained a common Person) is reckoned to all the Posterity that descend from him by Carnal Generation, because they were in him, and of him, and one with him, Rom. 5. 15, 16, 17, 18, 19.

Secondly, That we all who are descended from Adam by Natural Generation, were in his Loins, and a part of him when he fell; and so by the Law of Propagation and Generation sinned in him, and in him deserved eternal Condemnation therefore. Even as two Nations are said to be in the Womb of Rebekah, Gen. 25. 23. and Levi to have paid Tithes to Melchizedek in the Loins of Abraham, Heb. 7. 9, 10. who was not born some hundred Years after. Thus we see that by the Act of Generation in Leprous Parents, the Parents Leprosy is made the Children's: And the slavish and villainous Estate of the Parents is communicated unto all their Offspring. For a Man being a Slave, his Progeny unto the hundred Generation, unless they be manumitted, shall be Slaves: And even so the natural Man, howsoever he thinketh himself free, yet in Truth he is sold under sin, and is the very Servant of Corruption, and in that State shall for ever remain, unless the Son make him free, John 8. 33, 34, 36. Rom. 6. 17, 19, 20. & 7. 14. 2 Pet. 2. 19. We see also that great Personages rebelling against the King, do not only thereby hurt and disgrace themselves, but also stain their whole Blood, and lose their Honor and Inheritance from themselves and from their Children. For by our Law, a Man being attainted of High Treason, the attaint of Blood reacheth to his Posterity, and his Children, as well as he, lose the Benefit of his Lands and Living for ever: Unless the King in favor restore them again, as God in Mercy hath done unto us.

Then it appeareth, that by Propagation from our last Parents we are become Partakers of the Transgression of our first Parents?
Even so: And for the same Transgression of our first Parents, by the most Righteous Judgment of God, we are conceived in Sin, and born in Iniquity, and unto Misery, Psal. 51. 5. For Men are not born as Adam was created: But Death does reign over them also that sinned not after the like manner of the Transgression of Adam, (Rom. 5. 14.) that is, over Infants, who are born in sin, and sin not by Imitation, but by an inherent Corruption of Sin. Even as we see the young Serpents and Wolves that never stung Men, or devoured Sheep, are notwithstanding worthy to die; because there are Principles of Hurtfulness and Poisonsomness in them.

How is it showed, that Babes new born into the World have sin?
In that they are afflicted sundrily, which they betray by their bitter Cries, and in that they come out of the Mother's Womb go straight into the Grave.

What is then the Natural Estate of Man?
Every Man is by Nature dead in Sin as a loathsome Carrion, or as a dead Corpse, and lieth rotting and stinking in the Grave, having in him the Seed of all sins, Ephes. 2. 1. 1 Tim. 5. 6.

For the fuller understanding of the State of Sin, and the Consequents thereof, declare first what Sin is?
It is defined in one word, 1 John 3. 4. to be ἀνομία, the Transgression of the Law: Namely, a swerving from the Law of God, making the Sinner guilty before God, and liable to the Curse of the Law, Gen. 4. 7.

Seeing by the Law Sin is, and the Law was not before Moses: (Rom. 5. 13.) it seemeth there is no Sin until Moses?
When it is said, the Law was not before Moses, it is to be understood of the Law written in the Tables of Stone by the Finger of God, and other Laws Ceremonial and Political written by Moses at the Commandment of God. For otherwise the Law (the Ceremonial excepted) was written in the Heart of Man; and for the Decay thereof through sin, taught by those to whom that belonged, from the Fall unto Moses.

Is every Breach of the Law of God Sin?
Yea: If it be no more but the least want of that which the Lord requires, Rom. 7. 7. Gal. 3. 10.

And does every Sin, the very least, deserve the Curse of God, and everlasting Death?
Yes verily: Because God is of infinite Majesty and Dignity, and therefore what so toucheth him, deserveth endless Wrath. Wherefore Purgatory and our own Satisfaction for small sins is vain.

How many sorts of Sins are there?
Sin is either Imputed, or Inherent: The one without us, the other with in us.

What is the Sin Imputed?
Our Sin in Adam; in whom as we lived, so also we sinned. For in our first Parents (as hath been showed) every one of us did commit that first sin, which was the Cause of all other: And so we all are become subject to the Imputation of Adam's Fall, both for the Transgression and Guiltiness, Rom. 5. 12, 18, 19. 1 Cor. 15. 22.

What Sins are Inherent in us?
They do either defile our Nature, or our Actions: The one called Original Sin, the other Actual, (Col. 3. 5, 8.) For every one naturally descending from Adam, beside the Guilt of that first Sin committed in Paradise; first, is conceived and born in Original

Corruption, Psal. 51. 5. Secondly, Living in this World, sinneth also actually, Gen. 6. 5. Isa. 48. 8. yea, of himself he can do nothing but sin, Jer. 13. 23. Mat. 7. 18. neither is there any thing pure unto him, Tit. 1. 15.

What is Original Sin?
It is a Sin, wherewith all that naturally descend from Adam are defiled, even from their first Conception: Infecting all the Powers of their Souls and Bodies, and thereby making them Drudges and Slaves of Sin. For it is the immediate Effect of Adam's first Sin; and the principal Cause of all other Sins.

How is this Sin noted out unto us?
In that other Sins have their special Names, where this is properly called Sin; because it is the Puddle and Sink of other Sins: And for that also the more it is pressed, the more it bursteth forth, (as mighty Streams are, that cannot be stopped) till God by his Holy Spirit restrain it.

Wherein does it specially consist?
Not only in the Deprivation of Justice, and absence of Good; but also in a continual Presence of an evil Principle and wicked Property, whereby we are naturally inclined to Unrighteousness, and made prone unto all Evil, Jam. 1. 14. Rom. 7. 21, 23. For it is the defacing of God's Image, consisting chiefly in Wisdom and Holiness, whereof we are now deprived: And the Impression of the contrary Image of Satan, (John 8. 41, &c.) called Concupiscence, (Rom. 7. 7. Jam. 1. 14.) consisting, first, in an utter Disability and Enmity unto that which is Good, (Rom. 7. 18. & 8. 7.) Secondly, In Proneness unto all manner of Evil, (Rom. 7. 14.) which also every Man hath at the first Minute and Moment of his Conception: Contrary to the Opinion of the Pelagian's, who teach that Sin cometh by Imitation.

Is the Image of God wholly defaced in Man?
No: If we take it in a large Acceptation. For Man remaineth still a reasonable Creature, and capable of Grace, having the same Parts and Faculties he had before; and in them some Relics of God's Image, Gen. 9. 6. James 3. 9. As in the Understanding some Light, John 1. 9. in the Conscience sometimes right Judgment, Rom. 2. 15. in the Will, some liberty to Good and Evil, in natural and civil Actions, Rom. 2. 14. and freedom in all things from Compulsion, &c.

Is there not a Power lest in Man, whereby he may recover his former Happiness?
Man hath still Power to perform all outward Actions; but not to change himself until he be changed by the Grace of God.

Is Man then able to perform the Law of God perfectly?
They that are not born again of God, * cannot keep it all, † nor in any one point, as pleasing God thereby in respect of themselves. For except a Man be born again of God, he cannot see the Kingdom of Heaven, nor enter therein; neither can he keep the Commandments of God. Moreover, all Men by Nature being conceived and born in Sin, are not only insufficient to any good thing, but also disposed to all Vice and Wickedness. * Gal. 3. 22. Rom. 8. 3. † Phil. 3. 9. Tit. 3. 5. Isa. 64. 6.

Can Man in this Estate do no good thing to please God, to deserve at least something of his Favor?
We have lost by this Sin all the Righteousness we had in our Creation: So as now if God should say to us, Think but a good thought of thy self, and thou shalt be saved; we cannot: But our Nature is as a stinking Puddle, which in it self is loathsome, and being moved is worse.

Ninth Head

But does not God wrong to Man, to require of him that he is not able to perform?
No: For God made Man so that he might have performed it: But he by his Sin spoiled himself and his Posterity of those good Gifts.

Is this Corruption of Nature in all the Children of Adam?
Yea, in all and every one that are mere Men, none excepted, (Rom. 3. 10, 23.) all Children, since Adam's Fall, being begotten in it, Psal. 51. 5.

How then does the Apostle say, That Holy Parents beget Holy Children? 1 Cor. 7. 14.
Parents beget Children as they are by Nature, not as they are by Grace.

How is Original Sin propagated and derived from the Father to the Son?
We are not to be so curious in seeking the manner how, as to mark the matter to be in us: Even as when a House is on fire, Men should not be so busy to inquire how it came, and seeing it there, to quench it. But this we may safely say, that what effect the committing of the first Sin wrought in the Soul of Adam, the same does the Imputation of it work in the Souls of his Posterity. As therefore the Committal of that Sin left a Stain behind it in his Nature: Being like a drop of Poison that once taken in, presently infecteth the soundest Parts; or like the dead Fly that marreth the most precious Ointment of the Apothecary: So in the Creation and Infusion of our Souls into our Bodies, God justly imputing the same Transgression unto us; the same Corruption of Nature (as the just Punishment of that Sin) must ensue in like manner.

Hath this inbred Sin, wherein every one is conceived, equally polluted all Men?
Yes: Though not altogether alike for Disposition and Motion to Evil. For Experience teacheth us, that some are by Nature more mild, courteous and gentle than others: Which difference notwithstanding is not so much in the Natures of Men, as in the Lord who represseth those Sins in some which he suffereth to rise up in others.

In what part of our Nature do this our Corruption abide?
In the whole Man (from the top to the toe) and every part both of Body and Soul, (Gen. 6. 5. 1 Thess. 5. 23.) like unto a Leprosy that runneth from the Crown of the Head to the Sole of the Foot. But chiefly it is the Corruption of the five Faculties of the Soul; which are thereby deprived of that Holiness wherein God created them in Adam.

Is not the Substance of the Soul corrupted by this Sin?
No: But the Faculties only depraved, and deprived of Original Holiness. For first, the Soul should otherwise be mortal and corruptible. Secondly, Our Savior took our Nature on him without this Corruption.

To come then to the special Corruptions of the five Faculties of the Soul: Show first, how this Sin is discerned in the Understanding.
The Mind of Man is become subject to, First, Darkness, Blindness in Heavenly Matters, and Ignorance of God, and of his Will, and of his Creatures, 1 Cor. 2. 14. Ephes. 4. 17, 18, 19. Secondly, Incapableness, Unableness, and Unwillingness to learn, though a Man be taught, Rom. 8. 7. Luke 24. 45. Thirdly, Unbelief, and doubting of the Truth of God, taught and conceived by us. Fourthly, Vanity, Falsehood and Error; to the embracing whereof Man's Nature hath great Proneness, Isa. 44. 20. Jer. 4. 22. Prov. 14. 12. & 16. 25.

What use make you of this Corruption of the Understanding?
That the Original and Seeds of all Heresies and Errors are in Man's Heart naturally without a Teacher: And therefore we should distrust our own Knowledge, to lead us in the Matters of God and Religion; and only be directed by God's Holy Word.

How is the Memory corrupted?
First, With Dullness, and Forgetfulness of all good things that we should remember; notwithstanding we have learned them often. Secondly, With readiness to remember that we should not; and to retain Errors and Vanities (as Tales and Plays) much more than Godly Matters.

What use make you hereof?
First, As to bewail the Defects of our Understanding, so to lament our Forgetfulness of good things. Secondly, To distrust the Faithfulness or Strength of our Memories in hearing and learning good things: And to use all good helps we can, as often repeating them, writing and meditating on them. Thirdly, Not to clog our Memories with Vanities; for which we should rather desire the Art of Forgetfulness.

How is the Will corrupted?
First, With a Disableness and Impotency to will any thing that is good in it self, Rom. 5. 6. Phil. 2. 13. Secondly, With Slavery to Sin and Satan: The Will being so enthralled, (Rom. 6. 20. & 7. 23.) and hardened, (Ephes. 4. 18.) that it only desireth and lusteth after that which is Evil, Gen. 6. 5. Job 15. 16. Thirdly, With Rebellion against God, and any thing that is Good, Rom. 8. 7.

What use are we to make hereof?
First, That we have no free Will left in us, since Adam's Fall, for Heavenly Matters. Secondly, That for the Conversion either of ourselves or any other, we must not look for it from Man, but pray to God to convert Man, who worketh in us both the Will and the Deed, (Phil. 2. 13.) as the Prophet saith, Convert thou me, and I shall be converted, Jer. 31. 18. Lam. 5. 21.

How are the Affections corrupted?
The Affections of the Heart, which are many, (as Love and Hatred, Joy and Sorrow, Hope and Fear, Anger, Desire, &c.) are subject to Corruption and Disturbance, Gal 5. 24. Jam. 4. 1. Job 15. 16.

First, By being set upon unmeet Objects: In affecting and being inclined to the things they should not be, and not to those they should. Thus we hate Good and love Evil, (1 Kings 22. 8.) and in a word, our Affections naturally are moved and stirred to that which is Evil to embrace, and are never stirred up to that which is Good, unless it be to eschew it. Secondly, By Disorder and Excess; even when we do affect good things: As for our own Injuries we are more angry, than for God's Dishonor: When we are merry, we are too merry; when sad, too sad, &c.

What use make you of the Disorder of the Affections?
First, To keep ourselves from all Occasions to incense them to sin, whereunto they are as prone as Tinder to the Fire. Secondly, To labor to mortify them in ourselves; that we may be in regard thereof, as pure Nazarites before God, Gal. 5. 24. Col. 3. 5.

How is the Conscience corrupted?
It is distempered and defiled, (Tit. 1. 15.) both in giving Direction in things to be done, and in giving Judgment upon things done.

How in the former?
It sometime giveth no Direction at all; and thereupon maketh a Man to sin in doing of an Action otherwise good and lawful, (Rom. 14. 23.) sometime it giveth Direction, but a wrong one; and so becometh a blind Guide, forbidding to do things which God alloweth, and commanding to do things which God hateth, 1 Cor. 8. 7. Col. 2. 21. John 16. 2.

How in the latter?
When it either giveth no Judgment at all, being left without feeling; or when it hath an evil Feeling and Sense.

How is it left without Feeling?
When it is so senseless, and benumbed with Sin, that it never checketh a Man for any Sin, (Ephes. 4. 18, 19.) called a Cauterized Conscience, 1 Tim. 4. 2. which riseth from the Custom of sinning, Heb. 3. 13.

How does it fail, when it hath a Feeling, but a naughty one?
Sometimes in Excusing, sometimes in Accusing.

How in Excusing?
First, When it excuseth for things sinful, making them no Sins, or small Sins; and so feeding the Mind with vain Comforts, Mark 10. 20. Gen. 3. 10. 12. Secondly, When it excuseth us for having a good Intent, without any Warrant of God's Word, 1 Chron. 13. 9.

How in Accusing?
First, When for want of true Direction and Lightning, it condemneth for doing Good, (as a Papist for going to Sermons) condemning where it should excuse, and so filling the Minds with false Fears. Secondly, When accusing for Sin, it does it excessively; turmoiling a Man with inward Accusations and Terrors, (Isa. 57. 20.) and drawing him to despair by such excessive Terror; as may be seen in Cain and Judas.

What use are we to make of this Confusion of the Conscience?
First, Seeing it does thus abuse us, we are never to make it a warrant of our Actions, unless it be directed by God's Word. Secondly, We are to fear the Terror of the great Judge of Heaven and Earth; when we are so often, and so grievously terrified with our little Judge that is in our Soul.

What Corruption hath the Body received by Original Sin?
It is become a ready Instrument to serve the sinful Soul: Having both a Proneness to any Sin the Soul affecteth; and likewise an eagerness to commit it, and continue in it, Rom. 6. 12, 19. Whereby it is come to pass, that the Bodily Senses and Members are, 1. Porters to let in Sin, Job 31. 1. Psal. 119. 37. Mat. 5. 29, 30. 2. The Instruments and Tools of the Mind for the Execution of Sin, Rom. 2. 13, 14, 15. & 6. 13.

What use are we to make of this Doctrine of Original Sin?
First, The due Knowledge thereof serveth to humble the Pride of Man; remembering that he is conceived in so sinful a sort, that howsoever that Branches of his Actions may seem green, yet is he rotten at the Root. Secondly, It should move him with all speed to seek for Regeneration by Christ; seeing he hath so corrupt a Generation by Adam.

What is Actual Sin?
It is a Violation of God's Commandments, done by us after the manner of Adam's Transgression, Rom. 5. 14. to wit, a particular Breach of God's Law in the Course of our Life; which proceedeth as an evil Fruit from our natural Corruption, and leaveth a Stain in the Soul behind it, (Jer. 13. 23.) which polluteth the Sinner, and disposeth him to further Evil.

How is such Sin committed?
Either Inwardly, or Outwardly.

How Inwardly?
First, By evil Thoughts in the Mind; which come either by a Man's own conceiving, Gen. 6. 5. Mat. 15. 19. or by the Suggestion of the Devil, John 13. 2. Acts 5. 3. 1 Chron. 21. 1. Secondly, By evil Motions and Lusts stirring in the Heart; against the Righteousness of the Law, which condemneth the very first Motions of Evil that ariseth from our corrupt Nature.

How Outwardly?
By evil Words and Deeds, (Isa. 3. 8.) which arise from the corrupt thoughts and motions of the Heart, when any occasion is given, Mat. 15. 19. So that the Imagination of Man's Heart, the Words of his Mouth, and the Works of his Hands, are all stained with Sin.

Be not Outward Sins more grievous than Inward?
Some be, and some be not. For if they be against the same Commandment, and the same Branch thereof, they are much more wicked and evil: Because, first, God is more dishonored outwardly. Secondly, Other Men are offended, if Godly; or enticed by their Example, if wicked. Thirdly, A Man does more engross himself in sin outward, than in a bare thought that he restrain, from outward Action.

But how may some Thoughts be more evil than Actions?
If they be of more wicked Matters: As the denying of God in heart, is worse than an idle Word.

What use are we to make hereof?
It serveth, first, to condemn the common sort, that say and hold that Thoughts are free, which are oft so sinful. Secondly, To assure us that many, though they lead an outward civil Life in Actions, yet if their Hearts be not cleansed by Faith, may be more odious in God's Sight that knoweth their Thoughts, than a godly Person that may be left to some outward Weakness in this Life.

What are the Degrees by which Men do proceed in the committing of Actual Sin?
Out of James 1. 14, 15. these four Degrees may be observed:

First, Temptation to Sin, Jam. 1. 14. 2 Sam. 11. 2. which then only is Sin to us, when it either ariseth from our own Corruption, or from outward Occasions to which we have offered ourselves carelessly. For if every Temptation to Sin offered unto us should be sin simply, then our Savior that was tempted, should have sinned. Therefore the outward or inward Temptations that Satan may offer, be not Sins to us, till they get some hold in us: Which is, when we are the occasion of them ourselves, by inward Corruption or outward Carelessness in venturing upon Temptations.

Secondly, concupiscence, bringing Sin to Conception, James 1. 15. which is done by these Degrees. 1. Entertaining the Sin whereunto we are tempted, and suffering it to have abode in the Mind or Thought. 2. Withdrawing the Heart from God (whom we ought to fear with all our hearts) and his Commandment, (Jam. 1. 14.) 3. Consulting whether that Sin (which we ought to hate) may be done or no. 4. Taking liking of it, and coveting it, and so being ensnared by it, Psal. 7. 14. Jam. 1. 14.

Thirdly, Consent of the Mind to commit Sin: Whereupon ensues the Birth of Sin, James 1. 15. by which it is brought forth into Act against God or Man.

Fourthly, Often Repetition of Sin: by Custom and Continuance, wherein the Heart finally is hardened, (Heb. 3. 13.) and Sin is come to a Perfection or Ripeness, (Jam. 1. 15.) which is the Strength that Sin getteth over Man, whom it ruleth as a Master does a Slave: In which Estate who so continueth, must look for eternal Death, Jam. 1. 15. for Sin then reigneth; which it never does in the Godly.

Ninth Head

Are these Actual Transgressions all of one sort?
No: For they are diversely considered, in respect of the Commandment broken, the Object offended, the Disposition followed, and the Degrees attained.

How for the Commandment?
The Breach of a Commandment that biddeth, is a Sin of Omission; but of one that forbiddeth, is a Sin of Commission. The one is an Omission of Duty required; the other a Commission of Evil forbidden: By the one, we offend in omitting those things which we should do; by the other, in committing those things which we should not do.

Which be the Inward Sins of Omission?
The not thinking so often or religiously of Heavenly Things, (respecting the first Table) or of good Duties to Man, as we should; but suffering our Minds to be a thorough fare for vain or wicked Thoughts to pass through, more than Good. Which Sin if it were thought of well, would make Men more humble before God, and to make more Conscience of their Hours Day and Night, to mark how their Mind is occupied.

What are Inward Sins of Commission?
All Actual Sins of the Mind and Thoughts, whether we be awake dealing with God or Man, or asleep dreaming. Examples of the first are against God; to think there is no God, (Psal. 10. 4.) or to have vile and base Conceits of Him or his Government, (Psal. 10. 11. 1 Cor. 2. 14.) and towards Man, every Inward Breach of the second Table.

But does Man commit Sin in the Night when he dreameth?
Yes surely: The Soul is never idle, but when it thinketh not of Good, it thinketh of Evil. And the Godly may mark, that after they have had many Dreams of things unlawful, their Heart is in a measure wounded, till they obtain Peace and Pardon from God.

What use are we to make thereof?
To pray earnestly that God would sanctify our corrupt heart, that it may be a Fountain of holy and not sinful Thoughts: And in the Night, 1. To commit ourselves specially to God, that because we having our Senses and Judgment bound and silent, are less able to resist and judge our sinful Thoughts, God would preserve us from them by his Grace. And, 2. That we avoid all Occasions thereof in the Day.

What he the Outward Sins of Commission?
Such as to the committing of them, beside the thought of our Mind, any part of our Body does concur; as our Tongue to Words, and other parts to Deeds.

How are Sins distinguished in regard of the Object offended?
Some Sins are more directly against God, some against Men, either public or private, and others against a Man's self.

How in regard of the Disposition followed?
Either as we partake with others Sins, (Isa. 6. 5.) or as we commit the Sin in our own Person.

What are the differences of partaking with other Sins?
First, When we conceal and wink at other Men's Sins, which we ought to reveal or rebuke: As Magistrates and Ministers oft do, 1 Sam. 3. 13. Secondly, When we further it by our Consent, Presence, or Counsel, Acts 7. 58. & 8. 1. & 22. 20. & 23. 14, 15. Rom. 1. 32. Thirdly, When we provoke others to sin, Mark 6. 25.

What difference of Disposition is there in those Sins which a Man does commit in his own Person?
Some Sins are committed of Ignorance, (1 Tim. 1. 13. Psal. 19. 12.) or of an erring Conscience, (1 Cor. 8. 7) which a Man does either not know, or not mark: Others are done of Knowledge.

Does not Ignorance excuse?
Affected Ignorance does rather increase, than diminish a Fault.

What are the differences of Sins of Knowledge?
1. Some are of Infirmity and Temptation, for fear of Evil, or hope of Good, Rom. 7. 19. Mat. 26. 69, 70. 2. Some of Presumption, Obstinacy, and stubbornness in sinning: Against which David earnestly prayed, (Psal. 19. 13. & 50. 21. Eccles. 8. 11.) And this may proceed (if Men have not the Grace of God) to obstinate and willful Malice against God and his Truth, and to the unpardonable Sin against the Holy Ghost, Heb. 6. 4, 5, 6. & 10. 20, 29. Mark 3. 29, 30.

What, is the Sin against the Holy Ghost the highest of all Sins?
It is a willful and malicious falling from, and resisting of the Gospel, after a Man hath been enlightened with it, and felt a Taste thereof, manifested in outward Action by some blasphemous oppugning the Truth of Set Hatred, because it is the Truth.

What are you to consider in this Sin?
The Nature thereof, and the Deadliness of the same.

What note you in the Nature?
The Reason why it is so called, and the Quality thereof.

Why is it called the Sin against the Holy Ghost?
Not because it is committed against the third Person only, (for it is committed against all three) but because it is committed against that Light of Knowledge, with which the Holy Ghost hath enlightened the Heart of him that committeth it, and that of set Malice. For every one that sinneth against his Knowledge, may be said to sin against the Holy Ghost, as Ananias and Sapphira were said to do, Acts 5. 3. but that is not this great Sin of set Malice, resisting the Truth because it is the Truth, but of Infirmity.

What Qualities and Properties hath this great Sin?
First, It must be in him that hath known the Truth, and after falleth away, Heb. 6. 5. Therefore Infidels and Heathens do not sin this Sin; neither any that are ignorant, though maliciously they blaspheme the Truth. Secondly, It must be done of set Malice, because it is the Truth; as the Pharisees did, (Mat. 12, 31. Heb. 6. 6.) Therefore Peter that cursed himself, and denied that he knew Christ, to save his Life, did not sin this Sin: Nor Paul that did persecute him, doing it of Ignorance. Thirdly, It must be against God himself directly, and his Son Christ Jesus, Mat. 12. 31. Heb. 6. 6. Therefore it is not any particular Breach of the second Table, nor a slip against any special Sin of the first.

Can these Qualities at any time befall the Elect, or Children of God?
No: And therefore they that feel in themselves the Testimony of their Election, need not fear their falling into this Sin, nor despair.

What is the deadliness of this Sin above other Sins?
First, God hath pronounced it shall never be pardoned: Not because God is not able to pardon it, but because he hath said he will not forgive it. Secondly, This Sin is commanded not to be prayed for; when Persons are known to be guilty of it, 1 John 5.

16. whereas we are bound to pray for all other Persons. Thirdly, This is the ordinary and first Sin of the Devil: And therefore is he never received into Mercy, no more than those than are guilty of it.

Thus much of the Sin against the Holy Ghost; show now the differences of Actual Sins in regard of the Degrees attained.
Some are only Sins, but others are Wickednesses, and some Beastlinesses, or Devilishness. For though Original Sin be equal in all Adam's Children, yet Actual Sins be not equal, but one much greater than another.

Are not Sins well divided into Venial and Mortal?
None are venial of their own Nature; but only to the Faithful they are so made, by the Mercy of God in Christ.

Do all natural Men alike commit all these kinds of Sins?
No: For though all are alike disposed unto all manner of evil, (Rom. 7. 14.) having in their corrupt Nature the Seeds of every Sin; yet does God, for the good of human Society, restrain many from notorious Crimes, by fear of Shame and Punishment, desire of Honor and Reward, &c. Rom. 13. 3, 4, 5.

How does God employ Men in this State of Sin?
First, He guideth them, partly by the Light of Nature, Rom. 2. 14, 15. John 1. 9. and partly by common Graces of the Spirit, Isa. 44. 28. unto many Actions, profitable for human Society, and for the outward Service of God. Secondly, He over ruleth their evil and sinful Actions; so that thereby they bring to pass nothing, but what his hand and counsel had before determined for his own Glory, Acts 3. 18. & 4. 27, 28.

What are the things that generally follow Sin?
They are two: Guilt and Punishment. Both which do most duly wait upon Sin, to enter with it; and cannot by any force or cunning of Man or Angel, be holden from entering upon the Person that sin hath already entered upon, both likewise do increase, as the sin increaseth.

What is the Guilt of Sin?
It is the merit and desert of Sin, (which is as it were an Obligation to the Punishment and Wrath of God) whereby we become subject to God's Debt or Danger; that is, to Condemnation, Rom. 2. 15. & 3. 9. For every Man by reason of his sin is continually subject to the Curse of God, Gal. 3. 10. and is in as great danger of everlasting Damnation, as the Traitor apprehended, is in danger of Hanging, Drawing, and Quartering.

Is there any evil in the Guilt before the Punishment be executed?
Very much; for it worketh Unquietness in the Mind: As when a Man is bound in an Obligation upon a great Forfeiture, that very Obligation it self disquieteth him; especially if he be not able to pay it, (as we are not): And yet more, because where other Debts have a day set for Payment, we know not whether the Lord will demand by Punishment his Debt this day before to Morrow.

What learn you from this?
That since Men do shun by all means to be in other Men's Debt or Danger, (as also the Apostle exhorteth, Rom. 13. 8. Owe nothing to any Man; and Solomon also counselleth in the matter of pledges, Prov. 6. 1, 2, 3, 4, 5.) we should more warily take heed, that we plunge not ourselves over head and ears in the Lord's Day; for if it be a terrible thing to be bound to any Man in Statute Staple, or Merchant, or Recognizance; much more to be bound to God, who will be paid to the utmost Farthing.

How else may the hurt and evil of the Guilt of Sin be set forth unto us?
It is compared to a stroke that lighteth upon the Heart and Soul of a Man; where the Wound is more dangerous than when it is in the Body, Gen. 44. 16. 1 Sam. 24. 4, 5, 6. And so it is also a sting or a bite worse than of a Viper; as that which bringeth Death.

Have you yet wherewith to set forth the evil of the Guilt?
It seemeth when the Lord said to Cain, if he sin against his Brother, his sin lieth at the door, (Gen. 4. 7.) that he compareth the Guilt to a Dog that is always snarling and barking against us: Which is confirmed by the Apostle, who attributeth a Mouth to this defect of sin to accuse us, Rom. 2. 15.

What is the Effect of this Guilt of Conscience?
It causeth a Man to fly when none pursueth; and to be afraid at the fall of a Leaf, Prov. 28. 1. Lev. 26. 36.

When a Man does not know whether he does sin or no, how can he be smitten or bitten, or barked at, or fly for fear? Therefore against all this Evil, Ignorance seemeth to be a safe Remedy.
No verily; for whether we know it or no, his Guilt remaineth: As a Debt is Debt, though a Man knoweth it not; and it is by so much the more dangerous, as not knowing it, he will never be careful to discharge it, till the Lord's Arrest be upon his Back, when his Knowledge will do him no good.

We may see many which heap sin upon sin, and know also that they sin, and yet for all that cease not to make good cheer, and make their hearts merry.
The Countenance does not always speak Truth; so that sometimes under a Countenance in show merry, there are stings and pricks in the Conscience, (Rom. 2. 15.) which yet is oftentimes benumbed, and sometimes through Hypocrisy it is seared as it were with a hot Iron, (1 Tim. 4. 2.) but the Lord will find a time to awaken and revive it, by laying all his sins before his face Psal. 50. 21.

When it is known, what is the Remedy of it?
It were Wisdom not to suffer our Guilt to run long on the Score, but reckon with ourselves every Night e'er we lie down to sleep, and look back to the doing of the Day: That in those things which are well done, we may be thankful, and comfort our own hearts; and in that which hath passed otherwise from us, we may call for Mercy, and have the sweeter sleep. For if Solomon willeth us in that case of Debt by pledge, to humble ourselves to our Creditor, and not to take rest until we have freed ourselves, (Prov. 6. 1, 2, 3, 4, 5, 6.) much more ought we to haste the humbling ourselves unto God; since the Blood of Christ is the only Sacrifice for sin.

Is the Guilt of Sin in all Men alike?
No: For as the Sin increaseth, so does the Guilt, both in regard of the Greatness, and of the number of our Sins: As appeareth out of Ezra 9. 6. whereas Sin is said to be gone above their Heads, so the Guilt to reach up to the Heavens.

When the Sin is gone past, is not the Guilt also gone and past?
Christ taketh away both the Guilt and the Sin of the Godly, (except Original Sin, which continueth during Life) but in the Wicked, when the Act of Sin is gone, the Guilt remaineth always; as the strong savor of Garlic when the Garlic is eaten; or as the Scar of a Wound, or the mark of a Burning, when the Wound or Burning is past.

Tenth Head

What is contrary to the Guilt of Sin?
The Testimony of a good Conscience, which is a perpetual Joy and Comfort, yea and a Heaven to him that hath walked carefully in God's Obedience, as the other is a Torment of Hell.

[10TH HEAD.]

So much of the Guilt: What is the Punishment?
It is the Wages of Sin sent for the Guilt, Rom. 6. 23. namely, the Wrath and Curse of God, by whose just Sentence Man for his Sin is delivered into the Power both of Bodily and Spiritual Death, begun here, and to be accomplished in the Life to come, Gen. 2. 17. John 3. 18, 19. & 5. 24, 28, 29. Lam. 3. 39. Isa. 64. 5, 6. Rom. 5. 12. Gal. 3. 10.

What do you understand by Bodily and Spiritual Death?
By the one I understand the Separation of the Soul from the Body; with all personal Miseries and Evils that attend thereon, or make way thereto: By the other, the final Separation of both from God; together with present Spiritual Bondage, and all fore-runners of Damnation.

Are all the particular Punishments expressed in the Word, which shall come for Sin?
They cannot wholly be laid down, they be so manifold and so divers: And therefore it is said they shall come, written and unwritten, Deut. 29. 20. & 28. 61.

Against what are these Punishments addressed?
Against the whole Estate of him that sinneth. For whereas Executions upon Obligations unto Men are so directed as they can charge either the Person alone, or his Goods and Lands alone; so as if the Creditor fall upon the one, he frees the other; as if he fall upon the Person he cannot proceed further than unto his Body: The Execution which goeth out from God for the Obligation of Sin, is extended to the whole Estate of the Sinner; both to the things belonging unto him, and likewise to his own Person.

What are the Punishments that extend to the things belonging to him?
Calamities upon his Family, Wife, Children, Servants, Friends, Goods, and good Name; the Loss and Curse of all these: An unhappy and miserable Posterity, (Mat. 15. 22. Psal. 109. 12.) hindrances in Goods, (Deut. 28.) in Name, Ignominy and Reproach: (Job 18. 17. Prov. 10. 7.) loss of Friends and Acquaintance, &c.

What are the Judgments that are executed upon his Person?
They are executed either in this Life, or after this Life.

What Punishments are inflicted in this Life?
They be partly Outward, partly Inward.

What are the Outward Punishments?
1. His want of Dominion over the Creatures: And the Enmity of the Creatures against him. Calamities by Fire, Water, Beasts, or other means. Disorder in the World, in Summer, Winter, Heaven, Earth, and all Creatures. 2. Shame for the Nakedness of Body. 3. All Hunger in Extremity, Thirst, Nakedness, Penury, Poverty of Estate, and want of bodily Necessaries. 4. Weariness; following his Calling in sweat of his Brows, with Trouble and Irksomeness, Gen. 3. 19. 5. Outward Shame and Infamy. 6. Servitude. 7. Loss of Limbs, or the use of his Senses: Deformities in Body. 8. Weakness of Being, want of Sleep, Pains of Body, Aches, Sores, Sicknesses and

Diseases of all sorts, (Deut. 21. 27.) even to the Itch, which few make account of, thereby to feel the Anger of God and Punishment of Sin. Hither is to be referred Pain in Child-bearing, Gen. 3. 16.

What are the Inward Punishments of this Life?
1. Sorrow and Anguish of Soul for these Plagues, and the like. 2. Madness. Frenzy, and Foolishness. 3. Blindness and Distemper of the Soul; when God striketh it with an ignorant Spirit, with want of Judgment to discern between Good and Bad, with Forgetfulness of Holy Things, or Hardness of Heart, (Ephes. 4. 17, 18, 19.) which although for the time they be least felt, yet are they more fearful and dangerous, than those where the Sense is presently sharp. 4. Terror and Vexation of Spirit, driving into Hell: Guiltiness and Horror of Conscience; the Fury of a despairing Soul, beginning even in this Life to feel Hell Torments, Deut. 28. 28. Heb. 10. 27. Isa. 33. 14. 5. Strangeness and Alienation from God. 6. Spiritual Bondage: Whereby sinful Man is become subject to the Lust of the Flesh, the Curse of the Law, the Rule of Satan, and the Custom of the World; yea, even Blessings are cursed, (Mal. 2. 2.) and Prosperity causeth Ruin, (Psal. 69. 22.)

In what sort is Man in Bondage unto Satan?
Both Soul and Body is under the Power of the Prince of Darkness: Whereby Man becometh the Slave of the Devil, and hath him to reign in his heart as his God, till Christ deliver him, Col. 1. 13. Ephes. 2. 2. 2 Tim. 2. 26. 2 Cor. 4. 4. Heb. 2. 14. Luke 11. 21, 22.

How may a Man know whether Satan be his God or not?
He may know it by this, if he give Obedience to him in his Heart, and express it in his Conversation.

And how shall a Man perceive this Obedience?
If he take Delight in the evil Motions that Satan puts into his Heart, and does fulfill the Lusts of the Devil, John 8. 44. 1 John 3. 8.

What is that slavery whereby a Man is in Bondage to the Flesh?
A Necessity of sinning (but without constraint) until he be born again by the Grace of God, Mat. 12. 33, 34, 35.

If we sin necessarily, and cannot but sin; then it seemeth we are not to be blamed.
Yes: The Necessity of sin does not exempt us from sin, but only Constraint?

What Punishments are inflicted upon sinful Man after this Life?
A Two-fold Death.

Which is the first Death?
Bodily Death, in the several kinds: Namely, the Separation of the Soul from the Body, Gen. 3. 19. Eccles. 12. 7. Rom. 5. 12.

Wherein consisteth the second Death?
1. In an everlasting Separation of the whole Man from the favorable Presence and comfortable Fellowship of God's most glorious Majesty, in whose Countenance is Fullness of Joy. 2. Perpetual Imprisonment in the Company of the Devil and Reprobates damned in Hell. 3. The most heavy Wrath of God, and unspeakable Torments to be endured in Hell Fire, World without end, 2 Thess. 1. 9.

How does this Death seize upon Man?
First, after this Life is ended, the Soul of the Wicked immediately is sent unto Hell, there to be tormented unto the Day of Judgment, Luke 16. 22, 23. Secondly, at the Day of Judgment, the Body being joined to the Soul again, both shall be tormented in Hell everlastingly, (Mat. 10. 28.) so much also the more as they have had more freedom Pain of Body, and Anguish of Soul, and loss of outward things in this Life.

Is the Punishment of all Sins alike?
No; For as the Guilt increaseth, so does the Punishment: And as the smallest Sin cannot escape God's hand; so, as we heap Sins, he will heap his Judgment, Joh. 19. 11. Mat. 11. 20, 21, 22, 23, 24.

But God is merciful.
He is indeed full of Mercy; but he is also full of Righteousness, which must fully be discharged, or else we cannot be Partakers of his Mercy.

Cannot we by our own Power make satisfaction for our Sins; and deliver ourselves from the Wrath of God?
We cannot by any means; but rather from day to day increase our Debt: for we are all by Nature the Sons of Wrath, and not able so much as to think one good thought; therefore unable to appease the infinite Wrath of God conceived against our sins.

Could any other Creature in Heaven or Earth (which is only a Creature) perform this for us?
No, none at all. For, first, God will not punish that in another Creature, which is due to be paid by Man. Secondly, None that is only a Creature can abide the Wrath of God against Sin, and deliver others from the same. Thirdly, None can be our Savior but God.

Could Man by his own Wisdom devise any thing whereby he might be saved?
No: For the Wisdom of Man can devise nothing but that which may make a further Separation betwixt God and him.

[11TH HEAD.]

What then shall become of Mankind? Is there no hope of Salvation? Shall all perish? Then surely is a Man of all Creatures most miserable. When a Dog or a Toad die, all their Misery is ended: But when a Man dieth, there is the beginning of his woe.
It were so indeed, if there were no means of Deliverance: But God in his infinite Wisdom and Mercy hath found out that which the Wisdom of Man could not, and provided a Savior for Mankind.

How then is Man delivered from this sinful miserable Estate?
Sin is repressed, and Misery assuaged, by many means natural and civil: But they are not removed, nor Man restored, but only by a New Covenant; the Old being not now able to give Life unto any, by reason of the Infirmity of our Flesh, Rom. 8. 3.

Why is the former Covenant (of Works) called the Old?
Because we not only cannot do it; but through the Perverseness of our Nature (and not by the fault of the Law) it maketh our Old Man of Sin elder, and more hasting to Destruction.

How are they convinced that seek Righteousness by this Covenant?
Because thereby they make God unjust: In that he should thus give the Kingdom of Heaven to Wicked Men, as those that cannot fulfill the Law.

Seeing the nature of a Covenant is to reconcile and join those together that are at variance, (as we see in the Example of Abraham and Abimelech, Gen. 21. 27. Laban and Jacob, Gen. 31. 44.) why is this called a Covenant, that can make no Reconciliation betwixt God and us?
Although it be not able to reconcile us, yet does it make way for Reconciliation by another Covenant: Neither is it meet strictly to bind God's Covenant with Men, to the same Laws that the Covenant of one Man with another are bound unto. For amongst Men, the weaker seeketh Reconciliation at the hand of the Mightier, (Luke 14. 31, 32.) but God (who neither can be hurt or benefited by us) seeketh unto us for Peace, 2 Cor. 5. 20.

Which of these two Covenants must be first in use?
The Law: To show us, first, our Duty, what we should do. Secondly, Our Sin, and the Punishment due thereunto.

How is that other Covenant called, whereby we are reconciled unto God, and recovered out of the State of Sin and Death?
The New Covenant, (so called, because by it we are renewed): The Covenant of Grace, of Promise, of Life and Salvation; the New Testament, the Gospel, &c. Jer. 31. 31, 32.

What is the Covenant of Grace?
God's second Contract with Mankind, after the Fall, for the restoring of him into his Favor, and to the State of Happiness, by the means of a Mediator, Gal. 3. 21, 22. and it containeth the free Promises of God made unto us in Jesus Christ, without any respect of what we deserve.

Who made this Covenant?
God alone: For properly Man hath no more Power to make a Spiritual Covenant in his Natural Estate, than before his Creation he had to promise Obedience.

How are they convinced by the giving of this second Covenant, which seek Righteousness in the Law, or old Covenant?
Because thereby they make God unwise, that would enter into a new and second Covenant, if the former had been sufficient, Heb. 8. 7.

When was this Covenant of Grace first plighted between God and Man?
Immediately after the Fall in Paradise, in that Promise given concerning the Woman's Seed, (Gen. 3. 15.) God in unspeakable Mercy propounding the Remedy, before he pronounced Sentence of Judgment.

Was it once only published?
It was sundry ways declared in all Ages: Partly by ordinary means, and partly by Prophets extraordinarily sent and directed by God.

What is the Foundation of this Covenant?
The mere Mercy of God in Christ: Whereby Grace reigneth unto Life, through the Obedience of one, which is Jesus Christ, Rom. 5. 21. For there being three Persons of the Trinity, the Father sent his Son to accomplish the Work of our Redemption, and both of them send the Holy Ghost to work saving Grace in our Hearts, and apply unto our Souls the Holiness purchased by the Son of God.

What is promised therein?
The Favor of God and everlasting Salvation, with the means thereof; as Christ, and in him Conversion, Justification, and Sanctification.

What is the Condition on Man's part?
The Gift being most free on God's part, nothing is required on Man's part, but the receiving of Grace offered; which is done in those that are of Capacity by Faith in Christ, John 1. 12. & 14. 1. Acts 16. 31. whence followeth new Obedience, whereby the Faithful walk worthy of the Grace received; and this also is by God's Grace.

What then is the sum of the Covenant of Grace?
That God will be our God, and give us Life everlasting in Christ, if we receive him, being freely by his Father offered unto us, Jer. 31. 33. Acts 16. 30, 31. John 1. 12.

How does this Covenant differ from that of Works?
Much every way. For first, in many Points the Law may be conceived by Reason: But the Gospel in all Points is far above the reach of Man's Reason. Secondly, The Law commandeth to do Good, and giveth no strength: But the Gospel enableth us to do Good, the Holy Ghost writing the Law in our Hearts, (Jer. 31. 33.) and assuring us of the Promise that revealeth this Gift. Thirdly, The Law promised Life only; the Gospel Righteousness also. Fourthly, The Law required perfect Obedience, the Gospel the Righteousness of Faith, Rom. 3. 31. Fifthly, The Law revealeth Sin, rebuketh us for it, and leaveth us in it: But the Gospel does reveal unto us the Remission of sins, and frees us from the Punishment belonging thereunto. Sixthly, The Law is the Ministry of Wrath, Condemnation and Death: The Gospel is the Ministry of Grace, Justification and Life. Seventhly, The Law was grounded on Man's own Righteousness; requiring of every Man in his own Person perfect Obedience, (Deut. 27. 26.) and in default, for Satisfaction, everlasting Punishment, (Ezek. 18. 21, 22. Gal. 3. 10, 12.) but the Gospel is grounded on the Righteousness of Christ; admitting Payment and Performance by another, in behalf of so many as receive it, (Gal. 3. 13, 14.) And thus this Covenant abolisheth not, but is the Accomplishment and Establishment of the former, Rom. 3. 31. & 10. 4.

Wherein do they agree?
They agree in this, that they be both of God, and declare one kind of Righteousness, though they differ in offering it unto us.

What is that one kind of Righteousness?
It is the perfect Love of God and of our Neighbor.

What thing does follow upon this?
That the severe Law pronounceth all the Faithful Righteous: Forasmuch as they have in Christ all that the Law does ask.

But yet they remain Transgressors of the Law.
They are Transgressors in themselves, and yet Righteous in Christ; and in their inward Man they love Righteousness, and hate Sin.

A Body of Divinity

[12TH HEAD.]

What are we to consider in the Covenant of Grace?
The Condition, first of the Mediator; and then of the rest of Mankind. In the former consisteth the Foundation of this Covenant; the Performance whereof dependeth upon Christ Jesus, (Acts 10. 43. Rom. 1. 3, 4.) to the latter belongeth the Application thereof for Salvation unto all that will receive it, 2 Cor. 5. 20. Mat. 6. 33.

When was the Mediator given?
First, if we regard God's Decree; from all Eternity, Ephes. 1. 4. Second, If the Virtue and Efficacy of his Mediation; as soon as need was, even from the beginning of the World, Rev. 13. 8. Third, If his Manifestation in the Flesh, in the fullness of Time, (Gal. 4. 4. 1. Tim. 2. 6.) from whence we reckon now 1677 Years.

Who is this Mediator between God and Man?
Jesus (Luke 2. 11. Mat. 1. 21. 1 Tim. 2. 5.) the Son of the Virgin Mary, the promised Messiah or Christ; whom the Fathers expected, the Prophets foretold, (John 1. 45. & 8. 56.) whose Life, Death, Resurrection, and Ascension, the Evangelists describe, (1 John 1. 1. Acts 1. 1.) whose Word preached unto this day, subdueth the World, (1 Tim. 3. 16. 2 Cor. 10. 4, 5.) finally, whom we look for from Heaven to be the Judge of the Quick and Dead, Acts 10. 42.

What do the Scriptures teach us touching Christ our Mediator?
Two things: First his Person, (John 1. 14. & 3. 33.) Secondly, His Office, (Isa. 61. 1, 2. Luke 4. 18)

What is his Person?
The second Person in the God-head, made Man, John 1. 14.

What have we to consider herein?
First, The distinction of the two Natures. Secondly, The Hypostatical or Personal Union of both, into one Immanuel.

What are those two Natures thus wonderfully united in one Person?
First, His Divine Nature or Godhead, which maketh the Person. Secondly, His Human Nature or Manhood; which subsisteth and hath his Existence in the Person of the Godhead. And so we believe our Savior to be both the Son of God, and the Son of Man, Gal. 4. 4. Luke 1. 31, 32. Rom. 1. 3, 4. & 9. 5. 1 Tim. 3. 16. Mat. 26. 24.

What say you of him touching his Godhead?
I believe that he is the only begotten Son of the most High and Eternal God his Father: His Word, Wisdom, Character, and Image; begotten of his Substance before all Worlds, God of God, Light of Light, very God of very God, begotten, not made; finally God Coessential, Coeternal, and Coequal with the Father and the Holy Ghost.

Why call you him the only begotten Son of God?
Because he is the alone Son of God by Nature, even the only begotten of the Father full of Grace and Truth, John 1. 14. & 3. 18. For though others be the Sons of God by Creation, as Adam was, and the Angels, (Job 1. 6.) others by Adoption and Regeneration, as the Saints; and the Man Christ Jesus in another respect, namely, by hypostatical Union: Yet none is his Son by natural Generation, but the same Christ Jesus; and that in regard of his Godhead, not of his Manhood: According to the

Apostle, who saith, that he is without Father according to his Manhood, and without Mother according to his Godhead, Heb. 7. 3.

But it seemeth that he is called the Son of God in respect of the Generation of his Human Nature; wherein it is said that the Holy Ghost did that which Fathers do in the natural Generation: Especially seeing he is therefore said to be the Son of the Highest, Luke 1. 35.
He is the natural Son of God only in regard of the eternal Generation; otherwise there should be two Sons, one of the Father, and another of the Holy Ghost: But he is therefore called the Son of the Highest, for that none could be so conceived by the Holy Ghost, but he that is the natural Son of God.

How is he said to be conceived by the Holy Ghost?
Because the Holy Ghost by his incomprehensible Power, wrought his Conception supernaturally, which Fathers do naturally in the begetting of their Children: Not that any of the substance of the Holy Ghost, which is indivisible, came to his Generation in the Womb of the Virgin.

Why is he called the Word? John 1. 1.
As for other Reasons, declared in the Doctrine of the Trinity, so also because he is he whom the Father promised to Adam, Abraham, and all the Holy Patriarchs; to make his Promises of Salvation sure unto them: As a Man that hath one word, thinketh himself sure of the Matter that is promised.

Why is the Word said to have been in the beginning? John 1. 1.
Not because he began then to be: But that then he was, and therefore is from all Eternity.

What gather you out of this that he is the Wisdom of God?
That our Savior is from Everlasting, as well as his Father: For it were an horrible thing to think that there were a time when God wanted Wisdom.

Why is he called the Character or Image of his Father? Heb. 1. 3.
Because God by him hath made himself manifest to the World in the Creation, and especially in the Redemption of it.

What learn you from hence?
That whosoever seeketh to come to the Knowledge of God, must come to it by Christ.

How is the Godhead of Christ proved?
Not only by abundant Testimonies of Scripture, (Isa. 7. 14. & 9. 6. & 25. 9. John 1. 1. & 20. 28. Rom. 9. 5. 1 John 5. 20.) but also by his Miracles, especially in the raising of himself from death, Rom. 1. 4. together with the Continuance and Conquest of the Gospel, Acts 5. 39. and that not by carnal Power or Policy, but only by the Power of his Spirit, Zech. 4. 6. and patient suffering of his Saints, Rev. 12. 11.

Why was it requisite that our Savior should be God?
Because, first, none can satisfy for Sin, nor be a Savior of Souls, but God alone, Psal. 49. 7. 1 Thess. 1. 10. For no Creature, though never so good, is worthy to redeem another Man's Sin; which deserveth everlasting Punishment.

Secondly, The Satisfaction for our sins must be infinitely meritorious: otherwise it cannot satisfy the infinite Wrath of God that was offended: Therefore, that the Work of our Redemption might be such, it was necessary our Savior should be God; to the end his Obedience and Sufferings might be of an infinite Price and Worth, Acts 20. 28. Heb. 9. 14.

Thirdly, No finite Creature was able to abide and overcome the infinite Wrath of God, and the Sufferings due unto us for our sins. Therefore must our Savior be God, that he might abide the Burden of God's Wrath in his flesh, sustaining and upholding the Manhood by his Divine Power; and so might get again and restore to us the Righteousness and Life which we have lost.

Fourthly, Our Savior must vanquish all the Enemies of our Salvation, and overcome Satan, Hell, Death, and Damnation: Which no Creature could ever do. Rom. 1. 4. Heb. 2. 14.

Fifthly, He must also give Efficacy to his Satisfaction; raising us up from the Death of Sin, and putting us in Possession of eternal Life.

Sixthly, He must give us his Spirit; and by it seal these Graces to our Souls, and renew our corrupt Nature: Which only God can do.

What Comfort have we then by this, that Christ is God?
Hereby we are sure that he is able to save, by reconciling us to the Father.

And what by this that he is the Son?
That uniting us unto himself, he may make us Children unto his Heavenly Father, Heb. 2. 10.

Being God before all Worlds, how became he Man?
He took to himself a true Body and a reasonable Soul; being conceived in time by the Holy Ghost, and born of the Virgin MARY, Heb. 1 6. Joh. 1. 14. Mat. 1. 18, 20. Luk. 1. 31, 32. & 2. 7. and so became very Man, like unto us in all things, even in our Infirmities, sin only excepted, Heb. 2. 7. In which respect he hath the Name of the Son of Man given unto him, Mat. 26. 24. because he was of the nature of Man according to the Flesh: And the Son of David, Mat. 9. 27. because he sprang of the Lineage and Stock of David.

How does it appear that he was true Man?
Besides manifold Predictions and clear Testimonies of Scripture, Gen. 3. 15. Heb. 2. 17. 1 Tim. 2. 5. &c. it is abundantly proved by plentiful Experiments: especially by his partaking of human Infirmities, his Conception, Birth, Life, and Death, 1 Pet. 3. 18. John 4. 6, 7. Luke 1. 31. & 2. 7. Heb. 2. 9, 14, 15.

How by his Conception?
Because according to the Flesh he was made of a Woman, and formed of her only Substance (she continuing still a pure Virgin) by the Power of the most High, Rom. 1. 3. Gal. 4. 4. Luke 1. 34, 35.

Why is he said to be born? Mat. 2. 1.
To assure us of his true Humanity, even by his Infancy and Infirmity, Luke 2 7.

Why was he born of a Virgin? Luke 1. 27.
That he might be Holy and without Sin: The natural course of Original Corruption being prevented, because he came not by natural Propagation.

What learn you from hence?
That God is faithful as well as merciful; ever making good his Word by his Work in due season, Luke 1. 20, 45. Acts 3. 18, 24.

Twelfth Head

Why is there mention of the Virgin by her Name Mary? Luke 1. 27.
For more Certainty of his Birth and Lineage, Mat. 1. 16. Heb. 7. 14. 2. Tim. 2. 8. as also to acquaint us with his great Humility in so great Poverty, Luke 2. 24. compared with Levit. 12. 8.

What gather you from hence?
The marvelous Grace of Christ, who being rich, for our sakes became poor; that we through his Poverty might be made rich, 2 Cor. 8 9.

Did he not pass through the Virgin Mary (as some say) like as Saffron passeth through a Bag, and Water through a Pipe or Conduit?
God forbid: He was made of the Seed of David, and was a Plant of the Root of Jesse: For he took human Nature of the Virgin; and so the Word was made Flesh.

If he was only made Flesh, it would seem that the Godhead served instead of a Soul unto him?
Flesh is here taken according to the use of Scripture for the whole Man, both Body and Soul: Otherwise our Savior should not have been a perfect Man; and our Souls must have perished everlastingly, except his Soul had satisfied for them.

Was not the Godhead turned into Flesh, seeing it is said he was made Flesh?
In no wise: No more than he was turned into Sin, or into a Curse, because it is said, He was made Sin, and made a Curse for us, 2 Cor. 5. 21. Gal. 3. 13.

If the Godhead be not changed into the Manhood; is it not at least mingled with it?
Nothing less: For then he should be neither God nor Man; for things mingled together cannot retain the Name of one of the Simples; as Honey and Oil being mingled together, cannot be called Honey, or Oil 2. The Properties of the Godhead cannot agree to the Properties of the Manhood, nor the Properties of the Manhood to the Godhead. For, as the Godhead cannot thirst, no more can the Mankind be in all or many Places at once. Therefore the Godhead was neither turned nor transfused into the Manhood, but both the Divine Nature keepeth entire all his Essential Properties to it self; so that the Humanity is neither Omnipotent, Omniscient, Omnipresent, &c. and the human keepeth also his Properties and Actions: Though oft that which is proper to the one Nature, is spoken of the Person denominated from the other: Which is by reason of the Union of both Natures into one Person.

The Glory of the Godhead being more plentifully communicated with the Manhood after his Resurrection; did it not then swallow up the Truth thereof, as the whole Sea one drop of Oil?
No: For these two Natures continued still distinct, in Substance, Properties and Actions, and still remained one and the same Christ.

Why did he not take the Nature of Angels upon him? Heb. 2. 16.
Because he had no meaning to save Angels; for that they had committed the Sin against the Holy Ghost, falling maliciously into Rebellion against God without Temptation.

Are not the Elect Angels any way benefited by the human Nature of Christ?
No: His Humanity only reacheth to sinful Mankind: For if he had meant to have benefited Angels by taking another Nature, he would have taken their Nature upon him.

How is it then said, Ephes. 1. 10. & Col. 1. 20. that he reconciled things in Heaven?
This is to be understood of the Saints then in Heaven, and not any way of the Angels: Although by the second Person of the Trinity the Angels were elected, and are by him confirmed, so that they shall stand for evermore.

Why was it requisite that our Mediator should be Man? Was it not sufficient that he was God?
No: It was further requisite that he should be Man also; because

1. Our Savior must suffer and die for our Sins: Which the Godhead could not do.

2. Our Savior also must perform Obedience to the Law: Which in his Godhead he could not do.

3. He must be Man of Kin to our Nature offending; that he might satisfy the Justice of God in the same Nature wherein it was offended, Rom. 8. 3. 1 Cor. 15. 21. Heb. 2. 14, 15, 16. For the Righteousness of God did require, that the same Nature which had committed the sin, should also pay and make amends for Sin; and consequently that only Nature should be punished which did offend in Adam. Man therefore having sinned, it was requisite for the appeasing of God's Wrath, that Man himself should die for sin: The Man Christ Jesus offering up himself a Sacrifice of a sweet-smelling Savor unto God for us; 1 Tim. 2. 5. Heb. 2. 9, 10. & 14, 15. Rom. 5. 12, 15. Ephes. 5. 2.

4. It is for our Comfort, that thereby we might have free access to the Throne of Grace, and might find help in our Necessities; having such an High Priest as was in all things tempted like unto ourselves, and was acquainted with our Infirmities in his own Person, Heb. 4. 15, 16. & 5. 2.

5. As we must be saved, so likewise must we be sanctified by one of our own Nature: That as in the first Adam there was a Spring of Human Nature corrupted, derived unto us by natural Generation; so in the second Adam there might be a Fountain of the same Nature restored, which might be derived unto us by Spiritual Regeneration.

What comfort then have you by this, that Christ is Man?
Hereby I am assured that Christ is fit to suffer the Punishment of my sin; and being Man himself, is also meet to be more pitiful and merciful unto Men.

What by this, that he is both God and Man?
By this I am most certainly assured that he is able most fully to finish the Work of my Salvation: Seeing that he is Man, he is meet to suffer for sin; as he is God, he is able to bear the Punishment of Sin, and to overcome the suffering: Being by the one fit, and by the other able to discharge the Office of a Mediator. Man's Nature can suffer Death, but not overcome it; the Divine Nature cannot suffer, but can overcome all things: Our Mediator therefore being Partaker of both Natures, is by the one made fit to suffer, by the other able to overcome whatsoever was to be laid upon him for making of our Peace.

Are these his Natures separated?
No verily: For though they be still distinguished (as hath been said) in Substance, Properties and Actions: Yet were they inseparably joined together in the first moment the Holy Virgin conceived, and made not two, but one Person of a Mediator, 2 Cor. 13. 4. 1 Pet. 3. 18. 1 Cor. 15. 27, 28. the Holy Ghost sanctifying the Seed of the Woman (which otherwise could not be joined to the Godhead) and uniting two Natures in one Person; God and Man in one Christ, Luke 1. 35, 42. Rom. 9. 5. 1 Tim. 2. 5. John 1. 14. a Mystery that no Angel, much less Man, is able to comprehend.

Why so?

For that the Manhood of our Savior Christ is personally united unto the Godhead: Whereas the Angels, of much greater Glory than Men, are not able to abide the Presence of God, Isa. 6. 2.

Was this Union of the Body and Soul with the Godhead, by taking of the Manhood to the Godhead, or by infusing the Godhead into the Manhood?

By a Divine and Miraculous assuming of the Human Nature (which before had no Subsistence in it self) to have his Being and Subsistence in the Divine; leaving of its own natural Personship, which in ordinary Men maketh a perfect Person. For otherwise there should be two Persons and two Sons, one of the Holy Virgin Mary, and another of God: Which were most prejudicial to Salvation.

What then is the Personal Union of the two Natures in Christ?

The assuming of the Human Nature (having no Subsistency in it self) into the Person of the Son of God, (John 1. 14. Heb. 2. 16.) and in that Person uniting it to the Godhead; so making one Christ, God and Man, Mat. 1. 23.

Can you shadow out this Conjunction of two Natures into one Person by some earthly Resistance?

We see one Tree may be set into another, and it groweth in the Stock thereof, and becometh one and the same Tree, though there be two Natures or Kinds of Fruit still remaining. So in the Son of God made Man, though there be two Natures; yet both being united into one Person, there is but one Son of God, and one Christ.

What was the Cause that the Person of the Son of God did not join it self to a perfect Person of Man?

1. Because that then there could not be a Personal Union of both to make but one perfect Mediator. 2. Then there should be four Persons in the Trinity. 3. The Works of each of the Natures could not be counted the Works of the whole Person: Whereas now by this Union of both Natures in one Person, the Obedience of Christ performed in the Manhood is become of infinite Merit, as being the Obedience of God: And thereupon, Acts 20. 28. God is said to have purchased his Church with his own Blood.

What gather you hence?

That his Name is Wonderful, Isa. 9. 6. and his Sacrifice most effectual, offering himself without spot unto God for us, Heb. 9. 14, 26.

What further Fruit have we by this Conjunction?

That whereas God hath no Shape comprehensible, either to the Eye of the Body or of the Soul, and the Mind of Man cannot rest but in a Representation of something, that his Mind and Understanding can in some sort reach unto: Considering God in the second Person in the Trinity, which hath taken our Nature, whereby God is revealed in the Flesh, he hath whereupon to stay his Mind.

How did the Jews then before his coming, which could not do so?

They might propose to themselves the second Person that should take our Nature, and the same also that had appeared sundry times in the shape of a Man, Gen. 18. 1, 2. & 19. 1, 2. Albeit our Privilege is greater than theirs; as they that behold him as he is, where they did behold him as he should be.

Hitherto of the Person of Christ. What is his Office?

To be a Mediator betwixt God and Man: And so to discharge all that is requisite for the reconciling of us unto God, and the working of our Salvation, 1 Tim. 2. 5. Heb. 9. 15.

John 14. 6. whence also he is called an Intercessor and an Advocate: Because he prayeth for us to the Father, and pleadeth our Cause before his Judgment Seat.

What one must he be that should undertake this Mediation?
One which is indeed a Man, (Heb. 2 14, 15, 16.) and perfectly Righteous without Exception, (1 John 3. 5.) and more mighty than all Creatures, that is, he which also is very true God, Acts 20. 28.

Can no bare Man be Mediator betwixt God and Man?
No verily: For Eli saith, 1 Sam. 2. 25. that a Man offending a Man, it may be accorded by the Judges; but if he offend against God, there is no Man can make his Peace.

Is there then any other Mediator to be acknowledged besides our Lord Jesus Christ?
None but he: Because, 1. There is but one God, and therefore but one Mediator between God and Man, 1 Tim. 2. 5. 2. He only is fit, as he only that partaketh both the Natures of God and Man; which is necessary for him that should come between both. 3. That is declared by the Types of Moses, who alone was in the Mountain: Of Aaron, or the High Priest, who only might enter into the Sanctum Sanctorum, or the Holy Place of Holy Places. 4. The same appeareth by the Similitudes wherewith he is set forth, Joh. 10. 9. I am the door; by me if any Man enter in, he shall be saved, &c. and Joh. 14. 6. I am the way: No Man cometh to the Father but by me. 5. He alone hath found sufficient Salvation, for all those that come unto him, Heb. 7. 25. John 10.

How cometh it then to pass, that this Office is given unto Moses, and unto others? Gal. 4. 19. Deut. 5. 31.
They are only Ministers of the Word, not Authors of the Work of Reconciliation, 2 Cor. 5. 19. Job 33. 23.

But is there no need of any other Mediator for us unto Christ?
No: For he is the next of Kin, (Job 19. 25.) most merciful, most faithful, (Heb. 2. 17.) and able perfectly to save all those that come to God through him, Heb. 7. 25.

How is our Savior graced by God, and commended unto us in his Office of Mediation?
First, In that he came not to it, but being called of God his Father in a special sort, Isa. 42. 1. Heb. 5. 4, 5. Secondly, In that being called, he discharged it most faithfully: In which respect he is compared to Moses, faithful in all the House of God; and preferred before him, as the Master before the Servant, Heb. 3. 2, 3, 5, 6.

What use are we to make of his Calling by God?
1. Hereby we learn, that none should presume to take a charge in God's Church, without calling; since he did not, Heb. 5. 4, 5. 2. There ariseth hereby great comfort unto us, in that he thrust not himself in, but came by the Will of God and his Appointment. For hereby we are more assured of the good Will of God to save us, seeing he hath called his Son unto it; and that he will accept of all that he shall do for us, as that which himself hath ordained.

What learn you from his Faithfulness?
That he hath left nothing undone, of things that belong to our Reconciliation.

What Names are given him in regard of this Office of Mediation?
The Name of Jesus and of Christ, Luke 2. 21, 26. Mat. 16. 16.

Twelfth Head

Why is he called Jesus?
He is called Jesus, that is, a Savior: Because he came to save his People from their sins, (Mat. 1. 21.) and there is no other means whereby we may in part or in whole be delivered from them.

What Comfort have you by this?
1. My Comfort is even the same which I have said, and the rather, because God from Heaven gave him his Name, and the Church on Earth hath subscribed thereunto. 2. That nothing can hurt me, so long as my Faith does not fail me, Mark 9. 23.

Why is he called Christ?
He is called Christ, that is, Anointed: Because he was anointed of God to be a Prophet, Priest, and King, for all his People, and for me, Isa. 61. 1, 2, 3, 4. Acts 4. 26, 27. Luke 4. 18. Psal. 45. 7. & 110. 1, 2, 3, 4. Heb. 1. 9. & 7. 1, &c.

Who was he that was thus Anointed?
Christ God and Man: Though the outward anointing, together with the Name of Christ, appertained to all those that represented any part of the Office of his Mediatorship; namely, to Prophets, Priests, and Kings, which were figures of him.

Was Christ anointed with material Oil, as they were?
No: But he was anointed with all Gifts and Graces of the Spirit of God needful for a Mediator, and that without measure, Isa. 61. 1. Luke 4. 18. John 3. 34.

What learn you from hence?
That all fullness of Grace dwelling in Christ, all true Christians shall receive of his Fullness, Grace for Grace, John 1. 14, 16.

Whereunto was Christ anointed?
Unto the Offices of his Mediation; by discharging whereof, he might be made an All sufficient Savior.

Wherein standeth his Mediation? And what are the parts thereof?
Being to be a Mediator between God and Man, (1 Tim. 2. 5.) the first part of his Mediation must be exercised in things concerning God, wherein consisteth his Priestly Office, (Heb. 2. 17. & 5. 1. & 7. 24.) the second in things concerning Man, wherein he exerciseth his Prophetical and Kingly Function.

Why must he be a Priest?
To offer Sacrifice for his Church, and to reconcile us unto God, Psal. 110. 4. Heb. 3. 1. & 4. 14. & 5. 5, 6. &c. & 7. 3, 17. & 8. 2, 3. & 9. 11, 14. otherwise we should never have been justified, nor sanctified, and so not have been at peace with God.

Why must he be a Prophet, Doctor or Apostle?
To teach his Church, Deut. 18. 15, 18. Acts 3. 22. & 7. 37. Luke 4. 18. otherwise we should never have known God, nor the things that belong unto him, John 1. 18.

Why must he be a King or Prince?
To rule and govern his Church, Psal. 110. 1, 2, 3. Luke 1. 33. otherwise we should never have been delivered from the Captivity of Sin and Satan, nor be put in Possession of eternal Life.

[13TH HEAD.]

What is his Priesthood?
It is the first part of his Mediation, whereby he worketh the means of Salvation in the behalf of Mankind; and so appeaseth and reconcileth God to his Elect, Heb. 5. 1, 5. &c. & 7. 1, 3, 13, 17. &c. & 13. 11, 12.

Where is the Doctrine of Christ's Priesthood especially handled?
In the Epistle to the Hebrews: And namely, in the seventh Chapter, from the 13th vers. to the end, wherein is contained a Declaration of his Office of Priesthood, being compared with the Priesthood of Aaron: The Apostle showing, 1. What manner of one he ought to be that hath this Office. 2. How he executeth it.

Wherein standeth the manner of him that shall have this Office?
Partly without him, and partly within himself. Without him: As first, that he has chosen of the Tribe of Judah, and not of Levi: To show that he was no Successor of Aaron, but rather was to abolish all that Ceremonial Service and Offices. Secondly, That the Priests of Levi were appointed by the Law of the fleshly Commandment; whereas Christ was appointed by the Law of the Power of Life. Thirdly, That he was installed in it by his Father, and appointed by an Oath for ever to be a Priest, after a new Order of Melchizedek.

What arenefit ariseth to us in that this was confirmed by an Oath?
It giveth unto us comfortable Assurance, that all the parts of his Priesthood be performed unto us, and that he paid the ransom for our sins.

Was not the Word of God sufficient for the Performance of this Promise, without the binding of it with an Oath?
Yes, doubtless: But the Lord in this Promise having to deal with weak Man, and willing more abundantly to show unto the Heirs of the Promise the Stableness of his Counsel, bound himself by an Oath, Heb. 6. 17.

Whereby is the Perpetuity thereof confirmed?
In that it did not proceed by Succession, as from Aaron to Eleazer, from Eleazar to Phinehas, and so by descent; but is everlasting, always abiding in him: Which is another difference of their Priestly Office.

What Profit cometh to us by the Perpetuity of his Priesthood?
That he continually maketh Intercession for us to God, and of himself alone is able to save us, coming to the Father through him.

So much of the Quality of him that is to be Priest, which is without him. What is that part which is within him?
1. That in himself he is Holy. 2. To others harmless and innocent. 3. Undefiled of others, or of any thing. And to speak in a word, he is separated from Sinners, (Heb. 7. 26.) In all which, he differeth from that of Aaron. For they are neither Holy in themselves, nor Innocent; neither undefiled; but polluted by others.

What is the Fruit we gather of this his Holiness, Innocence, and Undefiledness?
That he being Holy, Innocent, Undefiled, and so consequently separated from Sinners; the same is attributed to the Faithful, and these his Properties imputed for theirs: And therefore he freeth them both from Original and Actual Sin: Contrary to their Doctrine who say, that he delivereth us from Original Sin only, and that we must make Satisfaction for Actual.

What is the difference touching the Execution of this Office?
1. That they offered first for themselves: He for the People only; for himself he needeth not. 2. He but once; they many times. 3. He offered himself: They something else than themselves.

What is the use of this?
To prove the Absoluteness, Perfection, and Excellency of this his Priesthood.

May not the Priesthood of the Papists be overthrown by all these Arguments, and proved to be a false Priesthood?
Yes verily. For, 1. they are not of the Tribe of Judah: And so cannot succeed our Savior. 2. They are not confirmed by an Oath from God: And therefore not perpetual. 3. They are not (as he was) Holy in themselves, but Unholy; neither Innocent, nor Undefiled, but defiling others, and being defiled of them; and so not separated from sinners, but altogether sinful and set in sin. 4. They offer first for themselves, than for the People likewise many times. 5. They offer Sacrifices, which are not themselves. 6. They bring a great disgrace to the Priesthood of Christ; by preferring themselves to him, as the Sacrificer to the Sacrifice, whom they say they offer. 7. Christ hath a Priesthood that passeth not away.

What comfort have we by the Priesthood of Christ?
Hereby we are assured that he is our Mediator; and that we also are made Priests.

What need was there of such a Mediator?
Between Parties so disagreeing, the one of finite Nature offending, the other of infinite Nature offended; the one utterly disabled to do any the least good, (2 Cor. 3. 5.) or satisfy for the least sin, (Job 9. 3.) the other requiring perfect Obedience, (Deut. 27. 26.) and satisfaction, (Mat. 18. 34.) what Agreement could there be without a Mediator? 1 Sam. 2. 25.

In this case what was the Mediator to do?
He was to work the means of our Salvation and Reconciliation to God. 1. By making satisfaction for the sin of Man. 2. By making Intercession, John 17. 19, 20. Heb. 7. 24, 25, 26, 27. Therefore Jesus Christ our High Priest, became obedient even unto the Death, offering up himself a Sacrifice once for all, to make a full Satisfaction for all our sins, and maketh continual Intercession to the Father in our Name: Whereby the Wrath of God is appeased; his Justice is satisfied, and we are reconciled.

Wherein then standeth his Satisfaction to God's Justice, which is the first part of his Priesthood?
In yielding that perfect Obedience, whereupon dependeth the whole merit of our Salvation, Dan. 9. 24. Ephes. 2. 14, 15, 16.

What is the effect thereof towards us?
Redemption, (Luke 1. 68, 69. Heb. 9. 24, 25, 26.) which is a Deliverance of us from Sin and the Punishment thereof, and a restoring of us to a better Life than ever Adam had, Rom. 5. 15, 16, 17. 1 Cor. 15. 45. For our Savior Christ hath, First, redeemed us from the Power of Darkness, (Col. 3. 13.) namely, that woeful and cursed Estate which we had justly brought upon ourselves by reason of our Sins. Secondly, Translated us into his own Kingdom and Glory, (Col. 1. 12, 13. 1 Cor. 2. 9.) a far more glorious and excellent Estate than ever our first Parents had in Paradise.

How hath Christ wrought this Redemption?
Having taken our Nature upon him, he hath in the same as a Surety in our stead made full Satisfaction to God his Father by paying all our Debts, and so hath set us free, Heb. 7. 22, 25.

What is this Debt which we owe unto God, which he hath paid for us?
This Debt is two fold. One is that perfect Obedience which we owe unto God in regard of that excellent Estate in which we were created, Deut. 12. 32. Mat. 5. 17, 18. The other is the Punishment due unto us for our Sins, in transgressing and breaking God's Covenant; which is the Curse of God, and everlasting Death, Deut. 27. 26. Rom. 6. 23. Gal. 3. 13. & 4. 4, 5. 2 Cor. 5. 21. All which is contained in the Law of God, which is the hand-writing between God and us concerning the Old Covenant, Col. 2. 14.

How was our Savior to make Satisfaction for this our Debt?
1. By performing that perfect Obedience which we did owe. 2. By suffering that Punishment due unto us for our sins: That so he might put out the hand-writing betwixt God and us, and set us free.

What then are the parts of Christ's Obedience and Satisfaction?
His Sufferings and his Righteousness, Phil. 2. 5, 6, 7, 8. 1 Pet. 2. 24. For it was requisite, that he should first pay all our Debt, and satisfy God's Justice, (Isa. 53. 5, 6. Job 33. 24.) by a price of infinite Value. (1 Tim. 2. 6.) Secondly, Purchase and merit for us God's Favor, (Ephes. 1. 6.) and Kingdom, by a most absolute and perfect Obedience, (Rom. 5. 19.) By his suffering he was to merit unto us the Forgiveness of our sins; and by his fulfilling the Law he was to merit unto us Righteousness: Both which are necessarily required for our Justification.

But how can one Man save so many?
Because the Manhood being joined to the Godhead, it maketh the Passion and Righteousness of Christ of infinite merit, and so we are justified by a Man that is God.

How hath Christ made Satisfaction for our Sins by his Sufferings?
He endured most grievous Torments both of Body and Soul; offering up himself unto God his Father, as a Sacrifice propitiatory for all our sins, 2. Cor. 5. 21.

In this Oblation who was the Priest or Sacrificer?
None but Christ, (Heb. 5. 5, 6.) and that as he was both God and Man.

Who was the Sacrifice?
Christ himself as he was Man consisting of Body and Soul, Isa. 53. 10.

What was the Altar upon which he was offered?
Christ as he was God, was the Altar on which he sacrificed himself, Heb. 9. 14. & 13. 10. Rev. 8. 3.

How often was he offered?
Never but once, Heb. 9. 28.

Whereunto was he offered?
Unto the Shame, Pain, Torment, and all the Miseries which are due unto us for sins. He suffering whatsoever we should have suffered, and by those grievous Sufferings making Payment for our sins, Isa. 53. Mat. 26. 28.

What Profit cometh by his Sacrifice?
By his most painful Sufferings he hath satisfied for the Sins of the whole World of his Elect, (Isa. 53. 5. 1 Pet. 2. 24. 1 John 2. 2.) and appeased the Wrath of his Father. So that hereby we receive Atonement and Reconciliation with God, our sins are taken away, and we are freed from all those Punishments of Body and Soul which our sins have deserved, Heb. 9. 26.

How cometh it then that Christ having born the Punishment of our sins, the Godly are yet in this World so often afflicted for them with grievous Torments both of Body and Soul; and that for the most part more than the Ungodly?
The Sufferings of the Godly are not by desert any Satisfaction for their sins in any part; but being sanctified in the most holy Sufferings of Christ, they are Medicines against Sin: Neither is their Affliction properly a Punishment, but a fatherly Correction and Chastisement in the World, that they should not perish with the World, (1 Cor. 11. 32.) whereas the Wicked the longer they are spared, and the less they are punished in this Life, their danger is the greater: For God reserveth their Punishment for the Life to come. Jer. 12. 3.

What gather you of this?
That we should not grudge at the Prosperity of the Wicked, when we are in trouble. For as the Sheep and Kine are put in fat Pastures, to be prepared to the Shambles: So they, the more they receive in this Life, the nearer and the heavier is their Destruction in the Life which is to come. Jer. 12. 3.

What are the more general things which Christ suffered in this Life?
Infirmities in his Flesh, Indignities from the World, and Temptations from the Devil, (Mat. 4. 2. Job. 4. 6, 7. & 8. 48, 52. Luke 4. 2.) Hitherto belong those manifold Calamities which he did undergo, Poverty, Hunger, Thirst, Weariness, Reproach, &c.

What arenefit does the Godly reap hereby?
All the Calamities and Crosses that befall them in this Life are sanctified and sweetened to them: So that now they are not Punishments of Sin, but Chastisement of a merciful Father.

What are the more special things which he suffered at or upon his Death?
The Weight of God's Wrath, the Terrors of Death, Sorrows of his Soul, and Torments of his Body, (Isa. 53. 4, 10. Mat. 26. 37, 38. Luke 22. 44. Mat. 26. 67.)

What learn you from hence?
To admire and imitate the Love of Christ, who being the Son of God, became a Man of Sorrows, even for the good of his utter Enemies, Ephes. 5. 2. 1 John 3. 16. Rom. 5. 7, 8.

What did our Savior Christ suffer in his Soul?
He drank the full Cup of God's Wrath filled unto him for our sakes; the whole Wrath of God due to the Sin of Man, being poured forth upon him, (Mat. 26. 27, 28. Luke 22. 44. Rev. 19. 15. John 11. 33, 38. Isa. 53. 5. 11.) And therefore in Soul he did abide most unspeakable Vexations, horrible Griefs, painful Troubles, fear of Mind, feeling as it were the very Pangs of Hell; into which both before, and most of all when he hanged upon the Cross, when he was cast; which caused him before his bodily Passion so grievously to complain.

What arenefit and Comfort receive you by this?
Hereby we have our Souls everlastingly freed from God's eternal Wrath: And herein are comforted, because in all our grievous Temptations and Assaults, we may stay and

make sure ourselves by this, that Christ hath delivered us from the sorrowful Griefs and Pains of Hell.

Now for our Savior's bodily Sufferings: Why is it said that he suffered under Pontius Pilate? 1 Tim. 6. 13.

For the Truth of this Story, and fulfilling of his own Prophecy, foretelling his Suffering under a foreign Jurisdiction and Authority, Mat. 20. 19. John 18. 31, 32. as likewise to teach us that he appeared willingly and of his own accord before a Moral Judge, of whom he was pronounced innocent, and yet by the same he was condemned.

What Comfort have you hereof?

That my Savior thus suffering, not any whit for his own sins, but wholly for mine and for other Men's sins, before an Earthly Judge; I shall be discharged before the Heavenly Judgment Seat.

What did he chiefly suffer under Pontius Pilate?

He was Apprehended, Accused, Arraigned, Mocked, Scourged, Condemned and Crucified, (Mat. 26. and 27 Chapters.)

What learn you hence?

That he that knew no sin was made sin for us, that we might be made the Righteousness of God in him, 2 Cor. 5. 21. 1 Pet. 2. 24.

Did Christ suffer these things willingly, as he suffered them innocently?

Yes: He laid down his Life meekly, as the Sheep does his Fleece before the Shearer, being obedient even unto the Death, Isa. 53. 7. Phil. 2. 8. Heb. 5. 8. 1 Pet. 2. 2. 22, 23.

Unto what Death was he so obedient?

Even unto the most reproachful, painful and dreadful Death, the Death of the Cross, Mat. 27. 30, 35, 38. Phil. 2. 8.

Why was Christ put unto this Death of the Cross?

Because it was not a common Death, but such a Death as was accursed both of God and Man: That so he being made a Curse for us, he might redeem us from a Curse due unto us, Deut. 21. 23. Gal. 3. 13.

What Comfort have you by this?

I am comforted in this, because I am delivered from the Curse which I have deserved by the Breach of the Law, and shall obtain the Blessing due unto him for keeping of the same.

Why was it requisite that our Savior's Soul should be separated from his Body?

Because we were all dead; that so he might be the Death of Death for us, 2 Cor. 5. 14, 15. Heb. 2. 14. 1 Cor. 15. 54, 55. For by Sin Death came into the World: And therefore the Justice of God could not have been satisfied for our Sins, unless Death had been joined with his Sufferings.

How could the Death and Suffering of Christ, which were but for a short time, be a full Satisfaction for us which have deserved eternal Death?

Although they were not everlasting, yet in regard of the Worthiness of the Person who suffered them, they were equivalent to everlasting Torments. Forasmuch as not a bare Man, nor an Angel did suffer them, but the eternal Son of God, (though not in his Godhead, but in our Nature which he assumed); his Person, Majesty, Deity, Goodness, Justice, Righteousness, being every way infinite and eternal, made that which he suffered, of no less force and value than eternal Torments upon others; yea, even upon all the World besides. For even as the Death of a Prince (being but a Man, and a sinful Man) is of more reckoning than the Death of an Army of other Men, because he is the Prince: Much more shall the Death and Sufferings of the Son of God, the Prince of all Princes, not finite, but every way infinite and without sin; much more, I say, shall that be of more reckoning with his Father, than the Sufferings of all the World; and the time of his Sufferings of more value (for the Worthiness of his Person) than if all the Men in the World had suffered for ever and ever. 1 Cor. 2. 8. Acts 20. 28. 2 Cor. 5. 16.

What use are we to make of Christ's Death and Passion?
First, The Consideration hereof may bring us to a sound Persuasion and feeling of our Sins: Because they have deserved so grievous a Punishment, as either the Death of the Son of God, or Hell Fire. Second, Hereby we reap unspeakable Comfort: Forasmuch as by his Stripes we are healed, by his Blood washed; by his Sacrifice God is satisfied, and by his Death we are saved and redeemed, 1 Pet. 2. 24. Rev. 1. 5. Heb. 10. 10, 12. Rom. 5. 8, 9, 10. Third, We learn from hence to die to our sins, and to live henceforth unto him that hath died for us, Rom. 6. 2, 6. 2 Cor. 5. 15.

What areset our Savior after his Soul was separated from his Body?
He was buried, Acts 13. 29, 30. and went to Hades, or (as we commonly speak) descended into Hell, Acts 2. 31.

Why was it needful that Christ should be buried?
First, To assure us more fully that he was truly dead, Mat. 27. 59, 60, 64, 65, 66. Acts 2. 29. Second, That even in the Grave, the very Fortress of Death, he might loose the Sorrows and Bands of Death, Acts 2. 24. 1 Cor. 15. 55.

What is meant by his descending into Hell?
Not that he went unto the place of the damned; but that he went absolutely unto the Estate of the dead, Rom. 10. 7. Ephes. 4. 9.

What do you call the Estate of the Dead?
That departing this Life, he went in his Soul into Heaven, (Luke 23. 43.) and was in his Body under the very Power and Dominion of Death for a season, Acts 2. 24. Heb. 2. 14. Rom. 6. 9.

What Comfort have you by Christ's Death, Burial, and lying under the Power of Death?
1. I am comforted, because my sins are fully discharged in his Death, and so buried, that they shall never come into Remembrance. 2. My Comfort is the more, because by the Virtue of his Death and Burial Sin shall be killed in me, and buried, so that henceforth it shall have no Power to reign over me. 3. I need not to fear Death, seeing that Sin which is the sting of Death is taken away by the Death of Christ, and that now Death is made unto me an entrance into Life.

Hitherto of his Sufferings: What is the other part of his Satisfaction?
His perfect Righteousness: Whereby he did that which we were not able to do, and absolutely fulfilled the whole Law of God for us, Psal. 40 7, 8. Rom. 3. 19. & 5 19.

Why was it necessary, that Christ should as well fulfill the Law, as suffer for us?
Because as by his Sufferings he took away our Unrighteousness, and freed us from the Punishment due to us for our sins; so by performing for us absolute Obedience to the whole Law of God, he hath merited our Righteousness, (making us just and holy in the sight of God) and purchased eternal Happiness for us in the Life to come, 2 Cor. 5. 21. Gal. 4. 4, 5. 1 Cor. 1. 30. Rom. 8. 3, 4. For as we are made Unrighteous by Adam's sin; so are we made fully and wholly Righteous, being justified by a Man that is God.

How manifold is the Righteousness of our Savior?
Two. fold: Original, and Actual.

What is his Original Righteousness?
The perfect Integrity and Pureness of his human Nature; which in him was without all Guile, and the least stain of Corruption, Heb. 7. 26.

Being very Man, how could he be without sin?
The Course of natural Corruption was prevented, because he was not begotten, after the ordinary Course, by Man; but was conceived in the Womb of a Virgin, without the help of Man, by the immediate Power and Operation of the Holy Ghost, forming him of the only Substance of the Woman, and perfectly sanctifying that Substance in the Conception, Luke 1. 34, 35, 41. So was he born Holy, and without Sin, whereunto all other Men by Nature are subject.

Why was it necessary that Christ should be conceived without sin?
First, Because otherwise the Godhead and Manhood could not be joined together. For God can have no Communion with Sin, much less be united unto it in a Personal Union. Secondly, Being our Priest, he must be holy, harmless, undefiled, and perfectly just without exception, Heb. 7. 26. 1 Joh. 3 5. For if he had been a Sinner himself, he could not have satisfied for the sins of other Men: Neither could it be, that an unholy thing should make us holy.

What Fruit then and Benefit have we by his Original Righteousness?
First, His pure Conception is imputed unto us, and the Corruption of our Nature covered from God's Eyes, whilst his Righteousness as a Garment is put upon us. Secondly, Our Original Sin is hereby daily diminished and fretted away, and the contrary Holiness increased in us.

What is his Actual Holiness?
That absolute Obedience whereby he fulfilled in Act every Branch of the Law of God; walking in all the Commandments, perfectly performing both in Thought, Word, and Deed, whatsoever the Law of God did command, and falling in no Duties, either in the Worship and Service of God, or Duties towards Men, Mat. 3. 15. Rom. 5. 18. & 4. 8.

What arenefit have we thereby?
1. All our Actual Sins are covered, while we are clothed by Faith with his Actual Holiness. 2. We are enabled by him daily to die unto Sin, and more and more to live unto Righteousness of Life.

But receive we no more by Christ, than those Blessings which we lost in Adam?
Yes. We receive an high Degree of Felicity by the second Adam, more than we lost by the first, Rom. 5. 1. For being by Faith incorporated into him, and by Communion of his Spirit inseparably knit unto him: We become the Children and Heirs of God, and Fellow heirs with Christ Jesus, (Gal. 4. 6, 7. 1 Cor. 12. 12, 13. Rom. 8. 9, 10.) who carrieth us as our Head unto the highest Degree of Happiness in the Kingdom of Heaven, where we shall lead, not a natural Life, as Adam did in Paradise, with Meat, Drink, and Sleep; but a Spiritual Life in an unspeakable manner and Glory.

There remaineth yet the second part of Christ's Priesthood: Namely, his Intercession. What is that?
It is that Work, whereby he alone does continually appear before his Father in Heaven to make request for his Elect in his own Worthiness: Making the Faithful and all their Prayers acceptable unto him, by applying the Merits of his own perfect Satisfaction

unto them; and taking away all the Pollution that cleaveth to their good Works, by the merits of his Passion, Rom. 8. 34. Heb. 9. 24. & 12. 24. 1 John 2. 1, 2. 1 Pet. 2. 5. Exod. 28. 36, 37, 38.

In how many things does this Intercession consist?
In five. First, In making continual request in our Name unto God the Father, by the virtue of his own Merits. Secondly, In freeing us from the Accusations of our Adversaries. Thirdly, In teaching us by his Spirit, to pray and send up Supplications for ourselves and others. Fourthly, In presenting our Prayers unto God, and making them acceptable in his sight. Fifthly, In covering our sins from the sight of God, by applying unto us the Virtue of his Mediation.

What Fruit then have we by his Intercession?
1. It does reconcile us to the Father for those sins which we do daily commit. 2. Being reconciled in him, we can pray to God with Boldness, and call him Father. 3. Through the Intercession of our Savior Christ, our good Works are of account before God.

How are we made Priests unto God, by our Communion with Christ?
Being sanctified by him, and our Persons received into favor, (Ephes. 1. 6.) we have Freedom and Boldness to draw near and offer ourselves, Souls, and Bodies, and all that we have, as a reasonable Sacrifice to God the Father. And so we are admitted, as a Spiritual Priesthood, (1 Pet. 2. 5.) to offer up the Sacrifices of our Obedience, Prayers and Thanksgiving: Which howsoever imperfect in themselves, (Isa. 64. 6.) and deserving rather Punishment than Reward, (Psal. 143. 2. Tit. 3. 5.) are yet, and our Persons, made acceptable unto GOD, and have Promise of Reward, (Mat. 10. 41, 42.) by the only Merit and Intercession of the same our High Priest.

[14TH HEAD.]

So much of our Savior's Priestly Office, which is exercised in things concerning God. How does he exercise his Office in things concerning Man?
By communicating unto Man that Grace and Redemption which he hath purchased from his Father, Rom. 5. 15, 17, 19. John 5. 21. & 17. 2, 6. Luke 4. 18, 19.

What parts of his Office does he exercise herein?
His Prophetical and Kingly Office, Acts 3. 22, 23. Psal. 2. 6, 7, 8.

What is this Prophetical Office?
The Office of instructing his Church, by revealing unto it the way and means of Salvation, and declaring the whole Will of his Father unto us. In which respect he was, he is, and ever shall be our Prophet, Doctor, or Apostle, Isa. 61. 1, 2, 3, 4. Psal. 2. 6, 7. Luke 4. 18. Mat. 17. 5. & 23. 8, 9, 10. Heb. 3. 1, 2. Acts 7. 37, 38.

For what Reasons must Christ be a Prophet?
First, To reveal and to deliver unto his People so much of the Will of God as is needful for their Salvation. Secondly, To open and expound the same, being delivered. Thirdly, To make them understand and believe the same. Fourthly, To purge his Church from Errors. Fifthly, To place Ministers in his Church to teach his People.

In what respect do you say that he is the only Teacher of his Church?
1. That he only knowing the Father as his Son, hath the Prerogative to reveal him of himself, and others by him to us. For no Man knoweth the Father but the Son, and he

to whom the Son will reveal him, Mat. 11. 27. 2. In that he is only able to cause our Hearts to believe and understand the Matter he does teach and reveal.

What were then the Prophets and Apostles?
They were his Disciples and Servants, and spake by his Spirit, 1 Pet. 1. 10, 11. & 3. 19. Nehem. 9. 30. Ephes. 2. 17.

What difference is there between the teaching of Christ, and of the Prophets and Ministers sent of him?
1. Christ taught with another Authority than ever did any other Minister before, or after him, Mat. 5. 22, 28, 32, 34, 44. & 7. 28, 29. Mark 1. 22. 2. By virtue of his Prophetical Office, he did not only bring an outward sound unto the Ear, but wrought (as he did before his coming, and as he does now by the Ministry of his Word) an Alteration of the Mind, so far as to the clearing of the Understanding.

How then does our Savior perform his Prophetical Office?
Two ways: Inwardly, and Outwardly.

How Inwardly?
By the teaching and Operation of the Holy Spirit, John 6. 45. Acts 16. 14.

How Outwardly?
By opening the whole Will of his Father; and confirming the same with so many Signs and Wonders.

How did he this?
Both in his own Person, when he was upon the Earth, (Heb. 2. 3.) as a Minister of the Circumcision, (Rom. 15. 8.) but with the Authority of the Lawgiver, (Mat. 7. 29.) and by his Servants the Ministers, (Mat. 10. 40. Luke 10. 16.) from the beginning of the World to the end thereof. Before his Incarnation, by the Prophets, Priests, and Scribes of the Old Testament, (Heb. 1. 1. 1 Pet. 1. 11, 12. & 3. 18, 19. 2 Pet. 1. 19, 20, 21. Hos. 4. 6, 7. Mat. 2. 5, 6, 17. & 23. 37.) and since to the World's end by his Apostles and Ministers, called and fitted by him for that purpose, (2 Cor. 4. 6. & 5. 19, 20. Ephes. 4. 8, 11, 12, 13.)

How does it appear that he hath opened the whole Will of his Father unto us?
Both by his own Testimony, John 15. 15. I call you no more Servants, because the Servant knoweth not what his Master does: But I call you Friends, because all which I have heard of my Father, I have made known unto you. And by the Apostles Comparison, Heb. 3. preferring him before Moses, though faithful in God's House.

In what respect is our Savior preferred before Moses?
1. As the Builder to the House, or to one Stone of the House. 2. Moses was only Servant in the House; our Savior Master over the House. 3. Moses was a Witness only, and Writer of things to be revealed; but our Savior was the end and finisher of things.

What learn you from hence?
1. That it is a foul Error in them, who think that our Savior Christ (so faithful) hath not delivered all things pertaining to the necessary Instruction and Government of the Church; but left them to the Traditions and Inventions of Men. 2. That since our Savior was so faithful in his Office, that he hath concealed nothing that was committed to him to be declared: The Ministers of the Word should not suppress in silence, for Fear or Flattery, the things that are necessarily to be delivered, and that are in their times to be

revealed. 3. That we should rest abundantly contented with that CHRIST hath taught, rejecting whatsoever else the boldness of Men would put upon us.

Did he first begin to be the Prophet, Doctor, or Apostle of his Church when he came into the World?
No, But when he opened first his Fathers Will unto us, by the Ministry of his Servants the Prophets, 1 Pet. 1. 10, 11. & 3. 19. Heb. 3. 7.

Is his Prophetical Office the same now in the time of the Gospel, that it was before and under the Law?
It is in substance one and the same: But it differeth in the manner and measure of Revelation. For the same Doctrine was revealed by the Ministry of the Prophets before the Law, by Word alone: After by Word written: And in the time of the Gospel more plainly and fully by the Apostles and Evangelists.

What have we to gather hence, that Christ taught and teacheth by the Prophets, Apostles, and Evangelists?
1. In what Estimation we ought to have the Books of the Old Testament; since the same Spirit spake then that speaketh now, and the same Christ. 2. We must carry ourselves in the hearing of the Word of God not to harden our hearts, Heb. 3. 8, 15. forasmuch as the careless and fruitless hearing thereof, hardneth Men to further Judgment. For it is a two edged Sword, to strike to Life, or to strike to Death: It is either the savor of Life to Life, or the savor of Death to Death, 2 Cor. 2. 16.

How does the Apostle press this? Heb. 3. 8, 9, 10, &c.
First, He aggravateth the refusal of this Office of our Savior against the Israelites: By the Time, forty Years; by the Place, the Wilderness; and by the multitude of his Benefits. Then he maketh an Application thereof, vers. 12, 13. consisting of two parts: 1. A removing from Evil. 2. A moving to Good.

What comfort have we by the Prophetical Office of our Savior?
1. Hereby we are sure, that he will lead us into all Truth, revealed in his Word, needful for God's Glory, and our Salvation.

2. We are in some sort Partakers of the Office of his Prophecy, by the Knowledge of his Will. For he maketh all his to prophesy in their measure, enabling them to teach themselves and their Brethren, by comforting, counseling, and exhorting one another privately to Good things, and withdrawing one another from Evil, as occasion serveth, Acts 2. 17, 18.

So much of the Prophetical Office of our Savior Christ. What is his Kingly Office?
It is the Exercise of that Power given him by God over all, (Psalm 110. 1. Ezek. 34. 24. John 17. 2.) and the Possession of all, (Mat. 28. 18. Psal. 2. 8, &c.) for the Spiritual Government and Salvation of his Elect, (Isa. 9. 7. Luke 1. 32, 33.) and for the Destruction of his and their Enemies, (Psal. 45. 5.)

For what Reasons must Christ be a King?
1. That he might gather together all his Subjects into one Body of the Church out of the World. 2. That he might bountifully bestow upon them, and convey unto them all the aforesaid means of Salvation: Guiding them unto everlasting Life by his Word and Spirit. 3. That he might appoint Laws and Statutes, which should direct his People, and bind their Consciences to the Obedience of the same. 4. That he might rule and govern them, and keep them in Obedience to his Laws. 5. That he might appoint Officers and a settled Government in his Church, whereby it might be ordered. 6. That he might

defend them from the Violence and Outrage of all their Enemies both Corporal and Spiritual. 7. That he might bestow many notable Privileges and Rewards upon them. 8. That he might execute his Judgments upon the Enemies of his Subjects.

How does he show himself to be a King?
By all that Power which he did manifest, as well in vanquishing Death and Hell, as in gathering the People unto himself which he had formerly ransomed, and in ruling them being gathered; as also in defending of them, and applying of those Blessings unto them which he hath purchased for them.

How did he manifest that Power?
First, In that being dead and buried, he rose from the Grave, quickened his dead Body, ascended into Heaven, and now sitteth at the right Hand of his Father, with full Power and Glory in Heaven, Ephes. 4. 8. Acts 2. 9. Secondly, In governing of his Church in this World, (1 Cor. 15. 25, 26, 27, 28.) continually inspiring and directing his Servants by the Divine Power of his Holy Spirit, according to his Holy Word, (Isa. 9. 7. & 30. 21.). Thirdly, By his last Judgment in the World to come, Mat. 25. 24, 31, 33, 34.

Why is Christ Jesus also called our Lord? 1 Cor. 1. 2.
Because he is the Lord of Glory and Life that hath bought us, our Head that must govern us, and our Sovereign that subdues all our Enemies unto us, Acts 3. 15. 1 Cor. 2. 8. 1 Pet. 1. 19. Ephes. 1. 22. Joshua 5. 14, 15. Heb. 2. 10, 14, 15.

How hath he bought us?
Not with Gold or Silver, but with his precious Blood he hath purchased us to be a peculiar People to himself, 1 Pet. 1. 18, 19.

What comfort have you by this?
Seeing he hath paid such a Price for us, he will not suffer us to perish.

What learn you from hence, that Christ is our Head to govern us?
To obey his Commandments, and bear his Rebukes and Chastisements, Luke 6. 46. John 14. 15. Col. 3. 23, 24.

In what place of Scripture is the Doctrine of Christ's Kingdom specially taught?
In Isa. 9. vers. 6, 7. For unto us a Child is born, and unto us a Son is given: and the Government is upon his Shoulder, and he shall call his Name, Wonderful Counselor, The Mighty God, The Everlasting Father, the Prince of Peace. The Increase of his Government and Peace shall have none end: And he shall sit upon the Throne of David, and upon his Kingdom, to order it, and to establish it with Judgment, and with Justice, from henceforth even for ever: The Zeal of the Lord of Hosts will perform this.

What are we here taught concerning Christ's Kingdom?
The Benefits that we receive by it, and the Cause of it.

How is the former set forth?
By Declaration, First, of his Person, that he is a Child born, namely, God made Man: Whereof hath been spoken. Secondly, Of his Properties; with the Effects of the same.

How are his Properties here expressed?
They are, first, generally set forth by Comparison of the Unlikelihood of his Kingdom with the Regiments of Worldly Potentates.

Fourteenth Head

What difference or Inequality is there?
That whereas other Kings execute Matters by their Lieutenants and Deputies, armed with their Authority: In our Savior's Kingdoms, although there be used Instruments; yet do they accomplish his Will and Purpose, not only by his Authority, but also by his Strength and Virtue.

What further Doctrine do you note hence?
That the Man of Sin, or Pope of Rome, is not the Ministerial Head of the Church, which is Christ's Kingdom: since he is himself present, yea, and that most notably by his Spirit; and more to the Advantage of his Church, than when he was bodily present, John 16. 7.

How are his Properties set forth more particularly?
First, That he should be called Wonderful: Not that it should be his proper Name, which was only Jesus; but that he should be as renownedly known to be Wonderful, as Men are known by their Names.

How is he Wonderful?
Partly in his Person, as is before-said: And partly in his Works; namely, First, In the Creation of the World. Secondly, In the Preservation, and especially in the Redemption of it.

What is the next that followeth?
It is showed more particularly wherein he is Wonderful; and first, That he is Wonderful in Counsel, and The Counselor.

What is here to be observed?
First, In the Government of a Kingdom, Counsel and Wisdom are the chief; as that which is preferred to Strength, (Isa. 9. 15. 2 Sam. 20. 16. Eccles. 7. 19. & 9. 16. Prov. 21. 22. & 24. 5.) and therefore that we may assure ourselves, that in the Kingdom of Christ all things are done wisely, nothing rashly; in which respect he is said to have a long Stoal, and a white Head, Rev. 1. 13, 14. Secondly, A great Comfort for the Children of God, that our Savior Christ is our Counselor, who giveth all sound Advice. Thirdly, That when we are in any perplexity, and know not which way to turn; yet we may come to our Savior Christ, who is given unto us for a Counselor.

By what means may we come to him for Advice?
By our humble Supplication and Prayer unto him.

How may we receive Advice from him?
By the Doctrine of God, drawn out of his Holy Word, which is therefore termed the Men of our Counsel, Psal. 119. 24.

What is the next Property?
That he is wonderful in might, and the strong God; having all sound strength.

What have we here to learn?
1. That as he is wise, and does all things pertaining to the good of his Church; so he is of power to execute all that he adviseth wisely. 2. That as there is in us no advice of ourselves, so there is in us no sound strength to keep us from any Evil; but that as he giveth good advice to his, so does he with his own Power perform and effect it, Phil. 2. 13. And therefore although we be as the Vine, of all other Trees the weakest; or as the Sheep, of all other Beasts the simplest; yet we have for our Vine a Gardner, and for our Shepherd Christ Jesus the mighty strong God. 3. That we should take heed how we depart from his obedience; for he will do what he listeth.

For if to obey be a good means to help us into the favor of our Earthly Princes; it will much more help us in the favor of the King of Kings.

What other Properties follow?
Two other, which are, as it were, the Branches and Effects of the former. 1. That he is the Father of Eternities. 2. The Prince of Peace.

Since he is called the Father of Eternities; is there not a confusion of Persons?
In no wise. For it is a borrowed speech, signifying that he is the Author of Eternity.

What do you here gather?
That where other Kingdoms alter, his is everlasting, Dan. 2. 44.

What Doctrine is thereof to be gathered?
First, That the Kingdom of our Savior Christ being perpetual, he dasheth and crusheth in pieces all other mighty Monarchies and Regiments that shall rise up against him: And therefore, that his Church and Subjects generally, and every particular Member, need not to fear any Power whatsoever.

Secondly, That whatsoever we have by Nature or Industry, is momentary, like unto the Grass that fadeth away; and whatsoever durable thing we have, we have it from Christ.

What is the second Property, arising out of the former?
That he is the Prince of Peace; that is, the Procurer, Cause and Ground of Peace; that causeth his Subjects to continue in peace and quietness.

Of what Nature is this Peace?
It is Spiritual (Rom. 5. 1. Ephes. 2. 14, 15, 16, 17). 1. When we have Peace with God. 2. When we have Peace in our Consciences. 3. When there is Peace between Men and Men: Which ariseth out of both the former.

Where should this Peace be established?
Upon the Throne of David, that is, in the Church of God.

What is the cause of all this?
The Love and Zeal of God, breaking through all Lets; either inward from ourselves and our own Sins, or outward from the enmity of the Devil and the World, Isa. 9. 7.

What Fruit receive we by the Kingly Office of our Savior Christ?
By it all the Treasures brought in by his Priestly and Prophetical Office, are dealt to us continually. For from it all the means of applying and making effectual unto us Christ and all his Benefits do come: Yea, without it all the Actions of his other Offices are to us void, fruitless and without effect.

What Comfort have we by this?
Hereby we are assured, that by this Kingly Power we shall finally overcome the Flesh, the World, the Devil, Death and Hell.

To whom will this Blessed King communicate the Means of Salvation?
He offereth them to many, and they are sufficient to save all Mankind: all shall not be saved thereby, because by Faith they will not receive them, Mat. 20. 16. John 1. 11. 1 John 2. 2.

Fourteenth Head

Are not the Faithful in some sort also made Partakers of this Honor of his Kingdom?
Yes verily. For they are made Kings to rule and subdue their stirring and rebellious Affections, and to tread Satan under their feet, Rom. 6. 12. & 16. 20. Rev. 1. 6. & 5. 10.

You have spoken of the two Natures, and three Offices of our Savior; show now, in what state did Christ God and Man perform this three fold Office?
In a two-fold estate: 1. Of Abasement and Humiliation, Phil. 2. 7, 8. 2. Of Advancement and Exaltation, Phil. 2. 9. Col. 2. 15. Eph. 1. 20, 21.

In the former he abased himself by his Sufferings for Sin: whereof we have heard largely in the declaration of his Priesthood. In the latter he obtained a most glorious Victory, and triumphed over Sin: thereby fulfilling his Priesthood, and making way to his Kingdom.

What was his Estate of Humiliation?
It was the base Condition of a Servant, whereto he humbled himself from his Conception to the Cross, and so until the time of his Resurrection, Phil. 2. 7, 8.

Wherein did this base Estate of the Son of God consist?
In his Conception, Gestation and Birth; and in his Life diversely: As in his Poverty, Hunger, Thirst, Weariness, and other Humiliations even unto Death. Of which heretofore hath been spoken.

What learn you from this, that Christ first suffered many things, before he could enter into his Glory? Luke 24. 26, 46.
That the way to reign with Christ, is first to suffer with him; and such as bear the Cross constantly, shall wear the Crown eternally, Rom. 8. 17, 18. 2 Tim. 2. 12. & 4. 8. Jam. 1. 12.

What is the State of Exaltation?
His glorious condition, (Phil. 2. 9. Heb. 2. 9.) beginning at the instant of his Resurrection, (Acts 2. 24, 31, 36.) and comprehending his Ascension (Ephes. 4. 8. Acts 2. 34. Heb. 9. 24, 25.) sitting at the right hand of God his Father, (Psal. 110. 1, 2, 5, 6. Mark 16. 19. 1 Pet. 3. 22.) and second coming in Glory to judge the World, Mat. 25. 31.

What is the first Degree of this Estate?
His glorious Resurrection. For after he had in his Manhood suffered for us, he did in the third day rise again by his own Power from the dead, Eph. 1. 19. Luke 24. 7, 46. 1 Cor. 15. 4. Mat. 16. 21. & 17. 23.

Was it needful that Christ being dead should rise again?
Yes it was: for his own Glory and our Good, Acts 2. 24. 1 Cor. 15. 21. 22.

How for his Glory?
That being formerly abased as a Servant, and crucified as a Sinner, he might thus be declared to be the Son of God, and exalted to be a Prince and a Savior, Phil. 2. 7, 8. Luke 23, 33. Isa. 53. 12. Rom. 1. 4. Acts 5. 30, 31.

How for our Good?
That having paid the Price of our Redemption by his Death, we might have good assurance of our full Justification by his Life, 1 Pet. 1. 19. Acts 20. 28. Rom 4. 25. 1 Cor. 15. 17.

What special Comfort ariseth from this, that the Lord of Life is risen from Death?
First, It assureth me that his Righteousness shall be imputed unto me for my perfect Justification; that he that had the Power of Death is destroyed, (Heb. 2. 14.) his

Works dissolved, (1 John 3. 8.) and that all our Misery is swallowed up in Christ's Victory, 1 Cor. 15. 54. Second, It comforteth me, because it does from day to day raise me up to Righteousness and Newness of Life in this present World. Third, It ministreth unto me a comfortable hope, that I shall rise again in the last day from bodily death.

What Fruits then are we to show from the Virtue of his Resurrection? Phil. 3. 10.
We are to stand up from the dead, to awake to Righteousness, to live unto God; and dying in him or for him, to look for Life again from him, Eph. 5, 14. 1 Cor. 15. 34. Rom. 6. 4, 11. Phil. 3. 20. 1 Thess. 4. 14. 1 Cor. 15. 22. Col. 3. 4.

Why is Christ said to raise himself?
To let us know, that as he had power to lay down his Life, so he had also to take it up again, John 10. 18.

What gather you hence?
That being Lord both of Quick and Dead, he can and will both quicken our Souls here to the Life of Grace, and raise our Bodies hereafter to the Life of Glory, Rom. 14. 9. John 5. 21. Phil. 3. 21.

Why did he rise the third Day?
Because the Bands of Death could no longer hold him; this being the time that he had appointed, and the day that best served for his glorious Resurrection, Acts 2. 24. Mat. 20. 17, 18, 19. & 12. 40.

Why did he not rise before the third Day?
Lest rising so presently upon his Death, his Enemies might take occasion of cavil, that he was not dead, Mat. 27. 63, 64. & 28. 13, 14.

And why could he not put it off till the fourth Day?
Lest the Faith of his Disciples should have been weakened, and their Hearts too much cast down and discouraged, Mat. 28. 1. Luke 24. 21.

What gather you hence?
That as the Lord setteth down the term of our durance, so does he choose the fittest time of our deliverance, Rev. 2. 10. Mat. 12. 40. Dan. 11. 35. Hos. 6. 2.

What is the second Degree of his Exaltation?
His Ascension, Mar. 16. 19. Eph. 4. 8, 9. For we believe that Christ in his human Nature (the Apostles looking on) ascended into Heaven.

What Assurance have you of Christ's Ascension?
The Evidence of the Word, the Testimony of Heavenly Angels and Holy Men, Luke 24. 51. Acts 1. 9, 10, 11.

Wherefore did Christ ascend into Heaven?
Because he had finished his Father's Work on Earth, (John 17. 3, 4, 5.) and that being exalted in our Nature, he might consecrate a way, (Heb. 10. 20.) prepare a place, (John 14. 2, 3.) and appear in the Presence of God to make Intercession for us, Heb. 9. 24.

What arenefits did he bestow upon his Church at his Ascension?
He triumphed over his Enemies, gave Gifts to his Friends; and taking with him a Pledge of our Flesh, he sent and left with us the Earnest of his Spirit, Ephes. 4. 8. Heb. 10. 12, 20. 2 Cor. 5. 5. Acts 2. 33.

What Comfort does hence arise to God's Children?
First, that our Head being gone before, we his Members shall follow after; Christ having prepared for us a place in Heaven; which now we feel by Faith, and hereafter shall fully enjoy, Eph. 1. 22, 23. 1 Cor. 15. 49. John 14. 3. & 17. 24. Second, that having such a Friend in Heaven, we need not fear any Foes on Earth, nor Fiends in Hell. Heb. 7. 25. Phil. 1. 28. Rom. 16. 20. Acts 20. 24. Rev. 2. 10.

What Fruits are we to show in our Lives, from the Virtue of his Ascension in our Hearts?
First, To have our Conversation in Heaven, whilst we be on Earth; placing our Hearts where our Head is, Col. 3. 1, 2. Phil. 1. 23. & 3. 20. Second, To look for the presence of Christ by Faith, not by Sight; in Spiritual, not in Carnal Things, Mat. 28. 20. 2 Cor. 5. 7. John 6. 63.

What is the third Degree of his Exaltation?
That he sitteth at the right hand of God the Father Almighty, Mar. 16. 19. Eph. 1. 20, 21, 22.

What is meant by this?
That Christ in Man's Nature is worthily advanced by the Father to the height of all Majesty, Dominion, and Glory; having authority to rule all things in Heaven and in Earth, Eph. 4. 10. Heb. 13. 8, 13. Mat. 28. 18.

How may this appear?
Because he is hereby exalted to be the King of Saints, (Rom. 15. 3.) the Judge of Sinners, (Acts 17. 31.) the Prince of our Salvation, (Acts 5. 31.) and the High Priest of our Profession, Heb. 8. 1.

What Comfort ariseth hence to all true Believers?
That 1. As our King, he will govern us, (Heb. 1. 8, 9. Luke 1. 33.) and that from him we shall receive all things needful for us under his gracious Government. 2. As our Judge, he will avenge us, (Rev. 6. 10. & 16. 5, 6.) and as our Prince, defend us, subduing all our Enemies by his Power, and treading them under our feet. 3. As our Priest, he will plead our Cause and pray for us, Heb. 7. 25. Rom. 8. 34.

Why is he said in the Creed, to sit at the right hand of God the Father Almighty?
That we may know he enjoyeth both the Favor and Power of God in full measure; the Father having committed all Judgment to the Son, Heb. 1. 13. Mat. 28. 18. John 5. 22.

What Duties are here required?
To honor the Son, as we do the Father: To cast our Crowns at his Feet, stoop to his Scepter, live by his Laws; so to follow him here, that we may sit with him in his Throne hereafter, John 5. 23. Rev. 4. 10, 11. Psal. 2. 10. James 4. 12. Rev. 3. 21.

Does he not now thus reign for the raising of his Friends, and ruin of his Enemies?
Yes; he does graciously by his Word and Works, (Heb. 1. 8: Rom. 10. 15, 16.) but he shall more gloriously when he cometh again to judge the Quick and the Dead, 2 Thess. 1. 10. Rom. 14. 9.

[15TH HEAD.]

Having thus declared that which concerneth the Mediator of the New Testament; what are you now to consider in the Condition of the rest of Mankind which hold by him?
Two things: 1. The Participation of the Grace of Christ, and the Benefits of the Gospel. 2. The Means which God hath ordained for the offering and effecting of the same.

To whom does God reveal and apply his Covenant of Grace?
Not to the World, but to his Church called out of the World, (Joh. 14. 22. & 17. 9. Mat. 11. 25. 1 Cor. 2. 8, &c.) that is, not to the Reprobate, appointed from everlasting to be Vessels of Wrath, but to the Elect and Chosen, upon whom he intended to show the Riches of his Mercy, (Rom. 9. 22, 23.) For howsoever the Light is come into the World, yet most Men rather love Darkness than Light, (John 3. 19.) and though the Proclamation of Grace be general, (1 Tim. 2. 4.) yet most Men refuse or neglect God's Goodness, by reason of the naughtiness of their Hearts. Neither are any saved, but such as God draweth to embrace his Mercy, and casteth as it were into a new Mould, John 6. 44.

It would seem by this, that the most part of the World be in no better estate than the Devil himself.
Most Men undoubtedly abide without recovery in the State of Sin and Death, (1 John 5. 19.) because the Lord does not grant unto them the Benefit of Redemption, and Grace of Faith and Repentance unto Life, but suffereth them to run on in Sin deservedly unto Condemnation, Mat. 13. 15. Acts 14. 18. & 17. 30.

How does God suffer them to run into Condemnation?
In a divers manner: Some Reprobates dying Infants, other of riper Years; of which latter sort, some are not called, others called.

How does God deal with Reprobates dying Infants?
Being once conceived, they are in the state of Death, (Rom. 5. 14.) by reason of the Sin of Adam imputed, and of Original Corruption cleaving to their Nature, wherein also dying they perish: As (for instance) the Children of Heathen Parents. For touching the Children of Christians, we are taught to account them Holy, 1 Cor. 7. 14.

How does God deal with those of riper years uncalled?
Being naturally possessed with Ignorance and Vanity, (Ephes. 4. 18, 19.) he giveth them up to their own Lusts to commit Sin without Remorse, with Greediness, in a reprobate Mind, (Rom. 1. 26, 28.) until the measure of sin being fulfilled, they are cut off, Gen. 15. 16. Psal. 69. 27.

How does God deal with such Reprobates as are called?
He vouchsafeth them the outward means of Salvation, (Heb. 4. 1, 2. 1 Cor. 10. 1, 2, &c.) giving farther to some of them some Illumination, (Heb. 6. 4, 5.) A temporary Faith, (Acts 8. 13.) some outward Holiness and taste of Heaven: Whom yet he suffereth to fall away, and the means of Grace to become a savor of Death unto them, (2 Cor. 2. 16.) yea some of these do fall, even to the Sin unpardonable, Heb. 6. 6.

So much of the Company of the Reprobate, which are not made Partakers of the benefit of Redemption: What is the Church of Christ, which enjoyeth this great benefit?
A Company of Men and Women, called out of the World to believe, and live in Christ; and endued accordingly with Spiritual Graces for the Service of God, (Gal. 3. 26, 27,

Fifteenth Head

28. John 1. 12. & 17. 14, 16. Ephes. 2. 10. 1 Tim. 3. 15. Tit. 2. 14.) or rather, the whole number of God's Elect, which are admitted into Fellowship with Christ Jesus, (Ephes. 1. 1. & 5. 23. Col. 1. 2, 27.) For all these being taken together are called the Church, that is, God's Assembly or Congregation: Which in the Scripture is likened to the Spouse of Christ, (Cant. 4. 9, 10. Ephes. 5. 23, 25.) which in the Creed we profess to believe, under the Title of The Holy Catholic Church, (Heb. 12. 22, 23. Ephes. 5. 27.)

Do you believe in the Catholic Church?
No. I believe that God hath a certain number of his chosen Children, which he does call and gather to himself: That Christ hath such a Flock selected out of all Nations, Ages and Conditions of Men, (Ephes. 5. 23. John 10. 16. Gal. 3. 28. Rev. 7. 9.) and that my self am one of that Company, and a Sheep of that Fold.

Why say you, that you believe that there is a Catholic Church?
Because that the Church of God cannot be always seen with the eyes of Man.

Why is this Church called Holy?
Because she hath washed her Robes in the Blood of the Lamb; and being sanctified and cleansed with the washing of Water by the Word, is presented and accepted as Holy before God, (Rev. 7. 14. Ephes. 5. 26, 27. Col. 1. 21, 22.) For though the Church on Earth be in it self sinful, yet in Christ the Head it is Holy, and in the Life to come shall be brought to Perfection of Holiness.

What learn you hence?
That if ever we will have the Church for our Mother, or God for our Father; we must labor to be Holy, as he is Holy, Gal. 4. 26. 1 Pet. 1. 13, 14, 15, 16, 17. Lev. 20. 7.

What is meant here by Catholic Church?
That whole universal Company of the Elect that ever were, are, or shall be gathered together in one Body, knit together in one Faith, under one Head Christ Jesus, Ephes. 4. 4, 5, 6, 12, 13. Col. 2. 19. Ephes. 1. 22, 23. For God in all Places, and of all sorts of Men, had from the beginning, hath now, and ever will have an Holy Church. Which is therefore called the Catholic Church, that is, God's whole or Universal Assembly; because it comprehendeth the Multitude of all those that have, do, or shall believe unto the World's end.

Do all these make one Body?
The whole number of Believers and Saints by calling make one Body, the Head whereof is Christ Jesus, (Ephes. 1. 10, 22, 23. Col. 1. 18, 24.) having under him no other Vicar. And so the Pope is no Head of the Church: For neither Property nor Office of the Head can agree unto him.

What is the Property of the Head?
To be highest: And therefore there can be but one, even Christ.

What is the Office of the Head?
First, To prescribe Laws to his Church, which should bind Men's Consciences to the Obedience of the same: And of such Law givers there is but one, Jam. 4. 12. Secondly, To convey the Powers of Life and Motion into all the Members, by bestowing Spiritual Life and Grace upon them. For as the natural Members take Spirit and Sense from the Head; so the Church hath all her Spiritual Life and Feeling from Christ, who is only able (and no Creature beside) to quicken and give Life. Thirdly, To be the Savior of the Body, Ephes. 5. 23. But Christ Jesus is only the Savior of the Church: Whom by this Title of the Head of the Church, Paul lifteth up above all Angels, Archangels,

Principalities, and Powers. And therefore if the Pope were the Successor of Peter; yet should he not be the Head of the Church: Which agreeth to no simple Creature in Heaven, or under Heaven.

So much of the Head. Where be the Members of this Holy Catholic Church?
Part are already in Heaven Triumphant, part as yet Militant here upon Earth.

What call you the Church Triumphant?
The blessed Company of those that have entered into their Master's Joy, (Heb. 12. 23. Rev. 7, 14, 16.) waiting for the fulfilling of the number of their Fellow members, and their own Consummation in perfect Bliss, Rev. 6. 9.

Why is it called Triumphant?
Because the Saints deceased have made an end of their Pilgrimage and Labors here on Earth, and triumph over their Enemies, the World, Death and Damnation.

Are the Angels of the Church Triumphant?
No. First, Because they were never of the Church Militant. Secondly, Because they were not redeemed, nor received Benefit by the Death of Christ. And therefore it is said, that he took not on him the Nature of Angels, but the Seed of Abraham, Heb. 2. 16.

What is the special Duty which the Church Triumphant in Heaven does perform?
Praise and Thanksgiving to God.

What is the Church Militant?
It is the Society of those, that being scattered through all the Corners of the World, are by one Faith in Christ conjoined to him, and fight under his Banner against their Enemies, the World, the Flesh, and the Devil: Continuing in the Service and Warfare of their Lord, and expecting in due time also to be crowned with Victory, and triumph in Glory with him, Rev. 1. 9. & 12. 11. 2 Tim. 4. 7, 8.

Who are the true Members of the Church Militant on Earth?
Those alone who as living Members of the Mystical Body, (Ephes. 1, 22, 23. Col. 1. 18.) are by the Spirit and Faith secretly and inseparably conjoined unto Christ their Head, Col. 3. 3. Psal. 83. 3. In which respect the true Militant Church is both invincible, Mat. 16. 18. and invisible, (Rom, 2. 29. 1 Pet. 3. 4.) the Elect not being to be discerned from the Reprobate till the last Day.

But are none to be accounted Members of this Church, but such as are so inseparably united unto Christ? Doubtless many live in the Church, who are not thus united unto him, and shall never come to Salvation by him?
Truly and properly none are of the Church, saving only they which truly believe and yield Obedience, (1 John 2. 19.) all which are also saved Howbeit God useth outward means with the inward for the gathering of his Saints; and calleth them as well to outward Profession among themselves, as to inward Fellowship with his Son, (Acts 2. 42. Cant. 1. 7.) whereby the Church becometh visible. Hence it cometh, that so many as partaking the outward means do join with these in League of visible Profession, (Acts 8. 13.) are therefore in human Judgment accounted Members of the true Church, and Saints by calling, (1 Cor. 1. 2.) until the Lord, who only knoweth who are his, do make known the contrary: As we are taught in the Parable of the Tares, the Draw-Net, &c. Mat. 13. 24, 47. Thus many live in the Church, as it is visible and outward, which are Partakers only outwardly of Grace: And such are not fully of the Church, that have entered in but one step, Cant. 4. 7. Ephes. 5. 27. 1 John 2. 19. That a Man may be fully of the Church, it is not sufficient that he profess Christ with his

Mouth; but it is further required, that he believe in him in heart. These do the one, but not the other; or if they believe in heart, they believe not fully. For they may generally believe indeed that Christ is the Savior of Mankind: But they know not whether themselves have part in him; yea, by the Works they disclaim any Interest in him.

What say you then of such?
They are Partakers of all good of the outward or imperfect Church; and therefore their Children also are baptized and admitted as Members of Christ's Church. These are like evil Citizens (as indeed the Church is God's City) who are in truth but Citizens in Profession and Name only. For they as yet want the chiefest Point, which only maketh a Man to deserve the true Name of a Citizen; which is to use the Place aright: And therefore have no part in those Rewards that are purposed for good and perfect Citizens; though they enjoy what outwardly belongeth to the City.

Are we then to acknowledge one Church or many?
One alone; as there is but one Lord, one Spirit, one Baptism, one Faith, Ephes. 4. 4. Cant. 6. 8. Gal. 3. 28. Howsoever (as hath been said) there is a begun, and a perfect Church. For the Church of God is one in respect of the Inward Nature of it; having one Head, one Spirit, and one final State: But Outwardly, there be as many Churches as there be Congregations of Believers knit together by special Bond of Order for the religious expressing of that Inward Nature, Rev. 1. 11. Yet, though there be many Visible Churches, there is but one Catholic and Universal Church; of which not one shall be lost, and out of which not one shall be saved, Acts 2. 47. Ephes. 5. 23. John 17. 12, 20.

What gather you hence?
That the Church of Rome is not the Catholic Church: Because it is Particular, not Universal; and because out of it many have been saved, and shall be saved, and in it some shall be damned, Rev. 18. 4 & 19. 20. 2 Thess. 2. 11, 12.

[16TH HEAD.]

What are the special Prerogatives, whereof all God's Children, the true Members of the Catholic Church, are made Partakers? John 1. 12.
In the Creed there are some principal Notes rehearsed.

1. The Communion of Saints, Heb. 12. 22, 23. Eph. 2. 19.
2. The Forgiveness of Sins, Rom. 8. 1, 33.
3. The Resurrection of the Body, 1 Cor. 15. 52. Acts 24. 15.
4. Life Everlasting, Rom. 6. 23.

There are four also recorded by the Apostle Paul in that Golden Sentence, 1 Cor. 1. 30. Ye are of him in Christ Jesus, who of God is made unto us Wisdom, and Righteousness, and Sanctification, and Redemption.

Why is Wisdom here set down by the Apostle as necessary to our Salvation?
Because it was necessary, that having absolutely lost all godly and saving Wisdom wherein we were first created, that it should be again repaired e're we could be Partakers of Life Eternal.

Why? have we no true Wisdom naturally able to bring us unto it?
No verily. For although we have Wisdom naturally engrafted in us to provide for this present Life, and sufficient to bring us to Condemnation in the Life to come: Yet we

have not one Grain of saving Wisdom able to save us, or to make us step one foot forward unto Eternal Life.

Where is this Wisdom to be found?
In the Word of God, Psal. 19. 7. 2 Tim. 3. 15.

How come we to it?
By Christ. For God dwelleth in Light which no Man hath approached unto, (1 Tim. 6. 16.) only the Son, which was in the Bosom of his Father, he hath revealed him, John 1. 18.

What does the Apostle mean by Righteousness?
As by the chief part thereof, our whole Justification: Which consisteth in the Remission of our Sins, and the Imputation of Christ's Righteousness.

How do you prove this Righteousness here to be meant of the Righteousness that is in Christ?
Because he speaketh afterward of Sanctification, which is the Righteousness within us.

What is Sanctification?
It is a freedom from the Tyranny of Sin into the Liberty of Righteousness; begun here, and increased daily, until it be fully perfected in the Life to come, Rom. 6. 14. Psal. 19. 13.

What is Redemption?
It is the happy Estate that the Children of God shall have in the Last Day, Eph. 4. 30. Rom. 8. 23. Luke 21. 28.

What is the Ground of all these Spiritual Blessings?
The whole Work of our Salvation must be ascribed to the Grace of God alone.

What is meant by the Grace of God?
1. And principally, that free favor which God does bear towards us. 2. Those Gifts and Helps that are in us, arising from that Fountain.

Is Man idle in this Work of Grace?
Man also worketh with God's Grace; but first he receiveth from God not only the Power to work, but also the Will and the Deed it self, Phil. 2. 13.

Is this Work of God only an offering of good things unto us?
God does not only offer Grace unto us, but causeth us effectually to receive it; and therefore is said not only to draw us, (Cant. 1. 4. John 6. 44.) but also to create a new heart in us, whereby we follow him, Psal. 51. 10.

What profit hath every one of God's Elect in Christ the Mediator, by the application of the Covenant of Grace?
Union and Communion, both with Christ himself and his whole Church: Whence ariseth the Communion of Saints; whereby nothing else is understood, but that Heavenly Fellowship which all the Faithful have with Christ their Head, and with the Members of his Body, all true Christians: The whole Church thus communicating with Christ, and every Member one with another, Heb. 3. 14. & 12. 22, 23. Eph. 2. 19, 20. & 4. 12. 1 John 1. 3.

What are the Bands of this Fellowship, and who is the Author of it?
The Spirit knits the Body to the Head by Faith, and the Members one unto another by Love, 1 Cor. 12. 11, 12, 27. Col. 3. 14. 1 Cor. 6. 17.

What Comfort have we by this?
1. That we are justified by that Faith, whereby Adam and Abraham were justified, which is tied to no time or place, and excludeth no Person. 2. That we are made Partakers of Christ and all his Merits by Faith, and of all the Blessings of the Church by Love.

What are the special Comforts of this Communion with Christ?
That we are sure to have all Graces and all good things from him: And that both our Persons are beloved, and our Services accepted in him, and for him, John 1. 16, 17. 1 Cor. 1. 30. Eph. 2. 4, 5, 13. 1 Pet. 2. 5.

And what especial Comforts do arise out of our Communion with Christians?
That we have a Portion in their Prayers, (Acts 12. 5.) a share in their Comforts, (Rom. 12. 13.) a room in their Hearts, (2 Cor. 7. 3. 2 Thess. 1. 3.) mutual bearing Infirmities, (Gal. 6. 1, 2.) furthering Duties, (Heb. 10. 24.) and relieving Necessities, (Rom. 12. 13. 1 John 3. 17.)

What Duty does this is Communion of Saints require of us? (Eph. 4. 7, 12.)
To renounce all Fellowship with Sin and Sinners, (2 Cor. 6. 17.) to edify one another in Faith and Love, (Jude ver. 20.) to delight in the Society of Saints, (Psal. 16. 3.) and to keep the Unity of the Spirit in the Bond of Peace, (Eph. 4. 3.)

Why are all Believers called Saints?
Because they are Partakers of Christ's Holiness, daily growing and increasing in the same: And to let us know, that none shall ever be Saints in Heaven, but such as are first Saints in Earth, Heb. 12. 10. 2 Pet. 1. 4. 2 Cor. 7. 1. 2 Thess. 1. 10.

For as much as the Point of our Union and Communion with Christ is of great Importance, and the very Foundation of all our Comfort, it is more largely to be stood upon. First therefore show how the Elect are united to Christ his Person.
They are incorporated, and made Members of the Mystical Body, whereof Christ is Head, Eph. 5. 30. which the Scripture figureth, as by other resemblances, so especially under the Similitude of Marriage, Eph. 5. 2. and the whole Book of the Canticles.)

How may we conceive of this our Marriage with Christ?
We are to conceive therein as in outward Marriage: First, The Consent of Parents and Parties. Secondly, The Manner of Conjunction.

What Consent of Parents is there in this Marriage?
Only God's Donation, who being the alone Parent of both Parties, (as in the Marriage of the first Adam, Gen. 2. 22.) giveth, first, Christ to us, (as a Savior, (John 3. 16. & 17. 6.) Secondly, Us to Christ, as a People to be saved by him, Heb. 2. 13.

What Consent of Parties is there?
First, Christ consenteth to take us for his own Spouse: Which he witnesseth especially by taking our Flesh upon him, (Heb. 2. 14.) that he might be our Emmanuel, or God with us, Mat. 1. 23. Secondly, We being drawn of God, (Joh. 6. 44.) and prepared by the Friends of the Bridegroom, (2 Cor. 11. 2.) do consent to take Christ as our Lord and Husband, (Cant. 7. 10.) as we profess by taking his Name, (Isa. 44. 5.) and Yoke, (Mat. 11. 29.) upon us.

What is the Manner of this our Conjunction?
Mystical; that is to say, Real, in respect of the things conjoined: Our very Nature, Body, and Soul being coupled to the Body and Soul of Christ, (so that we are Members of his

Body, of his Flesh, and of his Bones, Eph. 5. 30.) and thereby also to the Divine Nature, (2 Pet. 1. 4.) Yet not Corporal, but Spiritual, in regard of the Means whereby this Conjunction is wrought.

What are the means of this Spiritual Conjunction?
On Christ's part, his only Spirit, (1 Joh. 3. 24. & 4. 13. 1 Cor. 2. 12. Rom 8. 9.) given by him unto every Member of his Body, in the very moment of Regeneration, (Gal. 4. 6. 1 Joh. 3. 24. & 4. 13.) as the Soul of Spiritual Life, and Fountain of Supernatural Grace, Gal. 5. 25. 1 Cor. 15. 45. in which respect, He that is joined to the Lord, is said to be one Spirit, 1 Cor. 6. 17.

What is the Spirit of Christ?
The Holy Ghost, truly residing, (1 Cor. 3. 16.) and powerfully working in all those that are Christ's, (Rom. 5. 5.) derived unto them from him (Rom. 8. 2.) and knitting them inseparably unto him, 1 Cor. 12. 13. Eph. 2. 18. & 4. 4.

Is the Holy Ghost given to none but such as are thus joined to Christ?
The Holy Ghost is considered three ways: First, As the Author of all Excellency, even in common Gifts of Nature and Reason; as Strength and Courage, (Judg. 14. 6.) Arts and Sciences, (Exod. 31. 3.) Policy and Government, (1 Sam. 11. 6.) &c. In which sense he is given to many which never heard of Christ. Secondly, As the Author of Spiritual Gifts, (1 Cor. 12. 1, 4.) so called, because being sanctified, they are Means of Edification: As the Power of working Miracles, Healing, Languages, &c. yea a taste of the Heavenly Gift, and of the good Word of God, and of the Powers of the World to come, (Heb. 6. 4, 5.) In which sense he is given to sundry Reprobates; that are called, as hath been showed. Thirdly, As the Author of the perpetual, effectual, and vital Influence of saving Grace from Christ the Head, to every true Member of his Body, John 6. 51, 57, 63. In which sense, the World cannot receive or know him, (Joh. 14. 17.) but he is bestowed on the Elect only, (1 Pet. 1. 2.) and those truly regenerated, and converted to the Lord.

But on our part, what Means is there of this Conjunction?
Only Faith: Which yet is not of ourselves, but the Gift of God, (Eph. 2. 8.) and of all other the first and most general Effect and Instrument of the Holy Spirit of Christ, (2 Cor. 4. 13. Gal. 5. 5.) disposing and enabling us so to embrace and cleave unto him, (Eph. 3. 16, 17.) as first to receive from God by him, whatsoever Benefits and Graces, (Rom. 5. 2.) Secondly, To return to God in him all holy and thankful Obedience, Col. 2. 7. Gal. 5. 6.

Is Faith absolutely required in every one that is united unto Christ?
It is absolutely required of all those, that are of Discretion and Capacity. But in those that are not capable of Knowledge (without which there can be no Faith) as some natural Fools and Infants, which are within the Covenant; we are not to proceed further than God's Election, and the secret Operation of his Spirit, Acts 2. 39. 1 Cor. 7. 14. & 12. 13.

[17TH HEAD.]

So much of our Union with Christ's Person: What is our Communion with him?
It is our Participation with him in the Benefits, flowing from his several Offices. Whereby, as he is made to us of God, Wisdom, Righteousness, Sanctification, and Redemption, (1 Cor. 1. 30.) so we also by him, after a sort become Prophets, (Acts 2. 17, 18.) Priests, and Kings, (1 Pet. 2. 9. Rev. 5. 10.) as in the unfolding of the several Functions of our Savior Christ, hath more fully been declared. For being made one with

him, we are thereby possessed of all things that are his: (Rev. 2. 28. Col. 2. 10.) As the Wife of the Wealth of her Husband, the Branch of the Sap of the Root, (John 15. 5.) and the Members of Sense and Motion from the Head, (Eph. 4. 15, 16.) In which regard, the whole Church is also called Christ, (1 Cor. 12. 12. Gal. 3. 16.) and the several Members Christians, Acts 11. 26.

What are the main Benefits which Christians receive by their Communion with Christ.
Justification and Glorification, Rom. 8. 30. By the one whereof we have our Persons accepted, and new Relations between God and us established; by the other, our Nature reformed, and new Obedience wrought in us. Whereof this latter is but begun in this Life, and is called Sanctification; and perfected in the Life to come; which most usually hath the term of Glorification: Of which in its proper place.

What is Justification?
Justification is that Sentence of God, whereby he of his Grace, for the Righteousness of his own Son, by him imputed unto us, and through Faith apprehended by us, does free us from Sin and Death, and accept us as righteous unto Life, Rom. 8. 30, 33, 34. 1 Cor. 1. 30. Phil. 3. 9. For hereby we both have a Deliverance from the Guilt and Punishment of all our Sins; and being accounted righteous in the sight of God, by the Righteousness of our Savior Christ imputed unto us, are restored to a better Righteousness than ever we had in Adam.

I perceive your Answer needs further explaining. First, Why call you Justification a Sentence?
That thereby we may be informed, that the word [to justify] does not in this place signify to make Just, by infusing a perfect Righteousness into our Natures; (that comes under the Head of Sanctification begun here in this Life, which being finished, is Glorification in Heaven): But here the word signifieth to pronounce Just, to quit and discharge from Guilt and Punishment: And so it is a Judicial Sentence opposed to Condemnation. Rom. 8. 34, 35. Who shall lay any thing (saith Paul) to the charge of God's Elect? It is God that justifieth; who shall condemn? Now as to condemn, is not the putting any evil into the nature of the Party condemned, but the pronouncing of his Person guilty, and the binding him over unto Punishment: So Justifying is the Judges pronouncing the Law to be satisfied, and the Man discharged and quitted from Guilt and Judgment. Thus God imputing the Righteousness of Christ to a Sinner, does not account his Sins unto him; but interests him in a state of as full and perfect Freedom and Acceptance; as if he had never sinned, or had himself fully satisfied. For though there is a Power purging the Corruption of Sin, which followeth upon Justification; yet it is carefully to be distinguished from it: As we shall further show hereafter.

This for the Name of Justification: But now for the thing it self; what is the matter first of our Justification?
The matter of that Justification, or that Righteousness whereby a Sinner stands justified in God's sight, is not any Righteousness inherent in his own Person, and performed by him, but a perfect Righteousness inherent in Christ, and performed for him.

What Righteousness of Christ is it, whereby a Sinner is justified?
Not the essential Righteousness of his Divine Nature: But, First, The absolute Integrity of our human Nature, which in him our Head, was without all guile, Heb. 7. 26. Secondly, The perfect Obedience which in that human Nature of ours, he performed unto the whole Law of God; but by doing whatsoever was required of us, (Mat. 3. 15.) and by suffering whatsoever was deserved by our sins, (1 Pet. 2. 24.) For he was made Sin, and a Curse for us, that we might be made the Righteousness of God in him, 2 Cor. 5. 21.

What is the Form, or Being, Cause of our Justification, and that which makes this Righteousness so really ours, that it does justify us?
The gracious Imputation of God the Father, accounting his Sons Righteousness unto the Sinner, and by that accounting, making it his to all effects, as if he himself had performed it.

But how can Christ's Righteousness be accounted ours? Is it not as absurd to say that we are justified by Christ's Righteousness, as that a Man should be fed with that Meat another eats? Or be warmed with the Clothes another weareth? Or be in Life and Health with the Life and Health of another?
No doubtless: Because this Righteousness is in Christ, not as in a Person severed from us, but as in the Head of our common Nature, the second Adam: From whom therefore it is communicated unto all, who being united as Members unto him, do lay claim thereunto, and apply it unto themselves, Rom. 5. 19. & 10. 4. For if the sin of Adam, being a Man, was of force to condemn us all, because we were in his Loins, he being the Head of our common Nature: Why then should it seem strange, that the Righteousness of our Savior Christ, both God and Man, should be available to justify those that are interested in him? Especially considering that we have a more strict Conjunction in the Spirit with him, than ever we had in Nature with Adam. And although it be not fit to measure Heavenly Things by the Yard of Reason; yet it is not unreasonable, that a Man owing a Thousand Pounds, and not being able of himself to discharge it, his Creditor may be satisfied by one of his Friends.

If Christ have paid our Debt, how then are we freely justified by Grace?
It is both of Grace that Christ is given unto us, and also that his Righteousness apprehended by Faith is accounted ours. It is true that the Justification of a sinner, considering the case as it is between the Father and Christ, no Man dare call it free; (no, the Price of our Redemption was the deepest purchase that the World ever heard of) but whatever it cost Christ, it cost us nothing: And so to us it is freely of Grace from Christ. Yea, and to us, it is freely Grace from God the Father too. Not because he acquits us without a full Satisfaction to his Justice, or accepts that for perfect Righteousness, which is not perfect Righteousness: But because he receives full Satisfaction from the hands of a Surety, and that Surety being his own Son; when as he might have challenged the uttermost Farthing at our hands, which were the Principals; and then there had been no Possibility for us to have been delivered.

What gather you from this Doctrine of Justification by CHRIST's Righteousness?
1. To condemn the proud Opinion of Papists, who seek Justification by their own Works and Righteousness, inherent in themselves: Whereas though being accepted, we must in Thankfulness do all we can for God; yet when all is done, we must acknowledge ourselves unprofitable Servants: The only matter of our Joy and Triumph both in Life and Death, must be the Imputation of Christ's Righteousness. Not our Persons, nor the best Actions of the Holiest Men, dare appear in God's Presence, but in his Name and Merit who consecrates all, the Lord Jesus.

2. We may here take notice, that there is no comfort to a Christian Soul, like that which floweth from this Well of Salvation, this sweet Doctrine of Justification. 1. Here we have Assurance of the Sufficiency of our Redemption. That Soul must be thoroughly acquitted, that is stated in such a Righteousness; that Debt must be fully discharged, that hath such a Price laid down for it: Our sins, though never so great, cannot weigh down his Righteousness and Merit, Rom. 8. 33. and God having accepted his Son's Righteousness for us, will not hold us any longer Trespassers, but he disables his own Justice from making any further demand. 2. Hence there is nothing comes upon the

Saints from God's Revenging Justice, but all our Corrections are Medicinal from God's Fatherly Love; to purge that sin out of our Nature, which he hath already pardoned to our Persons. 3. Lastly, This Doctrine may be great Comfort to weak Christians in the midst of their troublesome Imperfections, and Sense of their weak measures of Sanctification: To consider that the Righteousness that is inherent in themselves, is not the matter of their Justification, or that which must appear before God's Presence to be pleaded. The Righteousness of Christ is complete and perfect; that is our main Joy and Crown of rejoicing to be found in Christ, not having our own Righteousness, but that which is in him, and made ours by God's gracious Account.

But how is this great Benefit of Justification applied unto us, and apprehended by us?

This is done on our part by Faith alone: And that not considered as a Virtue inherent in us, working by Love; but only as an Instrument or Hand of the Soul stretched forth, to lay hold on the Lord our Righteousness, Rom. 5. 1. & 10. 10. Jer. 23. 6. So that Faith justifieth only Relatively, in respect of the Object which it fasteneth on; to wit, the Righteousness of Christ, by which we are justified: Faith being only the Instrument to convey so great a Benefit unto the Soul, as the hand of the Beggar receives the Alms.

Forasmuch as it standeth us much in hand, to know what this Faith is, whereby we have profit by Christ's Redemption: Declare how many ways the Word Faith, is taken in the Scriptures?

Sometimes it is taken for true and faithful dealing between Man and Man, both in Word and Deed; called Fidelity or Faithfulness: (as Mat. 23. 23. Acts 2. 10. 1 Tim. 5. 12. 1 Pet. 5. 12.) But of that Faith we are not here to speak. Sometimes it is taken for the Faith (or Fidelity) of God towards Man: But that also is besides our purpose. Here we are to entreat of Man's Faith toward God: And that word Faith is also taken two ways.

1. For the Object to be apprehended, or things to be believed; even the whole Doctrine of Faith, or Points of Religion to be believed: As Acts 6. 7. & 13. 8. Rom. 1. 5. & 3. 31. & 12. 3, 6. & 16. 26. Gal. 3. 2, 5, 23. 1 Tim. 1. 2. & 4. 1. Jude vers. 3.

2. For the Action apprehending, or believing the same, viz. That Work of God in Man, whereby he giveth Assent or Credence to God in his Word; yea, and applieth that which any way concerneth him in particular, how otherwise general soever it be: (as Rom. 10. 17, &c.) And this Faith is set out by two Names, Heb. 11. 1. The Substance of things hoped for, and the evidence of things not seen: By the first meaning, That whereas God in his Word, hath made Promise of things which are not presently enjoyed, but only hoped for; they being not in Esse, but in Posse: Yet Faith does after a sort, give them a present subsisting or being, as if they were in Esse; by the second meaning, that whereas many of the Promises are of things so far out of the reach of Man, that they are both invisible to the Eye, and unreasonable, or impossible to the Sense or Understanding of Man: Yet Faith is the very Evidence of them, and that which does so demonstrate them unto us, that by it (as through a Prospective Glass) we as clearly discern them, as if they were even at hand.

How many kinds of Faith be there?

Although there be but one true saving Faith, (Eph. 4. 5.) yet of Faith there are two sorts. 1. Such as is common to all; which all Men have, or may have. 2. That which no Man hath, or can have, but the Elect: It being proper to them, 2 Thes. 3. 2. Rom. 11. 32. Tit. 1. 1. 2 Cor. 13. 5.

How many sorts be there of the common Faith?
Two: Ordinary, and Extraordinary. And of the Ordinary, two also: That which we call Historical, and that we call Temporary Faith.

What is an Historical Faith?
It is a Knowledge and Persuasion of the Truth of God's Word, concerning the Letter and Story of it: As that there is one only God, and in the God head a Trinity in Unity; that Jesus Christ is the Savior of the World, &c.

What is a Temporary Faith?
It is a joyful entertaining of the Promises of the Gospel, with some seeming Confidence: Which yet is but vanishing, uncertain, and not rooted; lasteth but for a time, and then comes to nothing, Mat. 13. 20, 21. Luke 18. 3, 14.

What is that common Faith which you call Extraordinary?
It is the Faith of Miracles: Which is the cleaving to some special and singular Promise; either for the doing of some extraordinary Effect, or for the receiving of some outward Good, after an extraordinary manner, 1 Cor. 13. 2. Mat. 21. 2. & 7. 22. Mark 9. 3. Acts 14. 9. Luke 17. 19.

By this kind of Faith, Judas might work Miracles as well as the other Disciples; and by this Faith many might be healed by our Savior in their Bodies, who were not healed in their Souls.

What now is true saving Faith, which none have but the Elect; it being proper to them?
It is such a firm Assent of the Mind to the Truth of the Word, as flows into the Heart, and causeth the Soul to embrace it as Good, and to build its Eternal Happiness on it.

What is that which you make the Object of saving Faith?
The general Object of true saving Faith, is the whole Truth of God revealed: But the special Object of Faith as it justifieth, is the Promise of Remission of sins by the Lord Jesus. For as the Israelites, by the same Eyes by which they looked upon the Brazen Serpent, they saw other things; but they were not healed by looking upon any thing else, but only the Brazen Serpent: So, though by the same Faith whereby I cleave to Christ for Remission of Sins, I believe every Truth revealed; yet I am not justified by believing any Truth but the Promise of Grace in the Gospel.

Open the Nature of this saving and justifying Faith somewhat more fully.
Justifying Faith may be considered two ways; either as God works it in Man's Heart, or else as Man's Heart works by it towards God again. For first God enables Man to believe; and then he believes by God's enabling.

In the first respect, Faith is said to be God's Gift, Ephes. 2. 8. Phil. 1. 29. And it is the Greatness of God's Power, that raiseth Man's Heart unto it, Ephes. 1. 19. In the second respect, Man is said to believe, Rom. 10. 10. and to come to Christ. But he believes by God's enabling him to believe; and he comes by God's causing him to come, John 6. 44. No Man can come unto me except the Father draw him, saith our Savior.

What does God work in Man when he gives him Faith?
First, He enlightneth the Understanding, to see the Truth and Preciousness of the rich Offers of Grace in the Lord Jesus, 1 Cor. 2. 11, 12, 14. John 1. 5. & 12. 40. & 6. 45. Mat. 16. 17. Acts 26. 18.

Secondly, He enables the Will to embrace them, and inclines all the desires of the Soul after them, and rests and builds eternal Comfort on them. The things of God, as they are Foolishness to Man's Natural Judgment; so they are Enmity to his Natural Will. And therefore when God gives Faith, he gives a new Light to the Understanding, and new Motions and Inclinations to the Heart. As the Covenant of Grace is; I will give them a new Heart, Ezek. 36. 26. It must be a mighty Power to turn the Heart of Man up side down, and cause him to pitch all the desires of the Soul upon a supernatural Object, John 6. 44.

What gather we from hence?
First, The Folly and Wickedness of the Popish Doctors, who persuade the Multitude to rest in a blind Faith, which they call implicit and folded up; telling them, that it is enough for them to believe as the Church believes, though they know not what the Church believes, nor who the Church is: Whereas the Scripture teacheth us, that Faith comes by hearing; that is, by hearing the blessed Promises of Grace offered to the People, Rom. 10. 14, 17. Faith does not consist in Darkness and Ignorance; but Knowledge of the Ingredients of it, John 12. 39. and therefore sometimes put for it, John 17. 3. Isa. 53. 11. Where God does work Faith, there he gives a saving Light to the Understanding, though in divers measures and degrees. As there are weak measures of Faith, so weak measures of Knowledge and Apprehensions in saving Mysteries: But no Man can build upon God's gracious Word and Promise, for the truth and reality of what he speaks, without he know what he speaks.

Secondly, We may here learn that Faith does not consist only in the Understanding, or only in the Will, but in the whole Soul: The whole intelligent Nature is the Seat of Faith. And therefore either Faith is not a supernatural Gift of God, or else they speak ungraciously of God's Grace in the Work of Faith, who attribute no more to God than the Renovation of Man's Understanding, and revealing those things to him, which by Nature he could not see; leaving the Action of consenting and embracing by Faith the things revealed to Man's Free will: So sharing the Business of Believing between God and Man; the enlightening of the Understanding shall be Gods, but the inclining of the Will must be a Man's own, any further than it may be invited by Moral Persuasion. But the Scripture every where shows Faith to be such a transcendent and supernatural Gift, as far exceeds all natural Power to produce to reach unto. God does all in this high Business by his powerful Spirit and supernatural Grace.

But how then is it said, That Man believeth, Man receiveth Christ, Man comes unto him?
These Phrases, and the like, show what Man does when Faith is wrought in him, how his Soul acts by it, and exerciseth this excellent Habit received. And it is thus: 1. By God's teaching him, he understands, by God's enlightening his Mind he sees the excellency of the Lord Jesus, and firmly assents unto the Word of Grace as true; that indeed Christ is the only Blessed Savior; and that all the Promises of God in him are Yea and Amen. 2. By God's changing and enabling his Will he wills; by God's sanctifying his Affections he loves and embraceth; by God's printing and sealing them on his Heart, he possesseth and closeth with Christ, and the precious Promises of Mercy in him, and embraceth the Tenure of the Gospel as the sweetest and happiest Tidings that ever sounded in his Ears, and entertains it with the best Welcomes of his dear Heart, and placeth his Eternal Happiness on this Rock of Salvation.

Put now all these together.
They all show that Faith is nothing else but a supernatural Action and Work of GOD in Man, whereby Man's Heart, that is, all the Powers of Man's Soul move as they are first moved by GOD. So that the Action of Man in believing, is nothing but his knowing of

Heavenly Things by God's revealing them, and causing him to know them; his willing them, and embracing them by God's enabling him to will and embrace them. Thus the motion of Man's Heart to Christ, being moved by God, is called Man's believing with the Heart: Even as a Wheel which of it self cannot move, yet being moved by a higher Wheel does move; which motion, though it be but one, yet is said to be the motion of two; that is, of the Mover, and of the thing moved.

It seems then that justifying Faith consists in these two things, viz. in having a mind to know Christ, and a will to rest upon him.
Yes: Whosoever sees so much Excellency in Christ, that thereby he is drawn to embrace him as the only Rock of Salvation, that Man truly believes to Justification.

But is it not necessary to Justification, to be assured that my Sins are pardoned, and that I am justified?
No: That is no Act of Faith as it justifieth, but an effect and fruit that followeth after Justification. For no Man is justified by believing that he is justified; for he must be justified before he can believe it: And no Man is pardoned by believing that he is pardoned; for he must be pardoned before he can believe it. But Faith as it justifieth, is a resting upon Christ to obtain pardon, the acknowledging him to be the only Savior, and the hanging upon him for Salvation, Mat. 16. 16. John 20. 31. Acts 8. 37. Rom. 10. 9. 1 John 4. 15. & 5. 1, 5.

It is the direct Act of Faith that justifieth; that whereby I do believe: It is the reflect Act of Faith that assures; that whereby I know I do believe, and it comes by way of Argumentation thus.

Maj. Whosoever relieth upon Christ the Savior of the World for Justification and Pardon; the Word of God saith, that he by so doing is actually justified and pardoned.

Min. But I do truly rely upon Christ for Justification and Pardon.

Concl. Therefore I undoubtedly believe that I am justified and pardoned.
But many times both the former Propositions may be granted to be true, and yet a weak Christian want strength to draw the Conclusion. For it is one thing to believe, and another thing to believe that I do believe: It is one thing for a Man to have his Salvation certain, and another thing to be certain that it is certain.

How then does the Soul reach after Christ in the Act of Justifying?
Even as a Man fallen into a River, and like to be drowned, as he is carried down with the Flood, espies the Bough of a Tree hanging over the River, which he catches at, and clings unto with all his might to save him; and seeing no other way of succor but that, ventures his Life upon it: This Man so soon as he had fastened upon this Bough is in a safe Condition, though all Troubles, Fears, and Terrors, are not presently out of his Mind, until he comes to himself, and sees himself quite out of Danger; then he is sure he is safe, but he was safe before he was sure. Even so it is with a Believer; Faith is but the espying of Christ as the only means to save, and the reaching out of the Heart to lay hold upon him. God hath spoke the Word, and made the Promise in his Son: I believe him to be the only Savior, and remit my Soul to him to be saved by his Mediation. So soon as the Soul can do this, God imputeth the Righteousness of his Son unto it, and it is actually justified in the Court of Heaven, though it is not presently quieted and pacified in the Court of Conscience: That is done afterwards, in some sooner, in some later, by the Fruits and Effects of Justification.

Eighteenth Head

[18TH HEAD.]

What are the Concomitants of Justification?
Reconciliation, and Adoption, Rom. 5. 1. John 1. 12.

What is Reconciliation?
It is that Grace, whereby we that were Enemies to God are made Friends, (Rom. 5. 10.) we that were Rebels are received into Favor; we that were far off, and Aliens from God, are now brought near through CHRIST, Eph. 2. 12, 13. & 18. 19. 1 John 13. Heb. 12. 22. 23.

What is Adoption?
Adoption is the Power and Privilege to be the Sons of God, (John 1. 12. Eph. 1. 5) derived unto us from Christ, who being the Eternal Son of God, became by Incarnation our Brother, that by him GOD might bring many Sons and Daughters unto Glory, Heb. 2. 10.

What are the Benefits that flow to us from our Adoption?
Some are privative Immunities, and freedom from many Grievances. As,

1. We are freed from the Slavery of Sin, Rom. 6. 14.

2. From Condemnation, Rom. 8. 1.

3. From all slavish Fears and Terrors, Rom. 8. 15. We have not received the Spirit of Bondage to fear again, but the Spirit of Adoption. 4. From the Law, not Ceremonial only, (Gal. 5. 1.) but Moral: Freed, I mean, from the Curse of it, freed from the Condemning Power of it, freed from the Coaction and Compulsion of it, freed from the rigorous Exaction and inexorable Demands of it, as it is a Covenant of Works: But not freed from the Doctrine of Holiness contained [in] it. The Justified and Adopted are every way freed from the Law, as it was an Enemy and against us, Luke 1. but not freed as it is our Guide and Director, containing the Rule of God's Holy Will. Our Sonship does not free us from Service, but from Slavery; not from Holiness, but to Holiness. There is a free Service, which benefits the Condition of a Son: God's Service is perfect Freedom.

Some are positive Dignities. As, 1. Free Access to the Throne of Grace, that we may come to God in Prayer as to a Father, Gal. 4. 6. Rom. 8. 15. 2. We have an Interest in God's particular and special Providence, 2 Cor. 6. ult. Rom. 8. 28. 3. We by our Adoption have a free and sanctified use of all God's Creatures restored; the right unto which we forfeited in Adam. For no Man hath any spiritual right to any thing, or a sanctified use of God's Creatures until he be in Covenant with God in Christ, and made a Son and Heir with him, and then all things are his, 1 Cor. 3. 21. Rom. 8. 32. 4. From Adoption flows all Christian Joy; which is called the Joy in the Holy Ghost, Rom. 14. 17. unspeakable and glorious, 1 Pet. 1. 8, 9. Rom. 5. 2. For the Spirit of Adoption is, first, a Witness, Rom. 8. 16. Secondly, A Seal, Eph. 4. 30. Thirdly, The Pledge and Earnest of our Inheritance, Eph. 1. 14. settling a holy Security in the Soul, whereby it rejoiceth even in Affliction in hope of Glory.

Do the justified Children of God always then rejoice?
Joy considered as a delightful apprehension of the Favor of God gladding the Heart, though it ought continually to be labored for, (Phil. 4. 4.) and preserved; yet it may be at times not only darkened and daunted, but for a time even lost, and to be restored, Psal. 51. 12. Yet it is, as all Spiritual Gifts of God, perpetual and without repentance: If we regard, First, The Matter of Rejoicing; which is God's unchangeable Love and

Grace, Mal. 3. 6. Second, The Causes and Fountains of Joy in the Regenerate; which are the never-failing Graces of Faith, (Luke 22. 32.) Hope, (Rom. 5. 5.) and Love towards God in Christ, 1 Cor. 8. Third, The Valuation (even in the deepest dismay) of our part and hope in Christ above the Pleasures of Ten thousand Worlds. Fourth, The pretence and claim of a faithful Heart, promising and challenging unto it self a comfortable Harvest of Joy for the present Seed time of Sorrow, Psal. 42. 5; 57. 11; 126. 5.

[19TH HEAD.]

So much of the first main Benefit which Christians receive by their Communion with Christ, viz. Justification. Now what is the second Benefit which is called Glorification and Sanctification?
It is the renewing of our Nature according to the Image of God, in Righteousness and true Holiness: Which is but begun in this Life, and is called Sanctification; and perfected in the Life to come, which therefore is most strictly called Glorification.

How far forth is our Nature renewed in this Life by Sanctification?
This renewing is of our whole Nature, 1 Thess. 5. 23. Rom. 12. 2. the Understanding being enlightened, the Will rectified, the Affections regulated, the outward Man reformed; but not wholly in this Life. And this is done by the powerful Operation of the Spirit of God; who having begun a good Work in us, will perfect it unto the Day of the Lord, Psal. 51. 10. Ezek. 36. 26.

What are the Parts of our Sanctification?
Two: Answerable to the two powerful Means whereby they are wrought. First, Mortification, or dying unto Sin, and thereby freedom from the Dominion thereof by the Death of Christ, Rom. 6. 6, 7. Secondly, Vivification, or quickening unto the newness of Life, by the Power of the Resurrection of Christ; in regard whereof it is also called our first Resurrection, Rev. 20. 6.

How does Sanctification differ from the former Grace of Justification?
In many main and material Differences: As,

1. In the Order; not of time, wherein they go together, (Rom. 8. 30.) nor of Knowledge and Apprehension, wherein this latter hath precedence, (1 Cor. 6. 11.) but of Nature, wherein the former is the ground of this latter, 2 Cor. 7. 1. Secondly, In the Subject: The Righteousness whereby we are justified being inherent in Christ for us; but this of Sanctification in ourselves from him, Rom. 8. 10. Thirdly, In the Cause: Our Justification following from the Merit; our Sanctification from the Efficacy of the Death and Life of Christ, Eph. 1. 19. & 2. 5. Fourthly, In the Instrument. Faith, which in Justification is only as an Hand receiving, in Sanctification is a co working Virtue, Acts 15. 19. Gal. 5. 6. Fifthly, In the Measure: Justification being in all Believers, and at all times alike; but Sanctification wrought differently and by degrees, 2 Cor. 3. 18. 2. Pet. 3. 18. Sixthly, In the end: Which being in both Eternal Life, (Rom 6. 23.) yet the one is among the Causes of Reigning, the other only as the High-way unto the Kingdom.

What is the Rule and Square of our Sanctification?
The whole Word of God, (John 17. 17.) Psal. 119. 9.) as containing that Will of his, (Rom. 12. 2.) which is even our Sanctification, 1 Thess. 4. 3. &c.

Nineteenth Head

How do you prove, that God's Word is such a Rule?
First, By express warrant of Scripture. 2 Tim. 3. 14, 17. Second, By the resemblances or things whereunto it is compared: As to the Way we are to walk in, (Jer. 6. 16. Mark 12. 14. Acts 18. 24, 25.) to a Light and a Lantern in a dark place, to guide our feet into the way of Peace, Psal. 119. 105. Prov. 6. 23. 2 Pet. 1. 19, 20. Luke 1. 77, 79.) to a Glass, (Jam. 1. 25.) to a Rule, Line, Square, Measure, and Balance, whereby must be framed, ordered, measured, and pondered, Isa. 28. 17. Gal. 6. 16. Phil. 3. 16. Third, Because they only are commended for a holy and righteous Life, who have framed it according to the Word, Luke 1. 6. and all others secluded, Isa. 8. 19, 20, Mat. 22. 29. Fourth, Because nothing can be counted holy and righteous, which God does not so account, and that in his Word. For as he only is righteous, and maketh this or that to be holy and righteous: So is Word only showeth us what that is which he so accounteth. And therefore it is called his Holy Word, Holy Scriptures, Righteous Laws, &c. Deut. 4. 8. 2 Tim. 3. 15, 16.

What mean you here by the whole Word of God?
Both the Law and the Gospel, the Old Testament and the New, Job 22. 22. John 17. 17.

How is the Gospel a Rule of Obedience, being the Rule of Faith?
As the Law requireth Obedience, (Jam. 2. 8.) so the Gospel directeth the Faithful how to perform it, (1 Tim. 1. 9, 10, 11. Eph. 4. 20, 21.) only with difference.

1. Of the Manner: The Law propounding God to be worshipped of us in himself, as our Creator; the Gospel in Christ, as our Savior, John. 5. 23. & 14. 1.

2. Of the End: The Law requiring all Duties, as for the procurement of our own Salvation; the Gospel in way of thankfulness for Salvation in Christ already bestowed, 1 Thess. 5. 18.

3. Of the Effect: The Law, (like Pharaoh, that required Brick, but allowed no Straw) demanding Obedience, but vouchsafing no Assistance; (supposing Man as in the state of Creation:) the Gospel both offering, and conferring to the Regenerate, that which it requireth, Rom. 10. 5, 6, 8. for it both requireth and conferreth Faith unto the Elect, and that not only as a Hand to lay hold on Christ, but also as a chief Virtue, working by Love in all parts of Obedience. Without which even the Gospel is Law, that is, a killing Letter (2 Cor. 3. 6.) to the Unregenerate; and with which the Law becometh as it were the Gospel to the Regenerate; even a Law of Liberty, Jam. 1. 25. & 2. 12. For as the Law saveth us not without the Gospel, so the Gospel saveth us not without the Law.

Does not the Gospel add other Precepts or Counsels to those of the Law?
Not any other, in substance of Action, but only reneweth and enforceth those of the Law, (1 John 2. 7, 8.) and specifieth some Duties, as of Faith in the Messiah, of the Sacraments, &c. which have their general ground from the Law. As for those that are propounded in form of Counsel, and do concern things indifferent, they are not therefore arbitrary Courses (Rev. 3. 18.) of higher perfection, much less meritorious of greater Glory: But as they are applied with due Circumstances, necessary Precepts, referred to some one or other Commandment of the Law; the rejecting whereof excludeth from the Kingdom of God, Mat. 19. 23.

What is that Law, which with the Direction of the Gospel, is the Rule of Sanctification?
The Moral Law, or Law of Nature, engraven by God himself first in the Heart of Man in his Creation, after in Tables of Stone (Deut. 10. 4.) in the days of Moses; and so published and committed unto the Church for all Ages, as the Royal Law for Obedience to God our King, Jam. 2. 8.

Why did God write that Law in Tables of Stone?
Partly to signify the perpetual use and continuance of them to the end of the World; partly to show the stony hardness of our Hearts, in which this Law was to be written, and to declare how hard it is to bring us to Obedience of them.

Why did none but God write this Law in Tables of Stone?
Because none but God can write his Law in our Hearts.

How was this Law delivered?
To show the Gloriousness of it, God delivered it in Fire. For the Mountain burned, the Trumpet sounded, the People fled, and Moses himself trembled.

What did this signify to them, and teach us?
1. That without Christ the Law is but Death. 2. That we should be very careful to perform Obedience to the same.

Did God give no other Law but the Moral Law only?
Yes, he added also the Ceremonial and Judicial Laws, as special Explications and Applications of the Law Moral, unto that present Church and People the Israelites, Rom. 9. 4.

What was the Ceremonial Law?
That Law which did set down Orders for Direction in Rites of outward Worship, shadowing the Grace of the Gospel, Heb. 10. 1. &c.

Are we bound to keep and observe those Laws?
No. For the Substance being now exhibited, those Shadows are utterly abolished by the Death of Christ; and therefore the use of them now would be a kind of Denial of his Death.

What call you the Judicial Law?
That wherein God appointed a Form of Politic and Civil Government of the Commonwealth of the Jews: Which therefore is ceased with the Dissolution of that State, for which it was ordained; saving only in the common Equity.

Is this Law utterly revoked and abolished by Christ?
No. For he came not to overturn any good Government of the Commonwealth; much less that which was appointed by God himself.

May not Christian Magistrates then swerve any thing from those Laws of Government, which were set down by Moses?
In some Circumstances they may: But in the general Equity and Substance they may not.

What Judicial Laws are immutably to be observed now of Christian Magistrates?
Those which have Reasons annexed unto them, and especially those wherein God hath appointed Death for the Punishment of heinous Offences.

What is the Moral Law?
That which commandeth the Perfection of Godliness and Righteousness; and directeth us in our Duties to God and Man, Deut. 5. 32. & 12. 32.

Are we not delivered from this Law by the means of Christ?
From the Burden of the Law exacting in our own Persons perfect Obedience, and from the Curse of that Law due unto Disobedience, we are delivered by Christ, Gal. 3. 10, 11, 12, 13. But from the Commandment as a Rule of Life, we are not freed, (James 2. 8.)

but contrariwise are inclined and disposed by his free Spirit, to the willing Obedience thereof, Psal. 51. 12. & 119. 32, 45. 1 John 5. 3.

To what end serveth the Law?
First, It is a Glass, to discover our Filthiness, and to show us our Sins, and the Punishment thereof: That thereby we may be driven unto Christ, to be purged by him, (Gal. 3. 24. Rom. 3. 20, 27.) For it layeth open all the Parts of our Misery, both Sinfulness, Accursedness, and Impotency or Unableness to relieve ourselves: So whipping and chasing us to Christ, that in him we may find Deliverance. Secondly, When we are come to Christ, and feel ourselves saved by him, it is a Guide to direct us in the way he have to walk in all our Life after, Mat. 5. 17. Luke 1. 6. Deut. 6. 6. For after the Law hath brought us to Christ, the feeling of the Love of God in him, maketh us to strive towards the Obedience of it: And then it is a Rule to direct us how to behave ourselves in all things that we do; teaching us how we are to live, in such sort, as whosoever walketh not accordingly cannot be saved.

What further use hath the Law in the Regenerate?
First, As a Light it directeth us. For the World being a dark Wilderness, and we naturally blind; we are in continual danger of falling, unless our steps be guided by the Lamp of the Law, Psal. 119. 105. Secondly, As a prick it inciteth us to Obedience; because God commandeth them. Thirdly, It frameth us to Humility; whilst by it we understand that we are far from fulfilling it.

What gather you of this?
First, What great reason there is why we should be well acquainted with the Law of God, seeing it is of so great use. Secondly, That every one should have a Warrant of all his doings out of this Law of God; whereby all the Creatures are sanctified for Man's use.

What is the contrary Vice?
Ignorance, whereof Christ saith, that the Blind fall into the Ditch, Mat. 15. 14.

So much of the use of Law: What is required for our profiting therein?
In the first place it is required, that we have the right Understanding of the Law: Without which it is impossible to reap any of the former Fruits; how can a Man acknowledge the Breach of that Law which he knoweth not? Or how can he serve God in the endeavour of the Performance of it, unless he understand his Master's Will?

What Rules are principally to be observed for the understanding and right interpreting of the Law?
Three especially. Rule 1: The Law is Spiritual. Rule 2: That the Law is perfect. Rule 3: In every Commandment there is a Synecdoche.

What is the first?
That the Law is Spiritual, reaching to the Soul and all the Powers thereof: And charging as well the Heart and Thoughts, as the outward Man, Rom. 7. 14. Deut. 6. 5. Mat. 22. 37. Mark 12. 30. Luk. 10. 27.

How does the Law charge all the Powers of the Soul?
It chargeth the Understanding to know every Duty, even all the Will of God. It chargeth the Judgment to discern between Good and Evil; and between two good things, which is the better. It chargeth the Memory to retain. It charges the Will to choose the better, and leave the worse. It charges the Affections to love things to be loved, and to hate things to be hated.

Does the Law require these alike of all?
No; but according to the Sex, growth in Age, and difference of Calling: as more of a Man than of a Woman, of a young Man than of a Child, of a public Person than of a private Man.

What is the second Rule?
That the Law is perfect, Psal. 19. 7. not only binding the Soul, but also the whole Soul, to discharge all the several Functions of her Faculties, perfectly. As the Understanding, to know the Will of God perfectly; the Judgment, to discern perfectly betwixt Good and Evil; the Memory, to retain and remember all perfectly; the Will, to choose the Good and leave the Evil perfectly; the Affections, to love the one, and hate the other perfectly. So in condemning Evil, it condemneth all Evil; and in commanding Good, it commandeth all Good; charging Man to practice the Good, and refuse the Evil perfectly: And that not only as it was commanded Adam before his Fall, but also according to the several times before, in, and after the Law.

What is the third?
That in every Commandment there is a borrowed Speech, whereby more is commanded or forbidden than is named.

What special Rules are comprehended under the third?
These three following. 1. Whatsoever the Law commandeth, it forbiddeth the contrary; and whatsoever it forbiddeth, it commandeth the contrary, Mat. 5. 21. 23, 24, 25. So where any Duty is enjoined, as in the affirmative Commandments, there we must understand the contrary Sin to be forbidden, (Mat. 4. 10. 1 Cor. 15. 34.) and where any Sin is forbidden, as in the Negative, there must we know the contrary Duty is required, Ephes. 4. 18.

2. Whatsoever the Law commandeth or forbiddeth in one kind, it commandeth or forbiddeth all the same kind, and all the degrees thereof. For under one kind manifest and plain are understood all things of like sort: And under one main Duty or Crime expressed, all degrees of Good or Evil in the same kind, are either commanded, or forbidden, Mat. 5. 21, 22. &c. 1 John 3. 15.

3. Whatsoever the Law commandeth or forbiddeth, it commandeth or forbiddeth the Causes thereof, and all the Means whereby that thing is done or brought to pass: So that with the thing forbidden, or the Duty enjoined, all Occasions and Provocations or Furtherances thereto, are consequently condemned or required, 1 Thess. 5. 22 Heb. 10. 24, 25. Mat. 5. 27, 30.

Besides the true Knowledge, what is further required for a profitable Course in the Law?
First, Remembrance: Without which our Knowledge is nothing, as that which is poured into a riven Vessel. And therefore in the fourth Commandment God using this word Remember, (to teach us how deeply Negligence and Forgetfulness of that Commandment is rooted in our Nature) does in one Commandment show what Remembrance we should have of all, and what Forgetfulness is (though not alike) in all. Secondly, Judgment to take heed that we do nothing rashly, and suddenly, but ever to examine our ways. Thirdly, The Will and Affections must be formed to an Obedience of the Commandments. Whereto also it may help to consider that God propoundeth the Ten Commandments in the second Person of the singular Number; saying, Thou shalt not, &c.

Why are the Commandments uttered in this sort; rather than by You, or No Man, or Every Man, &c.
First, Because God being without Partiality, speaketh to all Men alike; as well the Rich as Poor, High as Low. Secondly, Because no Man should put the Commandments of God from himself, as though they did not concern him: But every particular Man should apply them to himself, as well as if God had spoken to him by Name.

What gather you of this?
That God wisely preventeth a common abuse amongst Men, which is to esteem that which is spoken unto all Men, to be (as it were) spoken to none. As you shall have it common amongst Men to say and confess, that God is just and merciful, and that he commandeth this, and forbiddeth that: And yet they usually so behave themselves, that they shift the matter to the general, as if it did no thing belong unto them in particular; and as if they notwithstanding might live as they list. And therefore every Man is to judge and esteem that God speaketh in the Law to him in particular; and is accordingly to be affected therewith.

That this Obedience may be more willing and cheerful; what is further to be thought upon?
We must set before our Eyes God's Benefits bestowed upon us; as the Lord did before the Israelites, in the Preface to the Ten Commandments.

What arenefits ought we chiefly to call to Mind?
First, Those which God does generally bestow upon all his Children; as out Election, Creation, Redemption, Vocation, Justification, Sanctification, continual Preservation: And then particularly such Blessings as God hath severally bestowed upon every one of us.

Are not the Judgments of God also to be thought upon for furtherance to this Obedience?
Yes verily; to make us fear to offend in our ways, Exod. 20. 5, 7. Psalm 119. 120

Remaineth there yet any more?
Good Company; which with David we must cleave unto, (Psal. 119. 63. Prov. 13. 20.) not the noblest or of greatest account, but the godliest. For if we will avoid such a Sin, we must avoid all Company that does delight therein; which is no less dangerous than good Company is profitable.

What gather you of this?
That whosoever maketh no choice of Company, maketh no Conscience of Sin: As those that dare keep Company familiarly with Papists, and profane Persons, thinking that they may keep their Conscience to themselves.

[20TH HEAD.]

Hitherto of the helps both of the Knowledge and Practice. In what part of the Scripture is the Moral Law of God contained?
It is handled at large throughout the whole Scripture: But is summarily contrived first into Ten Words or Ten Commandments, Exod. 20. (Deut. 4. 13. & 10. 4.) and then into Two, (Mat. 22. 37, 40. Luke 10. 27.) comprehending the Sum of the whole Law. Which are now to be spoken of.

Why hath God given Ten Commandments and no more? Deut. 5. 22.
First, That no Man should either add any thing to, or take any thing from the Laws of God. Secondly, That we might be left without excuse, if we learned them not; seeing they be but Ten, and no more.

How are these Ten Commandments propounded?
Sometime Affirmatively, as the fourth and fifth; others Negatively, as all the rest: Some with Reasons annexed, as the five first; some without, as the five last; and all of them in the time to come, and in the second Person singular.

Why they are laid down in the second Person singular, you have showed before: And why some have Reasons added unto them, we shall hear a little after. Declare now, why God hath propounded all the Commandments in the time to come; saying, Thou shalt not, &c.
Because it is not enough for us, that we have kept the Commandments of God heretofore, except we continue in keeping of them to the end of our Lives.

Why are there more of the Commandments Negative, telling us what we should not do; then Affirmative, telling us what we should do? All of them, except two, being set down negatively.
1. To put us in mind of our Corruption; which needeth greatly to be restrained. Whereas if Adam had continued in Integrity, Sin had not been known; and then Virtue only had been propounded to us to follow. 2. Because our Souls being full of Sins must have them plucked forth, before we can do any thing that is good. 3. Because the Negative bindeth more strongly. For the Negative Precept bindeth always and to all moments of time; the Affirmative bindeth always, but not to all moments of time.

How are the Ten Commandments divided?
Into Two Tables, (Deut. 4. 13. & 10. 1, 4.) which Christ calleth the Two Great Commandments, Mat. 22.

What does the first contain?
Our Duty to God; in the four first Commandments.

What does the second?
Our Duty to Man; in the six last.

What is the Sum of the first?
Thou shalt love the Lord thy God with all thy Heart, and with all thy Soul, and with all thy Strength, and with all thy Mind, Deut. 6. 5. Mat. 22. 37, 38. Luke 10. 27.

What is the Sum of the second?
Thou shalt love thy Neighbor as thy self, Levit. 19. 18. Mat. 22. 30. Luke 10. 27.

What is the Sum of this Sum?
Love; which consisteth in two Heads (as we have heard); to wit, the Love of God, and our Neighbor, Luke 10. 27. 1 John 5. 2. 1 Tim. 1. 4, 5.

What use is there of this short Sum?
Very great: Both to show the marvelous Wisdom of God, and also for singular Profit that redoundeth to us thereof.

Twentieth Head

Wherein appeareth this Wisdom of God?
That since it was great Cunning to contrive the whole Will of God into. Ten Words; it must needs be more wonderful to bring all into Two.

What is the Profit that redoundeth unto us?
It furthereth us in the two fold use of the Law before spoken of. For, first, it is a means the more to humble us, and so the more effectually to drive us unto Christ. Secondly, It helpeth us much in our Obedience to Christ and his Commandments.

What profit ariseth of the first use concerning Humiliation?
That Men being brought to a nearer sight of their Sins, might be the more earnest to come unto Christ.

How shall that be?
That when all our Sins are gathered into one heap, and mustered into one Troop, they may appear the greater, and cast us down the more. As a Man owing sundry Debts unto divers or unto one Man, in the particulars, is confident of his ability to pay all, as long as he heareth they are but small Sums:

But hearing the whole Sum, he despaireth of the Payment of it. Or when as there be many Soldiers coming against their Enemy, but yet here and there scattered, they do not affect us with so great fear, as when they be gathered and ranged in order, and are all under one sight or view.

How is this showed in our Love towards God?
In that it should be done in simple Obedience of the whole Man, that is, of all the Powers both of Soul and Body; which is impossible for any Man to do.

What are they of the Soul?
Two, of the Mind, and of the Will.

What are they of the Mind?
The understanding and Judgment; unto both which Memory is annexed.

How are these charged?
Our understanding should perfectly comprehend all things that God would have us to know: In Judgment we should think aright of them; and the Memory accordingly should retain them. But we are ignorant of many things; and those which we know, we know but in part; and that which we know, we judge not aright of, nor remember as we ought.

How stand the Will and Affections charged?
Hereby must we love perfectly all known Good, and perfectly hate all known Evil; of which we come a great deal shorter than of the other.

What are they of the Body?
All the Members, Parts, and Graces of the Body, (as Beauty, Strength, &c.) should be wholly employed in the Service of God, and in the doing of his Will. But the wandering of our Eyes in the hearing of the Word, and other parts of God's Service, does easily betray our great negligence, and the small obedience and conformity of the rest of the Members and Parts of the Body.

Show the same in our Love towards our Neighbor.
In that we must love him as our self: Which as it is so much the less than the former, as Man is inferior to God; so we being not able to accomplish it, are much less able to fulfill the other.

How shall that be tried?
By Examination of ourselves in some particulars. As for example, Whether we love a Stranger, or our utter and most deadly Enemy, as ourselves; which no Man ever did; nay, a common Man, or to be plainer, even our dearest Friend, as we do ourselves; which cannot be found, Deut. 28. 53, 56, &c. And therefore the Righteousness of the Papist is a rotten Righteousness, and such as will never stand before the Judgment Seat of God.

What profit ariseth of the second use?
That by it, as by a Glass, we may the easier see, and being shortly contrived, we may the better remember our whole Duty both to God and Man; it being as a Card, or Map of a Country, easily carried about with us.

Seeing then that the whole Sum and main End of the Law is Love, what gather you thereof?
That which the Apostle exhorteth unto, viz. To leave all idle Questions as unprofitable, and to deal in those Matters only which further the Practice of Love, 1 Tim. 1. 4, 5.

Why is the Love of God called the first and greatest Commandment? Mat. 22. 38.
Because we should chiefly, and in the first place, regard our Duties to God, and be most careful to understand his Will, and to worship him, 1 Joh. 4. 20. In which respect the first Table is put before the second; as being the principal.

How may it appear that our Duties to God are to be preferred before the other towards our Neighbor?
First, By the inequality of the Persons offended: Because it is worse to offend God than Man, Acts 4. 19. Secondly, By the Punishments assigned in the Scripture. For the breaches of the first Table are to be more severely punished, than the Breaches of the second. As he that revileth the Magistrate, shall bear his Sin; but he that blasphemeth God shall be stoned to death, 1 Sam. 2. 25.

What gather you of this?
The crafty Practices of Papists, who would make Men believe, that the chiefest Godliness, and most meritorious Good Works of all, required in the Law of God, are the Works of the second Table, as Charity, Alms-deeds, &c. thereby deceiving the People to enrich themselves.

Are all the Duties of the first Table greater than all the Duties of the second?
No, unless the Comparison be equally made. For the Moral Duties of the second Table being perpetual, are greater than the Ceremonial Duties of the first being temporal: Whereunto agreeth, that God will rather have Mercy than Sacrifice, Hos. 6. 6. Mat. 9. 13.

When do you count the Comparison equal?
When they are compared in like degrees and the chief Commandment of the first Table with the chief of the second, the middle Duties of the one with the middle Duties of the other; and the last and least of the former, with the last and least of the latter. Thus if we compare the greatest with the greatest, and the meanest with the meanest; the Duties and Breaches of the first Table, are greater than the Duties and Breaches of the second. But though the principal Service of the one, be greater than the principal

Service of the other; if the Comparison be not made in the same degrees, as if (for example) the Murder of a Man be compared with the least abuse of the Name of God; or Adultery with the least breach of the Sabbath; these of the second Table are greater.

Why is the second Table said to be like unto the first? Mat. 22. 39.
For that they go so hand in hand together, that no Man can perform the one, unless he accomplish the other: As St. John plainly teacheth in his first Epistle, the fourth and fifth Chapter . For whosoever keepeth the first Table well, cannot but keep the second; and whosoever keepeth the second, must needs keep the first.

What is to be said then of those that seem to keep the one, and care not for the other?
If they will seem to serve God, and are not in Charity, they are mere Hypocrites: And if they will seem to deal uprightly with their Neighbors, and have not the Love of God in them, they are profane Politics, and very Atheists.

Wherein else do the Tables agree?
First, In that they are both perpetual. Secondly, In that they are both perfect.

Wherein do the Commandments of the first Table agree?
In this principally; that they concern the Worship of God, and contain our whole Duties towards him.

How are they divided?
They either respect the Root of this Worship, as the first; or the Branches thereof, as the three following. For the Fountain Worship of God is prescribed in the first Commandment: The means of his Service, in the other three.

Why did God enjoin his Worship in four Commandments?
That we might the better know and retain them in mind: Or otherwise might be left the more without excuse.

What is common to these four Commandments of the first Table?
That every one hath his several Reason annexed: Yet with this difference, that the first hath his Reason going before the Commandment, and the other three have it following.

Have not the Commandments of the second Table their Reasons also?
Yes verily in the Scripture; but for Brevity they are omitted in the Decalogue.

Why are the Reasons of the Commandments of the first Table rather set down than of the second?
First, That we might know, that there is less Light left in us of the Worship of God, than of the Duties we owe to our Neighbor. Secondly, To teach us, that as all Obedience should be grounded upon Reason and Knowledge; so especially that which concerneth God's Worship.

What gather you of this?
That those are greatly deceived, who think it sufficient, if they have the Commandments by heart, or can say them by rote.

Why is the reason of the first Commandment set before, which in all the other cometh after?
Because it serveth not only for a Reason of this Commandment, but also for a Preface to all the Ten. For it hath a reference to them all, and is a reason to urge the Observance of every one of them.

In what Words is it expressed?
In these Words of God, Exod. 20. 2. I am the Lord thy God, which brought thee out of the Land of Egypt, out of the House of Bondage.

How prove you this to be a Reason, and not a Commandment? As some do think?
First, Because it is commonly used for a Reason of other Commandments, Ezek. 20. 5. 7. Lev. 19. 36, 37. Secondly, Because it hath not the form of a Commandment. Thirdly, since the other three Commandments have their Reason added, it is unlikely that the first and chiefest should have none.

How is this Preface set as a Reason to enforce the Observation, both of the first Commandment, and of all the rest?
Thus: If I be the Lord thy God which brought thee out of the Land of Egypt, thou must take me for the Lord thy God alone, and keep all my Commandments. But I am the Lord thy God which brought thee out of the Land of Egypt. Therefore thou must take me for thy God alone, and keep all my Commandments.

What ground of Obedience is there laid in this Reason?
That this Law is to be obeyed; because it proceedeth from him, who is not only the Lord our Maker, (Psal. 100. 3.) but also our God and Savior, (1 Tim. 4. 10.) Psal. 36. 6.

Whence is the latter?
From the Covenant of Grace, whereby he is our God, the Savior of them that believe, (1 Tim. 4. 10.) assuring them of all gracious deliverances, by virtue of that his Covenant, from all Evils and Enemies, both Bodily, and especially Spiritual: A Proof whereof is laid down in that famous deliverance of the People of Israel out of the Slavery of Egypt; which was so exceeding great, that by reason thereof they were said to be in an Iron Furnace, Deut. 4. 20.

How can this belong to us which are no Israelites?
Though we be not Israel in Name, or according to the flesh; yet we are the true Israel of God, according to the Spirit and Promise.

Why does the Lord make choice of that benefit, which seemeth nothing at all to belong unto us; rather than of any other, wherein we communicate with them?
1. Because it is the manner of God, to allure the Israelites, to whom the Law was given at first, as Children, with temporal Benefits, (Levit. 26. 4, 10. Deut. 28. 13.) having respect to their Infirmity and Childhood: Whereas we are blessed of God with greater Knowledge, and therefore, in respect of them, are (as it were) at Man's Estate.

2. Because it was fittest to express the Spiritual Deliverance from Satan by Christ, which was thereby figured and represented; and so it belongeth no less (if not more) to us than to them.

3. Because we having been freed from the slavery of our Bloody Enemies, whereunto we were so near more than once, and unto whom we justly have deserved to have been enthralled; and it being the common case of all God's Children, to be in continual

danger of the like, and to feel the like Goodness of God towards them; we may also make use of this Title, and esteem it a great Bond also for us unto God.

4. Because it was the latest Benefit, the Sweetness whereof was yet (as it were) in their Mouth. And herein the Lord had respect unto our corrupt Nature, who are ready to forget old Benefits, how great soever.

What is there in this Reason, to set forth the true God whom we worship; and to distinguish him from all Idols whatsoever?
1. The Name Jehovah; which betokeneth that he only is of himself, and all other things have their being of him. Whereby we are taught, that there is but one true God, whose Being no Creature is able to conceive: And that he giveth Being to all other things, both by creating them at first, and by preserving and directing of them continually. 2. The Name Elohim, or God; which in the Hebrew is of the plural number, to signify the Trinity of the Persons in Unity of the Godhead. 3. That he is both Omnipotent, that is, able to do all things; and also willing to employ his Power to the Preservation of his People: Proved from an Argument of the Effects, in the Deliverance of the Israelites out of Egypt.

[21ST HEAD.]

So much of the Preface. What are the Words of the first Commandment?
Thou shalt have no other Gods before me. Or, Thou shalt not have any strange God before my face. Exodus 20. 3.

What is the Scope and Meaning of this Commandment?
1. That this Jehovah, one in Substance and three in Persons, the Creator and Governor of all things, and the Redeemer of his People, is to be entertained for the only true God, in all the Powers of our Soul, Mat. 22. 37.

2. That the inward and spiritual Worship of the Heart, (Prov. 23. 26.) wherein God especially delighteth, (Deut 5. 29.) and which is the ground of the outward, (Prov. 4. 23. Mat. 12. 35.) is to be given to him, and to none other: And that sincerely, without Hypocrisy, as in his sight, who searcheth and knoweth the Heart, (Jer. 7. 10.) For this word, Before me, or Before my Face, noteth that inward Entertainment and Worship whereof God alone does take notice. And thereby God showeth, that he condemneth as well the corrupt thoughts of Man's Heart concerning his Majesty, as the wicked Practice of the Body. For our Thoughts are before his Face.

What is forbidden in this Commandment?
Original Corruption, so far forth as it is the Fountain of Impiety against God, (Rom. 8. 7.) with all the Streams thereof.

What is required in this Commandment?
That we set up, embrace, and sanctify the Lord God in our Hearts, (Isa. 8. 13.) yielding unto him in Christ, that inward and spiritual Worship, which is due unto his Majesty.

Wherein does this consist?
First, In knowing of God, in Himself, in his Properties, and in his Works. For it should be the Joy of every Christian Soul, to know the true God, and whom he hath sent, Christ Jesus, John 17. 3. Second, In cleaving unto him, Deut. 11. 22. Josh. 23. 8. Acts 11. 23.

How is that to be done?
1. We must be persuaded of God's Love to us, and so rest upon him for all we want; being assured that he both can and will abundantly provide for us, here and for ever.
2. We are to love him so heartily, as to be loath to offend him, and delight to please him in all things.

So much of this Commandment in general:
What are we to consider of it in particular?
First, The several Branches of it. Secondly, The Helps and Hindrances of the Obedience thereof.

What are the several Branches of this Precept?
There is here commanded; 1. The having of a God: And herein Religion. 2. The having of one only God, and no more: And herein Unity. 3. The having of the true God, and none other, for our God; and herein Truth.

To what end does God command us to have a God; seeing we cannot choose but have him for our God, whether we will or not?
Because, albeit all Men of necessity must have a God above them: Yet many either know him not, or care not for him; and so make him no God, as much as in them lieth.

What is it then to have a God?
To know and worship such an infinite Nature as hath his being in himself, and giveth being to all other things; wholly to depend upon him, and to yield absolute Obedience unto his Will.

What is it to have no God?
In heart to deny either God himself or any of his Properties; or so to live, as if there were no God at all.

What things are to be considered in this first Branch of the Commandment?
Such as do concern the Faculties of the Soul, and the several Powers of the inward Man: Namely, the Understanding, Memory, Will, Affections, and Con science?

What is the Understanding charged with, in being commanded to have a God?
First, to know God, as he hath revealed himself in his Word and in his Works, 1 Chron. 28. 9. John 17. 3. Second, to acknowledge him to be such an one as we know him to be. Third, to have Faith, both in believing the things that are written of him, and applying to ourselves his good Promises.

What are we to consider in the Knowledge of God?
First, The Knowledge of God himself: And secondly, of the things belonging unto him.

Wherein is God himself to be considered?
In the Unity of his Essence, and Trinity of his Persons.

What are the Things belonging unto God?
His Properties, and his Actions: Whereby only we can know him, his Substance being past finding out of Man or Angel.

What are his Properties?
His Wisdom, Omnipotence, Justice, Goodness, &c. which are in him all essential.

What are his Actions?
His determining, and executing of all things.

What are the things forbidden in this Commandment, as repugnant to this Knowledge of God?
They either fail in defect or in excess.

What are those that fail in defect?
First, Ignorance of God and of his Will: which being a breach of God's Commandment, does therefore deserve Damnation, 2 Thess. 1. 8. Hos. 4. 1, 6. Second, Incapableness of Knowledge. Third, Atheism: Which is a Denial of God.

How many sorts of Ignorance are there?
Three: 1. Simple Ignorance; such as Children and Fools have. 2. Wretched Ignorance; when a Man may learn, and will not. 3. Willful Ignorance; when a Man would fain be ignorant of that he knows.

What is that which faileth in excess?
Curious searching into the secrets of God, Deut. 29. 29.

What Vice is contrary to that Faith which is here commanded?
Infidelity and Doubtfulness, Psal. 116. 11.

Hitherto of the Understanding: What is required in the Memory?
The Remembrance of God and good things; especially of those which most concern us, and chiefly at that Instant when we should make use of them.

What is the contrary Vice?
Forgetfulness.

What is required in the Will?
That we serve God with a perfect Heart, and with a willing Mind, 1 Chron. 28. 9.

What is the contrary to this?
Unwillingness to good things, principally to the best.

What Affections be there here ordered?
1. Affiance. 2. Love and Hatred. 3. Fear. 4. Joy and Sorrow.

What are we commanded in regard of the first of these?
To put our whole trust and confidence in God; and continually to depend upon him, Psal. 22. 4, 5, 8, 9. & 73. 25. Esther 4. 14.

What Vices are condemned repugnant to this?
1. In defect: Want of dependence upon God; and distrust of his Power, Mercy, Promises and Providences. 2. In excess: Presuming of God's Mercies, though we live as we list; and tempting him when we so depend upon him, that we neglect the use of the means which he hath appointed, Mat. 4. 6, 7.

What Virtues do arise of this affiance and trust in God?
Patience and Hope.

What is Patience?
That Virtue, whereby we willingly submit ourselves to the pleasure of God in all things; and with alacrity go through those Troubles which he sendeth upon us, like obedient Children meekly enduring the Correction of our Heavenly Father, 1 Sam. 30. 6. Heb. 12. 7, 8, 9, &c.

What Vices are condemned as repugnant to Patience?
1. In defect: Murmuring and Impatience, in grudging to bear whatsoever Cross the Lord shall lay upon us. 2. In excess: Stupidity, in not being touched with, nor profiting by the Hand of God, when it is upon us.

What is Hope?
That Virtue, whereby we expect all good things from God, and patiently attend for all things that we need at his hands, (Psal. 22. 4, 5. & 37. 7.) not only when we have the means, but also when we want all apparent means, (as the Israelites did in the Desert); yea, when the means seem contrary, as the three Companions of Daniel, and Daniel himself did, (Dan. 3. 17, 18.) and Job professed he would do, saying, I will trust in God although he kill me, Job 13. 15.

What is contrary to this?
Despair of God's Mercies, Gen. 4. 13.

What is required in the Affections of Love and Hatred?
First, That we love God above all, and all things that are pleasing unto him. Secondly, That we hate Ungodliness, and every thing that God hateth.

Upon what is our Love of God grounded?
Because we know and believe that he is Good, yea, the chiefest Good; we love him above all things, Deut. 6. 5. which is so excellent a Virtue, that it is accounted the end of the Law.

What contrary Vices are here condemned?
1. Coldness of Affection towards God; and little Love of Goodness, of God's Servants and Service. 2. Want of hatred of our own and others Sins. 3. Hatred of God and Godliness, Psal. 20. 3, 4. Rom. 1. 30.

Is it possible that any Man should be a Hater of God?
None indeed will confess this: Yet by this mark he may be known; when he is a Despiser of the Worship and Service of God.

And how may one that loveth God be discerned?
When a Child does love his Father, his only desire will be to do such things as please his Father, and to abstain from those things which might displease him: Yea, his chiefest felicity will be, to be always in his favor, and in his presence; and in his absence he will be always thinking and speaking of him. Such then as be the Children of God by Grace, as long as they are absent from their Father, will talk, and muse, and meditate upon him; in all things they do, they will desire to be well thought of by him; they will be always careful to please him, and by their honest Callings to glorify him.

What Duties then do arise from the Love of God?
1. To love his Word and Commandments, (John 14. 15, 21, 23. Psalm 119. 97.). 2. To yield absolute Obedience to his whole Will. 3. To bestow all our care, pains, and diligence in pleasing him; and so to consecrate ourselves unto him, never being weary of his Service.

What Vices are repugnant to this?
1. In defect, Profaneness: When a Man is without all Care and Conscience of glorifying God. 2. In excess, Superstition: When a Man would give more Worship unto God than he requireth.

What other Duties appertain to the Love of God?
1. To esteem of his Favor above all things. 2. To give him the praise of all his Benefits bestowed upon ourselves and others; and to be thankful unto him for the same, 1 Thess. 5. 18.

What is contrary to this?
Ingratitude, and Unthankfulness unto God for all his Benefits, Rom. 1. 21.

Upon what is our fear of God grounded?
Because we know and believe that he is most powerful and just above all; we stand in such a godly fear, as not to do any thing, but which makes for his Glory, (Mat. 10. 28. 1 Pet. 1. 17. & 3. 2, 6. Heb. 12. 28. Psal. 103. 13. Isa. 66. 2.) For this is not a Servile Fear, whereby one is afraid to be damned; but an awful Fear, whereby we are afraid to offend our Maker.

What then is required in this Fear?
That we do not the good we do only or principally for fear of danger from Men, but for fear of God.

What is the Vice contrary to this?
The want of the Fear of God, and Contempt of his Majesty.

What Sin is joined with the want of the Fear of God?
Carnal Security, whereby a Man does flatter himself in his own Estate, be it never so bad.

What Virtues arise from the Fear of God?
Reverence and Humility.

What is the former?
The Reverence of the Majesty of God, in regard whereof we should carry such a holy shamefacedness in all our Actions, that no unseemly Behavior proceed from us, that may any ways be offensive unto him, Heb. 12. 28. Of which if Men be so careful in the presence of Princes, who are but mortal Men; how much more careful ought we to be thereof, in the presence of the Almighty, and most glorious God?

How was this prefigured in the Ceremonial Law?
That when Men would ease themselves, (according to the Course of Nature) they should go without the Host, and carry a Paddle with them to cover their Filth; because, saith the Lord, I am in the midst of you: Whereby the Filthiness and Impurity of the Mind was forbidden, more than of the Body: and the Equity hereof reacheth also unto us, Deut. 23. 12, 13, 14.

What is contrary to this Reverence of the Majesty of God?
Irreverence and Profaneness of Men to God-ward.

What is Humility?
That Virtue whereby we account ourselves vile and unworthy of the least of God's Mercies; and casting ourselves down before his Majesty, do acknowledge our own

emptiness of Good, and insufficiency in ourselves. For so all our Behavior should be seasoned with humility.

What Sins are repugnant to this Virtue?
1. Counterfeit Humility; when a Man would seem more lowly than he is. 2. Pride, Vainglory, and Presumption; whereby we boast and glory of ourselves, and our own strength and goodness.

Who are to be accounted proud?
1. They that would be thought to have those good things in them which they want.
2. They that having a little goodness in them, would have it seem greater than it is.
3. They that having any goodness in them, do think that it cometh from themselves.
4. They that think they can merit from God, and deserve his Favor.

What is that Godly Sorrow which is required in this Commandment?
Spiritual Grief and Indignation against our own and others Transgressions: As also lamenting for the Calamities of God's People, private and public. The want of both which, here is condemned.

What Spiritual Joy is here enjoined?
Joying in God, and rejoicing in all our Afflictions, with Consideration of the Joy prepared for us before the beginning of the World, Luke 1. 47. Rom. 5. 3. Jam. 1. 2. the defect of which Spiritual Joy is here condemned.

So much of the Affections. What is required of us in respect of our Conscience?
That we live in all good Conscience before God, Acts 23. 1. Heb. 13. 8.

What Sins are here condemned?
1. Hardness of Heart, and Benumbedness of Conscience. 2. Hellish Terrors and Accusations, proceeding from doing things either without or against the Rule of the Word.

So much of the first Branch of this Commandment: What is required in the second Branch thereof?
Unity in Religion; because we are commanded to have but one God, and no more.

What things are required of us, that we may come to this Unity?
Four principally: 1. An upright and single Heart, ready to embrace the true Religion, and no other. 2. Constancy and Continuance in the Truth. 3. A Godly Courage to stand to the Truth, and withstand the Enemy. 4. An Holy Zeal of the Glory of God.

What contrary Vices are forbidden?
1. Indifference in Religion; when a Man is as ready to embrace one Religion as another. 2. Inconstancy and wavering in Religion. 3. Obstinate and willful Continuance in any Religion without good ground. 4. Rash and blind Zeal; when a Man, without Knowledge or Judgment, will earnestly maintain either Falsehood or Truth by wicked Means.

To what end does God will us to have no other God but himself, seeing no Man can have any other God, though he never so much desire it?
Because, howsoever there be but one God, yet many do devise unto themselves divers things which they place in God's stead, and to which they give that Honor which is proper unto God, 1 Cor. 8. 4, 5. & 10. 20.

What Sin then does God condemn, by forbidding us to have many Gods?
All inward Idolatry, whereby Men set up an Idol in their Heart instead of God, (Ezek. 14. 3.) ascribing thereunto that which is proper to him, or giving unto it any part of spiritual adoration.

Show how this is done in the Understanding.
When Men do think that other things have that which is proper unto God: As Papists, when they believe that the Sacrament is their Maker; that the Saints know their Hearts; that the Pope can forgive Sins; which none can do but God.

How does the Memory fail here?
In remembering of evil things, especially of those which most corrupt us; and chiefly then, when we should be most free from the thought of them.

What is the fault of the Will?
Readiness unto, and willfulness in Evil, especially the worst.

Show the like in the Affections: And first in sinful Confidence.
There is here condemned, Trust in the Creatures more than in God, and all fleshly Confidence in ourselves, or in our Friends, Honor, Credit, Wit, Learning, Wisdom, Wealth, &c. thinking ourselves the better or more safe, simple for them, Prov. 18. 11. Psal. 62. 10. Jer. 17. 5. 2 Chron. 16. 12. whence ariseth Pride, (Acts 12. 23.) and Security.

What is our Duty concerning these things?
1. To esteem of them only as good means given us of God, whereby to glorify him the better. 2. To trust in God no less when we have them, than when we want them, Job 13. 15.

What is further here condemned?
1. To ascribe the Glory of any good thing, either to ourselves, or any other than the Lord. 2. To seek for help of the Devil by Witches or Wise Men.

Wherein standeth inordinate Love?
In loving of Evil, or in loving of ourselves or any other thing more than God, of whose favor we ought more to esteem, than of all the World besides. Here therefore is condemned all carnal Love of ourselves, our Friends, our Pleasure, Profit, Credit, or any worldly thing else, for whose sake we leave those Duties undone, which God requireth of us, (2 Tim. 3. 4. 1 John 2. 15. 1 Sam. 2. 29.) whereas the true Love of God will move us, with Moses and Paul, to wish ourselves accursed, rather than that the Glory of God should any thing at all be stained by us, Exod. 32. 32. Rom. 9. 3.

What Fear is here condemned?
All carnal Fear, and especially the fearing of any thing more than God, Isa. 7. 2. & 8. 12, 13. & 5. 12, 13. Mat. 10. 28.

How may a Man know that he is more afraid of God than of any other thing?
If he be more afraid to displease God than any other, and this fear of God be stronger to move us to good, than the fear of Men to move us to evil.

What disorder in Joy and Sorrow is here condemned?
1. Immoderate carnal Mirth. 2. Abundance of worldly Sorrow, Shame and Discontentments.

What is required in the third and last Branch of this Commandment?
True Religion; because we are commanded to have the true God, and none other for our God.

What is contrary to this?
The having of a false God, and a false Religion.

How many things are required of us that we may come to true Religion?
Three. 1. We must labor earnestly to find out the Truth. 2. We must examine by the Word whether it be the Truth which we have found. 3. When by Trial we have found out the Truth, we must rest in it.

What is here forbidden?
1. All Errors and Heresies, especially concerning God and his Properties, and the three Persons in the Trinity. Where we must take heed, we imagine no likeness of God: For as much as we set up an Idol in our Hearts, if we liken him to any thing whatsoever, subject to the sense or Imagination of Man. For the better Avoidance whereof, we must settle our Minds upon Christ, in whom only God is comprehensible. 2. To believe any Doctrine concerning God without Trial. 3. Not to believe that which God hath revealed concerning himself in his Word.

We have spoken hitherto of the several Branches of the first Commandment. What are the Helps of the Obedience?
The only means to settle and uphold us in this Spiritual Worship of God, is to endeavour to attain and increase in the Knowledge of him in Jesus Christ, (2 Pet. 3. 18.) to consider what great things he hath done for us, (Psal. 116. 1, 12. 1 Sam. 12. 24. 1 John 3. 1.) yea, in all our ways to take Knowledge of his Presence, Promises, and Providence, Prov. 3. 6.

What are the means whereby we may attain to this Knowledge?
Principally Twelve. 1. Prayer. 2. A simple Heart, desirous of Knowledge. 3. Hearing of the Word. 4. Reading of the Word and Holy Writings. 5. Meditation in the Word. 6. Conference. 7. Diligence in Learning. 8. Remembrance of that we learn. 9. Practice of what we learn. 10. Delight in Learning. 11. Attentive marking of that which is taught. 12. Meditation on the Creatures of God.

What are the hindrances of the Obedience of this Commandment?
The neglect of the Knowledge of God, (Hos. 4. 1. & 8. 12.) and not considering his Word and Works, (Isa. 5. 12. & 26. 10, 11.) are the ground of all Impiety, and Spiritual Idolatry here forbidden, Isa. 1. 3, 4.

What things are forbidden as means of this Ignorance?
Five: First, Curiosity: When a Man would know more than God would have him know. Secondly, Vanity of Mind: When the Mind is drawn away and occupied upon vain and unprofitable things. Thirdly, Pride of our own Knowledge: When we think we know enough already. Fourthly, Forgetfulness of God and his Will. Fifthly, Weariness in learning, and talking of God and his Will.

[22ND HEAD.]

Hitherto of the first Commandment, concerning the entertaining God in our Hearts. What is enjoined in the other three?
The means of his Service. For as in the first Commandment we are required to have, so in the other we are required to serve the Lord our God.

What are the Branches of this Service?
Either they are such as are to be performed at all times, as occasion shall require: Or such as concern a certain Day, wholly set a part for his Worship. The Duties of the former kind are prescribed in the second and third; of the latter in the fourth and last Commandment of the first Table.

How are the Duties of the former kind distinguished?
They do either concern the solemn Worship of Religion, prescribed in the second Commandment: Or the Respect we should carry to God in the common course of our lives, laid down in the third.

What do you consider in the second Commandment?
Two things: 1. The Injunction. 2. The Reasons brought to strengthen the same.

What are the Words of the Injunction?
Thou shalt not make to thy self any Graven Image; nor any likeness of things that are in heaven above, nor in the Earth beneath, nor in the Waters under the Earth: thou shalt not bow down to them, nor worship them. Exod. 20. 4, 5.

What is the scope and meaning of this Commandment?
To bind all Men to that solemn Form of Religious Worship which God himself in his Word prescribeth: That we serve him not according to our Fancies, but according to his own Will, Deut. 12. 32.

What is generally forbidden herein?
Every Form of Worship, though of the true God (Deut. 12. 31.) contrary to, or diverse from the Prescript of God's Word, (Mat. 15. 9.) called by the Apostle Will-worship, (Col. 2. 23.) together with all Corruption in the true Worship of God, (2 Kings 16. 10.) and all lust and Inclination of Heart unto superstitious Pomps and Rites in the Service of God.

What are the parts of that Will-worship?
Either the Worship of any besides God; or of God himself, any otherwise than he hath commanded. For both Vices are here forbidden; either to worship the true God falsely, or to worship those things that are not God at all.

Who do chiefly offend in this kind?
The Papists: Which give Religious Worship unto Creatures; and serve God, not according to his Will prescribed in the Word, but according to the Pope's Decrees, and the Traditions of Men.

Why does the Lord forbid all these Corruptions under one instance of Images?
Because therein he foresaw there would be greatest abuse.

What does he expressly forbid concerning them?
1. That we make no Image to worship it. 2. That we worship it not when it is made.

What is meant by making of Images?
All new Devices and Inventions of Men in the Service of God: Whereby we are forbidden to make any new Word, new Sacraments, new Censures, new Ministries, new Prayers, new Fastings, or new Vows, to serve him withal. Also all Representations of any Grace of God, otherwise than God hath appointed, or may be allowed by his Word. As Christ condemned the Pharisees washing.

What by worshipping of them?
All use in God's Service of any new devised Inventions, (or practicing of them) and all abuse of things commanded.

What is generally required in this Commandment?
That we worship and serve God in that holy manner which he in his Word requireth.

How is that to be done?
First, We must use all those Holy Exercises of Religion, public and private, which he commandeth. Secondly, We must perform all the parts of God's Worship prescribed with Reverence, and Diligence; using them so carefully as may be, to God's Glory and our Good, Eccles. 5. 1.

What observe you by comparing the second Commandment with the first?
That the inward and outward Worship of God ought to go together. For as in the first Commandment the Lord requireth, that we should have no other Gods before him, that is, in the secret of our Heart, whereof he alone taketh notice: So in the second, by the words, Make, Bow, Worship, he forbiddeth any outward Service of Religion, to be given unto any other.

Wherefore must God be worshipped both by our Bodies and our Souls?
Because he is the Lord and Maker of them both, 1 Cor. 6. 20.

What gather you from hence?
That such as dare to present their Bodies to a Mass, or to any other gross Idolatry, and say that they keep their Hearts to God, are here convicted of Falsehood and Hypocrisy.

So much of the second Commandment in general. What are the particular Branches of it?
There is here first required, that all solemn Religious Worship should be given to the true God: And secondly, that it be given to him alone, and not communicated unto any thing which is not God. So that the sum of the first part is, Thou shalt worship the Lord thy God: Of the second, Him only shalt thou serve, Mat. 4. 10.

How are we to worship the Lord our God?
By those means only which himself approveth in his Word: According to the saying of Moses; Do that which I command thee, and do no more, Deut. 4. 2. & 12. 32.

What is here required?
First, That we give unto God that Worship, which he himself hath prescribed in his Word. Secondly, That we give him that alone, without Addition or Alteration.

What is forbidden?
First, The neglect of God's Worship, or any of his Ordinances: When we condemn, or despise, or leave undone that Service which he hath commanded us to perform unto him. Secondly, The adding any thing unto, or taking any thing from the pure Worship of God: When we serve him by any other means than that which he himself hath commanded.

Twenty-second Head

What are we to consider in the pure Worship of God, which he hath prescribed in his Word?
1. The parts of it. 2. The right manner of using of it.

What are the parts of it?
They are partly such as we give unto God; and partly such as God giveth unto us.

What is required of us touching these kinds?
1. That we use those things that God hath given us, to that end that God hath given them for. 2. That neither in giving to God, nor taking from him, we devise any thing of our own to serve him withal.

What are the things God giveth us to serve him by?
His Creatures in the first place; also his Word, Sacraments, Ministry, Discipline and Censures of the Church: Which we must use according as they are instituted of God.

What Duties are here required?
Our presence at these Exercises of Religion. The Preaching, Hearing, and Reading of the Word of God: Together with Meditation, Conference and all other means of increasing our Knowledge therein. The administering and receiving of the Sacraments, &c. Acts 2. 42.

How do we worship God in these?
In the Creatures, by beholding his Glory in them: In his Word, by diligent hearing of it, and careful believing and practicing of it; in his Sacraments, by receiving them duly; in the Ministry and Censures, by submitting ourselves unto them.

What are the things that we give unto God?
They are either more or less Ordinary.

What are the more Ordinary?
1. To pray to God, publicly and privately. 2. To praise God, both alone and with others.

Are these Duties required of all Christians?
Yea: Every true Christian must offer this Sacrifice to the Lord every day. For in all Ages, and at all times, it hath been the practice of God's Saints, to offer unto God the Sacrifice of Prayer and Praise: As we may see by the practice of David, Daniel, Peter, (who went up at noon to pray, Acts 10. 9.) and Isaac, who went out at Eventide to pray in the Fields, Gen. 24. 63.

What are the Parts of Prayer?
Three: First, Confession: Which is the Sacrifice of a broken Heart and wounded Soul, Psal. 51. 17. Second, Petition, for such things as we lack. Third, Thanksgiving for such things as we have received.

What are the things less Ordinary?
First, Fasts, public or private, Joel 2. 12, 15. Second, Solemn Thanksgiving for special Blessings, (Psal. 50. 14.) whereunto Feasting also is joined, when special occasion of Joy is given us. Third, Making and performing Holy Vows unto God.

What is Fasting?
An Abstinence for a time from all the Commodities and Pleasures of this Life; so far as comliness and necessity will suffer, to make us more apt to Prayer, and more able to serve God.

What is a Vow?
A solemn Promise made unto God of some things that are in our Power to perform: Which we do, to declare our Thankfulness, to strengthen our Faith, and to further us in doing our good Duties, wherein we are backward; or abstaining from some Evil whereunto we find ourselves specially inclined.

So much of the Parts of God's Solemn Worship. What is required to the right manner of using the same?
Our careful, sincere, and diligent Behavior in all his Service: That every thing there may be done as he hath appointed, and no otherwise.

What are the things required hereunto?
They are partly Inward, partly Outward: The former whereof concerneth the Substance, the latter the Circumstance of God's Worship.

What are the Inward?
All the Powers of the Soul are charged to join together, as (by the first and great Commandment) in the entertaining and loving, so (by this) in performing all Acts of Solemn Worship to the true God. Therefore herein there must be a concurrence, as well of the Understanding, that we have knowledge of the particular Service which we do, (Rom. 14. 5. 1 Cor. 14. 14, 15.) as of the Will and Affection, that we may worship God in Spirit and in Truth, John 4. 22.

What things are requisite in the performance of this?
Three: 1. A diligent Preparation and Advisedness, before we come to any Holy Exercise. 2. A right disposition of the Mind in the Action it self. 3. A comfortable departure, upon the sensible feeling of the Fruit thereof.

What is required in the Preparation before the Action?
at we bethink ourselves before-hand, about what things we come: And dispatch ourselves of all the things that hinder us in the Service of God. Which since we must do in things otherwise lawful, much more in things unlawful.

What is further to be observed herein?
That every Preparation be answerable to the Exercise whereunto we are called: As in the parts of Prayer; for Example:

1. In Confession, we must have a true feeling of our former Sins. 2. In Petition, we must have the like Sense of our Wants; and bethink ourselves what need we have of the things we ask, and strive against our staggering and doubting of God's Promises. 3. In Thanksgiving, we must call to mind at least the Kinds of God's Benefits bestowed upon us, and consider the Greatness of them. And so in all other Services of God.

What Disposition of the Mind is required in the Action?
1. A reverent, diligent, and earnest Attentiveness to the Thing, with all the Powers of our Souls; thereby to fasten our Minds, and so to hold them during the Exercise, that no idle or vain Thoughts withdraw us from the same.

2. Zeal in the Action: With such Affections as are answerable to the Matter in hand. As in Prayer, we must have a sure Confidence in God, that we shall obtain the Things we ask agreeable to his Will: In Thanksgiving, we must have a sweet feeling of the Benefit that God hath given us: In the Word and Sacraments, we must come with Affection to them, &c.

Twenty-second Head

What is required of us after the Action?
That we feel the Fruit of it; that is, some increase either of knowledge of true fear, or comfort, for strengthening of us in the Duties we perform. So every one must examine himself herein, and all those that belong unto him: Else they are like unto them, that having eaten a good Meal, by warm Water do give it up again.

What are the Outward Things that do accompany God's Worship?
1. Ecclesiastical Ceremonies, making for Order and Decency, 1 Cor. 14. 40. which are left to the appointment of the Church; being of that nature, that they are varied by Times, Places, Persons, and other Circumstances. 2. All comely and reverent Gestures of the Body: As Kneeling, lifting up the Hands and Eyes to Heaven, Silence in the Service of God, and such-like. For the Gestures of Religious Adorations being here forbidden to be given unto Images, are therein commanded to be given unto the God of Heaven.

Is there any use of our Bodily Behavior before God, since he is a Spirit, and looketh to the Heart?
Yes verily. For, 1. The whole Man, and consequently the Body it self, oweth Duty unto God. 2. It is a Glass, wherein the Affections of the Mind are beheld. 3. The Mind is the better holden in the thing affected, and the better holden and furthered in the Inward Worship, when both Body and Mind are joined together. Notwithstanding the Mind must always precede in Affection: Else it is shameful Hypocrisy.

What Gestures are most convenient for the Body?
Divers, according to the divers Exercises of Religion: As at the reading of the Word, standing; at Prayer, kneeling, and therein to witness our Humility, by casting down our Eyes, our Confidence by lifting them up; or with the Publican, to knock our Breasts, &c. except our Infirmities, or the like Lets, hinder us therein.

So much of the right use of God's Ordinances.
Wherein standeth the abuse of them?
1. In all rash, negligent, and careless dealing in any particular Point of the Worship of God. 2. In using any thing that God hath commanded for his Worship, otherwise than he himself hath appointed, 1 Chron. 15. 13. For the Brazen Serpent abused, was worthily broken in pieces, (2 Kings 18. 4.) and the Israelites for Carting the Ark, were worthily punished, 2 Sam. 6. 3, 7, 8.

What special Abuses of the Word are here condemned?
To hang pieces of St. John's Gospel about Men's Necks, or to use any other Gospel to heal Diseases, or for any Man to charge a Devil to go out of one, as the Apostles did.

What may be lawfully done in this Case?
We may and must pray only unto God, that he would command the Devil to depart: For he is the Master that authorized him to go thither.

What special Abuses of the Sacraments are condemned?
The receiving them unworthily, (1 Cor. 11. 27, 29.) and making them to be Sacrifices, as is done in Popery.

What of the Ministry?
The turning of that which is given to edify in Christ, to other ends than those for which it was ordained: As when Ministers exercise tyrannical Lordship over their Flock, or their Fellow-Servants; as the Bishops of the Church of Rome use to do, (Luke 22. 25. 1 Pet. 5. 2, 3.) Or when in the execution of their Function, they seek themselves, and not the Edification of God's People, &c.

What of the Discipline and Censures?
When they are used in another Manner, and for other Causes than God hath ordained, Isa. 66. 5.

What of Prayer?
To ask evil things, or to pray for such things as God hath made no Promise of, or for such Persons as he hath made no Promise unto: As when Men pray for Souls departed; or for those that sin to death, (1 John 5. 16.) to pray in a strange Tongue which we do not understand; to pray on Beads, and use much Babbling, &c. as also to aim more in our Requests at the relieving our Necessity, than at the advancement of God's Glory.

What of Thanksgiving?
To thank God for Things unlawfully gotten or come unto us.

What of Fasting?
To make it a matter of Merit, or to use superstitious choice of Meats, as is done in Popery.

What of Vows?
To undertake rash Vows: To break, or else to delay and defer the paying of our lawful Vows; as also to perform Vows that are unlawful, Psal. 66. 13. & 76. 11. Eccles. 5. 1, 5. Gen. 35. 1.

What defects are condemned, that concern the inward things required in the performance of all these parts of God's Worship?
1. Want of Understanding, when we do good Duties ignorantly, or think that we can please God by meaning well, when that which we do is evil. 2. Want of Zeal and Affection in performing God's Service. 3. Hypocrisy, when Men make greater show of the Service of God outwardly, than they have a desire to serve him inwardly. 4. Hearing, Reading, Meditating, Conferring, singing of Psalms, and receiving the Sacrament without Preparation, Attention, Reverence, Delight, and Profit. 5. Praying without Faith, Feeling, Reverence, Fervency, not waiting for Answer, &c.

What defects that concern the outward Worship?
1. All irreverent and unbeseeming Gestures. 2. All Ecclesiastical Ceremonies and Rites of Religion, which are repugnant to God's Word, or not warrantable by the general Grounds thereof: Such as are not for Order, and Comeliness, and Edification.

So much of the Parts of God's Worship prescribed, together with the right use and abuse thereof. What say you of such Forms of Worship as are not prescribed by God in his Word?
We are commanded to serve God, not according to the Traditions of Men, but according to his Will revealed in the Scripture, Col. 2. 18, Mat. 15. 9.

What followeth hereupon?
That no Power must be admitted in the Church to prescribe other Forms of Worship, not appointed by God himself in his Word.

What is then to be observed herein?
We must observe the Apostle's Rule and Practice, 1 Cor. 11. 23. where he saith, That which I have received, I delivered unto you. For if he might add nothing to God's Ordinance, much less may we.

What is here forbidden?
In general, all Will Worship; whereby we make any thing a part of God's Service, which he hath not commanded. For how great a show soever it have, yet in that it leaneth to Man's Wisdom, it is unlawful, Col. 2. 23. In particular, to ordain any other Word or Sacraments, than those which God hath appointed; to devise any other Ministry than that which God hath ordained; to place any Religion in Meat, Drink, Apparel, Time, Place, or any other indifferent thing.

What caution must we keep in the use of things indifferent?
1. We are to maintain that Christian Liberty which Christ hath purchased for us. 2. We must yet be careful not to abuse the same to the hardening, ensnaring, or preventing, or just grieving of any.

Remaineth there any thing else to be spoken of the first main Branch of this Commandment?
Yes: The Helps that may further us in performing this pure Worship of God.

What are they?
1. That all Men labor for Knowledge of the express Will of God touching all parts of his Worship, (Mich. 6. 6, 7, 8.) and that they increase therein every day more and more, by reading the Scriptures; using also for that end Meditation, Conference, good Books, and good Company.

2. That they Marry, and make Leagues of Friendship only with such as profess the true God, and therefore no Professor of the true Worship of God may join himself in Marriage with one of another Religion, or an apparent profane and irreligious Person; but with such only as are Godly, at least in show.

3. That we give no Toleration to Superstition, (2 Chron. 15. 13.) but show our Hatred and Detestation of all false Worship, so far as we may within our Calling.

4. That we join together, with order and decency, in the Performance of God's Worship, 1 Cor. 14. 40.

5. That such whom it concerneth, take care that faithful and able Ministers be ordained in every Congregation, (Tit. 1. 5.) and that sufficient maintenance, for Encouragement be allotted, 1 Tim. 5. 17, 18. 2 Chron. 31. 4.

6. That places for public Assemblies be erected and preserved, Luke 7. 5, 6.

7. That Schools and Universities be founded and maintained, 2 Kings 6. 1, &c.

8. That Books of necessary Use and Edification, (especially, the Holy Book of God) be set forth and divulged, Rev. 1. 3.

9. That, as occasion requireth, Synods and Councils be called and assembled, Acts 15. 6.

10. That such whose Calling and Ability reacheth no further, do yet afford the help of their Prayers unto all these, Mat. 9. 38.

What is required in the second main Branch of this Commandment?
That all Religious Worship and Reverence be given unto God alone, and not imparted to those things which are not God's at all.

What sins are here condemned?
Magic and Idolatry: Both of which are condemned by the Name of Spiritual Adultery, Lev. 20. 5, 6.

Who are guilty of the first of these sins?
First, The Practicers of all Diabolical Arts, Levit. 20. 27. Deut. 18. 10, 11. Second, Such as seek after them, (Lev. 20. 6. Isa. 8. 19, 20. 1 Sam. 28. 7. 1 Chron. 10. 13, 14.) by going to Witches, or consulting with Star-gazers, or the like: To whom Moses opposeth a Prophet, as the only lawful Minister of God, and warrantable means to know his Will by, signifying thereby, that to seek secret things or strange Ministries is abominable.

Who are guilty of the latter of these sins?
1. Such as worship those things that are not God. 2. Such as countenance them, or do any thing that may tend to the furtherance of Idolatry.

What Worship is here forbidden to be given unto those that are not God?
All Religious Service: As,

1. Praying, Isa. 44. 17.
2. Thanksgiving, Judges 16. 23, 24. Dan. 5. 4.
3. Offering of Sacrifice, 2 Kings 17. 35.
4. Burning of Incense, Jer. 18. 15. & 44. 17.
5. Vowing.
6. Fasting.
7. Building of Temples, Altars, or other Monuments unto them, Hos. 8. 14. & 12. 11.
8. Erecting of Ministries, (1 Kings 12. 31, 32.) or doing any Ministerial Work for their honor, Amos 5. 26. with Numb. 4. 24, 25.
9. Preaching for them, Jer. 2. 8.
10. Asking Counsel of them, Hos. 4. 12.
11. Outward Religious Adoration of them, Acts 10. 25, 26. Rev. 22. 8, 9.

To whom must this Worship be denied?
To every thing that is not God: As the Sun and Moon, &c. Angels, Saints, Relics, Images, and such trash as Rome alloweth, Deut. 4. 17, 19. Col. 2. 18. Rev. 19. 10. & 22. 8, 9. Acts. 10. 25, 26.

What is there in this Commandment expressly forbidden concerning Images?
First, The making of them. Secondly, The bowing unto them, or worshipping them.

Why is the first of these so largely set forth?
To meet with the Corruption of Men, that by Nature are exceeding prone unto Idolatry.

What Men are forbidden to make Images?
All Men, which have not some special warrant from God to make them.

But though I do not make Images my self; may I worship them that another Man makes?
No. For that is likewise forbidden. Exod. 32. 1. &c.

Is it not lawful to put them in Churches, or in public Places, if they be not worshipped?
No.

Twenty-second Head

Why then did Moses make the Cherubim, and the Brazen Serpent?
For so doing he had a special Commandment from God; who may dispense with his own Laws when he will.

To what end did God command them to be made?
The one, to signify the crucifying of Christ, (John 3. 14.) the other, to signify the Angels readiness to help God's Children in all distresses.

Is all manner of making Images forbidden?
No: But only in matters of Religion, and God's Service. For in Civil Matters they may have a lawful and commendable use, (Mat. 22. 20.) but to make them for Religious Ends and Uses, is altogether unlawful, Amos 5. 26. with Acts 7. 43.

What gather you of this?
That the Popish Doctrine of Images, that they are all Lay-men's Books, is directly contrary to the Word of God; and therefore as false and erroneous, to be detested of all God's Children, Hab. 2. 18. Jer. 10. 8, 14. Isa. 44. 10.

What kind of Images are we forbidden to make?
All kinds: Whether hewn, engraved, cut or carved, (which in the Commandment is expressed): molten, embroidered, painted, printed, or imagined, Hos. 13. 2. Ezek. 8. 10. Acts 17. 25, 29.

Of what things are we forbidden to make Images?
Of things which are in the Heavens above, or in the Earth beneath, or in the Waters beneath the Earth.

What is meant by things which are in the Heavens?
GOD, CHRIST, the Angels, and the Saints, which are in the highest: The Sun, Moon, and Stars, which are in the middle; and the Fowls which are in the lowest Heaven, Deut. 4. 17, 19.

Is it not lawful to make the Image of God?
To represent him by any shape, is most of all forbidden and condemned. For it is a great sin to conceive or imagine in our hearts, that he is like any thing, how excellent soever we think it, (Acts 17. 29.) but it is much worse so to set him out to the view of others, considering that the Mind can conceive a further Beauty than the hand of the Artificer can express. And therefore the Children of Israel did sin grievously, and were worthily condemned, for making God like a Calf, Exod. 32. 4, 9, 10, 27, 28.

How may it further appear that it is unlawful to make the Image of God?
First, Because God being Infinite and Invisible, cannot without a Lie be resembled to any finite or visible thing, Acts 17. 20. Secondly, God by such Images is, as it were mocked, Rom. 1. 23. Thirdly, When the Law was delivered by God himself unto the Israelites, he appeared in no shape unto them, lest they should make a likeness of him, and fall to Idolatry. And therefore Deut. 4. 10, 12. he forewarned them, that as they saw no Image of him, when he gave the Law, but only heard a Voice; they should learn that the Knowledge of God cometh by hearing, and not by seeing, Isa. 40. 17, 18.

But what moved the Papists to paint God like an Old Man?
The false expounding of that place in Daniel, where God is described to be the Ancient of days, (Dan. 7. 9, 13.) whereby is meant his Eternity, that he was before all times, Deut. 27. 15. but whatsoever Property in God it be, that they set forth by an Image, it is execrable so to do.

May we then paint Christ, for remembrance of his Death?
No verily. For, 1. It is a part of the Worship here forbidden: Because his Body is a Creature in Heaven; therefore not to be represented by an Image in the Service of God. 2. An Image can only represent the Man-hood of Christ, and not his Godhead, which is the chiefest part in him. Both which Natures being in him inseparable; it were dangerous by painting the one a-part from the other, to give occasion of Arrianism, Apollinarism, or other Heresies. 3. since that in all the Scriptures, which speak so much of him, there is no show of any Portraiture or Lineament of his Body; it is plain that the Wisdom of God would not have him painted. 4. since by preaching of the Gospel, and Administration of the Sacraments, Christ is as lively painted out, as if he were crucified again amongst us, (Gal. 3. 1.) it were to no purpose to paint him to that end.

What lastly may be added to these former Reasons?
That although the painting of Christ were both lawful to do, and profitable for remembrance; yet because it hath been so much abused, and no where in the Scripture commanded, it is now not to be used. As Ezechias worthily brake the Brazen Serpent being abused; although Moses had set it up at the Commandment of the Lord; and might have served for a singular Monument of God's Mercy, after the proper use thereof, had not the superstitious Opinion thereof been.

What is meant in this Commandment by things in the Earth?
The likeness of Man or Woman, or of Beasts, or creeping things, Ezek. 23. 14. Deut. 4. 16, 17, 18. Isa. 44. 13. Rom. 1. 23.

What by things in the Waters, under the Earth?
The resemblance of any Fish, or the like, Deut. 4. 18.

So much for the making of Images. What is meant by the bowing unto them, and worshipping them?
That we must not give the least token of Reverence, either in Body or in Soul, unto any Religious Images, Psal. 97. 7. Hab. 2. 18. Isa. 44. 15. Exod. 32. 4. For that is a further degree of Idolatry; as to shrine, clothe, and cover them with precious things; to light Candles before them; to kneel and creep to them, or to use any Gestures of Religious Adoration unto them, 1 Kings 19. 18. Wherein, although the gross Idolatry of Popery may be taken away from amongst us, yet the Corruption cleaveth still to the Hearts of many: As may be seen in them that make curtsy to the Chancel where the high Altar stood, and give the right hand unto standing Crosses and Crucifixes, &c.

But though we do not reverence the Images themselves; may we not worship God in or by the Images?
No. For the Israelites are condemned, not for worshipping the Golden Calf as a God, but for worshipping God in the Calf.

How does that appear?
In that they said, Let us make a Feast to morrow to Jehovah, Exod. 32. 5. And that Moses otherwise might seem not to have done well in making them to drink that against their Conscience, which they judged to be God, vers. 20.

Wherein did they sin so grievously?
In tying the presence of God to the work of their own hands, and coupling him with their Idols; which he cannot endure. For God saith by his Prophet Hosea, You shall no more call me Baal, Hos. 2. 16. So impossible it is truly to serve God by an Idol, as the Papists do.

Twenty-second Head

What kind of Images are here forbidden to be worshipped?
All kinds: Whether such as are made with Man's hands, (of which Isaiah speaketh, saying, One piece of Wood is cast into the Fire, and another of the same Tree is made an Idol, Isa. 44. 15, 17.) or such as in themselves are the good Creatures of God, as those which Hosea speaketh of, saying, They worship their Gold and Silver, Hos. 8. 4. Yea, of whatsoever things it may be said, That they have Eyes and see not, Mouths and speak not, Ears and hear not, Noses and smell not, Feet and go not, (Psal. 115.) unto them is this Worship forbidden to be performed.

What gather you of this?
That the Popish Idolatry is here flatly condemned. For although they worship not Jupiter, Mars, and such-like Heathen Idols, but the Holy Saints (as they say) in and by their Images; yet that worship of theirs is alike with the other; because these Places of Scripture do agree as well to the one as to the other: And therefore it is impious and abominable Idolatry.

So much for the practicing of Idolatry.
What is forbidden for the countenancing of it?
All the means and occasions of and to Idolatry; and giving the least allowance or liking that can be thereunto. As,

1. Urging by Authority, or Toleration of Idolatry, 2 Chron. 15. 16.

2. Approbation thereof by Speech, (praising and extolling these Inventions of Men) by silence, or any Gesture.

3. Presence at Idolatrous Worship: As going to Mass, and communicating with false Service, 1 Cor. 10. 18, 20, 21. & 2 Cor. 6. 16, 17.

4. Contributing towards the Maintenance thereof, Numb. 7. 3, 5. Nehem. 10. 32, 39.

5. Making a gain thereby: As those Merchants do, which sell Beads and Crosses; and those Painters, which take Money for Religious Images, Acts 19. 24, 25.

6. Retaining and preserving any superstitious Relics or Monuments of Idolatry; as Images, (2 Kings 18. 4.) Books, (Acts 19. 19.) Names, (Psal. 16. 4.) and such-like.

7. Keeping Company with Teachers of Idolatry, 2 Epistle of John, vers. 10, 11.

8. Making Leagues of Familiarity, Society, and Friendship with Idolaters, 2 Chron. 19. 2.

9. Joining in Marriage and Affinity with them, 2 Cor. 6. 14. Nehem. 13. 25, 26, 27. Deut. 7. 3, 4.

What Reasons does God use to strengthen this Commandment withal?
They are taken partly from his Titles, and partly from his Works.

What are we to learn from hence?
That if we consider aright of the Titles and Works of God; it will be a notable means to keep us from sin.

How is the Reason drawn from God's Titles laid down?
In these words: For I the Lord thy God am a jealous God.

Which is the first Title that is here mentioned?
JEHOVAH: Which noteth the Essence of God, and the Perfection thereof.

What have we to learn from hence?
That Idolaters are so far from worshipping the true God, that they deny his Being and Perfection.

What is the second Title?
Thy God: Whereby the Covenant of Grace is signified; which on our part is by no Sin so directly violated, as by Idolatry, called therefore in Scripture Spiritual Adultery, Jer. 3. 8.

What does this teach us?
That Idolaters are most miserable, in forsaking the true God, who is all Happiness to his People.

What is the third Title?
El: That is, a mighty or strong God; and therefore perfectly able to save and destroy.

What does this teach us?
That there is no Power so great, which can deliver Idolaters or Sinners from the Wrath of God.

What is the fourth Title?
Jealous: Whereby the Nature of God is signified, loving Chastity in his Spouse, with a most fervent Love; and abhorring spiritual Whoredom with most extreme hatred.

What are we to learn from hence?
That the Lord can no more abide Idolatry, than a married Man can brook it, that his Wife should commit Adultery. For his Wrath is compared to the Rage of a jealous Husband, upon the unchaste Behavior of his Wife, Prov. 6. 34, 35.

Declare this Comparison more at large.
The jealous Man finding the Adulterer with his Wife, spareth neither the one nor the other. So if any that by profession hath been espoused to Christ, and joined unto God in him, and hath promised in Baptism to serve him alone; yet notwithstanding shall forsake him, and worship others, how good soever they be (whether Saints or Angels) they shall not escape God's Wrath. For if Corporal Adultery be so severely punished, much more shall Spiritual.

What do the Reasons drawn from the Works of God contain?
A just Recompense to the Breakers of this Law; and a gracious Reward to them that keep it: God showing himself in this Case to be jealous, 1. By punishing Sin in many Generations. 2. By extending his Mercy in a far more abundant manner to them that keep his Law.

So the former Reason containeth a Threatening, to restrain from Disobedience; the latter, a Promise to allure to Obedience.

How is the former of these Reasons laid down?
In these words: Visiting the Iniquities of the Fathers upon the Children, unto the third and fourth Generation of them that hate me.

What is the Sum of this Reason?
That he will visit such as (how soever pretending Love) do thus declare their hatred of him; and punish them, both in themselves, and their Children, to many Generations.

What does God mean when he saith, That he will visit the Sins of the Fathers upon the Children?
Two things: 1. That he will inquire and search whether he can find any of the Parents Sins, and especially their Idolatry, in their Children. 2. That having found Children continuing in their Father's Sins, he will remember the same in the punishment of them.

What are we to learn from hence?
1. That howsoever God for a time does seem not to regard our sins, yet he does both see them, and in his due time will punish them, if we do not repent. 2. That neither the Example of our Parents, nor any other that do amiss, can be a sufficient warrant to us to commit any Sin. 3. That all Parents are carefully to take heed how they commit any sin; because in so doing, they bring God's Judgments not only upon themselves, but also upon their Children. 4. That Children are to sorrow for being born of Idolatrous Forefathers.

But how does that agree with the Righteousness of God, to punish the Children for the Sins of their Fathers?
Very well. For if Princes (whose Judgments are shallow in Comparison of Gods, the Depths whereof are past finding out) do with Equity disinherit and put to shame the Posterity of Traitors: The Lord may much more justly do the like with the wicked Child which followeth his Father's steps, and is a Traitor himself; having both his Father's Sin and his own upon his Head. For God here only threatens to punish those Children, which continue in their Father's Sins: And therefore as they have part in their Father's Sins, so it is reason they should have part in their Parents Punishments.

What does God mean by the third and fourth Generation?
He meaneth that not only the next Children, but the Children of divers and many Generations shall smart for their Father's Sins. As in Amos: For three transgressions and for fear; that is, for many.

Why then does he specially name three or four Generations?
Because Parents live so long oft times, that they see their Posterity for four Generations following punished for their Sins.

Why does God say of them that hate me?
To show, that not all the Sons of the Wicked, but only such as continue in their Father's Wickedness, shall be punished for their Sins, Ezek. 18. 4, 10, 13, 14, 17.

But is there any that hate God?
Yes verily, (John 15. 18. Rom. 1. 29, 30. & 5. 10. & 8. 7. Col. 1. 21.) so many as worship him otherwise than himself hath commanded, do hate him. For although every Idolater will say, that he loveth God; yet here God witnesseth of him that he is a Liar, and that he hateth God, in that he hateth the Worship that he commandeth; in the love whereof, God will have the experience of his love, 2 Chron. 19. 2. Mich. 2 8.

In what Words is the second Reason laid down, which is drawn from the Clemency of God?
Where it is said, that he showeth Mercy unto thousands of them that love him and keep his Commandments.

What is the Sum of this Reason?
That God will bless the Obedient unto many Generations, both in themselves, their Children and Posterity, and in whatsoever belongeth unto them: thus extending his Mercy unto thousands of such, as show their Love of him by Obedience to this his Law.

Why does the Lord say, That he will show mercy to them that love him, and keep his Commandments?
To teach us that the best Deeds of the best Men cannot merit or deserve any thing at God's hands; but had need to be received of him in mercy.

Wherefore does he say, That he will show mercy to thousands; seeing he said, that he would visit only the third and fourth Generation of them that hate him?
Because he is more willing and ready to exercise his Mercy than his Anger.

But will God be merciful to all the Children of the Godly?
No: But only such as love him, and keep his Commandments.

Is this Blessing proper to the Godly?
Not altogether neither. For God rewardeth the Prosperity of the Wicked with outward Benefits oftentimes, according to their outward Service: As appeareth by the Succession of Jehu.

[23RD HEAD.]

So much of the second Commandment. What is the third?
Thou shalt not take the Name of the Lord thy God in vain: For the Lord will not hold him guiltless that taketh his Name in vain. Exod. 20. 7.

What is contained in these words?
1. The Commandment. 2. The Reason.

What is the sum of this Commandment?
That we impeach not, but by all means advance the Glorious Name of God, in all things whereby he maketh himself known to Men, (Psal. 29. 2.) and carefully endeavour in our whole Life to bring some honor to God, Mat. 5. 16.

What do you observe herein?
The high honor that God showeth unto us, who being able without us to maintain his own Name and Glory; either by him, or by his Angels; hath notwithstanding committed the maintenance thereof unto us: Which should teach us to be very chary of it, and careful to discharge our Duty faithfully, in walking worthy of this honor and defense of his Name which he vouchsafeth us.

What is the meaning of those words; Thou shalt not take?
Thou shalt not take up, upon thy Lips or Mouth, (as this Phrase is opened in Psal. 16. 4. & 50. 16.) that is, not speak, use, or mention. For the Tongue is here specially bound to good speech.

Why was it needful to have a special Commandment for the Direction of the Tongue in God's Service?
Because it is an untamed Evil and unbridled, (James 3. 8.) and therefore a whole Commandment cannot be employed amiss for the Direction of it, in the use of the

Name of God. And seeing, in the second Table, there is a Commandment tending almost wholly to restrain the abuse of our Tongues towards our Neighbor, there is much more need of a Precept, both for direction and restraint of it, in the matters concerning God and his most Glorious Name.

What are we to understand by the Name of God?
The Speech is taken from the manner of Men, who are known by their Names; to signify God himself, both in his Essence and Majesty, (Isa. 26. 8. Exod. 3. 13, 14. & 34. 5, 6, 7.) and in all things, whereby he hath made himself known unto us: As is holy.

1. Titles and proper Names: As Jehovah, Elohim, Jesus, &c. Exod. 3. 14. & 6. 2, 3. Psal. 68. 4.

2. Properties and Attributes: As Love, Wisdom, Power, Justice, &c. Exod. 33. 18, 19. & 34. 5, 6, 7, 14.

3. Works and Actions, Psal. 8. 1, 9. & 145. 10.

4. Word: Both Law and Gospel, Psal. 138. 2. Deut. 18. 19, 22. & 32. 2. Acts 9 15. Whence, the Law of Christ, Isa. 42. 4. is expounded to be his Name, Mat. 12. 21.

5. Sacraments, Mat. 28. 18, 19. Acts 2. 38.

6. Censure, 1 Cor. 5. 4, 5. Mat. 18. 20.

7. Prayer, Gen. 4. 26.

8. The whole Worship of God, with all the Ordinances pertaining thereto; and whatsoever he is honored, reverenced, and glorified by, Deut. 12. 5. Mal. 1. 11, 12. Mich 4. 5. Acts 21. 13.

What is meant by this word, in vain?
All abuse of them; and all rash, negligent, and careless dealing therein:
where mentioning the smaller Fault, he declareth the heinousness of the greater. For if the taking of his Name in vain only be a sin; how heinous a sin is it, when it is blasphemed, or used for Confirmation of a Lie?

What is then forbidden in this Commandment?
Every wrong offered to the Glory of God; and doing of ought that may any way reproach the Lord, to cause him to be less esteemed, Mal. 1. 6, 12. All irreverent and unholy use of his Name: And profaning of his Titles, Properties, Actions and Ordinances, either by Mouth or by Action, Levit. 21. 23.

What are the parts of the prohibition?
Two: 1. The mentioning or using God's Name, in Word, or Deed, when it should not be used, and when there is no just cause so to do. 2. The using of it amiss, and abusing it; when Duty bindeth us to use it with Fear and Holiness.

What is required in this Commandment?
That we sanctify God's Name as it is holy and reverend, (Mat. 6. 9. Psal. 111. 9.) and labor by all we can to lift it up, that others may be moved by us more to love, serve and honor him. That we use the things aforesaid with all Reverence and Circumspection, to such uses as they are appointed to by God. In a word, that we have a careful and

attentive watch to all things that may advance God's Glory: And use all sincere and diligent Behavior therein.

What is that wherein this our Carefulness is required?
1. A diligent Preparation and Advisedness before we meddle with any of these Holy things: That we bethink ourselves before-hand what we are to do; and consider both of the cause that should move us to speak of them, and of the reverent manner of using them. 2. A reverent disposition in the Action it self: That we use earnest attentiveness therein: And seriously think how powerful God is, to punish the taking of his Name amiss; as also how able and ready to bless them, who shall reverently and holily behave themselves in the right use thereof. For which cause we are to remember, that the Name of God is Fearful; as it is written, Psal. 99. 3. Deut. 28. 58.

Declare now what particular Duties are contained in this Commandment?
1. The honoring of God, and his Religion, by our Holy Conversation, Mat. 5. 16. Tit. 2. 10. The contrary whereof, is, Profession joined with Hypocrisy, (Tit. 1. 16. Mat. 15. 7, 8, 9.) Profaneness and an evil Life, whereby the Name of God and the Profession of Religion is dishonored, Rom. 2. 24.

2. Confession of Christ unto Suffering, yea Martyrdom, if cause be, Rev. 2. 13. the contrary whereof, is, shrinking in case of Peril, and denying God the honor of our suffering for him, Mat. 10 33.

3. Honorable and reverent mention of God and his Titles, Properties, Attributes, Works, Word and Ordinances, Psal. 19. 1, 2. & 71. 15.

What Vices are repugnant to this?
All irreverent mention, or an unadvised, sudden, and causeless speaking of any of these; and all abusing of the Names and Titles of God.

How is that done?
First, By saying in our common talk; O Lord, O God, O Jesu, &c. or in wondering wife; Good God! Good Lord! &c. in matters light and of no moment. For such Foolish Admirations, and taking of God's Name lightly upon every occasion, is here condemned. Second, By idle Wishes. Third, By Imprecations and Cursings, Gen. 16. 5. 2 Sam. 16. 8, 9. Fourth, By Blaspheming. Fifth, By the abuse of Oaths, Jam. 5. 12.

Is there any true use of Oaths?
Yes. In matters of Importance, that cannot be decided but by an Oath; it is good and lawful to swear by the Name of God, and a Duty specially commanded, Deut. 6. 13. & 10. 20. so that it be done, truly, advisedly, and rightly. For so is the Commandment, Jer. 4. 2. Thou shalt swear, The Lord liveth, in Truth, in Judgment, and in Righteousness?

How are we to swear in Truth?
Affirming what we know to be true: And verifying by Deed what we undertake, Psal. 15. 4. & 24. 4.

What is here meant by Judgment?
A due Consideration, both of the Nature and Greatness of an Oath; wherein God is taken to witness against the Soul of the Swearer, if he deceive; and of the due calling and warrant of an Oath, whether public, being demanded by the Magistrate, without Peril to the Swearer, (Gen. 43. 3.) or private, in case of great Importance, when the Truth cannot otherwise be cleared, Exod. 22 11. 1 Sam. 20. 17. 2 Cor. 1. 23.

Twenty-third Head

What Considerations are then to be had in taking of an Oath?
1. Whether the Party we deal with, doubt of the thing we speak of, or not? 2. If the Party doubt; whether the Matter whereof we speak, be weighty and worthy of an Oath? 3. If it be weighty, whether the Question or Doubt may be ended with Truly and Verily, or such-like naked Asseverations? Or by doubling our Asseveration, as our Savior Christ did: For then, by his Example, we ought to forbear an Oath, Mat. 5. 37. 4. Whether there be not yet any other fit means to try out the Matter before we come to an Oath. 5. Whether he for whose cause we give the Oath, will rest in it, and give credit unto it: For otherwise the Name of God is taken in vain, Heb. 6. 16. 6. When the Matter is of Importance, and there is no other Trial but an Oath: And we must have our Minds wholly bent to sanctify the Name of God by the Oath we take; and think upon the Greatness of God's Power to punish Oaths taken amiss, and to bless the true use of them.

How are we to swear in Righteousness?
1. In a due form: Which must be no other than God's Word alloweth, viz. by God alone, not by any Creature or Idol, Deut. 6. 13. Isa. 65. 16. Zeph. 1. 5. Jer. 12. 16 Mat. 5. 34, &c. Although in lawful Contracts with an Infidel or Idolater, we may admit of such Oaths, whereby he sweareth by his false Gods. 2. To a right end; which is the Glory of God, (Isa. 45. 23. with Phil. 2. 11.) the good of his Church, and Peace amongst Men, Heb. 6. 16.

What Persons may lawfully take an Oath?
Such only as have weighty Matter to deal in: And therefore it is altogether unlawful for Children to swear; as also, because they cannot think sufficiently of the Dignity of an Oath. No Atheist or profane Man should swear; because they either believe not, or they serve not God, Rom. 1. 9. In Women Oaths should be more seldom than in Men; in Servants than in Masters; in poor Men than in Rich, because they deal not in so weighty Matters.

What are the special abuses of an Oath?
1. The refusing of all Oaths, as unlawful: Which is the error of the Anabaptists.

2. A rash and vain Oath, where there is no cause of swearing; when upon every light occasion we take up the Name of God, and call him for a Witness of frivolous things, by usual swearing, Mat. 5. 34. James 5. 12. Jer. 23. 10.

3. A Superstitious or Idolatrous Oath: When we swear by an Idol, or by God's Creatures, Zeph. 1. 5. Amos 8. 14. as by the Mass, our Lady, &c. Bread, Salt, Fire, and many fond trashes. Whereas God never appointed the Creatures for such uses.

4. A counterfeit and mocking Oath.

5. Passionate swearing, whereby we call God for a Witness of our furious anger, 1 Sam. 14. 39. 2 Kings 6. 31.

6. Outrageous and blasphemous swearing.

7. Perjury; when God is called for a Witness of an Untruth, by forswearing, Isa. 48. 1. Zech. 5. 4. which is, first, when one sweareth that which he himself thinketh to be false, Levit. 19. 12. Secondly, When he sweareth, and does not perform his Oath, 2 Chron. 36. 13.

8. Taking a lawful Oath without due Reverence and Consideration.

So much for the right use and abuse of an Oath. Declare now further, how the Name of God is taken in vain, in regard of his Properties and Attributes.
First, by seldom or never breaking forth into such Confession and Declaration of God's Power, Wisdom, Justice, Mercy, &c as ourselves and others might thereby be stirred up the more to be thankful unto him, and to stay upon him, Psal. 40. 9. Second, by abusing his Properties; and by carnal, careless, or contemptuous speaking of them, 2 Kings 7. 2.

How is God's Wisdom touched here?
By calling it into question; and prying into the hidden Counsels of God. As when a Man undertaketh to foretell future things and events, &c.

How is his Justice?
1. By passing over his Judgments without notice. 2. By Cursings and Imprecations; whereby we make ourselves Judges, and attribute that to ourselves which is due to God. 3. By misconstruing and perverting his Judgments.

How is his Mercy?
First, By passing over of his Benefits, without due notice taken; and not observing and recounting, what special Mercies he hath vouchsafed us in particular, Psal. 66. 16. & 103. 2, 3, &c. Second, By presuming upon his Mercy, to harden our Hearts in sinning, Deut. 29. 19.

How is the Name of God taken in vain, in respect of his Works and Actions?
By, 1. not seeing God in his Works, Acts 17. 27.

2. Lightly passing over of God's great Works, of Creation, Preservation, Redemption; as also other his Mercies and Judgments, and not glorifying God for that which may be seen in them.

3. Vain and foolish Thoughts concerning the Creatures: Whereby a virtue is attributed unto them, which God never gave unto them. As all guessing of future things by the Stars, or a Man's Face and Hands: The counting it a prodigious Token, that a Hare should cross our way, &c.

4. Not using the Creatures as we ought; not receiving them to God's Glory, with Thanksgiving. As when a Man giveth not thanks to God for his Meat and Drink, but does think them to come without God's Providence: Which is a fearful taking of God's Name in vain.

5. Faultfinding at the Doctrine of Predestination, (Rom. 9. 19, 20.) and not admiring the depth of his Counsels, Rom. 11. 33, 34.

6. Murmuring at God's Providence, under the names of Fortune, Chance, and Fate, &c. Job 3. 2, 3, &c.

7. Evil thoughts towards our Brethren, which are afflicted. As when we see one visited by God, either in Body, Goods, or both; we are always ready to think the worse of him; viz. that God executeth these Punishments on him for his sin. When as God may do it either to exercise the Faith and Patience of the Party afflicted, as in Job; or to stir others to Compassion and Pity: or else to set forth his own Glory, as we may see verified in the Example of the blind Man in the Gospel, John 9. 2, 3.

8. Abuse of Lots, Esther 3. 7. Prov. 16. 33.

How is God's Name taken in vain, in regard of his Word?
1. By not speaking of it at all, Deut. 6. 7. Psal. 37. 30.

2. By foolish and fruitless speaking of it; or abusing any part thereof unto idle and curious questions, 2 Pet. 3. 16.

3. By abusing it to profane Mirth, by framing Jests out of it, or against it, (Psal. 22. 13.) also by making Plays and Interludes thereof.

4. By maintaining Error, Sin and Profaneness by it, Mat. 4. 6. Isa. 66. 5.

5. By applying it to Superstition, and unlawful Arts: To Magical Spells, Sorceries, and Charms, for the healing of Diseases, finding out Theft, &c. Deut. 18. 11. Acts 19. 23.

How is God's Name taken in vain, in regard of the Sacraments and other Holy Mysteries and Ordinances of God?
When they are unworthily received, and profanely used, Mal. 1. 11, 12. 1 Cor. 11. 27, 29. Jer. 7 4, 10.

So much of the chief particulars forbidden in this Commandment. What are the helps or hindrances of the Obedience thereof?
1. That we both inure our Hearts to fear and reverence the great and dreadful Name of the Lord our God, (Deut. 28. 58. Eccles. 9. 2.) and keep a careful watch over our Lips and Lives, lest by any means we dishonor him, Psal. 39. 1.

2. That we avoid, both the Company of profane Persons, who set their Mouth against Heaven, (Psal. 73. 9.) and all unnecessary dangers, whereby divers have been occasioned to deny the Lord, Mat. 26. 69. &c.

What is contained in the Reason annexed to the Commandment?
A dreadful Penalty: That the Lord will not hold him guiltless that taketh his Name in vain.

What is the sum of this Threat?
That God will not leave this sin unpunished, (1 Kings 2. 9.) but will grievously punish the Breach of this Commandment: Whereby he threateneth extreme Miseries and Judgments to the Transgressors. For it being our Happiness to have our sins covered, and not imputed, (Psalm 32. 2.) it must needs be extreme Unhappiness, to have them reckoned and imputed unto us.

What is implied herein?
A fit Opposition: That howsoever Man's Laws take not hold of offending in this kind; yet God will not acquit them, (Psalm 1. 5.) nor suffer them to escape his righteous and fearful Judgments, (Zech. 5. 3. Jer. 5. 12.) Neither shall the Transgressor escape unpunished, although the Magistrate and Minister also would pronounce him innocent. And although the Malefactor flatter himself, as if all dangers were past; nay, the more free, that (usually) he escapes the Judgments and Punishments of Men: The more heavy Plagues and Vengeance will surely light upon him from God, except he repent.

[24TH HEAD.]

Hitherto of the Commandments concerning that Service which is to be performed to God at all times, as occasion shall require. What is that which concerneth the special time, wholly to be bestowed in his Worship?
The fourth and last Commandment of the first Table; which setteth forth a certain Day, especially appointed by the Lord himself, to the practice of the Worship prescribed in the three former Commandments: For therein consisteth the chief Point of the sanctifying of that Day.

What are the Words of this Commandment?
Remember that thou keep holy the Sabbath-Day, &c. Exod. 20. 8, 9, 10, 11.

What are we to observe in these Words?
First, The Commandment; and then the Reasons annexed thereunto.

What is the meaning of the Commandment?
It challengeth at the hand of every Man, one day of seven in every Week, to be set apart unto a holy Rest, and requireth all Persons to separate themselves from their ordinary Labor, and all other Exercises, to his Service on the same: That so being severed from their worldly Businesses, and all the Works of their Labor and Callings concerning this Life, they may wholly attend to the Worship of God alone, Nehem. 13. 15, 22. Isa. 58. 13, 14.

Why do you add these Words [apart] and [separate?]
To make a difference between the Sabbath-Days, wherein we must wholly and only serve God; and the Exercises of the other Six Days, wherein every Man must serve him in his lawful Calling.

What need is there of one whole Day in every Week to serve God; seeing we may serve him every Day?
That is not enough. For,

1. To the end that we should not plunge ourselves so deeply into the Affairs of the World, as that we should not recover ourselves; the Wisdom of God hath thought it fit, that one Day in Seven there should be an intermission from them: That we might wholly separate ourselves to the Service of God, and with more freedom of Spirit perform the same.

2. A whole Day is needful for the performance of all the parts of God's Service and Worship: As hearing of Public Prayer, and the Word preached, Catechizing, Administration of the Sacraments, Exercise of Holy Discipline, and Consideration of the Glory of God in the Creatures.

3. If Adam in his Perfection had need of this Holy-Day; much more have we, who are so grievously corrupted.

4. If the Lord in Love and Wisdom, considering our Necessities both of Soul and Body, hath set out a Week's-time for both of Provision: That as every Day we set apart some time for Food, and spend the rest in Labor, so we set one Day in the Week aside for our Spiritual Food, and bestow the other Days on our Earthly Affairs. So that this day may in comparison be accounted the Soul's Day: Wherein yet we must have some care of our Bodies; as on the Six Days we must have some care of our Souls.

What is forbidden in this Commandment?
The unhallowing or profaning of the Sabbath, either by doing the Works of our Calling, and of the Flesh, or by leaving undone the Works of the Spirit.

But is not this Commandment Ceremonial, and so taken away by the Death of Christ?
No: But is constantly and perpetually to be observed, and never to cease 'till it be perfectly consummated in the Heavenly Sabbath, Heb. 4. 9, 10.

How perceive you that?
1. Because it is placed in the number of the perpetual Commandments. Otherwise the Moral Law should consist but of Nine Words or Commandments; which is contrary to God's Word, Deut. 4. 13.

2. Because this Commandment (among the rest) was written by the Finger of God, (Exod. 31. 18.) whereas no part of the Ceremonial Law was.

3. For that it was written in Tables of Stone, as well as the other, (Deut. 5. 22.) as to signify the hardness of our Hearts, so to signify the continuance and perpetuity of this Commandment, as well as the rest.

4. Because it was before any Shadow or Ceremony of the Law; yea, before Christ was promised, whom all Ceremonies of the Law have respect unto. For the Sabbath was first instituted in Paradise, before there was any use of Sacrifices and Ceremonies, Gen. 2. 1, 2, 3.

5. The Ceremonies were as a Partition-Wall betwixt the Jews, and the Gentiles: But God does here extend his Commandment, not only to the Jews themselves, but also to the Strangers, Exodus 20. 10. Nehem. 13. 15, 16, &c.

6. Our Savior Christ willing his Followers, which should live about forty Years after his Ascension, to pray that their Flight might not be on the Sabbath Day, to the end that they might not be hindered in the Service of God; does thereby sufficiently declare, that he held not this Commandment in the account of a Ceremony, Mat. 24. 20.

But it sometimes shadoweth our Sanctification, and our eternal Rest, (Col. 2. 16, 17. Exod. 31. 13.) and is therefore Ceremonial.
That followeth not. For, 1. There is no Commandment which hath not some Ceremonies tied unto it: As in the Commandment touching Murder, to abstain from strangled Things and Blood. And the whole Law had the Ceremony of the Parchment Law. So by that reason the whole Law should be Ceremonial: Which is absurd. 2. The Ceremonial Representation of our Eternal Rest, came after the Commandment of the Rest, and therefore is accessory and accidental. For which cause, the time of Correction and Abolishment of Ceremonies being come, (Dan. 9. 7. Mat. 11. 13. Acts 15. 6. Col. 2. 13, 14. Heb. 10. 14. Gal. 5. 2.) that use may well fall away, and yet the Commandment remain; it being not of the substance of the Commandment.

What is the special Day of the Week, which God hath set apart for his Solemn Worship?
The first Day of the Week, called the Lord's Day, 1 Cor. 16. 2. Rev. 1. 10. Acts 20. 7.

Was this Day set apart thereunto from the beginning?
No. For from the first Creation 'till the Resurrection of Christ, the last Day of the Week, commonly called Saturday, was the Day that was appointed thereunto, and that which the People of God constantly observed.

And why so?
Because upon that God ceased from the Work of Creation, Gen. 2. 2. Exod. 31. 17.

How came this Day to be changed?
By Divine Authority.

How does that appear?
By the Practice of our Savior Christ, and his Apostles, John 20. 19, 26. Acts 2. 1. and 20. 7. which should be a sufficient Rule unto us; especially the Apostle's having added a Commandment thereunto, 1 Cor. 16. 1, 2. There is no reason why it should be called the Lord's Day, Rev. 1. 10. But in regard of the Special Dedication thereof to the Lord's Service: For otherwise all the Days of the Week are the Lord's Days, and he is to be served and worshipped in them.

What was the cause why the Day was changed?
Because it might serve for a thankful Memorial of Christ's Resurrection. For as God rested from his Labor on the last Day of the Week: So Christ ceased from his Labor and Afflictions on this Day, Mat. 28. 1. Gen. 2. 1, the one therefore was specially sanctified in regard of the Creation of the World: So was the other, in respect of the Restoration and Redemption of the World; which is a greater Work than the Creation.

Can this Day then be altered?
No Power of any Creature in Heaven or Earth can alter it, or place another Seventh Day in the place and stead thereof.

Does not this Commandment directly require the Seventh Day from the Creation?
No; but the Seventh Day in general.

Does not the Reason annexed, where the Lord in six Days is said to make Heaven and Earth, and to rest the Seventh Day, and therefore to hallow it, confirm so much?
No, not necessarily. For it does not hence follow, that we should rest the same Day the Lord rested; but that we should rest from our Work the Seventh Day, as he rested from his: Which Seventh Day, under the Law, he appointed to be Saturday. So nothing hindreth, but by his special appointment under the Gospel it may be Sunday, and yet the substance of the Commandment nothing altered.

Why does not the New Testament mention this change?
Because there was no Question moved about the same in the Apostles time.

When then does this our Sabbath begin, and how long does it continue?
This Day, as all the six, is the space of Twenty-four Hours, and beginneth at the Dawning; though we ought in the Evening before to prepare for the Day following.

Why does our Sabbath begin at the Dawning of the Day?
Because Christ rose in the Dawning, and to put a difference between the Jewish, and the true Christian Sabbath. For as the Jews begun their Sabbath in that part of the Day, in which the Creation of the World was ended, and consequently in the Evening: So the Celebration of the Memory of Christ's Resurrection, and therein of his Rest from his special Labors, and the renewing of the World, being the ground of the change of that Day into this; it is also, by the same proportion of Reason, to begin when the Resurrection began, which was in the Morning.

Can you see this by Example?
Yea. Paul being at Troas, after he had preached a whole Day, until Midnight, celebrated the Supper of the Lord the same Night, which was a Sabbath Days Exercise: And therefore that Night following the Day, was a part of the Sabbath. For in the Morning he departed, having stayed there Seven Days: By which it is evident, that that which was done, was done upon the Lord's Day, Acts 20. 7, 10.

Is the Lord's Day only to be separated to God's Service?
No. For of this manner also are all Holy Fasts observed for the avoiding of some great Evil, present or imminent, (Lev. 23. 27. Joel 2. 12.) and Holy Feasts, for the thankful remembrance of some special memorable Mercies obtained, Zech. 8. 19. Esther 9. 17, 18, 19.

To what Commandment do you refer the Churches meeting on the Working days?
That is also, by a manner of Speech of one part for the whole, contained in this Commandment: Yea, it reacheth to the times which the Family appointeth, or that every one for his private good proposeth; although the Bond to that time is not so strict, as is the Bond to observe the Days of Rest.

So much of this Commandment in general.
What do you note therein in particular?
1. The Entrance, in the word Remember. 2. The Parts of the Commandment.

What is to be observed in the Word Remember?
That although all the Commandments are needful diligently to be yet this more specially.

Why so?
1. Because this Commandment hath least Light of Nature to direct us to the Observation of it. 2. For that naturally we are most negligent in it, suffering ourselves to be withdrawn by our worldly Business from the Lord's Service, upon the Lord's Day, and therefore such a special Warning is needful to be added.

What things are we hence to remember?
1. To look back unto the first Institution of the Sabbath Day in Paradise, Gen. 2. 2, 3. before all Sacrifices and Ceremonies. 2. So to bear it in mind, as to live in continual Practice of the Duties we learned the Sabbath Day last past. 3. To bethink ourselves before of the Works of the Sabbath; and so to prepare ourselves and our Affairs, (Luke 23. 54.) that we may freely and duly attend on the Lord in the Sabbath approaching.

What should be done in this Preparation of the Sabbath?
1. We should so compass all our Businesses within the six working Days, that our Worldly Affairs enter not, or encroach into the possession of the Lord's Day: Not only willingly, but not so much as by any Forgetfulness. As when through want of Fore-fight, or Fore-casting, the Payment of Money due by Obligation, or any such Businesses that might be prevented, shall fall out on that Day. 2. We should sanctify ourselves, and those that are under us, to keep that Day.

What is contrary to this?
The neglect of Preparation for the Sabbath before it come, and of fitting our Hearts for Holy Services when it is come.

What are the Parts of this Commandment?
They are two. First, To keep the LORD's Rest. Secondly, To sanctify this Rest. For it is not sufficient that we rest from Worldly Businesses; but it is further required, that it be

Holy Rest. The first showeth, what Works we are to decline upon this Day; the other, what Duties we are to perform.

What are the Works we are to decline, and leave undone on the Lord's Day?
Not only the Works of Sin, which we ought to leave undone every Day: But also Works of our ordinary Callings concerning this Life, and bodily Exercise and Labors; which upon other Days are lawful and necessary to be done, Mark 3. 4. Ezek. 23. 37, 38. Numb. 15. 32, 33. Exod. 31. 10, 11, 12, 13, 14. & 34. 21. Nehem. 13. 15, &c. Isa. 58. 13.

What Instances have you in Scripture of the Performance hereof?
The Israelites ceased both from those Works which were of the least importance, as gathering of Sticks, (Numb. 15. 32.) and from such also as were of greatest Weight, as working of the Tabernacle, and building the Temple on the Sabbath Day: And consequently all other Works, betwixt these extremes, as buying and selling, working in Seed time or Harvest, were forbidden unto them, Exod. 31. 14, 15, 16. & 34. 21.

Are we strictly bound to rest from all outward Businesses, and to forbear all worldly Labor upon this day, as the Israelites?
Yea, so far forth as the Morality of the Commandment reacheth. But by the Ceremonial Law, there was enjoined unto the Jews a more exact observation of outward Rest, which to them was a part of that Ceremonial Worship; whereas unto us the outward Rest is not properly any part of the Sanctification of the Day, or the Service of God; but only a means tending to the furtherance of the same. Even as in Fasting and Prayer; Fasting of it self is no part of God's Service, but a thing adjoined thereunto, and so far forth only acceptable in the Worship of God, as it maketh a way and readier passage for the other, 1 Cor. 8. 8.

What did that most strict Observance of outward Rest signify unto the Jews?
Their continual Sanctification in this World, (Exod. 31. 13. Ezek. 20. 12.) and their endless Rest in the World to come; whereof this was a Type no less than the Land of Promise, Heb. 4. 4, 5, 10.

How was the latter of these specially typified?
In this World God's Children are subject unto the fiery Trial, (1 Pet. 4. 12.) but after these Troubles, Rest is provided for them, (2 Thess. 1. 7.) and no Fire to be feared in that after-world. For a more lively Representation, there was a charge laid upon the Children of Israel, that no Fire might be kindled throughout all their Habitations upon the Sabbath Day, (Exod. 35. 3.) though it were for the very preparing of the Meat which they should eat, (Exod. 16. 23.) which was allowed unto them even in the two great solemn Days of the Passover, Exod. 12. 16.

Is it then lawful for us to make a Fire and dress Meat upon the Lord's Day?
Yea certainly. Because these were proper unto the Pedagogy or manner of Government of the Children of Israel under the Law: As may appear by this, that there was no such thing commanded before the Law was given by Moses; and consequently being not perpetual, must necessarily follow to be Ceremonial. Now after the Sabbath that Christ our Lord rested in the Grave, this Ceremonial Sabbath lieth buried in that Grave, together with those other Rites which were shadows of things to come, the Body being in Christ, (Col. 2. 16, 17.) Therefore we being dead with Christ from these Ceremonies, are no more to be burdened with such Traditions, (ibid. v. 20.) nor to be brought under the Bondage of any outward thing. It is a Liberty purchased unto us by Christ, and we must stand fast unto it: That Blessed Hour being come, wherein the true Worshippers are to worship the Father in Spirit and Truth, John 4. 23.

Twenty-fourth Head

To leave then the Ceremonial Sabbath, and to come to the Moral: How is the Rest required therein laid down in the fourth Commandment?
By a Declaration. First, Of the Works from which there must be a Cessation. Secondly, Of the Persons that must observe this Rest.

How is the former of these expressed?
In these words: In it thou shalt not do any work, Exod. 20. 10.

What is required of us hereby?
That for the Space of that whole Day, we cease in Mind and Body from all Worldly Labors; yea, from the Works of our lawful Calling, and all other earthly Businesses whatsoever, more than needs must be done, either for God's Glory or Man's Good.

What gather you of this?
That all Exercises that serve not in some degree to make us fit to the Lord's Work, are unlawful upon the Lord's Day.

Why do you say that we must rest in Mind and Body?
Because this Rest must be of the whole Man, in Thoughts, Words, and Deeds, Isa. 58. 13.

Is it merely unlawful to do any bodily or outward Business on the Lord's Day?
No. For first such Works are accepted as are presently necessary, either for common Honesty or Comeliness. Secondly, The Actions of Piety, requisite for the Performance of God's Service on that Day, Mat. 12. 5. Acts 1. 12. Thirdly, Extraordinary Exigents of Charity, for the Preservation of the Common-Wealth, 2 Kings 11. 9. Fourthly, The Preservation of our own or others Life, Health, and Goods, in case of present necessity, or great danger of their perishing if they were not saved on that day, Mat. 12. 1, 10, 11. Mark 3. 4. Luke 13. 15, 16.

What are the special breaches of this part of the Commandment?
1. The making of the Sabbath a common Day through common Labor in our ordinary Callings, (Nehem. 13. 15, &c.) vain Speech and talking of our worldly Affairs, (Isa. 58. 13.) thinking our own thoughts, or other, but a common use of the Creatures.

2. The making it a Day of carnal Rest unto Idleness, Feasting, Pastimes, &c. which draw our Minds further from God, than our ordinary Labors, Exod. 32. 6. Whither are referred all Recreations which distract us; as also excessive eating and drinking, which causeth drowsiness and inaptness unto God's Worship and Service.

3. The making it a Day of Sin, or the Devil's holy Day; by doing that on the Lord's Day which is no Day lawful, (Mark 3. 4.) but then most abominable, Ezek. 23. 37, 38.

4. The keeping a piece of the Day, not the whole; or giving liberty to ourselves in the Night, before the whole Sabbath be ended.

5. The forbearing ourselves, but employing others in Worldly Businesses; for preventing of which sin, God is so large in naming of the Persons which in this Commandment are forbidden to work.

Why is there a particular Rehearsal of these Persons in this Commandment?
To take away all Excuses from all Persons. For the Lord did see, that such was the Corruption of Men, that if they themselves did rest upon this Day from Labors, they would think it sufficient; not caring how they toiled out and wearied their Servants at

home with continual Labor, as many do: So that it were better to be such Men's Oxen than their Servants; so small Care they have of their Souls.

What is the special use of this Rehearsal?
To teach us that all sorts and degrees of Persons are bound to yield this Duty unto God: And that the Sabbath is to be kept both by ourselves and those that do belong unto us.

Was it not ordained also for the rest and refreshing of Men and Beasts; especially Servants, which could not otherwise continue without it?
That also was partly intended, (as may appear by Deut. 5. 14.) but not principally. For the things here contained do concern the Worship of God; but that wearing and toiling out of Servants and Beasts is against the Sixth Commandment: And working is here forbidden, that Men might be the more free for the Worship of God; and therefore though Servants had never so much Rest and Recreation upon other Days, yet they ought to Rest upon this Day in that regard.

Why is there mention made of allowing Rests to the Beasts?
First, That we may show Mercy even to the Beast, Prov. 12. 10. Secondly, To represent after a sort the everlasting Sabbath, wherein all Creatures shall be delivered from the Bondage of Corruption, Rom. 8. 20, 21. Thirdly, Because of the whole Employment of Men in the Lord's Service: For Beasts cannot be traveled or used in any Work upon that Day, unless Man be withdrawn from God's Service: Yea, though the Beast could labor without Man's attendance, yet his Mind would sometime or other be carried away and distracted thereby, that it would not be so fit as it ought to be for God's Service.

To whom especially is the Charge of this Commandment directed?
To Householders and Magistrates; who stand charged in the behalf, both of themselves, and of all that are under their Roof and Government, Jos. 24. 15. Neh. 13. 15, &c.

What is the Charge of the Householder?
That not only himself keep the Lord's Day, but also his Wife, Children, and Servants, as much as may be. For as they serve him in the Week Days; so he must see that they serve God on the Lord's Day.

What gather you of this?
That a Householder should at least be as careful of the Lord's Business, as of his own. And if he will not keep such a Servant as is not careful in his ordinary Work, much less should he keep any that will not be careful in the Lord's Work, how skillful soever he be in his own.

What is the Magistrate's part?
To see that all within his Gates keep the Lord's Day, (Jos. 24. 15.) even Strangers, though Turks and Infidels, (Nehem. 13. 15.) causing them to cease from Labor, and restraining them from all open and public Idolatry, or false Worship of God; much more all his own Subjects, whom he ought to force to hear the Word, 2 Chron. 34. 33.

So much of the first part of this Commandment, touching our rest from all worldly Businesses. What followeth in the next place?
The second and greater part of this Commandment: Which is the sanctifying of this Rest, and keep it holy unto the Lord; by exercising ourselves wholly in the Service of God, and performing the Duties of the Day.

Twenty-fourth Head

Are we as strictly bound to these Duties as the Jews?
Yes verily, and more than they: Because of the greater measures of God's Graces upon us, above that which was upon them.

What is required of us herein?
To make the Sabbath our delight; to consecrate it as glorious unto the Lord, (Isa. 58. 13.) and that with joy and without weariness, (Amos 8. 5. Mal. 1. 13.) and that also with care and desire of profit we bestow the whole Day (as Nature will bear) in holy Exercises.

What are these Exercises?
They are partly Duties of Piety, (Acts 13. 13, 15. & 20. 7. Psal. 92. 1.) as hearing and reading the Word, Prayer, singing of Psalms, and feeding ourselves with the Contemplation of the Heavenly Sabbath: Partly of Mercy, (1 Cor. 16. 2. Nehem. 8. 12.) as visiting and relieving the Sick and Needy, comforting the Sad, and such like.

How are these Duties to be performed?
Partly publicly in the Church; where the Solemn Worshipping of God is the special Work and proper Use of the Sabbath: Partly privately out of the Church; and that either secretly by ourselves alone, or jointly with others.

What if we cannot be suffered to use the Public Means?
Such as are necessarily debarred from the Public Duties, must humble themselves before God, mourning and sorrowing for this restraint, (Mat. 24. 20: Psal. 42. 6. & 84. 1, 2, 3.) and with so much more care and earnestness use the private means, Psal. 63. 1, 2.

What is the first Duty we are to perform in the Public Assembly?
To join in Prayer with the Congregation: Which is an excellent Duty. For if, as Christ saith, When two or three are gathered together in his Name, he will grant their Requests: How much more will he hear his Servants, when two or three hundred are gathered in his Name?

What is the second?
To hear the Word of God read, Luke 4. 16. Acts 3. 16. & 15. 20. for blessed is he that readeth, and they that hear the Word, Rev. 1. 3.

What is the third?
To hear the Word preached, Luke 4. 16, 22. Acts 13. 14, 15. & 15. 21. & 20. 7.

What is the fourth?
To communicate in the Sacraments: By being present when the Sacrament of Baptism is administered unto others; and by receiving the Sacrament of the Lord's Supper ourselves (after a decent order) in the appointed time, Acts. 20. 7. 1 Cor. 11. 20.

Why should a Man be present at Baptism?
First, That he may give Thanks to God for adding a Member to his Church. Secondly, That he might be put in mind of his own Vow made to God in Baptism, by seeing the Child baptized.

What is the fifth Duty to be performed in the Congregation?
Singing of Psalms.

What is the sixth?
Exercise of the Discipline of the Church against Offenders, 1 Cor. 5. 4.

A Body of Divinity

What is the seventh?
Collection for the Poor, and Contribution for Relieving the Necessities of the Saints of God, 1 Cor. 16. 1, 2. where we are to give according to our Wealth, and the Blessing of God upon the Week going before.

What are the private Duties that are to be performed out of the Church?
Such as we perform either in secret by ourselves alone, or in common with our Families at home, or others abroad: Both before the Public Exercises in the Church, the better to perform them; and after, the more to profit by them.

What are they in particular?
First, Private Prayer. Secondly, reading of the Word. Thirdly, Holy Conference touching the Word of God, and familiar talk of things that belong to the Kingdom of Heaven, Luke 14. 7, 19. Fourthly, Examination of ourselves, and those that belong unto us, what we have profited by the hearing of the Word, and other Exercises of Religion. Fifthly, Catechizing of our Families. Sixthly, Meditation upon God's Word, Properties, and Works, as well of Creation as of Providence; especially that which he exerciseth in the Government of the Church, Psal. 80. and 92. Seventhly, Reconciling such as are at variance. Eighthly, Visiting the Sick, relieving the Poor, &c. 1. Cor. 16. 2. Neh. 8. 12. For these also are Works of the Sabbath.

What proof have you of this continual Exercise and Employment of the whole Day in Holy Services?
First, In the Law, every Evening and every Morning were Sacrifices; which on the Sabbath where multiplied, Numb. 28. 9. Second, The 92 Psalm (entitled, A Psalm for the Sabbath) appointed to be sung that Day, declareth, that it is a good thing to begin the praises of God early, in the morning, and continue the same until it be night.

That we may know then how to spend a Sabbath well: declare more particularly how we may bestow the whole time in exercises of Holiness, and first begin with the evening Preparation.
Our care must be over-night, that having laid aside all our earthly Affairs, we begin to fit ourselves for the Lord's Service: that so we may fall asleep, as it were, in the Lord's Bosom, and awake with him in the morning.

What must be done in the Morning when we awake?
We are to put away all earthly Thoughts, and to take up such Meditations as may most stir up our Hearts with reverence and cheerfulness to serve the Lord the whole Day after. Wherein, first, we are to consider the great benefit of the Lord's Sabbath, and so cheer up our Hearts in the expectation to enjoy the same. Secondly, To covenant with the Lord, more religiously to sanctify the whole Day after.

In making of ourselves ready, what are we to do?
Rising as early for the Lord's Service, as we do for our own Businesses, and bestowing no more time nor care about our Apparel, and such like, than needs must: we may then occupy our Mind about such matters as be most fit for that time; which ordinarily may be these two.

1. To think upon God's goodness in giving us such Apparel, and other necessaries, which many others want: so that we may judge all things we have rather too good for us, than be discontented with any thing we enjoy. 2. Considering how well our Bodies be appareled, and provided for, to seek more to have our Souls better appareled with Christ Jesus.

Twenty-fourth Head

Being up and ready, what are we to set ourselves to?
We must set ourselves to morning Sacrifice, either alone, or with others, if it may be: some short Prayer for our preparation being used.

What Meditations must we here enter into?
Two especially: the one, for that which is past; the other, for that which is to come.

What for that which is past?
To cast our weeks account at least, how God hath dealt with us in Benefits and Chastisements; and how we have dealt with him in keeping or breaking his Commandments: that by both we may find matter to comfort and humble us, to move us to thankfulness for Mercies received, and to earnest suit and labor for pardon of our trespasses, and supply of all necessities.

What for that which followeth?
To prepare ourselves for the public Ministry, and as it were to apparel ourselves, and make ourselves fit to go to the Court of the Lord of Hosts, with his Children, and before his Angels.

What things are necessary hereunto?
1. A due regard whither we go, before whom, what to do, and to what ends, wherewith to honor God, and to receive Grace from him.
2. An earnest hunger so to use the means to God's honor and our good.
3. True Faith, that she shall enjoy our desire.
4. Joy and thankfulness in the hope of such blessings.
5. Humility, in regard of our unworthiness.
6. Unfeigned purpose of amendment of life.

What must be added unto these?
To the Meditations, fervent Prayer must be joined, and Reading, for our furtherance in God's Service: and such as conveniently can, are to join together in a Christian Family, to read, pray and confer; and Governors to instruct their Families in such matters as are then befitting.

Having thus spent the time privately, what is to be done in public?
We are to go to Church in all comely sort, before the public Ministry is begun, and then with all diligence to attend, and to give consent thereunto; and so to take to heart whatsoever shall be brought unto us, that by all the holy Exercises, we may be edified in all needful Graces.

The public Ministry ended, what are we to do?
We are to occupy our Minds on that we have heard, and when we come to place and time convenient, to set ourselves more especially to make use of it to ourselves and others pertaining to us; and to water it with our Prayers, that it may grow and bring forth Fruit.

What say you to our Diet, and refreshing of our Nature on this Day?
Care would be had, that it be such as every way may make us fitter for Holy Duties. And to this end, we are to season it with Meditation and Speeches of Holy Things.

How is the Afternoon to be spent?
1. The time before the Evening Sacrifice we are to bestow, either alone or with others, in such Exercises as may best quicken in us God's Spirit. 2. For the Evening Sacrifice, in all respects, to behave ourselves as in the Morning, and to continue to the end. 3. The public Ministry fully ended, to keep our Minds (in like sort as before) on that we

have heard; and so being come home, either alone or with others, to enter into examination of ourselves for the whole Day.

How are we to end the Day?
1. With thanks for God's Blessings on our Labors. 2. Humble suit for pardon of all our Faults escaped. 3. Earnest desire of Grace, to profit by all; that we may persevere unto the end, and be saved.

Do you make any difference between the Sabbath Nights and other Nights?
Yes: we should lay ourselves down to rest in great quietness that Night, upon the sense and feeling of the former Exercises: so that our sleep should be the more quiet, by how much the former Exercises of that Day have been more holy: otherwise we should declare, that we have not kept the whole Day so holy to the Lord as we ought.

What are the sins condemned in the second part of this Commandment?
Generally, the omission of any of the former Duties: and in particular: 1. Idleness: which is a sin every Day, but much more on the Lord's Day. 2. Profane absence from, or unfaithful presence at, God's Ordinances. 3. Neglect of calling ourselves to a reckoning after holy Exercises. 4. Being weary of the Duties of the Sabbath; thinking long till they be ended. Amos 8. 5. Mal. 1. 13.

What are the helps or hindrances to the keeping of this Commandment?
1. We must add to the aforementioned Duty of Remembrance, an ardent endeavour to taste the sweetness of Holy Exercises, (Psal. 24. 3. and 84. 1, &c.) that so we may come to make the Sabbath our delight. 2. We must avoid and abhor all profane Opinions, either disannulling the necessity of the Sabbath, or equaling any other Day to it; together with such Meetings and Companies, Exercises and Occasions, whereby we shall be in danger to be drawn to the unhallowing of the Sabbath Day, Ezek. 22. 26.

So much of the Commandment. What Reasons are used to enforce the same?
Four.

Whence is the first taken?
From Equity; by a secret reason of comparison of the less. That forasmuch as God hath allowed us six Days of seven for our Affairs (to do our own Business in; whether it be Labor, or honest Recreation) and reserved but one for himself; when as he might most justly have given us but one of seven, and have taken six to himself: we ought not to think it much, to spend the whole seventh Day in his Service.

What learn you from hence?
The unequal and wretched dealing of most Men with God, who by the grant of this Commandment urge usually at their Servants hands the Work of a whole Day in every of the six days; yet upon the Lord's Day think it enough, both for themselves and those under them, to measure out unto the Lord three or four hours only for his Service: using one measure to mete the Service due unto themselves, and another to mete the Service due unto God: which is a thing abominable before God, (Prov. 11. 1.) and so much the more as the things are greater and of more value, which they mete with lesser measure.

Whence is the second Reason taken?
From God's own right; who made the Sabbath; and is Lord of it. For the Seventh Day is the Sabbath of the Lord thy God. This Day is his, and not ours.

Whence is the third?
From the example of God. That as God, having made all things in the six days, rested the seventh Day from creating any more; so should we rest from all our Works. God himself ceasing from his Work of Creation on that Day, and sanctifying it; with what joy ought we to imitate our God herein? Gen. 2. 2, 3. Exod. 31. 17.

Did God cease from all Works on the Seventh Day?
No verily: he did then, and still continueth to do a great Work, in preserving the things created, John 5. 17.

What learn you from this?
1. That we be not idle on the Lord's Day, seeing God's Example is to the contrary; but attend upon the Lord's Service. 2. That as the Lord preserved on the Sabbath Day things created in the six days before, but created none other new, so by his example, we may save things on that Day, which otherwise would be lost; but we may not get or gain more.

Whence is the fourth and last Reason drawn?
From hope of blessing. Because God ordained not the Sabbath for any good it can do to him, but for the good of unthankful Man: and therefore he blessed and Sanctified it; not only as a Day of Service to himself, but also as a time and means to bestow increase of Grace upon such as do continually observe the same, Exod 31. 13. Isa. 56. 6, 7.

What is meant by sanctifying it?
The setting it apart from worldly Business to the Service of God.

What by blessing?
Not that this day in it self is more blessed than other days: but as the acceptable time of the Gospel is put for the Persons that receive the Gospel in that time: so by blessing this Day, he meaneth that those that keep it shall be blessed; and that in setting it apart, and separating it by this Commandment from other days, to be kept holy by public Exercises of his Holy Worship and Service, God hath made it an essential means of blessing to them that shall sanctify it as they ought.

Wherein shall they be blessed that keep the Sabbath Day?
1. In all the Holy Exercises of the Sabbath: which shall serve for their further increase, both of the knowledge and fear of God, and all other Spiritual and Heavenly Graces accompanying Salvation. 2. In matters of this Life, we shall not only not be hindered by keeping the Sabbath, but more blessed than if we did work that Day: as on the other side, the gain on the Lord's Day shall (by the curse of God) melt and vanish away, what show of profit soever it have; and bring some curse or other upon our labors in the week days, which in themselves are lawful and honest.

[25TH HEAD.]

So much of the first Table, concerning our Duties to God, the due performance whereof is called Piety: wherein God (as a King or as a Father of an Household) does teach his Subjects or Family their Duties towards himself. What is taught in the second Table?
Our Duties to ourselves and our Neighbors: the performance whereof is commonly called Justice or Righteousness; wherein God teacheth his Subjects and Family their Duties one towards another.

What is the sum of the Commandments of the second Table?
Thou shalt love thy Neighbor as thy self, Levit. 19. 18. Mat 22. 39. Or, As you would that Men should do unto you, do you unto them likewise, Mat. 7. 12. Luke 6. 31.

What general things do you observe belonging to this Table?
1. That it is like unto the first, Mat. 22. 39. and therefore that according to the measure of our profiting in the first Table, we profit also in this. In which respect the Prophets and Apostles do commonly try the sincerity and uprightness of profiting under the first Table, by the forwardness in the second.

2. That the Works thereof are in higher or lower degree of Good or Evil, as they are kept or broken towards one of the Household of Faith, rather than towards a Neighbor simply; 1 Cor. 6. 8. & 10. 32. Gal. 6. 10. Deut. 22. 2, 3.

3. That out of our Bond to our Neighbor, we draw all our Duties to all Men, (1 Thess 3. 12. & 5. 15.) reaching them even to the Wicked, so far forth as we hinder not God's Glory, nor some great Duty to others, especially the Household of Faith. For sometime it may so fall out, that that which Men require (and that which otherwise is right) may not be given? As Rahab, though subject to the King of Jericho, might not reveal the Spies, but should have failed in her Duty, if she had betrayed them at the King's Commandment: and therefore in this case she did well, in preferring the Obedience she owed to God, before the Duty she owed to Man, Jos. 2. 3. In like case also Jonathan, revealing his Fathers Counsel unto David, and preferring the greater Duty before the lesser, did well, 1 Sam. 19. 3. So we owing a greater Duty to our Country, than to our natural Kindred, must rather refuse to relieve them, if they be Traitors, than suffer any hurt to come to our Country.

But what if two have need of that which I can give but to one only?
I must then prefer those that be of the Household of Faith before others, (Gal. 6. 10.) and my Kinsmen, and those that I am tied unto by a special Bond, before Strangers. Joh. 1. 41. Acts 10. 24.

What are we specially forbidden to do by the Commandments of the second Table?
To do any thing that may hinder our Neighbors Dignity, in the fifth; Life, in the sixth; Chastity, in the seventh; Wealth, in the eighth; or good Name, in the ninth; though it be but in the secret motions and thoughts of the Heart, unto which we give no liking nor consent: for unto that also the last Commandment does reach.

How are these six Commandments of the second Table divided?
Into such as forbid all practice or advised consent to any hurt of our Neighbors; and such as forbid all thoughts and motions of evil towards our Neighbor, though they never come to advised consent of the Will. The first five Commandments do concern such things as come unto consent, and further; the last, such as come not unto consent at all.

How are those five Commandments of the first sort divided?
Into those that concern special Duties to special Persons; and those that concern general Duties to all. Those Duties which concern special Persons, are commanded in the first: those that generally concern all Men, either in their Life, Chastity, Goods, or good Name, are enjoined in the four Commandments following.

What gather you hence?
That we are to distinguish between Duties and Duties, and Sin and Sin, done towards Men; and that to offend principal Persons, and such unto whom we are in special

manner obliged, is a greater sin; because God hath singled out this one Commandment for these Persons.

What are the words of this Commandment, which is the fifth in order?
Honor thy father and the mother, that thy days may be long upon the Land which the Lord thy God giveth thee. Exod. 20. 12.

What is to be considered in these words?
1. The Commandment. 2. The Reason.

What is the meaning and scope of the Commandment?
That the quality of Men's Persons and Places, in whatsoever estate, Natural, Civil, or Ecclesiastical, and with whatsoever relation to us, be duly acknowledged and respected. For it requireth the performance of all such Duties as one Man oweth unto another, by some particular bond; in regard of special callings and differences. which God hath made between special Persons.

What are these special Persons?
Either Inequals, as Superiors and Inferiors; or Equals: For this Commandment enjoineth all due carriage of Inferiors to their Superiors; and by consequent also of Superiors to their Inferiors; and likewise by analogy of Equals among themselves; under the sweet relation betwixt Parents and Children, or betwixt Brethren of the same Family, and the general duty of Honor.

Who are Equals?
They that be equal in Gifts, either of Nature or Industry; as Brethren in a Family, Citizens in a Common-Wealth, Pastors in a Church, &c.

What is required of Equals?
That they live equally amongst themselves; loving one another and affording due respect to each other, Rom. 12. 10. That they live together sociably, and comfortably; preferring each other before themselves; and striving to go one before another in giving honor, 1 Pet. 2. 17. and 5. 5. Ephes. 5. 21. Phil. 2. 3. That they be faithful one to another: and Friends, be secret.

What is here forbidden?
Want of love; incivility, strife, and vain-glory; whereby they seek to advance themselves one above another, and to exalt themselves above their Fellows, Phil. 2. 3. Mat 23. 6.

Who are Superiors?
They be such as by God's Ordinance have any preeminence, preferment or excellency above others: and are here termed by the Name of Parents, (2 Kings 2. 12. & 5. 13. & 6. 21. & 13. 14. 1 Cor. 4. 15. Col. 3. 22.) to whom the first and principal Duties required in this Commandment do appertain, Ephes. 6. 1, 2.

Why are all Superiors called here by the name of Parents?
1. For that the Name of Parents being a most sweet and loving Name, Men might thereby be allured the rather to the Duties they owe; whether they be Duties that are to be performed to them, or which they should perform to their Inferiors. 2. For that at the first, and in the beginning of the World, Parents were also Magistrates, Pastors, School-Masters, &c.

How does this agree with the Commandment of Christ, (Mat. 23. 8, 9. 10.) that we should call no Man Father or Master upon Earth?
Very well. For there our Savior meaneth only, to restrain the ambitious Titles of the Pharisees in those days; who desired not only so to be called, but that Men should rest in their Authority alone, for matters concerning the Soul.

Who are Inferiors, comprehended here under the Name of Children?
Such as (by the Ordinance of God) are any way under Superiors; and who are principally and in the first place, to perform the Duties required in this Commandment.

What is the Commandment conceived in the Name of Inferiors?
Because the Duties are hardest obeyed in all estates.

What is here contained under the Name of Honor?
Not only Cap and Knee, but every particular Duty, according to their particular Estates, Mal. 1. 6.

Why are these Duties comprehended under the word Honor?
Because it adds an Ornament and Dignity unto them.

What is the Honor that all Inferiors owe to all Superiors in general?
First, Reverence in Heart, Word, and Behavior, Levit. 19. 3. Ephes. 6. 1, 2, 5. For the reverence of the Mind is to be declared by some civil behavior, or outward submission; as of rising before them, and of giving them the honor of speaking first, &c. Levit. 19. 32. Job. 29. 8. & 32. 6, 7. Second, Obedience to their Counsels. Third, Prayer to God for them, with giving of thanks, 1 Tim. 2. 1, 2. Fourth, Imitation of their Virtues and Graces, 2 Tim. 1. 5. Phil. 4. 9.

What contrary sins are here forbidden?
First, Want of reverence, inward or outward. Second, Despising of Superiors, Jude v. 8, 9, 10. Prov. 30. 11. Third, Neglect of Prayer, and other Duties.

What is the Duty of all Superiors toward their Inferiors?
That they answerably afford unto them love, blessing according to the power they receive from God, (Heb. 7. 7. & 11. 20. Gen. 9. 25, 26, 27.) good example for their Imitation, (Tit. 2. 7.) and that they so carry themselves, as that they may be worthy the honor that is given them, Ephes. 6. 4, 9. &c.

What are the contrary Vices?
Want of Love, failing in Prayer, and in giving good example; dishonoring their places, by unseemly and indiscreet carriage, Tit. 2. 15. 1 Sam. 2. 23.

How many sorts of Superiors are there?
Two: without Authority, and with Authority.

Who are Superiors without Authority?
Such as God hath by Age only, or by some supereminent Gifts, lifted above others: whether they be of the Body as Strength and Beauty; or of the Mind, as Wit and Learning, (which are most to be honored;) or of outward State, as Wealth, (1 Sam. 25. 8.) and Nobility, in which respect, although Brethren be equal, yet by Age the elder is Superior to the younger: and the Man in regard of his Sex is above the Woman: and he that is skillful, before him that hath no skill.

Twenty-fifth Head

Who are Inferiors to such?
They who are younger, and of meaner Gifts, whether of Nature or of Grace, or of such as are gotten by Exercise.

What is our Duty towards such Superiors?
To acknowledge the things wherein God hath preferred them before us, and to respect and regard them according to their Graces and Gifts.

What is the Duty of them that are Superiors in years?
They are by grave, wise, and godly carriage of themselves, to procure reverence unto themselves: on one side avoiding lightness and variableness, on the other, too much severeness and austerity.

What are the Duties to be performed towards Aged Persons?
To rise up before the Hoary Head, and honor the Person of the Aged, (Levit. 19. 32.) to give them the way, &c. in regard their Age is honorable. Yet Men that have a place of preeminence given them of the Lord, may keep their places.

What is the contrary sin forbidden?
Despising or disregarding of the Aged.

What is the Duty of such as are our Superiors in Knowledge and other Graces?
Superiors in Knowledge, To use their skill and other Graces so, as others may be benefited by them, 1 Pet. 4. 10.

What is our Duty towards them?
To give them the due approbation; to wait for their words, and give ear unto their Speeches, (Job 32. 11, 16.) as being wiser than ourselves: to profit by their Gifts, and to make our benefit of their good Graces, so far as our Calling will suffer.

What is the contrary sin?
Not acknowledging, nor reverencing, nor imitating the Graces of their Superiors.

Who are the Superiors with Authority?
Such as by special Office and Calling have charge over others.

What are the Inferiors?
Such as be committed unto their charge.

What general duty is there between the Superiors and Inferiors of this sort?
To pray more especially one for another 1 Tim. 2. 1. Psal. 20, and 21. Gen. 24. 12. Psal. 3. 8. and 25. 22. & 28. 9.

What is required of the Inferiors?
Besides thankfulness and fidelity, (Tit. 2. 10.) there is specially required Subjection and Obedience, Rom. 13. 1.

What is Subjection?
An humble and a ready mind to submit ourselves to their Government who are set over us; in acknowledging the necessity of their power in governing us, Rom. 13. 1. Tit. 3. 1. 1 Tim. 6. 1.

What is Obedience?
A voluntary and hearty doing of that which the Superiors command, (Eph. 6. 1, 5, 6, 7. Col. 3. 20. Heb. 13. 7.) or patient suffering of that they shall inflict upon them; albeit it should be either without just cause, or somewhat more excessively than the cause requireth. Heb. 12. 9, 10. 1 Pet. 2. 19, 20.

Is there no restraint of this Obedience?
None, saving that which we owe unto God; in regard whereof, our Obedience to them must be in the Lord, that is, only in lawful things: otherwise we are with reverence to refuse and allege our duty unto God for our Warrant, Ephes. 5. 24. and 6. 1. 1 Sam. 22. 17.

What contrary sins are here condemned?
Disobedience: and neglect of humble submission to our Superiors Commandments, and Corrections, Rom. 1. 30. Judg. 8. 6, 8, 9.

What is the duty of Superiors in Authority towards their Inferiors?
To protect and support such as are committed unto them, (Eph. 5. 23. Rom. 13. 4.) to provide good things for the Body and the Soul, (Mat. 7. 9, 10.) to command things that are good and profitable for the Inferiors; governing them prudently, and after an holy manner. Not as Tyrants, but as those which have a Governor above them, to whom they shall give an account, (Ephes. 6. 9.) and as those who rule over such as have a Title unto, and shall be partakers of, the same Glory, which themselves look for, 1 Pet. 3. 7.

In what things does this Government consist?
In two: Direction, and Recompense or Reward.

Wherein consisteth Direction?
In Word, and in Deed.

What must be done by Word?
They must instruct and command them in the things which pertain to God, and to their special Callings, Ephes. 6. 4. Gen 18. 19.

Must every Superior in Authority, be careful for the instruction of those that be under him, in the things of God?
Yes verily: and herein God hath declared his singular care of the everlasting good of Men, who hath therefore commended the care of Religion to so many, to the end they might be so much the more assuredly kept in the fear of God.

What is Direction by Deed?
Good example; whereby in their Life, Conversation, and Experience, they are to go before their Inferiors, that thereby they may be provoked to follow them.

What is Recompense?
It is either a cheerful reward for Well-doing, or a just chastisement for Evil, both which should be answerable in proportion to the deed done.

What is the sin contrary hereunto?
Abuse of this Authority, through too much lenity, (1 Sam. 2. 23) or severity, (Ephes. 6. 4, 9.)

How many kinds of Superiors are there with Authority?
Two: Private and Public; and consequently so many Inferiors.

Who are private Superiors, and Inferiors?
They are either in the Family, or in the Schools.

What is the duty of Superiors in a Family?
First, To provide for the Household the things belonging to their Soul, by a familiar catechizing and examination; and to go before them in Prayer accordingly; the Householder being therein to be the Mouth of his Family. Second, To provide the Necessaries belonging to this present Life; as Food and Raiment, both sufficient and agreeable to every ones place and estate, (Gen. 18. 6, 7, 8. Prov. 27. 23, 24, 25. & 31. 15. 1 Tim. 5. 8.) with convenient Government.

What is the duty of Inferiors in a Family?
To submit themselves to the Order of the House: and according to their Places and Gifts, to perform that which is commanded by the Governors thereof, for the good of the Household, Gen. 39. 2, 3, 4.

What are the differences of Superiors and Inferiors in a Family?
They are either natural, as Husband and Wife, Parents and Children: or otherwise, as Masters and Servants, Ephes. 5. & 6. Col. 3. & 4.

What are the common duties of the Husband and Wife each to other?
Mutual and conjugal love one towards another: yet so, as the Word presseth love at the Husband's Hands more than at the Wives; because Men are commonly more short of that Duty, Ephes. 5. 25.

Wherein must this Conjugal Love be declared?
First,. By mutual help, Gen. 2. 18. Second, By due benevolence, (1 Cor. 7. 3.) except by consent for a time, that they may give themselves to Fasting and Prayer, 1 Cor. 7. 5. 2 Sam. 11. 11.

What are the sins common to the Husband and the Wife?
1. Want of Love. 2. Betraying one another's Infirmities. 3. Discovering each others Secrets. 4. Jealousy. 5. Contention.

What is the duty of the Husband towards his Wife?
First, An entire love unto her, to cherish her, as he would cherish his own Flesh, and as Christ does his Church, Ephes. 5. Second, To provide for her that which is meet and comely during his Life: and then also that she may be provided for after his Death, if it so fall out. Third, To protect her, and defend her from all Evil. Fourth, To dwell with her, as one of Knowledge, 1 Pet. 3. 7. Fifth, To give honor to her, as the weaker Vessel, (Ibid.) that is, to bear with her infirmities. Sixth, To govern and direct her.

What are the special sins of the Husband?
1. Not dwelling with his Wife. 2. Neglect of edifying her by Instruction and Example. 3. Denying her comfortable Maintenance, and Employment.

What is the Duty of the Wife to the Husband?
First, Subjection, in a gentle and moderate kind and manner, Eph. 5. 22. For albeit it be made heavier than it was from the beginning, through the transgressions: yet that Yoke is easier than any other domestic subjection. Second, Obedience: wherein Wives are oft short, as Husbands in Love, Ephes. 5. 33. 1 Pet. 3. 1-6. Third, She must represent (in all Godly and commendable Matters) his Image in her behavior, that in her a Man may see the wisdom and uprightness of her Husband, 1 Cor. 11. 7. Fourth, She must be an helper unto him, (Gen. 2. 18.) as otherwise, so by saving that which he bringeth in, Prov. 31.

11, 12. 1 Tim. 3. 11. Finally, She must recompense her Husbands care over her, in providing things necessary for her Household; and do good for her Husband all the days of her Life, (Prov. 31. 12.) that so he may be unto her, as it were, a veil and covering before her eyes. Gen. 20. 16.

What are the sins of the Wife, in respect of her Husband?
1. Failing in reverence: which appeareth in forward looks, speeches, or behavior. 2. Disobedience in the smallest Matters. 3. Disregarded of her Husband's Profit.

What Duties come in the next place to be considered?
Those of Natural Parents, who are specially mentioned in this Commandment: whereunto also are to be reduced all in the right Line ascending, and their Collaterals; as also Fathers in Law, and Mothers in Law.

What are the Duties of Natural Parents towards their Children?
They are either common to both Parents, or in particular to either of them.

What are the common Duties of both of Parents?
They do either respect the things of this Life, or of that which is to come.

What care are they to have of the Souls of their Children, to fit them for the Life to come?
1. To make them Members of the visible church by Baptism. 2. They are to catechize and instruct them in Religion, as they are able to receive it: and to bring them up in nurture and the fear of God, Ephes. 6. 4. 3. They are to pray to God to bless them, and guide them in his Fear.

What is required of them for the things of this Life?
First, To mark the wits and inclinations of their Children; and as far as their own ability will reach to apply them accordingly, in due time, to some good, honest, and godly Calling: that so being trained up in such a Trade as they are fittest for, they may not afterwards live idly without any Calling, Gen. 4. 2. Prov. 20. 11. & 22. 6. Second, To provide for them a Godly Marriage (if it please God) in time convenient, 1 Cor. 7. 36. Third, Not only to maintain them, during their abiding in their House, but also to lay up and provide somewhat for them, that they may live honestly afterward. And therefore are they to distribute their Goods among their Children: and what they have received from their Ancestors, to leave the same (where it may be done lawfully) to their Posterity, 2 Cor. 12. 24. 2 Chron. 21. 3. Prov. 19. 14.

What special regard is here to be had by Parents to the Eldest Son?
That since God hath honored him with that dignity, as to be their strength, (Gen. 49. 3.) he should also be honored by them (at the least) with a double portion, (Deut. 21. 17.) as by the rest of the Brethren, with honor: yet so, as he fall not from his honor by some horrible sin, Gen. 49. 4.

What are the common sins of Parents?
1. Negligence in not instructing their Children early in life. 2. Not correcting them till it be too late: or doing it with bitterness, without Compassion, Instruction, and Prayer. 3. Giving them ill example. 4. Neglect of bringing them up in some lawful Calling. 5. Not bestowing them timely, and religiously in Marriage. 6. Light behavior before them, and too much familiarity with them; whereby they become vile in their eyes. 7. Loving beauty, or any outward parts, more than God's Image in them.

Twenty-fifth Head

What is required of the Father in particular?
To give the name unto the Child, Gen. 35. 18. Luke 1. 62, 63. For notwithstanding the Mothers having sometimes given the Name, yet that hath been by the Father's permission.

What special Duty is laid upon the Mother?
To nurse the Child if she be able, Gen. 21. 7. 1 Sam. 1. 23. Lam. 4. 3, 4. 1 Thess. 2. 7, 8. 1 Tim. 2. 15. & 5. 10.

So much of the Duty of Parents to their Children. What is the Duty of Children to their Parents?
It is either general or special, viz. in the case of Marriage.

What are the generals Duties?
First, To reverence them: and to perform careful obedience to them in all things that they command: by the example of our Savior, who was subject to his Parents, Luke. 2. 51. Second, To pray for them. Third, So to carry themselves, while they are under their Parents tuition, and after they are departed from them, as they may cause their Parents (in their good bringing up) to be commended, Prov. 10. 1. & 17. 25. & 31. 28. Fourth, To be an aid unto them, as well as they be able, and to help them with their Bodies, when they are in distress, Ruth. 1. 16. & 2. 17, 18. Fifth, To repay their Parents care over them, by being ready to relieve them, if they stand in need of relief, and want any thing wherewith God hath blessed them, 1 Tim. 5. 4. Gen. 45. 11. & 47. 12.

What are the contrary sins of Children, in respect of their Parents?
1. Disobedience. 2. Murmuring at their Parents Chastisements. 3. Condemning them for any default of Body or Mind. 4. Unthankfulness, in not relieving them, not standing for their deserved credit, &c.

What is the special Duty of Children to their Parents, in case of Marriage?
That they ought not so much as or attempt to bestow themselves in Marriage, without their Parents direction and consent; especially Daughters, Gen. 24. & 21. 21. & 27. 46. & 28. 9. Judg. 14. 2. 1 Cor. 7. 36, 37, 38.

What Reason have you to persuade Children to this Duty?
That seeing their Parents have taken such great pains and travel in bringing them up, they should reap some Fruits of their Labors in bestowing of them. Besides, they should give them this honor, to esteem them better able, and more wise to provide for their comfortable Marriage, than themselves are.

Is this Duty required only of Children to their Natural Parents that beg at them?
No: It is also in some degree required of Children to their Uncles and Aunts; or to any other under whom they are, and that be instead of Parents unto them, when their Parents are dead, Esther 2. 10, 20. Ruth. 2. 18, 23.

What is the Duty of Masters towards their Servants?
1. To deal honestly and justly with them, leaving of threatening; remembering they have a Master in Heaven, Col. 4. 1. Ephes. 6. 9. 2. To have a care to instruct and catechize them, and to teach them the Fear of the Lord. 3. To teach them their Trades and Occupations; that they may be bettered for being in their Family. 4. To allow them that fit Wages which they have covenanted with them for; that they may live honestly: for the Laborer must have his Hire. 5. To reward them plentifully, and to recompense their Service when they part from them, according as the Lord hath blessed them by their Labor, Deut. 15. 13, 14. & 24. 14, 15.

What are the sins of Masters?
1. Unadvised entertainment of sinful Servants. 2. Negligence in not instructing them, (in the Fear of God, and in some lawful Calling) and not using Religious Exercises with them. 3. Not admonishing nor correcting them, or doing it in an ill manner: grieving more when they fail in their Business, than when they are slack in God's Service;
4. Giving them ill example, and using light behavior before them. 5. Detaining their Wages from them; and not recompensing their Labors, by giving them a due reward, when they are with them, and when they part from them. 6. Neglect of them in Sickness: unjust stopping of their Wages for that time. 7. Not relieving them (if they be able) in their Age, who have spent their youth in their Service.

What is the Duty of Servants to their Masters?
1. To reverence and obey them in all things agreeable to the Word. 2. To pray for them, that God would guide their Hearts. 3. To learn all good things from them. 4. To be faithful, and not prodigal in spending their Goods. 5. With care and faithfulness (as in the presence of God) to bestow themselves wholly (at the times appointed) in their Master's Business; doing their Work, not only faithfully and with a single eye, but also diligently, Gen. 24. 10, 11, &c. Ephes. 6. 5, 6, 7.

What are the sins of Servants, in respect of their Governors?
1. Contempt and Disobedience. 2. Murmuring at their Corrections, though justly deserved. 3. Idleness in their Calling. 4. Unthriftiness and unfaithfulness in dealing with their Master's Goods and Affairs. 5. Stealing, and privy defrauding of them. 6. Eye-service, Ephes. 6. 6.

Who are Superiors and Inferiors in the Schools?
Tutors and School Masters are the Superiors; Pupils and Scholars the Inferiors. Whose Duties are to be gathered by proportion out of those of Fathers and Children, Masters and Servants, in the Family.

Hitherto of Superiors and Inferiors, which are more Private. Who are the Public?
Such as Govern and are governed in Church and Common-Wealth.

What is the Duty of Superiors?
To procure the common good of those of whom they have received the charge; forgetting (to that end) themselves, and their own private good, so oft as need shall require, Exod. 18. 13. 2 Sam. 24. 17. Mat. 11. 2. 1 Thess. 2. 7, 8, 11.

What is the Duty of Inferiors to their public Superiors?
To minister Charges, and other things necessary for the execution of their Offices; and to their Power to defend them in the same, Rom. 13. 6, 7. Gal. 6. 6. 1 Tim. 5. 17, 18. 1 Cor. 9. 4-10, 11, 13.

How many sorts be there of Public Superiors?
Two: Ecclesiastical, and Civil. The former whereof are (as it were) Divine, the other are called Human Creatures, 2 Kings 2. 3. 1 Tim. 2. 2. 1 Pet. 2. 13, 14.

Why do you call the Ministers of the Church Divine Creatures?
Because they are precisely in their Kinds, Number, and Order, set down in the Word of God.

Why call you the other Human Creatures?
Because, notwithstanding they are appointed of God, and such as without them, neither Church nor Common-Wealth can stand; yet are not their Kinds, and Number, and Order so appointed of God, but that Men may make more or fewer, of greater

authority or less; according as the occasion of Places, Times, or the dispositions of People do require.

Who are the Superiors in the Church?
All Ecclesiastical Governors, and Ministers of the Word especially. 1 Tim. 5. 17.

Who are under their Government?
All Christians, and professors of Religion.

What is the Ministers duty to the People?
First, To be faithful and painful in dispensing to them the will of God (and not their own fancies, or the inventions of men) instructing them sincerely in the way of Salvation, and breaking unto them the daily bread of life. 2. Tim. 4. 1, 2. Acts 20. 26. Second, To comfort and strengthen the weak. Third, To be an example unto all in life and conversation. 1 Tim. 4. 12.

What are the sins of Ministers?
1. Slackness in preaching. 2. Unprofitable or hurtful teaching. 3. Giving ill Example.

What is the duty of the people to their Ministers?
First, To hear them willingly. Mat. 10. 14. Second, To Submit themselves to all that they shall plainly and directly teach them out of the Word of God, Heb. 13. 7, 17. Third, Frankly and freely to make provision for them, that there be no want. Gal. 6. 6. 1 Tim. 5. 17, 18. 1 Cor. 9. 4, 5, &c.

What are the sins of the people in regard of their Ministers?
1. Disobeying and opposing against their Doctrine. 2. Denying them competent maintenance. 3. Not standing for them when they are wronged.

Who are Superiors in the common-wealth?
All civil Magistrates: Whether they be Supreme, as Emperors and Kings, or Inferior Governors under them. 1 Pet. 2. 13, 14. Whereunto are to be referred, the General in the Field, and Captains in War: As also in Courts, Advocates are Fathers to their Clients.

Who are under the Government of the Civil Magistrates?
All persons and subjects in the Realm, City or State, where they are Governors, Rom. 13. 1.

What are the duties of Kings and inferior Magistrates in the Commonwealth?
They are two-fold. First in respect of God's matters. Secondly in regard of civil affairs. 1 Tim. 2. 1, 2. The former whereof regardeth the good of the souls, the latter of the bodies of their subjects.

What is the civil Magistrate to do in God's matters, and for the souls of the subjects?
1. He should pray for them, that God would make their hearts obedient unto him. 2. He should see that God be honored in his dominions: That abuses in Religion be reformed, and the truth promoted and maintained, After the example of David, Solomon, Hezekiah, Josiah, and other good Kings. 2. Chron. 14. 3, 4. & 15.12-15. & 17. 6-9. 3. He should plant the sincere preaching of the word among his subjects; that so they may be more obedient unto him: and take care that the good things already taught and established may be done as God hath appointed. He is not to make new Laws of his own for Religion; but to see those ordinances of Religion which are grounded upon the word of God, duly established and practiced: That so God may be truly served and glorified, and the Churches within his Realms, and under his government, may under him lead a

quiet and peaceable Life, in all godliness and honesty, 2 Tim. 2. 2. For he who neglecteth this duty to God, shall never perform his duty to men; how politic soever he seem to be.

What is the Magistrate specially to perform, in respect of civil affairs?
1. He must look to the peace of the Common-Wealth, over which he is set: (1 Tim. 2. 2.) defending his subjects from their Enemies, and preserving their lives in War and Peace; by suppressing Murderers, Robbers, and all outrageous persons. 2. He must not only maintain Peace, but also Honesty. That by him we may not only lead a peaceable life, but also an honest. 1 Tim. 2. 2. Where specially he is to provide; that all uncleanness be removed. 3. He must see that Justice be duly executed: (Psal. 72. 24.) and that the Ministers thereof give judgment speedily in matters belonging to their judgment. 4. He must take order, that every man may enjoy his own. Psal. 72. 4. 5. He must cherish the good, and discountenance the bad: and take order that malefactors may be punished, and well-doers may be encouraged. Psal. 72. 4, 7. Rom. 13. 3, 4.

What is the sin of Magistrates?
Carelessness in performing those former duties.

What is the duty of Subjects to their Magistrates?
First, To pray for them, that God would rule their hearts by his holy Spirit, that under them we may lead a quiet and peaceable life in all godliness and honesty. 1 Tim. 2. 1, 2. Second, To help them with our goods: Paying willingly all customs, Taxes, and Tribute due to them. Mat. 22. 17, 21. Rom. 13. 6, 7. which condemneth the Popish Clergy, that detract this Tribute. Third, To Adventure our lives for them, in War and Peace. 2 Sam. 21. 16, 17. & 23, 15. 16. Fourth, When they do us wrong, not to rebel, but endure it patiently. For it is better to suffer for well-doing, than for evil. Fifth, To be obedient and dutiful unto them, and to obey their Laws in the Lord.

Do their Laws bind the Conscience?
As far as they are agreeable with the laws of God, they do: But otherwise they do not. For there is but one Lawgiver, who is able to save and to destroy. Jam. 4. 12.

What learn you out of the former?
That Drunkards, Thieves, Murderers, &c. break both this Commandment, and that other under which those sins are principally contained.

What out of the Latter?
That the Papists are to be condemned, who hold that the Popes Laws do bind the conscience.

What are the sins of subjects?
1. Disobedience, and Rebellion. 2. Refusing and repining to pay dues.

Hitherto of the duties of Superiors, Inferiors, and Equals. Show now what are the helps of the obedience of this Commandment?
They are either common to all; or proper to Inferiors and Superiors.

What is common to all?
There must be endeavour to nourish and increase natural affection, (Rom. 12. 10.) Humility, (Rom. 12. 16.) and Wisdom to discern what is fitting for our own and other places. Rom. 13. 7.

What is proper to the Inferior?
He must see God in the place and authority of his Superiors: (Rom. 13. 1, 2.) setting before his eyes the dreadful threatenings, and examples of God's vengeance on the seditious and disobedient. Eccl. 10. 8, 20. Prov. 24. 21, 22.

What is proper to the Superior?
He must be the same to his Inferior, that he would have Christ to be unto himself: (Ephes. 6. 9.) remembering the Tragic ends of Tyrants and Usurpers.

What hindrances of these duties are to be avoided?
First, Self-Love: Which maketh men unfit, either to rule or to obey. 1. Tim. 3. 2, 3, 4. Second, Partial inquiry into the duties of others towards us; joined for the most part, with the neglect of our own. Eccl. 7. 23, 24. Third, The company of seditious persons, and despisers of government, Prov. 24. 21. 22.

What is the reason annexed to this Commandment?
That thy days may be prolonged, and that it may go well with thee, in the Land which the Lord thy God giveth thee. Deut. 5. 16.

What is taught in this reason?
That God moveth the hearts of Superiors to promote the good estate of Inferiors: (for so also do the words sound, Exod. 20. 12. that they may prolong thy days) besides the providence of God to the obedient, which is far above all experience of men's provision.

What is the sum of this promise?
The blessing of long life and prosperity, to such as, by keeping this Commandment, shall show that they regard the Image and Ordinance of God. (Ephes. 6. 1, 2, 3. Rom 13. 1, 2.)

Have not the other Commandments this promise?
No, not expressly: Which showeth, that a more plentiful blessing in this kind followeth from the obedience of this Commandment, than of the other that follow. Hence it is called by the Apostle, the first Commandment with promise: Ephes. 6. 2. it being the first in order of the second Table, and the only Commandment of that Table that hath an express promise; and the only Commandment of the ten, that hath a particular promise.

But how, is this promise truly performed; seeing some wicked men live long, and the godly are taken away in the midst of their time?
The Lord performeth all temporal promises, so far forth as it is good for us: and therefore, the godly are sure to live so long as it shall serve for God's glory, and for their own good; but the wicked, live to their further condemnation. Isa. 65. 20.

It is enough that the promises of this life be performed for the most part. What loseth the obedient Child, and what injury is done unto him who being taken out of this Life, is recompensed with a better? Or what breach of promise is in him, that promiseth Silver and payeth with Gold, and that in greater weight and quantity? As for the wicked, they gain nothing by their long life, receiving (by means thereof) greater judgment in Hell.

Does not the Lord oftentimes revenge the breach of this Commandment, even in this life?
Yes: 1. Upon the Parents, who having been ungracious themselves, in giving unto them ungracious and disobedient Children. 2. Upon the Children themselves; who are sometimes immediately stricken from Heaven, and sometimes punished by the hand of the Magistrate.

[26TH HEAD.]

So much of the fifth Commandment concerning all special duties, to special persons. What are the general duties, in the Commandments following, which come at least to consent?
They are either such as concern the person it self of our Neighbor in the sixth: or such as concern the things that belong to his person; as his Chastity in the seventh, his goods in the eighth, and his good name in the ninth Commandment.

What are the words of the sixth Commandment?
Thou shalt not murder. Exod. 20. 13.

What is the sum and meaning of this Commandment?
That the life and person of man (as bearing the Image of God) be by man not impeached but preserved. (Gen. 9. 5.) and therefore that we are not to hurt our own persons, or the person of our Neighbor, but to procure the safety thereof; and to do those things that lie in us, for the preservation of his and our life and health. 1 Tim. 5. 23.

What is forbidden in this Commandment?
All kind of evil tending to the impeachment of the safety and health of mans person: with every hurt done, threatened, or intended, to the soul or body, either of ourselves or of our neighbors.

What is required in this Commandment?
All kind of good tending to the preservation of the welfare of mans person: that we love and cherish both the soul and body of our Neighbor; as we would and ought to do our own. Heb. 3. 13. Jam. 1. 27. Phil. 2. 12. Eph. 5. 29. For some of the duties here enjoined concern our own persons, some the person of our neighbor.

What are those duties that do concern our own persons?
They are either such as ought to be performed by us in our own life time, or when we are ready to depart out of this World.

What are the duties we are to perform towards our own persons in our lifetime?
They respect either the welfare of our Souls or of our bodies.

What are the duties that respect the welfare of our Souls?
First, To use the means of Grace. 1. Pet. 2. 2. Second, With diligence to finish our salvation (Phil. 2. 12.) and to make our election sure by the fruits of faith. 2 Pet. 1. 10. Third, To reject evil counsel and approve that which is good. Psal. 1. 1. Prov. 1. 10. 15. Fourth, To imitate the example of good men, and not to take scandals given by others. Fifth, To follow our Vocation diligently.

What are the contrary vices forbidden?
Cruelty to our own souls: by First, Rejecting the food of spiritual life; by not hearing, (Prov. 28. 9.) or not obeying the word. Jam. 1. 22. Second, Corrupting or perverting it, by itching ears. 2 Tim. 4. 3. or unstable minds. 2. Pet. 3. 16. Third, Want of knowledge: (Prov. 4. 13. & 8. 35, 36. Hos. 4. 6.) especially when people have had the ordinary means appointed of God for obtaining the same, either of their own, or of others, which they might have been partakers of. Fourth, Sin, especially gross sins. (Prov. 6. 32. & 8. 36) and obstinacy in sinning, Rom. 2. 5. Tit. 3. 11. Fifth, Following of evil counsel, and evil examples, and taking of scandals. Sixth, Neglecting of our Vocation.

Twenty-sixth Head

What are the things that respect the welfare of our Bodies?
First, Sober and wholesome diet. 1. Tim. 5. 23. Second, Help of Physic when need is: so that it be after we have first sought unto God. 2 Chron. 16. 12. Third, Using honest recreation, whereby health may be maintained, Judg. 14. 12. Fourth, Preventing unnecessary dangers. Fifth, Giving place to the fury of another: as Jacob did to Esau, by his Mothers counsel. Gen. 27. 43, 44.

What are the contrary sins forbidden?
First, Immoderate worldly sorrow: which (as the Apostle saith) worketh death. 2 Cor. 7. 10. Second, Malice and envy, which maketh a man a murderer of himself, as well as of his Neighbors. For (as the Wise man noteth) Envy is the rottenness of the bones. Prov. 14. 30. Third, Neglect either of wholesome diet, or of exercise and honest recreation, or of Physic to preserve or recover health. For we must not think that there are no more ways to kill a mans self, but with a knife, &c. Fourth, Drunkenness and surfeiting, eating and drinking out of time: (Prov. 25. 16. Eccl. 10. 16, 17.) or spending ones self by unchaste behavior. (Prov. 5. 11. and 6. 26. and 7. 22, 23.) All which are enemies to the health and life of man. Fifth, Lancing or whipping our own flesh; (1 King. 18. 28. Col. 2. 23. Eph. 5. 29.) as Idolaters use to do: or otherwise wounding ourselves. Sixth, Capital crimes, 1 Kings 2. 23. Seventh, Unnecessary dangers. Eighth, Not giving place to the fury of another. Ninth, Refusing the means of life. Tenth, Self murder. 1 Sam. 31. 4. 2. Sam. 17. 23. Mat. 27. 5. Acts 16. 27, 28.

What are we to do at the time of our departure out of this life?
First, With willingness we must receive the sentence of death, when God shall utter it. 2 Cor. 1. 9. Second, We must then resign our charge in Church, Commonwealth, or Family, into the hands of faithful men. Num. 27. 16. 1 Chron. 28. from 1 to 9. Third, We must resign our soul to God in Christ: (Psal. 31. 5.) with confidence of his love, though he kill us; (Job. 13. 15.) of the remission of our sins, and our resurrection unto immortality. Job. 19. 25, &c. Fourth, We must leave our body to the earth as a pledge, in time to be resumed: giving order for the comely and Christian burial thereof. Gen. 49. 29. 1 King 13. 31.

Hitherto of the duties that concern our own persons. What are they that do respect our neighbor?
They likewise are to be performed unto him, either while he is alive, or after his death.

What are the duties belonging to our Neighbor while he liveth?
They are partly inward, partly outward.

What are the inward?
To love our neighbor as ourselves, to think well of him, to be charitably affected towards him, and to study to do him good: In respect that we are all the creatures of one God, and the natural children of Adam. For which end we are to cherish all good affections in our hearts.

What are those good affections here required?
First, Humility and kindness, Proceeding from a loving heart to man, as he is man. Rom. 12. 10. Eph. 4. 32. Second, A contentment to see our brother pass and exceed us in any outward or inward gifts or graces: with giving of thanks to God for endowing him with such gifts. Third, Compassion and fellow-feeling of his good and evil. Rom. 12. 15, 16. Heb. 13. 3. 2 Cor. 11. 29. Fourth, Humility. Fifth, Meekness. Sixth, Patience, long-suffering and slowness to anger. Ephesians 4. 26. 1 Thes. 5. 14. Seventh, Easiness to be reconciled, and to forgive the wrong done unto us. Eph. 4. 32. Eighth, A peaceable mind; careful to preserve and make peace. Rom 12. 18. 1 Thes. 5. 13. Mat. 5. 9.

What is required for preservation of peace?
First, Care of avoiding offences. Second, Construing things in the best sense. 1 Cor. 13. 7. Third, Parting sometime with our own right. Gen. 13 8, 9. Fourth, Passing by offences: and patiently suffering of injuries, lest they break out into greater mischief.

What are the inward vices here condemned?
The consenting in heart to do our neighbor harm, with all passions of the mind which are contrary to the love we owe him.

What are those evil passions?
First, Anger, either rash or without cause; or passing measure, when the cause is just. Mat. 5. 21, 22. Eph. 4. 26, 31. Second, Hatred and malice: which is a murder in the mind. 1 Joh. 3. 15. Third, Envy: whereby one hateth his brother (as Cain the murderer did) for some good that is in him. Jan. 3. 14. Prov. 14. 30. 1 Joh 3. 12. Fourth, Grudging and repining against our Brother, which is a branch of envy. 1 Tim. 2. 8. Fifth, Unmercifulness, and want of compassion. Rom. 1. 31. Amos 6. 6. Sixth, Desire of revenge. Rom. 12. 19. Seventh, Cruelty. Psal. 5. 6. Gen. 49. 5, 7. Eighth, Pride: which is the mother of all contention. Prov. 13. 10. Ninth, Uncharitable suspicions. (1 Cor. 13. 5, 7. 1 Sam. 1. 13, 14.) yet godly jealousy over another is good, if it be for a good cause. Tenth, Forwardness, and uneasiness to be entreated. Rom. 1. 31.

What use are we to make of this?
That we should kill such affections at the first rising; and pray to God against them.

So much of the inward. What are the outward?
They respect, either the Soul principally; or the whole man, and the Body more specially.

What duties are required of us for preservation of the Souls of our Neighbors?
First, The ministering of the food of spiritual life. Isa. 62. 6. 1 Pet. 5. 2. Acts 20. 28. Second, Giving good counsel, and encouraging unto well doing. Heb. 10. 24, 25. Third, Walking without offence: which the Magistrate ought to be careful of in the Common-wealth, the Minister in the Church, and every one in his calling. For the Rule of the Apostle reacheth to all: Give none offence, neither to the Jews, nor to the Gentiles, nor to the Church of God. 1 Cor. 10. 32. Fourth, Giving good example, and thereby provoking one another to love and good works. Mat. 5. 16. 2 Cor. 9. 2. Heb. 10. 24. Fifth, Reproving our Brothers sins, by seasonable admonition. Levit. 19. 17. 1 Thes. 5. 14. Psal. 141. 5. Sixth, Comforting the feeble minded, and supporting the weak. 1 Thes. 4. 28. & 5. 14.

What are the contrary vices here condemned?
1. When the food of spiritual life is with-holden. (Prov. 29. 18. Amos 7. 13.) which charge specially lieth upon such Ministers, as are either Ignorant shepherds and cannot: or Idle, and will not feed the flock committed to their charge, or for the most part neglect their own, and busy themselves elsewhere, without any necessary and lawful calling. Ezek. 3. 18. and 13. 19: Jer. 48. 10. Isa. 56. 10. Acts 20. 26, 27, 28.

2. When the Word is corrupted by erroneous, or vain and curious expositions. 1 Tim. 1. 4

3. When Magistrates procure not, so much as in them lieth, that the people under their government do frequent the hearing of the Word read and preached, and receiving of the Sacraments, in the appointed times.

4. When men command, or tempt others to things unlawful. 1 Kings 12. 28.

5. When men give offence, either by evil example of life, (Prov. 29. 12.) or by unseasonable use of Christian liberty. 1 Cor. 8. 10, 11.

6. When we rebuke not our neighbor, being in fault; but suffer him to sin. Lev. 19. 17.

7. When the blind lead the blind, (Mat 15. 14.) and those that be seduced, seduce others. Mat. 23. 15. 2 Tim. 3. 13.

So much of that which concerneth the Soul of our Neighbor principally. Wherein consisteth that, which respecteth his whole person, and his Body more specially?
In Gestures, Words and Deeds.

What are required in our Gestures?
A friendly countenance, (that we look cheerfully upon our Neighbors) and an amiable behavior. Phil. 4. 8. Jam. 3. 13.

What is here forbidden?
All such Gestures as declare the scornfulness, anger, or hatred of the heart, with all forward and churlish behavior. 1 Sam. 25. 17. So that here is condemned, 1. A scornful look; and any disdainful sign, expressed by the gestures of the head, nose, tongue, finger, or any other member of our body: as nodding the head, putting out the tongue, pointing with the finger, and all manner of deriding of our neighbor. (Mat. 27. 39. Gen. 21. 9. compared with Gal. 4. 29.) 2. A fallen countenance, (such as was in Cain, Gen. 4, 5, 6.) snuffing, (Psal. 10. 5.) frowning, &c. which, as sparks, come from the fire of wrath and hatred.

What does this teach us?
That we are to look to our very countenance, that it betray not the filthiness of our hearts: For God hath so adorned the countenance and face of man, that in it may be seen the very affections of the heart. 1 Cor. 11. 7.

What is required in our words?
That we salute our Neighbor gently, speak kindly, and use courteous and amiable speeches unto him, which (according to the Hebrew phrase) is called a speaking to the heart one of another. Eph. 4. 32. Ruth. 2. 13.

What are the contrary vices here forbidden?
1. Evil speaking of a brother; although the matter be not false in it self; when it is not done either to a right end, or in due time, or in a right manner.

2. Disdainful speaking, when words are contemptuously uttered, whether they carry with them any further signification or no. As to say Tush; or to call our Brother Raca, (Mat. 5. 22.) and such like.

3. Bitter and angry words, or speeches wrathfully uttered, by any evil or vile terms, as Fool, and such like. Mat. 5. 22.

4. Mockings, for some want of the body (Lev. 19. 14.) especially for piety. (Gen. 21. 9. 2 Sam. 6. 20.) instead that they ought to be an eye to the blind and a foot to the lame. (Joh. 29. 15.) yet Gods children may sometimes use mocking in a godly manner: as Elias did to the Priests of Baal. 1 Kin. 18. 27.

5. Grudging, and complaints one of another, Jam. 5. 9.

6. Brawling, threatening, and provoking of others. Tit. 3. 2.

7. Crying: which is an unseemly lifting up of the voice. Eph. 4. 31.

8. Despiteful words, reviling and cursed speaking. Prov. 12. 18. Yet men in authority may use such terms, as the sin of those with whom they deal does deserve.

What use are you to make of all this?
That according to the counsel of St. Paul, we see that no corrupt communication proceed out of our mouth, but that which is good, to the use of edifying, that it may minister grace unto the hearers. Eph. 4. 29. that our speech be always gracious, seasoned with salt, that we may know how we ought to answer every man. Col. 4. 6. For as flesh in the Summer, if it be not powdered with salt will smell: so it will be with them that have not their hearts seasoned with the word of truth. And thence for want of care, proceed angry, wrathful, and loathsome speeches against our brother: which are in the Scripture compared to Juniper coals, which burn most fiercely; (Psal. 120. 4.) or to the pricking of a sword, or a razor, which cutteth most sharply. (Prov. 12. 18. Psal. 52. 2.) Whereupon the tongue is by St. James said to be an unruly evil, set on fire of Hell. Jam. 3. 6, 8. We ought therefore to govern our tongues by the Word of God, and take heed of vile speeches.

So much of our Gestures and Words. What is required in our Deeds?
1. That we do good unto our Neighbor, so far as our power and calling will suffer.
2. That we visit and comfort him in sickness and affliction. Mat. 25. 36. Jam. 1. 27.
3. That we give meat, drink, and cloth to the poor and needy.
4. That we give relief to the distressed, and succor to the oppressed Job. 29. 15; &c.
5. That we foresee and prevent mischiefs before they come.
6. That we rescue our Neighbor from danger, and defend him with our hands, if we can, if we may.

What are the contrary sins forbidden?
First, Oppression and cruelty, in withdrawing the means of life: (Jam. 5. 4.) as by usury, and by letting out of land so that men cannot live by it, &c. Second, Not looking unto the sick, and those that be in distress. Third, Neglect of Hospitality; especially to the poor, which by the commandment of God must be provided for. Fourth, Not preventing mischiefs and turning away strokes from our Neighbor, so much as in us lieth. Fifth, Extremity and cruelty in punishing: when the correction is excessive; (Deut. 25. 3. 2 Cor. 11. 24.) or is not inflicted in love of justice. Deut. 16. 19, 20. Sixth, All angry and despiteful striking, how little soever it be. Seventh, Fighting, smiting, wounding, or maiming of the body of our brother or neighbor. Jam. 4. 1. Lev. 24. 19, 28. Eighth, The endangering or taking away of his life.

How is this done?
Either directly, or indirectly.

How indirectly?
First, when one defendeth himself with injury, or purpose of revenge, or to hurt his adversary, and not only to save himself. Rom. 12. 21. Exod. 22. 2, 3. Second, when women with child, either by misdiet, or strain by reaching, violent exercise, riding by Coach or otherwise, and much more by dancing; either hurt the fruit of their womb, or altogether miscarry. Third, when children begotten in fornication or adultery, are committed to them to keep, which have no care of them. Fourth, when those to whom it appertaineth, do not punish the breach of this Commandment Numb. 35. 31, 32. Prov. 17. 15. Fifth, Keeping of harmful beasts, Exod. 21. 29. Sixth, All dangerous pastimes,

&c. Seventh, When things are so made, that men may take harm by them; or much care is not had of them as ought to be. As when the high ways and Bridges are not mended: or when stairs are so made, that they are like to hurt either Children, Servants, or others: Or when Wells or Ditches (or any such like dangerous places) are not covered, or fenced. Exo. 21. 33. whereunto belongeth that the Lord commandeth the Israelites to have battlements upon their Houses. Deut. 22. 8.

How directly?
When a man (without a calling) does actually take away the life of his Brother; (Gen. 9. 6.) otherwise then in case of public justice, (John 7. 19.) just War, (Deut. 20. 12, 13.) or necessary defense. Exo. 22. 2.

How many sorts of this direct killing are there?
Three: First, Chance-medly. Secondly, Man-slaughter. Thirdly, Willful murder.

What is that which we call Chance-medly?
When it is simply against our will, and we think nothing of it: as he which felleth a Tree, and his Ax head falleth, and hurteth, and killeth a man. Deut. 19, 45. Which is the least sin of the three, and by mans Law deserveth not death: and therefore by the Law of Moses, in this case the benefit of sanctuary was granted. Exod. 21. 13.

But how appeareth it to be a sin at all?
1. Because by the Law of Moses, the party that committed this fact, was to lose his liberty, until the death of the high Priest, to signify, that he could not be freed from the guilt thereof, but by the death of Jesus Christ the great high Priest. 2. Because it is a fruit of the sin of our first Parents: who if they had stood in that integrity wherein God created them, such an act as that should never have happened. 3. Because there is some imprudency in him that does it, and want of consideration.

What should this teach us?
To take heed of all occasions, that may make us guilty of this sin.

What do you account Man-slaughter?
When one killeth another in his own defense. Whereunto also may be referred: if one should kill a man at unawares, in hurling stones to no use; or if a Drunkard in reeling should fell another, whereof he should die. For this is different from that which cometh by Chance-medley, when a man is employed in a good and lawful work.

What think you of killing one another in quarrelling, and challenges to the field?
It deserveth death, by the law of God and man.

What is willful Murder?
When a man advisedly, wittingly, and maliciously, does slay or poison his Neighbor. Which is a sin of a high nature, and at no hand by the Magistrate to be pardoned: because thereby the Land is defiled. Gen. 9. 5, 6. Hos. 4. 2, 3. Numb. 35. 31, 33, 34. Deut. 21. 2, 7, 8, 9.

What reasons are there to set out the detestation of this sin?
First, If a man deface the Image of a Prince, he is severely punished: how much more if he deface the Image of God? Gen. 9. 6. Second, By the Law of Moses, if a beast (an unreasonable creature) had killed a man; it should be slain, and the flesh of it (although otherwise clean) was not to be eaten. Exod. 21. 28. Third, by the same Law, if this sin go unpunished; God will require it at the place where it was committed, and at the Magistrates hands. Numb. 35. 33.

Hitherto of the duties of this Commandment belonging to the person of our Neighbor while he is alive, What are they after his death?
They either concern himself, or those that pertain to him.

What are the duties that concern himself?
First, Friends and Neighbors should see that his body be honestly buried, and Funerals decently performed. Gen. 23. 4, 19. & 25. 9. 1 Sam. 25. 1. Psal. 79. 3. Second, Moderate mourning is to be used for him. Eccle. 12. 7. 1 Thes. 4. 13. Third, We are to report well of him, as he hath deserved. Fourth, We are to judge the best of him.

What is that which concerneth those that belong unto him?
To provide for his Wife, children and posterity; that he may live in them. Ruth 2. 20. 2 Sam. 9. 7.

So much of the respect which we do owe our Neighbors. Is it not required also, that we should show mercifulness unto our beasts?
Yes. A righteous man is to regard the life of his beast. Pro. 12. 10. And all hard usage of the creatures of God is forbidden, (Deut. 22. 6, 7. and 25. 4.) yet not so much in regard of them, (1 Cor. 9. 9, 10.) as that thereby the Lord would train us forward to show mercy to our Neighbor. For it being unlawful to use the dumb creatures cruelly; it is much more unlawful to use men so.

What are the breakers of this Commandment to expect?
The Apostle James teacheth that, when he saith: Judgment without mercy shall be upon those that are merciless. James. 2. 13.

Of how many sorts are those judgments?
They either concern this life, or that which is to come.

What are those that concern this life?
First, severe punishments (by the Law) are to be inflicted upon the body; as limb for limb, eye for eye, hand for hand, tooth for tooth, wound for wound, blood for blood, life for life: (Exod. 21. 23. Jud. 1. 5, 6, 7.) although it were a beast, if it were known to be a striker. Exod. 21. 28. Second, short life. Psal. 55. 23. Blood-thirsty men live not out half their days. Third, magistrates, that should punish Murderers, if they spare them, their lives are in danger to go for the offenders: as Ahab's did for Benhadad's. 1 Kin. 20. 42. David was exceedingly punished for sparing blood-thirsty men, (such as was his son Absalom) and not punishing them. 2 Sam. 13. 28, 29. & 14. 33. & 16. 11. Fourth, God threatneth; that he will not only revenge the blood of the slain upon the Murderer himself, but also upon his issue and posterity, in unrecoverable diseases. 2 Sam. 3. 29.

What is the punishment that concerneth the life to come?
First, That their prayers are not heard. Isa. 1. 15. 1 Tim. 2. 8. Second, Everlasting death both of body and soul, in the bottomless pit of Hell. And as the degrees of sin are, so shall the punishment be.

What helps are we to use for the furthering us to the obedience of this Commandment?
It behooveth us to consider, that first, all men are made in the image of God; (Gen. 9. 6.) and of one blood with us; (Acts 17. 26.) and all Christians in the image of Christ also, in whom we are all one body. 1 Cor. 12. 27.

Secondly that God hath appointed the Magistrate to punish proportionally every offender in his kind: (Gen. 9. 6. Levit. 24. 20, 21.) yea himself also extraordinarily bringing Murderers to light and punishment. Gen. 4. 9. Prov. 28. 17. Acts 28. 4.

What must we avoid as hindrances to the obedience of this Commandment?
First, The false opinion of the World, placing manhood in revenge and bloodshed, Gen. 4. 23, 24. Second, The company of furious and unmerciful men. Proverbs 22. 24, 25. Third, Greedy desire of gain. Pro. 1. 19. Mich. 3. 3. Fourth, Pride. Pro. 13. 10. Fifth, Riot and drunkenness. Pro. 23. 29.

Hitherto of the general duties that belong to the person of Man, contained in the sixth Commandment, what followeth?
The duties which we owe to Man, in regard of the things which belong unto him: the first whereof concerneth those that be most dear unto him; namely his family and his wife especially, who is nearest unto him, and as himself; being one flesh with him. In respect whereof, Temperance and Chastity is required in the next Commandment.

[27TH HEAD.]

What are the words of the seventh Commandment?
Thou shalt not commit Adultery. Exod. 20. 14.

What is comprehended under this name of Adultery?
All sins of that sort, committed either in the body or in the mind of persons, whether married or unmarried, are signified by this name; to show the vileness of the breach of this Commandment.

What then is the meaning and scope of the Commandment?
That all uncleanness and impurity be avoided, and chastity by all means preserved. 2 Cor. 7. 1. 1 Thes. 4. 3, 4, 5.

What is required?
All purity, honest behavior, continent and chaste usage, towards ourselves and towards our neighbor. 1 Thes. 2. 3. & 5. 23. 1 Cor. 7. 34.

What are the special breaches of this Commandment?
They are either Inward, or Outward.

What is the Inward?
The unchastity and dishonesty of the mind: with all filthy imaginations, and inordinate lusts, Mat. 5. 28. Col. 3. 5.

What are the special branches of this inward impurity?
1. The desire of strange flesh, with resolution to have it, if he could. Col. 3. 5. 1 Thes. 4. 5. For a lust after a strange Woman, with consent of heart, is forbidden in this; (Mat. 5. 28.) as lust without consent is in the last Commandment. Not that the bare affection is of it self a sin, being rightly directed to a true and good object: but the abuse of the affection, the right subject, manner and measure being not observed.

2. Inward boiling and burning in affection: Whereby godly motions, as with a fire, are burnt up, and a mans mind is so carried away, that he is hindered in all other things belonging to his calling. This is an high degree of corruption, which if it be not restrained, will break forth into further mischief: (Jam. 1. 15.) and therefore we are earnestly to pray to God against it; and if we can no otherwise prevail, we must use the remedy of Marriage prescribed by God himself: for it is better to marry then to burn. 1 Cor. 7. 9.

3. Evil thoughts and cogitations in the mind, arising from foolish and vain talk, but first and principally from our own concupiscence, when a man suffers as it were, his soul to be trampled under foot with impure imaginations. Jam. 1. 14. 15.

4. Jealousy in the mind, betwixt two persons, upon no just occasion or good ground: which is contrary to that entire love and affection, which a man should have towards his wise. Numb. 5.

What is the inward virtue here commanded?
The virginity and continency of the mind; and the chastity and purity of the heart. 1 Cor. 7. 34. 1 Thes. 4. 3, 4. & 5. 23.

What is the outward breach of this Commandment?
Such uncleanness, as being once seated in the mind, after showeth it self outwardly.

Wherein does it show it self?
Either in things that belong to the body, or else in the body it self.

How in those things that belong to the body?
In the abuse either of Apparel, or of Meat and Drink.

How is this Commandment broken in the abuse of apparel, and the ornaments of the Body?
First, By excess: when it is above our estate, or ability. Mat. 11. 8. Isa. 3. 16. Second, By lightness: when it is wanton and lascivious. Whence some apparel is called by the Holy Ghost, whorish: (Pro. 7. 10.) which is a great occasion of lust and uncleanness. Third, By immodesty, and wearing of such attire as does disfigure the body. Fourth, By new fangledness: when it is not according to the custom of the Country, City, or Town where we dwell, 2 Sam. 13. 4, 18. Fifth, When it is otherwise than belongeth to the sex: as if a man put on woman's apparel, or a woman a mans. Which is abominable to God, Deut. 22. 5.

What are the reasons hereof?
First, God would have every sex hereby maintained; that the man should not become effeminate, nor the woman mannish. Second, To avoid a most notorious occasion of a shameless and nameless sin. For if a man may be inflamed with a wanton Picture painted: much more with a lively Image, and portraiture of the sex. Third, It is a dishonor for a man to belie his sex, and to spoil himself of the dignity God hath given him; and presumption for a woman to desire the reputation of a better sex then God hath set her in.

May not women in their apparel submit themselves to please their Husbands?
They must seek to please them by lawful means, and therefore by clothing themselves in decent apparel, with sobriety; and for their success, to put their trust in God, who is able by modesty in apparel, without any such indirect means, to maintain their husbands love towards them. 1 Pet. 3. 5.

What apparel are we then to use?
Such as cometh under the rule of the Apostle; namely, such as may witness our godliness and modesty, 1 Tim. 2. 9. Tit. 22. 3. And therefore, although some (exceeding this measure) say they do it not to allure any: yet it others be allured by it, it is a sin in them; although not so grievous and great as in the other, who propound to themselves (by their wanton apparel) to allure.

Twenty-seventh Head

How is this Commandment broken in the abuse of meat and drink?
Either in regard of the quality or quantity thereof.

How in regard of the quality?
First, When we seek for too much daintiness. Deut. 14. 21. Luke 16. 19. Second, When we seek such kinds of meat and drink, which provoke this sin.

How in regard of the quantity?
By excess, and intemperance in diet: when we seed to fullness, and give ourselves to surfeiting and drunkenness. Ezek. 16. 49.

What are the contrary duties here commanded?
First, Temperance, in using a sober and moderate diet; (Eccl. 10. 16.) according to our ability, and the use of the Country where we be. Second, Convenient abstinence. 1 Cor. 9. 27.

So much of the breach of this Commandment in the abuse of those things which belong to the body. Wherein consisteth the abuse of the body it self?
Partly in the gestures and carriage of the body; partly in speech and words; partly in act and deed.

How is the wantonness of the heart manifested by the countenance, gestures and carriage of the body?
First, by impudence or lightness in countenance, gesture or behavior. Pro. 6. 13, 7, 10. Second, by wanton looks: when the eye (which is the seat of Adultery, or of Chastity) is suffered to wander without regard; and either giveth occasion to others to commit adultery, or is so fixed to behold the beauty of another, or else lascivious and wicked pictures (wherein many set their delight) and the like things, that the heart is inflamed to lust, and allured to filthiness thereby, 2 Pet. 2. 14. Mat. 5. 28. Gen. 39. 7. Job 31. 1. Ezek. 23. 14. Third, by uncovering of the nakedness of the breasts, and other parts of the body, for the allurement of others. Whereunto may be referred the Apostles Commandment for women to be covered: (1 Cor. 11. 6.) and the example of Rebekah, who for modesty put a veil upon her face. (Gen. 24. 65.) not as many do now a days, for other respects. Fourth, by painting the face, and counterfeiting the complexion: as wicked Jezebel did, who was afterwards (by the just judgment of God) eaten up of dogs. Fifth, by mincing and tinkling with the feet; by wanton dancing of men and women together, (which is a great enticement to this lust) and all other lascivious motions. Isa. 3. 16. Mar. 6. 22. Sixth, by dalliance; and abuse of any parts of the body to the provocation of others unto lust, or suffering them to wander in wantonness.

What are the contrary virtues here commanded?
Chastity in the eyes, countenance, and all the parts of the body; modesty, and gravity in behavior: (Tit. 2. 2, 3.) that we make a covenant with our eyes; (Job. 31. 1.) and pray that the Lord would turn them away from seeing vanity: (Psal. 119. 37.) finally that we so carry and direct all the members of the body, as that they be not weapons of uncleanness. Rom. 6. 13, 19.

How is this Commandment broken by evil Words?
First, by vain and wanton speeches, corrupt and rotten communication: whereby not only the speakers heart, but also the hearts of the hearers are inflamed. Eph. 4. 29. and 5. 3, 4. 1 Cor. 15. 33. Second, by giving ear to filthy words, and taking delight in hearing dishonest things; although (for our credit) we will not speak them. 1 Cor. 15. 33. Third, by making of love Epistles, amorous Books, lewd Songs and Ballads, and such like. Fourth, by reading or hearing of wanton Poems, naughty Songs, and bad

Books; and much more by learning of them: whereby the memory is cloyed, and so better things kept forth.

What is contrary to this?
Chastity in tongue and ears: speech favoring of sobriety and grace, (Thes. 4. 23.) modest and chaste talk. Where we are to follow the example of the Holy Ghost, who speaking (by necessity) of matters unseemly to be spoken plainly of, useth chaste speech: as, he knew her, he covered his feet, &c. Judg. 3. 24. 1 Sam. 1. 19.

What say you here to Interludes, and Stage-plays?
They offend against many branches of this Commandment together, both in the abuse of apparel, tongue, eyes, countenance, gestures, and all parts almost of the body. For besides the wantonness therein used, both in attire, speech, and action; the man putteth on the apparel of the woman, (which is forbidden, as a thing abominable (Deut. 22. 5.) much filthiness is presented to the beholders, and foolish talking, and jesting, which are not conversant: lastly, fornication and all uncleanness (which ought not to be once named amongst Christians) is made a spectacle of joy and laughter. (Ephes. 5. 3, 4.) Therefore they that go to see such fights, and hear such words, show their neglect of Christian duty, and carelessness in sinning, when as they willingly commit themselves into the snare of the Devil. 1 Cor. 25. 33.

There remaineth now the breach of this Commandment in Act and Deed.
What is that?
Fleshly pollution, and impurity in action: of which the unlawful Vows of continency are nurses. Heb. 13. 4. 1 Tim. 4. 1, 3.

What is the contrary virtue?
The possessing of our vessels in holiness and honor: (1 Thes. 4. 4.) for the preservation of which purity, holy wedlock is commanded to such have not got the gift of continency 1 Cor. 7. 9.

How does a man exercise uncleanness in act?
Either by himself, or with others.

How by himself?
By the horrible sin of Onan; (Gen. 38. 9.) lustful dreams, and nocturnal pollutions, (Deu. 23. 10.) rising from excessive eating, and unclean cogitations, or other sinful means, Jude v. 8. 2. Pet. 2. 10. Gal. 5. 19. Col. 3. 5.

How is it with others?
Either in lawful conjunction, or unlawful separation.

What are the kinds of unlawful conjunction?
It is either with those that are of diverse, or of the same kind.

What is the filthiness, which consisteth in the conjunction of divers kinds?
It is either Bestial, or Diabolical?

What is the Bestial?
When a man or woman committeth filthiness with a beast. Which is a most abominable confusion. Levi. 18. 23. & 20. 15, 16.

Twenty-seventh Head

What is the Diabolical?
When a man or a woman hath company with an unclean spirit, under the shape of a man or woman. Thus witches sometimes prostrate their bodies to the Devil, who to fulfill their lusts, does present himself unto them in an human form,

How is sin committed betwixt those of the same kind?
When men do carnally company with others out of marriage, or otherwise than the laws of holy marriage do require.

What is common to those unlawful mixtures?
That they all be either voluntary in both, or by force in the one. To the former may be referred the maintenance of Stews, which are permitted and defend in Popery: to the latter, the case of Rape.

How do you prove the unlawfulness of Stews?
First, they are so far from being the remedies of uncleanness, that they be the special nourishers thereof. For the acting of sin does not extinguish, but increase the flame of concupiscence. Second, they are expressly forbidden in the Law of God. Lev. 19. 29. Deu. 23. 17. Third, the Kings are commended in Scriptures, who took away such filthiness out of the land. 1 King. 15. 12. 2. King. 23. 7. Fourth, by them, not fornication only, but Adulteries, yea Incests also were committed, when as both married, and unmarried came thither; and oftentimes some of the same blood and affinity, committed villainy with one whore. Ezek. 22. 11.

What do you say to the case of Rape?
Herein the party forced is to be holden guiltless: but the offence of the other is highly aggravated hereby. Deut. 22. 25, 26. 2 Sam. 13. 14.

Of how many sorts are these unlawful mixtures?
They are either of one sex with the same sex; or of both sexes, the one with the other.

What is that of one sex with the same sex?
Sodomy, or Buggery: when man with man, or woman with woman, committeth filthiness Lev. 18. 22. & 20. 13. Deu. 23. 17. Rom. 1. 26, 27.

What are the unlawful mixtures of both Sexes, the male and female together?
They are either more unnatural, or less contrary to nature.

What are the more unnatural?
1. When there is a mixture of those bodies that are within the degrees of kindred and alliance, forbidden by the Law of God. (Lev. 18. 6. &c.) whether it be in marriage, or otherwise. 2 Sam. 13. 14. Gen. 38. 16. which sin is called Incest.

Of what sorts are Incests?
They are either in degrees of Consanguinity, or Affinity.

What is the incest of Consanguinity?
Confusion of blood, either in the right line upward, as Father with Daughter; Collateral, as Brother with Sister; or crosswise and oblique, as Son with Aunt, Daughter with Uncle

May Cousin-Germans (being in the second degree) marry by the Law of God?
Yea: but in divers respects it is unnecessary and inconvenient.

What are the Incests of Affinity?
There is the same prohibition of Affinity as of Consanguinity: as for a man to have his Sister in Law, &c.

What use make you of this?
It condemneth the Pope, who dispenseth with the degrees prohibited by God, and prohibiteth many degrees which God alloweth: making that to be sin, which is no sin, and that which is no sin to be sin.

What are the unlawful conjunctions of man and woman, that are less contrary to nature?
They are either betwixt strangers, or betwixt man and wife.

What are the kinds of the former?
Fornication and Adultery. Heb. 13. 4.

What is Fornication?
When two single persons come together out of the state of Matrimony. Deut. 22. 28, 29. Eph. 5. 3.

What is Adultery?
When a man or a woman, whereof the one at least is contracted in marriage, commit filthiness together.

How manifold is this Adultery?
Either Single or Double.

What call you single Adultery?
When the one party is single, and the other married or espoused.

What is the double?
When two persons married or contracted, do company together: which is a most high degree of offence, as being committed against four persons.

What is the unlawful conjunction between man and wife?
It is either betwixt one and many, or betwixt one and one.

What is the former?
Polygamy, and the having of many wives at once: which was ever unlawful in conscience, however for a time it was born with of God, (in regard of the increasing of the World and Church,) and not punished by the positive Law. Gen. 4. 24. Lev. 18. 18. Malac. 2. 15, 16. 1 Cor. 6. 16. & 7. 2.

What is the latter?
When the holy laws of Matrimony, and the order which God hath appointed in his word, are not observed.

What are those Laws and orders?
They do either concern the entrance into Marriage, or the holy use thereof, after it is consummate.

What is required in the entrance?
1. That the persons be joined in wedlock, meditate of the ends of Matrimony: that it is ordained for procreation sake, and for their own mutual comfort and preservation, not

for fulfilling of lust only. 2. That they use prayer for a blessing upon them. 3. That they look to the degrees of Consanguinity and Affinity prescribed. 4. That they look that either of them be free from any former Contracts. 5. That they be of the same Religion. 6. That they have consent of Parents, and those which have charge over them. For Parents have as great interest in their children, as in any of their goods. 7. That there be due consent likewise betwixt themselves. Where Parents must have a care to marry them, when they have understanding and discretion. 8. That due respect be had to the age of the parties. 9. That there be espousals before marriage; and that the parties espoused join not themselves together before the marriage be confirmed by the prayers of the Congregation. According to the example of Joseph and Mary. Mat. 1.

What are the contrary abuses?
First, when Meditation and Prayer are neglected. Second, when nearness of blood and kindred is not respected. Third, when either of the parties is formerly married, or contracted to some other. Malac. 2. 15. Fourth, when they are of a divers Religion. Gen. 6. 2. Fifth, when there wanteth consent of Parents. Exod. 22. 16, 17. Where stealing away of men's daughters cometh within the compass of Adultery, and is condemned in this Commandment. Sixth, when there is not due consent between the parties themselves, Gen. 29. 23. Where untimely marriages come to be condemned; which are the causes of many discords, and so great dissention between Husbands and Wives, when they are come to discretion and age. Seventh, when there is great disparity of age in the parties contracted. Eighth, when espousals are neglected, or the parties espoused come together before the consummation of the marriage. Both which are breaches of God's Ordinance.

What is required in the Holy use of marriage?
1. An holy and Christian conversation together, during the whole term of their life. 2. The sober use of the marriage bed.

What is required in the former?
That there be mutual delight, (Prov. 5. 19.) fidelity (Rom. 7. 2.) and confidence each in other. Prov. 31. 11.

What in the latter?
That they render due benevolence one to the other; (1 Cor. 7. 3, 4, 5.) and abuse not the marriage bed, either unseasonably, or intemperately.

How unseasonably?
In not observing the time, either of natural separation, (Lev. 18. 19.) or of solemn humiliation; wherein (with consent) they are to give themselves unto Fasting and Prayer. Which though it be not strictly commanded, is yet permitted. 1 Cor. 7. 5, 6, 7.

How intemperately?
When the honorable and chaste estate of Matrimony is used to wantonness, and not with moderation and seemliness. 1 Thes. 4. 4, 5. For as a man may commit a fault in excess of wine, although it be his own: so may he sin in abusing his body with his own wife.

Hitherto of the unlawful conjunction. Wherein does unlawful separation consist?
Either in the utter abjuration of marriage, or in the breach of conjugal society.

How is the former sin committed?
By the unlawful vows of continency: where we must abhor the doctrine of devils, depraving and denying holy marriage. 1. Timothy 4. 1, 3.

How is the latter committed?
Either when the party is present, or when he is absent.

How when the party is present?
When due benevolence is not yielded, although there be aptness thereunto, not any hindrance by consent, in respect of extraordinary prayer. 1 Cor. 7. 3, 4.

How when the party is absent?
Either privately, or publicly.

How privately?
When the party withdraweth it self in dislike, or loathsomeness; or else by long and unnecessary journeys of traveling, of merchandise, wars, &c. or maketh a desertion for hatred of Religion. 1 Cor. 7. 12, 13, 15.

How publicly?
When separation hath been made by the Magistrate, without lawful cause.

Is there any lawful cause of divorce?
Yes. Adultery is a lawful cause of separation: but not contention, or discord, or any thing beside. Mat. 5. 32.

So much of the Commandment. What are the punishments of the breach of it?
1. When many other sins are hid, this is most commonly discovered. Num. 5. 13, &c. Prov. 5. 11, &c. John 4. 16.

2. The sin is a judgment of it self, Prov. 22. 14. Eccl. 7. 27, 28. Rom. 1. 24.

3. God judgeth them oftentimes in this world, always in the world to come. Heb. 13. 4. 1 Cor. 6. 9, 10. Num. 25. 8. Gen. 12. 17. 1 Cor. 10. 8. Gen. 34, 25. Judg. 19. 29. Prov. 7. 23, 26, 27. Job. 31. 9, 10, 11, 12. 2 Sam. 13. 14, 28.

4. More particularly; whipping for Fornication, and death for Adultery and other unlawful mixtures. Lev. 20. 10.

5. It spendeth the goods. Prov. 15. 10. & 6. 26.

6. It hurteth, wasteth, and consumeth the body, Prov. 5. 11.

7. It bereaveth a man of his understanding and judgment. Hosea. 4. 11.

8. It not only reacheth to the offenders themselves, but also to their children; who are the children of Adultery. And by Moses' law, the Bastard (to the tenth generation) might not enter into the Sanctuary. Deut. 23. 2.

9. He sinneth against his wife and lawful children, whilst thereby he oftentimes maketh a stews of his house: as David did by the Adultery he committed with the wife of Uriah. 2 Sam. 16. 21.

10. Barrenness in his wife. Lev. 20. 20.

11. Children begotten in horrible incest were to be burnt or slain in their mothers womb.

What are the helps to the obedience of this Commandment?
Unto the fore-mentioned helps there must be added: First, care to keep a good Conscience. Eccl. 7. 28. Second, labor in our vocations. Third, watchfulness over our own spirit. Mal. 2. 16. Fourth, a Covenant with our eyes. Job. 31. 1. Fifth, love of God and of his wisdom. Prov. 2. 10. &c. Sixth, Prayer. Psal. 119. 37. Seventh, Holy meditations.

What are the hindrances to be avoided?
Beside the unlawful vows of continency, and other provocations unto this kind of sin, before noted: we must beware of.

First, idleness: in ceasing from doing any profitable thing Ezek. 16. 49. 2 Sam. 11. 12. 1 Tim. 5. 11, 13. Gen. 34. 1. &c. Second, the breach of peace with God. Prov. 22. 14. Third, running on in sin; (Eccl. 7. 28.) especially superstition and Idolatry: (Rom. 1. 25. 26.) in which cases God giveth men over to vile lusts. Fourth, lewd company. Prov. 5. 20. & 7. 25. Fifth, idle and unwarrantable exercises. Gen. 34. 1. &c.

[28TH HEAD.]

So much of the seventh Commandment, where Chastity is commanded. There follow the general duties which we do owe to man in other things appertaining unto him. What are they?
They either regard the preservation of his goods, as the eighth; or his good name, as the ninth Commandment.

What are the words of the eighth Commandment?
Thou shalt not steal. Exod. 20. 15.

What does it contain?
A charge of our own and our Neighbors goods: that we show love and faithfulness therein, and not only not impeach or hinder, but by all means preserve and further the same.

What special matter do ye learn from hence?
The gross error of the Anabaptists, that hold community of goods: which by the whole drift and scope of this Commandment is manifestly overthrown.

What is forbidden in this commandment?
Whatsoever is prejudicial to our own or our Neighbors wealth: that we no way hinder, diminish, or abuse the same.

What is required?
Whatsoever may further and prosper our own or our Neighbors wealth: that we give to every one that which is his, and do our best (as far as our callings and means will suffer) to preserve his goods, and (as occasion serveth) help to increase them; by all lawful courses, (Eph. 4. 28.) and honest dealing (Tit. 2. 10.)

What is the end of this Commandment?
It is divers. First, in respect of God: that the goods which he hath bestowed on us should be conserved and employed to those uses for which he hath entrusted them unto us: and principally to the setting forth of his glory who gave them.

Secondly, in respect of the Church. For whatsoever is given unto any member thereof, whether it be either spiritual or external good, it is given for the common benefit of the whole body. And therefore he that taketh away the goods of any member, or refuseth to employ for the common profit what he hath, he neglecteth this communion; and consequently sinneth against this Commandment.

Thirdly, in respect of the Common-wealth: for the preservation whereof justice is required, in giving unto every one that which is his own; which being neglected great Kingdoms are great Thieveries.

Lastly, in respect of every singular person: that every man may freely and quietly enjoy those his goods which God hath given him.

What was the occasion of this Commandment?
It was that covetousness which naturally adhereth unto us; whereof it cometh to pass, that we are not contented with our estate and means, but lust and long after other men's and use all our endeavors to compass them whether it be by right or wrong. And from hence arise injuries, oppressions, thefts and robberies: by which means what is gotten does naturally more delight and please us, than that we get in our lawful callings. Prov. 9. 17. & 20. 17.

What is here forbidden?
Theft in all the kinds thereof.

What is theft?
It is the fraudulent embezzling or taking away of those goods which belong to another man, without the knowledge or against the will of the owner: or the unjust detaining of it from him, when we know that in right it belongeth unto him.

What things are chiefly to be here considered?
Two. First, the Objects, about which it is chiefly exercised: and Secondly, the virtues and Vices commanded and forbidden.

What are the Objects?
Our own and our Neighbors goods; or as they commonly speak, Meum & Tuum, mine and thine. For whereas he forbiddeth theft, and commandeth beneficence, he employeth and requireth, that there should be distinct properties and possessions: for otherwise there could be no theft, nor exercise of bounty and beneficence. For a man cannot steal but that which is another's, nor give but that which is his own.

What are the Virtues commanded, and the Vices forbidden in this Commandment?
The Apostle hath comprised all in a brief sum, Ephes. 4. 28. Let him that stole steal no more, but rather labor, working with his hands the thing which is good, that he may have to give to him that needeth. Of which the Apostle propoundeth himself for an example; Acts 20. 33, 34, 35.

What then are the parts of this Commandment?
Two. First, the negative, forbidding all Theft. Secondly the affirmative, enjoining the just getting, and the just and liberal use of our goods.

What understand you by stealing or Theft?
All vices of the same nature and kind, whereby we any ways hinder or hurt ourselves, or our neighbors in our goods. And as Theft it self is here forbidden, so also the cause

and root of it, which is covetousness; together with the means and signs of it, and the procuring of it in others: as also the contrary virtues hereunto are required.

How must we proceed in handling of them?
From the generals to the more special.

What are the degrees of general duties?
They are three. First; to abstain from all injuries and injustice, whereby we hurt or hinder ourselves or our neighbor, in our own or his goods. Secondly, that we use our best endeavour to preserve by all lawful means, both our own and his. Thirdly, that we cheerfully communicate our goods to the relieving of our neighbors necessities.

What are the vices opposite hereunto?
They are three. First, injuriously to hurt or hinder ourselves or neighbors in our goods. Secondly, to be wanting in any means whereby they may justly be preserved. Thirdly to be wanting to our neighbors in relieving them when their necessities require our help. For we are not absolute owners of the things which we possess: but God's Stewards, who are enjoined to employ his Talents to such uses as he requireth; and particularly to the benefit of our fellow servants Luk. 16. 2 Luke 19. 13. Mat. 25. 14, 15. 19.

What is the second general duty respecting our own and our neighbor's goods?
That we use our best endeavour to preserve them. First, our own. For though we may not set our hearts upon them (Psalm 62. 10.) yet seeing they are Gods gifts, and are to be employed for his glory and our own and neighbors good, if we should willfully or negligently suffer them to perish, we should be worse then the unprofitable servant, who kept the Talent committed unto him, though he did not increase it. Mat. 25. 25.

Secondly, we must do our best to conserve our neighbors goods; seeing they have not by chance come unto them but by the wise disposing of God's providence: whose wise dispensation we resist, if by our best endeavour we do not preserve them for their use. And to this end that Law concerning our neighbors Cattle tendeth Deut. 22. 1, 2, 3. Exod. 23. 4, 5.

What are the special duties here required?
They are of two sorts: the first, respect the just getting and possessing; the other, the right using and employing of our goods.

What are the duties which are referred to the former?
They are either internal, or external.

What are the internal?
They are chiefly four: First, little or no love and desire of money. Secondly, self-contentedness. Thirdly, a lawful measure of our appetite; or moderate concupiscence and desires. Fourthly, lawful providence without taking care; or a laudable study and endeavour in getting goods.

What do you mean by little or no love of money?
When we do not set our hearts upon riches and worldly wealth: (Psal. 62. 10.) But first seek Gods Kingdom and righteousness. Matthew 6. 33.

What is opposite hereunto?
Love of money: that is, when we set our hearts upon riches and worldly things; which should be devoted unto, and fixed upon God.

By what arguments may we be dissuaded from this vice?
By divers; especially these that follow.

Because it is a foolish vice: seeing riches to those that immoderately love them, are not only vain, but also hurtful and pernicious. Hab. 2. 6. 1 Tim. 6. 9.

Secondly, because it is unseemly. For we are Pilgrims in this world, and Citizens of Heaven: and therefore we should not set our hearts and affections on earthly, but on heavenly things, Phil. 3. 20. Col. 3. 1, 2.

Thirdly, because it is impious. For 1. He that loveth the world loveth not God: (1 Joh. 2. 15. Jam. 4. 4.) neither can we serve God and Mammon. (Mat. 6. 24.) 2. Because a lover of money is an Idolater. Ephe. 5. 5. For that is our God on which we set our hearts.

Fourthly, Because it is pernicious. For, he that soweth unto the flesh shall of the flesh reap corruption, Gal. 6. 8. and their end is destruction who mind earthly things. Phil. 3. 19. 1 Tim. 6. 9.

Fifthly, because the love of money is the root of all evil, and exposeth men to all temptations. 1 Tim. 9. 9, 10.

What is the second special virtue here commanded?
Self-contentedness: when a man is contented with that estate and condition which God in his wise providence hath allotted unto him; and does not covet either that which is another mans, or that which is unnecessary and superfluous. Phi 4. 11. And this springeth partly from the neglect of money and contempt of worldly things; and partly from our affiance in God, resting it self upon his promises, providence, goodness, and all-sufficiency.

What motives may induce us to embrace this virtue?
1. By the consideration of the vanity of worldly things, and the profit which ariseth from piety and the love of divine excellencies, 1 Tim, 6. 6, 7, 8. Godliness is great gain with contentment. For this abundantly supplieth all our wants. 1 Tim. 4. 8 Psal. 34. 10, 11. & 37. 16. Mat. 6. 33. Prov. 15. 1. 6 Better is a little with the fear of the Lord, than great treasures and trouble therewith.

2. Of God's providence; who is our provident and loving Father. And therefore seeing we are his sons, we ought to be content with our portion which our gracious Father hath allotted unto us; and to say with David. Psal. 16. 6. The lines are fallen unto me in pleasant places. For he best knoweth what we stand in need of. (Mat. 9. 32.) Therefore let us submit ourselves to his will and providence.

Thirdly, Let us meditate on Gods promises, Heb. 13. 5, 6. Be content with such things as you have; for he hath said, I will never leave nor forsake thee. And therefore let us cast our care upon God, for he careth for us, 1 Pet. 5. 7. Psal. 55. 22. Cast thy burden upon the Lord, and he shall sustain thee, &c.

What is the vice opposite to this virtue?
Not to be contented with our present State and condition but immoderately to desire more and greater things; and to afflict ourselves with distracting, and carking cares in getting and compassing them.

Who are most addicted to this vice?

Those who will not live according to the proportion of their means which God hath given them. For these wanting more than is needful, their ordinary comings in and lawful means do not suffice them, but they desire and seek things superfluous by unlawful means; as food and raiment above their state and ability.

But is it then unlawful, in a mean and poor condition to use means to improve and better our estate?

Our affiance in God, and self-contentedness do not hinder us from using all lawful means to better our condition, nor make us slothful in our callings; so that our desires be moderate, and the means we use be lawful, we in the mean time resting upon God's just and wise providence with contentment.

What is the third internal duty, respecting the lawful getting and possessing of earthly things?

The lawful measuring of our appetite, and the moderating of our concupiscence.
For all appetite and desire is not unlawful, but that only which is inordinate and immoderate: For that desire which tendeth to the necessary sustentation of ourselves and others is commendable.

What things are here considerable?

Two things. First, what is necessary. Secondly, when the appetite is lawful. Concerning the former, things are said to be necessary, in respect of the necessity, either of ourselves or others.

What things are to be reputed necessary in respect of ourselves?

There may be a threefold necessity: in respect of Nature, Person, or Estate. Those things which are required to the sustaining of nature, as we are men; that is, food and raiment. 1 Tim 6. 8.

What is necessary in respect of Person?

When we have sufficient for ourselves, and those that belong unto us. 1 Ti. 5. 8.

What is necessary in respect of State?

When we have that which is sufficient to maintain us according to our rank, place, and calling; whether it be Magistrates, Ministers, or ordinary men.

What is necessary in respect of others?

It is either private, or public.

What is that necessity which respecteth the private?

When we have wherewith to relieve the necessities of private men: after which ability all ought to labor. For it is a more blessed thing to give, than to receive. Acts 20. 35.

What in respect of the public?

It either concerneth the Church or Common-wealth: unto both which we must be serviceable, as being born not only for ourselves, but also for them. Therefore we may justly desire and labor after such abilities, as that we may not be wanting in either of them, when their necessities require our help.

When is the appetite lawful?

When it is ordinate and moderate.

When is it ordinate?
When it is subordinate to our study and desire of God's glory, and our own salvation. Mat. 6. 33. and contrariwise it is inordinate and preposterous, when earthly things are more affected and desired than heavenly.

Who do sin in this kind?
Those who seek worldly things by sinful and unlawful means, to the hazard of their souls, and their eternal salvation. Such are more foolish than Esau, that sold his birth-right for a mess of pottage. Mark. 8. 36. Heb. 12. 16.

What is a moderate appetite or desire?
When we desire only things necessary; and these also so, as that we can be content, though we cannot get them. An example whereof we have in Paul, Phil. 4. 11, 12. and in Agur, Prov. 30. 8. And Christ hath taught us to pray, Give us this day our daily bread; that is, food convenient and necessary.

What are the extremes opposed hereunto?
They are two: The first is voluntary affectation of poverty; as in the begging Friars among the Papists, commending that for a virtue and a degree of perfection, which the spirit of God hath taught us to pray against, Prov. 30. 8. and hath enjoined us not to beg, but to labor with our hands, that we may be helpful unto others. Ephes. 4. 28.

What is the other extreme?
The immoderate affectation of riches and honors; and that in a greater measure than is needful for us. The former we call Covetousness; the other Ambition.

What is Covetousness?
An immoderate desire of Riches: In which these vices concur.

First, an excessive love of Riches, and the fixing of our hearts upon them. Second, a resolution to become rich, either by lawful or unlawful means. 1 Tim. 6. 9. Third, too much haste in gathering riches, joined with impatience of any delay. Prov. 28. 20, 22. & 20. 21. Fourth, an insatiable appetite which can never be satisfied: but when they have too much, they still desire more, and have never enough. Eccl. 4. 8. like the Horseleech Prov. 30. 15. The Dropsy and Hell it self, Prov. 27. 20. Fifth, miser like tenacity; whereby they refuse to communicate their goods either for the use of others or themselves. Sixth, cruelty, Prov. 1. 18, 19. exercised both in their unmerciful ness and oppression of the poor.

What do you think of this vice?
That it is a most heinous sin. For it is Idolatry, and the root of all evil, (Col. 3. 5. 1 Tim. 6. 10.) a pernicious Thorn that stifleth all grace, and choketh the seed of the word, (Mat. 13. 22.) and pierceth men through with many sorrows, 1 Tim. 6. 10. and drowneth them in destruction and perdition, ver. 9.

What is ambition?
An immoderate love and desire of honors: which is a vice compounded of Covetousness and Pride; in which concur all those vices in covetousness before spoken of. As an immoderate love of honors, a resolution to aspire unto honors, either by lawful or unlawful means, too much haste in aspiring unto honors, not waiting upon God for preferment in the use of lawful means, insatiableness in aspiring higher, and higher and enlarging of the ambitious mans desire like unto Hell. Heb. 2. 5. Unto which may be added Arrogance, whereby he coveteth to be preferred before all others, and Envy, whereby he disdaineth that any should be preferred before him.

What is the fourth and last vice here forbidden?
Immoderate and carking care in the pursuing of these earthly things, riches and honors. As contrariwise, moderate appetite and desires of having, and moderate care of procuring them, is approved and required; that we may not be burdensome but rather helpful unto others. 2 Cor. 12. 13. Eph. 4. 28.

What are the extremes opposed to the former virtue?
They are two. The first is carelessness and neglect of our goods and state: For as he is commended who gathereth in seasonable times: so he is condemned, who neglecteth those opportunities, (Prov. 10. 5. & 6. 6.) and is censured by the Apostle to be worse than an Infidel. 1 Tim. 5. 8.

What is the other extreme?
Anxious and solicitous care, which distracteth the mind that it cannot be wholly intent to Gods service. And this does partly arise from Covetousness, and partly from diffidence in God's Promises and Providence.

What are the reasons that may dissuade from this vice?
They are chiefly two. First, because it is impious, Secondly, because it is foolish.

Why is it impious?
Because it chargeth God either with ignorance, that he knoweth not our wants, (contrary to that, Mat. 6. 32.) or of carefulness, that he neglecteth us; or of impotency, that he is not able to supply our wants. Whereas he is omniscient, and knoweth our necessities; omnipotent and able to relieve us; (Eph. 3. 20.) and our most gracious Father, and therefore willing and ready to help us in time of need. Secondly, because it divideth the heart betwixt God and Mammon; and we cannot at once serve these masters. Mat. 6. 24. 1 John 2. 15. Jam. 4. 4. Thirdly, Because it is heathenish. Mat. 6. 32.

Why is it foolish?
Because it is both superfluous and vain. Superfluous, because God hath undertaken to provide for us; and therefore in the use of lawful means we must cast all our care upon him. 1 Pet. 5. 7. Psal. 55. 22.

How is it vain?
Because it is Gods blessing only that maketh rich: (Prov. 20. 22. Deut. 8. 18.) and by our own care we can no more add to that stint of state which he hath allotted unto us, than we can thereby add one cubit to our stature Mat. 6. 27.

You have spoken generally of the internal duties: what duties are externally, and more specially?
They respect either the just acquisition and getting of our goods; or the just retention and possessing of them. Unto which is opposed the unjust getting and keeping of them: which are here forbidden under the name of Theft.

What is required to just getting?
That we get them by just and lawful means. For riches are thorns: which are not to be hastily caught, but to be handled warily and with much caution; that they do not pierce the soul, and wound the conscience.

What may move us hereunto?
First, by considering, that a little justly gotten is better then abundance gotten unjustly, Prov. 16. 8. Psal. 37. 16. Secondly, that what is justly gotten is the gift of God, and a pledge of his love; but that which is gotten unjustly, is given in his wrath, and is a snare

A Body of Divinity

of the Devil to our destruction. Thirdly, that as goods justly gotten are Gods gifts, which he blesseth unto us; (Prov. 10. 22.) so that which is ill gotten, is liable to his curse. Pro 13. 11. Heb. 2. 9.

How many ways are goods lawfully gotten?
Two ways. First, without Contracts Secondly, by Contracts Of Contract, either such as are gotten by ourselves, or received from others.

How gotten by ourselves?
Either ordinarily, or extraordinarily, Ordinary getting is by the sweat of our brows in our lawful callings. So that here two things are required. First, a lawful calling: and Secondly, that we labor in it. Eph. 4. 28.

What is a lawful calling?
It is the setting apart of singular men unto some lawful labor and employment, according to the variety of their gifts, and inclinations, whether they be public or private.

What is in the second place required of every man?
That they diligently labor in their lawful calling, (2 Thes. 3. 10.) and that variously, according to every mans condition, and the variety of their several callings. For if Adam was not to be idle in the state of Innocence; (Gen. 2. 15.) much less we after the fall Gen. 3. 19.

What do you call extraordinary getting?
That which is acquired by the Law of nature, or the law of Nations: as that which is gotten by the law of Arms, or that which is casually found, being lost of another; unto which men have right, when as by diligent inquiry the owner cannot be known.

How are goods justly gotten as they are retained from others?
When as by a civil right we retain them from others, who are the true and lawful owners: and that either by free gift, or by succession and inheritances; whether it be given unto us by the Testators will, or by law and right do fall unto us.

What are the vices opposite to the former virtues?
All means and kinds of unjust getting, opposite to just acquisitions; whether ordinary or extraordinary.

What is opposite to ordinary just getting?
Inordinate walkings; 2 Thes. 3. 6, 7, 11. which is opposed either to a lawful calling, or to labor required in it.

What is opposed to a lawful Calling?
Either no Calling at all, or such a Calling as is unlawful. They who have no Calling, are unprofitable burdens to the Common-wealth, and like pernicious humors in the body.

Who are those?
First, sturdy beggars and rogues, who can work and will not, but live upon other men's labors: which kind of people are not to be suffered in a Common-wealth. For though we shall have the poor always; (Deut. 15. 11. Mat. 26. 11.) yet there ought to be no beggars, and inordinate walkers, who eat and labor not. 2 Thes. 3. 10. 12. Secondly, idle and superfluous Gentlemen; who having no Calling spend all their time in pleasure, hunting, hawking, reveling, gaming, &c. Thirdly, such as thrust themselves into such Callings for which they have no right.

What are unlawful callings?
Those that have no warrant out of Gods Word, or the Laws of the Land: as those that live by unlawful Arts; as Whores, Bawds, Deu. 23. 17, 18. Witches, Wizards, Deut. 18. 11, 12. Stage-players, Bear-wards, Gamesters, and the like.

What is opposed to lawful labor in our Calling?
An idle life: which as it is condemned in the seventh Commandment, as being a cause and incentive of lust; so here, as a companion and cause of theft. Eph. 4. 28. Prov. 18. 9. For sloth causeth beggary; and this, stealing. Pro. 6. 11. & 28. 19. & 30. 9.

What are the kinds of unjust getting out of Contract?
They are two: 1. Theft. 2. Rapine or Robbery. Lev. 19. 13. Both which men may commit either as principals, or accessories.

What is Theft?
The fraudulent taking of another mans goods, against the knowledge or the will of the owner. Which is the sin that is chiefly forbidden in this Commandment, and comprehendeth under it all the rest; and is a great sin, strictly forbidden by God, Lev. 19. 11. and severely punished, Zech. 5. 3, 4. 1 Cor. 6. 10. and by our Laws also made Capital.

What are the kinds of Theft?
They are either Domestic, and in the Family, or out of the Family. Thefts in the Family, are either of the wife, or children, or of servants.

What is the Theft of the Wife?
When she purloineth her Husbands goods, either without his knowledge, or against his will. For howsoever she hath a right unto them in respect of use; yet the propriety belongeth only to the Husband.

What is the Theft of the Children?
When they take away their Parents goods, either without their consent, or against their will. For howsoever children think this to be no Theft; yet Solomon saith otherwise. Pro. 28. 24. Who so robbeth his Father or his Mother, and saith it is no transgression; the same is the companion of a destroyer.

What is the Theft of Servants?
When they are unfaithful, or wasteful. Unfaithful, when as they purloin their Masters goods, Joh. 12. 6. Tit. 2. 10. or are idle or negligent in their service; or run away from them, as did Onesimus, Philem. 12. or give away their goods without their knowledge and consent, though it be to good uses. Wasteful, when as they wastefully and riotously consume their Masters substance.

How is Theft that is committed out of the Family distinguished?
It is either of goods, or of persons. Of goods, either common or sacred: and those, either private or public. Private are such goods as belong to private men; whether it be Cattle, money, or any thing that is money-worth.

What is the Theft of public things?
When things are stolen which belong to the public State or Body of the Common-Wealth: which is more heinous and capital then that which is committed against a private man. And in this kind enclosures of Commons are to be reputed as theft. Prov. 23. 10, 11.

What is the Theft of sacred things?
When things consecrated to an holy and sacred use, are purloined and embezzled: which we usually call Sacrilege. As when the utensils and instruments of divine worship are stolen; when the Lands or Tithes devoted unto God for the maintenance of his Ministers are diminished, withheld, or taken away. Mal. 3. 8. In which kind, the chief offenders are corrupt Patrons, who having only the right of presentation of fit persons, do encroach upon part of the Tithes, or sell Church livings for money; and also Proprietaries, who seize upon Church livings devoted to the maintenance of the Ministry, and convert them to their own proper and private use: and finally, the Court Harpies, who seize upon the revenues of the Church, by preferring of unworthy, idle, and ambitious men.

What do you think of this sin?
That it is most heinous: seeing such as commit it, rob God himself; (Mal. 3. 8.) and thereby bring his heavy curse upon them, v. 9. As we see in the example of Achan, Nebuchadnezzar, Belshazzar, Ananias, Sapphira, and the rest.

What is the Theft of Persons?
It is an heinous sin punished by the Law of God with death: (Exod. 21. 16. Deut. 24. 7.) being so much worse than the theft of goods, as the persons of men are better than they. Mat. 6. 25. And this is committed by such as steal men or children, to sell them for slaves; and by lustful or covetous wooers, who steal men's daughters to make them their wives.

You have spoken of Theft so properly called. What is the other kind which is more improper?
Rapine: which is a violent taking away of another mans goods. And this is done, either under the pretext of Authority and legal power, or else without it. The former are public Thieves, of which Solomon speaketh, Prov. 12. 7. which are worse than common thieves, and shall be more severely punished, Wis. 6. 6. because their sin is aggravated by the abusing of their Authority; and because commonly violence and cruelty is joined with it. Zeph. 3. 3. Ezekiel 22. 27. Mic. 3. 2, 3. Isa. 3. 14, 15.

What is this Theft called?
Oppression, and extortion: when a man spoileth his neighbor under color of law; as Ahab and Jezebel did Naboth. 1 Kin. 21.

What is that rapine which is committed without any pretext of Authority?
It is either in War or in Peace. In War, either by Land, when Soldiers being not content with their pay, do spoil and plunder, not only their enemies but also their friends. Deut. 2. 5, 6. Luke 3. 14. Or by Sea, when as Pirates they rob and spoil all they meet with and can master.

What is that rapine which is exercised on the Land?
It is either robbery by the high way; (Luke 10. 30. Joh. 18. 40.) or Burglary, when as they break open houses that they may rob the inhabitants.

Are there no others to be esteemed thieves but those only who act theft themselves?
Yes, They also who are accessories, Psal. 50. 18. and do consent to the theft of others. And these thefts are either common to all, or proper to Superiors. The former is committed before, with, or after the theft.

How is a man an accessory before the theft?
When he counselleth or provoketh another unto it: as Jezebel did Ahab. 1 Kings 21. Prov. 1. 11, 13, 14.

How with, or in the Theft?
Either when he aideth the Thief, or does not hinder him when as it is in his power.

How after the Theft?
First, When he receiveth, and concealeth what is stolen; or hideth, or keepeth the Thief from being apprehended. Secondly, When he partaketh with him in the stolen goods. Prov. 29. 24. And this is done, 1. When he taketh the goods from the Thief that he may keep them to himself. 2. When he knowingly buyeth stolen goods, which ought to be restored to the owners. 3. When by silence he concealeth the Thief.

How are the Superiors accessory?
When they do any ways encourage, or do not punish them: especially when they do acquit them for a bribe.

So much of that acquisition, and getting of goods which is out of Contract Now show that which is in, or by Contracts And first what a lawful contract is, and what is required in it?
A Contract is an agreement between parties, by mutual consent, about the alienation of goods from one to another, upon some just and honest conditions. And this either respecteth the things themselves, or their use for a time.

What is required in a lawful Contract?
That it be done in simplicity add integrity without guile and deceit. Unto which three things are required: First, truth in our words. Secondly, fidelity in our promises. Thirdly, justice in our deeds. Psal. 15. 4. Zech. 8. 16.

What is opposed hereunto?
First, All collusion and deceit; whereby one seeketh to circumvent another. 1 Thes. 4. 6. which is a vice odious unto God, (Ezek. 22. 12.) and severely punished. Psal. 5. 6. & 55. 23. Mic. 7. 2. Secondly, lies in contracting the bargain; (Prov. 21. 6.) and most of all when they are confirmed by oaths. Thirdly, Perfidiousness in promises; when convenants are not kept. Lastly, Injustice in Contracts; when equality is not observed.

What are the sorts of the things gotten by Contract?
They are either of things alienated, or committed to trust: and the former is either liberal or illiberal.

What is liberal alienation?
It is either for ever, or only for a certain time. For ever, as when things are given absolutely, or upon certain conditions.

What is liberal alienation for a time?
When as things are lent for a time; either to be restored in the same, or in the like kind; as money, corn, and such like.

What is opposed hereunto?
When the Borrower being able does not pay all, or not at the appointed time; or does not do his best endeavour to pay it. Psal. 37. 21.

What is that acquisition which you call illiberal alienation?
That which is made by way of recompense, or exchange: which is either of the thing it self, or the use of it, or of labor and industry. In which the general rule to be observed is, that there be an equal and just proportion in the recompense or exchange, between the things exchanged: as between the price and thing prized, the industry, labor and reward.

What is opposite hereunto?
When as this just proportion is not observed.

What are the kinds of the alienation of the thing it self?
They are two: either that which is for ever, or that which is only for a certain time.

What do you call alienation for ever?
Merchandise; which consisteth in buying and selling: and it is a commutation either of money for ware, which is buying; or of ware for money, which is selling.

What do you think of it?
I hold that Merchandise is a lawful calling, but liable to much danger of sin in the managing of it. Eccl. 2.26. 1, 2. Hos. 12. 7. Mat. 21. 12, 13.

What is selling?
A contract about the alienation of goods for ever at a certain price agreed upon between the seller and the buyer, without any fraud or guile.

What is required in just selling?
First, in respect of the person: that he be the just owner, or by him appointed to sell in his right. Secondly, in respect of the goods: that it be saleable, and neither sophisticated by mixture, nor base and corrupt in respect of the substance. Thirdly, in respect of use: that it be profitable for necessity of life, or for ornament and delight. Fourthly, in respect of the manner of selling: that it be without any deceit. Fifthly, that it be sold in a just and equal price, according to the worth: respect being had both to the use of the thing it self, and also to the necessary pains and danger which the Seller hath been at in getting of it.

What is required to the manner of lawful selling?
That it be done with simplicity and integrity; and that we do not in bargaining defraud and over reach one another. 1 Thes. 4. 6. Levit. 24. 14.

What are the vices and corruptions in selling, opposite hereunto?
They are many: and concern either the Seller himself, The Ware or things sold, the price or the manner of selling.

What are the vices which respect the person of the seller?
First, when as he selleth that which is not his own. Secondly, when as he selleth that which is not vendible. As, first, when it is defective and faulty, or not useful. Secondly, when as it is such a thing as ought not to be sold: as Gehazi, 2 Ki. 5. 20. did with the miracle of healing, wrought by divine power; and when Magistrates for bribes sell justice. Amos. 2. 6. Isa. 5. 23. & 1. 23. Thirdly, when men by lying and false-witness-bearing sell the truth; in which rank Lawyers are chiefly to be numbered, who wittingly for fees plead ill causes.

How does the seller offend in respect of the price?
When as he observeth not a just and equal proportion between the price, and the worth of the thing sold. And this is the vice either of private men, or of whole societies. Private men

who thus offend, are those which we call Regraters, Monopolists, hoarders up of Corn, and other commodities, to raise the Market by making a dearth and scarcity. Prov. 11. 26.

How do whole societies in this kind offend?
First, when as they of the same Trade and Craft agree together to sell their wares at an unequal rate above the true worth. Secondly, not to finish the work which another hath begun, though he dealeth deceitfully and unjustly with his work-Master.

What are the sins committed by the Seller in respect of the manner?
They may be referred to two heads; either his Words or Deeds.

How offendeth he in Words?
First, when as he immoderately praiseth his wares above their true worth; and concealeth the faults and defects in them which he well knoweth. Secondly, when as he asketh much above the worth, and protesteth that he cannot afford it better cheap.

How does he offend in his Deeds?
Either in respect of the kind, quality, or quantity of his wares. In respect of the kind, when as he selleth one thing for another, or one color for another; presuming on the ignorance of the buyer.

How in respect of the quality?
When as he deceitfully selleth old for new, that which is corrupt and sophisticated for that which is pure and simple, and bad for good. To which end he useth many arts, and false lights, and showing course and bad wares, to commend those for the best which he showeth after, though they be but a little better.

How in respect of the Quantity?
When he detracteth from the just and equal proportion, by using false weights and measures not agreeable to Standard; using less and lighter when they sell, and larger and heavier when they buy: which God forbiddeth as abominable. Lev. 19. 35, 36. Deut. 25. 14, 15. Prov. 11. 1. & 20. 10, 23. Hos. 12. 2. Amos 8. 5, Mic. 6. 10, 11.

You have spoken of Selling. Now what is that alienation which is by buying?
Buying is a contract, whereby money or a just price is alienated and parted with for wares of proportionable worth.

What is required in buying?
Things answerable to those before spoken of in selling: and respect; first the person buying. Secondly, the thing bought. Thirdly, the price given. And fourthly, the manner of buying.

What is required in respect of the person buying?
That he buy only of him whom he thinketh to be the right owner of the thing sold. For he that buyeth known stolen goods, communicateth in the theft.

What in respect of the thing?
That he buy that only which he knoweth may be lawfully bought and sold.

How do men sin in this respect?
When as they offer to buy, with Simon Magus, spiritual gifts and graces, or things consecrated to divine worship; that they may alienate them from their right use; pardons, and Indulgences, sacred Ordination, Benefices, and the like. Secondly, they which buy justice, and much more injustice, by bribery. Thirdly, they that buy lies and false testimonies to prevent justice.

What is required of the buyer in respect of the price?
That according to his knowledge and judgment he give a just, equal, and proportionable price, according to the true value of the things sold, and bought. Especially when he buyeth of the poor, who are by present necessity enforced to sell, whether it be wares or labor: upon which if any take advantage to bear down the just price, they grievously oppress the poor. Amos 8. 6. & 2. 6. Mic. 2. 2, 3.

What is required of Buyers in respect of the manner?
That they use all simplicity, and upright dealing; and shun all injustice and deceit, both in their words and deeds.

How in words?
First, that they do not offer much under the true value of the wares they buy according to their knowledge and judgment. Secondly, that they do not undeservedly dispraise it, and without cause, to beat down the price; yea, even when they inwardly like and approve it. Prov. 20. 14.

How in deeds?
When as they do not pay at all, or less than the price that was agreed upon. And this deceit respecteth either the quality, when as they put off in payment base and adulterate money; or in quantity, when as they pass for payment clipped many, (Gen. 33. 16.) or such as is defective in weight or number: And to these private thefts in buying, we may add one that is more public; when as the buyer buyeth up and engrosses a whole commodity; that having all in his own hand, he may raise the market, and sell at what rate he listeth.

Hitherto of that liberal alienation which is for ever.
What is that which is only for a time?
It is called pawning. Which is a contract whereby the dominion and right of a mans goods is alienated from the owner to another man, only for a time, upon some condition agreed upon between the parties: which condition being not observed, the right of the thing belongeth to the receiver, at least so long till it be performed. And this pawning is either of moveables, and is called properly pawning; or of immoveables; and is called mortgaging.

What is his duty who layeth a thing to pawn?
First, to provide, that the thing pawned be at least of equal worth to that for which it is pawned. Secondly, that he redeem it at the appointed time.

What is his duty that receiveth a pawn?
First, that if the party be poor, and the thing pawned necessary to the preservation of life; that either he do not receive it, or that he do restore it to the owner when his necessity requireth it. Deut. 24. 6. and 24. 10, 11, 12, 13, 14, 15. Exod. 22. 26. Secondly, that if the borrower be not able to restore it at the appointed time, he do not use extremity, nor take advantage upon his necessity, to make him forfeit the thing pawned; but at the most, provide only for his own indemnity. Ezek. 18. 7, 12. & 33. 15.

So much of the illiberal Alienation of the thing it self. Now what is the illiberal Alienation only of the use?
This contract of Alienation concerning only the use, is either location and letting, which is the alienation of the thing for hire: or hiring and conduction, which is the alienation of the hire for the use of the thing.

What is Location or Letting?
It is a contract, whereby only the use of a thing, and not the interest and dominion, is alienated from the owner to another, for hire and wages agreed upon, and that only for a certain time. And therefore, by this contract, the same individual is to be returned.

What is his duty that letteth?
1. That he require an equal and proportionable price for the thing he letteth. 2. That he letteth only such things as are useful to him that hireth them. 3. That he do not exact any recompense for any hurt with happeneth to the thing hired, which cometh not by the fault or negligence of him that hireth it. Exod. 22. 11,

What is conduction or hiring?
It is a contract whereby a man getteth the use of a thing for a certain time, for a just price or reward.

What is the duty that thus hireth any thing?
First, that he use the thing hired only for that end and purpose to which he hired it. Secondly, that he use it no worse than if it were his own. Thirdly, that he restore it to the owner at the time agreed upon. Lastly, that he restore whole and sound the thing hired; or if through his fault or negligence it have received any hurt, that he give to the owner a valuable recompense. Exod. 22. 12.

What is that we call Usury?
It is a lending in expectation of certain gain.

What do you think of it?
If you speak of that properly, which the Scriptures forbid and condemn; it is a wicked and unlawful contract, into which as a common sink, the filth of many other sins and unlawful contracts do run: a fruitful womb, in which many vices and corruptions are bred; and by which if we live and die in it without repentance, we are excluded out of the Kingdom of Heaven. Psal. 15. 5. & Ezek. 18. 8. & 22. 13.

But there is much question what this Usury is, which the Scripture condemneth?
Therefore it shall be our wisdom in matters concerning our salvation to take the surest and safest course: and that is, wholly to forbear it, and not to put our souls, which are of more value than the whole world, upon nice disputes and subtle distinctions. Mark. 8. 36.

You have spoken of that alienation which is in illiberal Contracts, in respect of the things themselves, or the use of them. Now what is that alienation which is for recompense of care, labor, and industry?
These Contracts are either public or private. The private are either in the Commonwealth, between the Magistrate and people; or in the Church, between the Ministers and people.

What is the Contract between the Magistrate and people?
That the Magistrates should receive from them their stipends, tribute, and maintenance; and the people from them, and by them, protection, direction, and peaceable government.

What then is the Magistrates duty to the People?
That he faithfully bestow all his labor and industry, his care and diligence, that he may in the Lord Govern the people committed to his charge; and direct, correct, and protect them for the common good. Rom. 13. 4. Psal. 78. 71, 72. And if they have their reward and neglect their duty, they are guilty of theft, and sin against this Commandment. Ezek. 34. 2, 3.

What is the peoples duty to them?
That they faithfully pay unto them their tribute and due, as an honorable reward of their pains and care. Mat. 22. 21. Rom. 13. 7.

What is the public Contract between Ministers and People?
That the Ministers receive their portion and maintenance from the people or rather from God himself, feed the people committed to their charge with the bread of life; faithfully preaching the Word and administering the Sacraments, and shining before them by an holy example and the light of a godly life, seeking rather them than theirs. 2 Tim. 4. 1, 2. 2 Cor. 12. 14.

What is this theft?
First, when he receiveth his reward, and neglecteth his duty. As when he presseth into his Calling uncalled, by the window and not by the door: (Joh. 10. 1.) being neither qualified with gifts, not willing to employ those he hath for the good of the people. Second, when he feedeth himself and not the people; eating the milk and clothing himself with the wool, but neglecting the flock. Ezek. 34. 2, 3. Zech. 11. 15. 17. Third, when for gain he either preacheth false doctrine, or concealeth the truth. Mic. 3. 11.

What is the duty of the people?
That receiving spiritual things from their Ministers, they communicate and impart unto them their carnal things. 1 Cor. 9. 10.

What is the peoples theft?
When receiving these spiritual things, they defraud them of their dues, and withhold from them their means and maintenance which the Laws of God and Man do allot unto them. Which is not only theft but even Sacrilege, and the robbing of God himself. Malac. 3. 8.

What is that alienation which is in private Contracts?
When as men employ others to do their work upon promise of reward; or any ways to use their gifts and abilities, their care, industry and labor, for a just recompense.

What is required of such as thus employ others?
First, that they give an equal and proportionable recompense to those whom they thus hire. 1 Tim. 5. 18. Second, that they pay it without delay: especially to the poor who are not able, nor willing to forbear it. Deut. 24. 14, 15. Lev. 19. 13.

What then is their Theft?
When either they give not an equal and just recompense, or delay to pay it to the poor who are unable to forbear it. Jam. 5. 4.

What are the duties of the mercenary or hireling?
1. That he require no more than such wages as is equal and proportionable to his skill care and labor. 2. That he do his work that hireth him, faithfully and diligently.

You have spoken of such Contracts as respect Alienation and change. Now what are those which are of things committed to trust?
They are either of things committed to others only for safe custody, or such as are committed to Fifes of trust for uses appointed, or such as by last will are entrusted to Executors.

What is the nature of things deposited?
When neither the dominion and right, nor the use of the thing is alienated, but only the safe custody is committed to a man.

What is his duty?
That he safely keep that which is committed to his trust, and willingly restore it to the owner when he calleth for it.

What is his Theft?
First, When he converteth the thing committed to his keeping unto his own use. Secondly, when he will not restore it to the owner when he desireth to have it.

But what if the things deposited were stolen, or become worse?
If it be by his default that had the keeping of them, he is to make it good: but if by oath he can clear himself of all unfaithfulness and negligence, the owner and not he must bear the loss. Exod. 22. 7, 8.

What is the duty of Fiduciaries and Executors?
That they faithfully discharge their trust, and do their will (and not their own) who have reposed confidence in them.

How do they offend?
When they fail in their trust; and aim more at their own profit, than at the performing of their will who have entrusted them, or the faithful discharge of their duty.

These are duties which respect things committed to trust. What say you of persons thus entrusted?
Those are Pupils, and children in their nonage: who being unable to govern, direct, protect, and order themselves, are by the Laws of God and man, committed to the care and tuition of others.

What is the duty of their Tutors and Guardians?
That they carry themselves towards them faithfully, according to the trust reposed in them; and like Parents aim chiefly at the good of their Pupils and Wards, and not their own gain and profit. Est. 2. 7. remembering that they shall one day be called to give an account of these persons committed to their charge and trust, and of all the goods belonging unto them.

So much of just getting goods. Now in the order propounded we are come to the just possession and retention of them. What is required unto this just possession?
Two things. First, the keeping of our own goods. Secondly, The restitution of that which justly belongeth to others.

What does this Commandment require of us in the former respect?
That we be not wanting to the just preservation, not only of our neighbors, but also of our own goods.

How prove you this?
Because our goods are Gods Talents, committed unto us; of which we must give an account to our great Lord and Master. And therefore if through our own fault and negligence we suffer them to be lost, or to be taken unjustly from us; we rob ourselves, and the poor also, who have right unto that which we can well spare from our own uses.

What does this Commandment require concerning restitution of other men's goods?
That we readily restore those goods, which either we have unjustly gotten from the right owners, or which we cannot justly retain.

How do you prove that goods unjustly gotten ought to be restored?
Both by Gods Precepts, the examples of the godly, and necessary reasons. For the first, God strictly requireth, that if any thing be unjustly gotten, as either by violence, or by fraud and deceit, or any other ways, restitution be made to the true owner. Levit. 6. 2. 3. 4. 5. Num. 5. 6, 7, 8.

By what examples do you evince it?
Before the Law, by the example of Jacob and his sons. Gen. 43. 12. 21. Under the law, by the profession of Samuel, 1 Sam. 12. 4. and the practice of Micah, Judges 17. 2. who though an Idolater, made conscience of it. And of the Jews, Nehem. 5. 11. 12. And under the Gospel we have the example of Zaccheus, Luk. 19. 8. Yea Judas himself being convinced of his sin, maketh restitution: so that they herein are worse than Judas who refuse to do it.

What reason have you for it?
Because it is a duty necessarily to be performed by all that hope for salvation. For without restitution we can neither have any true faith to persuade us that our sin of theft is remitted, nor any sincere Repentance. For God pardons no sin which we will pertinaciously retain and live in, Prov. 28. 13. But he that restoreth not ill gotten goods, liveth still in his theft, and repenteth not of it: seeing restitution is an inseparable fruit of repentance. Ezek. 33. 15.

But what is to be considered in this restitution?
Four things. First, who is to make it: namely every man who hath gotten any thing unjustly, either by force or fraud, by contract or out of contract, by calumny, and false accusation, by lying, oppression, or any other evil course. Luke 19. 8. Numb. 5. 6. Levit. 6. 2, 3.

Secondly, to whom restitution is to be made: namely, to him who is wronged, defrauded, or oppressed. Lev. 6. 5. or to his kindred if he be dead, or if none such can be found, to pious uses.

Thirdly, how much ought to be restored: to wit, all the whole that is unjustly gotten if he be able, or at least so much to the uttermost as he is able. Yea the law of God required, that to the principal a fifth part should be added. Lev. 6. 5. Numb. 5. 7. And even equity it self requireth, that beside the principal it self, so much more should be added as the party is damnified by this unjust detention of his goods.

Fourthly, when this restitution ought to be made: namely, not at the end of our lives or after our death; but as soon as we repent, and desire at God's hands that our sin should be forgiven. We must confess, bewail and forsake our sin, that God may be reconciled unto us: and then we must make satisfaction to our wronged neighbor. Mat. 5. 23, 24.

What are the things, which though they be justly gotten, yet are unjustly detained?
Such things as others having lost, we have found. For such things come unto us by the disposing of God's providence, and we may justly keep them till we can find out the true owners: so that we make diligent inquiry after them, with a resolution to restore what we have thus found, when we know to whom they belong. Deut. 22. 3. Exod. 23. 4.

Hitherto of the duties which belong to just getting and possessing of goods. Now what is required to the right use of them?
Two things: Fruition, in respect of ourselves; and Communication, in respect of others. Prov. 5. 15, 16.

What is required to the former?
That we thankfully and comfortably enjoy God's blessings, which he hath bestowed on us. Eccles. 5. 17, 18.

How must this be done?
By exercising two virtues. The first is Parsimony or thriftiness: whereby we honestly keep and preserve our goods, that they be not vainly and unprofitably misspent. John 6. 12. Prov. 27. 23, to 28. The second is Frugality: whereby we dispose of our goods justly and honestly gotten, to fit and necessary uses, in a sober and moderate manner.

What virtues then must here concur in the right use of our goods?
These four: 1. Justice in getting them. 2. Thriftiness in keeping them. 3. Frugality in enjoying them. 4. Liberality in communicating them.

For without justice, parsimony degenerateth into covetousness; Frugality without liberality, into sordid miserliness; Liberality without parsimony and frugality, into prodigality.

What vices are opposed to these virtues?
Two: First, Tenacity, or sordid gripingness. Secondly, profusion and wastefulness.

What is Tenacity?
A kind of covetousness which restraineth men, both from communicating their goods to others, and from enjoying themselves. Eccl. 6. 2. & 6. 10. 11.

Wherein do such offend?
By committing a double theft. First against their neighbors: seeing God hath not made them absolute owners of their riches, but Stewards, who must dispose of them also for the good of others; which if they do not, they rob them of their right. Jam. 5. 1, 2, 3. Secondly, against themselves: in defrauding their own souls of the use of those blessings which God hath allowed them, Eccl. 4. 8.

What do you think of such Misers?
First, that none are more wicked; seeing they are neither good for themselves, nor others. Eccles. 4. 8. & 5. 12, 13, 14. Secondly, more poor; seeing though they possess much, yet they enjoy nothing: and want as well what they have, as what they have not. Thirdly, none more foolish; seeing they want for fear of wanting, and live poor that they may die rich. Fourthly, none more wretched; seeing they deprive themselves both of the comforts of this life, and the joys of the life to come.

What is the other extreme?
Profusion and wastefulness. And this is two fold: either in spending above their means in unnecessary expenses; whereby they either ruin their estates, or expose themselves to the devils temptations, in using unlawful means to recover that which they have wastefully misspent.

Or secondly, in wasting their goods in dishonest and riotous courses, tending to luxury and riot; whereby they necessitate themselves to use all unlawful means to get so much more wealth as may serve to maintain their riotous expenses. And so luxury becometh the mother of Covetousness; and Covetousness the nurse of Luxuriousness.

What is the use of goods respecting others?
It is by communication or liberal alienation of them for the use and benefit of others.

What virtues are hereunto required?
Two: Liberality and Justice. Liberality; whereby we communicate our goods with a ready and cheerful mind. Justice; whereby we thus communicate that only which is our own. And these must go hand in hand; and are therefore conjoined by Solomon, Proverbs 21. 21.

What are the kinds of liberal alienation?
They are two. For it is for a certain time only, or for ever.

What is that which is only for a certain time?
It is either a liberal alienation of the use only of a thing for a certain time, or of the dominion also, and that freely, without any expectation of recompense.
For both these ought to be liberal, respecting only the profit of the receiver: and secondly, just; to which is required that which is lent be his own who lendeth it, and fit for his use who borroweth it, And this duty is commended, Psal. 112. 5. and commanded, Deut. 16. 7. 8. Mat. 5. 42. Luke. 6. 35.

What is that alienation which is for ever?
It is free giving: when as goods are alienated from the true owner unto another liberally, and without expectation of any recompense. 2 Cor. 9. 7. Act 20. 35.

What is further required to it?
That it be not only free, but also just; giving that only which is a mans own and not another's, which were no better than theft. As when a man by lavish giving defraudeth his children of their inheritance, or giveth his goods or lands from his daughters to strangers, or remote kindred of his name, because he hath no sons to continue it. Secondly, that we make good choice of those upon whom we confer benefits, either for their worth or indigency; but especially we must give and do good to those who are of the household of faith. Gal. 6. 10.

What are the uses unto which we must freely contribute?
They are either public or private: and the public are either Civil or Ecclesiastical.

What are the Civil?
When as we freely give our goods for the service, preservation and benefit of the Commonwealth, both in the time of Peace and War. To which uses we must give freely, to the uttermost of our ability: yea, even above it, when the necessity of the State requireth it; seeing the good of the whole body must be preferred before the good of any particular member. 2 Sam. 17. 27, 28, 29.

What are the Ecclesiastical?
When as we give freely for the maintenance of the Ministry, and means of Gods Worship, tending to the Salvation of our souls. To which uses we must give so much the more cheerfully, as the soul is to be preferred before the body, or outward estate. Luk. 10. and last. Prov. 3. 9. An example whereof we have in the Israelites, Exod. 36. 5, 6. 1 Chro. 29. 9. And if they were so free and liberal in giving towards the building of the Tabernacle and Temple: how much more should we towards the building of God's spiritual Houses and Temples for the holy Ghost?

What are the private uses?
For the benefit and relief of private men, whose necessity does require it of us according to our abilities. And these are those Alms-deeds, and other works of mercy, unto which the Apostle exhorteth, Heb 13. 16. and are partly fruits of mercy, and partly of brotherly love and Christian Charity.

[29TH HEAD.]

Hitherto you have spoken of the duties respecting our own and our neighbors person, both in regard of life in the sixth, and of Chastity in the seventh; as also our own and their goods in the eighth. Now what is the ninth Commandment?
Thou shalt not bear false witness against thy Neighbor. Exod. 20. 16.

What is the main scope and end, at which God aimeth in this Commandment?
The conservation of truth amongst men, and of our own and our Neighbors fame and good name.

Why does God so much regard truth?
Because it is most dear unto him. For he is the God of truth, Deut. 32. 4. Psal. 31. 5. yea truth it self, Joh. 14. 6. Therefore Christ came into the world, that he might bear witness unto the truth, Joh. 18. 37. and by speaking the truth God is glorified. Josh. 7. 19.

Why does he respect so much our fame and good name?
Because it is his own good gift; and therefore he taketh care to preserve that unto us, which himself hath given.

What was the occasion of this Commandment?
First, our natural corruption, which maketh us prone to lying Psa. 58. 3. Ro. 3. 4. as appeareth hereby, in that we no sooner speak than lie, and not only for advantage, but without any cause, out of mere vanity. Secondly, out of a natural disposition men are ready to trespass against the fame and good name of others; and this ariseth out of mere envy and pride, which maketh us ready to abase others to advance ourselves.

What is the thing that is here chiefly forbidden?
That we should not in legal proceedings and Courts of justice give a false testimony concerning our neighbors: as appeareth by the words expressly used, Thou shalt not answer a false testimony concerning thy Neighbor; which implies a precedent question or examination. Unless we will say that answering is here used for speaking or saying, as it is oftentimes; Mat. 11. 25. Luk. 14. 3, 5. Mat. 28. 5. and then the meaning is, that we must not give a false testimony of our neighbor either publicly or privately, whether it be with or against him. Or if we had rather take it of legal testimonies in Courts of Justice, then by a Synecdoche we must under this one kind understand all other kinds of false testimonies: but this is here named as the chief, and of all the rest most hurtful and pernicious, to comprehend under it all the rest, as it is in the other commandments.

What then is the negative part of this Commandment?
It generally forbiddeth all false, vain, and offensive speeches concerning our neighbor; whether it be for or against him, whether in Judgment or out of Judgment: although principally here are forbidden all false testimonies which tend to the prejudice of the fame or state of our neighbors; or more briefly, it forbiddeth all falsity and untruth; especially that which is prejudicial to our neighbor in any respect, or to ourselves.

What does the affirmative part require?
Two things: the conservation of the truth, and of our own and neighbors good name; with all duties of the tongue homogeneal and of the same nature and kind, with all helps and means tending hereunto.

Why are our words and speeches so much to be regarded, seeing they are but mind, as is commonly supposed?
Great care is to be had of our speech, seeing it is an excellent faculty peculiar to man; and being a special gift of God, it must not be abused to God's dishonor and our own destruction. Neither are words slightly to be regarded, seeing we must give account of every idle word; and by our words we shall be justified or condemned. And the wise man telleth us, that death and life are in the power of the tongue, Prov. 18. 21. and that a wholesome tongue is a tree of life, whereas an evil tongue is an unruly evil, and full of deadly poison, Jam, 3. 8. which if we do not subdue and rule, whatsoever profession we make of Religion, it is all in vain. Jam. 1. 26.

What is the sum of the duties of the tongue here required?
That our speeches be both true and charitable: for these must inseparably go together. For charity rejoiceth in truth, 1 Cor. 13. 6. and the truth must be spoken in love, Ep. 4. 15. For truth without love savoreth of malice; and charity without truth is false, vain, and foolish.

Unto what heads then are these duties of the Tongue required in this Commandment, to be referred?
Unto two: 1. The conservation of truth amongst men. 2. The conservation of our own and our neighbors fame and good name.

What have you to say concerning truth?
Two things. First, what the truth is. Secondly, the means of conserving it.

What is to be considered in truth it self?
Three things. First, what it is. Secondly, whether it be to be professed. Thirdly, after what manner.

What is truth or veracity?
It is an habit of speaking that which is true from our hearts Psal. 15. 2.

What is required hereunto?
Two things. First, that our speech be agreeable to our minds. Secondly, that our minds be agreeable to the thing. For though we speak that which is true, yet if we think it false, we are liars; because our tongue agreeth not with our minds: and if that we speak be false, and yet we think it true, we do not speak truly. For though truth be in our hearts, yet a lie is in our mouths: and though we cannot be called liars, because we speak as we think, yet may we be said to tell a lie, because that we say is false.

What great necessity is there of this truth?
Very great. For if speech be necessary, (as all confess) then also speaking truth; without which there would be no use of speech. For take away truth, and it were better that we were dumb, than that we should be endued with this faculty of speaking.

What other motives are there to embrace it?
Because it is both commended and commanded in the Scripture. It is commended as a virtue which God greatly loveth; as a note of a Citizen of heaven, Psal. 15. 2. and of one who shall be established for ever, Prov. 12. 19. It is commanded, Eph. 4. 25. Zech. 8. 16, 19.

Is it only sufficient to know the truth and believe it?
No: we must also upon all fit occasions profess it with our mouths. Rom. 10. 9, 10. Mat. 10. 32, 33.

Twenty-ninth Head

How must the truth be professed?
Freely and simply.

How it is done freely?
When as we profess it willingly and undauntedly; so far forth as the matter, place, and time do require. So Dan. 3. 16, 17, 18. Acts 4. 8, 10, 13.

How is it done simply?
When as it is done without guile and dissimulation, shifts or shuffles.

What are the vices opposite to truth?
They are two. First, falsity and lying. Secondly, vanity, or an habit of lying.

What is lying?
It is twofold, First, when we speak that which is false. Secondly, when we speak that which is true, falsely, and with a mind to deceive.

What is it to speak that which is false?
When as you do not speak as the thing is; whether we think it true or false.

What is it to speak falsely?
When as we do not speak as we think; whether the thing be true or false.

What are the reasons which may dissuade from lying?
1. Because God is true and the Author of truth; and the Devil a liar, and the Father of lies: and as truth maketh us like unto God, so lies make us like unto the Devil.

2. Because it is strictly forbidden in the Scriptures. Exod. 23. 7. Col. 3. 9. Eph. 4. 25.

3. Because the liar sinneth grievously, not only against his Neighbor, but also against God himself. Lev. 6. 2.

4. Because the Scriptures condemn lying as the spawn of the old serpent, Joh. 8. 44. and as a thing abominable and odious unto God. Prov. 12. 22. & 6. 16, 17.

5. Because it perverteth the use of speech, taketh away all credit and faith between man and man, and quite overthroweth all human society; which cannot stand without contracts and commerce, nor they without truth.

Lastly, because God severely punisheth lies, Prov. 19. 5, 9. Psal. 5. 6. Acts 5. 1, 2, 3. &c. and that both in this life with infamy and disgrace; (for it maketh a man esteemed base and of no credit; so that the usual liar is not believed when he speaketh truth, Ecclus. 34. 4.) and in the life to come. For it excludeth out of Heaven, Rev. 22. 15. and casteth men into that lake which burneth with fire and brimstone. chap. 21. 8.

How are lies usually distinguished?
Into three sorts: Pernicious, Officious, Merry.

What are merry lies?
Such as are spoken only to delight the hearers, and make sport.

Are such to be condemned as sinful, seeing they do no man hurt?
Yes verily. For first, the Scriptures condemn not only false, but also all vain speeches, Mat. 12. 36. Secondly, Because they are against truth; and cannot be spoken without

impeaching of it. Thirdly, lies must not be spoken to delight Princes, who have most cause of care and trouble. Hos. 7. 3. Fourthly, lies must not be spoken for profit; and therefore much less for delight.

What are officious lies?
Such as are spoken either for our own or our neighbors profit, and do not hurt any man.

Are such lies unlawful likewise?
Yes surely, and upon the same grounds. For though we may buy the truth at a dear purchase; yet we must not sell it at any rate. Prov. 23. 23. And if it be unlawful to lie in the cause of God, because it hath no need to be supported by our lies: (Job. 13. 7, 8.) much less for our own or our neighbors profit.

What do you call vanity in lying?
When men by a corrupt custom are so habituated to lying, that they will lie for every cause; yea even for no cause, and when they might attain their ends as well and easily by speaking truth.

What vices are opposite to freedom and liberty in speaking the truth?
They are either in the excess, or in the defect.

What in the excess?
Unseasonable and indiscreet profession of the truth, with the danger or loss of ourselves or others; when neither the glory of God, nor our own or our neighbors good does require it. And in such cases our Savior himself would not profess the truth; though he were pressed unto it by his malicious enemies: (Joh. 18. 20, 21.) because he should thereby have but cast Pearls before Swine; contrary to his own doctrine. Mat. 7. 6.

What is opposite in defect?
When either out of a cowardly fear, or some other sinister respect, we deny the truth in our words, or betray it by our silence. Of the former we have an example in Peter, Mat. 26. of the other in those weak Christians. 2 Tim. 4. 16.

But it is not sometime lawful to conceal the truth?
Yes surely: when neither the glory of God, nor our own or our neighbors good do require the profession of it; but yet with this caution, that we do not speak any untruth to conceal it. 1 Sam. 16. 2, 5.

What is opposed to simplicity in speaking the truth?
Simulation or double dealing. Which is two-fold: either in our words, or deeds.

What is that in our words?
When we speak one thing, and think another; or speak with an heart and a heart in the Scripture phrase, Psalm 12. 2. This is called a deceitful tongue and mouth, Zeph. 3. 13. and a tongue that frameth deceit, Psal. 50. 19. as it is described. Psal. 52. 2. Jer. 9. 8, 9. The which is to be avoided, Psal, 34. 13. and Christ's example to be imitated. 1 Pet. 2. 22.

What is simulation in our Deeds?
When as one thing is pretended, and another thing is intended. So Joab killed Abner and Amasa, under pretence of friendship. But howsoever this is esteemed policy with men, yet it is odious to God. Psal. 5, 6. and punished with immature death. Psal. 55. 23.

Twenty-ninth Head

You have spoken of truth it self, and the opposites unto it, now show what are the means of it?
They are of two sorts. First, that it may be amongst men. Secondly, that it may have a profitable being.

What is required to the being of it?
Two things. First, that it may be known. Secondly, that being known, it may be preserved.

What is required to the knowing of it?
Two things. First, a love of the truth. Secondly, teachableness.

What is the love of truth?
First, when as men are so affected towards the truth; that they study with all their endeavour to get it, but will not sell it at any price. Prov. 23. 23. Secondly, when as they are willing to defend it upon all occasions. Eccles. 4. 33.

What is opposite to the defense of truth?
First, love of lies: which excludeth out of heaven. Rev. 22 15. Secondly, voluntary ignorance. 2 Pet. 3. 5.

What is teachableness?
A fruit of the love of truth: when as men are ready and willing to admit the truth, and to give place to better reasons. Acts 17. 11.

What is further required to the preserving of truth?
That we be constant, and not carried away with every wind of doctrine, Eph. 4. 14. And these two virtues must concur: for teachableness without constancy degenerateth into levity and vain credulity; and constancy without teachableness into pertinacy.

What are the means of the profitable being of truth amongst men?
Profitable speech: which is accompanied and furthered with courtesy and civility, and remedied with silence.

When is our speech profitable?
First, when it advanceth God's glory, either in respect of the matter of it, or the end. The matter; when as we praise God, and celebrate his glory, Psal. 50. 23. Eph. 5. 4. Jam. 5. 13. And God's glory is the end of our speech; when as it is chiefly referred thereunto.

How do our speech tend to our neighbors profit?
First and chiefly, when it tendeth to his spiritual good and edification; as instructing the ignorant, counseling them that need counsel, comforting the afflicted, strengthning the weak, exhorting the sluggish, admonishing them that err, and rebuking them who willfully offend.

Secondly, when it tendeth to his temporal profit: either for his honest delight in a witty and facetious way called Urbanity; (which may be called the sauce that seasoneth truth, 2 Cor. 12. 15) or for his profit, when as it hath some necessary use for the good of his body or state.

What is the means of furthering this profitable truth in our speeches?
Courtesy and affability: which is a virtue whereby we are easily drawn to communicate with others, by talking with them in a human and courteous manner, with expressions of love and good-will. An example whereof we have in Christ. Joh. 4. 7, 10. who for this cause was said to be a friend to publicans and sinners.

What is the remedy against the contrary vice?

Taciturnity, or seasonable silence: which is a virtue that keepeth counsel, and restraineth us from uttering secrets, or any unprofitable, unnecessary, and unseasonable speeches. Which in the Scriptures is made a note of a wise man, Prov. 17. 28. & 10. 19. Jam. 1. 19. and is commended to all; especially to women, 1 Tim. 2. 11, 12. and young men in the presence of their elders and betters, Ecclus. 32. 9. And these two virtues, taciturnity and affability, must go together. For affability without seasonable silence degenerateth into vain babbling; and silence without affability into Cynical sullenness and sour churlishness.

What are the opposites to these virtues, and namely to profitable speech?

They are two. First, speech unprofitable. Secondly, that which is hurtful.

What is unprofitable and vain speech?

That which is not referred either to God's glory, or our own or our neighbors good. Which is condemned in the Scripture, Psal. 12, 2. Deut. 5. 20. Tit. 3. 9. Prov. 30. 8. and accountable at the day of judgment. Mat. 12. 36.

What is hurtful speech?

First, that which tendeth to God's dishonor; as imprecations, blasphemies, rash and false oaths. Secondly, that which tendeth to our own and our neighbors hurt, and is opposed either to edification, or the temporal good of his person, name, or state.

What is speech opposite to edification?

Rotten and unsavory speech, Eph. 4. 29. which is called rotten, because it springeth from a rotten and poisonous fountain, and is also apt to infect and poison the hearers. 1 Cor. 15. 33.

What are the kinds of this rotten speech?

They are many: as by our words to mislead men, to give evil counsel, grieve the afflicted, to encourage men to run on in sin, to praise men in their evil courses, and the like.

What vices are opposed to Urbanity?

There are divers; some in the excess, as witty speeches wantonly wicked, scurrility, talkativeness, and vain babbling. In the defect, such speeches as are foolish and unsavory.

What vices are opposite to Affability?

In the excess, counterfeit Complements. 2 Sam. 15. 5. Secondly, lightness, and idle talk. And in the defect, Morosity, and churlish speeches.

What vices are opposed to seasonable silence?

First, Prating and immoderate and unseasonable multiplying of words. Pro. 10. 19. Psal. 140. 11. Secondly, futility; when men can hold in no secrets, but unseasonably vent out all that is in their minds. Prov. 15. 28. & 12. 23. & 29. 11. Thirdly, unseasonable suppressing of truth with silence.

You have spoken of conserving of truth: now speak of our fame and good name; and first show why it is to be respected;

We ought to have singular care of preserving of our own and our neighbors good name; because it is no less dear to a good man than his life. Prov. 15. 30. & 22. 1. Eccles. 7. 1, 2.

Twenty-ninth Head

What is required to the conserving of our neighbors good name?
First, an internal disposition, care, and study of preserving it: which we shall show by these fruits. First, when we are glad of it, and rejoice in it; (Rom. 1. 8. Col. 13. 4.) and are grieved when as it is blacked and blemished.

What other fruits are there of it?
They respect either our hearing, judgment, or reports.

Our hearing; First, when as we shut our ears to whisperers and slanderers, for their detractions and slanders cannot hurt our neighbors good name, if we will not hear and believe them. Prov. 25. 23. And this is a note of a Citizen of heaven. Psal. 15. 3. Secondly, when as we willingly and cheerfully hear the praises of our neighbors: which is a sign of an honest heart, that is free from self love and envy.

What is required in the judgment?
A candid and ingenuous disposition to preserve our neighbors fame, and in all things doubtful to judge the best of his words and deeds.

What are the fruits thereof?
First, not to nourish hard conceits of him; but when they arise to suppress them, if the grounds of them be not very probable. Secondly, not to believe rashly any evil of our neighbor. Thirdly, to take and construe all things well done and spoken by him in the best sense. Fourthly, to interpret and take things doubtful in the better part.

What are the fruits respecting reports?
Silence and secrecy. For it is a Christian duty to keep secret our neighbors faults, which proceed from infirmity and human frailty: unless it be to amend him by admonition or seasonable reproof. Lev. 19. 17. Mat. 18. 15, 16. Gen. 37. 2. 1 Cor. 1. 11. or to give warning to the hearer, that he may prevent some evil that is intended against him. Jer. 40. 14. Acts 23. 16. or to preserve him that he be not infected with the contagion of his sin, with whom he converseth: or finally, when himself is necessitated to discover another's faults and crimes, lest by silence he become accessory unto them; as in case of Felony, Murder or Treason.

What are the vices opposite to these virtues?
To the care of preserving our neighbors name is opposed, First, carelessness, as if it did not concern us: which argueth defect of love. Secondly, a study and desire to contract from his fame, and to lessen his credit and estimation: which is a fruit of hatred and envy. Mat 12. 15.

What are the vices opposite to those virtues which respect the means?
They are referred either to hearing, the judgment or report.

What are those which respect hearing?
First, to have itching ears after such rumors as tend to our neighbors infamy and disgrace: forbidden, Exod. 23. 1. Prov. 17. 4. which was Saul's sin. 1 Sam. 24. 10. Secondly, to have our ears open to hear calumnies and reproaches, and shut to our neighbors praises: which is a fruit of envy and self-love.

What are the vices which respect the judgment?
They are vices opposite to candid ingenuity. As first, suspiciousness: when we suspect evil of our neighbor without just cause, and upon every slight occasion; (1 Tim. 6. 4.) which is a false testimony of the heart.

Secondly, to believe rashly rumors reported from others, tending to the disgrace of our Neighbors, which have no sure ground: which was Potiphar's fault, Gen. 39. 19. and David's. 2 Sam. 16. 3, 4.

Thirdly, hard and uncharitable censures: either in respect of their sayings and doings, sinisterly interpreting things well spoken or done, or taking things doubtful in the worst sense; or in respect of their persons, censuring and condemning them rashly, when as we have no just cause. 1 Sam. 1. 13. Acts 2. 13. Luke 7. 39. & 13. 1. Acts 28. 4.

What vice respecteth report?
First, when as men raise false reports against their neighbors. Secondly, when as they discover uncharitably their secret faults; especially arising from infirmity, and human frailty. Prov. 10. 18.

What is opposite to the external profession of truth, concerning our Neighbor, which ought to be charitable?
First, a malicious testimony, though true, which ariseth from malice and envy, and tendeth to a sinister and evil end. 1 Sam. 22. 9. Psal. 52. 3, 4. Secondly, a false testimony: which is either simply false, as that 1. Kin. 21. 13. Acts 6. 13. or true in the letter of the words, but false in the sense; as that against Christ. Mat. 26. 60, 61. John. 2. 19.

Into what sorts are testimonies spoken of in this Commandment to be distinguished?
They are either public, or private: and the public, either in the Courts of Justice or out of them.

Of which does this Commandment principally speak?
Of public and legal testimonies: which are to be regarded above others, because it is the judgment of God rather than man, Deut. 1. 17. 2 Chron. 19. 6. and therefore he that perverteth this judgment, maketh God himself, as much as in him is, guilty of his sin of injustice.

What are the kinds of legal testimonies?
They are either of the Judge, or of the Notary, or the Parties suing, contending and pleading, or of the Witness.

What is the testimony of the Judge?
It is the sentence which he giveth in the cause tried before him.

What is herein required of him?
First, that before he give sentence, he thoroughly examine and find out the truth and equity of the cause; Deut. 13. 14. & 17. 4. & 19. 18, according to God's own example. Gen. 3. 9, 10, & 18. 21. Secondly, that in passing sentence he judge according to truth, justice, and equity. For Judges must be men of truth, Exod. 18. 21. Secondly, just and righteous. Deut. 1. 16. & 16. 18, 19, 20. Lev. 19. 15. And thirdly, not just in a rigid and extreme way, according to the letter of the Law; but so as when there is just occasion he must moderate the rigor of the Law with equity; which is the true sense and life of the Law.

But is not the Judge to give sentence according to things legally alleged and proved?
Yes ordinarily. But if he undoubtedly, upon his own certain knowledge find that things are otherwise then they seem to be by Testimonies, pleadings and reasons alleged; he must judge according to known truth, and defend the cause, being just, which is oppressed by false evidences and reasons: or otherwise he shall sin against his own knowledge and conscience. Prov. 31. 8, 9.

What are the vices opposite hereunto?
They are two: Rash and Perverse judgment.

What is rash judgment?
It is done divers ways. First, when as the Judges pronounce sentence before the cause be sufficiently examined and known. Prov. 18. 13. Secondly, when as they condemn any man before they have heard his cause. Acts 25. 15, 16. Thirdly, when as they pronounce sentence, having heard one part only. So David. 2 Sam. 16. 4. Let such remember that of Solomon. Prov. 18. 17. Fourthly, when as they in matters concerning life and death give sentence upon the single testimony of one witness. Deut 17. 6.

What is perverse judgment?
When as truth is oppressed, and justice and right is perverted; whereby the wicked is acquitted, and the just condemned. Prov. 17 5. which for the most part happeneth, because the Judge is corrupted with bribes, or accepteth persons: both which are forbidden and condemned, Deut. 16. 19. Exod. 23. 8. Prov. 24. 23, 24. & 28. 21. Lev. 19. 15. Deut. 1. 16, 17.

What must Judges do to avoid this?
They must ever remember that in the Seat of Justice they represent God himself, and in that regard are called Gods. Exod. 28. 21. Psa. 28. 1, 2. and therefore they must Jade as God would if he were present, 2 Chron. 19. 6. which if they do not, they must expect that woe threatened. Isa. 5. 22, 23. Neither must they protract suits, but put as speedy an end unto them as the cause will permit. Exod. 18, 7, 23.

What is the duty of the Notary?
That he commit things truly to writing, conserve them truly, and truly recite them.

What are the persons suing and contending in Law?
They are either the principal, or less principal. The principal are the Plaintiff and Defendant: to both which these common duties do belong. 1. That they do not contend in Law, unless in their consciences they are persuaded that, their cause is good and just; yea and necessary also. 2. That in pursuing of it they do no say or do any thing that is false and unjust.

What are the vices opposite hereunto?
First, to commence suits out of a love and desire of contention. Secondly, to produce false instruments, writings, proofs, seals, and suborn false witnesses.

What are the special corruptions of the Plaintiff?
First; to calumniate upon a false or uncertain ground. Deut. 19. 16. So Haman. Esth. 3. 8. So Acts 25. 7. Secondly, when prevaricating and trifling in the cause, they conceal and let pass weighty matters and heinous crimes, and insist upon those which are light, feigned, and impertinent; so as they may seem to daily trifle with their adversary, rather than to contend in a legal manner. Thirdly, when as they fall off, and hang back from a just accusation once undertaken.

What are the special sins of the defendant?
To defend himself in a false way: which is done in a various manner. First, by false speaking; in denying the fault whereof he is accused, and standing guilty, as it is usual amongst us: where as we should give glory unto God by confessing our sin, (Jos. 7. 19. Job. 31. 33.) and not by denying the truth; to add sin unto Sins. Secondly, by concealing and hiding the truth, which he ought to confess. Thirdly, by answering indirectly; and so waving a just accusation. So Adam Gen. 3. 12.

How else does the Defendant?
First, by making an unjust appeal to protract the suit. Secondly, by resisting a just sentence: which is to resist God's ordinance in a lawful power instituted by him, and so to make himself liable to damnation Rom. 13. 2.

Who are the Persons that are less principal?
The Lawyers who plead the cause of the parties and principals.

What are their duties?
First, to undertake the defense of such causes only as in their judgment appear to be good and just. Secondly, to defend them in a true and just manner.

What are the corruptions opposite hereunto?
First, wittingly to undertake the defense of ill and unjust causes: Wherein they sin; first, against God, whilst they labor to overturn truth and judgment. Eccles. 5. 6, 33. Secondly, against our neighbor: as, First, against the Judge; in seeking to corrupt his Judgment, that he may pass an unjust sentence. Secondly, against his Clients; by encouraging him in a sinful course, if he prevail; or defrauding him of his money, if he do not. Thirdly, against his adversary; whom he woundeth, either in his body, goods, or fame. Pro. 25 18. Thirdly, against his own soul. First, in a sinful defense of an unjust cause. Exod. 23. 1. 2. 2 Chron. 19. 2. Rom. 1. 30. 32. Secondly, by setting his tongue to sale to speak lies for fees. (Pro. 21. 6.) and with their tongue their souls also.

What other vice do Lawyers commit by handling of their causes in an evil manner?
They handle them ill; First, by lying either for their Client or against their adversary: in both which they are guilty of a false testimony. Secondly, by prevarication, in betraying the cause of their Client, whilst they seem to defend it: and this is the worst kind of trickery and theft.

What is the testimony of the witness which this Commandment specially respecteth, and what is required unto it?
Two things. First, that he be ready and willing to give his testimony when need requireth. Secondly, that we do give a true testimony.

When does need require it?
Either when lawful authority calleth for it; or when thereby he can do his neighbor good. Prov. 24. 11. Psal. 82. 4. Prov. 14. 25.

What are the vices opposite hereunto?
First, to detract and withhold a true testimony. Secondly, to give a false testimony.

What do you think of this sin?
That it is odious, and abominable to God. Prov. 6. 16, 19. and therefore God made choice of this sin as most heinous, to comprehend under it all sins of the like kind; as in the other Commandments forbidding murder, adultery, theft. Secondly, because he addeth perjury to his false testimony. Thirdly, because he sinneth against the Judge, whom he laboreth to pervert; against the Plaintiff and the Defendant; (Prov. 25. 18.) and most of all against his own soul; as before, Prov. 19. 5. 9. & 21. 18. Deut. 19. 16, 19. Rev. 21. 8. & 22. 15.

You have spoken of public testimonies in Courts of Justice. Now what are these which are given out of the Courts?
They are either open and manifest, or else hid and secret.

What are those that are open and manifest?
They are either in the public Ministry of the word, or in public Writings, or in Elections.

How in the public Ministry?
He giveth therein a false testimony, who preacheth false doctrine, which is repugnant to God's glory, or hindreth mans salvation, which God hath appointed to be punished with death, Zech. 13. 3. And the same is to be said of those who in their public writings broach errors, or oppose the truth.

How in elections?
When those are not preferred that are worthy, but those that are unworthy: for in elections men testify their excellency that are chosen before others.

What are the false Testimonies that are hidden and in secret?
They are either infamous Libels, which by the Civil Law disable a man from giving any testimony; or the spreading of false rumors and scandalous reports, tending to the disgrace of our neighbors. Exod. 23. 1.

You have spoken of public testimonies: now what are private testimonies, or the private profession of the truth with charity?
It is either of the virtues or vices of our neighbors.

What is the duty which respects the virtues of our neighbors?
It is willingly to acknowledge, and ingenuously to commend, the virtues and good parts of our neighbors, both absent and present; to the glory of God that gave them, and the increase of virtue in him that hath received it. 1 Cor. 11. 2.

What is that duty which respecteth the vices of our neighbor?
It is freely to admonish and reprove him being present: (Mat. 18. 15. Lev. 19. 17. Prov. 27. 5, 6. Psal. 141. 5.) and in his absence to cover his faults, as far as will stand with justice and charity. 1 Pet. 4. 8.

What are the opposite vices?
They are two: Flattery, and Evil speaking.

What is Flattery?
It is fair and fawning speech, whereby a man is falsely and unworthily praised.

How does the Flatterer offend?
First, in respect of the object; when they commend another either for a thing doubtful and uncertain, whether it be good or evil; or for a known evil. Prov. 28. 4. & 24. 24, 25. Secondly, in respect of the manner: and that either in dissimulation, (Prov. 27. 14.) or above measure (Acts 12. 22.).Thirdly, in respect of the end: and that either for their own profit, as Parasites do; or for his hurt and ruin whom they flatter. Prov. 29. 5. Jer. 9. 8. Mat. 22 15, 16.

What is the second opposite vice?
It is evil speaking. And this is either against one present, by railing and reproachful words tending to his discredit and disgrace; (Mat. 5. 22. 1 Cor. 6, 10.) and by scoffing and mocking, which is a kind of persecution: (Gen. 21. 9. Gal. 4. 29.) or else against one absent, which is whispering, or slander, or detraction.

What evils are in the vice of whispering?
Whisperers defame their neighbors, by discovering their faults and failings; dissolve all friendship between man and man. (Prov. 16. 28.) and sow dissentions between them. Prov. 26. 20. Secondly, they spoil their neighbors of their good name, (which is better than riches. Prov. 22. 1. and more sweet than a precious ointment. (Eccl. 7. 1.) and also of their friends, by sowing discord among them. Prov. 6. 19.

What is Obtrectation?
The blacking and branding of our neighbors good name by secret and malicious words: and that either by detracting from his virtues, or by malicious discovering of his vices.

What do you think of this vice?
That it is a grievous sin: for it deeply woundeth our Neighbor in his life, goods and fame. In which regard it is compared to Bows and Arrows that shoot in secret, Jer. 9. 3, 8. Psal. 64. 3, 4. to coals of Juniper, Psal. 120. 4. to a Sword, Psal. 64. 3. Prov. 12. 18. to a Razor, Psal. 52. 2. to the tongue of a Serpent, Psal. 140. 3. Eccl. 10. 11.

How should we keep ourselves from it, being naturally addicted to it?
By considering that the Scriptures forbid it, Lev. 19. 16. James 4. 11. and condemn it as an heinous sin, Psal. 50. 20. Ezek. 22. 9. Rom. 1. 30. Secondly, because it is a sign of an hypocrite; who will declaim against the sins of others, that himself may be thought religious. Jam. 1. 26. Thirdly, because above other sins it maketh them like unto the devil; who hath his name from slandering, being a slanderer from the beginning. 2 Tim. 3. 3. Tit. 2. 3. Lastly, because God's heavy judgments and punishments are denounced against it. Psal. 50. 20, 21. Ezek. 22. 9, Psal. 15. 3. & 52. 4.

But is it not lawful to speak truly of our neighbors faults?
There are few detracters and back-biters do so; but either devise calumnies of things that are not, or add something that is untrue of their own. But though a man speak truth, yet if it be maliciously to do hurt, or out of a vain custom to keep their tongue in practice; he is a slanderer, and offendeth, if not against truth, yet against charity.

What is the chief cause of detraction?
To be curious in prying into other men's lives and manners, and negligent in looking into our own and judging ourselves.

You have spoken concerning our Neighbors fame: now what is required to the conserving of our own?
Two things. First, that every one have a care of preserving his own good name. Secondly, that every one give a true testimony of himself.

What is to be considered in the former?
Three things. First, what this good fame is. Secondly, how highly to be esteemed, that hereby we may be moved to this care of preserving it. Thirdly, by what means it may be attained unto and kept.

What is good Fame?
It is a good opinion and esteem which men conceive of others for their virtues and deeds well done. And this is highly to be valued, Prov. 22. 1. Eccl. 7. 1. as being not only profitable to ourselves, but also unto others, who are refreshed with the smell of this fragrant ointment, and studiously to be sought after. Phil. 4. 8.

Wherein does the care of conserving our good name consist?
First, in prosecuting and using the means of getting it. Secondly, in avoiding the means of both vain-glory, and also infamy.

What are the means of getting and conserving our fame and good name?
First, and above all things to seek God's glory, his kingdom, and righteousness; and to glorify him by our serious study, to walk before him in holiness of life, and the exercise of all good works. Mat 6. 33. & 5. 16. Psal. 112. 6. 1 Sam. 2. 30. Prov. 10. 7.

Secondly, we must avoid the means of vain-glory, whereby men seek more the praise of men than of God. John 5. 44. & 12. 43.

Thirdly, to prefer the testimony of a good conscience before the applause of men. 2 Cor. 1. 12.

Fourthly, to look more to the inward than the outward man, and take more care to be good than to seem good, and to approve our hearts unto God than our outward actions unto men Rom. 2. 29.

Fifthly, to avoid hypocrisy and dissimulation: which though for a time it may gain the praise of men, yet at length God will pull off this false mask, and expose the hypocrite to shame and contempt.

Sixthly. Go shun that glory which men seek to gain by vanity and vice: (2 Sam. 18. 18.) which were to glory in our shame.

Seventhly, to abhor flatterers, and parasites; and to love those who faithfully admonish us when we err, and reprove us when we offend. 1 Kings 22. 18.

Eighthly, to be severe in judging ourselves, and charitable in censuring others. Mat. 7. 1, 2. For if we think well of others, they likewise will think well of us.

Lastly, not to undertake great matters above our strength, to gain an opinion of our great parts and abilities; but to be lowly in our own eyes. Psal. 131. 1. Luke 14. 28, 29.

But may we not at all in our good actions seek the praise of men?
We may not principally, and in the first place aim at this end in performing our duties; but rather God's glory, and the adorning of the Gospel which we profess; yet if God cast upon us this blessing of a good name and praise of well-doing, as a vantage unto the bargain, it is not to be neglected; seeing contempt of others opinion of us, especially those that are good, argueth both arrogance and desperate dissoluteness. We must seek God's glory by good report and evil report (2 Cor. 6. 8.) but if he be pleased to bless us with unaffected fame, let us thankfully accept it, and use it as an encouragement in well-doing. Phil. 4. 8. Rom. 13. 3. 1 Pet. 2. 14.

What are the means of infamy from ourselves?
All manner of sin. For as sin is the cause of shame, so shame the punishment of sin. Therefore all sin is to be avoided of him that would preserve his fame. As first, open sins: (Eccles. 10. 1.) yea not only the sin it self, but all appearance of it. 1 Thes. 5. 22. Rom. 14. 16. Secondly, secret sins: which if they be not repented of, God will discover them to our shame, (2 Sam. 12. 12.) if not in this life, yet at Christ's coming before men and Angels. Luke 12. 2. Mat. 25. 31. Luk. 8. 17. 1 John: 2. 28.

What are the means of infamy from others?
Either the opprobrious obloquies of Railers, or the rumors and whisperings of Backbiters and Sycophants, against which we are bound to preserve our fame by speaking, writing, and (it need be) by the authority of the Magistrate: especially if we be public persons, whose infamy may prejudice the Church and Common-wealth.

You have spoken of conserving our fame: what say you to the second thing propounded, that is, a true testimony of ourselves?
Every one is bound by this Commandment to give a true testimony of himself, as occasion is offered. For as we must speak nothing but truth to our neighbors, so also of ourselves.

How is this done?
Either by modest acknowledging that which is good in us, or ingenuous confessing that which is evil; or by denying a false good attributed unto us modestly and humbly, or a false evil wisely and warily.

What is opposite hereunto?
When as we give a false testimony of ourselves, by denying any truth; to affirm any thing false concerning ourselves, whether it be good or evil.

May we then acknowledge that which is good in ourselves without vanity?
Yes if we do it with modesty, and chiefly to God's glory, from whom we have received all that is good in us. 1 Cor. 15. 10.

What is opposite to the profession of truth concerning ourselves?
First an ironical speech, whereby true good in ourselves is denied. Secondly, boasting or bragging; whereby it is falsely arrogated.

How is the former vice committed?
Either out of simplicity, when in an humble conceit of themselves men speak as they think, though it he not true; and therefore do not properly lie, because their words agree with their mind, who are not wholly to be justified, because they speak that which is not true: yet their falsity is no more to be condemned then their humility to be commended. And such was the excuse of Moses, Exod. 3. 11. & 4. 10, 13 and of Jeremy, Jer. 1. 6. Or secondly, they speak worse of themselves then they are in their own opinion: and that either out of modesty, to avoid bragging; (which though it cannot be wholly excused from being sinful, because it is ingratitude to God to deny his gifts, and so derogatory to his glory and bounty, and not free from lying; yet it is extenuated by modesty and humility:) or else it proceedeth from a dissembling and counterfeit modesty and pride of heart, when men deny the good that is attributed unto them in a slight manner, to draw on double praise; and so men offend both in opposing truth by lying, and humility also by seeking praise in a cunning way.

What is the other opposite?
Boasting and arrogance. For as we must truly profess the good that is in us or done by us, to God's glory, when need requireth, in a modest manner; so must we carefully shun all vain bragging, in arrogating unto ourselves that good which belongeth not to us, or extolling it above due measure: seeing it cannot stand with modesty, (Prov. 27. 2.) and is opposite to God's glory from which we so much detract as we arrogate to ourselves. 1 Cor. 4. 7. Joh. 5. 13.

In what respect does the arrogant boaster offend?
Three ways. First, in respect of the object. Secondly, the manner. Thirdly, the end.

How in respect of the object?
When that he boasteth of that which is not truly good, but evil: which argueth desperate wickedness; as in Doeg, Psal. 52. 1 Phil. 3. 19. Gen. 4. 23. 24. And such are those who glory in their drinking and whoring.

How in respect of the manner?
When this boasting is contrary to truth or charity, To truth; either in respect of the thing it self, or of opinion.

How in respect of the thing it self?
When he boasts to himself the good he hath not, or in a greater measure then it is So. Mat. 26. 33, 35.

How in respect of opinion?
Either his own when he boasts that to himself which in his own opinion belongeth not to him: or the opinion of others, when his boasting exceedeth that merit and worth, which men truly conceive is not his due, or above that measure that he deserveth.

How does he sin against charity?
Both in respect of God and his Neighbor. In respect of God: either openly and professedly, as when he arrogates to himself that which is due only to him; (Ezek. 28. 2. Exod. 5. 2. Isa. 36. 20. Dan. 3. 15,) or else more covertly and cunningly, when he spoils God of his glory, by attributing the praise of the good things he hath given him unto himself. Isa. 10. 15. Secondly, in respect of his neighbor, when as his own praises tend to the disgrace of others. Luke. 18 10, 11.

How do men sin in respect of the end?
When as they boast and brag; either for their glory, which usually is accompanied with shame; (Rom. 1. 22. Prov. 26. 12.) or for their gain, as when they glory in their skill to draw on profit; which is the practice of Empericks and Mountebanks. Acts 8. 9.

What is the confession of truth concerning the evil that is in us, or done by us?
It is either before God, or man. Before God we must confess our sins; if we expect to have them pardoned. Pro. 28. 13. 1 Joh. 1. 9. Psal. 32. 5.

How are they to be confessed before men?
So far forth as the glory of God requireth it, (Josh. 7. 19. John 1. 20.) or the good and salvation of our neighbors, or our own profit and necessity, (Jam. 5. 15, 16.) otherwise it is not necessary that we should lay them open to our own shame. But however we may conceal that which is evil in us, yet when it is questioned we must not deny that which is true, nor confess that which is false in us. For by denying the truth, we lie, and add sin unto sin (Gen. 18. 15.) and by confessing that evil falsely which is not in us we also lie and expose ourselves to disgrace and dangers; (2 Sam. 1. 10. compared with 1 Sam. 31. 4. 5.

[30TH HEAD.]

What is the tenth Commandment?
Thou shalt not covet thy neighbors house, thou shalt not covet thy neighbors Life, &c. Exodus 20. 17.

What is the sin chiefly here forbidden?
Concupiscence, that is, those secret and internal sins, which go before consent of will, and are the seeds of all other vices: of which sort are wicked and corrupt inclinations thoughts, desires, which are repugnant to charity.

What is the end of this Commandment?
It respecteth either God, our Neighbors, or ourselves.

What is the end which respecteth God?
That he might show the perfection of that Charity which in His Law He requireth of us, and the excellency of it above all other human laws. For human and divine laws differ, as the Law-givers themselves. And as God is a Spirit, who is omniscient and searcheth the heart, so He requireth spiritual obedience, Rom. 7 14. and bindeth by his Law, (which is spiritual, like Himself) not only the hand, tongue, and out-ward man, as men do by human laws; but even the most inward, hidden, and secret thoughts and desires of the mind and heart.

What is the end respecting our Neighbors?
That we might not think or desire any thing tending to their hurt; but that with all the powers of our souls, we exercise charity in doing them good, not seeking our own good only but theirs also. 1 Cor. 13. 5.

What is the end of this Commandment respecting ourselves?
That it might discover unto us our corruption, and how far we are from that perfection which Gods law requireth. Rom. 7. 7, 13, 24. Prov. 20. 9. Psal. 19. 11, 12. and secondly, that it might be unto us a perfect rule of spiritual obedience; and might teach us chiefly to observe our hearts, (Prov. 4. 23.) to suppress the first and inward motions of sin, and to aspire to that original purity, that we had by creation.

What was the occasion of this Commandment?
Three-fold: first, the depravity of our hearts and thoughts: Gen. 6. 5. and 8. 21. Secondly, the blindness and stupidity of our minds and hearts; which could neither see nor feel their own depravity and corruption. Rom. 7. 7, 8. Thirdly, the error of our judgments; which suppose that our thoughts be free, and that concupiscence and first thoughts are not sins till they have our consent, because they are not in our power to restrain them.

What is the difference between the spiritual obedience required in this and the other Commandments?
In that it not only requireth the internal obedience of the heart, with the outward man, as the rest do; but also restraineth the first motions and inclinations, which go before consent. If we had not rather say, that it is added to the other, as a full and more clear explication of that spiritual obedience which is required in all the rest.

Now show the meaning of this Commandment: and first, what is that concupiscence which it here spoken of?
There are two sorts of concupiscence, or of the affections of the heart: the first called Irascible, conceived against things evil which we shun, as anger, hatred, fear, grief. &c. the other called Concupiscible, conceived towards things good and desirable, as love, joy, delight, &c. And these are things either truly evil or good, or else so only in appearance.

Is all concupiscence here forbidden?
No: for there is some good and lawful, some evil and unlawful; the one commanded, the other forbidden.

Thirtieth Head

What is lawful concupiscence?
It is either natural, or spiritual. Natural, that which desireth things good and necessary to our being or well-being; as food, clothing, and other lawful comforts of this life. Spiritual, which lusteth and fighteth against the flesh, (Gal. 5. 17.) and affecteth and coveteth after spiritual things Psal. 119. 40.

What is opposite hereunto?
Unlawful and evil concupiscence, (Col. 3. 5.) which is also called concupiscence of men, (1. Pet. 4. 2.) concupiscence of the flesh, (Gal. 5. 16, 17.) worldly concupiscence, (1 Tit. 2. 12.) lusts of the Devil. (Joh. 8. 44)

What are the kinds of this concupiscence?
Either habitual, or actual. Habitual, is an evil inclination and proneness to that which is evil; or an evil desiring of it, which is a part of original injustice. Rom. 8. 6, 7.

What is that evil concupiscence which is actual?
It is distinguished into two kinds. First, in respect of the form. Secondly, in respect of the object.

What is that which respecteth the form?
It is either inchoate and imperfect, which is an act of sensuality only, and the first and sudden motions of concupiscence; which go before the act of reason and the will, tickling the mind and heart with a kind of delight: or it is formed and perfected, having also the act of the will joining with it, and consenting to it. 1 Thes. 4. 5.

What are the degrees of that inchoate concupiscence?
They are three. First, an evil motion cast into our minds, by either the Devil, the World, or our own Flesh, corrupting the sense, memory, or fantasy; whereby we have an hanging and hankering appetite after that which is our neighbors, as thinking it fit and convenient for us. Secondly, a longing after it, and wishing for it, following that motion. Thirdly, a tickling delight, arising from a conceit of the pleasure or profit which we should have in the enjoying of it. Jam. 1. 13, 14, 15.

How then does sin grow from its first conception to its full growth?
Saint James in respect of the degrees of it compareth it to the conception growth and birth of an Infant, in and from the womb. James 1. 14, 15.

The first is, the abstraction of the mind and heart from good to evil, by the evil motion and appetite: which may be called the carnal copulation between the heart and sin and Satan. The second, infection and enticing of the heart with delight and consent unto it; as it were the retention of the seed. The third, consent to the acting of it; which may be called the conception of it. The fourth, deliberation after this consent, by what means and how it may be acted; which is the articulation and shaping of the parts and members. The fifth is the acting of sin it self, that is the birth of it; which being born causeth death. Which degrees and growth of sin may be observed in the example of Eve, Ahab, and David himself.

How many evil concupiscence be distinguished in respect of the Object?
Into three kinds. First, Of pleasure; which is the lust of the Flesh. Secondly, of profit; which is the lust of the eyes. Thirdly, of honor and glory; which is the pride of life. 1 John 2. 16

What are the parts of this Commandment?
Two. First, the Affirmative: Secondly, the Negative. The first is here to be understood; the other is plainly expressed.

What is forbidden in the Negative?
Evil concupiscence: which is twofold, either original or actual.

What is original concupiscence?
Original sin: which is the corruption and disorder of all the powers and faculties of soul and body, disposing them to all that is evil. It is also called habitual concupiscence: which is nothing else but an evil inclination and proneness to the transgression of Gods Law, which by corrupt nature is bred with us.

How is it called in the Scriptures?
The old man, (Eph. 4. 22. Col. 3. 9.) Sin inhabiting and dwelling in us, the Law of sin, the Law of the members warring against the Law of the mind, the flesh, the encompassing of sin, &c. Rom. 7. 23. Gal. 5. 17, 24. Heb. 12. 1.

Is this to be reputed sin?
Yes; and a great sin: as may appear by these reasons. First, because it defileth and corrupteth the whole man, soul and body, with all their faculties, powers, and parts: as the mind, will, memory, heart, affections, appetite; with all the members of the body, which it maketh to be the instruments of evil. Second, it polluteth all our words and works, and maketh them all repugnant to the law of God. Third, it is the root and fountain of all our actual sins; from which they grow and spring. Fourth, because it continually warreth against the Spirit, and choketh and quencheth the good motions of it Gal. 5. 17. 1 Pet. 2. 11. Fifth, because it maketh a man the slave of sin and Satan. Rom. 7. 14, 23 Sixth, because it joineth with the Devil and the World, and betrayeth us to their temptations. Eph. 2. 2, 3. Seventh, because it is an incurable evil; seeing it so hangeth upon us that we cannot shake it off. Heb. 12. 21. Eighth, because it is but the more irritated by the Law of God, which should suppress it Rom. 7. 8. Lastly, because it maketh us children of wrath, and liable to everlasting condemnation; although dying in child-hood, we should never commit any actual transgression. For death and damnation reigneth even over them which had not sinned after the similitude of Adam, that is by actual transgression. Rom. 5. 14.

But does this Commandment extend to the prohibition of Original sin in the whole body, and all the parts of it?
No, For it forbiddeth sins committed against our Neighbors only, like all other Commandments of the second Table, as appeareth by the words themselves, and the Apostles epitomizing of this whole Table, in those words; Thou shalt love thy neighbor as thy self, Rom. 13. 9. And therefore, all original injustice, wicked inclination, thoughts, and affections are here only forbidden; as they respect our neighbors, and are opposite to charity: but as they respect God, and are repugnant to the love of him, they are forbidden in the first Table.

What are actual concupiscences?
They are evil motions which are repugnant to charity.

What are the kinds of them?
They are either such as are vain and unprofitable, or such as are hurtful and pernicious.

How are they unprofitable?
So far forth as they fasten men's minds to earthly things, and thereby withdraw them from heavenly.

In what respect are they hurtful?
First, because they are instruments of sin: as they are fit objects to every sin in its kind. For if any objects are offered to the mind or senses; which self-love causeth them to think to be profitable, pleasant and desirable; concupiscence presently apprehendeth and catcheth at them to satisfy worldly lusts. Secondly, they choke the seed of the Word in the hearts of Carnal men. Mark. 4. 19. Thirdly, they make men insatiable; knowing no end or measure in pursuing worldly things. Fourthly, they cast men headlong, in whom they reign, into sin. (Eph. 2. 3.) and give them up to vile lusts, and reprobate minds. Rom. 1. 24. (Psal. 81. 12.). Fifthly, they fight against the Soul; and if they overcome, bring it to destruction. 1 Pet. 2. 11.

How many ways are these motions evil?
Two ways either in respect of the fantasy and cogitations of the mind or in respect of the affections and imaginations of the heart,

When are the thoughts evil?
Then and so far forth, as they solicit and incline us unto evil.

Why do men think that thoughts are free, and not to be charged upon men. or called to account?
Foolish men think and say so: but the Scriptures say otherwise, and affirm them to be sins. Prov. 24. 9. as being repugnant to charity, 1 Cor. 13. 5. and therefore forbid them. Deut. 15. 9. enjoin us to confess them, and to crave pardon for them. Isa. 55. 7. Acts 8. 22. And though we slight them, yet God taketh notice of them; (Psa. 94. 11. 1 Chro. 28, 9. Ezek. 11. 5. Psal. 139. 2.) yea, he hateth evil thoughts, as abominable, (Prov. 15. 26. Zech. 8. 17.) and severely punisheth them, as we see in the example of the old world. Gen. 6. 5. & 8: 21.

Whence do those evil thoughts arise?
They are either injected by Satan; or else arise from original concupiscence: and both of them befall men either walking or sleeping.

How are they injected by Satan?
Either immediately by himself, (1 Chron. 21. 1. John 13. 2.) or mediately by his instruments, as of old by the serpent. And that he may the more easily insinuate into his mind whom he tempteth he often induces those that are nearest and dearest unto us to be his Instruments: as we see in the example of Job's wife, and Peter. Joh. 2. 9. Mat. 16. 22, 23.

But are these temptations to be reputed our sins?
Not if we reel and extinguish them, as fire in water: for Christ himself was tempted, yet without sin. (Heb. 4. 15.) But if we admit them, and do not presently reject them, they infect our minds and hearts with their poison, and become our sins.

How else do evil thoughts arise in us?
From our natural corruption, and habitual concupiscence. Luk. 34. 38. Gen. 5. Mat. 15. 19. 2 Cor. 3. 5.

How are these motions evil, in respect of the affections of the heart?
These though they have not the consent of the will to act them, yet are they sinful in respect of the sins which arise from them; of which also they are the first degrees: as we see in the first boiling of anger in the heart and of lust and unclean motions; which proceed from the defect of that charity and purity which God requireth in us and afterwards produce the acts of murder and fornication, when the will consenteth unto them. Mat. 5. 22, 28.

Are there no degrees of those evil affections and perturbations of the heart?
Yes: for they are to be considered either in their first beginnings, as they are the first motions of concupiscence, by which the mind is first withdrawn from its rectitude, and then the heart suddenly affected; or else, when by the pleasure and delight in those first motions, they are tickled and enticed to retain them still, that they may enjoy a greater and more full measure of delight.

What followeth this pleasure thus retained and continued in the mind and heart?
Consent to the acting of the sin, which in God's light is all one with the sin it self: seeing he regards the will for the deed, whether it be in good or evil. 2 Cor. 8. 12. Mat. 5. 28.

Why then it seemeth that it were as good for a man to act sin, as to consent to the acting of it?
Not so: For though they be both sins, the one as well as the other, yet not equal, and in the same degree: but as the one is more heinous then the other, and more defileth the conscience, so maketh it a man liable to a deeper degree of hellish condemnation.

You have spoken of the degrees of evil affections: now show what are the kinds?
They are either concupiscible, about things affected and desired, or irascible, about things which they abhor and shun; as sudden and rash anger, and the first motions of envy, &c.

How are the concupiscible distinguished?
By the Objects. For it is either the lust of the eyes, the lust of the flesh, or the pride of life, 1 John 2. 16. all which are forbidden in the first Commandment, as they are repugnant to the love of God, and in this Commandment, as they are opposite to the love of our neighbors; and so far forth as they are more secret and covert, and the first motions of concupiscence, and the first principles and degrees of the sins against our neighbors forbidden in the other Commandments.

You have showed what concupiscence is in the generals: now show what is that special kind of it which is here expressly forbidden?
The concupiscence of the eyes: which is varied and diversified by the removing of divers objects.

But why is this rather forbidden, than any other kind?
Because it is the worst of all and most pernicious, and therefore fittest to comprehend under it all the rest: as it is done in the other Commandments.

Why is it the most pernicious?
First, because it is the root of all the vices forbidden in the other Commandments, either in begetting or nourishing them. Secondly, because it extinguisheth charity towards God, by turning the heart from him after earthly things: (Eph. 5. 5. Col. 3. 5.) and towards our neighbors by disposing men's hearts to cruelty, lust, and covetousness; and making them averse to charity, mercy and Christian beneficence. Thirdly, because it is insatiable. Eccl. 4. 8. Fourthly, because it is unquiet and restless; vexing the covetous mind and heart as it were hellish furies. 1 Tim. 6. 10. 1 Kg 21. 4. Fifthly, because it is joined with self love and envy. Lastly, because it betrayeth men unto Satan's temptations, to their destruction. 1 Tim. 6. 9.

But is all concupiscence here forbidden as unlawful?
No: but that only which is repugnant to charity towards God and our neighbors; that which is inordinate, and that which by unlawful means seeketh to be satisfied and tendeth to an evil end, James 4. 3. Finally, that which is either immoderate, having no bounds; or else unjust, coveting that which is another mans, against their will and profit.

What are the objects which are here removed?
They are infinite and innumerable: but for examples sake, he insisteth upon some which men more usually and ardently covet after.

What meaneth he by the house of our neighbor?
Both his place of habitation, and his Family. (Gen. 17. 72.) for a house is necessary to him that hath a family. Which convinceth them of a great sin, that for every slight cause thrust their Tenants out of their houses. Isa 5. 8.

What are the parts of the Family here numbered?
The wife, servant, maid, &c. The wife of another must not be coveted: for such is the union in marriage between man and wife, that it is unlawful to covet another mans wife; not only to commit adultery with her, but to enjoy her for his own, though by lawful means, and after the others death.

What are the other parts of the Family?
Servants, men and maidens: whom we are here forbidden to covet, or to use any means to entice them from their masters to come to us. For though this were a greater sin amongst the Jews, because they had propriety in them, their servants being part of their goods: yet it is a sin also amongst us, as being against charity and the common rule of Justice, which enjoineth us to let every one have his own, and to do to another as we would have him do unto us.

What other things does this Commandment forbid to covet?
Our neighbors Ox, or Ass: which are here named, to comprehend all other goods, immoveable or moveable; because they are of most necessary use for mans life. And lest we should think it lawful to covet any other thing not here named, he includeth all in the last words; Nor any thing that is thy neighbors: whether it be for necessity, profit, or delight.

What do you further gather from hence?
First, that those things are our neighbors which God hath given him. Secondly; that by this gift of God every man hath a propriety and distinct right in that he possesseth by virtue of this tenure. Thirdly, that he ought to be contented with that portion which God hath given him, and not to covet another mans: and consequently, that the doctrine and practice of the Familists is erroneous and wicked.

You have spoken hitherto of the Negative part: now show what is the Affirmative?
Here is commanded a pure, charitable, and just heart towards our neighbors; (1 Tim. 1. 5.) unto which, though none can attain in a legal perfection, yet ought all to desire and aspire unto it.

Wherein does this purity consist?
In two things; First, in original justice, and internal perfect charity, in which we were created. Secondly, in spiritual concupiscence.

What is original Justice?
Not only an exact purity from all sports of unrighteousness, but also a disposition to perform cheerfully all Offices of Charity and Justice.

What is spiritual Concupiscence?
It contains two things; First, good motions of the Spirit. Secondly, a fight of the Spirit against the lust of the Flesh.

What are those good motions of the Spirit?
Charitable and just motions, thoughts, desires, and affections; that all which we think or desire may be for our neighbors good. And this we must do frequently and constantly.

What is the fight against fleshly lusts?
When as being regenerate, and assisted by Gods Spirit, we make war against the flesh, and the lusts thereof; and in all we may, labor to mortify, crucify, and subdue them, because they make war against our souls and spiritual part. Gal. 5. 17. 1 Pet. 2. 11. Rom. 7. 23.

What are the means moving and enabling us to perform the duties required in this Commandment?
They are either general and common; or else more special and proper.

What are the general means?
Such as tend to the conserving of the heart in purity, that it may shun all sinful concupiscence. As first, to walk with God, and so to demean ourselves at all times, and in all things, as being always in his presence, who searcheth the heart and reins. Secondly, to observe and set a watch over our hearts. Prov. 4 23. And first, that it do not admit any evil concupiscence. Secondly; that if it be admitted, it be not retained. And this care must be taken both when we be awake, that we keep our minds intent unto lawful and good things; and when we go to sleep, that by hearty prayer we commend them to Gods keeping.

But what if the heart have admitted evil concupiscences?
We must strive and fight against them, and never be at rest, until we have cast them out and extinguished them.

What further is required to the conserving of the heart in purity?
In the third place we must observe our senses, that they do not bring into our minds such objects as being apprehended, will stir up in us evil concupiscence. Gen. 3. 6. & 6. 2. Josh. 7. 21. 2 Sam. 11. 2. Mat. 5. 28. Joh. 31. 1. Psal. 119. 37.

What are the special means to suppress or take away the concupiscence of the eyes?
First, we must mortify self-love, and not seek our own, but every man another's wealth. 1 Cor. 10. 24. Secondly, we must pull out the eyes of envy. Thirdly, we must labor after contentment. Phil 4. 11. And to this end consider: First, how many want those good things, which thou enjoyest, who are far more worthy of them. Secondly, thine own unworthiness of the least of Gods benefits. Thirdly, meditate on Gods providence and fatherly care, who provideth all things necessary for thy good and salvation.

What do you learn from this Commandment thus expounded?
That it is most impossible for any man to keep it. For who can say, that his heart is clean from the first motions of sin, and concupiscence, that go before consent? Prov. 20. 9.

To What purpose serveth the knowledge of this impossibility?
To humble us in the light and sense of our sins, which have made us subject to the wrath of God, and the curse of the Law: that so despairing in our own merits, we may be driven out of ourselves, and with more ardent desire flee unto the mercies of God in the satisfaction and obedience of Jesus Christ.

What other use are we to make of it?
That being by Christ freed from the curse of the Law, we study and endeavour to conform ourselves, or souls, and lives according to the prescript rule of this holy and

most perfect law: (Mat. 5. 48.) and that mortifying the flesh, with all the carnal concupiscences and lusts of it, we be daily more and more renewed unto the Image of God in all holiness and righteousness, and walk worthy of our high calling, as it becometh Saints. Eph. 4. 1.

[31ST HEAD.]

Hitherto we have treated of the rule and square of our Sanctification, viz. The Ten Commandments. Now wherein is the effect or exercise of Sanctification seen?
In unfeigned repentance, and new obedience springing from thence. For the fruits of Sanctification, are; First, inward virtues, whereby all the powers of the mind are rightly ordered. Secondly, the exercise of the same, by putting those heavenly and sanctified abilities to holy use and service.

If then the exercise of Sanctification be first seen in repentance: what is Repentance?
An inward and true sorrow for sin, especially that we have offended so gracious a God, and so loving a Father; together with a settled purpose of heart, and a careful endeavour to leave all our sins, and to live a Christian life, according to all Gods Commandments. (Psal. 119. 57. 112.) Or, A turning of ourselves to God, whereby we crucify and kill the corruptions of our nature, and reform ourselves in the inward man, according to Gods will.

What is it to crucify the corruption of our nature?
It is truly and with all our hearts to be sorry that we have angered God with it and with our other sins, and every day more and more to hate it and them, and to fly from them.

How is this wrought in us?
It is wrought in us, partly by the threatening of the Law, and the fear of Gods judgments; but especially increased by feeling the fruit of Christ his death, whereby we have power, to hate sin and to leave it. For when the sinner once humbled with the terrors of the Law, flieth to the comforts of the Gospel; he there sees in Christ crucified, not only the mercy of God discharging him of all his sins; but also how deep the wounds of sin are, wherewith he hath pierced his Savior, (Zech. 12. 10.) and how severe the wrath of God is against sin, even to the slaughtering of his own Son; and hence (1 Pet. 4 1.) cometh he to hate his sins, (Psal. 97. 10.) as God hateth them, and to look back thereon with godly sorrow; (2 Cor. 7. 10.) resolving for ever after to forsake them all.

How is the reformation of ourselves to newness of life wrought in us?
Only by the promise of the Gospel, whereby we feel the fruit of the rising again of Christ.

What does ensue hereof?
Hereby we are raised up into a new life, having the Law written in our hearts, and so reform ourselves.

Wherein then does Repentance properly consist?
In a through changing of our purpose and desires from the evil which Gods Word rebuketh in us, to the good which it requireth of us, Rom. 12. 1. Psal. 1. 1, 2.

What is required in respect of the evil we turn from?
First, a knowledge of the evil, then a condemning of the same, together with a judging of ourselves for it: and then with godly sorrow for that which is past, a hatred of it for ever, and all this because it is sin, and displeaseth our God.

What is required in regard of the good we turn unto?
First, a knowledge and approbation of good to be done, with a purpose of heart to do it: then, an earnest love of the same, showed by care, desire and endeavour.

Can men repent of themselves, or when they list?
No: for it is the gift of God, given unto them that are born again.

Is it sufficient once to have repented?
No: we must continue it always in disposition, and renew it also in act, as occasion is given by our transgressions, and Gods displeasure: for there is none of Gods Saints but always carrying this corruption about them, they sometimes fall and are far from that perfection and goodness which the Lord requireth: and therefore stand in need of Repentance as long as they live.

When then is this repentance to be practiced of us?
The practice of Repentance ought to be a continual abhorring of evil, and cleaving unto that which is good, (Rom. 12. 9.) for as much time as we remain in the flesh after our conversion: (1 Pet. 4. 2, 3.) yet at times there ought to be a more special practice and renewing thereof; as after grievous falls, (Psal. 51.) in fear of imminent judgments, (Amos, 4. 12.) or when we would fit ourselves to receive special mercies. (Gen. 35. 2, 3, &c.)

In what manner must the special practice of Repentance, in such cases, be performed?
There must be:

1. A serious search and inquiry after all sins, (Lam. 3. 60.) as Traitors against God; but especially special sins, (Jer. 8. 6. Psal. 18. 23.) as the Arch-rebels.

2. Humble confession of sins: and that,

> 1. Of necessity unto God, with shame of face, and true sorrow of heart. Prov. 28. 13. Jer. 31. 18, 19.
>
> 2. Unto men conditionally: viz. if either
>
>> 1. The Church; for satisfaction of the public offence, do enjoin open acknowledgment. 2 Cor. 26.
>>
>> 2. Some personal wrongs demand private reconciliation. Luke 17. 4.
>>
>> 3. The weakness of the laboring conscience do require the secret assistance of a faithful, and able Minister or Brother. James 5. 16.

3. Fervent and faithful prayer (Psal. 51. 1, 2. &c.) to God in Christ, both for pardon of what is past (verse. 7.) and for supply of renewing grace for the time to come. (ver. 10.)

4. Promise of amendment; and satisfaction to such as we have endamaged.

Seeing many do falsely pretend that they repent; how may we know that our repentance is true?
1. From the generality of it viz. if it extend to the abhoring and shunning of all sins (Psal. 119. 128. & 139. 24.) and to the love and practice of all duties without reservation. Psal. 119. 6.

2. From the thorough performance of each part: viz.
    1. Of hatred of sin: in spiritual warfare against it; and that even unto blood if need be, Heb 12. 4.

    2. Of the love of righteousness: in bringing forth fruit worthy amendment of life, (Mat. 3. 8.) to wit, good works.

[32ND HEAD.]

What is the spiritual warfare?
The daily exercise of our spiritual strength, and amour, against all adversaries, with assured confidence of victory. For the state of the faithful in this life is such, that they are sure in Christ, and yet fight against sin: there being joined with repentance a continual fighting and struggling against the assaults of a mans own flesh, against the motions of the Devil, and enticements of the world.

How shall we overcome these enemies?
By a lively faith in Christ Jesus.

What is then our principal strength?
The powerful assistance of God in Christ, 2 Cor. 12. 9. Phil. 4. 13. who hath loved us: whereby we become more than Conquerors. Rom. 8. 37.

What is our spiritual Amour?
The complete furniture of saving and sanctifying graces; called therefore the Amour of righteousness, (2 Cor. 6. 7.) and the Panoply or the whole Amour of God. Eph. 6. 11, 14.

1. The girdle of verity or sincerity. 2. The breast-plate of righteousness, that is, holiness of life and a good Conscience. 3. The shoes of the preparation (or resolution to go through with the profession) of the Gospel of peace. 4. The Shield of faith. 5. The helmet of the hope of Salvation. 6. The Sword of the Spirit, which is the (sound knowledge and wise application of the) Word of God. 7. Finally, continual, and instant prayer in the Spirit.

Who are our adversaries in the spiritual conflict?
They are either our friends proving us, or our enemies seducing and endangering us.

Who is that friend of ours, that for our probation entereth into conflict with us?
God himself: who though he tempt no man unto evil, (no more then he can himself be tempted; Jam. 1. 13.) yet as a Master of defense inureth us to the conflict by contending with us, even in his own person; viz. sometimes by probatory commandments, (Gen. 22. 1.) or sensible apparations: (Gen. 32. 24.) but more ordinarily by striking our hearts with his terrors, (Job 6. 4.) withdrawing the comfort of his gracious presence, (Psal. 77. 7.) leaving us for a time to ourselves, (2 Chr. 32. 31.) that by our falls we may acknowledge our own weakness: finally exercising us under the cross and yoke of outward afflictions, Heb. 12. 5, 6. Rev. 3. 19.

How must we contend with God?
No otherwise, then Jacob, (Hos. 12. 3, 4.) and other holy men have done, that is, by obedience, humility, patience, and fervent prayer unto God; who only enableth us to prevail with himself, giving us the blessing and name of Israel, Gen. 32. 28.

[33RD HEAD.]

What are those enemies of ours that seek to seduce and endanger us?
Whatsoever marcheth under the banner of Satan, the God and Prince of the darkness of this world, (2 Cor. 4. 4. Eph. 6. 12.) who sometimes immediately assaileth us with impious and odious suggestions, (2 Cor. 12. 7. Zech. 3. 1.) but more usually employeth his forces or attendants, namely, the World, (1 Joh. 2. 15.) and the flesh; (Gal. 5. 24.) So that the faithful in this life have battle both without, by the temptations of Satan and the World; and within, by the battle of the flesh against the Spirit.

How do these enemies fight against our souls?
By implying all force and fraud, to draw us by sin from the obedience and favor of God, unto damnation. 1 Joh. 2. 15.

What must we do being thus assaulted?
We must stand fast, being strong in the Lord, and in the power of his might, and taking unto us the whole amour of God, (Ephes. 6. 10, 11, 12.) that we may be able to resist in the evil day, and to lead our captivity captive.

How shall we overcome?
By a lively faith in Jesus Christ.

To come then to those enemies in particular. What call you Satan?
The adversary or enemy of God and his people.

How may we be able to stand against his assaults?
First, we must labor to inform ourselves, that we may not be ignorant of his enterprises or stratagems. 2 Cor. 2. 11.

Secondly, we must boldly resist. (Jam. 4. 7. 11 1. Pet. 5. 9.) that is, give no place or ground unto him. (Eph. 4. 27.) or admit any conference with him, but rather neglect and despise his suggestions.

Thirdly, we must take the shield of faith in Christ, and his assistance (setting him on our right hand who is mighty to save, (Psal. 16. 8. Isa. 63. 1.) whereby we may quench all the fiery darts of the wicked one. Eph. 6. 16.

Fourthly, we must brandish against him the sword of the Spirit, that is, the word of God; (Eph. 6. 17.) after the example of our Savior; (Mat. 44. &c.) keeping ourselves to that only, which God revealeth to us, and requireth of us.

What is the first assault of Satan against us?
By subtlety he allureth us to sin: and therefore he is called a Tempter, and a Serpent.

Thirty-fourth Head

How shall we overcome him in these temptations?
First, by faith in Jesus Christ, who overcame all Satan's temptations in his own person, that so we might overcome in him. Secondly, by resisting the inward motions and outward occasions of sin.

How shall we do that?
By believing that we are baptized in the death and resurrection of Christ.

What is the second assault of Satan against us?
He lieth fearfully to our charge our sins committed: and therefore he is called the Devil, an accuser.

How shall we overcome him in these accusations?
First, by faith in Jesus Christ, who hath justified us from all the sins for which Satan can accuse us. Secondly, by all those comfortable promises of forgiveness of sins, which in Christ's name are made unto us.

What is the third assault of Satan against us?
He seeketh by manifold inward terrors, and outward troubles; to swallow us up: and therefore is called a roaring Lion.

How shall we overcome him in these terrors and troubles?
First, by faith in Jesus Christ; who was heard in all his troubles; to give us assurance, that we shall not be overcome in them. Secondly, by faith in Gods providence; whereby we know that Satan can do no more harm unto us then the Lord does direct him for our good.

[34TH HEAD.]

So much of Satan the first enemy: what call you the World?
The corrupt state and condition of men, and of the rest of the Creatures, which Satan abuseth as his store house and armory of temptations, 1 Joh. 2. 15.

How does the world fight against us?
By alluring us and withdrawing us to the corruption thereof.

What means does it use?
First it allureth us to evil, with hope of false pleasures, gain, and profit preferment and glory of this world, from our obedience to God. 1 John 2. 16. Secondly, otherwhiles with fear of pains, troubles, losses, reproaches, &c. it discourageth us from our duty, and allureth us to distrust Gods promises. Joh. 16. 33.

How may we withstand the temptations of the World?
By our faith, (1 Joh. 5. 4.) which setteth a better world, even God's heavenly kingdom, before our eyes; and so enableth us both to condemn, (Heb. 11. 24. &c.) and crucify (Gal. 6. 14.) the love of this present world; and to endure manfully the threats and wrongs thereof. (Heb. 11. 36, 37.) both confessing Christ in peril, and suffering martyrdom for his sake, if we be thereto called. Rev. 12. 11.

How are then the pleasures, profits, and glory of this world to be overcome?
First, by a true faith in Jesus Christ, who despised all these things to work our salvation, and to make us overcome them. Secondly, by faith in Gods word, that feareth us from doing any thing that is against his will.

And how shall we overcome the pains, losses, and reproaches of this world?
First, by a lively faith in Jesus Christ, who suffered all these things to work our salvation, and to enable us to suffer them. Secondly, by a stedfast faith in Gods promises and providence, that we shall want no good things and that all things seeming hurtful shall be turned to the furtherance of our salvation.

[35TH HEAD.]

So much of the World, the second enemy: what call you the Flesh?
The corruption of our nature, wherein we were born and conceived.

Does that remain after Regeneration?
Yea: it dwelleth in us, and cleaveth fast unto us, so long as we carry the outward flesh about us.

How does the flesh fight against the Spirit?
As a treacherous part without us, being by Satan stirred up, and inveigled with the baits of the world, or discouraged with the evil entreaty thereof, it fighteth on his side against our soul, (1 Pet. 2. 11.) that is, our spiritual life and welfare; by continual lusting against the Spirit, Gal. 5. 17.

How is that?
First, by hindering or corrupting us in the good motions, word and deeds of the Spirit. Secondly, by continual moving us to evil motions, words, and deeds.

What call you the Spirit?
The holy Spirit which God in Christ hath given us, whereby we are begotten again.

Do we not receive the Spirit in full measure, and in perfection at the first?
No: but first we receive the first fruits, and afterwards daily increase of the same unto the end, if the fault be not in ourselves.

How does the Spirit fight in us?
By lusting against the flesh.

How does it lust against the flesh?
First, partly by rebuking and partly by restraining in us the evil motions and deeds of the flesh. Secondly, by continual enlightening and affecting us with thoughts, words, and deeds, agreeable to God's will.

How may we withstand the temptations of our flesh?
By setting before our eyes the pattern of the death of Christ, and arming ourselves with the same mind, that it behooveth us also to suffer in the flesh, ceasing from sin; (1 Pet. 4. 1.) hereto craving and employing the power of the same death of Christ, to subdue and crucify our carnal lusts and affections (Rom. 6. 2. &c. Whereunto also belongeth the help of Abstinence for the repressing of the inordinate desires of nature. 1 Cor. 9. 26. &c.

So much of the spiritual fight. What followeth after a man hath gotten the victory in any temptation or affliction?
Experience of God's love in Christ, and so increase of peace of conscience, and joy in the Holy Ghost. Rom. 5. 3. 2 Cor. 1. 5.

Thirty-sixth Head

What follows if in any temptation he be overcome, and through infirmity fall?
After a while there will arise godly sorrow; which is, when a man is grieved for no other cause in the world but for this only, that by his sin he hath displeased God, who hath been unto him a most merciful and loving father. 2 Cor. 7. 8, 9. Mat. 26. 75.

What sign is there of this sorrow?
Repentance renewed afresh. 2 Cor. 7. 11.

By what signs will this repentance appear?
By seven. (2 Cor. 7. 11.) 1. A care to leave the sin whereunto he is fallen. 2. An utter condemning of himself for it with a craving of pardon. 3. A great anger against himself for his carelessness. 4. A fear lest he should fall into the same sin again. 5. A desire ever after to please God. 6. A zeal of the same. 7. Revenge upon himself for his former offences.

[36TH HEAD.]

Thus far of Repentance, and the spiritual warfare accompanying the same. What are those good works wherein our new Obedience is exercised?
That which proceeding from a person acceptable, is something of God commanded, performed in right manner, and directed unto a good end; namely, whatsoever thing is done of us, not by the force or conduct of nature, (2 Cor. 3. 5.) but by the power of the spirit of Christ dwelling in us, (Rom. 8. 10.) and according to the rule of the known will of God, (Rom. 12. 2.) unto the glory of God, (1 Cor. 10. 31.) the assurance of our Election, (2 Pet. 1. 10. &c.) and the edification of others. 1 Cor. 10. 23.

How many things then are needful for the making of our actions good? and what properties are to be required in good works?
Five: 1. They that do them must be such as are engrafted into Christ, and continue in him; that so their persons may be acceptable unto God. 2. They must be agreeable to the Law of God: and he that does them must know that he hath a warrant for his action from the commandment of God. 3. He that does them must not only have a warrant for his action, and know that it is lawful; but he must also do it in that manner which God hath appointed. 4. He that does them must be persuaded in his heart that God alloweth them. 5. They must be done to that holy end for which God hath commanded them: namely to glorify God, and to assure our own salvation.

Cannot all men do good works?
No, but only the regenerate: who are for that purpose created a new, and endued in some measure with the spirit of Christ, and power of his Resurrection, and carry the Image of God in them. Eph. 2. 10. 2 Tim. 2. 21.

What say you then of the good works of the unregenerate?
They do no good works: because they neither are as yet members of Christ, nor do offer them to God in the name of Christ, and therefore are the evil tree, which bringeth forth only evil fruit. Mat. 7. 17, &c. Jer. 13. 23.

Is there no difference between those men, though unregenerate, which keep themselves to their own wives, and those that take other men's? or between him that stealeth, and him that liveth of his own labor?
Yes verily. For the former actions are civilly good, and profitable for the maintenance of the society of men, and before God not so abominable as those which are committed against civil honesty: yet coming from some other cause (either of vain-glory, or of

servile fear, or opinion of merit) than from faith, and consequently the love of God, they are no better than sins, what show of goodness soever they have.

Is there no concurrence of nature in the doing of a good work?
Taking nature (in the common sense of Scripture) for that hereditary corruption that cleaveth to all the sons of Adam, (Eph. 2. 3. 1 Cor. 2. 14.) no good work hath any ground or help from nature, but is altogether contrary thereto: (Rom. 8. 7.) But if we understand by nature, (as Rom. 2. 14.) the created abilities of soul and body, as the light of reason, liberty of will, motion of the bodily members, &c. we acknowledge nature not to be the principal mover or guide, (Mat. 16. 17.) but the thing moved and guided by grace, in well doing. 1 Thes. 5. 23.

Do not our good works make us worthy of eternal life? or in some part justify us? or any whit merit and deserve the favor of God?
No; because, 1. We are ten thousand times more indebted to God, than all our good works or ourselves are worth. 2. We can do no good thing but that which cometh from God. 3. The righteousness which is able to stand in the judgment of God, must be perfect in all respects. But in many things we sin all: and again, our best works are imperfect, corrupt and defiled with sin; and therefore can deserve nothing at the hands of God, who being perfect righteousness it self, will find in the best works we do, more matter of damnation than of salvation; wherefore we must rather condemn ourselves for our good works, than look to be justified before God thereby. Psal. 143. 2. Isa. 64. 6. Job 9. 3.

Is there no work of man perfectly good?
No work of a sinful man is wholly free from sin: neither is there any good work perfect, no not for the most perfect in this life, by reason of the remainders of corruption; (Isa. 64. 6. Gal. 5. 17.) but only the work of Christ, in whom alone there was no mixture of sin. 1 Pet. 2. 22.

But when our sanctification here begun shall be perfect in the world to come; shall we not then be justified by an inherent righteousness?
No, but by the imputed righteousness of our Savior Christ, which being once given us, is never taken away from us.

How is pollution conveyed into the good works which God worketh in us?
There is (beside the work of his own hand, through the operation of his holy Spirit) a pollution in us, and an infection of ours, which cometh from the sin that dwelleth in us: as clear water put into an unclean Vessel, or running through a filthy channel, receiveth some evil quality thereof.

Wherein do our good works fail of Gods justice?
Partly in the instrumental causes, from whence they proceed; and partly in the final cause, or end whereunto they aim.

What are the instrumental causes hindering the perfection of our works?
1. Our Understanding; in that the work is not done with knowledge absolute and thoroughly perfect. 2. Our Memory; in that our remembrance is enfeebled, and does not so fully retain that which the Understanding conceiveth. 3. Our Will and affections; in that they are short of their duty. 4. Our Body; in that it is not so apt and nimble for the execution of good things, as is required.

Express this by a Similitude.
We are in the instrumental causes like to a common laborer, which being hired by the day, worketh with one hand, whereas both are required; or worketh a piece of the day, being hired for the whole.

What is the final end wherein good works fail?
In that we have not so direct an eye to God's glory, or the good of our neighbor, as is required: but look asquint (as it were) at those duties which are enjoined us. Like to those Artificers, who prefer their own credit in their skill, before their Masters profit.

If then it be so that sin cleaveth to our best works, are not our good works sin, and are not all evil works equal?
No doubtless: be it far from us to think of it; For their imperfection is sinful, but the good work is not a sin: and even in bad actions (as hath been said some are better, that is, less evil and hurtful than others.

But seeing our ways are thus corrupt, how can they please God? and why does he promise a reward unto them?
First, the reward that God does promise, is not for the desert of our works, but of his own grace and mercy. Secondly, the corruption and pollution that cleaveth unto our good works is taken away by the intercession of our Savior Christ, for whose sake God covering their imperfection, accepteth and accounteth of them, and so rewardeth, them, as if they were perfect. 1 Pet. 2. 5. Exod. 28. 36, 37, 38.

What Doctrine is hence to be gathered?
A doctrine of great comfort to the children of God to stir them up to abound in good works, since they are so acceptable to God in Christ Jesus; for when men know any thing to be delightsome to their Prince, they will with all endeavour strive for it: how much more then ought we to be pricked forward to the service of God, who quencheth not the smoking flax, nor breaketh the bruised Reed, (Mat, 12. 20.) yea, which forgetteth not a cup of cold water given in faith, and for his sake? Mat. 10. 42.

Declare now the ends for which good works are to be done?
1. That by them God's glory may be advanced. 2. That by them we may show our thankfulness unto God for all his benefits. 3. That by them we may be assured of our faith and election. 4. That by our good works we may edify others.

How may we edify others?
1. By encouraging and strengthning those that are good. 2. By stopping the mouths of the wicked, and of those that are incorrigible.

It is not lawful to seek our own praise, and merit by our good works?
No: for all our good works are imperfect, and salvation is only merited by the death and obedience of Christ; as hath been said.

But will not this doctrine make men careless of well doing?
No: for they that are engrafted into Christ, must needs bring forth good works: and good works are necessary (as hath been declared) though not for merit, yet for God's glory, the edification of others, and our own assured comfort.

Are good works so needful that without them we cannot be saved?
Yea: for although good works do not work our salvation in any part; yet because they that are justified are also sanctified, they that do no good works declare that they neither are justified nor sanctified, and therefore cannot be saved.

Then they must much more be condemned which commit sin and lie in it?
Yea, for such are not only pronounced to be accursed by the law, but also the Gospel hath denounced, that they shall not inherit the Kingdom of heaven.

What considerations may draw us to be zealous in good works?
That if we do well, we shall have well; as the old saying is.

But that is a hard thing to be persuaded of.
So it is indeed: because our hearts are naturally distrustful in the promises of God; as also our flesh, the world and the devil do suggest unto us, that it is a vain thing to do good. Mal. 3. 14.

What remedy is there against these assaults?
That it shall be well with them that do well; by the testimony of God himself commanding the Prophet Esaiah to say so to the righteous: (Isa. 3. 10.) which ought to teach all men, that laying aside all their own opinions, and whatsoever seemeth good in their own eyes, they should rely wholly on the direction of God.

What may be gathered of this?
That it is better to endanger ourselves with obedience to God, then with disobedience to rid ourselves out of appearance of trouble.

But why did the Lord thus charge the Prophet?
Because the wicked (as saith Malachi) wearied God with their blasphemies, saying that he delighted in their wickedness. Mal. 21. 7.

How secondly is that point confirmed?
By a continual practice and experience from time to time, as the friends of Job do well reason thereupon.

What is the third proof?
That first the Lord must do either good for good, or evil for good; and that it is absurd, yea blasphemous, to say, that God does evil for good it must needs follow, that he will do good for good. For if a reasonable honest man would not requite kindness with unkindness; it can much less fall into the nature of God so to do: especially seeing he did then show kindness unto us, when we were enemies unto him.

How fourthly is it confirmed?
In that God is said to write up the good deeds of his servants into his book of records; as the Kings of the earth are wont to do, Mal. 3. 16, 17, 18.

But this seemeth not so; since the wicked do so triumph over the godly, as if there were no difference?
A difference shall specially appear at the day of Judgment, when by the sentence of the great Judge the wicked like stubble shall be consumed with fire, and the Sun of righteousness shall shine upon the just. Mal. 4. 1, 2.

Is there no difference at all in this life?
Yes, inwardly. For the godly in doing well have always a good conscience, howsoever earthly things go with them: so that the green salad of herbs, or dry bread, is better to them then all the rich man's wealth: because the grace of God goeth with them whithersoever they go; whereas the wicked have a hell in their conscience, how well soever they fare outwardly.

Thirty-seventh Head

[37TH HEAD.]

So much of good works in general: What special good works are commended to us in the Word of God?
The things which we give unto God, prescribed in the first Table: and the giving of alms to our needy Neighbor; touching which among all the duties of the second Table, our Savior giveth special direction in the 6. of Matthew, where he entreateth of Prayer and Fasting.

What are those things that we give unto God?
Prayers and Vows: Psa. 50. 13, 14. & 66. 13, 14. which being special parts of Gods worship, may not be communicated unto any other. Isa. 42. 8. & 48. 11.

What is Prayer?
It is a familiar speech with God, in the name of Christ, (Joh. 5. 14.) opening the desires of our hearts unto him: and so lifting up of the mind, and a pouring out of the heart before God; for the more ample and free fruition of the good things we have need of. Psal. 50. 15. Jer. 33. 3. Lam. 2. 19. Phil, 4. 6.

What gather you hence?
That we can never honor God aright in calling upon his name, unless we bring faithful and feeling hearts before him. Jam. 1. 6, 7. 1 Sam. 1. 16.

Describe Prayer yet more largely?
It is a religious calling upon God alone, in the name of Christ, by the titles wherewith in the Scripture he is set forth unto us; as well thereby to do service and homage unto the Lord, as to obtain those further things and graces that are necessary for us. Or thus. It is the holy request of an humble and sanctified heart together with thanksgiving, (Phil. 4. 6.) offered by the power of the Spirit of prayer, (Rom. 8. 26.) as a special service unto God. (Psal. 50. 15.) in the name of Christ, (John 14. 14.) in behalf of ourselves and others, (Ep. 6. 18.) with assurance to be heard, in what we pray for, according to the will of God. Joh. 5. 14. Jam. 1. 6.

Why do we call it a request with thanksgiving?
Because in all our Prayers, there must be both Petition of the good things we need; and thankful acknowledgment of those we have obtained; (1 Thes. 5. 17, 18.) As for those forms which contain neither supplication nor giving of thanks, (as the Articles of the Belief, the Decalogue, &c.) they may and ought, for other good purposes, be committed to memory and rehearsed; (Deut. 6. 7.) but to use them as Prayers, savoureth of deep ignorance, if not of superstition. Mat. 6. 7.

Why do you call it the request of the heart?
Not to exclude the use of bodily gesture, much less of the voice and tongue, in the action of Invocation; (therefore called the Calves of the Lips, Hos. 14. 2.) but to show, First, that the heart i, on our part, the principal mover and speaker in prayer; from whence both voice and gesture have their force and grace, 1 Cor. 14. 15. Psal. 45. 1. & 8. 108. Secondly, that Prayer on sudden occasion may be secretly and powerfully offered, and is of God heard and accepted, when neither any voice is uttered, nor any bodily gesture employed. Exod. 14. 15. Neh. 2. 4.

Why do you add, of an humble and sanctified heart?
Because as in general, none can pray or do any thing acceptably, (Psal. 109. 7.) but such as are truly regenerate, and sanctified unto this and every good work: (Psal. 51. 15.) so in special (and for the present action of prayer) it is required as the Sum of all

sacrifices, that the heart be humble and contrite, (Psal. 51. 17.) acknowledging its own unworthiness, by reason of sin, (Dan. 9. 8, 9.) feeling the want of Gods grace and mercy. (Psal. 143. 6.) and submitting it self unto him, willing to be beholding for the least degree of favor. Luk. 15. 18, 19.

What then is required of us that our prayers may be holy?
1. That we pray with faith and assurance that God for Christ's sake will hear us. 2. That we pray with fear and reverence of God. 3. That we pray with humility and a lively sense of our own unworthiness to obtain any thing at Gods hands. 4. That we pray with a true feeling of our own wants, and an earnest desire to obtain those things for which we pray. 5. That our affections be agreeable to the matter for which we pray. 6. That we purpose to use all good means for the obtaining of those things for which we pray.

In brief: these be the special properties of true Prayer. It must be,
1. In faith, without wavering, Jam. 1. 6.
2. In truth, without feigning, Psal. 145. 18.
3. In humility, without swelling, Luk. 18. 13.
4. In zeal. without cooling, Jam. 5. 16.
5. In constancy, without fainting, Luk. 18. 1.

What learn you hence?
That even they which are most frequent and fervent in this duty, had need to pray to God to forgive their prayers, in conscience of their own frailties and infirmities. Isa. 38. 14, 15. Psal. 77. 9, 10. & 32. 3, 5.

What is the spirit of Prayer?
An especial grace and operation of the holy Ghost, Jude. 20. called therefore the spirit of grace and supplication, Zech. 12. 10. enabling us to pour out our souls unto the Lord (Psalm 62. 8.) with sighs that cannot be expressed. (Rom 8 26.) For the holy Ghost must be our helper in prayer, to teach us both what to pray and how to pray. Rom. 8. 26.

To whom must we pray?
To God alone and to none other. For he alone as the searcher of the hearts, heareth the voice, and knoweth the meaning of the spirit of prayer. Psal. 65. 2. Rom. 8. 27. Second, he is able to grant whatsoever we demand. Eph. 3. 20. Third, he challengeth our faith and confidence, without which we cannot pray. Rom. 10 14.

Wherefore seeing he alone hears all prayer, heals all sins, knows all suitors; (Jer. 31. 18.) 2 Chron. 7. 14. & 6. 30. 1 Chron 28. 9. Psal. 44. 21.) he alone hath love enough to pity all, and power enough to relieve all our wants and necessities: to him alone we are to pray, and to none other.

What learn you hence?
That seeing the Scripture forbiddeth us to communicate Gods honor to any other; (Isa. 42. 8. & 48. 11.) such as pray either to Saint or Angel, (Col. 2. 18.) have forgotten the name of their God. Psal. 44. 20. Which condemneth those of the Church of Rome, who would have as to pray to Angels and Saints departed.

Whether must we direct our prayers to the Father, or the Son, or to the Holy Ghost?
We must pray to the Trinity of the Persons in the Unity of the Godhead; this is to say, to one God in Trinity.

In whose name, or for whose sake must we pray to God?
In the only name and for the only sake of his Son, our Lord Jesus Christ, (Dan. 9. 17. Joh. 16. 23, 24.) the alone Mediator between God and Man. (1 Tim. 2. 5.) as of propitiation, so of intercession; (1 Joh. 2. 1, 2. Rom. 8. 34) who through the veil of his flesh, and merit of his blood, hath prepared for us a new and living way, whereby we may be bold to enter into the holy place: (Heb. 10. 19.) in whom alone we are made the children of God, and have liberty to call him Father; (Gal. 4. 6.) finally in, with, and for whom, God giveth all good things to his Elect. Rom. 8. 32.

Who are condemned by this doctrine?
They of the Church of Rome, who teach us to pray in the name of Saints, and make them to be mediators between God and us.

For whom are we to pray?
For ourselves and others; us and ours: in a word, First for all men, (1 Tim. 2. 1.) even our enemies (Mat. 5. 44.) because they bear the common Image of God, (Jam. 3. 9.) and blood of mankind, whereof we are all made; (Acts 17. 26.) unless it be apparent that any one hath committed the unpardonable sin: (1 Joh. 5. 16.) but principally, for such as are our Brethren in Christ and of the household of faith. Eph. 6. 18. Gal. 6. 10. Secondly, for all sorts and degrees of men; especially public persons, as Rulers, and such as are in authority: (1 Tim. 2. 2.) Ministers, that watch over our souls; (Eph. 6. 19. Col. 4. 3.) &c.

What assurance have we, that we shall be heard in what we pray for?
Because we pray to that God that heareth prayer, (Psal. 65. 2.) and is the rewarder of all that come unto him; (Heb. 11. 6.) and in his name, to whom God denieth nothing: (Joh. 11. 42.) (and therefore howsoever we are not always answered at the present, (Psal. 77. 3.) or in the same kind that we desire, (2 Cor. 12. 9.) yet sooner or later, we are sure to receive, even above that we are able to ask or think, if we continue with constancy, patience, and importunity, to sue unto him according to his will. Luk. 11. 5. to 9. & 18. 1. 1 Joh. 5. 14.

What things must we come to God in prayer for?
Not for trifles and toys, but for things needful and necessary, and such as God hath made us promise of: some whereof do immediately concern the glory of God, others the necessity of man; either in things belonging to this present life, or those especially which belong to the life to come.

But how can we remember all the promises that God hath made, thereon to ground our petitions; especially being unlettered?
There are general promises, that whatsoever we shall ask according to his will, it shall be given us, 1 Joh. 5. 14. Again, whatsoever we read or hear that the servants of God have demanded in the Scripture uncontroledly, or without special calling, that is a good warrant for us to demand at the hands of God.

Where then is that will of God revealed, according whereto we must direct our prayers?
Throughout the whole book of the Scriptures of God; which inform us, as concerning other duties, so especially concerning this of prayer; recording also for this purpose many excellent prayers, as of Moses, David, Daniel, Nehemiah, Paul, &c. but most absolutely in that passage or portion delivered by our Savior himself, and therefore commonly called the Lord's Prayer?

What learn you from hence?
That for help of our weakness and rudeness in prayer, we are to look unto the prayers of the holly men of God set down in Scripture, according as the estate wherein they were at the time of those prayers may best sort with the special cases wherein we are when we pray. But especially and above any other, yea above all of them together, we are to look to that most absolute prayer, which our Savior Christ hath taught us in the Gospel.

What is the special end and use of prayer?
To recover our peace, and to nourish our communion with our God, Dan. 9. 9. Phil. 4. 6, 7. Joh. 17. or 1 John 1. 3, 4.

What gather you hence?
That such as have least care, and make least conscience to call upon him, have also least acquaintance and acceptance with him. Psal. 14. 4.

How farther is the necessity of Prayer considered?
Prayer is a key to open the Store houses of all God's treasures unto us: and as by knocking we enter into the place we desire to go to, so by Prayer we obtain those things we need. Also as men provide gifts to make way for favor: (Prov. 17. 8.) so Prayer is a gift to appease God's anger towards us; and as a hook to reach those things that are above our reach, and to put by those things that stand in our way and let us. Add hereunto, that it is so necessary, as without it the use and enjoying of the things we have is unlawful. 1 Tim. 4. 5. For as if we take any thing that is our neighbors without asking him leave, we are accounted Thieves; so to take any thing of Gods (whose all things are) without asking them at his hand, is Felony. Finally, Prayer is a principal means serving for the strengthning and increasing of Faith, and for the further advancing, and more plentiful effecting of the outward means of salvation. Jude 20. 1 Thes. 5. 17, 18. Psal. 4. 6, 7. And therefore the Apostles did not only say unto Christ, Increase our faith; Luke 17. 5. but also, Lord teach us to pray, as John also taught his disciples, Luke. 11. 1.

What is the excellency of this duty?
It setteth head, and heart, and all our best affections to work; giving God the praise of his Majesty and Mercy, Goodness and Greatness both together. 1 Sam. 1. 10, 13. Jam. 5. 13, 14. Psal. 50. 23. And therefore it is compared to Incense or sweet perfumes; (Psal. 141. 2.) for that it is acceptable to the Lord, as perfumes are to men: and to the drops of honey, as it were dropping from the lips of the Church, as from an honey-comb. Cant. 4. 11. Thy lips, & my Spouse, drop as the honey-comb: honey and milk are under thy tongue.

How can God so infinitely wise, take delight in our prayers that are so rude?
Because in Christ he taketh us for his children: and therefore as Parents rather take pleasure to hear their children stammer, than some other to speak eloquently; so does the Lord take pleasure in the weak prayers of the Saints.

Hitherto of Invocation and Prayer in general. What are the parts thereof?
Two principally: (Psal. 63. 15, 23. 1 Thes. 5. 17, 18. 1 Tim. 2. 1. Phil. 4. 6.) Petition or Request (properly called Prayer,) whereby we crave things needful; and Thanksgiving or Praise, whereby we magnify the goodness of God, and give thanks for benefits received. To the which is annexed Confession of sins, and of the righteous judgment of God against them; at the view whereof we being humbled, may come more preparedly to prayer in both kinds.

What is Petition?
Petition (or Prayer properly so called) is a religious calling upon the name of God by suit or request, in which we desire and beg all things necessary. Luk 11. 1, 2, 3. Phil. 4. 6, 7. Psal. 50. 15. And it is either for things of this present life, with this exception, so far forth as the same shall be thought good unto the wisdom of God; or (and that especially) for the things of the life to come, without exception. Mat. 8. 2. 2 Sam. 15. 25, 26.

What learn you of this, that it is a religious calling upon God?
First, that we may not rush unadvisedly into Gods presence, but approach his Throne with fear and reverence. Heb. 12. 28. Eccl. 5. 1. Secondly, that the best hearing is in heaven, and readiest help from God's hand. 2 Chron. 7. 14.

What do you mean by calling upon God?
Not the calling of the tongue, but the cry of the heart: as Hannah called upon God, when her voice was not heard; (1 Sam. 1. 13.) and Moses cried unto the Lord when he spake not a word, Exod. 14. 15.

What gather you hence;
That the heart without the tongue may pray with fruit and feeling: (1 Sam. 1. 10.) but the tongue without the heart is nothing but vain babbling. Mat. 6. 7.

What do you mean by the name of God?
God himself considered in his Attributes and Properties, whereby (as men by their names) he is known unto us. Exod. 34. 5, 6, 7.

What learn you hence?
First, that neither any may claim, nor we may yield this duty, but where we may find the power and properties of the Deity. Psal. 44. 20, 21. Secondly, that it is a good ground of prayer to stay our hearts on such of God's properties, as are best suiting with our necessities: 2 Chron. 20. 6, 7, 8, 9. Neh. 1. 5. Thirdly, that they that will not settle their hearts on God alone by faith can never lift up their hearts to him alone in prayer. Rom. 10. 14. Psal. 44. 20. Lam. 3. 41. Fourthly, that in every state and condition, they that pray best, speed best, and live best. Dan. 9. 13, 14, 23. Psal. 50. 15. & 66. 18, 19.

It seemeth to be of no use to make our petitions unto God; seeing he both knoweth what we need, either for his glory or our good, and hath determined what to bestow upon us?
Yes verily, we must ask, and that continually (that is, at set times, without intermission) by the Commandment of Christ himself, bidding us ask and we shall receive, seek and we shall find, knock and it shall be opened to us: (Mat. 7. 7.) wherein we should rest. For as God hath foreappointed all necessaries to be given us; so hath he also appointed the means whereby they should be brought to pass, whereof Prayer is a chief.

What other reason have you for this?
We should therefore pray for the things we have need of, that having received them, we may be assured we had them of God, and not by accident or fortune as natural men do say.

Does not God oftentimes bestow his benefits without prayer?
Yes: both upon the wicked, (either to provoke them to repent or to make them inexcusable: and upon his own children. Even as a loving Father in regard of his ignorant, or sometimes negligent child, does give things unasked; even so does God toward his.

Why will the Lord have us beg his blessing of him?
To exercise our faith in seeking, (Mat. 7. 7.) and our Patience in waiting: (Jam. 5. 10, 11.) as also to stir up a feeling of our wants, (Mat. 15. 22.) and to quicken our affections unto good things. Phil. 4. 6.

What gather you hence?
That where the heart is faithless, the prayer must needs be fruitless: for according to our faith it shall be unto us. Luk. 18. 11, 14. Jam. 1. 6, 7.

But why does not he answer when we ask, but delays to help us when yet he sees and hears us?
Because we are sometimes too haughty and he will humble us; sometimes too hasty and he will curb us. 2 Cor. 12. 7, 8, 9. Sometimes we fail in matter, asking we know not what: sometimes in the manner, asking we know not how: and sometimes in the end, asking we know not wherefore Jam. 4. 2, 3.

Does he not sometimes delay us, when yet he purposeth to answer us?
Yes he does: First, because he loves to hear the voice of his own spirit in us. Rom. 8. 26. 27. Secondly, because the suit may be good, and yet the season not so meet for us. Rev. 6. 10, 11 Acts 1. 7. Thirdly, he takes pleasure in our constancy, being a fruit of faith and fervency. Luk. 18. 1. Mat 15. 27, 28. Fourthly, because such blessings as are won by long and strong prayers, are always esteemed very highly, received in humility, enjoyed in sobriety, and employed faithfully for mans good and God's glory. 1 Sam. 1. 10, 21. 1 Chro. 29. 14, 15.

What gather you hence?
That if we faint not in praying, we shall in due season be sure of a blessing (Luk. 18, 7. 8.) and that when our God denies us or delays us in that which seems good unto us, even then he gives us that which he knows is better for us. 2 Cor. 12. 8, 9.

What good means may we use to obtain the gift of prayer in some measure?
First, to get some true feeling for our Misery: for the sense of Misery breeds suit for mercy. Mat. 15. 22. Second, bring hungering and thirsty souls after grace and good things, Psal. 42. 1, 2. when the soul panteth most, the heart prayeth best. Third, gather principles of knowledge: that the head may guide the heart. 1 Cor. 14. 15. for what we know is worth the having, he will not lose for the asking. Fourth, consider the examples of God's servants in like sorrows, and make like suits. Dan. 9. Nehem. 9. Be thou as they were to him and he will be to thee what he was to them. Fifth, be well persuaded of Christ's ordinance, Master teach us to pray; (Luk. 11. 1.) and of God's acceptance, reckon of him as of our Father: (Mat. 6. 5, 9.) for according to our faith it shall be unto us. Sixth, be resolute against sin, neither living in grosser iniquities, nor allowing lesser infirmities: (Rom. 7. 15.) and so he will never shut out our prayers, nor withhold his mercies from us Psal. 66. 19, 20. Seventh, in reading or hearing, turn Precepts into Prayers; Lord give what thou commandest, and command what thou wilt. Duties enjoined, graces commended blessings promised, and curses threatened, do all quicken us to prayer, and furnish us with matter for the same. Mat. 5. 6, 7. Rom. 12. Eph. 6.

But when for all this our Prayers are few and faint, cold and weak? what special help may we then have against our infirmities?
None better then to pray for the Spirit of Prayer, which helpeth and healeth our infirmities, and teacheth us both for manner, measure, and matter, to lay open all our necessities. Rom. 8. 26. Luk. 11. 13. And secondly, call others which are best acquainted with the practice and power of prayer, to pray with us being present. (Jam. 5. 14.) and for us being absent from us. Rom. 1. 9.

What are the signs of a sound Prayer?
1. To use all other good means carefully. Acts 27. 23. 31.
2. To seek God's glory principally. Exod. 32. 11, 12.
3. To desire the best things most earnestly. Col. 1. 9. 10, 11.
4. To ask nothing but what God's Word warranteth us. 1 John. 6. 14.
5. To wait patiently till he hear and help us. Psalm 40 1. James 5. 10, 11.

What motives may we have to stir up our hearts to this duty?
Many and good, because prayer is the voice of God's spirit in us. (Rom. 8. 26.) a Jewel of grace bequeathed by Christ unto us, (Luk. 11. 2.) It is the Hand of Faith, the Key of God's treasure, the Souls Solicitor, the Hearts Amour-bearer, and the Minds Interpreter. Mat. 7. 7. Ephes. 6. 18. It procureth all blessings, preventeth curses, (2 Chr. 7. 14.) sanctifieth all creatures, that they may do us good. (1 Tim. 4. 5.) seasoneth all crosses, that they can do us no hurt. Lastly, it keeps the heart in humility, the life in sobriety, strengtheneth all graces, overcometh all temptations, subdueth corruptions, purgeth our affections, makes our duties acceptable to God, our lives profitable unto men, and both life and death comfortable unto ourselves. Acts 9. 11. Eph. 6 18, Jude. 20. Acts. 4. 24. & 7. 59.

What are the lets and hindrances of prayer?
There be some which hinder the power of it, as our ordinary Infirmities: (Mark. 9. 23, 24.) other, which hinder either the practice or the fruit of it, as our customary and grosser Iniquities. Psal. 66. 18.

What are the Infirmities that weaken the Power of Prayer?
Roving imaginations, inordinate affections, dullness of spirit, weakness of faith, coldness in feeling, faintness in asking, weariness in waiting, too much passion in our own matters, and too little compassion in other men's miseries. Psal 32. 3, 4. Mar. 9. 24. Isa. 38. 13, 14. Jonah 4. 2. 3.

What are the customary Iniquities which hinder the Practice of Prayer?
First, The profaneness of the Atheists, in not calling upon God. Psal. 14. 4. Second, The sottishness of the Papists, lifting up their hearts and hands to base Idols. Psa. 44. 20. Third, The sensuality of the voluptuous, drowning all his desires in delights, and his prayers in pleasures. 2 Tim. 3. 4. Fourth, The stupidity of worldlings, that think they have no need of praying, but of carking and caring, toiling and moiling in the world. Luk. 12. 17, 18. Phil 3. 19. Fifth, The foolishness of the malicious, which because they will not forgive their brother an hundred pence, cannot pray to God to forgive them their ten thousand Talents. Mat. 18. 32.

What are the gross sins which shut the ears of the Lord and hinder the fruit of our Prayers?
First, Graceless hypocrisy, drawing near with our lips, but having our hearts far from him. Isa. 29. 13. Second, Shameless impiety, when turning our ears from his precepts he turneth away his from our prayers. Prov. 28. 9. Third, Senseless impenitency, when the cry of our sins unrepented of, drowns the vice of our prayers that are offered. Zech. 7. 13. Fourth, Merciless cruelty, when we either cause or suffer the afflicted to cry without hearing; the Lord hearing us cry in our affliction, without helping. Gen. 42. 22.

What is the general subject of our requests?
Good, or evil. Good to obtain it, and Evil to remove or prevent it. Col. 1. 9. 2 Thes. 3. 1, 2. That wherein we pray for good things is called Supplication. (1 Tim. 2. 1. 2. That wherein we pray against any evil, is called Deprecation.

What do you mean by good or Evil?
Whatsoever is helpful or hurtful either for soul or body: goods and graces, sins and sorrows, mercies or judgments in spiritual or in carnal things. Phil. 1. 9. Luk. 18. 13. Dan. 9.

What gather you hence?
First, That as Prayer is the key of our heart to open all our necessities unto God, (Lam. 2. 19.) so is it also the key of his treasury to obtain his mercies from him. Mat. 7. 7. Second, That the gift of Prayer is a pledge and earnest penny of all other good gifts and graces whatsoever; (Rom. 8. 26, 27, 32.) and that so long as we can pray, the greatest evil cannot hurt u, (Jonah 2. 1. &c. 2 Cor. 12. 7, 8). nor the greatest good without Prayer be ever profitable unto us. 1 Tim. 4. 5.

Are we only bound to pray for ourselves by request for Good, and against Evil things?
No: we are also bound to pray likewise for others; which kind of prayer is called Intercession. 1 Tim. 2. 1. 2.

What is Intercession?
It is the suit of the heart unto God for the good of others. As Abraham prayed for Abimelech, (Gen. 20. 17.) Jacob for his sons, (Gen. 49.) Paul for the people, (1 Thes. 1. 2.) and they for him.

Why does the Lord require this duty of us?
1. For communicating our gift and his graces. Jam. 5. 14, 15. 2. For nourishing our love. 3. For increase of our comforts. 4. For mutual support and relief in all Crosses.

What gather you hence?
That all such persons as are linked together in nearest bonds of society are also mutually bound to discharge this duty 1 Tim. 2. 1, 2. As first, in the household of faith, the stronger is to pray for the weaker that he fail not, (Phi. 1. 9.) and the weaker for the stronger that he fall not. 2 The. 3. 1, 2.

Secondly, the Sovereign for the Subject that he may obey in piety and loyalty, (2 Chron. 6 13. 14. the Subject of the Sovereign that he may rule in righteousness and religious policy: (1 Tim. 2. 1. 2.) and so in all societies, whether of public assemblies, or of private families. Job. 1. 5. Deut. 33. 6. 1 Chr. 29. 11.

What followeth of all this?
Strong consolation: that when we find small power or comfort in our prayers, the Lord hath ordained that we may seek and find both, in the prayers of his Church and children. Jam. 5. 14, 15. Acts 12. 5, 7.

You have now spoken of the first part of Invocation, namely Petition: What followeth?
The second, which is Praise and Thanksgiving. 1 Thes. 5. 18.

What is this Praise or Thanksgiving?
It is reverent calling upon the name of God, wherein the heart being cheered with some taste of his goodness, acknowledgeth all from his Mercy, and purposeth all for his Glory. Luke 10. 20. 1 Chro. 29. 10, 11, 12, 13. And it is either in praising all his goodness wisdom, power, mercy, and generally for the government of his Church; or for those particular favors, that by Petition we have received from his merciful hand.

Thirty-seventh Head

Whence does this duty of Praise arise?
As Petition ariseth from the feeling of our misery: so Praise from the feeling of God's mercy. Petition beggeth what we want, and praise acknowledgeth what and whence we have it. Rev. 15. 3. 1 Chron. 29. 12.

What gather you hence?
That when the Lord hath granted unto us our Petitions, we are forthwith bound to render unto him his due praises. Exodus 15. 1. Psal. 66. 19, 20.

Wherein does this duty of Praise especially consist?
First, in emptying ourselves of all worthiness. Gen. 32. 10. Second, in acknowledging him the author of every good gift, and fountain of living waters. Jam. 17. 17. Jer. 2. 13. Third, in speaking good of his name to others, Psal. 40. 9, 10. Fourth, in rejoicing before him in all his mercies. Deut. 26. 11. Fifth, in resolving to bestow all for his honor and service. 1 Chron. 29. 2, 3.

Wherefore does the Lord require praise and thanksgiving at our hands?
First, because it is the fairest and sweetest fruit of true piety. Psal. 92. 1. Secondly, it entirely preserveth God's glory. Thirdly, it boweth the heart of true humility. Fourthly, it is the condition of the Covenant, when he gives and we receive any mercy. Psal. 50. 15. Fifthly, it provoketh others to faithfulness and cheerfulness in God's service. Psal. 95. 1. Sixthly, it maintaineth the intercourse of mercies and duties betwixt God and man.

What are the properties of true praise?
First, it must be faithful without, glozing, with a single not with a double heart. Psal. 145. 18. Second, it must be plentiful. Psalm. 18. 1, 2, If God gives his mercies by showers we may not yield our praises by drops. Third, it must be cheerful. 1 Chron. 29. 14. he gives freely and we must offer, willingly: for he loves a cheerful giver. 2 Cor. 9. 7. Fourth, it must be powerful in the best measure, with the best member. Psal. 81. 1, 2. Fifth, it must be skillful, in the best manner, suiting his several properties with their due praises according to the nature of the present blessings. Exod. 15. 2, 3. Psal. 144. 1, 2. Sixth, it must be continual, as long as his mercy endureth and life lasteth Psal. 146. 2. 1 Thes. 5. 18.

What means may we use to attain unto this duty?
First, a serious consideration of the great things he hath done for us so vile creatures. 1 Sam. 12. 24. Second, to desire to taste God's love in the least of his mercies. Gen. 28. 20, 21. Third, to give him a taste of our love in the best of our services. Psalm 116. 12. Fourth, to rest content with our allowance and estate wherein he hath set us Phil. 4. 11. Fifth, to compare our estate with many of God's Saints who want several of those comforts which we enjoy, and feel many sorrows which we feel not. Psal. 147. 20. Sixth, to be faithful in all talents and fruitful in all graces, will be great means to make us praise God in all his mercies, Mat. 25. 23. Phil. 1. 11.

What motives have we to provoke us to praise?
First, it is a good, comely, and pleasant thing to praise God. Psal. 147. 1. Second, it is his will thus to be honored. 1 Thes. 5. 18. Third, it is a duty of Saints and Angels, both here and hereafter. Luk. 2. 13, 14. Fourth, it spreadeth abroad religion, magnifieth and sanctifieth him that is most High and most Holy Psal. 145. 1, 2. 3. Isa. 8. 13. Fifth, it keeps the heart from swelling, and the soul from surfeiting with God's blessings. Sixth, it fits the heart for further graces, and provokes the Lord to fresh mercies.

What are the special signs and marks, of one that desires to be thankful, and unfeigned to praise God in all things?
First, Contentedness Phil. 4. 11. Second, Cheerfulness in the use of God's blessings. Deut. 26. 11. Psal. 63. 5. Third, Faithfulness in our duties, both of our persons and places. Fourth, Readiness to draw others into the fellowship of God's praises. Psal. 66. 16. & 135. 1. Fifth, Rejoicing in God, even in the midst of many crosses. Job. 1. Sixth, Fruitfulness in good words and works. John 15. 8. Seventh, a conscionable carefulness to take all occasions and use all means to seal up our love, and set forth God's glory.

So much of the principal parts of Invocation, Petition and Thanksgiving. Are we limited and bound in certain words, how and wherein to pray?
No verily: but we have a prescript rule and perfect pattern of Prayer of all kinds, left us in that Prayer which our Savior Christ taught his Disciples, (and in them all succeeding ages) called the Lord's prayer.

What is the Lord's prayer?
It is an absolute prayer in it self, and a Prayer giving a perfect direction to frame all other prayers by.

It is thought by some not to be a Prayer, but only a platform to direct all our prayers by.
It is both a Prayer, which we both may and ought to pray; and also a platform of Prayer, whereunto we are to conform, and by which we ought to square all ours. And therefore as St. Matthew biddeth us pray after this sort; (Mat. 6. 9.) so St. Luke biddeth us say; Our Father, &c. (Luk. 11. 2,) the one propounding it as the most perfect platform to be imitated; the other. as the most excellent form, to be used of all Christians.

What is the platform propounded in this Prayer, whereunto we ought to look?
It teacheth both the manner how to pray, and the matter for which to pray. It teacheth us in all our prayers to whom, and through whom, and for what to pray; also what difference to make of the things we ask, and with what affection we are to come unto God in Prayer.

What are the words of the Lord's Prayer?
They are thus set down in the sixth Chapter of the Gospel according to St. Matthew: After this manner therefore pray ye: Our father which art in heaven, &c.

What do you observe here in general?
That Prayer is to be made in a language which we understand, for our Savior Christ taught his disciples here in a tongue which they understood, and not in an unknown language. Which condemneth the practice of the Church of Rome, which teach the people to pray in an unknown tongue: contrary to Christ's practice here, and the will of God who commandeth us to serve him with all our hearts, and therefore with our understanding as well as our affection.

What are the parts of this Prayer?
They are three. 1. Preface of compellation, for entrance into prayer; in the first words, Our Father which art in heaven? 2. A body of Petitions, containing the matter of Prayer in the words following. 3. A conclusion (or shutting up) for the confirmation and close of prayer; in the last words, For thine is the kingdom, &c.

What gather you of this, that there is a preface?
That Christian men are not to come impudently or rashly, but with preparation. Eccl. 5. 1. Psal. 26. 6. Exod. 3. 5. For the Angel of the Lord standeth at the entry, to strike with

hardness and blindness, &c. those that come not with preparation. And if we make preparation before we come to an earthly Prince, and bethink us of our words and gesture: how much more ought we to do it, when we come before the Prince and Lord of heaven and earth?

How are we to prepare ourselves?
Not only to put off our evil affections. (1 Tim. 2. 8.) but even our honest and (otherwise in their due time) necessary cogitations; as the cares and thoughts of our particular vocations, as of house or family.

What does the preface put us in mind of?
1. Of him to whom we pray. 2. Of our own estate in prayer: That we come unto God as to our Father, with boldness and yet with reverence of his Majesty that filleth the heavens.

What are we taught concerning him to whom we must pray?
That God and God only (not any Saint or Angel) is to be prayed unto. Psal. 73. 25: For although there be other fathers besides God, and others in heaven besides him: yet there is none which is our father in heaven but God alone. Beside that this being a perfect platform and pattern of all prayers, it is evident that all prayers (as in other things so in this) must be framed unto it.

Why do you here name the Father?
Because discerning the persons, we pray to the Father secretly understanding that we do it in the mediation of his Son, by the working of the holy Ghost; and so come to the first person in the Trinity, by his Son, through the holy Ghost, which form is to be kept for the most part, although it be also lawful to pray unto Christ, or to his blessed Spirit particularly: (Acts 7. 59. 2 Corin. 13. 14.) if so be that in our understanding we do conjoin them, as those which cannot be separated in any actions, either belonging to the life to come, or pertaining to this life.

Why must we pray to the Father in the mediation of Jesus Christ his Son?
Because God being displeased for sin, we can have no dealing with him, but only by the means of his Son, in whom he is well pleased; (Mat. 3. 17.) and in whom alone we have liberty to call him Father. Gal. 4. 5.

Why is it required that we pray by the working of the Holy Ghost?
Because the Holy Ghost assureth us that he is our Father: and whereas we know not what to pray, nor how to pray, the Holy Ghost does teach us both.

What must we be persuaded of, and how must we be affected in Prayer?
Partly concerning

Ourselves:
    1. We must be truly humbled: which is wrought in us, with a certain persuasion.
        1. Of our sinful misery and unworthiness to be helped.
        2. Of the glorious Majesty of God in heaven that must help us.
    2. We must have a certain confidence we shall be heard: and this is wrought in us by faith, being persuaded that
        1. God loveth us as his own Children in our Lord Jesus Christ.
        2. Our Father being God Almighty, he is able to do whatsoever he will in heaven and in earth.

Others:
    1. That all God's people pray for us.

2. We must be persuaded, that it is our bounden duty to pray for others as well as ourselves.

Why does our Savior direct us to give such Titles unto God in the entrance of our Prayers?
That thereby we may increase and strengthen our faith in God; considering what he is to us, to whom we are about to pray. Heb. 11. 6.

What are we taught to consider from this, that we are taught to call God Father?
That God in Christ is become our Father, and giveth us both the privilege, (John 1. 12.) and spirit of sons, (Gal. 4. 6.) so to call him.

What ariseth from hence?
First, confidence in his fatherly love and compassion towards us, as his children; (Psal. 103. 13.) with assurance of obtaining our suits and desires. 1 Joh. 5. 14. 15. For as young children desire to come unto their Fathers bosom or to sit upon the knee or in the Mothers lap, so we by prayer do creep into the Lord's bosom, and (as it were) do stand between the Lord's legs: [Deut. 33. 3.] coming with boldness to him, as to our merciful Father, whose bowels are larger in pitiful affection than any parents, yea than the mothers towards the most tender child; if we come with faith and assurance that he, will grant what we require. For if parents will give good things to their children when they ask them; much more will the Lord give his spirit to them that ask it of him without doubting. Mat. 7. 11. Luk. 11. 13. And this doubting is the cause why many go away so often from prayer without profit and comfort. James 1. 5. Which overthroweth the long and idle prayers of the Papists, who have not assurance of God's love towards them in the thing they demand.

Secondly, necessity of duty, on our parts; that we both reverence, (Mal. 1. 6.) and imitate him, (Mat. 5. 45.) as our Father. Eph. 5. 1. 1. Pet. 1. 17.

Thirdly; that to come in any other name than our Savior Christ's, is abominable: which was figured in Moses, (Exod. 24. 2. & 19, 20. 21. & 20. 19.) and Aaron, (Levit 16. 17.) but is notably set forth of the Apostle, 1 Tim. 2. 5. Therefore it is abominable to come by Saints, as in Popery they do.

What is to be considered by this, that we are directed to call him [our] Father?
The nature of faith, which is to apply it home to himself. Joh, 20. 28. Gal. 2. 20. Mat. 27. 46. Also that our Savior Christ is the natural Son, as we his sons by grace and adoption.

May not a man say in his prayer, My Father?
Yes verily: and that with warrant of our Savior Christ's example. Mat. 26. 39, 4, 2.

Why then are we taught here to say, Our Father?
As the word Father directeth us to meditate upon the relation between God and ourselves: so the word Our directeth us to meditate upon the relation between ourselves, and so many as are or may be the Children of the same Father with us.

What does this put us in mind of?
First, that we must at all times maintain or renew, love and peace one with another: but especially when we make our prayers, we must come in love, as one brother loveth another; and therefore reconcile ourselves, if there be any breach 1 Tim. 2. 8. Isa. 1. 15. Mat. 5. 23. &c. Secondly, that we are bound to pray, and to be suitors to our God and Father one for another, as well as for ourselves: (Jam. 5. 16.) that every one

praying for all, and all for every one, we may jointly increase and enjoy the benefit of the common stock of prayers laid in the hands of God.

Whereto do the words following direct us, when we say, Which art in Heaven?
To the meditation of the glory, powerful providence, wisdom, and holiness of God; in which regards he is said to dwell in the high and holy place: (Psa 11, 4 Isa. 57. 15.) not that he is excluded from earth, or included in heaven or any place, (who filleth all places. Jer. 23. 24. yea, whom the heaven of heavens is not able to contain: 1 Kings 8. 27.) but First, because his wisdom, power, and glory appeareth most evidently in the rule of the heavens, as of the most excellent bodily creatures by which inferior natures are ruled. Psa. 19. 1, & 8. 3. & 104. 1, &c.

Secondly, for that in heaven he does make himself, and his goodness known to the Angels and blessed Spirits of men immediately, and without the helps and aids which we have.

Thirdly, because he communicateth himself and his goodness more powerfully to them than to us: and so God is said to be present in the Temple, and in the Elect.

Fourthly, because there, and not on earth, we should now seek him (Psal. 123. 1. Col. 3. 1, 2.) where also we hope, another day to dwell with him in the same happy fellowship, which now the holy Angels and blessed souls do enjoy: Which teacheth us not to have any fleshly conceit, but to have our cogitations above any worldly matter.

Fifthly, to teach us that as we are to come boldly unto him as to a Father, so we also are to come with humility, and reverence of his Majesty, who is so high above us: we wretched men being as worms crawling upon the earth and he sitting in great Majesty in the highest heavens. Eccl. 4. 16. & 5. 1.

Sixthly, to teach us to pray not only reverently, but also fervently before him, so directing and lifting up our hearts to Almighty God that our prayers may ascend into heaven. 2 Chron. 32. 20.

Seventhly, to increase our confidence in him, who is both ready and able to do all things for us. That acknowledging him to ride on the heavens for our help, able (as in heaven) to do for us whatsoever (as a father) he will; (Psa. 115. 3.) we may with full confidence in his power and love, ask every good thing of him. Psa. 2. 8. Luk. 11. 13.

Thus much of the Preface: now are we come to the prayer it self, What is general unto it?
That our affections, with zeal and earnestness ought to wait and attend on prayer: which appeareth by the shortness of all the petitions.

What is declared hereby?
The great affection we should have to the things we come for, which giveth a check to our cold prayers, where the understanding is without the affection, and (as it were) the sacrifice without the heavenly fire to lift it up and make it mount into heaven, both in public and private prayers.

[38TH HEAD.]

So much of the attention general to the Prayer. What are the parts thereof?
A form of Petition and of Thanksgiving.

What is taught hereby?
First, that whenever we come unto God in Petition, we are also to give him thanks. (Phil 4. 6. Luk. 17. 17, 18.) things not to be severed, and means to make way for further graces and benefits to be obtained. Secondly, that it is a fault of us (when we are distressed) in public prayer to come unto God in Petition, but not to return thanksgiving for our benefits received.

How many Petitions are there in the Lord's Prayer?
Six (equally divided, as it were, into two Tables:) whereof three do concern God, as does the first Table of the Law; three do concern ourselves and our neighbors, as does the second Table. For in the three first we make request for those things that concern God's Majesty, whose glory and service we are to prefer before our own good: (John 12. 27. 28.) in the three latter, for those things that concern the necessity of man, and our own welfare, which we must refer to the former. (Psal. 50. 15.) So that by the very order of the Petitions we learn this instruction; that we must and ought first to think upon God's glory before any thing that appertains or belongs to us: and that we should seek the service of God before our own good; (Joh. 12. 27, 28.) yea, and prefer the glorifying of the name of God before our own salvation: (Rom. 9. 3.) as also by the order of the Commandment, which being divided into two Tables, the first concerneth the worship of God, the second ourselves.

What observe you from this?
Our hypocrisy: for were it not for ourselves, and our wants, we would not come to God at all in prayer: as in Popery, all their prayers are for themselves, and their salvation &c. Whereas this word (thy) in all these Petitions, does shut forth the consideration of ourselves, to the end that we might have our minds altogether fastened upon the service of God.

What further observe you proper to those Petitions that concern the glory of God?
That as they must be begged in the first place, so must they likewise be performed with further zeal of spirit and earnestness of affection; as may be gathered, in that they are propounded without any band or coupling of one with another.

How are these three Petitions divided?
Thus: the first concerneth God's glory it self: the other two the things whereby God is glorified; as when this Kingdom cometh, and his Will is done.

What are the words of the first Petition?
Hallowed be thy Name. Mat. 6. 9. Luke 11. 2.

What is the sum of this Petition?
That in all things God may be glorified. That he, who in himself, his word and works, is most holy and glorious; may be acknowledged and honored for such, by us. Psa. 96. 8. 1 Pet. 2. 9.

Why is this Petition set before all?
Because it is that which ought to be dearest unto us; and for that all things are to be referred unto it. Prov. 16. 4. 1 Cor. 10. 31.

What is to be considered for the further opening of this Petition?
First, the meaning of the words apart; then of them together.

What is meant by the word, Name?
By the Name of God, we are to understand God himself, (1 Kings 5. 5. Isa. 26. 8.) as he maketh known to us the fame and glory of his nature, otherwise unconceivable (Gen. 32. 29.) For the Name of God in the Scripture signifieth God himself (because the nature of a thing is taken for what it is the name of: as (Acts 1. 15.) is Essence, and all things by which he is known unto us.

What are those Names, whereby God is made known unto us?
First, his Titles: as Jehovah, Elohim, the Lord of Hosts, and such like. Exod. 3. 14. and 6. 3. Secondly, his Attributes and Properties; as his wisdom, power, love, goodness mercy, justice, truth (Exod. 33. 18, 19, &c. & 34. 5, 6, &c) which being essential in him, are for our capacity expressed under the name of such qualities in us and are called the names of God, because as names serve to discern things, by, so God is known by these things. Thirdly, his memorials; signified by his name, because he getteth glory by them.

What are those Memorials?
First, the works and actions of God: as the Creation and Government of the world, (Psal. 104.) but especially, the work of Redemption. Psal. 19. 14. Secondly, the things that belong unto God: as his Worship, Word, Sacrament and discipline, but especially his Word (Psal. 138. 2. & 19. 7, &c.) which is the book of grace, and the box of ointment, out of which the sweet savor of his name is most effectually poured. Can. 1. 2, 3.

What is meant by the word; Hallowed?
Sanctified and reverenced. For to hallow, is to set apart a thing from the common use to some proper end: and therefore to hallow the name of God, is to separate it from all profane and unholy abuse, to a holy and reverend use.

Can any man add any thing unto God's holiness?
No we cannot add any holiness unto God, or take any from him. But as God is holy in his Proprieties and Actions, and also in his Ordinances, both in the Church and Common-wealth; so we desire they may be (and that not only by ourselves, but also by all men) acknowledged and reputed as they are worthy in themselves to be reputed and accounted. And in this respect only are we said to hallow his name, when we acknowledge it and honor it for such: (Psal. 96. 7, 8.) thereby (as it were) setting the Crown of holiness and honor upon the head of God. Contrariwise, failing so to do, we are guilty of the profanation of God's holy name: not that he can receive any pollution from us, but only as the man that lusteth after a chaste woman, is said by our Savior to be guilty of adultery with her, though she remaineth in her self spotless and undefiled. Mat. 5. 28.

May none else be glorified but the name of God?
When it is said, Hallowed be thy name: there is noted, that no glory or honor should be given to any thing in the world, but to the name of God, (Isa. 42. 8. 48. 11) further then they are instruments, whereby we may arise to the glorifying of it: for God will not give his glory to any other thing, no not to the manhood of our Savior Christ.

What is to be considered in the words together?
That it is a singular benefit of God to admit us to the sanctifying of his name and (as it were) to set the Crown (which is his glory) upon his head, and to hold it there: especially seeing he is able himself alone to do it; and when he would use others thereto he hath so many Legions of Angels to do it, yea, can raise up stones to do it.

What do you then ask of God in this Petition?
That as God is glorious in himself, so he may be declared and made known unto men. That therefore God would have himself known and acknowledged by all men, but especially by my self, to be most holy. That whether we speak, think, or any way use his name, properties works or Word, we may do it holily and with all reverence. That his Wisdom, power, goodness, mercy, truth, righteousness, and eternity, may more and more be imparted unto me and other of God's people. That he may be acknowledged just, wise, &c. in all his works, even in his ordaining of some to eternal life, and other some to everlasting damnation. That his infinite justice, and infinite mercy over all his creatures (but especially over his Church) may be reverenced and adored by all men, but specially by my self. That the name of God may be reverently and holily used of all men, but especially of my self. That when the glory of God cometh in question between my self and any thing that belongeth unto me, I may prefer that unto this. Finally, that God would vouchsafe to plant and increase in me and others such grace whereby his name may be glorified.

What are those graces for which we pray here in particular?
1. Knowledge of God: (Psal. 100. 3. & 67. 2.) that God would give us the knowledge of himself, his Word, and Works; for we cannot glorify his name unless we know it.

2. Belief of his Word: that we and others may sanctify God in believing his word, how unlikely soever. John. 3. 33. Wherefore Moses and Aaron are said not to have sanctified the name of God, in that they believed not. (Num. 20. 12.) Contrariwise Abraham glorified God in believing. Rom. 4. 20.

3. Fearing the Lord alone, and not men. That the Lord be our fear Isa. 8. 12, 13. 1 Pet. 3. 14, 18.

4. Humility (for ourselves and others) without which we cannot glorify God, as it is meet. Psal. 115. 1. 2 Sam. 7. 18 Psal. 8. 4. 5. and 144. 3. Luk. 1. 48.

5. Patience, (arising from thence:) whereby we do willingly submit ourselves unto the correcting hand of God, as Eli, (1 Sam. 3. 18) and Hezekiah. (Isa. 39. 8.)

6. Thankfulness: that we may praise him for his benefits more particularly. Where we are to hallow God's name, as well by praising it for the benefits we have received, as for the wonderful works in the creation, and government of the world, the Church especially.

7. Lips opened, and tongues tuned to speak of him with reverence. Psal. 51. 15. & 44. 1. & 45. 1.

8. A life so ordered, that men may say, he is a holy God, who by his grace maketh us an holy people. Mat. 5. 16. 1 Pet. 2. 9. Tit. 2. 10. That, according as we know the virtues of our good God, so the fruits of them may appear in ours and all God's peoples lives; that so his name may be honored and praised, and he may get glory by the godly conversation of us and others.

What do we pray against in this Petition?
We pray against all ignorance of holy things we should know, (Hos. 8. 13.) against infidelity and want of good works, whereby God wants of his glory. We pray against all lofty and high things, that hinder that God only cannot be exalted; (Isa. 2. 11, 12, 13, 14, 15.) especially the pride of our hearts, which we are to confess and lament. (Prov. 8. 13.) We pray against all false Religion, all Profaneness, impatience, unthankful

ness, (Rom. 1. 21.) &c. those tongue-worms of swearing, blasphemy, and irreverent speaking of God; (Exod. 20. 7.) together with all wickedness and ungodliness, whereby God's name is dishonored. In a word, we pray that God would remove, and root out of our hearts, tongues and lives, all such vices, by and for which his name is dishonored, especially an evil and scandalous life, for which the name of God, and his religion, is evil spoken of in the world. Rom. 2. 23. 24.

What does this teach us?
Our dullness is hereby condemned; who by nature are so ill disposed to glorify God, and to use his name holily and reverently.

What is to be considered in the second Petition?
Let thy Kingdom come. Mat. 6. 10. Luke. 11. 2. One of the means how to have the name of God sanctified; which is a dependence of the former Petition.

What is the sum of this Petition?
That God may reign in our hearts and not sin: and that the Kingdom of our Lord Jesus Christ, both by the inward working of his spirit, and also by the outward means, may be enlarged daily until it be perfected at the coming of Christ to judgment. That the Kingdom of sin and Satan being more and more abolished, (Acts 26. 18. Col. 1. 13.) Christ may now reign in our hearts by grace, (Col. 3. 15, 16.) and we with him for ever in glory. 2 Tim. 2. 12.

What is meant here by Kingdom?
That government which our Savior Christ exerciseth, first in this world, then in the last day, both in the whole Church and in every member thereof. For by the Kingdom of God we must understand here, not so much that universal sovereignty which, as Creator, he exerciseth over all creatures, disposing them all to their proper ends for his glory: (Isa. 6. 5. Psalm. 95. 3. &c. as the spiritual regiment (Psalm. 110. 2. 1 Cor 15. 25.) of the Church (and of all things for the good of the Church) wherein God hath appointed Christ to be the King (Psal. 2. 6. Hos. 3. 5) the Saints his Subjects, Revel 15. 3.) the word his Law, (Job. 22. 22.) the Angels and all creatures his servants, (Heb. 1. 6) the Ministers his Heralds and Ambassadors; (2 Cor. 5. 20.) finally, the Devils kingdom. (Mat. 12. 26.) that is, wicked Angels and men (enemies to the Kingdom of Christ, Luk. 19. 17.) his footstool. Psalm. 110. 1.

How is this Kingdom said to come?
First, in regard of means, where the word of the Kingdom is published. Mat. 12. 28. & 13. 19 Mark. 4. 15. Second, in regard of efficacy, where from the heart obedience is yielded. Rom. 6. 17. Third, in regard of perfection it hath these degrees:

> 1. Increase of grace in the time of this life. Mat 13. 8.
> 2. The translation of blessed souls into heaven, in the moment of death. Luk. 23. 42, 43.
> 3. Finally, the full redemption and glorification of the Saints in soul and body, in the life to come Mat. 25, 34.

What do we then desire concerning the Kingdom of God, in this Petition?
We pray either for that he exerciseth in this world, or for that he exerciseth in the world to come, called the kingdom of glory.

How many sorts are there of that Kingdom he exerciseth in this world?
Two. First, that he exerciseth over all men, and other creatures, called the Kingdom of power. Secondly, that he exerciseth over the Church; called the Kingdom of grace.

What desire we of God concerning the government he exerciseth over all Creatures?
That he would govern all the creatures, both in the natural course of things, and in the civil and domestic government of men, yea, in the rule of the Devils themselves, in such sort as they may serve for the good of his Church. Psal. 97. 1. Mat. 6. 13. John 17. 2.

What desire we concerning his government in the Church?
That it may be here in this world enlarged, and that it may be accomplished in the last day. Psal. 122. 6. Isa. 62. 7.

What do we desire for the enlargement of it in this world?
That by Christ the head of the Church, God would govern his people to the perfect salvation of the elect, and to the utter destruction of the reprobate, whether open rebels, or feigned and hollowed-hearted Subjects.

What great need is there that we should pray for the Kingdom of God?
For that being taught that we should pray that the Kingdom of God may come, hereby we are put in mind of another Kingdom of Satan and darkness, which opposeth strongly against his Kingdom Mat. 14. 24, 25. 1 Cor. 6. 14, 15, 16.

Why, all men do naturally abhor Satan, even to the very name of him.
They do in words and show: but when they do his will, live under his laws, delight in his works of darkness, subject themselves to the Pope and other his instruments; they are found indeed to love him as their father, and honor him as their Prince, whom in words they would seem to abhor. For as the same men are affirmed by our Savior Christ to approach unto God with their lips and to have their hearts far from him: (Mat. 15. 8.) so are they in their lips far from Satan, but near him in their hearts.

What other oppositions are there against God's Kingdom?
The flesh, and the world. Gal. 5. 16, 17.

What are the means we ought to pray for, that our Savior Christ may govern his Church in this world thereby?
Inward, and outward.

What inward things do we pray for?
That God would give his holy Spirit, as the chief and principal means whereby our Savior Christ gathereth and ruleth his Church, conveying his Spirit of knowledge and good motions into his people: and consequently, we pray against the motions and temptations of Satan and of our own flesh.

What are the outward things we pray for?
The means whereby the Spirit is conveyed: namely, the Word, and the dependence thereof, the Sacraments and Censures.

What pray we for concerning the Word?
That it being the scepter of Christ's Kingdom, the rod and standard of his power (Psal. 110. 2, Isa. 12. 4, 10.) and called the word of the kingdom, (Mar. 1. 14) and the kingdom of heaven; (Mat. 13.) may have free passage every where, (2 Thes. 3. 1.) and be gloriously lifted up and advanced: and, it only having place, all not agreeable thereunto, all traditions and inventions of men may be rejected.

What pray we for concerning the Sacraments?
That as they are the Seals of God's promises and the whole Covenant of grace: so they may be both ministered and received in that pureness and sincerity, which is according to this Word; and all false Sacraments and sacrifices put under foot.

What pray we for concerning the Censures?
That not only private persons, but the whole Church may be ruled by the line of God's Word; that so well doers may be advanced, and evil doers censured and corrected, according to the degree of their fault: and therefore that all either impunity or tyrannous tortures of conscience, may be taken away.

What further do we pray or?
That God would furnish his Church with all such Officers as he approveth; that being endued with special gifts may be both able and willing to execute their charge diligently and faithfully.

What further desire you in this Petition?
That where these things are only begun, they may be perfected; and that every Church may be polished and garnished, that Zion may appear in her perfect beauty; and so the Jews may be called, and so many of the Gentiles as belong unto Christ; and the contrary enemies may be either converted or confounded.

What do we pray for, in respect of every member of the Church?
Even as poor captives are always creeping to the prison door, and laboring to get off their bolts; so we, out of a sorrowful feeling of the spiritual bondage we are in to Satan and sin, pray that the kingdom of Christ may come, and be advanced in every one of our hearts, in justice, righteousness, peace, and joy in the Holy Ghost: (Rom. 14. 17.) that as Kings unto God, we may subdue within us all those either opinions or affections that rise up and rebel against God.

What then are the particulars concerning the kingdom of grace, that we do crave of God, in this Petition?
1. That Satan's kingdom may be abolished, (Acts 26. 18.) the bands of spiritual captivity loosed, (2 Tim. 2. 26. Col. 1. 13) the power of corruption that maketh us like well of our bondage, abated, (Gal, 5. 24) the instruments of Satan's tyranny (as the Turk, and Pope, and all such out-laws from Christ) defeated. 2. Thes. 2. 8.

2. That it would please God to gather out of every part of the world those that belong to the election.

3. That God for the gathering of them would raise up faithful and painful Ministers in every part of the world where there are any which belong to his election. That all loiterers, and tongue-tied Ministers being removed. (Isa. 56. 10; 11.) faithful and able watchmen may be set over the flock of Christ, (Mat. 9. 38.) with sufficient encouragement of maintenance, countenance, protection, &c. and the word of God may be freely preached every where. 2. Thes. 3. 1.

4. That it would please God with the blessing of his Spirit to accompany the word; so that it may be of power to convert those that belong unto him.

5. That it would please God every day more and more to increase the holy gifts, and graces of his holy Spirit in the hearts of those whom he hath already called effectually.

6. That the Lord, by his Word and Spirit, would rule in the hearts and lives of his Saints, (Col. 3. 15. 16.) making them Kings, in part, by overcoming the corruption, which is in the world through lust. 2 Pet 1. 4

7. That God would raise up godly and religious Magistrates, which should further and countenance his worship as much as in them lieth.

8. That the eyes of all men, especially Princes, may be opened to see the filthiness of the whore of Babylon, (Rev. 17. 16.) and the true beauty of pure Religion, and of the Spouse of Christ, Isa. 60. 3.

9. That God would banish and root out of his Church all those things which may hinder the proceeding of his kingdom in the hearts of those that belong unto him.

10. Finally that he would finish the Kingdom of grace, calling his elect uncalled, (Gen. 9. 27. Rom. 9. 25, 26.) confirming such as stand, (2 Thes. 2. 17.) raising the fallen, (Jam. 5. 15, 16.) comforting the afflicted, (Isa. 61. 3.) and hasten the kingdom of glory.

What do we desire of God in this Petition concerning the Kingdom of glory, and our good in the world to come?
First, that God would be pleased to take us in due time (so soon as he does see it to make for his glory and our good) out of this sinful and conflicting life, into peace with Christ, and translate us unto the kingdom of heaven. Phil. 1. 23. Second, that the number of the elect being accomplished, the final dissolution of all things may come: That God would hasten the second coming of his Son to judgment for the elects sake, who with singular love and affection long for it, saying Come Lord Jesus, come quickly: Revel. 22. 20. 2 Tim. 4. 8.) that we, and all his chosen, may obtain; full salvation; and enjoy the fruition of that glory prepared for us before the beginning of the world. Third, that God would get himself glory by the final confusion of his enemies.

What are the words of the third Petition?
Thy will be done in earth as it is in Heaven Mat. 6. 10. Luke 11. 2:

What is the sum of this Petition?
That God would grant us that we may voluntarily and willingly subject ourselves unto him, and his providence: that renouncing the will of Satan, and our own corrupt inclination, 2 Tim. 2. 26. 1 Pet. 4. 2.) and rejecting all things that are contrary to the will of God, we may do his will; not as we will, nor grudgingly, but readily. (Psal. 119. 60. and heartily, (Col. 3. 23.) following in our measure the example of the Angels and Saints that are in heaven: (Psa. 103. 20.) finally, that obedience may be given to Christ, in ruling us, until we be as the holy Angels.

What is meant by this word [Thy:]
Hereby we exclude all wills opposed to, or diverse from the will of God; whether the will of Satan, (2 Tim. 2. 26.) or our own (1 Pet. 4. 2.) naturally corrupt and enthralled to Satan; yea, whatsoever lawful intentions or desires, repugnant to the secret will of God. (2 Sam. 2. 7. James 4. 15.) For when we pray for obedience to God's will, we pray that all wills of wicked Angels (Zac. 3. 3.) and men. (Psa. 140. 8.) as contrary to the will of God, may be disappointed: we desire also the suppression of our own will, as that which being prone to all sin, as a match to take fire, is naught and repugnant to the will of God; so far are we from having any free-will naturally to do that which is good (Psa. 86, 11. & 119. 37. Ge. 6. 5. & 8. 21. Rom. 8. 6. & 7. 24.) Which we must bewail both in ourselves and others: (2 Pet. 2. 7. Ezek. 9. 4.) freely acknowledging, that we

cannot of ourselves do the will of God but by his assistance; and desiring grace, that we may obey his will, and not the lusts of our flesh.

How manifold is the will of God?
Twofold: (Deut. 29. 29.) First, his secret and hidden will; whereof the Scripture speaketh thus, If so be the will of God, (1 Pet. 3. 17.) Whereunto are to be referred his eternal counsel, the events of outward things, (Prov. 27. 1.) times and seasons, &c. Acts 1. 7. Second, his manifest will, which is revealed and made known unto us in the Word; both in his Promises, which we are to believe, and in his Precepts and Commandments, which (as conditions of obedience, in way of thanksgiving annexed unto the promises) we are to perform.

What will are we to understand in this Petition?
Not so much that part, which God keepeth secret from us, as that part hereof, which he hath revealed in his Word, wherein is set down what we ought to do, or leave undone.

How does that appear?
First, because it is unlawful to search or inquire into the secret will of God, and impossible for man to know it until it come to pass: whereas to the doing of this will, knowledge is requisite. Second, no man can resist or withstand God's secret will, neither is it any thank for us to accomplish it. Acts 4. 28. Third, there are no promises for the performing the secret will of God: seeing a man may do it and perish; as Pilate, &c. Fourth, God purposeth many things in his secret will, for which it is not lawful for us to pray.

What then must we especially pray for in the secret will of God?
That when God bringeth any thing to pass by his secret will, which is grievous to our natures, we may with patience and contentment submit our wills to his will. Acts 21. 14.

What do we ask of God in this Petition, concerning his revealed will?
First, that we may know his will; without the which we cannot do it. Second, that we may do his will, being known, and show ourselves obedient to our heavenly Father and Lord. Third, that he would bestow upon us the gifts and graces of his Spirit; that so our hearts being by grace set at large, strengthened, and directed, (Psa. 119. 32, 36.) we may be enabled to do his will. Fourth, that he would remove from us all things that shall hinder us from knowing his will and putting it in execution: as ignorance of the revealed will of God, (Psa. 119. 18.) rebellion, disobedience, murmuring, &c. (1 Sam. 15. 22, 23.) all pretences and dispensations, or powers presuming to dispense with the will of God. In a word, that so many as are subjects in the kingdom of Christ may do the duty of good subjects, and be obedient to the revealed will of God, seeking his kingdom and his righteousness. (Mat. 6. 33.) so that there is a mutual relation of this petition to the former, where we pray that God may rule; as here, that his rule may be obeyed.

What understand you in this petition by Doing?
Not a good intent only in the heart, or profession of obedience in word and pretence: (Mat. 21. 30.) but an actual and thorough performance of what is required of us. James 1. 25. And therefore we pray here, that the will of God may not only be intended and endeavored, but also accomplished, although it be with grief and smart. Phil. 2. 13. Acts 20. 24.

What is here meant by Earth and Heaven?
By Earth, those that are in earth; and by Heaven, those that are in heaven. For here we propound to ourselves the patterns of the Angels and blessed souls, who being freed from all mixture of corruption, do in their kind perfectly obey God. (Psal. 103. 20, 22.)

Whereby we learn, that our obedience should be done most humbly, willingly, readily, cheerfully, and wholly; (not doing one, and leaving another undone) even as the will of God is done by the Angels: (Mat. 18. 10.) who therefore are set forth winged, to show their speediness. Isa. 6. 2 and round footed, to express their readiness to all and every Commandment of God. Ezek. 1. 7.

But seeing we are sinful, and the Angels; holy how can we imitate them?
We desire to imitate them in the manner, though we know we cannot equal them in measure and degree of obedience. And hereby we are taught that we should endeavour to the like holiness, and so grow therein daily more and more till we be like unto them: not that we can perform it to the full as they do. As also in this regard God himself saith; Be ye as I am holy: (Levit. 11. 44. 1 Pet. 1. 16.) and yet it were absurd to say or think, that any man could come to the holiness of God, whose holiness he is commanded to follow. And this answereth to our desire of hastening the Lord's coming in the former Petition.

What then do we desire here for the manner of performance of God's will?
That we may (after the heavenly pattern aforementioned) willingly without constraint or repugnancy, (Psal. 110. 3.) speedily without delay, (Psal. 113. 60,) sincerely without hypocrisy, (Deut. 5. 28, 29. fully without reservation (Psa. 119. 6.) and constantly without intermission (Psal. 119, 112.) believe the promises of mercy, and obey the precepts of holiness. And so all unwilling, and by law only enforced obedience is here condemned: and we enjoined to perform our service with delight, Joy and alacrity.

[39TH HEAD.]

Thus far of the three first petitions, for things concerning God. To come to the three latter, that concern ourselves, and our neighbors: what are we generally to note in them?
First, the order and dependence they have from the former three concerning God: whereby we are taught, that there is no lawful use of these Petitions which follow, or any of them, unless we first labor in the former Petitions concerning the service of God. For we are then hallowed, and not till then, (Luk. 17. 7. &c.) to seek good things for ourselves, when we have first minded and sought those things that concern the glory of God: because unto godliness only the promises of this life and that which is to come, are entailed. 1 Tim. 4. 8.

What further?
That as in the former the word [Thy] did only respect God: so in these following, by these words [Our and Us] we learn to have a fellow-feeling of the miseries and necessities of others; and therefore in care to pray for them; which is one trial of the true spirit of prayer.

Is there any else common to them all.
That in all these Petitions, under one thing expressed, other things are figuratively included; and under one kind all the rest, and all the means to obtain them, are comprehended: as shall appear.

How are these petitions divided?
The first concerneth mans body and the things of this life the two last concern the soul and things pertaining to the life to come. For all which we are taught to depend on God: and namely, according to the order observed in the Creed, (called the Apostles,) 1. On

the providence of God the Father, our Creator, for our nourishment, and all outward blessings. Second, On the mercy of Christ, our Savior, for pardon of our sins. Third, On the power and assistance of the holy Spirit, our sanctifier, for strength to resist and subdue all temptations unto evil.

What observe you out of the order of these Petitions?
That we have but one Petition for outward things, as less to be esteemed: but for spiritual things two, as about which our care is to be doubled: (Mat. 6. 33.) To teach us how small earthly things are to be accounted in regard of heavenly: and therefore that our prayers for the things of this life should be short, and further drawn out for the things that belong to the life to come.

Why then is the Petition for the temporal things put before the Petitions for the spiritual?
The first place is given to outward things, not because they are chiefest: but because,

First, it is the manner of the Scriptures, commonly to put things first that are soonest dispatched. Secondly, that outward things may be helps to enable us to spiritual duties: (Gen. 28. 20, 21.) and that in having aforehand earthly things, we may be the more ready and earnest to entreat for heavenly things: so our Savior Christ healed the bodily diseases, to provoke all men to come unto him for the cure of the spiritual. Thirdly, that outward things may be as steps or degrees, whereby our weak faith may the better ascend to lay claim and hold on spiritual graces: (Acts 17. 27. 28.) that by experience of the smaller things, we may climb up to higher. Whereby their hypocrisy is discovered, which pretend great assurance of forgiveness of sins, and of the keeping from the evil one; whereas they are distrustful for the things of this life. Fourthly, God hath a consideration of our weakness; who are unapt to perform any duties or service to God, if we want the things of this life and that which is requisite to sustain and suffice nature.

To proceed in order: What are the words of the fourth Petition, which concerneth the things of this life?
Give us this day our daily bread. Mat. 6. 11. Luke 11. 3.

What is the sum of this Petition?
That God would provide for us competent means, and such a portion of outward blessings, as he shall see meet for us; (Pro. 30. 8.) not only for our necessities, but also for our Christian and sober delight, according to our calling, and his blessing upon us. Likewise, that he would give us grace to rely ourselves upon his providence for all the means of this temporal life, and to rest contented with that allowance which he shall think fit for us. Phil. 4. 11, 12.

What is meant by Bread?
All outward things, serving both for our necessity, and sober delight: (Pro. 27. 27. & 31. 14.) as health, wealth, food, physic, sleep, raiment, house, &c. together with all the helps and means to attain them; as good Princes, Magistrates, Peace, seasonable weather, and such like: as also the removal of the contrary; as war, plague, famine, evil weather, &c. and the blessing of God upon those creatures which he bestoweth upon us.

What is here to be observed?
That we must desire Bread: not Quails or delicates, not riches and superfluity; (James 4. 3. Num. 11. 4. 5, 6.) but a proportion of maintenance, credit, liberty, &c. convenient for us: (Prov. 30. 8. 1 Tim. 6. 8.) and that with condition;

If God shall see it good for us, or so be his good pleasure: (Mat. 8. 2. Jam. 4.15. 2. Sam. 7. 27.) which exception is a caution proper to this petition for outward things.

What need is there of asking these things?
The frailty of our nature, not able to continue in health scarce one day without these helps, and as it were props to uphold this decayed and ruinous cottage of our mortal bodies; less able to forbear them than many beasts. For seeing there was a necessary use of our meat in the time of innocence, the necessity by our fall is much greater.

What learn you from the word [Give?]
First, that from God all things come: (Psal. 104 27, 28, 29, 30. Acts 14. 17.) which we are ready to ascribe, either to the earth, called the nurse; or to our money, wherewith we buy them; or to our friends, that give them us. As if we should look upon the Steward only, and pass by the Master of the Family; or upon the breast that giveth suck, and neglect the nurse and bottle we drink of, and pass by the giver.

What next?
That although in regard of our labor or buying any thing, it may be called ours: yet we say, Give Lord, both because we are unable by any service or labor to deserve the least crumb of bread or drop of water, (much less the kingdom of heaven and salvation) at the hands of God; (Luk. 17. 10. Gen. 32. 10.) and because our labor and diligence cannot prevail without God's blessing.

What learn you further?
That seeing God giveth to whom he will, and what he will; we learn to be content with whatsoever we have received. Moreover to be thankful for it; seeing all things in regard of God are sanctified by the Word and in regard of ourselves by prayer and thanksgiving (1 Tim. 4. 5.) And last of all, not to envy at other men's plenty, being God's doing. Mat. 20. 15.

What reason is there that they should pray for these things of God, which have them already in their Garners, Cellars, &c. in abundance?
Very great. Because. 1. our right unto the creatures being forfeited in Adam, we have now nothing to plead, but only God's Deed of gift made unto us in Christ, the second Adam, and heir of all things; in whom and with whom all things are conveyed to us; (Psal. 8. 7, 8, 9. Heb. 1. 2. Rom. 8. 32. 1 Cor. 3. 22.) so that although we possess them, yet are we not right owners of them but by faith, which is, declared by prayer for them.

2. The things we do possess, we may easily a hundred ways be thrust from the possession of them, before we come to use them: according to the proverb, that many things came between the cup and lip. 1 Sam. 30. 16, 17. Dan. 5. 5. 2 Kings 7. 17.

3. Although we have the use of them, yet will they not profit us, neither in feeling nor clothing us, unless we have the blessing of God upon them; yea, without the which they may be hurtful and poisonable unto us. Isa. 3. 1. Haggai 1. 6. Prov. 12. 22. Dan. 1. 13, 14, 15. Psal. 78. 30, 31. By all which reasons it may appear, that the rich are as well to use this petition as the poorest: praying therein, not so much for the outward things as God's blessing upon them.

Why do we say give [Us?]
Hereby we profess ourselves petitioners for all men, especially the household of faith: that for the most part every one may have sufficient, and where want is others may be enabled to supply it out of their abundance. 2 Cor. 8. 14.

Thirty-ninth Head

Why do we say, This day, or For this day?
That we are to pray for bread for a day and not for a month, or year, &c. it is to teach us to restrain our care, that it reach not too far: but to rest in God's providence, and present blessing; and therefore not to be covetous. Exod. 16. 19, 20, 21. Prov. 30. 8. So that hereby we profess the moderation of our care, and desire of earthly things: (Mat. 6. 34) with our purpose every day, by labor and prayer, to seek these blessings at the hands of God.

Is it not lawful to provide for children and family?
Yes verily, not only lawful, but also needful. Gen. 41. 34, 35. Acts 11. 28, 29. 2 Cor. 12. 14. 1 Tim. 5. 8. But here our affections are only forbidden to pass measure; as to have a carking and troubling care, seeing the vexation of the day is enough for itself: (Mat. 6. 34.) but to commit our ways unto the Lord, and to roll our matters upon him, who will bring them to pass. Psal. 37. 5. Prov. 16. 3.

Why is bread called ours; seeing that God must give it us?
To teach us, that we must come unto it by our own labor, (Gen. 3: 17. Psal. 128. 1, 2. 1 Thes. 4. 11.) in which respect, he that will not labor, should not eat, (2 Thes. 3. 8. 9. 10.) For that is called our bread, which cometh to us by the blessing of God on our lawful labors, (2 Thes. 3. 12.) so that neither God, nor man can justly impeach us for it.

What is the reason of the word Daily?
By daily bread, or bread instantly, or such as is to be added to our substance we understand such provision, and such a proportion thereof, as may best agree with our nature, charge and calling. Prov. 30, 8. For this word in the Evangelists, (Mat. 6. 11. Luk. 11. 3.) and in the proper language of the spirit of God, is the bread fit for me, or agreeable to my condition. Which is a special lesson for all estates, and callings, to keep them within their bounds not only of necessity, but of Christian and sober delight, and not to ask them for the fulfilling of our fleshly desires. Psal. 104. 15. Prov. 30. 8. 1 Tim. 6. 8. Rom. 13. 14. Jam. 4. 3. Hereby also we are taught, that every day we must require these blessings at God's hands.

What do we beg of God in this Petition?
First, that it would please God to preserve this mortal life of ours, so long as he sees good in his wisdom that it maketh for his glory and our good. Second, that he would bestow upon us all good things needful for the preservation of this life. Third, that he would give us care and conscience to get those needful things by lawful means. Which condemneth: First those that use wicked and unlawful means towards men. Secondly those that go to the Devil. Fourth, that he would give us grace to use painfulness and faithfulness in our callings: that laboring with our hands the thing that is good, we may eat our own bread. Eph. 4. 28. 2 Thes. 3. 12. Fifth, that we may add unto our labor prayer, (that it would please God to bless our labors in getting those things) and thanksgiving, (for them being gotten;) as whereby, on our part, all God's blessings are assured and sanctified unto us. 1 Tim. 4. 4, 5. Sixth, that we may put our confidence not in the means, but in God's providence, and contain ourselves within the care for the means, leaving events unto God's only disposition. Phil. 4. 6. Psa. 37. 5. Seventh, that it would please God to give us faith and grace, as well in want as in abundance, to depend on his providence for outward things. Phil. 4. 12. Eighth, that we may be contented with, and thankful for, that portion of temporal blessings which it shall please the Lord to measure out unto us, as his gift; (Heb. 13. 5. Psa. 16. 6.) not envying such to whom he giveth more.

So much of the Petition for things belonging to this life. What do we desire in those two which belong unto the life to come?
Perfect salvation: standing in the deliverance from the evils past, contained in the former, and those to come, comprised in the latter. By the former we pray for Justification, and by the latter for Sanctification.

To begin then with the former: What are the words of the fifth Petition?
And forgive us our debts, as even we forgive them that are debtors unto us Mat. 6. 12. Luk. 11. 4. Where we are to observe: 1. The Petition for the forgiveness of our sins. 2. The reason added for the confirmation thereof, or, a reason of the persuasion that they are forgiven.

What is the sum of this Petition?
That we may be justified, and be at peace with God. That God giving us a true knowledge and feeling of our sins, would forgive us freely for his Son's sake; and make us daily assured of the forgiveness of our sins, as we are privy to ourselves of the forgiveness of those trespasses which men have offended us by. Job 33. 24. Psal. 35. 3. Jer. 14. 7. Col. 3. 13.

What is meant here by debts?
The comparison is drawn from debtors, which are not able to pay their creditors to whom all we are compared, for that we have all sinned. Therefore by debts we must understand sins (as Saint Luke expoundeth the Metaphor:) and that not in themselves, as branches of the Law of God, (for who would say that we owe and are to pay sin unto God?) but with respect to the punishment, and satisfaction due to God's justice for the offence of sins. For our debt being properly obedience, whereto we are bound under penalty of all the curses of the Law, especially eternal death; (Rom 8. 12. & 13. 8. Gal. 5. 3.) we all in Adam forfeited that bond, whereby the penalty became our debt, and is daily increased in us all by sinning. Luk. 13. 4. Mat. 18. 24 &c. Rom. 6. 23.

What learn you from hence?
Here hence two things are implied: One, a frank and humble confession, that we have sinned both originally and actually; Another that there is no, power in us to make satisfaction for our sins.

What use is there of confession?
Great: for that we have naturally a senselessness of sin; or else being convinced thereof, we are ready to lessen it, and make it light: the contrary whereof appeareth in the Children of God. 1 Joh. 1. 8, 9. Psal. 32. 3, 4. Prov. 28. 13. Job 31. 33. 1 Sam. 15. 19, 20. Psa. 51. 3, 4, 5. 6. Acts 22. 3, 4, 5. 1 Tim. 1. 13, 15,

How can a man confess his sins, being not known, and without number?
Those that are known we must expressly confess; and the other that are unknown, and cannot be reckoned, generally, Psal. 19. 12.

How appeareth it that we are not able to pay this debt?
Because by the Law, as by an obligation, every one being bound to keep it wholly and continually, (Deut. 27. 26. Gal. 3. 10.) so that the breach thereof even once, and in the least point, maketh us debtors presently; (as having forfeited our obligation) there is no man that can either avoid the breach of it, or when he hath broken it, make amends unto God for it: considering that whatsoever he does after the breach, is both imperfectly done; and if it were perfect, yet it is due by obligation of the Law, and therefore cannot go for payment, no more than a man can pay one debt with another.

Thirty-ninth Head

What does it draw with it, that causeth it to be so impossible to be satisfied?
The reward of it, which is everlasting death, both of body and soul, Rom. 6. 23. The greatness, and also number whereof, is declared by the parable of ten thousand talents, which no man is able to pay, being not able to satisfy so much as one farthing.

But are we not able to satisfy some part of it, as a man in great debt is sometimes able to make some satisfaction, especially if he have a day given him?
No, And therefore we are compared to a child new born, red with blood, and not able to wash himself, nor to help himself: (Ezek. 16. 4, 5.) and to captives close shut up in prison and fetters, kept by a strong one; (Luk. 4. 18. Mat. 12. 29.) so that there is as small likelihood of our deliverance out of the power of Satan as that a poor Lamb should deliver it self from the gripes and paws of a Lion.

What is the means to free us from this debt?
By this petition Christ teacheth us, that being pressed with the burden of our sin, we should flee unto the mercy of God, and to entreat him for the forgiveness of our debt, (Mat. 11. 28. Isa. 55. 1.) even the canceling of our obligation, that in Law it be not available against us. In which respect, the preaching of the Gospel is compared to the year of Jubilee, when no man might demand his debt of his brother, Luk. 4. 19.

How shall we obtain this at God's hands?
By the only blood and suffering of Christ, as the only ransom for sin. Contrary to the Papists, who confessing that original sin is taken away by Christ in Baptism, do teach that we must make part of our satisfaction for our actual sins: and therefore some of them whip themselves, as if their blood might satisfy for sin; which is abominable to think.

What do you then understand here by forgiveness?
Such remission, as may agree with God's justice, which will not endure him to be a loser. Wherefore it is forgiveness of us, by taking payment of another. (Job. 33. 24.) even of our surety Jesus Christ, in our behalf. 1 Joh. 2. 2.

What mean you by saying, Us, and Ours?
We include with ourselves, in this petition, as many as are in Christ enabled by a true faith to lay hold on him, and to plead his payment and satisfaction. Psal. 130. 7, 8. & 51. 18.

Do we here pray for the sins of this day, as before for the bread of this day?
Not only for them, but also for all that ever we have done at all times before; to the end, that we might be the further confirmed in the assurance of the remission of all our sins.

What is further to be considered in this Petition?
That as in the former by Bread more was understood, so here under one part of our Justification, to wit, the Remission, or not imputation of sins unto death, by means of the satisfaction of Christ's sufferings, we do also conceive the other part, which is the imputation of his holiness unto life eternal, implied under the former, and inseparably annexed thereto. For as Christ hath taken away our sins by suffering, so he hath also clothed us with his righteousness, by fulfilling of the Law for us. Dan. 9. 24. 2 Cor. 5. 21.

What do we then ask of God in this Petition?
Six things. 1. Grace feelingly to know and frankly and tremblingly to confess without excuse or extenuation, the great debt of our sins, (Psal. 51. 3.) and our utter inability to satisfy for the same, or for the least part thereof. Psal. 103. 3. & 143. 2.

2. That God would bestow upon us Christ Jesus; and for his sake remove out of his sight all our sins, and the guilt and punishment due unto us for the same.

3. The power of saving faith (Luk. 17 5.) to lay hold on the meritorious sufferings and obedience of our Lord Jesus Christ unto our full Justification Isa. 53. 5.

4. The spirit of prayer: that with grief and sorrow for our sins, we may crave pardon for sins and increase of faith. Zech. 12. 10. Mark. 9. 24.

5. An assurance of the forgiveness of our sins: by the testimony of the spirit of Christ, (Ro. 8. 15, 16.) exemplifying, and applying the general pardon of sins, once for all granted unto us at our conversion, unto the several sins and debts of every day and moment of our life.

6. We pray for remission of sin, not as intending, ourselves, to undergo the punishment, or any part thereof, (Jer. 14. 7.) but contrariwise, the whole debt (which is properly the punishment, as hath been showed) may be accepted at the hands of Christ our surety, and we fully discharged and acquitted; so that nothing may remain on our account, but the righteousness of Christ (Phil. 3. 8, 9.) whereby the favor and kingdom of God is purchased for us.

So much of Petition: What is set down in the reason?
A true note to certify us, whether our sins are forgiven us, or not; by that we forgive, or not forgive others that have offended us.

Does this reason bind God to forgive us?
No otherwise than by his gracious and true promise: this being a necessary consequent and fruit of the other, and not a cause. For when we say, As we, or, for we also forgive. &c. we argue with the Lord, not from merit, but from the model of God's grace in us; (Mat. 6. 14, 15.) which being incomparably inferior to the mercy and love of God, and yet disposing us to forgive and let fall (in regard of hatred, or private revenge,) (Rom. 12. 19.) any wrongs and injuries of our brethren against us, may both stir up the compassion of the Lord toward us his children, (Neh. 5. 19.) and assure us of the attaining of this our request. Jam. 2. 13. And therefore that we may not be destitute of so important an argument, (Mar. 11. 25. 1 Joh. 3. 14.) both to plead for mercy with God, and to assure ourselves of success; we desire of God a portion of that mercy, which is so abundant in him, that we may be tenderly affected one towards another, forgiving one another, even as God for Christ's sake forgiveth us. Eph. 4. 32. Col. 3. 13.

But seeing God alone forgiveth sins, Mat. 9. 2. Mat. 2. 7. Job. 14. 4. Isa. 43. 25.) here understood by the word Debt: how is it said that we forgive sins?
We forgive not the sin so far as it is sin against God, but so far as it bringeth grief and hindrance unto us, we may forgive it.

Are we hereby bound to forgive all our debts?
No verily; we may both crave our debts of our debtors, and if there be no other remedy, go to law, in a simple desire of Justice; (yea, in lawful war we may kill our enemies, and yet forgive them) being free from anger and revenge: yet so, that if our debtors be not able to pay, we are bound in duty to forgive them, or at least to have a conscionable regard to their inability.

How is the reason drawn?
From the less to the greater, thus. If we wretched sinners upon earth can forgive others; how much more will the gracious God of heaven forgive us? Mat. 5. 7. & 6. 14,

15. If we, having but a drop of mercy, can forgive others, how much more will God, who is a sea full of grace? 1 Joh. 2. 10. & 3. 14. especially when we by forgiving, sometimes suffer loss; whereas from God by forgiving us nothing falleth away.

Wherein appeareth the inequality between our debt unto God, and mans debt unto us?
First, in the number: our debts to God's being compared to ten thousand; men debts to us, to one hundred. Secondly, in the weight: our debts to God being compared to ten thousand talents, men's debts to us to an hundred pence.

How riseth this great inequality in the weight?
From the great inequality between God and man. For if to strike a King be much more heinous than to strike a poor boy: what is it then to strike God, who is infinitely greater than all the Kings of the earth?

What is to be gathered out of this reason?
That we should daily pray unto God, that he would work in us a merciful affection, and give us loving and charitable hearts towards all men, free from malice and revenge, and make us desirous of their salvation. And that as this is a testimony to our hearts, that God will forgive us, if we for his sake can heartily forgive such as have offended us: so on the other side, if we can show no favor unto others, we can look for none at the hands of God. And therefore to pray without forgiving such as have offended us, were not only a mere babbling, but also a procuring of God's wrath more heavily against us. Which condemneth the hypocrisy of many which assuring themselves in great confidence of the forgiveness of their sins, yet cannot find in their hearts to forgive others; and so by mocking the Lord, bring a curse upon themselves in stead of a blessing: seeing heart, hand, and mouth should go together.

What further learn we by this reason?
That as our forgiveness is nothing, unless the danger of imprisonment be taken away, which inability of paying the debt does draw with it; so it availeth us nothing to have our sins forgiven us of God, unless the punishment also be forgiven. Contrary to the Papists, who teach that sin and the guilt thereof is taken away by Christ; but that we must satisfy for the temporary punishment of it. Wherein they make God like unto those hypocrites (here also condemned,) who will seem to forgive, and yet keep a pique and quarrel in their hearts, watching all occasions of advantage; which say, they will forgive, but not forget.

So much of the former Petition belonging to the life to come. What are the words of the latter; which is the sixth and last Petition of the Lords prayer?
And lead us not into temptation, but deliver us from evil. Mat. 6. 13. Luk. 11. 4.

What is the sum of it?
In it we pray for Sanctification, and strength against our sins. That sin may not only be pardoned unto us but daily mortified in us: (Rom. 6. 1, 2.) and we are either kept by the providence of God from temptations, (Pro 30. 8. 2 Cor. 12. 8.) or preserved by his grace from being hurt thereby: (1 Cor. 10. 13. 2 Cor 12. 9.) And as we pray, that by the power of God we may be strengthened against all temptations: so do we also pray, that by the same power we may be raised up to new obedience. For under one part of sanctification, that is, the avoiding and mortifying of sin, is implied the other part also, which is ability unto new obedience. 2 Cor. 7. 1. Rom. 6. 11.

What is here to be observed in regard of the order; that this Petition consequently followeth upon the former?
That therefore to strengthen our faith for the obtaining of this Petition, we must be assured of the former. That seeing God hath forgiven us our sins. he will be pleased also to mortify our flesh, and quicken our Spirit: which are the two parts of Sanctification, and never severed from true Justification.

What learn you of this?
That we cannot rightly desire God to forgive us our sins, unless we crave also power to abstain from the like in time to come: else our prayer is but babbling. So that here we would be stirred to pray for strength to avoid those sins whereof we craved pardon for before: so far is it, that men should think that they are justified, when they have not so much as a purpose to leave their sin. For who being delivered from a great disease will return to it again, and not rather desire a diet whereby he may escape it? Swine indeed after they are washed, and dogs after their vomit, return, the one to their mire the other to their vomit; (Pro. 26. 11. 2 Pet. 2. 22.) as do also the Papists, who after auricular confession being discharged in their opinion, will go to their sins afresh: but those that are truly washed with the blood of Christ, will never give themselves over to their sins again.

If they cannot return to their vomit, what need have they to pray?
Yes, very great: because God hath ordained prayer one means of keeping them from revolt. And they ought to be so much the more earnest in prayer as they are more subject to be beaten and buffeted with temptations, then others Zech. 1. 11. Luk. 11. 21,

What learn you from hence?
Much comfort in temptations; in that it is a token of God's favor and of pardon of our sins, that we are subject to temptation.

What other cause is there to pray, that we be not led into temptation?
For that the condition of them that are called to the hope of life, will be worse than the state of those that never tasted of the good word of God, if they give themselves to evil: as a relapse in diseases is more dangerous than the first sickness was. Joh. 5. 14. 2 Pet. 2. 22. Mat. 12. 43.

May we pray simply and absolutely against all temptations?
No verily. For first, the best men that ever were (yea, the Son of God himself) were subject to temptations. Secondly, all temptations are not evil, but some are trials of our faith and hope, and oftentimes make for our good. In which regard, they are pronounced blessed that fall into divers temptations. And therefore ought we not to pray simply and without exception to be delivered from them; (Jam. 1. 2. Deut. 8. 2. & 13. 3.) but only from the evil of them.

What then do we pray for concerning them?
That if the Lord will be pleased to take trial of the grace he hath bestowed upon us, either by afflictions, or by occasion of temptation to sin offered us; that we be not given over to them, or overcome by them; but that we may have a good issue, and escape from them: (1 Cor. 10. 13.) and that if either we must go under trouble, or offend the Lord, we may rather choose affliction than sin: Joh. 36. 21.

Why are they called Temptations?
Because by them God trieth our obedience, to notify our faith and patience, both to ourselves and others, whether we will follow him or not: and therefore we may be assured, that so often as we beat back or overcome the temptations, we have as many undoubted testimonies of his love.

Thirty-ninth Head

What is here meant then by the word Temptation?
Sin, and whatsoever things, by the corruption of our nature, are occasions to lead us into sin; as prosperity, adversity, &c. (Prov. 30. 9.) which otherwise simply are not to be numbered among these temptations we desire here to be delivered from.

How many ways may a man be tempted?
Three: 1. By God. 2. By Satan and his wicked instruments. 3. By a man's own corruption.

How may God be said to tempt?
Though God tempteth no man unto evil, as he is tempted of none, (James 1. 13.) yet sometimes he leadeth men into temptations of probation: (Mat. 4. 1. & 6. 13.) and that first, by unusual probatory precepts: as when he commanded Abraham to kill his son. Gen. 22. 1. &c. Secondly, by sending an extraordinary measure of prosperity or adversity. Deut. 8. 16. Thirdly, by letting loose Satan (his band-dog) to buffet and molest the godly, as Saint Paul, (2 Cor. 12. 7.) or to seduce the wicked, as Ahab's Prophets. 1 King. 22. 22. Fourthly, by desertion, leaving men to themselves: whether for a time, (Hos. 5. 15.) as Hezekiah in the business of the King of Babylon's Embassage; (2 Chr. 32. 31.) or utterly, as those whom he justly giveth up to their own lusts. Rom. 1. 26, 28.) and the power of Satan. Acts 5. 3.

How agreeth it with the goodness of the Lord, to lead thus into temptation?
When all things are of him and by him, it must needs follow, that the things that are done are provided and governed of him; yet in such sort, as none of the evil which is in the transgressors cleaveth unto him.

But how can that be without stain of his righteousness?
It is a righteous thing with God to punish sin with sin, and to cast a sinner into further sins by way of just punishment. Therefore we desire God not to give us over to ourselves, by withdrawing his spirit from us. As when men do delight in lies, he giveth them over to believe lies: (2 Thes. 2. 11.) and for idolatry, he justly punisheth them with corporal filthiness in the same degree. (Hos. 4. 14. Rom. 1. 24.) Now being naturally prone to sin when by the just judgment of God we are left to ourselves, we rush into all evil, even as a horse into the battle to whom we put the spurs, or as an Eagle flyeth to her prey.

May not earthly Magistrates thus punish sin?
No verily: it were a cursed thing in Magistrates so to do. But God is above all Magistrates; who even for our natural corruption may justly give us over to all naughty affections.

Why do the Papists say? [And suffer us not to be led into temptation?]
In a vain foolish fear of making God to be guilty of sin, if he should be said to lead us into temptation: and therefore they lay the Lords words (as it were) in water, and change his tongue, and set him to the Grammar School to teach him to speak, which teacheth all men to speak. Whose folly is so much the greater, as it is the usual phrase of Scripture. Exod. 4. 21. & 9. 16. 1 Kings 22. 20, 21, 22. Rom. 1. 24, 26, 28. 2 Thes. 2. 11.

What inconvenience followeth upon this addition?
Very great For by this bare permission of evil they rob God of his glory, (working in the most things that are done of men) yea even of the best things, the doings whereof is attributed to his permission. Heb. 6. 3.

May we not offer ourselves unto temptation, as Christ did?
In no wise. For he was carried extraordinarily by the power of his Godhead into the desert, to be tempted for our sakes; that in his victory we might overcome.

What learn you of this?
1. That no godly man should choose his dwelling among those of a sinful profession; as a chaste man among stews, or a temperate man among drunkards, belly-gods, &c. 2. If we fall into such companies or occasions at unaware; (as did Joseph, Gen. 39. 12. and David, 1 Sam. 25. 13, 22.) that we pray God for his assistance, to carry ourselves godly, and in no wise to be infected by them.

What is meant by [deliver us from evil?]
This expoundeth the former by a flat contrary, as thus; [Lead us not into Temptation] but pull us out of it (even when we fall into it by our own infirmity) and that with force. For by delivering here is meant a forcible rescuing of our nature, (Rom. 7. 24) neither able nor willing to help it self out of these dangers,

What does this teach us?
That men are deeply plunged into sin, as a beast into the mire, which must be forcibly pulled out: although a beast will help it self more, than we can do ourselves of ourselves. Not that there is not a freedom and willingness in that which is well done: but, as that force cometh from that which is without, so the grace conteth not from us, but from God. Therefore the Church saith, Cant. 1. 4. Draw me, we will run; and Christ, Joh. 6. 44. No man can come unto me, except the Father which hath sent me draw him. Whence we learn, that to have this desire of being drawn out, is a singular favor of God.

What is God's hand to pull us out of this evil?
The Ministry of the Word, whereby he frameth our wills through the power of his Spirit to yield to his work.

What gather you of this?
That we kick not at the Ministers for reproving our sins, seeing that they strive to pluck us out of the mire; but that we rejoice and yield to their exhortation.

What is meant here by Evil?
First, that evil one, (1 John 5. 18, 19.) Satan, (who pretendeth to have power over us) and in him, all his instruments and provocations to sin. Then secondly, the effects of temptation, which without the special grace of God is extremely evil; to wit, sin and damnation. 1 Tim. 6. 9.

Is not the Devil the author of all evil?
Yes, he is the first Author: but properly those evils are called his, which in his own person he suggesteth.

From how many kinds of evils then desire we deliverance?
From two: First, the inward concupiscence of our hearts, which are our greatest enemies, James 1. 14, 15. Second, the outward, as the Devil, and the World, which do work upon us by the former: and therefore if we can subdue the inward, these outward cannot annoy us.

From what evils should we desire principally to be delivered?
Those whereunto we are most bent and naturally inclined, or wherein our Country especially, or our neighbors amongst whom we converse, (Mat, 8. 28.) do most delight: that we make the hedge highest, where Satan striveth most to leap over; who, although he knoweth not our secrets, yet seeing his subtlety and sharpness of discovering us even by a beck or countenance is very great, we must desire wisdom of God to discern his temptations, and power also to resist them.

Fortieth Head

Show now briefly, as you have done in the rest, what things we pray for in this last Petition.

1. That seeing we cannot be tempted without the will of God (Job 1. 10) nor resist without his power; (2 Cor. 12. 9.) if it be his blessed will, he would give us neither poverty nor riches, (Pro 30. 8.) nor any such thing as may endanger our spiritual estate, but remove those causes away which lead us into temptation.

2. That he would tie up Satan, and restrain his malice and power, (2 Cor. 12. 8.) or else make us wise to know and avoid his stratagems: (2 Cor. 2. 11.) preserve us from the evil that is in the world, (Joh. 17. 15.) and abate the power of the corruption that is within us Rom. 7. 24, 25.

3. That in our trials (if he see good to prove us) he would keep us from charging him with any injustice or hard measure: (Job 1. 22.) and that he would give us grace to behold his holy hand therein, and to make that holy use of them for which he hath sent them. Isa. 27. 9.

4. That he would not take his holy spirit from us in our trials, but give us sustentation in our temptations, and always stand by us with his grace, to keep us from falling, and not suffer us to be overcome by the temptations, 1 Cor. 10. 13 Jude verse 24.

5. That, leaving us at any time to our own weakness for our humiliation, he would graciously raise us up again, with increase of spiritual strength and courage. Psal. 51. 12.

6. That he would keep us from all carnal security, from despair, and presumption of his mercies.

7. That he would put an end to all trials, and to these days of conflict, in his own good time, treading Satan, with his forces, for ever under feet. Rom. 16. 20.

8. That he would increase and perfect the work of his grace in us enabling us to every good work, (Heb. 13. 21.) and, instead of temptations to the contrary; affording us all helps unto well-doing, and all things that may further us in holiness; as good company, godly examples, holy counsel and encouragements, &c.

[40TH HEAD.]

Hitherto of the Petitions. There remaineth the Conclusion; containing both the Thanksgiving, (Which is the second part of Prayer) and a Confirmation of the former requests. What are the words of this close of the Lord's Prayer?
For thine is the kingdom, and the power, and the glory, for ever: Amen Mat. 6. 13. Which words, though they be not repeated by St. Luke, yet are expressly mentioned by St. Matthew: and therefore causelessly, and without warrant omitted by the Church of Rome.

What observe you therein?
Their Sacrilege, who steal away this Thanksgiving from prayer, as if it were no part of it. So that it is no marvel that in Popery, all the whole body of their doctrine is of the salvation of men; God's glory being buried in a deep silence.

Whence is this form of Thanksgiving drawn?
Out of Daniel 7. 14. and 1 Chron. 29. 10, 11, 12, 13. where David useth the like phrase in praising of God. But that which David enlargeth there, our Savior shortneth here; and yet comprehendeth the marrow of all.

What is the sum thereof?
That we ground our assurance of obtaining our prayers in God; from whom all things we ask do come, and to whom therefore all glory must return.

What observe you in this?
That Christ maketh this Thanksgiving, consisting in the praise of God, to be a reason of all the Petitions going before; and therefore a further assurance of obtaining our suits: for so good men in praying for new blessings, do always join thanksgiving for the former.

What do you here understand by [Kingdom?]
God's absolute Sovereignty and right over all things; 1 Chro. 29. 11. which answereth to the second Petition. And therefore this reason, of God's right and authority over all, ought to move us to pray to him, and to him alone, as to one that hath only right to any thing we have need of.

What is meant by [Power?]
The omnipotence of God, whereby he is able to do all things. Luke 1. 37.

That besides his right, noted in the former word, he is also able to bring to pass whatsoever he will: both which concur in God, though not always in earthly Princes. Which seemeth to answer unto the third Petition, and ought to give us encouragement to pray unto him, who is able to effect any thing we pray for according to his will; and to strengthen us to any thing which in duty we ought to do, although there be no strength in us.

What is meant by [Glory?]
That due, which rising from the two former, of Kingdom and Power, does rightly belong unto God, as following upon the concurrence of the other two. For if whatsoever we desire be granted unto us, in that he reigneth powerfully; it is reason, that from the establishing of his kingdom and power, all glory and praise should return unto him again, Therefore hereby we do thankfully refer and return all good things to the honor and service of God that giveth them. Psalm. 65. 1, 2. otherwise we have nor comfort of our prayers. And it answereth to the first Petition, and ought to move us to pray unto him, and to assure us that our prayers are granted; seeing by our prayers duly made and granted, he is glorified. And it is one of the most powerful reason, that the servants of God have grounded their confidence of being heard, that the name of God therein should be glorified.

What mean you by the word [Thine?]
Here by these titles of Kingdom, Power, and Glory, are appropriated unto God, to whom they do belong; and all creatures excluded from fellowship with him in these attributes. For howsoever, Kingdom, Power and Glory, are communicated unto some creatures (namely Kings and Princes, Dan. 2. 37.) as God's instruments, and Vice-gerents: Psalm 82. 6. yet God alone claimeth them originally of himself, and absolutely without dependence or control; others have them not of themselves, but as borrowed, and hold them of him as Tenants at will. Rom. 13. 1. Prov. 8. 15. Job 33. 13.

What is meant by the words, [for ever, or, for ages?]
By ages, he meaneth eternity: Dan. 2. 4. and thereby putteth another difference between the Kingdom, Power, and Glory of God, which is eternal, without any beginning or end; 1 Tim. 1. 17. and that in Princes, whose Kingdoms, powers and glory fade.

How is this a close of confirmation to our requests?
Because we do not only in general ascribe Kingdom, Power, and Glory unto God, as his due, but also with respect unto our prayers and suits believing and professing, that he, as King of heaven and earth, hath authority to dispose of all his treasures; Rev. 3. 7. as omnipotent, is able to do exceeding abundantly above all that we can ask or think; Eph. 3. 20. finally, as the God of glory, is interested in the welfare of his servants for the maintaining of the honor of his name, Psa. 35. 27. and truth of his promises Psal. 119. 49. Therefore there are here contained three reasons to move God to grant our Petitions. Because,

First, he is our King; and so tied to help us, who are his Subjects. Secondly, he hath power; and therefore is able to help us. Thirdly, The granting of our Petitions will be to his glory and praise. Whereupon we firmly believe, that God the mighty and everlasting King, 1 Tim. 1. 17. can, and for his own glory will grant the things we have thus demanded. Eph. 3. 20. Jer. 14. 7. Ezek. 36. 22.

What is understood by the last word [Amen?]
Not only, So be it, as commonly men say; but also, So it is or shall be, as we have prayed. (Rev. 22. 20, 21.) For it is a note of confidence and declaration of Faith, (without which our prayers are rejected: whereby we assure ourselves, that God will grant those things which we have prayed to him for.

Why are we taught to conclude with this word?
There being two things required in prayer, a fervent desire, (James 5. 17.) and Faith, (Jam. 1. 6.) which is a persuasion, that these things which we truly desire, God will grant them for Christ's sake: this is a testimony both of our earnest affection of having all those things performed, which in this prayer are comprehended, and the assurance of our faith to receive our desires, at least so far forth as God sees good for us. And so hereby we do not only testify our earnest desire that so it may be, but also express our full assurance that so it shall be, as we have prayed, according to the will of God: and being already let in (Mat. 7. 8.) by the key of faithful prayer into the rich treasure of his mercies, we also set our seal (John 3. 11.) in the word of faith, Amen.

Is it lawful to use no other form of words, than that which is set down in the Lord's Prayer?
We may use another form of words: but we must pray for the same things, and with like affection, as is prescribed in that prayer.

This form being so absolute, what need we use any other words in praying?
Because, as to refuse this form savoureth of a proud contempt of Christ's ordinance, so to confine ourselves to these words alone, argueth extreme idleness in this duty, wherein variety of words is required for the pouring out of our souls before the Lord, (Hos. 14. 3.) and oftentimes according to the occasion some one Petition is more than the rest to be insisted on and importuned. (Mat. 26. 44.) Wherefore our blessed Savior hath commended this form unto us, as an excellent copy or lesson, to be both repeated, and imitated, or at the least, aimed at by us his Scholars: for which cause, both he himself, (Joh. 17. 1, &c.) and his Apostles, (Acts 4. 24, &c.) are recorded to have prayed in other words, which yet may be referred to these. Finally the liberty which the Lord affordeth us is not to be abridged, or despised, who admitteth all languages,

words and forms, agreeable to this pattern, whether read, rehearsed by heart, or presently conceived; (2 Chron. 23. 30. Psal. 90. & 92. in the Titles. Num. 10. 35, 36.) so be it we pray both with spirit and affection, and with understanding also. 1 Cor. 14. 15.

May there not then besides this prayer of the Lord, be now under the Gospel a set form of Prayer in the Church?
Yes verily: so that it be left at the liberty of the Church (not of private men without consent of the Church) to alter it.

Wherefore is it necessary or convenient that there be a set form of Prayer?
To help the weaker and ruder sort of people especially: and yet so as the set form make not men sluggish in stirring up the gift of Prayer in themselves according to divers occurrences; it being incident to the children of God, to have some gift of Prayer in some measure. Zech. 12. 10.

Remaineth there yet any thing necessary to be considered of prayer?
Something would be spoken of the Kinds and Circumstances thereof.

What kinds are there of Prayer?
Prayer is either public or private: and both of them, either ordinary or extraordinary. Acts 6. 4. &c. 1 Tim. 2. 12. Mat. 6. 6. Acts 10. 4. Joel. 2. 15. Jonah 3. 6, &c.

What is public Prayer?
It is prayer is made of and in the Congregation, assembled for the service of God. Psa. 84. 1, &c.

What is private Prayer?
It is that Prayer which is made out of the Congregation, and it is either less private; as when the whole Family, or private friends, meet in that exercise: (2 Sam. 6. 20. Esth. 4. 16.) or more private; when either one of the members of the family, (Nehe. 1. 4, 5, 6. Gen. 25. 21.) or some by reason of special duty they have, jointly together make their prayers. 1 Peter 3. 7.

Is it not enough for every one in a family to make prayers with the rest of the body of that household?
No: it is required also that we pray solitarily by ourselves. Mat. 6. 6. For as every man hath committed special sins, which others in the family have not; and hath special defects; and hath received special favors, that others have not: so in these regards it is meet that he should have a special resort unto God in Confession, Petition, and Thanksgiving.

What is ordinary Prayer?
It is that prayer which is made daily upon ordinary occasions. Psal. 55. 17. Dan. 6. 11.

What is the extraordinary?
That which is made upon some special occasion, or extraordinary accident falling out; by reason whereof it is both longer and more fervent. Psal. 119. 62. Acts 12. 5. Joel 2. 15. Jonah 3. 6.

Are the same persons always to keep the private extraordinary Prayers that keep the public?
No, not such persons as are under the commandment of others; unless it be public, or with consent of their commanders. Numb. 30. 13, 14, &c.

Forty-first Head

What are the ordinary circumstances of Prayer?
Gestures, Place, and Times.

What arehavior and gestures must we use in praying?
We must use such holy behavior and comely gestures of body, as are beseeming the Majesty of God with whom we have to deal, and so holy an exercise which we have in hand: namely, such as may best express and increase the reverence, humility, fervency, and affiance, that ought to be in our hearts. As the bowing of our knees, (Eph. 3. 14.) lifting up of our hands and eyes to heaven, (La. 3. 41. Joh. 17. 1.) &c. which yet are not always or absolutely necessary, (Luk. 18. 13.) so our hearts be lifted up, (Psa. 25. 1. & 143. 8.) and the knees of our conscience bowed before the Lord, (Phil. 2. 10.) and nothing done unbeseeming the company, with whom we pray, and the kind of prayer.

Is not the behavior all one, in every kind of prayer?
No. In private prayer it sufficeth that we use such words, gestures, &c. as may express our reverence and faith towards God: (1 Cor. 14. 2.) in public prayer our behavior must be such, as may also witness our communion one with another, and desire of mutual edification. (1 Cor. 14. 4, 17, 40.) When we pray by ourselves, we have more liberty of words and gestures, than in company. (1 Kings 18. 42.) In extraordinary prayers the public must be done with open show of affection, either sorrow or joy, (Isa. 1. and 58. Joel 2. 13.) which in the private must be covert and secret. Mat. 6. 17.

Where must we pray?
Generally all places are allowed, (1 Tim. 2. 8.) the ceremonial difference of places being removed, (John 4. 21.) and Christ our propitiatory every where present before us (Mat. 18. 20.) Notwithstanding, according to the kinds before mentioned, the public place of resort, for the worship of God, be fitteth common prayers, (Isa. 56. 7. Joel 2. 17.) and the private house, or closet is most convenient for private supplication: (Mat. 6. 6.) howsoever the sudden lifting up of the heart in secret unto God, may be as occasion is, (with out gesture) in any place or company. Neh. 2. 4.

When must me pray?
Continually; as the Apostle enjoineth, 1 Thes. 5. 17. For the whole course of a Christian is a perpetual intercourse with the Lord: either suing for mercies, or waiting for the answer of his suits, or rendering thanks for graces received. (Psal. 5. 3. Luke 2. 37.) Nevertheless ordinarily the Sabbath among the days of the week, Psal. 92. Title: and morning and evening among the hours of the day ibid. verse 2. are to be preferred, whereto such times may be added, wherein we enter into any business. Col. 3. 17. Prov. 3 6. or receive any of the creatures or blessings of God: 1 Cor. 10. 31. 1 Tim. 4. 4, 5. Extraordinarily other days, or hours, must also be set apart for prayer, especially in cases requiring longer continuance therein. Psal. 55. 17. & 119. 62, 164.

[41ST HEAD.]

What circumstances are annexed unto such extraordinary prayers?
An holy fasting; or feasting. 1 Cor. 7. 5. Zac. 8. 18. Neh. 8. 10. the one, to further our Zeal in Petition; the other in Thanksgiving.

What mean you by Fasting?
Not any natural abstinence, arising from sickness: nor medicinal, used to prevent or remove the same; nor civil, enjoined sometimes by authority, as in case of death; sometimes enforced by necessity, as in siege, 2 Kin. 6. 25. seafaring, &c. not yet

moral, for subduing of carnal concupiscence, 1 Cor. 9. 27. and preservation of chastity, required especially in some constitutions by virtue of the seventh Commandment: but religious, Joel 1. 14. that is, referred to religious ends, for the furtherance of the special practice of repentance, and the enforcing of our prayers.

Is fasting a good work?
Fasting is not properly a good work, but an help, and assistance thereto; namely to Prayer: neither is the outward exercise thereof a certain mark of a godly name. The Pharisees which fasted, Luk. 5. 33. came not to our Savior Christ to learn of him, (as the disciples of John did, Mat. 9. 24. although it were in weakness) but to discredit him; namely, to make the world believe that he was a belly god: as the Church of Rome does charge the children of God now, to open a school to all liberty to the flesh, following the steps of their old fathers the Pharisees.

What is an holy Fast?
The chastising of our nature, and laying aside the delights of the senses for a time; Joel 2. 16. 1 Cor. 7. 5. to the end thereby to humble ourselves, and to make us more apt to prayer. Or more fully: Fasting is a religious abstinence, commanded of God, whereby we forbear the use not only of meat and drink, but also of all other earthly comforts and commodities of this life, so far as necessity and comeliness will suffer, to the end that we being humbled and afflicted in our souls, by the due consideration of our sins and punishment, may, grounded upon the promises of God, more earnestly and fervently call upon God, either for the obtaining of some singular benefit or special favor we have need of; or for the avoiding of some special punishment or notable judgment hanging over our heads, or already pressed upon us. Acts 16. 30, 31, 32. & 14. 23. 2 Chron. 20. Joel 1. & 2. 12, 16.

Is there any necessity of this exercise of Fasting?
Yes verily, in that it is necessary to humble ourselves under the mighty and fearful hand of God; and to afflict our souls with the consideration and conscience of our sins, and the punishment due unto them; unto which this outward exercise of Fasting is a good aid. For howsoever the kingdom of God consisteth not properly in the matter of meat and drink, whether used or forborn; (Rom. 1. 4. 17.) yet fasting, as an extraordinary help unto the chief exercises of piety, hath the warrant and weight of a duty, as well from precepts as examples, both out of the old Testament, (Lev. 23. 27. &c. Joel. 2. 22. Isa. 22. 12.) and the new. (Mat. 9. 14, 15. Acts 13. 3.) And our Savior Christ (Luk. 5. 35.) does expressly say, that the time shall come, when his disciples shall fast, where both by the circumstances of the persons, and of the time, the necessity of fasting is enforced.

How so?
By the persons; for that the Apostles themselves have need of this help of fasting for their further humiliation. And by the times; for that even after the Ascension of our Savior Christ, when the graces of God were most abundant upon them, they should have need of this exercise.

What is gathered hereof?
That it is a shameful thing for men to say, that Fasting is Jewish or Ceremonial.

What do you gather in that our Savior would not have his disciples to fast till after his Ascension?
His singular kindness, in that he would not suffer any great trouble, or cause of fast to come unto them, before they had strength to bear them, or were prepared for them.

When is the time of Fasting?
As oft as there are urgent and extraordinary causes of prayer; either for the avoiding of some great evil or notable calamity, (1 Sam 7. 6. Est. 4. 16.) or for the obtaining of some great mercy or special benefit at the hand of God. (Neh. 1. 4. Acts 10. 30.) For in that our Savior Christ teacheth, (Luk. 5. 34) that it must not be, when he, who is as it were the Bridegroom, is with his disciples, to furnish them with all manner of benefits they had need of: we are taught, that the time is, when any great calamity is hanging over us, or fallen upon us, whereby the gracious presence of Christ is taken from us; or when there is any weighty matter to be taken in hand.

What gather you hereof?
That the fast in Popery is foolish, which is holden at set times, whether the times be prosperous, or not prosperous; whether the affairs be common and ordinary, or whether they be special and extraordinary.

When then is this Religious exercise of Fasting to be performed of Christians?
When God calleth upon us for this duty by the occasions, arising from his providence, and our own necessities. Mat. 9. 15.

What are those occasions, whereby the Lord calleth us to fasting?
There are generally two: (as hath been noted;) viz. First, evils which, being felt or feared, we desire to remove, or to prevent; as sins, (1 Sam. 7. 6. 1 Cor. 5. 2.) and the judgment of God for sin, Est. 4. 16. Jonah 3. 7. Mat. 17. 21. Second, good things, spiritual (Acts 10. 30.) or outward, (Neh. 1. 4.) which we desire to enjoy; and therefore do thus seek them, and prepare ourselves for the receiving of them.

When is this Fast to begin and end?
As in all holy rests, after preparation, (Luk. 23. 54.) it is to begin in the morning of the day of the Fast, and to continue to the morning of the day following; Mark 16. 2. Luke 24. 1.

It seemeth by this that the law of Fasting will not suffer a man to sup the night of that day when the Fast is holden.
The Fast is so long continued as hath been said: but so, as there be that refreshing, whereby health may be preserved. For such as be sick or weak, or to take somewhat for their sustenance, thereby to be better able to serve God in the Fast; provided that they do not abuse this to license of the flesh.

Is it of necessity, that the Fast should always begin in the morning, and continue until night?
No. It may be from morning till evening; (Judg. 20. 26. 2 Sam. 3. 35.) or from evening till evening again. (Lev. 23. 32) And according to the greatness of the affliction, the Fast is to be prolonged, even to the space of three days; as appeareth by the examples of the Jews, Est. 4. 16. and Paul, Acts 9. 9.

What are the kinds of Fasting?
It is either public or private.

What is the public Fast?
It is when for a general cause the Churches do fast: viz. when the Governors and Magistrates, (Joel. 2. 15.) stirred up by consideration of common sins, (Neh. 9. 1. &c.) calamities, (Jonah. 3. 7, 8.) necessities, or businesses of great importance, do in the name of God blow the trumpet, and call a solemn assembly, or assemblies; in which case he that obeyeth not, is culpable before God and man. Lev. 23. 29. And it is either

more public, when all Churches fast generally; or else less public, when some particular Churches are humbled in fasting:

What is the private Fast?
When upon the view either of public causes, not considered by such as are in authority, (Ezek. 9. 4. & 13. 17.) or of the like, but more private occasions (as domestic or personal, &c.) a Christian is moved either with his family, or special friends, (Zech. 12. 12. 1 Cor. 7. 5.) or by himself solitarily, (Mat. 6. 17.) to humble himself before the Lord. For it is more or less private: less private, as when a particular house; more private, when a particular person is humbled in fasting.

Is there any difference in the manner of holding a public and private Fast?
Yes. In a public Fast, the sorrow and grief ought to be declared openly to the view of all: which ought to be covered, as much as may be, in the private Fast; wherein the more secrecy is used, the greater proof is there of sincerity and hope of blessing. Wherefore our Savior Christ reproveth the private fast of Hypocrites, that would outwardly appear to men to fast; and commandeth the contrary. Mat. 6. 16, 17, 18.

Whom does God call to this exercise of fasting?
All Christians, enabled by understanding, and grace, to judge, and to perform aright this weighty duty: (Zech. 12. 12. &c.) unless any be exempted by present debility; (Mat. 12. 7. 1 Sam. 14. 29, 30.) but differently according to the divers occasions of fasting, and kinds thereon depending, (whereof before hath been spoken.)

May those that are under the government of their Parents or Masters fast, without leave of them?
No: but in the public all may fast.

Are all persons meet for this exercise of fasting?
By the unfitness of his own Disciples for it, our Savior Christ teacheth, that they that meet for this exercise must not be Novices in the profession of the truth: no more than he that is accustomed with the drinking of old wine, can suddenly fall in liking of new wine, Luk. 5. 33.

Is it so hard a matter to abstain from a meals meat, and such bodily comforts for a short time; which the young sucking babes, and the beasts of Nineveh did, and divers beasts are better able to perform than any man?
No verily. But hereby appeareth, that there is an inward strength of the mind required, not only in knowledge of our behavior in this service of God, but also of power and ability to go under the weight of the things we humble ourselves for: which strength if it be wanting, the fast will be to those that are exercised in it, as a piece of new cloth sewed into an old garment, which because it is not able to bear the stress and strength of, hath a greater rent made into it, than if there were no piece at all.

What gather you hereof?
That it is no marvel, if where there is any abstinence and corporal exercise in Popery; yet that the same makes them nothing better, but rather worse: having not so much as the knowledge of the service of God; much less any spiritual strength and ability to perform it with.

What then are the parts of a true Christian Fast?
They are partly outward, partly inward. First, Bodily exercise, serving to the inward substance, 1 Tim. 4. 8. Second, An inward substance, sanctifying the bodily exercise, and making it profitable unto the users.

Forty-first Head

What is the bodily exercise in fasting?
It is the forbearing of things, otherwise lawful and convenient, in whole or in part, for the time of humiliation: so as nature be chastised but not disabled for service; and the delights of the sense laid aside, but yet without annoyance and uncomeliness.

What are those outward things that are to be forborn during the time of the fast?
First food: Esther 4. 16. Jonah 3. 7. from whence the whole action hath the name of Fasting: and the word does signify an utter abstinence from all meats and drinks, and not a sober use of them, which ought to be all the times of our life. Wherefore this outward exercise is thus described. Luk. 5. 33. The disciples of John and the Pharisees fast; but thine eat and drink.

What is here to be considered?
A charge upon Popery. For the greater sort of people among them, in the day of their Fast, fill their bellies with bread and drink; and the richer sort with all kind of delicates, (flesh, and that which cometh of flesh only excepted:) so that the fastings of the one and the other is but a fullness; and the latter may be more truly said to feast than fast.

It seemeth you make it unlawful for those that fast to eat any thing during their fasting.
Not so; if for help of weakness, the taking of meat be moderately and sparingly used, as before hath been observed.

What other things are outward?
The ceasing from labor in our vocations, on the day of the Fast; (Num. 29. 7.) to the end we may the better attend to the holy exercises used in fasting: in which respect such times are called Sabbaths (Levit. 23. 32.) the laying aside of choice apparel, or whatsoever ornaments of the body, and wearing of homely and courser garments. (Exod. 33. 4, 5. Jonah 3. 5, 6.) The forbearing of Sleep, Music, Mirth, Perfumes, &c. (Dan. 6. 18. & 10. 2, 3.) And this abstinence is required of all that celebrate the Fast. But of married persons there is further required a forbearance of the use of the marriage bed, and of the company each of others. 1 Cor. 7. 5. Joel 2. 16.

What is the meaning of the abstinence from these outward things?
By abstinence from meat and drink, by wearing of courser apparel, by ceasing from labor in our callings, and by separation in married persons for the time; we thereby profess ourselves unworthy of all the benefits of this present life, and that we are worthy to be as far underneath the earth as we are above it; yea, that we are worthy to be cast into the bottom of hell: which the holy Fathers in times past did signify, by putting ashes upon their heads; (Job 2. 12. Est. 4. 3. Jer. 6. 26. Ezek. 27. 30. Dan. 9. 3.) the truth whereof remaineth still, although the ceremony be not used.

What is the spiritual substance of duty, whereto the bodily exercise serveth?
It is an extraordinary endeavour of humbling our souls before the Lord, and of seeking his face and favor; (Ezra 8. 21.) wherein that inward power and strength, whereof we speak, is seen.

Wherein does it consist?
First, in the abasing of ourselves, (Joel 2. 13.) by examination, confession, and hearty bewailing of our own, and the common sins: Ezra, 9. 3, 4. &c. Neh. 9. 1, 2, &c. Dan. 9. 3-5. Second, in drawing near unto the Lord by faith, Luk 15, 18, 21.) and earnest invocation of his name; Jona. 3. 8. Isa. 58. 4.

The former is grounded upon the meditation of the Law and threats of God: the latter upon the Gospel and promises of God, touching the removing of our sins and God's judgments upon us for them.

How agreeth this with the Popish Fast?
It faileth in both parts. For instead of humbling themselves and afflicting their souls, they pride themselves, and lift up their minds, in thinking they deserve something at God's hand for their fasting: which is great abomination. Neither have they upon the days of their fast any extraordinary exercise of Prayer, more then upon other days Of all which it may appear, how small cause they have to boast of their fasting, which in all the warp thereof hath not a thread which is not full of leprosy.

What is required in our humiliation?
Anguish and grief of our hearts, conceived for our sins, and the punishment of God upon us, for which we ought to be humbled in fasting. For the effecting whereof, we are to set before our eyes:

1. The glass of God's holy Law, with the bitter curses threatened to the breakers thereof. 2. The examples of vengeance on the wicked. 3. The judgments new felt, or feared of us. 4. The spiritual contemplation of our blessed Savior, bleeding on the Cross, with the wounds which our sins have forced upon him, Zech. 12. 10, &c.

What is required in our drawing near unto the Lord by Faith?
Not only fervently and importunately to knock at the gate of his mercy for the pardon of our sins, removal of judgment, and grant of the graces and blessings we need: (Psal. 51. 1, 2, &c and verse 14.) but also to make a sure Covenant with his Majesty, (Nehem 9. 38. Ezra 10. 3, 5.) of renewing and bettering our repentance thence forward, in a more earnest and effectual hatred of sin, and love of righteousness. Isa. 55. 7. Jonah 3. 8.

What fruit or success may we look for, having thus sought the Lord?
Who knoweth whether by this means we may stand in the gap, and cause the Lord to repent of the evil intended, and to spare his people? (Joel 2. 14, 18, &c. Jona. 2. 9, 10.) At the least, for our particular, we shall receive the mark and mercy promised to such as mourn for the abominations generally committed; (Ezek. 9. 4, 6.) together with plentiful evidence of our salvation, and assurance of the love of God towards us; (Mat. 6. 18. Prov. 28. 13. 1 Joh. 1. 9.) strength against temptations; patience and comfort in afflictions; with all other graces, plentifully vouchsafed (especially upon such renewing of acquaintance) by him who is the rewarder of all that come unto him; (Heb, 11. 6.) so that we need not doubt, but that as we have sown in tears, so we shall reap in joy: (Ps, 126. 5.) and as we have sought the Lord with fasting and mourning so he yet again will be sought, Ezek. 36. 37. and found of us, with holy feasting and spiritual rejoicing.

What is an holy feasting?
A comfortable enjoying of God's blessings, to stir us up to thankfulness and spiritual rejoicing. Or, (to describe it more largely) It is a solemn Thanksgiving unto God for some singular benefit, (or deliverance from some notable evils either upon us, or hanging over us;) which he hath bestowed upon us, especially after that in fasting we have begged the same at his hands. Zech. 8. 19. Esther. 9. 17, 11 20, 21, 22, 30, 31. for this is a duty specially required for the acknowledgment of such mercies, as we have by the former course obtained: (Psa. 30. 11, 12 & 50. 51. Esther 9. 22.) and so answering thereto, that from the one, with due reference, the other may be conceived.

What ought especially to be the time of this duty?
That time that is nearest unto the mercy and benefit which we have received: as we see in the story, Esth. 9. where the Jews that were in the country, and in the provinces, did celebrate their feast on the 14, day of the month Adar, because they had overthrown their adversaries the 13, day before: and the Jews in Shushan, because they made not an end of the slaughter of their enemies before the 14. day was past, they celebrated it the 15. day. Look 2 Chro. 20. 29. and the example of Jacob, checked for deferring the payment of his vow at Bethel. Gen. 35. 1. 3. with 20. 28.

Wherefore ought we to take the time that is next the deliverance?
Because we being most strongly and thoroughly affected with the benefit we receive the first time it is bestowed upon us, especially where there is not only notable benefit befallen unto us, but thereby also we are freed from some notable evil that was upon us, or near unto us, we are then most fit to hold a feast unto the Lord.

Why is the ordinance of a yearly feast by Mordocheus, rather commanded upon the day after the slaughter of their enemies, than the day of the slaughter?
To set forth that rejoicing ought not to be so much for the destruction of our enemies, as that thereby we obtain peace to serve God in.

Wherein does this feast consist?
The scope and drift of it is, to rejoice before the Lord; and to show ourselves thankful for the benefit received: not only in that we are delivered, but that we are delivered by prayer that we have made unto God; whereby our joy increases, and whereby it differeth from the joy of the wicked, which rejoice that they are delivered, as well as we.

How may that be best performed?
Partly by outward and bodily exercises; and partly by spiritual exercises of godliness.

What are the outward exercises?
A more liberal use of the creatures, both in meat and apparel, than is ordinary.

May we eat and drink on that day more than on others?
No: the exceeding is not in the quantity of meat and drink, but in a more dainty and bountiful diet than ordinary. (Neh. 8. 10.) Which yet is to be referred to the exercise of godliness; and therefore ought to be used in that moderation and sobriety, as men may be made more able thereunto: even as the abstinence in fasting is used to further humiliation of the mind, and affecting of the soul.

What is the exercise of godliness?
It is either in piety and duty unto God, or in kindness unto men.

What is the duty unto God?
To lift up our voice in thanksgiving unto him, as for all other his mercies (whereof this benefit should cause the remembrance; as one sin causeth the, remembrance of others; (Psalm 51.) so for that present benefit, and for that purpose to call the remembrance, and to compare the former evils which either we were in, or were near unto, with the present mercy, and every part of the one with the members of the other.

What other duty of Piety is to be performed unto God?
By a diligent meditation of the present benefit, to confirm our faith and confidence in God; that he that hath so mightily and graciously delivered us at this time, will also in the same or the like dangers deliver us hereafter, so far as the same should be good for us.

What is the kindness we should show towards men?
An exercise of liberality according to our power, out of the feeling of the bountiful hand of God towards us.

To whom must that be showed?
To our friends in presents, and as it were in New-years-gifts, (Rev. 11. 10.) and portions to be sent to the poor and needy. Neh. 8. 10.

What remaineth further of these holy Feasts?
The sorts and kinds of them; which are, as before we have heard of Fasts.

Hitherto of Prayer, and the extraordinary circumstances thereof, Fasting and Feasting. What is a vow?
A solemn promise made unto God by fit persons, of some lawful thing that is in their choice and power to perform.

It is thought that vows are Ceremonial, and not to pertain to the times of the Gospel?
They are indeed good, yea excellent persons, that think so; which carry so much the more a dislike of Vows, because they have been abused in Popery. Howbeit, it appears by the fiftieth Psalm, verse 14, 15. That it is a constant and perpetual service of God, as shall appear.

What is the proper end and use of a Vow?
It is twofold: First, to strengthen and confirm our faith. Gen. 28. 28. Judg. 11. 30. 31. 1 Sam. 1. 11. Secondly, to testify our thankfulness unto God: but no way to merit any thing at God's hand. So that whereas the exercise of a Fast is in adversity, and of a Feast in prosperity; the Vow may be in both.

Who are the fit persons that may Vow?
Such as have knowledge, judgment, and ability to discern of a Vow, and of the duties belonging to the performance of the same. Numbers 30. 6.

Are all such bound to vow?
Not simply, all (for it is no sin not to vow: Deut. 23. 22.) but those only, which either being in distress feel a want of feeling of God's assistance, thereby to strengthen their faith for necessary aid: or they, who being delivered from some necessary evil, or have received some singular good, where no vow hath gone before should witness their thankfulness. Deut. 23. 21, 22, 23. Numb. 30. 2. & 6. 2, &c.

What have we herein further to consider?
That the Vow must be of lawful things: else it is better not to pay the vow, then to pay. As Herod, and the forty mentioned in Acts 23. 24. and as the Monks, Friars and Nuns vow willful poverty, perpetual abstinence from Marriage, and Canonical obedience, and the peoples pilgrimage.

May we vow any thing which is lawful to be done?
We may not vow any vile or base thing: as if a wealthy man should vow to give to the poor some small value, far under his ability. For what either token of thankfulness can that be; or what comfort in his troubles can he take of the performance thereof?

What have we secondly to consider?
That the vow must be of such things as are in our choice to perform.

Forty-first Head

How many ways fail men against this?
Two ways: 1. In vowing that which we are not able to perform. 2. In vowing that which otherwise by the law of God we are bound to perform.

Who be they which vow that they cannot perform?
They are either they whose strength does fail through the common frailty of all men (as those that vow perpetual continency) whose lets come from themselves: or they which cannot perform it, by reason of subjection unto others; as wives unto their husbands, children to their parents, servants to their masters, &c. In whose power they are, to perform their vows, or not to perform them, Num. 30. 3, 4, &c.

Why may not a man vow such things as he is otherwise bound to do?
For that they are due unto God without the service of a vow, and therefore it were a dalliance with God, to make show of some special and extraordinary service, where the common and ordinary is only performed: as if a man would present as a gift unto his Lord, the rent of his house due for the occupation thereof.

What may we then lawfully vow?
An increase of God's service: as to pray more often every day than ordinarily is used: or to be more liberal to the poor with some strain of our ability; building of Colleges, Alms-houses, &c.

What is the duty of those that have vowed?
First, to have a diligent care to perform their vows: Eccles. 5. 3, 4. Deut. 23. 21, 22, 23. For if it be a reproachful thing to deal with God as with a man: it is more reproachful to deal worse with God than we dare deal with many men. Second, not to delay the performance of it. Eccles. 5. 3. For God corrected sharply in Jacob the deferring of the payment of his vows: (Gen. 35. 1.) 1. By his daughters deflowering. 2. By the rage and murder committed by his sons.

Is the necessity of performing vows so great, that they may no ways be omitted?
Not so: for to the performance of a greater duty a man may omit his vow for a time, and after a time return, and be not a Vow-breaker. As the Rechabites for safety of their lives came and dwelt in Jerusalem, notwithstanding a former vow, that they would not dwell in a house; (Jer. 35. 9, 10, 11.) and yet God witnesseth, that the vow was not broken thereby: so to help our neighbors in some present necessity, we may cease from any vowed duty at that time, and not sin. Wherein the Papists greatly fail, who having vowed unlawfully, yet think they may not intermit their vows.

If a man in vowing, does not consider sufficiently the greatness of the matter; may he not break that vow that he hath not so advisedly made?
No: the vow being otherwise lawful, that rashness is to be repented, but the vow must be kept.

What have we to learn of all this?
That we be advised in that we do, and not to inquire after we have vowed, to find some starting hole where to go out; but either not to vow at all; or if we vow, to have a good remembrance of it, and a diligent care in the due time to perform it. Prov. 20. 25.

[42ND HEAD.]

Having spoken of those good things which we do give unto God: let us proceed to that which we do give unto our needy Neighbor. What is Alms?
It is a duty of Christian love, whereby such as have this worlds good, do freely impart to such as are in want, 1 John 3. 17. 1 Tim. 6. 17, 18. Mat. 5. 42.

How can it be both a duty, and withal free?
First, that it is a duty, appeareth by many formal precepts touching this matter. (Deut. 15. 7. &c. Heb. 13. 16.) in that it is called our justice, or righteousness; (Psal. 112. 9. Mat. 6. 1.) in that every man is a steward of God's blessings for the benefit of others; (1 Pet. 4. 10) finally, in that according to the performance, or neglect, even of this duty, men shall be judged at the last day. Mat. 25. 35, 42. Second, it is free, not as being left by God unto our choice, whether we will do it or no, but as proceeding from an heart freely and cheerfully performing this obedience to God, and relief of our brother, without compulsion of human law, &c. 2 Cor. 9. 7.

Who are to give Alms?
Whosoever hath this worlds good, (1 Joh. 3. 17.) that is such a portion out of which by frugality something may be spared, though it be but two mites (Lu. 21. 2, 3.) And therefore not only rich men and householders are to give; 1 Tim. 6. 17. but also such as labor with their hands, (Ep. 4. 28.) out of their earnings; servants out of their wages; children out of their parents allowance; wives out of any portion they have in several without their husbands, or allowance from their husbands or out of the common stock they enjoy with their husbands: provided the husbands consent in whom the possession fundamentally remaineth be either expressed, or by silence, or not gainsaying implied: Finally, even they that live upon liberal alms, must spare something unto those that have little or no supply. 2. Cor. 8. 2, 24.

May there not be some cases, wherein such as are accountable to others may give without their knowledge, yea against their will?
Yes; as appeareth in the wise and commendable example of Abigail, (1 Sam. 25. 3. &c.) to wit, when the life and whole estate of the giver or receiver, may be now or not at all, thus or not otherwise preserved. For extreme necessity dispenseth with the ordinary course of duty, both to God and man. Mat. 12. 7.

Whereof must we give Alms?
Of that good thing, (Ne. 8. 10.) that is wholesome and profitable to the receiver, which is justly our own, not another mans; unless in case of extremity before mentioned. For otherwise of goods evil gotten, or wrongfully detained, not alms, but restitution must be made, Luke 19. 8.

How much must we give?
We must sow liberally, that we may reap also liberally; 2 Cor. 9. 6. Gal. 6. 7. Prov. 11. 25. notwithstanding, in the quantity and proportion of alms, respect be had;

First, as to the ability of the giver (Luke 3. 11. 1 Cor. 16. 2.) who is not bound so to give, as utterly to impoverish himself, (2 Cor. 8. 13.) and to make himself of a giver a receiver; (Acts 20. 35.) that in a common and extreme necessity of the Church, every one must be content to abate of his revenues that the rest may not perish; (2 Cor. 8. 1, 2, 9. Luke 12. 33.) and some whose hearts God shall move, may voluntarily and commendably sell all, and put it into the common stock: (Acts 4. 34, 35. with Acts 5. 4.) yea, it is unlawful so to give unto some one good use, as to disable ourselves for the service of the common-wealth, Church, or Saints in general, or for the relief of our Family or kindred in special. 1 Tim. 5. 8. Second, to the condition of the receiver, that his necessity may be supplied; (2 Cor. 9. 12. Job 31. 17, 18. &c. Jam. 2. 15, 16.) not as to make him of a receiver a giver: for this is to give a patrimony, not an alms; and belongeth rather to Justice, binding men to provide for those of their own household, than to mercy.

To whom must we give?
To such as are in want; (Mat. 5. 42. Ro. 12. 10.) but with this difference; first, in present extremity, we must preserve life in whomsoever, without inquiring who or what an one the party be. Luke 10. 33. with John 4. 9. Second, in cases admitting deliberation (Ps. 41. 1.) we must confine our alms to such as God hath made poor: (Deu. 15. 7, 11.) as Orphans, Aged, Sick, Blind, Lame, the trembling hand, (Lev. 25. 35.) &c. Wherein such gifts are most commendable, as extend unto perpetuity; as the erecting or endowing most commendable, as extend unto perpetuity; as the erecting or endowing of Churches, (Luk. 7. 5.) Schools of good Learning, (2 King. 6. 1. &c. 2 Chr. 34. 22.) Hospitals, &c. But as for such as turn begging into an art or occupation, they are by order to be compelled to work for their maintenance: (2 Thes. 3. 10, 11, 12.) which is the best and greatest alms.

What order must we observe in giving?
We must begin with such, as are nearest to us in regard of domestic, (1 Tim. 5. 8. Mat. 15. 5, 6.) civil, (Deut. 15. 7.) or Christian (Gal. 6. 10.) neighborhood, according as the laws of Nature. Nations and Religion direct us, unless other circumstances, as the extremity of want, or the dignity of the person to be relieved, 1 Kings 17. 31. do dispense: and so proceed to such as are farther off, according as our ability can extend.

What are the times, and places fittest for this duty?
For public alms the fittest time is, when we meet together for the solemn worship of God; (1 Cor. 16. 2.) Likewise the fittest place where provision is made for public collections. (Luk. 21. 1.) For private, when, and wherever the necessity of our poor brother offereth it self unto us. Joh. 31. 16. Prov. 3. 28.

With what affection must we do alms deeds?
First, with pity and compassion on our needy brother. Psal. 112. 4. Second, with humility, and secrecy, not seeking praise from men, but approving ourselves to God. Mat. 6. 1. &c. Third, with cheerfulness; (Rom. 12. 8.) because God loveth a cheerful giver. 2 Cor. 9. 7. Fourth, with simplicity, (Rom. 12. 8.) not respecting ourselves, but the glory of God, and the good of our fellow members. 2 Cor. 8. 4, 5.

How many ways may alms-deeds be performed?
For only by giving; but also, First, by lending, (Deut. 15. 8. Mat. 5. 42.) to such as are not able to lend to us again, Luke 6. 34. Psal. 37. 26. (some being no less relieved by lending, than others by gift:) provided we take nothing for the loan, (Exo. 22. 25.) yea, in some cases either remit part of the loan; (Neh. 5. 12.) or commit it into the hands of our poor brother without assurance to receive from him the principal again. Luk. 6. 35. Secondly, by selling when we do not only bring forth the commodity, as of corn, &c. which others keep in: (Prov. 11. 26.) but also in a merciful commiseration of our poor brother abate somewhat of the extreme price. Thirdly, by forbearing whatsoever is our right in case of great necessity. Nehem. 5. 18.

What fruit may we expect out of this duty?
Not thereby to merit at the hands of God: (1 Chro. 29. 14) but yet,

First, to make God our Debtor, (Pro. 19. 17.) according to his gracious promise; who also in Christ will acknowledge and requite it at the last day. Mat. 10. 42. & 25. 35. 2 Tim. 1. 18. Second, to seal the truth of our Religion. Jam. 1. 27. Third, to assure our salvation. Heb. 6. 9, 10. 1 Joh. 3. 14. 1 Tim. 6. 19. Fourth, to make amends to men, for former covetousness and cruelty. Dan. 4. 24, 25. Luk. 19. 8. Fifth, to sanctify our store (Luk. 11. 41.) and bring a blessing on our labors (Deut. 15. 10.) yea & upon our posterity after us. Ps. 11. 2. 2. & 37. 26. 2 Tim. 1. 16.

[43RD HEAD.]

We have spoken at large of the participation of the grace of Christ, and the benefits of the Gospel: Now we are to come unto the means whereby God does effect these things.

Show therefore how, and in what manner, God does offer and communicate the Covenant of grace unto mankind.
By Vocation, or Calling, (Rom. 8. 30. Heb. 3. 1.) when God, by the means of his Word and Spirit, acquainting men with his gracious purpose of salvation by Christ, inviteth them to come unto him; (Hos. 2. 14.) and revealing unto them his Covenant of grace, (Mat. 11. 27. & 16. 17. Joh. 14. 21. Psa. 25. 14.) bringeth them out of darkness to light. Acts 26. 18.

Is this calling of one sort only?
No, there is an external gathering common to all, together with some
light of the Spirit, and certain fruits of the same, attained unto by some that are no heirs of the promise: for many are called with this outward and ineffectual calling, who are not chosen. Isa. 48. 12. Mat. 22. 14.

And there is an internal and effectual calling, peculiar to those few that are elect, whereby unfeigned faith and true repentance is wrought in the heart of Gods chosen; and God become in Christ their Father, does not only outwardly by his word invite, but inwardly also and powerfully by his Spirit allure and win their hearts to cleave to him inseparably unto salvation. Gen. 9. 27. Ps. 25. 14. &. 65. 4. Joel. 2. 32. Acts 2. 39.

How do both these kinds of Callings differ?
Howsoever we are to judge charitably of all outwardly called, (1 Cor. 1. 2.) because who among them are also inwardly called is only known to God; (2 Tim. 2. 19.) yet does this outward calling differ from the inward.

First, in that it is wrought only by outward means and common illumination, (Heb. 4. 2.) without the spirit of regeneration, (Jude verse 19.) or any portion of saving faith. Luk. 8. 13. Second, in that they are admitted only to an outward and temporary league of formal profession, (Acts 8. 13. Rom. 9. 4, 5.) not to that entire fellowship with Christ, required unto salvation. 1 John 2. 19. 1 Cor. 1. 8, 9.

What are the means which God hath appointed to call us by?
They are partly inward, and partly outward, 1 Thes. 5. 19, 20. Acts 10. 44.

What are the inward?
The spirit of God, which is given by the outward things. Gal. 3. 2, 3. 1 Tim. 1. 14.

Forty-third Head

What mean you by the spirit of God in this place?
That power of God which worketh in the hearts of men things which the natural discourse of reason is not able to attain unto.

Being incomprehensible, how may we come to some understanding and sense of it?
By the things whereunto it is compared. 1. To wind, Acts 2. to show the marvelous power of it in operation. 2. To oil, that is of a hot nature, that pierceth and supplieth. 3. To water, John 4. that cooleth, scoureth, and cleanseth. 4. To fire, Mat. 3. Acts 2. that severeth dross and good metal.

How is the operation of it?
Divers: as softening and hardening, enlightening, and darkening; which it worketh after a diverse manner, by the word, in the hearts of the elect and reprobate, according to the good pleasure of God's secret will only; and after that, according to the good pleasure of his revealed will. So, that the lawful use thereof is rewarded with a gracious increase of blessing; and the abuse punished with further hardness to condemnation.

What then does the spirit work in the wicked?
Finding them heard, it hardeneth them more (by with-holding of grace) to their further condemnation.

What does the same spirit work in the Godly?
Faith; whereby they take hold on Christ, with all his benefits. Eph. 2. 8.

What are the outward things which God hath given to call us by?
They are either common to the whole world, or proper to the Church.

What are the things common to the whole world?
God's works, not unprofitably given, although not sufficient to salvation.

Is not the knowledge of the wisdom, power and goodness of God in the Creation and government of the Heaven and Earth, with the things that are in them, sufficient to make us wise to salvation?
No. First It serveth rather to further condemnation, without the word: Rom. 1. 19, 20, 21. Secondly; as by, and with the word the due meditation and consideration of God's works is a good help to further us in religion, and in the graces of God's spirit. 1 Cor. 1. 21, 22.

Since then God does not reveal the Covenant of grace, nor afford sufficient means to salvation to the whole world, but only to the Church: explain here what you mean by the Church.
We speak not here of that part of God's Church which is triumphant in glory: who being in perfect fruition, have no need of these outward means of communion with him: (Rev. 21, 22, 23.) but the subject here is the Church militant. And that we consider also, as visible in the parts of it; consisting of divers assemblies and companies of believers, making profession of the same common faith: how it is many times, by force of persecution, the exercise of public ordinances may for a time be suspended among them.

But are none to be accounted members of this Church, but such as are true believers, and so inseparably united unto Christ their head?
Truly and properly none other. (1 John 2. 19.) How beit, because God does use outward means with the inward, for the gathering of his Saints; and calleth them as well to outward

profession among themselves, (Acts. 2. 42. Cant. 1. 7.) as to inward fellowship with his Son, whereby the Church becomes visible: hence it is, that so many as partake of the outward means, and join with the Church in league of visible profession, are therefore in human judgment accounted members of the true Church, and Saints by calling, (1 Cor. 1. 1.) until the Lord (who only knoweth who are his) do make known the contrary. As we are taught in the Parable of the Tares, Mat. 13. 24, 47, &c. and of the draw-net, and the threshing floor, where lieth both good corn and chaff, Mat. 3.

Hath Christ then his Church visible upon earth?
Yea, throughout the world, in the particular congregations of Christians, (Rom. 3. 3.) called to the profession of the true faith and obedience of the Gospel. In which visible assemblies, and not else where, the true members of the true Church invisible, on earth, are to be sought (Rom. 11. 5.) and unto which therefore all that seek for salvation must gladly join themselves. Isa. 60. 4.

Does the visible Church consist of good and bad, or of good only?
It consisteth of good and bad: as at the beginning we may see it did in Cain and Abel. Whereupon our Savior compareth the Church to a net, in which are fishes good and bad; and to a field, which in it hath wheat and cockle. Mat. 13. 24, 47, &c.

What are the marks and infallible notes whereby to discern a true visible Church, with which we may safely join?
First and principally, the truth of Doctrine which is professed and the sincere preaching of the Word; together with the due administration of the Sacraments, according to the Commandment of Christ our Savior, Mat. 28. Secondarily, the right order which is kept; with a sincere and conscionable obedience yielded to the word of God.

Why do you make the first to be the principal mark of visible profession?
Because they are the only outward means, appointed by God for the calling and gathering of the Saints; and which prove the Church to be a Pillar of truth. 1. Tim. 3. 15.

Can the Church want these, and yet be a Church?
Yea; it may want them in the time of war or persecution: and in such a time we may safely join ourselves to a company which allows of the public ministry of the word of God and administration of the Sacraments, howsoever the exercise of the same by reason of those confusions be wanting for a time.

Are we to join with all Churches, that have these marks?
Yea: neither must we separate from any, farther then they separate from Christ, Phil. 1. 18. Cant. 1. 5. as shall be showed.

What say you to the other notes that are commonly given of the Church?
Either they are accidental, and in great part separable; or utterly impertinent, and forged for the upholding of the Romish Synagogue.

But is not Antiquity a certain note of the Church?
No: for errors are very ancient; and the Church when it began, was a Church, yet had no antiquity.

Is not Multitude a note?
No: for Christ's flock is a little flock; (Luk. 12. 32.) and Antichrist's very great. Rev. 13. 3, 48. & 18. 3.

Forty-third Head

Are not Miracles a mark of the Church?
No: for beside that wicked people may work them, (Mat. 7. 22, 23.) the Church of Christ hath been without miracles; and the coming of Antichrist is foretold to be with all power, and signs, and lying wonders: (2 Thes. 2. 9. Apo. 13. 13, 14.) such as those are whereof the Papists brag and boast, which are indeed no true miracles

May the Church err, and be corrupted, or fall, and become no Church?
First, we must distinguish of errors. Some are fundamental, such as raze the foundation of the Church (as the denying that Christ came in the flesh, or the denying of the resurrection:) and in these the Church cannot err. Others are of less moment; and in these it may err.

Secondly, the Catholic Church considered in her true members, can never utterly fall: (Mat. 16. 18. Phil. 1. 6. 1 Thes. 5. 24.) howsoever no Congregation be so pure, that it may be said at any time to be free from all corruption, (Cant. 1. 4, 5.) or so constant, but that, at times it may be shaken in the very foundation of truth; as may appear by the Churches of Corinth, Galatia, &c. 1 Cor. 15. 12, 13, 33. Gal. 3. 1. &c.

Thirdly, the Church being considered with respect to the place; God does not always continue a succession of true believers within the same limits and borders: and hence we say, that divers Churches are fallen, as those of Asia, &c. Neither is any place so privileged, but that for sin the Candlestick may in time be thence removed. Rev. 2. 5.

How may we judge of a Church corrupt, or ceasing to be a Church?
Where God utterly taking away the means of his Word and Worship, (Acts 13. 46.) hath apparently given the bill of divorce, (Es. 50. 1.) there are we not to acknowledge any Church at all: as at this day in Jerusalem, once the holy City. But where these means are yet continued, we are to acknowledge a Church of Christ, (Rev. 2. 12, 13.) howsoever more or less corrupt according to the greater or less abuse of God's Word and Worship.

Since Churches may be so diversely corrupted; from which, and how far are we to separate?
From Churches mortally sick of heresy (Tit. 3. 10, 11.) or Idolatry as it were a contagious plague or leprosy, we are to separate: (Rev. 18. 4.) howbeit, while there is yet any life, rather from the scab or sore, then from the body; that is, from the prevailing faction, maintaining fundamental errors, and forcing to Idolatrous worship. Such is our separation from the present Church of Rome, not from such therein, who either meaning well in general, are ignorant of the depth of Satan. (Rev. 2. 24.) or secretly dissent from these damnable corruptions; (1 Kin. 19. 18.) with whom, as a body yet retaining life, we desire to join, (Phil. 1. 18.) so far, as we may with safety from the foresaid contagion.

Are we to continue fellowship with all other Churches, not so deadly and dangerously corrupt?
From Churches holding the foundation, in substance of faith and worship, though otherwise not free from blemish, we are not to separate (1 Kin. 15. 14. & 22. 43.) farther then in dislike and refusal of that wherein they do apparently separate from Christ, in respect either of manners, doctrine, or form of public worship.

What are the enemies of the Church?
Besides these spiritual wickednesses, which sight against our souls; there are outward enemies also, that visibly oppose the Church of Christ.

How does Christ defend his Church against those enemies?
This is partly to be done by the Civil Magistrate, to whom it belongeth by civil means to maintain the Church in that truth and liberty, which Christ hath given unto it: and partly by the breath of Christ's own mouth in the preaching of the Gospel; yet not perfectly, but by the brightness of his coming in the latter day.

What is the estate of the Church, when these enemies do prevail?
The Church is often oppressed and darkened so by them, that it does partly degenerate, and is partly hid; but never wholly destroyed, nor altogether invisible.

Is not the Church always visible in her parts?
The persons are always visible. for Christ hath, and ever had from the beginning, his Church visible upon earth, (Rom. 11. 1, 2, 3, 4.) that is, some companies of Believers making profession of the same common faith. Yet the persecution may be such, that the visible Church may not appear thoroughly for a time: the professors being forced thereby to hide themselves from the eye of the world, (Rev. 12. 14.) and happily by the rage of the enemy so scattered, that (as in the days of Elias, 1 Kin. 19. 10, 14, 18.) they can hardly be known or have intercourse between themselves: And hence it is that the Church is compared to the Moon, sometimes in the full, and sometimes in the wane.

What distinction is there of the numbers of the visible Church?
Generally, they are all the family of Christ. (Eph. 3. 15.) which as sheep of his flock, are to hear his voice and follow him: (Joh. 10. 2, 3, 4) but more specially out of these Christ the chief Prince and Shepherd, hath instituted some to be above, some to be under; ordaining some to have preeminence and government, others to be governed and guided by them. Heb. 13. 17.

Whom hath Christ appointed to be governors and guides unto the rest?
1. Church officers and ministers, appointed to teach and govern the flock of Christ, and to feed it with the wholesome food of the Word and Sacraments. 1 Cor. 12. 18. 1 Tim 5. 17. Joh. 21. 15. 1 Pet. 5. 2.

2. Princes and Civil Magistrates, whom Christ hath charged to see to the ways of his household, (and so to rule and order it outwardly) that all, both Ministers and People, do their office and duty, even in things concerning God, Psal. 78. 71, 72. 2 Chron. 35. 2, &c. & 34. 32, 33.

What are the parts of the Ministry, committed to the officers of the Church?
The Word: (Rom. 10. 17. Joh. 5. 25. & 6. 68.) and the dependents thereof, viz. Sacraments, (1 Cor. 10. 1, 2, 3, 4.) and Censures. Mat. 18. 15. 1 Cor. 5.

What is the Word?
That part of the outward Ministry which consisteth in the delivery of Doctrine. (2 Chron 17. 9. Acts 2. 40, 41. & 11. 20. 1 Cor. 4. 15.) And this is the ordinary instrument which God useth in begetting of faith. Joh. 17. 20. Rom. 10. 17. Eph. 1. 13.

What order is there used in the delivery of the Word, for the begetting of Faith?
First, the Covenant of the Law is urged, to make sin and the punishment thereof known: whereupon the sting of conscience pricketh the heart with a sense of God's wrath, and maketh a man utterly to despair of any ability in himself to obtain everlasting life. After this preparation, the promises of the Gospel are propounded: whereupon the sinner, conceiving hope of pardon, goes to God for mercy; and particularly applieth to his own soul those comfortable promises which in the word are propounded. Rom 3 19.

& 7. 9, 10. Gal. 3. 22, 23. Acts 2. 37. Mat 15. 24. Gal. 2. 19, 20. Heb. 4. 16. Hosea 14. 2, 3. Rom. 8. 15, 16.

What is the inward means for the begetting of Faith?
The holy spirit of God.

Is it not lawful to separate the inward means from the outward?
In no case: for those things which God hath joined together no man may separate, Mat. 19. 6.

How does it appear, that God hath joined both these means together?
Because he saith by the Prophet, Isa. 59. 21. that this is the Covenant that he will make with his people; to put his Spirit and Word in them, and in all the posterity of the Church. The Apostle in like manner, 1 Thes. 5. 19, 20. joineth these two together: Quench not the Spirit, and Despise not prophesying.

It would seem by these words of the Apostle, that the spirit of Adoption and Sanctification, proper to the faithful, may be lost; whilst he exhorteth that we should not quench the Spirit.
By no means: but as God does assure the faithful of their continuance in him, so he does declare by these exhortations, that the only means whereby we should nourish this holy fire in us, is to take heed unto the preaching of the Word.

Is by the word prophesying only meant the preaching of the Word?
No: but by a figurative speech, all those outward means whereby God useth to give his holy Spirit, as are the Sacraments and the discipline of the Church; over and above the preaching of the Word, which being principal of all, is here set down for the rest.

Why does the Apostle set the Spirit before the preaching of the Word, meant by Prophesy: considering that by and after preaching of the Word the Lord giveth his Spirit?
1. Because the Spirit is the chief of the two: the Word being but the instrument whereby the Spirit of God worketh. 2. For that the work of the Spirit is more general, and reacheth to some to whom the preaching of the Word cannot reach. 3. For that the Word is never profitable without the Spirit: but the Spirit may be profitable without the Word, as after will appear.

What do you learn of this, that the means of God's Spirit and Word are usually conjoined together?
That no man is to content himself with this fantasy, to think that he hath the Spirit, and so to neglect the Word: because they go together.

Who are by this condemned?
The Anabaptists, Papists and Libertines, which ascribe to the spirit that which they like, although wickedly: seeing the Spirit does not ordinarily suggest any thing to us, but that which it teacheth us out of the Word. Joh. 14. 26.

What other sort of men are here condemned?
The Stancarists, who esteem the Word to be fit to catechize, and to initiate or enter us in the Rudiments of Religion; but too base to exercise ourselves continually in it: whereas the Prophets and Apostle, most excellent men did notwithstanding exercise themselves in the Scriptures. Mar. 4. 1, 2, &c. compared with Isa. 2. 1, 2, &c. 2 Pet. 3. 15, 16.

Are none saved without hearing of the Word?
Yes. For first, children which are within the Covenant, have the Spirit of God, without the ordinary means of the Word and Sacraments, Mat. 2. Ro. 8. 9, 14. Secondly, some also of age in places where these means are not to be had. Thirdly, some also which live in places where such means are, yet have not capacity to understand them; as some natural fools, mad men, or deaf born, to show that God is not tied to means.

What must we here take heed of?
That we presume not upon this, since that notwithstanding this secret working of God, yet it is as impossible to come to heaven, if having the means and capacity of receiving them, we condemn the means; as it is impossible to have a harvest, where no seed time hath gone before; (Mat. 13.) or to have children without the Parents seed: (1 Pet. 1. 23.) seeing amongst such the Spirit of God works faith only by the preaching of the Word. Indeed where the Lord placeth not the preaching of the Word, there he can and does work faith without it: but where he hath placed it, he will not do it without. In times and places where Popery hath prevailed, many were, (and may be so at this day in Spain and Rome) converted by the very bare reading of the Word, yea without the reading of the Word: but not so among them who have or may have it, either by going from home to it, or fetching it home to them.

How is the divers working of God's Spirit, by the Ministry of the Word, set out unto us?
By the parable of the seed, three parts whereof fell into barren and unprofitable ground, one into good and fruitful. Mat. 13. 3, 9, 18, 19, 24.

Are not three parts of the four in the Church likely to be condemned by this Parable?
No, in no case. For it is both curious, and uncomfortable doctrine: it being a far different thing to have three sorts of wicked men in four sorts and to have thrice as many of one sort.

What is the first thing you observe here common to the Godly with the wicked?
To understand something of the word of grace; and to give consent unto the same.

If they understand it, how is it that the first sort of unfruitful hearers are said not to understand? Mat. 13. 19.
They have some understanding, but it is said to be none, because it is no clear knowledge, (whereof they can give a reason out of the Word) nor effectual. Which ariseth from hence; for that they come without affection, and go away without care.

What are we here to learn?
1. To take heed not to deceive ourselves in a bare profession or light knowledge of the Word; and that we come to hear it with zeal, and depart with care to profit. 2. To be ware of the great subtlety of Satan, who as a swift bird, snatcheth the Word out of unprepared hearts; even as also does a thief, which taketh away whatsoever he findeth loose.

What observe you in the second sort, common to the Godly with the wicked?
To have some kind of delight in the Word, and a glimpse of the life to come. Mat. 13. 20. Heb. 6. 5.

What difference is there between a godly joy and this?
1. This is like the blaze of the fire, and is never full and sufficient: whereas the Godly joy is above that in gold and silver. 2. The wicked's delight is for another purpose, than

is the Godly's. For it is only to satisfy a humor desirous to know something more than others: whereas the Godly's joy is to know further, to the end they may practice.

Why is it said they have no root? Mat. 13. 21.
Because, though they understand the things, yet are they not grounded upon the reasons and testimonies of the Word, nor transformed into the obedience of the Gospel: and therefore when persecution cometh, they wither away.

Proceed to the third sort.
They are they which keep it, (it may be with some suffering of perfection:) yet the thorns of covetousness, or of worldly delights, overgrow the good seed, and make it unfruitful.

So much of the three sorts of unfruitful soil, and therein of the things common to the godly with the wicked. What are the things proper to the godly; signified by the good and fruitful ground?
1. The receiving of the seed in a good heart. 2. The bringing forth of fruit with patience. Luk. 8. 15.

What is there meant by receiving the seed into a good heart?
By the seed, is meant, the word of promise; whereby God hath said he will be merciful to us in Christ. By receiving it into a good heart, is meant, the receiving it by faith in Christ.

Where it is said, that the Word must be received into a good heart; it may seem that a man hath a good heart before he receiveth that seed?
Doubtless naturally they are all alike, and there is never a barrel better herring (as they say:) but as the face answereth the face in the glass; so one of the sons of Adam is like another in their nativity they have by their parents, till they be regenerated. And therefore it is called a good heart, in respect of God's changing of it by the engrafted word. (Ja. 1. 21.) And by these words he putteth difference between the fruits of the three former, and the fruits of this last: for that there is no difference in the outward show of fruits but only in regard that those fruits proceed from an unclean heart, and those from a heart that is cleansed.

How may we know that we have true faith; and so approve ourselves that we are good ground?
By good fruits, which are the effects of faith.

What are the effects of faith?
Reconciliation, and Sanctification. (Rom. 8. 1, 2, 3. Eph. 2. 6. Col. 2. 1, 2, 3,) The fruits of the former are set down, Rom. 5. 1, 2, 3, 4. The fruits of the latter, are Repentance and new Obedience: which have been already declared.

What special tokens observe you out of the former whereby we may discern a justifying faith from the faith of worldlings?
The end of our faith being the salvation of our souls, which shall be at the day of judgment, if we can willingly forsake father and mother, sister and brother, wife and children, and abandon the world, and say; Come Lord Jesus, come quickly: we may assure ourselves we are in a happy case.

What special marks of a justifying faith observe you out of the latter?
1. To be zealous of God's glory. 2. To love God's children. For these be the special effects of our holy Faith.

What is the Word farther compared with, and likened unto?

The Apostle Peter, 1 cap. 2. v. 1, 2. compares it unto milk: As new born babes desire the sincere milk of the word, that you may grow thereby. Teaching us, that the word is not only of use for our begetting unto God; but for our daily nourishment, that we may grow in grace, and in the knowledge of our Lord Jesus Christ. 2 Pet. 3. 18. So it is called a light, a lantern; and is appointed to be our guide, our Counselor, our Comforter, &c.

Is this meant only of the word preached?

Doubtless, the blessing of God does in an especial manner wait upon that ordinance. Whence it is said, that when Christ ascended up on high, he gave gifts to men, some Apostles, and some Pastors and teachers, for the gathering of the Saints, far the edifying of the body of Christ, (Ep. 4. 12.) yet withal, the reading of the Word with prayer and diligence, is of singular use and benefit, and commended unto us by our Savior, Search the Scriptures? Joh. 5. 59. and how readest thou? Luk. 10. 26. and by the example of the Bereans, who searched the Scriptures daily, and examined the things they heard in the public ministry of them. Acts 17. 11.

[44TH HEAD.]

So much of the Word. What are the dependants annexed to it?

Sacraments, (1 Cor. 10. 3, 4.) and Censures: (Mat. 18, 15. 1 Cor. 5.) the one, sealing the promises; the other, the threatenings of the Gospel.

What are Sacraments?

Seals of the promise of God in Christ: wherein by certain outward signs,
(and sacramental actions concerning the same) commanded by God, and delivered by his minister, Christ Jesus with all his saving graces is signified, conveyed, and sealed unto the heart of a Christian. For Sacraments are seals annexed by God to the word of the Covenant of grace; (Rom. 4. 11. 1 Cor. 11. 23.) to instruct, assure, and possess us of our part in Christ and his benefits, (Gal. 3. 27.) and to bind us to all thankful obedience unto God in him Rom. 6. 4.

Was not God's Word sufficient? What need have we of Sacraments?

This argues our infirmity, and manifesteth God's great love and mercy: who for the furthering of our understanding hath added visible signs to his Word, that our ear might not only be informed of the truth, but our eyes also might more plainly see it; and for the greater strengthening of our faith, vouchsafe to confirm the covenant of grace unto us not only by promise, but also by outward seals annexed thereunto. The like means had Adam himself in Paradise, to put him in remembrance of God's will. And if he in perfection needed a token of God's favor, (which was the tree of life,) how much more we that are corrupt and sinful? If we were Spirits or Angels, we should not need these helps: but since God knowing our frailties and what is best for us, hath given us these seals to our further comfort, let us use the receipt of so skillful a Physician, unless we will hasten our own deaths.

How does God by the Sacraments assure us of his mercies in Christ?

By exhibiting to the worthy receiver, by such outward signs, (whether Elements, or Actions) as himself for the relief of our weakness hath prescribed, whole Christ, God and man, with all his benefits; (1 Cor. 10. 4.) in whom all the promises of God are yea and Amen. 2 Cor. 1. 20.

Forty-fourth Head

Do they seal nothing else but the promise of God unto us?
Yes: they seal our promise unto God, that we take him only for our God and Redeemer; whom alone by faith we rest on, and whom we will obey.

How do they bind us unto God?
We receiving them as pledges of his infinite love in Christ, do thereby profess ourselves bound to express our thankfulness, by all duties to his Majesty; (Col. 2. 6, 7.) and for his sake one to another. Eph. 4. 3, 4, 5.

Describe yet more largely what a Sacrament is.
A Sacrament is an ordinance of God, wherein by giving and receiving of outward elements, according to his will, the promises of the Covenant of grace, made in the blood of Christ, being represented, exhibited and applied unto us, are further signed and sealed betwixt God and man. Or, It is an action of the whole Church, wherein by certain visible signs and outward things done according to God's instruction, inward things being betokened, Christ with all his benefits is both offered unto us, and received by us: offered (I say) to all in the Church, but exhibited only to the faithful, for the strengthening of their faith in the eternal Covenant, and the bringing them more effectually to the practice of God's Commandments. Ex. 12. 6. Luk. 1. 59. & 3. 3, 16. 1 Cor. 11. 23. Mat. 26. 26. Rom. 4. 11. & 6. 4. 1 Pet. 3. 21.

Why call you it an action?
Because it is not a bare sign alone, but a work. 1 Cor. 11. 24, 25.

Why call you it an action of the whole Church?
Because it is a public action, and appertaineth to the whole Church: and therefore ought to be done in the presence of the congregation, by the example of John, (Mat. 3. 11, 12.) and commended of Paul, 1 Cor. 11. 18, 20, 22. it being a greater indignity for the Sacraments to be administered privately, than for the civil judgment, which is open and public; that we say nothing of the Sacrifices under the Law, which were not so excellent as these; and yet it was not lawful to offer them in private. Which reproveth the disorder of the Papists, who turn the Communion into a private Mass, and minister the Lord's Supper to one alone without the presence of the Congregation.

But may not the Sacraments be so administered upon necessity; as namely to a sick man ready to depart out of this life?
There is no such necessity. For a man believing, wanting that opportunity of coming to the Lord's Supper, wanteth not the effect thereof: seeing the Lord promised by Ezekiel, that he would be a Tabernacle to his people, being banished from it. (Eze. 37. 27.) And therefore the want of the Sacraments does not hurt, when with convenience a man cannot enjoy them; but the contempt or neglect of them, when they may conveniently be come unto.

What then is the fittest time and place for the administration of the Sacraments?
The fittest time, is the Lord's day or some other day of public meeting: The most convenient place is the Church and usual place of the assembly of the Congregation.

Did not Abraham minister the Sacrament of Circumcision in his private house?
His house was at that time the Church of God, and therefore not private. And so in the time of persecution, the Godly did oft-times meet in Barns and such obscure places; which were indeed public, because of the Church of God there: the house or place availing nothing to make it public or private. Even as wherever the Prince is, there is the Court also said to be although it were in a poor Cottage.

What difference is there between a Sacrament and a Sacrifice?
In a Sacrifice, there is an offering made to God; in a Sacrament, there is an offer made by God to us. In the Sacrifices Christ was signified as given for us, in the Sacraments as given to us: the Sacrifices were only signs, the Sacraments seals also.

Who is the author of a Sacrament?
God alone; because he only can bestow those graces which are sealed in a Sacrament.

How does God ordain a Sacrament?
By his Word.

How many parts of God's Word are there, whereby he does institute and ordain a Sacrament?
First, a commandment to do it. Secondly a promise of a blessing upon the right using of it.

Was not the Rainbow a Sacrament, being a sign ordained by God?
No. For though it were a sign, yet it was no sign of salvation by Christ.

What is the matter and substance of every Sacrament?
One and the same Jesus Christ although diversely communicated in divers Sacraments, and in some more forcibly than in others; because of some Elements communication with or taking hold of, or reaching to more of our senses.

What things then are required in a Sacrament?
Three. First, the outward signs; and sacramental actions concerning the same. Secondly, the inward things signified thereby: viz. Christ Jesus, with his saving graces and spiritual actions concerning the same. Thirdly, a similitude betwixt them both. As in Baptism for example; that as water does wash the body, so does the blood of Christ wash away the spots of the soul.

What signs are used in Sacraments?
Some only representing, as water, bread and wine: some applying; as washing, eating, drinking, and such like.

What are the things signified?
First, Christ Jesus and his merits: and secondly, the applying of the same unto us in particular.

Wherein do the signs and the things signified differ?
1. In Nature. 2. In the manner of receiving. 3. In the parts which do receive them. 4. In the necessity of the receiving of them.

Wherein do they agree?
In this, that the sign does so fitly represent the things signified thereby, that the mind of a Christian is drawn by the sign to consider of the things signified.

What then is the Sacramental union, betwixt the signs and the things signified?
Such as betwixt a sealed will, and the things conveyed in the same. From whence it is, that the names, effects, and properties of the one are given to the other.

What is the cause that moved the Lord to grace the outward signs in the Sacraments, with the names of the things signified?
The outward elements have the names of the spiritual things they set forth: 1 because of their fit proportion and agreement, in regard of the resemblance and similitude of the

elements and the things signified; in which respect they are called Signs. 2. To show the inseparable conjunction of the things signified with the sign, in the worthy receiver; in which regard they are called Seals: as in the person of Christ his two natures are so inseparably united, that often times the properties and effects of the one are attributed to the other.

What is the ground of this sacramental union?
In general, the institution of Christ, whereby fit things are appointed so to be used, with a promise annexed. In special, the applying of that word unto certain special signs with prayer. In particular and unto me the ground is, my reverent and worthy receiving.

What is the use of Sacraments?
God hath ordained them, to the end that by comparing and conferring the outward things with the inward, they might help,

First, our understanding; in which regard they are as it were Images and glasses. Gal. 3. 1. Second, our remembrance; in which respect they are monuments. Luk. 22. 19. 1 Cor. 11. 24. Third, and specially, the persuasions of our hearts; by reason whereof they are seals and pledges. Rom. 4. 11. For they are appointed by God to strengthen us in the promises of salvation, which God hath not only made to us in word, but also confirmed the same by writ: and left that we should any ways doubt (as naturally we are inclined) he hath set to his seals, according to the manner of men; that nothing might be lacking which should increase our strength.

What doctrine is here to be gathered?
1. What root of blindness, of forgetfulness, and especially hardness of heart to believe, is in us; that the Word and Oath of God is not sufficient to pluck up, but that we must have such aids. 2. The mercy of God, that applieth himself to our weakness. 3. What miserable men they are that refuse the Sacraments.

Repeat the principal ends, for which God hath instituted the Sacraments?
To help our insight as clear glasses; to relieve our memories as lasting monuments; and to confirm our faith, as most certain feals and pledges: from whence they become our bonds of obedience, and the marks and badges of our profession. So the ends for which they are appointed are these four.

First, the clearing of our knowledge. Second, the helping of our memories. Third, the strengthening of our faith. Fourth, the quickening of our obedience.

How may we more clearly consider of those things which are ministered in the Sacraments?
By considering distinctly, the things given and received, and the persons giving and receiving.

What are the things given and received?
They are partly outward, and partly inward.

What are the outward?
The visible creatures, ordained for signs and figures of Christ: as under the time of the Gospel, Water, Bread, and Wine.

Why hath God made choice of these creatures?
Both in respect they are for their natural properties most fit to represent the spiritual things: as also for that they are most generally used of all nations in the world.

What are we to learn from hence?
The wonderful wisdom of God, that hath chosen base and common things, for so high and singular mysteries: whereas he might have chosen things more rare and of greater price, to set out such excellent benefits as are offered to us in the Sacraments. Wherein there is great difference between the time of the Law and of the Gospel.

What are the inward things?
The invisible and spiritual: Graces namely, Christ, with all his benefits.

What learn you of this?
Not to stick to the outward elements, but to lift up our hearts unto God; accounting the elements as a ladder, whereby to climb up to those celestial things which they represent.

So much of the things, what are the persons?
The Giver, and the Receiver.

How many Givers are there?
Two: the outward, giving the outward; and the inward, giving the inward things.

Who is the inward Giver?
God himself: even the holy Trinity, God the Father, God the Son, and God the holy Ghost.

What are the actions of God in a Sacrament?
They are principally two: 1. To offer and teach forth Christ and his graces. 2. To apply them to the heart of the faithful communicant.

Who are the outward givers?
The Ministers especially, representing unto us the Lord, whose stewards they are. Mat. 28. 19. 1 Cor. 4. 1.

What is the Ministers office herein?
To consecrate the elements, and then to distribute them.

Wherein consisteth the consecration of the elements?
Partly in declaring the institution of the Sacraments, and partly in going before the Congregation in prayer unto God. First in praising God, who hath ordained such means for the relief of our weakness: then in suing to God, that he would please to make those means effectual to that end, for which they were ordained.

Is not the substance of the elements changed by this consecration?
No verily: only the use is altered in that they are separated from a common to a holy use: which change and alteration continueth only while the action is in hand.

Does the Minister with the signs give the thing signified also?
No: he only dispenseth the signs: but it is God that giveth and dispenseth the things signified. Mat. 3. 11.

Is God always present to give the thing signified to all them that the Minister giveth the sign?
No, not to all: for some in receiving the signs, receive together with them their own judgment. (1 Cor. 11. 29) Yet he is always ready to give the thing signified to all those that are fit to receive the Sacraments: and to such persons the signs and things signified are always conjoined.

Forty-fourth Head

Who are the persons that are to receive the Sacraments?
All Christians that are prepared thereunto.

Is there any special preparation required to the receiving of the Sacraments?
Yes verily: for seeing men ought to come with preparation to the hearing of the Word alone; they ought much more to come when the Sacraments are administered also, wherein God does offer himself more familiarly and visibly to us. Exod. 3. 5. 1 Cor. 11. 28.

What is the preparation that is required in them that come to receive the Sacraments?
There is required in those that are of years of discretion, to a worthy participation of the Sacraments, knowledge, faith, and feeling, both in the Law, and in the Gospel.

Seeing no man is able to attain the knowledge of the Law and the Gospel perfectly, much less the simple and common people: tell me, how far is this knowledge, faith and feeling, necessary?
First, concerning the Law, it is necessary that the receiver of the Sacrament be able to understand and believe the common corruption of all men, both in the bitter root of original sin, and in the poisoned fruits thereof, together with the curse of everlasting death due thereunto; and that he be able to apply both these, that is, the sin and wages thereof, to himself.

Secondly, concerning the Gospel, that he be able (in some measure) to understand the Covenant of grace, which God in Christ hath made with the sons of men; and then that by faith he be able (in some measure) to apply the same to himself.

What ariseth from this knowledge, faith, and feeling, to a further preparation thereunto?
A true and earnest desire to be made partaker of the Sacraments; with a conscionable care to perform special duties, in and after the action of receiving. Mat. 3. 13. Acts 8. 36. Luk. 22. 15.

What duties in the action of receiving are to be performed?
First, a grave and reverent behavior, befitting such holy mysteries. Secondly, an attentive heedfulness in comparing the outward signs and actions in the Sacraments, with the inward and spiritual things which they betoken.

What duties are to be performed after the partaking of the Sacraments?
If we have a sense and feeling of the gracious work of God by them, we are to rejoice with thanksgiving; if not, we are to enter into judgment with ourselves, and to humble, ourselves for want therein. And though we ought to be humbled, if we feel not the work of God in us, in or after the Sacraments: as that which argueth want of preparation before, or attention in receiving of them; yet ought we not therefore to be altogether dismayed: for as the sick man feeleth not the nourishment of his meat, because of his malady, and yet notwithstanding is nourished; so it is in such faithful ones, as do not sensibly feel the working of God in and by the Sacraments, through the weakness of their faith. And although we cannot feel it immediately, yet after (by the fruits thereof) we shall be able to discern of our profiting thereby.

How many kinds of Sacraments be there?
Two. The first of the Admission of God's children into the Church there to be partakers of an everlasting communion with Christ. The second of their Preservation and nourishment therein; to assure them of their continual increase in Christ. (1 Cor. 10. 1, 2, 3, 4. Exod. 12. 48.) In which respect the former is once only; the latter often to be administered.

A Body of Divinity

[45TH HEAD.]

Hath the administration of the Gospel been always after the same manner?
For substance it always hath been the same: but in regard of the manner proper to certain times, it is distinguished into two kinds; the Old and the New. Heb. 11. & 13. & 13. 8. Acts 10. 43. & 15. 11. &c. 26. 6, 7. Luke 16. 16. Joh. 1. 17. Heb. 11. 2. & 8. 8, 9, 10, 13. & 9. 9, 10, 11. 2 Cor 3. 6, 7, 8.

What call you the old Ministry?
That which was delivered unto the Fathers, to continue until the fullness of times; wherein by the coming of Christ it was to be reformed. Heb. 1. 1. & 9. 10. Acts 7. 44. 2 Cor. 3. 7, 11.

What were the properties of this Ministry?
First, the commandments of the Law were more largely, and the promises of Christ more sparingly and darkly propounded: these latter being so much the more generally and obscurely delivered, as the manifesting of them was further off. Malachi. 4. 4, 5. Jer. 31. 32, 33. Heb. 11. 13. 2 Cor. 3. 13, 18.

Secondly, the promises of things to come were shadowed with a multitude of types and figures; which when the truth should be exhibited, were to vanish away. Heb. 8. 9, 13. & 9. 1, 8, 9, 10. 2 Cor. 3. 11, 13. Gal. 4. 3, 4. Col. 2. 16, 17.

What were the chief States and Periods of this old Ministry?
The first from Adam to Abraham; the second from Abraham to Christ.

What were the special properties of the latter of these two Periods?
First it was more specially restrained unto a certain Family and Nation. Luke. 1. 54, 55. Psalm. 147. 19, 20. Rom. 9. 4. Acts 13. 17. Deut. 4. 1, 6, 7, 8. & 14. 2. & 26. 18, 19. Secondly, it had joined with it a solemn repetition and declaration of the first Covenant of the Law. John 1. 17. Exod. 24. 7, 8. Deut. 4. 12, 13. & 5. 2, 5. & 27. 26. Rom. 10. 5. Thirdly, besides the ceremonies, (which were greatly enlarged under Moses) it had Sacraments also added unto it. Heb. 9. 1, 2, 3. Acts 7. 44, 45, 46, 47.

What were the ordinary Sacraments of this ministry?
The Sacrament of Admission into the Church was circumcision instituted in the days of Abraham: (Gen. 17. 9, 10. John 7. 22. Exod. 12. 48. Deut. 30. 6, 7, 8. Acts 7. 8. Rom. 2. 28, 29. & 4. 11. Col. 2. 11.) The other of continual Preservation and nourishment, was the Paschal Lamb, instituted in the time of Moses. Exod. 12. 3, 4. Num. 9. 11, 12. Deut. 16. 2. 1 Cor. 5. 7. 1 Pet. 1. 19. John 19. 36. with Exod. 12. 46.

[46TH HEAD.]

What is the new administration of the Gospel?
That which was delivered unto us by Christ: which is to continue unto the end of the world. Joh. 1. 17. Heb. 1. 2. & 2. 3, 4. & 3. 5, 6. & 12. 25, 26, 27, 28. 2 Cor. 3. 11.

What are the properties thereof?
First it is propounded indifferently to all people, whether they be Jews or Gentiles; and in that respect is Catholic or universal. Isa. 54. 1, 2, 3. & 60. 3, 4, 5. & 65. 1. & 66. 12, 19, 20. Mat. 18. 19, 20. Rom. 16. 25, 26. Eph. 3. 5, 6, 8, 9. Col. 1. 5, 6. Secondly, it is full of

grace and truth; bringing joyful tidings unto mankind that whatsoever was formerly promised of Christ, is now performed, and so instead of the ancient types and shadows, exhibiteth the things themselves; with a large and clear declaration of all the benefits of the Gospel. Joh. 1. 17. & 17. 21, 25. Rom. 1. 1, 2, 3. 1 Pet. 1. 10, 11, 12. 1 Cor. 1. 23, 24. & 2. 9, 16. 2. Cor. 3. 11, 13, 14, 18.

What are the principal points of the Word of his ministry?
That Christ our Savior (whom God by his prophets had promised to send into the world) is come in the flesh, and hath accomplished the work of our Redemption. That he was conceived of the Holy Ghost, born of the Virgin Mary, suffered under Pontius Pilate, was crucified, and died upon the Cross. That the body and soul being thus separated, his Body was laid in the grave, and remained there under the power of death, and his Soul went into the place appointed for the souls of the righteous; namely, Paradise, the seat of the blessed. That the third day, body and soul being joined together again, he rose from the dead, and afterwards ascended into Heaven; where he sitteth at the right hand of his Father, until such times as from thence he shall come unto the last Judgment. Rom. 1. 35. Joh. 1. 14, 15. & 19. 28, 30. Heb. 9. 12, 26, 28. 1 Tim. 3. 16. Luke 1. 35. Matt. 1. 18, 19, 20, 21, 22, 23. & 27. 2, 26. verse ad. 50. & 12. 40. & 27. 59, 60. Rom. 6. 9. Luke 23. 43, 46, 47. Mat. 16. 21. & 28. 19, 17. 1 Cor. 15. 4, 5, 6. 2 Tim. 2. 8. Mar. 10. 19. Acts 1. 2, 3, 9, 10, 11. Ephes. 4. 10. Heb. 1. 3. 2 Tim. 4. 1.

How do the Sacraments of the new Testament differ from those of the Old?
In respect, not of the Author, God; the substance, Christ; or the receivers, the people of God; which are in both the same: (Rom. 4. 11. 1 Cor. 10. 2, 3, 4.) But of continuance. (Mat. 28. 19, 20.) evidence, (1 Cor. 11. 26.) easy performance, and efficacy; in all which those of the new Testament have great preeminence; (2 Cor. 3. 9.)

What Sacraments be there of the New Testament?
Only two: to wit, Baptism, succeeding in the place of Circumcision; and the Supper of the Lord, answering to the Passover. (Rom. 4. 1. Gen. 17. 11, 12. 1 Cor. 10. 1, 2, 3. and 12. 13. Mat. 26. 26. and 28. 19.) By the former we have our admission into the true Church of God: by the latter we are nourished and preserved in the Church after our admission.

How may it appear, that there be no more then two Sacraments of the New Testament?
First, when the number of Sacraments were most necessary (as under the law) they had but two: whereof we need require no more. 1 Cor. 10. 1, 2, 3.

Secondly, having meat, drink and cloths, we ought therewith to be content. (1 Tim. 6. 8.) Now by the Sacrament of our entrance, our spiritual clothing is sealed unto us: (Gal. 3. 27.) and by that of our growth is sealed our feeding. (1 Cor. 10. 16.)

Thirdly, these two seals assure us of all God's graces; as of our regeneration, entrance and engrafting into Christ, so of our growth and continuance in him: and therefore we need no more. (1 Cor. 12. 13.) For there are as many Sacraments, as there be things that need to be betokened to us about our justification. Now they be two; our birth in Christ, and our nourishment after we are born: as in the bodily life we see that we need no more, but to be born, and then to have this life preserved. The Sacrament of Baptism showeth us the first; the Sacrament of the Lord's Supper the second.

Therefore those five other Sacraments, of Confirmation, Penance, Matrimony, Orders and extreme Unction, joined by the Papists, are superfluous. Because some of them have no warrant at all out of the Word of God, and God hath not promised a blessing upon the using of them; others of them, though they be agreeable to the Word, yet are without the nature and number of Sacraments.

[47TH HEAD.]

What is Baptism?
It is the first Sacrament of the New Testament by the washing of water (Eph. 5. 26.) representing the powerful washing of the blood and spirit of Christ; (1 Cor. 9. 11. Heb. 10. 22.) and so sealing our regeneration or new birth, our entrance into the Covenant of Grace, and our engrafting into Christ, and into the body of Christ, which is his Church. (John 3. 5. Tit. 3. 5. Acts 8. 27.) The word Baptism signifieth in general any washing: but here is specially taken for that sacramental washing which sealeth unto those that are within God's covenant, their birth in Christ and entrance into Christianity.

How was this Sacrament ordained and brought into the Church, in the place of Circumcision?
At the Commandment of God, (Joh 1. 33.) by the Ministry of John, therefore called the Baptist: (Mat. 3. 1.) after sanctified and confirmed by our Savior Christ himself, being baptized by John, (Mat. 3. 13.) and giving commission to his Apostles and Ministers, to continue the same in his Church unto the end. (Mat. 28. 18, 19.)

Why call you it the first Sacrament?
Because Christ gave order to his Apostles, that after they have taught, and men believe they shall baptize them; that so they might be enrolled amongst those of the household of God, and entered into the number of the Citizens and Burgesses of the heavenly Jerusalem.

What abuse does this take away?
That which sometimes the ancient Church was infected withal: namely, that they baptized men at their deaths, and let them receive the Lord's Supper twice or thrice a year; whereas this is the first Sacrament of the Covenant.

What are the essential parts of this Sacrament of Baptism?
As of all other Sacraments, two: the outward signs, and the inward things signified. Where also is to be considered, the proportion and union which is between those two parts, which is as it were the very form and inward excellency of a Sacrament.

What are the outward signs in Baptism?
They are the outward elements of water, and the outward sacramental actions performed about it.

What are those Sacramental actions?
First, the Ministers blessing and consecrating the water. And secondly, the right applying it so consecrated, to the party to be baptized.

May none but a lawful Minister baptize?
No. For Baptism is a part of the public Ministry of the Church, and Christ hath given warrant and authority to none to baptize, but those whom he hath called to preach the Gospel: Go, Preach and Baptize. Mat. 28. 19. those only may stand in the room of God himself, and ministerially set to the seal of the Covenant. And it is monstrous presumption for Women, or any other private persons, (who are not called) to

meddle with such high Mysteries; nor can there be any case of necessity to urge, as will appear afterwards.

Touching the first action of the Minister; how is he to bless and consecrate the water?
First, by opening to them that are present the doctrine of Baptism, and the right institution and use of it; what inward mysteries are signified and sealed up by those outward signs. So did John, when he baptized: he preached the doctrine of Repentance, and taught the people the inward baptism of the Spirit, signified by his baptizing with water. Mat. 3. 11.

Secondly, by acknowledging in the name of the congregation mans natural pollution that we stand in need of spiritual washing; by giving thanks to God the Father for giving his Son for a propitiation for our sins, and appointing his blood to be a fountain to the house of Israel, to wash in; and for ordaining of this service to be a Sacrament and seal of so great a mystery.

Thirdly, by making profession of Faith in God's promises in that behalf, and praying that they may be made good unto the party that is to receive the seal thereof. For as every thing is sanctified by the Word of God and prayer: so in especial manner the Sacramental water in Baptism is blessed and consecrated by the Word of institution, and prayer to God for a blessing upon his own Ordinance.

What is the second Sacramental action?
The action of washing, that is, of applying the Sacramental water unto the party to be baptized; diving or dipping him into it, or sprinkling him with it, In the name of the Father, the Son, and of the Holy Ghost.

Is the action of diving, or dipping, material and essential to the Sacrament? Or is there absolute ground and warrant for sprinkling; which is most commonly practiced with us in these cold Countries? Mat. 28. 19.
Some there are that stand strictly for the particular action of diving or dipping, the baptized under water, as the only action which the institution of this Sacrament will bear; and our Church allows no other, except in case of the child's weakness, and there is expressed in our Savior's baptism, both his descending into the water and rising up: so that some think our common sprinkling to be (through ease and tenderness) a stretching the liberty of the Church further than either the Church would, or the symbolism of the outward sign with the thing signified can safely admit, it typifying our spiritual burial and resurrection. Rom 6. 8.

Others conceive the action of sprinkling of water upon the face of the baptized very warrantable; especially in young children, to whom further wetting may be dangerous, and the grounds are these.

First, it seems that neither dipping is essential to the Sacrament of Baptism, nor sprinkling; but only washing and applying water to the body, as a cleanser of the filth thereof.

Secondly, then as in the other Sacrament, a spoonful of wine is as significant as a whole Gallon; so here, a handful of water is as significant as a whole River.

Thirdly, the action of sprinkling bears fit resemblance with the inward as well as dipping and hath authority in the Scriptures. Read 1 Pet. 1. 2. and Heb. 12. 24. Where is speech of the sprinkling of the blood of Christ, and the blood of sprinkling speaking better things than the blood of Abel.

Fourthly, it is not unlikely that the Apostles baptized as well by sprinkling or pouring upon, as by diving and dipping into; since we read of divers baptized in houses, as well as others in rivers. However the washing the body by water is essential (Ephes, 5. 26.) though whether way it be done, seem not to be essential; so water be applied to the body for the cleansing of it.

Thus much of the Sacramental element, and Sacramental actions, which are the outward part of Baptism: What now is the inward part?
Those spiritual things which are signified and represented, and exhibited in and by the outward element and actions. As the water signifies the blood of Christ, the Ministers consecrating the water signifies God the Father's setting apart his Son for the expiation of the sins of the world by his blood; the Ministers applying the water to the body of the baptized to cleanse it, signifieth God's applying the blood of his Son to cleanse the soul for justification and remission of sins: and not only to signify but to seal up unto the believer, that the inward part is effected as well as the outward.

How come these visible things to signify such invisible mysteries?
There is a natural fitness and aptness in the outward things to express the inward. As for water to be a resemblance of the blood of Christ; thus they agree. First, water is a necessary element; the natural life of man cannot be without it: and the blood of Christ is as necessary to his spiritual life.

Secondly, water is a comfortable element; as the Hart panteth after the water brooks. Psal. 42. 1. The thirst of the body cannot be quenched but by water: whence the height of misery is described by a barren and dry ground where no water is, Psal. 63. 1. So the thirst of the soul cannot be quenched but by the blood of Christ. John 4. 13, 14.

Thirdly, water is a free element: as it is necessary, useful, and comfortable, so it is cheap and easy to come by without cost. So is the blood of Christ. Isa. 55. 1. Ho, every one that thirsteth, come ye to the waters.

Fourthly, water is a common element: none are barred from it, any may go to the river and drink. And the blood of Christ is offered as generally to all, rich and poor, high and low, bond and free; every one may lay claim unto him, come and have interest in him, John 1. 12. Whoever receiveth him, whoever believeth, the proposals is without restraint; none can say I am shut out or excepted.

Fifthly, water is a copious and plentiful element; there is no less in the River for thy drinking of it, there is enough for all men. So is the blood of Christ all-sufficient, it can never be drawn dry: of his fullness we may all receive, and yet he never the more empty. Hence the Scripture speaks of plenteous redemption.

Sixthly, lastly and especially, water is a cleansing and a purifying element: and it resembles the blood of Christ fitly in that; for 1 John 1. 7. The blood of Christ cleanseth us from all sin.

And here we may also observe the symbolism between the Sacramental action of washing, and the inward grace signified.

First, nothing is washed but that which is unclean: even so the Sacramental washing implies our natural pollution: Whosoever submits to this Sacrament of Baptism, does by so doing acknowledge himself to be defiled; whoever brings a child to be baptized, does by so doing make confession of original corruption and sinfulness, as John's hearers were baptized of him in Jordan confessing their sins. Mat. 3. 6.

Secondly, as the applying of the water to the body washeth and cleanseth; so it is with the blood of Christ; it cleanseth not the soul, but by being applied to it, in the merit and efficacy of it, by the sanctifying Spirit; of which the outward ministerial washing is a sign and seal. 1 Cor. 6. 11.

What is there besides the natural fitness of the outward things to express the inward?
There is also considerable God's divine institution, ordaining and appointing these things to typify to the soul Christ crucified in his cleansing quality. For otherwise though there were never such aptness in the creature; yet it hath nothing to do to meddle with a Sacrament, unless the Lord do specially appropriate it to serve for such a purpose. And then with God's institution there goeth a blessing and a special virtue and power attends on a divine Ordinance. That which makes the outward signs significant, is God's Word and appointment.

But is Christ and the cleansing power of his blood only barely signified in the Sacrament of Baptism?
Nay more: the inward things are really exhibited to the believer as well as the outward; there is that sacramental union between them, that the one is conveyed and sealed up by the other. Hence are those phrases of being born again of water and of the Holy Ghost, John 3. 5. of cleansing by the washing of water, Ephes. 5. 26, &c. so, Arise and be baptized, and wash away thy sins, Acts 22. 16. so Rom. 6. 3. We are buried with Christ by Baptism, &c. The Sacraments being rightly received, do effect that which they do represent.

Are all they then that are partakers of the outward washing of Baptism, partakers also of the inward washing of the Spirit? Does this Sacrament seal up their spiritual engrafting into Christ to all who externally receive it?
Surely no. Though God hath ordained these outward means for the conveyance of the inward grace to our souls; yet there is no necessity that we should tie the working of God's Spirit to the Sacraments more than to the Word. The promises of salvation, Christ and all his benefits are preached and offered to all in the Ministry of the Word; yet all hearers have not them conveyed to their souls by the Spirit; but those whom God hath ordained to life. So in the Sacraments, the outward elements are dispensed to all, who make an outward profession of the Gospel, (for in infants their being born in the bosom of the Church is instead of an outward profession) because man is not able to distinguish corn from chaff: but the inward grace of the Sacrament is not communicated to all, but to those only who are heirs of those promises whereof the Sacraments are seals. For without a man have his name in the Covenant the Seal set to it confirms nothing to him.

What is the advantage then or benefit of Baptism to a common Christian?
The same as was the benefit of Circumcision to the Jew outward, Rom. 2. 28. Rom. 3. 1, 2. there is a general grace of Baptism which all the baptized partake as of a common favor; and that is their admission into the visible body of the Church, their matriculation and outward incorporating into the number of the Worshippers of God by external communion. And so as Circumcision was not only a seal of the righteousness which is by faith but as an excess God appointed it to be like a wall of separation between Jew and Gentile: so is Baptism a badge of an outward member of the Church, a distinction from the common rout of Heathen; and God thereby seals a right upon the party baptized to his ordinances, that he may use them as his privileges, and wait for an inward blessing by them. Yet this is but the porch, the shell, and outside: all that are outwardly received into the visible Church, are not spiritually engrafted into the mystical body of Christ. Baptism always is attended upon by the general grace, but not always with this special.

To whom then is Baptism effectual to the sealing up this inward and special grace?

We must here distinguish of persons baptized. The Church does not only baptize those that are grown and of years; if any such being bred Pagans be brought within the place of the Church, and testify their competent understanding of Christianity, and profess their faith in the Lord Jesus and in God's precious promises of remission of sins by his blood; and their earnest desire to be sealed with Baptism for the strengthning of their souls in this faith: but the Church also Baptized her infants such as being born within her bosom of believing parents are within the Covenant; and so have right unto the seal thereof.

Does the inward grace always accompany the outward sign in those of years baptized?

No; but only then when the profession of their faith is not outward only and counterfeit, but sincere and hearty; they laying hold on Christ offered in the Sacrament by a lively faith, which is the hand to receive the mercies offered. Acts 8. 37 If thou believest with all thy heart, thou mayst be baptized; saith Philip to the Eunuch. For it were absurd to extend the benefit of the seal beyond the Covenant. Now the Covenant is made only in the faithful, John 1. 12. Mark. 16. 16. He that believeth and is baptized shall be saved; but he that believeth not, whether he be baptized or no, shall be condemned. Simon Magus (Acts 8. 13.) and Julian, and thousands of Hypocrites and Formalists shall find to help in the day of the Lord by the holy water of their baptism, without it be to increase their judgment.

But what say you of Infants baptized that are born in the Church; does the inward grace in their baptism always attend upon the outward sign?

Surely no: the Sacrament of baptism is effectual in Infants, only to those and to all those who belong unto the election of grace. Which thing though we (in the judgment of charity) do judge of every particular Infant, yet we have no ground to judge so of all in general: or if we should judge so, yet it is not any judgment of certainty; we may be mistaken.

Is every elect Infant then actually sanctified and united unto Christ in and by Baptism?

We must here also distinguish of elect Infants baptized, whereof some die in their Infancy, and never come to the use of reason; others God hath appointed to live and enjoy the ordinary means of faith and salvation.

What is to be thought of elect Infants that die in their infancy, and have no other outward means of salvation but their baptism?

Doubtless in all those the inward grace is united to the outward signs; and the Holy Ghost does as truly, and really, and actually apply the merits and blood of Christ in the justifying and sanctifying virtue unto the soul of the elect Infant, as the Minister does the water to its body, and the invisible grace of the Sacrament is conveyed by the outward means.

But how can an Infant be capable of the grace of the Sacrament?

Very well. Though Infants be not capable of the grace of the Sacrament by that way whereby the grown are, by hearing, conceiving, believing yet it followeth not that Infants are not capable in and by another way. It is easy to distinguish between the gift conveyed, and the manner of conveying it. Faith is not of absolute necessity to all God's elect, but only to those to whom God affords means of believing. It is the application of Christ's righteousness that justifieth us, not our apprehending it: God can supply the defect of faith by his sanctifying Spirit, which can do all things on our part which faith should do. Do we not know that the sin of Adam is imputed to children, and they defiled by it, though they be not capable to understand it; even so the righteousness of Christ may be, and is, by God's secret and unknown way to elect Infants: and so to those that are born deaf, and fools, not capable of understanding. For though God tieth us to means, yet not himself: he that hath said of Infants, to them belongs the kingdom of God, knows how to settle upon them the title of the kingdom. And we have no reason to think, but that even before, or in, at or by, the act of Baptism, the Spirit of Christ does unite the soul of the elect infant to Christ, and cloth it with his righteousness, and impute unto it the title of a son or daughter by Adoption, and the image of God by sanctification; and so fit it for the state of glory.

But what is to be thought of the effect of Baptism in those elect Infants whom God hath appointed to live to years of discretion?
In them we have no warrant to promise constantly and extraordinary work to whom God intends to afford ordinary means. For though God do sometimes sanctify from the womb, as in Jeremy and John Baptist, sometime in Baptism as he pleases; yet it is hard to affirm (as some do) that every elect Infant does ordinarily before or in Baptism receive initial regeneration and the seed of faith and grace. For if there were such a habit of grace then infused, it could not be so utterly lost or secreted as never to show it self but by being attained by new instruction. But we may rather deem and judge that Baptism is not actually effectual to justify and sanctify, until the party do believe and embrace the promises.

Is not Baptism then for the most part a vain empty show, consisting of shadows without the Substance, and a sign without the thing signified?
No: it is always an effectual seal to all those that are heirs of the Covenant of grace: the promises of God touching Justification, Remission, Adoption are made and sealed in Baptism to every elect child of God; then to be actually enjoyed, when the party baptized shall actually lay hold upon them by faith. Thus Baptism to every elect Infant is a seal of the righteousness of Christ, to be extraordinarily applied by the holy Ghost, if it die in its infancy; to be apprehended by faith, if it live to years of discretion. So that as baptism administered to those of years is not effectual unless they believe; so we can make no comfortable use of our Baptism administered in our infancy until we believe. The righteousness of Christ and all the promises of grace were in my Baptism estated upon me and sealed up unto me on God's part: but then I come to have the profit and benefit of them, when I come to understand what grant God in Baptism hath sealed unto me, and actually to lay hold upon it by faith.

Explain this more clearly.
We know that an estate may be made unto an Infant, and in his infancy he hath right unto it, though not actual possession of it until such years. Now the time of the child's incapability, the use and comfort of this estate is lost indeed; but the right and title is not vain and empty, but true and real, and stands firmly secured unto the child to be claimed what time soever he is capable of it. Even so Infants elect have Christ and all his benefits sealed up unto them in the Sacrament of Baptism; yet through their incapableness they have not actual fruition of them, until God give them actual faith to apprehend them. Is Baptism lost then which is administered in our infancy? Was it a vain and an empty Ceremony? No, it was a complete and effectual Sacrament; and Gods invisible graces were truly sealed up under visible signs. And though the use and the comfort of Baptism be not for the present enjoyed by the Infant; yet by the parent it is, who believes God's promises for himself and for his seed, and so by the whole Congregation: and the things then done shall be actually effectual to the Infant, when ever it shall be capable to make use of them.

But are there not some who utterly deny the baptizing of Infants to be warrantable?
Yes; but not to insist upon answering their weak arguments, sufficient and clear ground for the practice of our Church in this behalf may both be picked out of that which hath been spoken before; and further evidenced by these following arguments.

The first we draw from the use of Circumcision in the old Testament, which answereth to Baptism: yet that was applied to the Infant the eighth day. There can be no reason given to deprive Infants of Baptism, but that which may be given against Circumcision; the main whereof is their incapableness of the grace of the Sacrament.

To them to whom the Covenant belongs to them belongs the seal of the Covenant that confirms the right unto them. But to the infants of faithful parents the Covenant belongs: To you and to your children are the promises made, saith Peter, Acts 2. 39. and to them belongs the Kingdom of God: if the thing it self, then the sign and seal of it. And the Apostle saith, Your children are holy, 1 Cor. 7. 14. there is a federal sanctity, or external and visible holiness at least in children of believing parents; and they are to be judged of the true flock of Christ, until they show the contrary.

Yea, but it is objected that they do not believe; which is in the Scripture required of those that are to be baptized, that they make profession of their faith.
The Scripture requiring faith in the party to be baptized, speaks of grown men. When the Apostle gives a rule that none should eat but those that labor, it were monstrous from thence to deny meat to children or impotent persons. Besides, it is not simply an improper speech to call the Infant of believing parents a believer. Our Savior reckoneth them among Believers, Mat. 18. 6. he took a child and said, Whosoever offendeth one of these little ones that believe in me. What do we deem of Christian Infants? is there no difference between them and Pagans? Certainly as it were hard to call them infidels, so it were not harsh to call them Believers. And further it is the received judgment of our Church, that the faith of the parents (or of those that instead of parents present the child in the Congregation) is so far the Infants, as to give him right unto the Covenant. And lastly, as we have said before, the Spirit of God in elect Infants supplies the room of faith: and however it be Adam's corruption cannot be more effectual to pollute the Infant, then Christ's blood and innocence is to sanctify them; and God's wisdom wants not means to apply it, though we cannot attain unto the manner.

But the Anabaptists urge, we have no rule in Scripture for baptizing Infants, nor example.
But do we read any thing in Scripture that may infringe the liberty of the Church therein? nay, do not the Scriptures afford many friendly proofs by consequence of it; we read of such an one baptized, and all his household, the house of Lydia, of the Jailor, of Crispus, of Stephanus, &c. why should we imagine that there were no infants there, or that they were left out? And if the Scriptures not expressing directly the baptizing of infants, were sufficient reason why that Sacrament should be denied them: then by the same reason the Sacrament of the Lord's Supper should be denied to women. For (to my remembrance) it is not expressed in all the new Testament, that any women did partake of it which thing yet were senseless to doubt of.

But is Baptism of absolute necessity to salvation?
Baptism, as we have seen, is a high Ordinance of God, and a means whereby he hath appointed to communicate Christ and his benefits to our souls; and therefore not to be neglected or slightly esteemed, but used with all reverence and thankful devotion when it may be had. Yet where God denieth it, either in regard of shortness of the infants life, or by any other unavoidable necessity, there comes no danger from the want of the Sacraments, but only from the contempt of them.

Who are here to be confuted?
First, the Papists; who have contrived in their own brains a room near hell which they call (Limbus infantum) a receptacle for the souls of infants which die without Baptism; and where, as they feign, they are deprived of God's presence, and never partake of joy and happiness.

Secondly, many ignorant people amongst us; who for want of better teaching, harbor in their minds such Popish conceits, especially that Baptism does confer grace upon all by the work done, (for they commonly look no higher:) and they conceive a kind of inherent virtue, and Christendom (as they call it) necessarily infused into children by having the water cast upon their faces. Hence the minister is oft posted for to baptize in a private chamber, to the dishonor of that Ordinance: and which is more intolerable, in case of the want of a Minister, women will undertake to be Baptizers; which is a monstrous profanation of so high a service.

How may these errors of opinion and practice be avoided?
They proceed from gross ignorance: and therefore the means to cure them is to be informed in the right nature and use of Sacraments, and in the extent and limitation of the necessity of them.

How may that be done?
We must know that Sacraments properly do not give us any right unto God and his Christ, but only seal up and confirm that right and interest which already we have in God's Covenant and promise. God promised to Adam life; and then he gave him the Tree of life to be a pledge of his promise: It was not the Tree of life that gave Adam life, but the promise. Adam might have lived by the promise without the Tree; but the Tree could do him no good without the promise. Thus God promiseth Christ and his benefits to the faithful and to their seed, and then he gives us baptism to seal these promises: it is not Baptism that saves us, but the promises; it is not water that purgeth our sins, but the blood of the Covenant.

Why then was the Sacrament added?
For our weakness, to be a strengthening to our faith; not to give any strength or efficacy to the Covenant made in the blood of Christ. God's Word is as sure as his bond, his promise is as sure and effectual as his seal and shall as surely be accomplished; the Sacraments only give strength to our faith in apprehending it.

What infer you from this?
That where God is pleased to dispense his seals and Sacraments, they are great comforts and pledges of his love; and to despise or slight them were a horrible slighting even of the Covenant it self. But where he denieth means and opportunity of enjoying the signs, the things signified are never the farther off, or less effectual. It is said, Gen. 7. 14. that the uncircumcised should be cut off from God's people, because he had broke the Covenant but it is meant only of voluntary and willful refusing of Circumcision. For the people of God in the wilderness were forty years without the outward sign of Circumcision; yet they were not without the inward grace. David's child died the seventh day, a day before the time appointed for Circumcision: and yet both his words and his carriage express that he doubted not of the salvation of it; the thief upon the Cross believing in Christ, was received with Christ into Paradise, though he were never baptized: he had the inward grace of Baptism, the washing of the blood of Christ, though not the outward sign. When God affordeth means, we must wait upon him for a blessing in them and by them: when he does not afford means, we must not tie the working of his grace to them. God who sanctifieth some in the womb, knows how to sanctify all his elect infants, and by his Spirit apply the merits of Christ unto them

without the outward water. Some have the outward sign and not the inward grace; some have the inward grace and not the outward sign, we must not commit Idolatry by deifying the outward element. The rule will hold. It is not the want of the Sacraments, but the contempt or willful neglect of them that is dangerous.

What other errors of opinion and practice do you observe about Baptism?

As some through ignorance and superstition have too high a concept of the outward signs, so others through ignorance and profaneness have too mean and base an opinion of them. Some there are who esteem of Baptism as of a mere Ecclesiastical ceremony and Church complement; as if there were no serious virtue or efficacy in it, or profit to be expected by it; or had no other use, but to give the child a name and there is an end, they look no further.

How does it appear that some have so slight an opinion of this Ordinance?

By their answerable practices: such as these and the like. 1. Often Baptism is deferred, and that upon every trifling occasion, as if it were a business of no great weight and moment, but might attend every ones leisure: and many times, through delay, the child dieth without it. Which though, it does nothing prejudice the child's salvation; yet it will lie heavy upon the parents conscience, for neglecting God's ordinance when he afforded opportunity.

2. Often the minister is sent for home to perform that service with few in a private chamber, when no imminent necessity urgeth; to the dishonor of so sacred a business, which ought to be a most solemn and public action of the whole Congregation.

3. Though the child be brought to Church, yet often some by-day is chosen, and not the Lord's Sabbath; and it is then done as if it were only women's work to be present at Baptism, who have most leisure to spend time about matters of smaller consequence.

4. If it be on the Sabbath; then the main care and preparation is about matters of outward pomp and state: every thing is fitted and prepared for the purpose, but only that which should chiefly be; viz. the hearts and minds of those that go about a business of that nature.

5. While the Sacrament is in performing, the demeanor of many showeth that they have a slight opinion of that service: some turning their backs upon it and going out of the Church so soon as Sermon is done, as if the word was worth the minding, but not the Sacrament; others prating and talking all the while, as if there were nothing for them to learn by, but no duty for them to perform in that action.

6. Lastly, Infants are brought to the Sacrament of Baptism in their infancy, but are never by their Parents taught the doctrine of Baptism when they come to years of understanding: Baptism is not made use of, as it ought, in the whole course of men's lives. These things show, that men commonly have a mean conceit of this Ordinance.

What is the best way to reform these irreligious practices?

A serious pondering and considering of the high dignity of this divine ordinance: which will cause a devout and reverent demeanor in that holy business.

1. Every one shall consider that it is no customary formality, but an honorable ordinance instituted by the lawful authority of God himself; who never imposed any service upon his Church in vain. It was honored by our Savior Christ himself, who sanctified it unto us by submitting unto it in his own sacred person; confirmed by his practice, by his precept, &c.

2. Every one should consider, that there are infinite mercies sealed up by it to the faithful, and to their seed. It is a visible admittance of thy child (if thou be a Parent) into the congregation of Christ's flock, signifying its interest in the heavenly Jerusalem which is above. Is this a business to be mumbled over in a corner? Christ came from Galilee to Jordan to be baptized. Is the receiving of thy child into the bosom of the Church in a full Congregation, no comfort unto thee? is it not mercy to see the blood of Christ ministerially sealed up unto thy Infant to purge it from that pollution which it hath brought into the world with it; which also thou makest confession of by presenting it to this mysterious washing? Is it not joy to thy heart, to hear the whole congregation of God's Saints pray for thy child: And that God hath honored thee so much, as to count thy very child holy and within this Covenant? think on these things.

3. Every one that is present at Baptism should consider, that that being a public action of the Congregation, every particular person ought reverently to join in it. Shall the whole Trinity be present at Baptism (Mat. 3.) and we be gone? Join ought every one in prayer to God for the Infant, join in praises to God for his mercy, that we, and our children are brought forth, and brought up within the pale of his Church (whereas the rest of the world are like a wilderness) and thank God for adding at the present a member to his Church. Join every one ought in meditation of the pollution of nature, of the blessed means of redemption by Christ, of the happy benefits that God seals up unto us in our Baptism, even before we knew them; of the vows and promises which we in our child-hood made by those who were undertakers for us: and finding our failings, every time we are present at Baptism, we should renew our Covenant with God, and labor to get new strength to close with his promises, which in our Baptism he made unto us. Thus if we were wife to make a right use of it; we might learn as much at a Baptism as at a Sermon.

4. Parents should always bear in mind the promises which their children have made to God by them, and they for their children; laboring to bring them up accordingly in the instruction and information of the Lord, teaching them (so soon as they understand) the meaning of that Sacrament, unfolding unto them God's precious promises, and their strict engagements. The negligence of parents herein, is a cause of monstrous profaneness in many: they bring children to receive Christ's badge, but bring them up to the service of the Devil: and God hath not so much dishonor by Heathens and Pagans, as by those who have taken upon them the name of Christians.

Lastly, Baptism should be of continual use through a Christians whole life. It is administered but once, but it is always lasting in the virtue and efficacy of it. Baptism loseth not it's strength by time. In all thy fears and doubts look back to thy Baptism, and the promises of God sealed up unto thee there; lay hold on them by faith, and thou shalt have the actual comfort of thy Baptism, and feel the effect of it, though thou never saw it. In thy failings, slips, and revolts, to recover thy self have recourse to thy Baptism: new baptism shall not need; the Covenant and seal of God stands firm, he changeth not: only renew thy repentance, renew thy faith in those blessed promises of grace which were sealed up unto thee in thy Baptism.

[48TH HEAD.]

So much for Baptism. What is the Lord's Supper?

It is the second Sacrament of the new Testament, wherein God by the signs of bread and wine signifieth, sealeth and exhibiteth to every faithful receiver, the body and blood of Christ, for his spiritual nourishment and growth in Christ: and so sealing unto him his continuance with increase in the body of Christ, which is his Church confirmeth him in the Covenant of grace. Or thus: It is a Sacrament of the Gospel, wherein by the outward elements of Bread and wine, sanctified and exhibited by the minister, and rightly received by the communicant, assurance is given to those that are engrafted into Christ, of their continuance in him and receiving nourishment by him unto eternal life.

Are there divers graces offered to us in Baptism and in the Lord's Supper?
No. The Covenant solemnly ratified in Baptism, is renewed in the Lord's Supper, between the Lord himself and the receiver: and the same graces offered again, but to divers ends: in Baptism, to the investing and entering of us into Christianity (for of that entrance Baptism is a seal:) in the Lord's Supper, to the nourishing and continuing of us in it; of which growth and continuance in Christianity, it is a seal. And therefore as unto the Sacrament of Baptism, so unto this of the Lord's Supper, the Popish feigned Sacrament of Confirmation is notably injurious.

Wherein then does Baptism differ from the Lord's Supper?
First, in regard of the thing signified. Baptism (as hath been said) is a seal of our entrance into the Church of God, the Supper of the Lord of our continuance in the same; the one of our new birth, the other of our spiritual food. The former is ordained to this end, that being out of Christ by nature, we might by the Sacrament of our new birth be engrafted into his body: (Tit. 3. 5. Joh. 3. 5.) the latter, that being in Christ by grace, we might continue and increase in him. 1 Cor. 10. 16. & 11. 23. 1 Pet. 3. 21. Second, in regard of the outward sign. Water in the one, bread and wine in the other. Third, in regard of the Communicants. Unto Baptism both Infants, and those that are of years of discretion are to be admitted; but unto the Supper of the Lord, only those of years of discretion. Fourth, in regard of the time. The Supper of the Lord is to be received as often as the Lord shall give occasion; Baptism but once.

Why is this called the Lord's Supper seeing we use not to make it a Supper?
It is called the Lord's Supper, (1 Cor. 11. 20.) not because he appointed it a supper to us; but because our Lord Jesus Christ sitting at his last Supper ordained it instead of our Passover. For in the night that he was betrayed, (1 Cor. 11. 23.) immediately after that he had eaten the Passover with his Disciples, he did both himself with them celebrate this holy Sacrament, (Mat. 26. 26. &c.) and withal, give charge for continuance of the same in the Church until his second coming. 1 Cor. 11. 26.

What may we learn by this? that both our Savior Christ and his Apostles likewise administered this Sacrament after Supper?
That we must not come unto it for our bellies, but have our minds lifted up from these earthly elements to our Savior Christ represented by them. For men after supper set not bread and wine, but banqueting dishes upon the Table. Which serveth to reprove.

1. Such profane persons, as come for a draught of Wine only. 2. Those that rest only in the outward Elements.

But does not the example of our Savior Christ and his Apostles tie us to administer this Sacrament in the night time?
No: because they had special cause so to do, which we have not.

What cause had our Savior so to do?
He was to administer it after supper. First, because it was to come in lieu and stead of the Passover; and therefore was presently after the eating of it. Secondly, that it might go immediately before his passion, the better to show whereunto it should have relation. Where also is another difference our Savior Christ's Supper representing his

death, which followed the Supper and was to come; our Sacrament representing the death of Christ already suffered and past.

What cause had the Apostles?
They did it in the night, because it was not safe for the Church to meet in the day for fear of persecution. Wherefore hearing the laudable custom of the Church of administering it in the Morning, when our wits and capacities are best, is to be followed. In which respect also there is some difference between this Sacrament, and the Sacrament of Baptism which may without any inconvenience be administered in the afternoon.

What is the fittest day for the administration of this Sacrament?
The Lord's day is the fittest day for the administration of the Sacraments. For although our Savior Christ did administer it on another day, (for the reasons before declared) yet he did not bid us so to do. But the Apostles example and religious practice herein is to be followed, which did celebrate the Supper of the Lord on the Lord's day.

So much of the time. Now for the nature of this Sacrament, how may it be known?
First, by the matter; and secondly, by the form of it.

What is the matter of the Supper of the Lord?
Partly outward, as the elements of bread and wine; partly inward, as the body and blood of Christ. Those outward elements signifying Christ and him crucified, with all the benefits of his death and passion; even whole Christ, with all the fruits of his mediation. Mat. 26. 26, 27. 1 Cor. 11. 24, 25.

Wherefore did the Lord make choice of Bread and Wine for the outward elements of this Sacrament?
Because meaning to set forth our spiritual nourishment by them, they are of all the means of our corporal nourishment the chiefest. Ps. 104. 15.

Why did he not content himself with one of these only?
He took both, that he might hereby show how plentiful and assured redemption we have in Christ, whom these do represent. Wherefore it is no marvel, that the Papists in the prohibiting of the cup, do answerably teach our salvation to be neither wholly in Christ, nor assuredly.

What argument do you observe, in the institution of the Sacrament against this robbery?
The foreseeing spirit of Christ, knowing the sacrilege that Popery would bring in for the robbery of the people of the use of the Cup, hath prepared a preservative against it; speaking here more fully of the cup (which he did not of the bread) Drink ye all of this. Mat. 26. 27.

What Bread used our Savior Christ?
Ordinary bread such as was used at the common Table, at that time. It was indeed unleavened bread: but it was so, because no other was then lawful at the feast of the Passover.

Are not the Bread and Wine, changed into the Body and Blood of Christ in this Sacrament?
No: they are not changed in nature, but in use (1 Cor. 10. 16.) For the words of eating and drinking do properly belong to the outward elements of bread and wine, and by a borrowed speech do improperly belong to the body and blood of Christ: to note unto us the communion we have with our Savior Christ, of whom we are verily partakers by a

lively faith, as of the bread and wine, by eating and drinking them. And thus we say that these elements are changed in use: because being separated from a common use, they are consecrate to sign and seal unto us our spiritual nourishment and growth by the body and blood of Christ Jesus. (Luke 22. 19. 1 Cor. 10. 3, 4.) For as the Sacrament of Baptism does seal to us a spiritual regeneration; so the Lord's Supper, a spiritual feeding: and even as well the body and blood of Christ, is in Baptism given us for clothing, as they are given in the Lord's Supper for nourishment: Therefore the bread and wine are not the true body and blood of Christ, but the signs and tokens of them, as in Baptism, the water was only a sign of Christ's blood, not the blood.

What further reasons have you to overthrow the carnal presence of Christ in the Sacrament?
1. If the bread were turned into Christ; then there should be two Christ's, one that giveth, another that is given: for our Savior Christ gave the bread, &c. 2. If the bread be the very body of Christ, there should then be no sign of the thing signified; and so no Sacrament. (Rom. 4. 11.) Where their miserable shift, that the whiteness is the seal and sign, is not worthy the answer. 3. The wicked receiver might then eat and drink Christ's body and blood as well as any true believer. Joh. 13. 2, 30. 4. The Minister cannot give the inward grace, but the outward element in the administration of the Sacrament. Luk. 3. 16.

What reason was there to more our Savior Christ to use such a borrowed speech in this so great a mystery?
Because it is ordinary and usual in the Scripture, to give the name of the thing signed and signified to the sign: as it is called the tree of life, which was but a sign of life. (Gen. 2. 6.) So in the Sacraments of the Old Testament, circumcision is called the covenant, (Gen. 17. 10.) that is, the token of the Covenant: (Verse 11.) and the Lamb or Kid the Passover, whereof it was a sign only. (Exod. 12.) The self same manner of speech is also used in the new Testament, of Baptism, called the new birth and washing away of sins, whereof it is only a seal. So that unless the Lord would in this Sacrament have departed from the wisdom of the Spirit of God accustomably received; he must needs here also tread in the same steps of a borrowed and figurative speech.

Howbeit, it may seem that to have used a more proper speech, would have been more meet for him, being near unto his death, and more convenient for their understanding?
He did after his last Supper use as figurative speeches as this in the 13 , 15, and 16 of John; and that without all danger of darkness of speech: there being often-times more light in a borrowed, than in a proper speech. And a trope of force must be yielded, when he faith, that the cup is the new Testament.

It maketh further for the corporal presence, that our Savior Christ saith in his Supper, that his body was then broken, and not that it should be broken after.
That it is also usual to the Scripture, for further certainty to speak of things to come, as of them that are present.

But there is nothing impossible unto God.
1. The question is here, not of the power, but of the will of God; what he will have done. 2. God cannot do these things, in doing whereof he should contradict himself: and therefore the Scripture feareth not, without dishonor to God, to say that he cannot lie, nor cannot deny himself. Tit. 1. 2. 2. 2. Tim. 2. 13.

Forty-eighth Head

Why is the cup called, the cup of the new Testament?
Because it is a seal of the promises of God touching our salvation in Christ, which being in old time under the Law shadowed by the shedding of blood of beasts, is now after a new manner accomplished in the blood of Christ himself.

Thus much of matter of this Sacrament: wherein consisteth the form thereof?
Partly in the outward actions both of the Ministers and of the receivers; partly in the inward and spiritual things signified thereby: these outward actions being a second seal, set by the Lord's own hand unto his Covenant.

What are the Sacramental actions of the Minister in the Lord's Supper?
Four. First to take the bread and wine into his hands, and to separate it from ordinary bread and wine.

What does this signify?
That God in his eternal decree had separated Christ from all other men to be our mediator: and that he was set apart to that office, and separated from sinners. Exod. 12. 5. Heb. 7. 26.

What is the second?
To bless and consecrate the bread and wine, by the Word and Prayer.

What does that signify?
That God in his due time sent Christ into the world and sanctified him, furnishing him with all gifts needful for a Mediator.

How are the Bread and Wine to be blessed and consecrated?
By doing that which at the first institution Christ did.

What is that?
1. He declared the doctrine of the mystery of the Sacrament unto his Apostles, which received it, by teaching the truth of that which these outward signs did signify. 2. He thanketh his heavenly Father for that he had so loved the world, that he gave him, which was his only Son, to die for it; through the breaking of his most holy Body, and shedding his most precious blood. Also he gave him thanks, for that he had ordained these outward elements, to seal our spiritual nourishment in Christ. 3. By a trope of the chief part of Prayer (which is thanksgiving) for the whole, the Evangelist giveth to understand; that our Savior Christ sued to God his heavenly Father, that his death, in it self sufficient to save, might by the working of his holy spirit, be effectual to the elect, and that those outward signs of Bread and Wine might, through the operation of his holy spirit, be effectual to the purposes they were ordained unto.

How shall it be known that he gave thanks, and prayer for these things; seeing there is no mention of these things in the Evangelists?
1. The very matter it self that is handled, does guide us to the knowledge of these things. 2. The like manner of speech in other places of Scripture; where there being no mention what words he used, yet must needs be granted that he gave thanks and prayed, proportionally to the prayer and thanks here used. For taking the barley loaves and fishes, and giving thanks; what can be understood, but that he giving thanks to God, that had given those creatures for the bodily nourishment, prayed that he would bless them, and make them effectual to that purpose and end? (Mat. 14. 19. and 15. 36. John 6. 11.) And as it is not lawful to eat and drink the common meat and drink, without such prayer and thanksgiving; so it is not lawful to communicate these elements without thanksgiving and prayer.

So much for the second action (which the Minister indeed performeth with the Communicants. But yet as chief in the action): What is the third?
To break the Bread and pour out the Wine.

What does it signify?
The passion and suffering of Christ, with all the torments which he endured for our sins both in body and soul: his blessed body being bruised and crucified, his precious blood shed (trickling and streaming down from all parts of him to the ground) and his righteous soul poured out unto death; (Isa. 53. 5, 10, 12. Heb. 9. 14.) That Christ himself of his own accord offered his body to be broken, and his blood to be shed, upon the Cross: and that as the Bread nourisheth not, if it remain whole and unbroken; so there is no life for us in Christ, but in as much as he died.

What is the fourth?
To give and distribute the Bread and Wine to the Receivers.

What does that signify?
That God giveth Christ, and Christ himself unto us: that Christ Jesus with all his merits is offered to all sorts of receivers; and that God hath given him unto faithful receivers, to feed their souls unto eternal life. John. 3. 14, 15 and 6. 50, 51.

What are the Sacramental actions of the Receivers?
They be two: first to take the bread and wine offered by the Minister.

What does that signify?
The receiving of Christ into our soul with all his benefits by faith. That they, and only they, have benefit by Christ crucified, which thus apply Christ to themselves by a true and lively faith. John. 1. 12.

What is the second?
To eat the bread and drink the wine; receiving them in the body, and digesting them, 1 Cor 11. 26.

What does that signify?
Our uniting unto Christ, and enjoying of him. That we must with delight apply Christ and his merits to all the necessities of our soul; spiritually feeding upon him, and growing by him. For the eating of the bread to strengthen our nature, betokeneth the inward strengthening of our souls by grace, through the merit of the breaking of Christ's body for us: and the drinking of the wine to cherish our bodies, betokens, that the blood of Christ shed on the Cross, and (as it were) drunken by faith, cherisheth our souls. And as God does bless these outward elements, to preserve and strengthen the body of the receiver: so Christ apprehended and received by faith, does nourish him, and preserve both body and soul unto eternal life. Joh. 6. 50, 51. 1 Cor. 10. 3, 11, 16, 17.

Is Christ's body and blood, together with the outward elements, received of all Communicants?
No. For howsoever they be offered by God to all, (Mat. 26. 26.) yet are they received by such alone, as have the hand of faith to lay hold on Christ. And these with the bread and wine spiritually receive Christ with all his saving graces. As for the wicked and those that come without faith they receive only the outward elements, 1 Cor. 11. 27. and withal judgment and condemnation to themselves: verse 29.

Forty-eighth Head

So much of the matter and form: Show now the special, ends and uses for which the Lord's Supper was ordained.
1. To call to mind and renew the memory and virtue of Christ's death. 1 Cor. 11. 24. 2. To increase our faith, begotten by the Word preached: and to confirm unto us our nourishment therein by the means of Christ's death. 3. To increase our love. 4. To increase our joy in the Holy Ghost, our peace of conscience, our hope of eternal life, and all other graces of God in us. 5. To stir us up with greater boldness to profess Christ, then heretofore we had done. 6. To quicken our hearts to all holy duties. 7. To show our thankfulness to God for his mercy bestowed upon us in Christ. 8. To make a difference betwixt ourselves and the enemies of Christ. 9. To knit us more near in good will one to another. 10. To preserve the public ministry of the Word and Prayer in Christian assemblies.

Who are to be partakers of this Sacrament?
All baptized who are of years and sound judgment to discern the Lord's body, ought to repair to this Sacrament. But those only come worthily, who professing the true faith, have duly examined and prepared themselves. (Isa. 66. 23. 1 Cor. 11. 27, 28.) Whereby all not of age and sound judgment, are shut from this Sacrament; which are not always from the other of Baptism.

May none be admitted by the Church to the Supper of the Lord, but such as have these things in them which God requireth at their hands?
Yes, Those who having knowledge, do make profession of Religion and are found guilty of no great error or crime unrepented of.

What if any thirst themselves to the Lord's Table, who are ignorant, or guilty of such crimes?
They are to be kept back by the discipline of the Church.

What is to be performed by every Christian, that he may worthily partake of the Lord's Supper?
There must be a careful preparation before the action, great heed in the whole action, and a joyful and thankful close and shutting up of it. All which must be performed as well by the Minister as the people. For there is great difference betwixt our Savior Christ, the first deliverer of this Sacrament, and all other Ministers. He having no battle of the spirit and flesh in him, but being always prepared unto every good work: had no need of these things: but other Ministers have as much need thereof as the people.

How are we to prepare ourselves to this Sacrament?
By due search and trial of our own souls, whether we can find in ourselves the thing which God does require in worthy communicants.

How may we perform that?
By fitting our minds, and framing our hearts thereunto. 1 Cor. 10. 15, 16. and 11. 28.

How may we fit our minds?
By examining our wisdom and knowledge both of God's will in general, and of the nature and use of this holy Sacrament in particular: whether we can give a reason of the representation of Christ in the bread and wine; and bring the resemblance and difference of the proportion of the bread and wine, with the body and blood of Christ; and of the eating and drinking of the elements, with the partaking of the spiritual things, Rom. 4. 11. 1 Cor. 18. 3, 4, 16, 17.

How may our hearts be framed for the feeling of the virtue and power of this Sacrament?

First, by weighing with ourselves what need we have of it, and what arenefit we may reap by it. Second, by examining of our Faith, (2 Cor. 13. 5. 1 Tim. 1. 5, 15.) and Repentance, (Heb. 10. 22. James 4. 8.) attended with true love of God, (Zech. 12. 10.) and of our brethren. 1 Cor. 16. 4. Third, by fervent Invocation, praying for a blessing upon this ordinance of God. Mat. 26. 26.

How may we find what need we have of this Sacrament?

Partly by our wretched estate by nature, and partly by our weak estate by grace.

What may we find by our estate by nature?

That being prone to all evil, we have need of this Sacrament to nourish and preserve the life of grace new begun, which otherwise by our own corruption might die or decay in us. 1 Cor. 10. 16.

What need have we of this Sacrament for relief of our weak estate by grace?

That being weak in understanding and feeble in memory, we may by the signs of Bread and Wine, have our understanding bettered, and our memory confirmed in the death of Christ. 1 Cor. 11. 24, 26.

What further need may we find of it?

That being frail in faith and cold in love, we may by the same creatures, as by seals and pledges, have our faith further strengthened and our love more inflamed to God and God's children.

What arenefit then may we reap by the Lord's Supper?

We see already the benefit is great: this Sacrament being as a glass for the mind, a monument for the memory, a support of faith, a provocation to love. a quickning to obedience, and a sign and seal of all the mercies of God in Christ Jesus.

How must the heart be prepared to find the power of this Sacrament for supply of these wants and obtaining of these benefits?

The heart must be purged by Repentance and purified by Faith. 1 Cor. 10. 14, 16, 21. Acts 15. 9.

How may the heart be purified by faith?

If I have not only knowledge what Christ hath done for his chosen, but a full assurance that whatsoever he hath done he hath done it for me as well as any other. 1. Cor. 2. 2. Joh. 17. 3. Gal. 2. 20.

What gather you hence?

That they only are to present themselves at the Lord's table, who after their baptism are able to make a profession of their true faith, and can find that they do truly believe in Christ: seeing ignorant and unbelieving persons do rather eat and drink their own judgment, then reap any benefit by this Sacrament. 1 Cor. 11. 29, 30, 31.

How may thy heart be purged by repentance?

If from my heart I do repent of my particular sins past, and judge my self for them, bewailing and forsaking them: and frame the rest of my life according to God's will. 1 Cor. 11. 30, 31. Gal. 6. 16.

What learn you hence?
That it is dangerous for such as remain in their old sins, or after the sacrament return unto them, once to offer themselves to the Lord's Table: forasmuch as by this means they procure the wrath of God against them and those that belong unto them; although not in condemnation in the world to come (which the faithful notwithstanding their unworthy receiving cannot come unto) yet to fearful plagues and judgments in this world.

Is it not meet that we be free from all malice in our hearts, when we come to the Lord's Supper?
Yes it is: for this Sacrament is a seal both of our conjunction with Christ, and of our society one with another: (1 Cor. 10. 17.) and we must know that true repentance purgeth out malice amongst other sins; and a sound faith worketh by love towards God and our Brethren. Mat. 5. 22, 23. James 1. 19, 20, 21. 1 Pet. 2. 1. Gal. 5. 6.

So much for Examination and Preparation required before the action:
What is to be done by the Communicants in the present action?
They are to use reverent attention, the better to apply the whole action: hearkening to the doctrine of the Sacrament delivered by the Minister, joining with him in his prayers, making use of all the sacramental actions, and so commemorating the Lord's death for the comfort and refreshing of their own souls, 1 Cor. 11. 17, 26.

According as it is commanded, all must take the Bread and Wine into their hands. Contrary to the superstition of divers, which will either have it thrust into their mouths, or else take it with their gloves: as if the hand of a Christian, which God hath both made and sanctified, were not as fit as the skin of a beast, which the Artificer hath tanned and sewed.

They must moreover, according to the commandment of Christ, eat and drink the Bread and Wine; not laying or hanging it up, or worshiping it, as the Papists do.

Lastly they must use thanksgiving: offering up themselves both souls and bodies as a sacrifice of thanks; (Rom. 12. 1.) in which regard this Sacrament is called the Eucharist.

What is to be done after the action?
1. We must by and by use joyful thanksgiving, with prayer and meditation: being so comforted in heart in the favor of God towards us, that we be ready with a feeling joy to sing a Psalm unto the Lord. Mat. 26. 30.

2. We must continually endeavour to find an increase of our faith in Christ, love to God and all his Saints, power to subdue sin and practice obedience, with all other sanctifying and saving graces: (1 Cor. 10. 16, 17. and 11. 21. Col. 2. 6, 7. 2 Pet. 3. 18.) For a true receiver shall feel in himself, after the receiving of the Sacrament, an increase of faith and sanctification; a further deadening of the old man, and so a greater measure of dying unto sin; a further strength of the new man, and so a greater care to live in newness of life, and to walk the more strongly and steadily in the ways of God all the days of his life. This being a Sacrament, not of our incorporation, as Baptism, but of our growth: which albeit one cannot always discern immediately after the action, yet between that and the next Communion it may be easily espied in our service towards God and men.

What if a man after the receiving of the Sacrament never find any such thing in himself?

He may well suspect himself, whether he did ever repent or not; and therefore is to use means to come to sound faith and repentance. For the Lord is not usually wanting to his ordinances, if men prepare their hearts to meet him in them. If we receive no good nor refreshment at this spiritual feast, if God send us away empty: either it is because we have no right unto his mercies, being not in Christ, and so not accepted; or because some secret unmortified lust remaineth in us, like Achan's wedge of gold. So some beloved sin (either not seen, or not sufficiently sorrowed for, and resolved against) lieth glowing in the heart, which causeth God to frown upon our services; and like a dead fly causeth the ointment to stink: and therefore in this case, a man should descend into himself, and make a more strict search into his conscience, that he may again come before the Lord with more humility, and better preparedness, and God will reveal himself in due time to everyone who unfeignedly seeks after him in his ordinances.

[49TH HEAD.]

So much of the Sacraments. What are the Censures?

They are the judgments of the Church, for ratification of the threats of the Gospel, against the abusers of the Word and Sacraments.

What do these Censures profit the Church of God?

Very much. For by them the godly having strayed from the course of sincerity, are through obedience brought home again; but the wicked are hardened by them through disobedience: whereof it is, that the wicked are properly said to be punished, the Godly only chastened and corrected.

But it seems that corrections rather belong to Magistrates then to Ministers?

The Magistrates by the laws of the Common-wealth punish some by death, others by other torments, and some by purse: which belongeth not to the Minister, who hath to do only with the soul. And these spiritual censures are of as necessary use in the Church (both to help the godly, and to restrain and root out the wicked out of the Church) as those penal laws of the Magistrate in the Common-wealth. They therefore who upon this pretence that God forceth no man to come unto him, suppose the censures to be unprofitable; are like unto children that will have no rod in the house.

Whereby does the necessity of Censures appear?

Easily. For since in the Church of God there be of all sorts, as in a net cast into the sea, which catcheth good and bad: it is impossible, without correction, to keep good order in the Church; especially to restrain the wicked hypocrites from offending and thereby slandering their profession.

If then there were no hypocrites, there were no use of Censures.

Not so: but they serve most of all for them that make no conscience of their calling. For the best man that is, having some sparks of his natural corruption remaining unregenerate, may fall and offend, and therefore must be chastened by the Church. But this is the difference: the godly falling by infirmity, by correction do amend; but the wicked offending purposely, by punishment are hardened:

What is to gathered of this?

That since censures are as needful in the Church, as the rod in the house, or the Magistrates sword in the common-wealth for offenders; (yea and of so much more use as these are for the body and this life, and the other for the soul and life to come) they that set themselves against them, care not what disorder there be in the Church, but seek to exempt themselves from punishment, that they might do what they list and make the Gospel a covert for all their wickedness: who are like to them in the second Psalm, that would not bear the yoke of Government.

So much for the use and necessity of Censures. Where is the doctrine of them especially delivered?
In the 18 chapter of Saint Matthew, from the 15 verse to 20. where both their Institution and Ratification is laid down. For first our Savior declareth the degrees of the censures ordained for such as are called brethren (which are generally corrections according to the greatness of the offences,) and then treateth of their power and authority.

What is to be observed in the degrees of the censures?
That the censures be according to the offences: as if the offence be private, the censure thereof must be private. Wherein the censurer is to deal circumspectly. 1. That he know the offence. 2. That he admonish the offender secretly. 3. That he do it in love, convincing his offence so to be by the word of God.

What further duty is required of us in this case?
First, that we run not to others to slander the offender: which Moses forbiddeth, Levit. 19. 16. Second, not to keep the injury in mind, of purpose afterwards to revenge it. Third, not to deal roughly with one, under pretence of seeking the glory of God. 4. Not to despise the offender, but by all means to seek his amendment.

Who are to be admonished openly in the Church?
Those that sin openly.

What if they will not amend by admonition?
Then they are by suspension to be barred for a time from some exercises of religion: and if by that they will not amend, then they are by excommunication to be cut off from the Church, and delivered unto Satan, as shall be declared.

How are the Censures ratified, and the authority of the Church confirmed by our Savior Christ?
That appeareth by his words unto the disciples, Mat. 18. 18. Whatsoever you bind on earth, (meaning according to the rule) shall be bound in heaven? and whatsoever you loose on earth; shall be loosed in heaven. Which is as much as if a Prince, giving authority to one of small reputation, should bid him execute justice, he would bear him out.

How is this further used?
It is further confirmed in the verse following, by a reason of comparison. If two or three shall agree upon any thing, and shall ask it in my name; it shall be granted. If Christ will ratify the deed of two or three, done in his name; how much more then, that which the whole Church shall do accordingly.

Why is it said; And shall ask it in my name?
To declare that by prayer unto God in the name of our Savior Christ all the censures of the Church, but especially Excommunication, should be undertaken as the Apostle faith. 1 Cor. 5. 4. When you are gathered together in the name of the Lord Jesus Christ, (that is, calling upon the name) deliver such an one unto Satan.

What need is there of this ratifying of the Churches authority in exercising the Censures?
Because some do condemn the Censures of the Church, as proceeding from men only, as if thereby they were no whit debarred from the favor of God: whereas nevertheless, whom the Church separateth from the outward seals, them also Christ depriveth of inward graces; banishing them from his kingdom, whom the Church hath given over to Satan.

What gather you of this?
That men should not slightly shake off, but with reverence esteem the censures of the Church as the voice of God himself: and although they be never so high and stout, yet are they to subject themselves to the judgment of God in the Church, unless they will set themselves against the Lord himself.

We have heard of the general doctrine of Censures. What are the kinds of them?
They are either of Sovereign medicine, (Mat. 18. 15, 16. 1 Cor. 5.) or of fearful revenge: (1 Cor. 16. 22. 2 Tim. 4. 14.) the former properly are corrections, the latter punishments.

What are the Medicinal Censures?
They are such as serve to bring men to repentance: the principal end of the next glory of God, being the salvation of his soul that is censured.

What things are required of them that do execute these Censures against any man?
Six. 1. Wisdom. 2. Freedom from the sin reproved. 3. Love. 4. Sorrow. 5. Patience. 6. Prayer for the party.

Of what sort are the Medicinal Censures?
They are either in Word or Deed.

What are they in Word?
The chidings or rebukes of the Church for sin: which we call Admonitions.

How many sorts of Admonitions are there?
Two: the first is private, betwixt brother and brother; (Levit. 19. 17. Mat. 18. 15, 16.) the other public, by the Minister assisted by the congregation, when the private will not prevail. Mat. 18. 17. 1 Tim. 5. 20.

What are we to observe in the private Admonitions?
That we should watch one another diligently, witnessing thereby our mutual love, which God requireth of us. As if any man seeing another (whose journey he knoweth) wander out of the way, if he should not admonish him, he might justly be accounted unnatural: much more we knowing all men think to journey toward heaven, if we see any go the wrong ways, (as by Robberies, Adulteries, Usury, Swearing, or Drunkenness) and do not admonish them, are even guilty of their wandering; especially since the other belongeth to the body, but this both to body and soul.

But it is not sufficient for men to watch themselves; seeing every man standeth or falleth to God?
Such was the wicked answer of Cain: and they that use it, are like unto him. But if God commanded in the law, to help our enemies Ox or Ass, having need of help; we are more bound by the law of charity to help himself. And unless we reprove him, we are partakers of his sin; (as hath been said;) which we ought not to be, because we have enough of our own.

Forty-ninth Head

What are the degrees of private admonition?
They be two. The former is most private, done by one; the other is private also, but more public then the first; and it is done by two or three at the most, whereof he that first admonished, must be one. Mat. 18. 15, 16.

Why hath our savior Christ limited us with these degrees?
By all means to win the offender, if it be possible: if not, that his condemnation may appear to be most just, after so many warnings.

How is the first degree of private Admonition expressed?
If thy brother offend against thee, or, in thy knowledge only; tell him between thee and him. Mat. 18. 15.

Are we bound to reprove all men of what profession soever?
No: but him that is of the same profession of Christianity that we be of, whom the Scripture terms a brother; (thereby shutting forth Jews, Turks, Heretics, and Atheists:) except we have some particular bond; as of a master to his servant; or a father to his child, or magistrate to his subject. &c.

What learn you thereby?
First, that we observe this in our admonitions; that he be a brother whom we admonish, and not such a one as is a scorner. Second, that we are not to make light of, or condemn the admonitions of others, but to accept of them and account of them as a precious balm.

How must we reprove our brothers fault?
First, we must be sure that it is a fault we reprove him for: and then we must be able to convince him thereof out of the word of God, so that he shall not be able to gainsay us, unless he do it contemptuously; it being better for us not to reprove him, then not to be able to convince him by the word of that we have reproved him in. Lastly, we ought to do it with all love and mildness, regarding the circumstances of persons, time, and place: not inconsiderately, nor of hatred, or to reproach him, or as one that is glad of somewhat to hurt his good name.

What is meant by, Tell him between thee and him? Mat. 18. 15.
That the good name and report of another man should be so regarded by us, that if his fault be private, we are not to spread it abroad: as some that think they be burdened, unless they tell it to others; which is not the rule of charity.

Why is this added, If he hear thee, thou hast gained thy brother?
As a notable means to encourage us in this duty. For if the bestowing of a Cup of cold water should not be unrewarded: how much more gaining of a soul from Satan?

What if our brother hear us not, and so we do not gain him?
Notwithstanding we lose not our labor: but our reward is laid up with God. Isa. 49. 4. For that which is done for God's cause, though it be never so evil taken or used, shall certainly be remembered of God; Who will recompense it plentifully, and lay it up among our good deeds. Also this shall serve against him that is reproved, in judgment, for refusing such a profitable means.

What is the second degree of Private Admonitions?
It is more public then the former. If thy brother hear thee not, take yet with thee one or two, Mat. 18. 16. For although he hear not the first admonition, yet love will not give him over: but as the case requireth, and the nature and the condition of the offender may be

discerned to be easy or hard to repent; the admonisher is to take with him one, or if need be two at the most, to assist him.

The first Admonition not availing, may we take whom we will to the second?
The choice is to be made which is likeliest to take effect. And therefore we may not take his enemy, or one that is not able to convince: but we must choose one or two such, whom either he reverenceth or at least favoreth, or otherwise may do most good with him, either by graciousness of speech, or ability of personage, or some other gift; in a word, such as be fittest both for gifts and authority to recover him; of whom the Pastor may be one; as he also may be the first.

May the first admonisher substitute another in his place the second time?
No. For our Savior Christ does not leave it free so to do; but will have him that did first admonish to be one; both for the better conferring of the former dealing with the latter; as also for keeping the fault of the offender in as much silence and secrecy as may be.

What is gathered hereby?
That great love and care of our Savior Christ towards him; as also what diligence we must use, and what care for our brother.

What may not one alone deal with him the second time?
Because that by the testimony of two or three he might be brought to reverence now, that which he would not at the first admonition: and further, that way may be made to the public judgment of the Church, yea to the others way before the Church, which under two testimonies at least cannot proceed further against him. For in the mouth of two or three witnesses every truth is confirmed. Mat. 8. 16.

Thus far of the private Admonitions. What is the public?
That which is done by the whole Church, or the Minister assisted by the Congregation (1 Tim. 5. 20.) For if the second warning serve not, our Savior would have the offender present to the Church, as to the highest Court, (Mat. 18. 19.) not of greatest personages, but of the most learned, and beautified with inward graces, whose presence he cannot choose but reverence. As in the book of Numbers, a wife suspected of adultery, was brought unto the priest in the house of God; that the reverence of the place and person might strike a fear in her heart, to cause her to confess the truth. (Num. 5. 15, 16.) Wherein appeareth a further step and degree of God's singular love and affection.

But the bringing of him to open shame seemeth rather hurtful then profitable?
Not to the godly, to whom it is prepared as a sovereign medicine for his diseases. For as a wealthy man being sick, assembleth a whole College of Physicians to consult of his disease and the remedy thereof, so the whole Church in the like case having Urim & Thummim, that is, treasures of knowledge, should consult upon the recovery of the offender; who therefore hearing their Admonition, is to be received, notwithstanding his former obstinacy. But the hearts of the wicked by the warning are the more hardened to their everlasting perdition.

Hitherto of the Corrections which are in Word: what are they in Deed?
Suspension, (Num. 12. 14. Exod. 33. 6, 7.) and Excommunication. Mat. 18. 17. 1 Cor. 5.

What is suspension?
A certain separation of him that will not amend by Admonition, from some holy things in the Church: as 1. the use of the Sacrament: 2. some offices in the Church.

Forty-ninth Head

What is Excommunication?
The casting of the stubborn sinner out of the Church, and delivering him unto Satan. Who being thus disfranchised of all the liberties, and deprived of all the benefits and common society of the church, is separated, as it were, from that protection and mercy which may be looked for at the hands of God.

What is the end of this casting out?
It is twofold: First in regard of God's glory; Secondly in regard of men.

How in regard of God?
Because that his holy Name and Religion should not be evil spoken of by suffering wicked and unclean persons, (as blasphemers, adulterers, &c.) in the Church; which should not be like unto a sty, but clean from all show of filthiness. For in houses of good report, a proud person, detracter, or liar, (much less a drunkard or filthy person) is not suffered: much less ought such an one to be in the church, which is the house of the living God, lest the Gospel come to reproach through such; in that godless persons would thereby take occasion to open their mouths against the truth.

How in regard of men?
That likewise is two fold: either respecting the good of the person excommunicated, or the rest of the church.

What is the regard that concerneth the Church?
That they be not infected with his naughtiness, and that they may keep themselves from the like offence. For that if he remain in the Church, and be not banished,

First, other men would be provoked to commit the like sins. For the Apostle comparing a sinful man to leaven, 1 Cor. 5. 6. teacheth, that as a little leaven will sour the whole batch; so one wicked man will infect the whole Church. Secondly, the weak would take occasion thereby of falling away from the truth; and others yet without, would be holden from coming unto it.

What is the regard that concerneth him that is cast out?
That he being shamed, may be brought to repent and turn unto the Lord. as the Apostle saith of the incestuous person; who should be cut off for the destruction of the flesh, that is, the natural corruption, and for saving of the spirit, that is the man regenerate. 1 Cor. 5. 5. 1 Tim. 1. 20.

If the severity of this censure be such as hath been declared; how then tendeth it to reformation?
They that are thus censured, are only delivered to Satan conditionally, if they repent not. So it is a means either to bring them to Christ, or send them to the devil: as a hand almost cut off, and hanging but by the skin, is in danger to be lost, unless some skillful Surgeon bind it up.

What is to be done to him if he repent?
He is to be received of the Church; whom as they loose in earth, our Savior Christ looseth in heaven. Yet he is not by and by to be admitted to all privileges of the Church, but to be suspended for a time, till the fruits of repentance may better appear. For if some in the Law, for a certain pollution in a lawful duty of burying the dead, were suspended from the Passover; (Num. 9. 6.) much more in the Gospel for such obstinacy.

How many sorts of Suspensions then are there?
Two: one going before Excommunication, and the other following the same, towards them that are penitent. Both which were shadowed in the Levitical law, in the case of Leprosy. For first in the 13. of Lev. we find that upon Suspicion of Leprosy a man was shut up for a time, not only from the worship of God, but also from all society of men: how much more then may it be lawful under the Gospel, to execute the censure of suspension after two admonitions upon a known offence? Secondly, it is set down in the 14. of Levit. That a man cleansed from his leprosy, was brought home unto the camp and placed in his tent, where he stayed for certain days; it being not lawful for him to come into the Tabernacle.

So much of the Medicinal censures. What is the last censure of fearful revenge?
The curse unto death called by S. Paul, Anathema Maranatha, 1 Cor. 16. 22. that is accursed until the Lord come, or everlastingly. Which is thought to have been executed upon Hymeneus and Alexander by Paul, (1 Tim. 1. 20.) and afterwards upon Julian by the Church then.

Against whom is this Censure to proceed?
This everlasting curse, which is the most fearful thunder-clap of God's judgment, is to be pronounced only against such as are desperately wicked, that have nothing profited by the former censures, and showed their incorrigibleness by their obstinate and malicious resisting all means graciously used to reclaim them: giving tokens even of that unpardonable sin against the Holy Ghost. Which fearful sin, by how much the more difficult it is to be discerned and known; by so much the more carefully is this heavy doom to be used by the church. Yet doubtless God does sometimes give clear tokens thereof in blasphemous Apostates, such as Julian and others, who maliciously oppose deride and persecute that truth of God which they have been enlightened in. And where God does set such marks upon them, the Church of God may pronounce them to be such, and carry it self towards them accordingly.

Who are the outward enemies that oppose themselves against the Church of Christ?
Some do under show of friendship, and some with profession of enmity.

Who are the open enemies?
Heathens, Jews, Turks (Muslims), and all that make profession of profaneness, by sitting down in the seat of scorners.

What enemies are they, that make show of friendship?
Such are all those, that bearing the name of Christians, do obstinately deny the faith, whereby we are joined unto Christ, which are called Heretics; or that break the bond of charity, whereby we are tied in communion one to another, which are termed Schismatics; or else add tyranny to schism, and heresy, as that great Antichrist, the head of the general Apostasy, which the Scriptures forewarned of by name.

Where are we forewarned of that Apostasy?
In 1 Tim. 4. 1. and 2 Thess. 2. 3. where the Apostle foretelleth, that there shall be a general Apostasy, or falling away from the truth of the Gospel, before the latter day.

Is it meant, that the whole Church shall fall away from Christ?
No: it were impossible that a perfect head should be without a body.

Why is it then called general?
Because the Gospel having been universally preached throughout the world; from it, both whole nations did fall, and the most part also even of those Nations that keep

the profession of it: howbeit still there remained a Church, though there were no settled estate thereof.

Is it likely the Lord would bar so many nations that lived under Antichrist and that so long, from the means of salvation?
Why not? and that most justly. For if the whole world of the Gentiles were rejected, when the Church was only in Jury, for some 1500 years and seeing even the Jews ten Tribes were rejected, and of the remainder, but a few were of the Church: with great reason might the Lord reject those nations and people for so many ages; seeing they rejected God's grace in falling away from the Gospel, which the Lord most graciously revealed unto them, rather then unto their Fathers before them.

Is this Apostasy necessarily laid upon the See of Rome?
Yes verily: as by the description that followeth may evidently appear.

What are the parts of this Apostasy?
The head and the body. For as Christ is the head of the Church, which is his body: so Antichrist is the head of the Romish Church which is his body.

Who is that Antichrist?
He is one who under the color of being for Christ; and under title of his Vicegerent, exalteth himself above, and against Christ; opposing himself unto him in all his offices, and ordinances, both in Church and Commonwealth: bearing authority in the Church of God; ruling over that City with seven Hills, which did bear rule over nations, and put our Lord to death: a Man of sin, a Harlot, a Mother of spiritual fornications to the Kings and people of the nations, a child of perdition, and a destroyer; establishing himself by lying miracles, and false wonders. All which marks together do agree with none but the Pope of Rome.

How does the Apostle in 2 Thess. 2. 3. describe this Antichristian head unto us?
First, he describeth what he is towards others: and then what he is in himself.

What is he towards others?
That is declared by two special titles the Man of sin, and Son of perdition: declaring hereby, not so much his own sin and perdition, which is exceeding great; as of those that receive his mark, whom he causeth to sin, and consequently to fall into perdition, as Jeroboam, who is often branded with the mark of causing Israel to sin. And he is so much more detestable then he; by how much both his Idolatry is more execrable, and hath drawn more Kingdoms after him, then Jeroboam did Tribes.

In what respect is he called the man of sin?
In that he caused many to sin: and this the Pope does in a high degree; justifying sin, not by oversight, but by Laws advisedly made; not only commanding some sins, which we are by our corrupt nature prone unto, as spiritual fornication, but also (to the great profanation of the holy name and profession of Christ) permitting and teaching for lawful such as even our corrupt nature (not wholly subverted through enormous custom of sin) abhorreth: as incestuous marriages, and breaking of faith and leagues, equivocating, and the like; which profane men (by the very light of nature) do detest.

In what sense is he called the child of perdition?
Not as the unthrift mentioned in the Gospel, (Luk. 15. 32.) neither as Judas, who is passively called the Son of perdition, (John 17. 12.) but actively, as it is other-where expounded, where he is called the destroyer, (Rev. 9. 11.) because he destroyeth many. And that the Pope is such an one, some of his own Secretaries make it good;

confessing that many who were well disposed persons before their entering into that See, became cursed and cruel beasts when once they were settled in the same, as if there were some pestilent poison in that seat infecting those that sit therein.

What learn you of this?
That the calling of the Pope is unlawful. For every office or calling which the Lord does not bless, or wherein none occupying the place groweth in piety, is to be esteemed for an unlawful calling: for in a lawful calling some (at the least) are found in all ages profitable to the Church or Commonwealth.

What is the use of all this doctrine?
That whosoever are partakers of the sins of Rome, are also under the same curse: and therefore such of us as have lived in Popery should examine ourselves if we have truly repented us of it; first, by the change of our understanding, as whether we have grown in the knowledge of the truth: and secondly, by the change of our affections, as whether we hate Popery, and love the truth unfeignedly; and so let every one judge himself, that he be not judged, and that with harder judgment, according as God hath been the longer patient towards us. Rom. 2. 4.

What further?
That there can be no sound agreement betwixt Popery and the profession of the Gospel; no more than betwixt light and darkness, falsehood and truth, God and Belial: and therefore no reconciliation can be devised betwixt them. For if the members of Antichrist shall be destroyed, we cannot in any sort communicate with them in their errors, unless we will bear them company in their destruction also.

Does every error destroy the soul?
No verily. For as every wound killeth not a man, so every error depriveth not a man of salvation: but as the vital parts being wounded or infected, bring death, so those errors that destroy the fundamental points and heads of faith bring everlasting destruction; in which kind is Popery, which sundry ways overthroweth the principles and grounds of our holy faith, and therefore is termed an Apostasy, or departing from the faith. 2 Pet. 2. 1.

Is it then impossible for a Pope to be saved?
No; it is not impossible, his sin being not necessarily against the Holy Ghost, to which only repentance is denied. For some (in likely hood) have entered into, and continued in that See ignorantly; and therefore may possibly find place to repentance. But if any be saved, it is a secret hidden with God: for concerning any thing that appears by the end of any Pope, since he was lift up into the Emperors chair, and discovered to be the man of sin, there is no grounded hope given to persuade that any one of them is saved.

So much of Antichrist, what he is towards others. What is he in himself?
That is set down in two points. First, in that (contrary to right, and by mere usurpation) he feareth himself in the Temple of God, as if he were Christ's Vicar, being indeed his enemy: both which the word Antichrist noteth. Secondly, in that he is expressly named an adversary, and one that is contrary to Christ.

Wherein is the Pope adversary unto Christ?
Every way; in life, and in office.

How in life?
In that Christ being most pure and holy, yea holiness it self; the Popes many of them are, and have been, most filthy and abominable in blaspheming, conjuring, murdering,

covetousness, whoring, and that incestuously and Sodomitically: and yet will they in their ordinary Titles be called holy, yea holiness it self; which is proper only to Christ.

How in office?
First, in his Kingdom. Christ's Kingdom is without all outward show or pomp: but the Popes Kingdom consisteth wholly in Pomp, and Shows, as imitating his Predecessors the Emperors of Rome in his proud, stately, and lordly offices, princely train, and outrageous expenses in every sort. Secondly, in his Priest-hood: in raising up another Sacrifice than Christ's, another Priest-hood than his, other Mediators than him. Thirdly, in his prophetical office: in that he teacheth clean contrary to him. Christ taught nothing but what he received of his Father: the Pope setteth out his own Canons and decrees of Councils; and in them he teacheth such doctrine as overthroweth the main foundation of that which Christ taught.

What is the second effect?
That he is exceeding lifted up against all that is called God.

How does this agree to the Pope?
More fitly than to any other person. For Christ being very God, abaseth himself unto the assuming of the nature of man: the Pope a vile man, advanceth himself to the Throne of God. Christ being above all secular power, paid tribute, and was taxed, and suffered himself to be crowned with a Crown of Thorns, and bear his own Cross: but the Pope, being under all secular power, exalteth himself above all secular powers, exacteth Tribute of Kings, setteth his foot on the neck of Emperors, carrieth a triple Crown of gold, and is born upon men's shoulders.

But he calleth himself the servant of servants?
Though he do, yet (by the confession of his own Canonists) he does it but dissemblingly and in hypocrisy, which is double iniquity; for they say, that he does in humility only say so; not that he is indeed so as he saith.

What are the effects of this his pride?
They are two. First, he sitteth in the Church as God. For he bindeth the consciences of men by his decrees, which no Prince's Law can do. For though men observe no such Laws, yet if they break them not of contempt, they are discharged, if they did bear the penalty prescribed in them.

By this it seemeth that the Church of Rome is yet the Church of God although corrupt; seeing it is said, that he sitteth in the Temple of God?
No verily: but it is so said, first, because it beareth the name of the Church: for the Scripture giveth the name to a thing according to that it hath been; as when Christ saith, The abomination of desolation shall stand in the holy place; he meaneth not that the Temple was then holy, which at that time, (being no figure nor shadow of Christ and his Church) was profaned, but that it had been holy: so we confess that there had been a true Church in Rome; which is now no Church of Christ, but the Synagogue of Satan.

Secondly, he is said to sit in the Temple of God, because he exerciseth his tyrannical rule in the Christian world, and is most busy in those parts where Christ hath his church, and the Gospel is professed; laboring in all places, either by himself or his wicked instruments, to overthrow or corrupt, poison or hinder the free course of the Gospel: so that in this regard he may be said to sit in the Temple of God, that is, to reign and tyrannize in the Church of God; though the city where he is, be Sodom, and the Church whereof he is head, the Synagogue of Satan.

What is the other effect of his pride?
He boasteth himself that he is God: as the Popes flatterers in the canon Law call him, Our Lord God the Pope. Neither does his pride stay there, but also he challengeth to himself things proper to God: as the title of Holiness, also power to forgive sins; and to carry infinite souls to hell without check or resistance, and to make of nothing something; yea, to make the Scriptures to be no Scriptures, and no Scripture to be Scripture, at his pleasure, yea to make of the Creature the Creator.

It may seem to be an impossible thing, that men should be carried away from the faith of the Gospel, by one so monstrous and directly, opposite to Christ?
It might seem so indeed, if at once at a sudden he had showed himself in such foul colors: and therefore by certain degrees of iniquity he raised himself to this height of wickedness, and did not at the first show himself in such a monstrous shape and likeness.

How does that appear?
By the Apostle, who in the 2 Thes. 2. 3. unto 13. showeth of two courses the Devil held to bring this to pass: one secret and covert, before this man of sin was revealed; the other when he was revealed and set up in his Seat.

What were the ways of Antichrists coming before he was revealed?
Those several errors which were spread, partly in the Apostles time, and partly after their time, thereby to make a way for his coming. And in this respect, this mystery of iniquity was begun to be wrought (as it were) under ground and secretly in the Apostle's time.

How was this mystery of iniquity wrought in the Apostles time?
By many ambitious spirits, (as it were) petty Antichrists, which were desirous to be Lord's over the church; and wicked Heretics, which then sowed many errors and Heresies, as justification by works: worshipping of Angels, and which put Religion in meats, and condemned marriage, &c. which were beginnings and grounds of Popery and Antichristianism. 2 John 9. Acts 5. 1. Gal. 1. 6, 7. & 2. 16. Col. 2. 18, 21. 1 Tim. 4. 3.

What gather you of this?
That those whom God hath freed from the bondage of Popery, should strive to free themselves from all the remnants thereof; lest if they cleave still to any of them, God in judgment bring the whole upon them again.

How shall Antichrist's Kingdom be continued and advanced after that he is revealed?
By the power of Satan, in lying miracles and false wonders.

What difference is there betwixt Christ's miracles and theirs?
Very great every way. For Christ's miracles were true: whereas these are false and lying and by legerdemain. Christ's miracles were from God: but theirs, where there is any strange thing and above the common reach of men, from the Devil. Christ's miracles were for the most part profitable to the health of man: but theirs altogether unprofitable, and for a vain show. Christ's miracles were to confirm the truth: but theirs to confirm falsehood.

What gather you of this?
That seeing the Popes Kingdom glorieth so much in wonders, it is most like, that he is Antichrist: seeing the false Christ's and the false Prophets shall do great wonders to deceive (if it were possible) the very Elect, and that some of the false Prophets Prophesies shall come to pass, we should not therefore believe the doctrine of Popery

for their wonders sake, seeing the Lord thereby tryeth our faith; who hath given to Satan great knowledge and power to work stranger things, to bring those to damnation who are appointed unto it. Moreover, whatsoever Miracles are not profitable to some good, neither tend to confirm a truth, they are false and lying. So that as the Lord left an evident difference between his miracles and the enchantments of the Egyptians; so hath he left an evident difference between the miracles of Christ and his Apostles, and those of the Romish Synagogue. Mat. 24. 24. Deu. 13. 1, 2, 3. Exod. 7. 12.

Are not miracles as necessary now, as they were in time of the Apostles?
No verily. For the doctrine of the Gospel being then new unto the world, had need to have been confirmed with miracles from heaven: but being once confirmed there is no more need of miracles; and therefore we keeping the same doctrine of Christ and his Apostles, must content ourselves with the confirmation which hath already been given.

What ariseth out of this?
That the doctrine of Popery is a new doctrine, which had need to be confirmed with new miracles; and so it is not the doctrine of Christ, neither is established by his miracles.

What force shall the Miracles of Antichrist have?
Marvelous great, to bring many men to damnation: God, in just revenge of the contempt of the truth, sending a strong delusion among them.

Hitherto we have heard Antichrist described by his effects and properties: now tell me, where is the place of his special residence?
That is the City of Rome.

How does that appear?
First, because he that letted at the time when Paul wrote, was the Emperor of Rome, who did then sit there and must be dis-seated, (as the Learned Papists themselves grant) e'er Antichrist could enter upon it. Secondly, John called the City where he must sit, the Lady of the world: (Rev. 17. 18.) which at that time agreed only to Rome, being the Mother City of the world. Thirdly, it was that City which was seated upon seven hills (Rev. 17. 9.) which by all ancient records belongeth properly to Rome. As for the occasion of the Popes placing there, it came by the means of translating of the seat of the Empire from Rome to Constantinople, from whence ensued also the parting of the Empire into two parts: by which division it being weakened, and after also sundered in affection, as well as in place, was the easier to be entered upon, and obtained by the Pope.

What do you further gather of that the Apostle saith, that he that letteth shall let?
That the Antichrist is not one particular man, as the Papists do fancy; for then by the like phrase he that letteth must be one particular man: where it cannot be that one man should live so many hundred years, as from Paul's time to the time of the translation of the Empire from Rome, much less until within two years and a half of the latter day, as they imagine the time of Antichrist. And therefore as by him that letteth is understood a succession of Emperors, not one man alone: so by Antichrist the man of sin is understood a succession of men, and not one only man: So in Dan. 7. 3, 17. the four beasts, and the four Kings, do not signify four particular men, but four governments; in every one whereof there were sundry men that ruled. So that the argument of the Papists, who upon the words (the man of sin) would prove, that the Antichrist the Apostle speaketh of, is one singular man, is but vain, and hath no consequence in it.

But how can Antichrist be already come, seeing, the Empire yet standeth?
The name of the Empire only remaineth, the thing is gone. For he hath neither the chief City, nor the Tribute: nor the command of the people: and therefore he can be no let to

the Antichrists coming; especially the Pope having gotten such an upper hand over him, as to cause him to wait at his gate barefoot, and to hold his stirrup.

What shall be the end of this Antichrist?
God shall confound him with the breath of his mouth, that is, with the preaching of his Word. Which serveth for another argument to prove the Pope to be Antichrist: for whereas he had subdued Kingdoms and Empires under his feet, he hath been of late mightily suppressed by the word preached, and not by outward force, as other Potentates use to be.

What learn you of this?
The marvelous power of God's word to suppress whatsoever riseth against it: for if the mightiest cannot stand before it, much less the smallest. And therefore it is expressed by a mighty wind, Acts 2. 2, 3. which carrieth all before it; and by fire, which consumeth all, and pierceth all. And it declareth a marvelous easy victory against the enemies, when it is said that with the breath of his mouth he shall consume his enemies.

What else shall be the overthrow of Antichrist?
The glorious appearance of the Son of God in the latter day.

What gather you of this?
That before the Last day he shall not be utterly consumed. Whereof notwithstanding it followeth not that the head should remain till then: for the Beast and the false Prophet shall be taken and cast into the fire before the latter day; but some shall retain a liking of him and his errors and superstitions, even till the last day.

Hitherto of the head of the general Apostasy. What are the members of it?
They are first described by their end, even a number of people that should perish: which accordeth with that name and property of the head, the Destroyer or Son of perdition; being truly verified in them, in regard of the fearful end he shall bring them to.

What is the use of this?
That as no poison can take away the life of an elect: so small occasions carry away such as are appointed to destruction.

How other wise are these members of Antichrist described?
By this that they never love the truth, although they understood and professed it.

How should a man love the truth?
For the truths sake; not for vain glory, fleshly delight or commodity.

How appeareth it that men love the word of God?
When they walk accordingly, and keep faith and a good conscience; which some losing by their wicked life, lost also their Faith, that is their Religion. 1 Tim. 1. 19.

How is it to be understood, that God giveth men up to strong delusions?
Because God is a just judge, which by them either punisheth or correcteth former sins, and especially the contempt of the Gospel: in which regard even amongst us now, some are cast into the sink of Popery, some into the Family of love; some become Arians, some Anabaptists; all which are (as it were) divers Gaols and Dungeons, whereunto he throweth those that are cold and careless Professors of the Gospel.

What learn you by this?
That they which imagine God favorable unto them notwithstanding their sins, because their life, or goods, or honors are spared, are foully deceived. For when the Lord ceaseth to reprove any, or to strive with them; then does he give them up into vanity of their own minds, to do their own wicked wills; which is the greatest judgment, and very usual with God to do. Rom. 1. 24, 26.

What is our duty in such cases?
To pray to the Lord to keep us from all error: but if for our trial, or further hardening of others, it please him to send errors amongst us, that it would please him to preserve us in that danger, that we talk not of that bait, whereby Satan seeketh to catch us.

What other cause is there of sending these errors?
That those may be damned, which believe not the truth: for as God hath appointed them to damnation, so betwixt his counsel in rejecting them, and the final effect of it, there must be sin to bring the effect justly upon them.

What reason is annexed of their just damnation?
Because they rest in unrighteousness, having their ears itching after error; which they drink in, as the earth drinketh up rain, or the fishes water. So that albeit they be powerfully sent to God in his Judgment; yet are they also greedily desired and affected of them.

[50TH HEAD.]

Having spoken at large of the Providence of God's disposing of men to this world: it followeth to speak of his Providence concerning mankind in the world to come. How does God then deal with men after this life?
He bringeth them all unto Judgment.

What is meant here by Judgment?
The pronouncing, and executing of the irrevocable sentence of Absolution or Condemnation.

How it that done?
Partly, on every man in particular at the hour of his death: (Heb. 9. 27.) but fully and generally upon all men, at the second coming of Christ (Act) 17. 31,) The death of every one severally goeth immediately before the particular Judgment. The general Resurrection of all goeth before the final Judgment which shall be at the last day.

Must all men then die?
Yea, all both good and bad: (Psal. 49. 10. Eccles. 2. 16.) save that unto some, namely such as shall be found alive at the coming of Christ a Change shall be instead of Death.

Death being the punishment of sin; how cometh it to pass that the righteous die, to whom all sins are forgiven?
Death indeed came on all mankind by reason of sin: (Rom. 5. 12.) but yet it is not in all things the same to the godly and to the wicked. For howsoever unto both it be the enemy of nature, as the end of natural life: (1 Cor. 15. 26. Psal 90. 3.) yet:

First, unto the godly it is a token of Gods love: unto the wicked of his anger: Psal. 37. 38. 6. Joh. 18. 13, 14. Second, unto the godly it is a rest from labor and misery: (Rev.

14. 13.) unto the wicked it is the height of all worldly evils. Luk. 12. 20. Third, unto the godly it is the utter abolishing of sin, and perfection of mortification: (Rom. 6. 7.) unto the wicked it is the conquest of sin and accomplishment of their spiritual captivity. Fourth, unto the godly it is so far from being a separation from Christ, that even the body severed from the soul, and rotting in the grave, is yet united unto Christ, and the soul freed from the body is with him in Paradise: (Luke 23. 43. Phil. 1. 23.) unto the wicked it is an utter cutting off from the favorable presence, and fruition of God. Fifth, unto the godly it is the beginning of heavenly glory; unto the wicked it is the entrance into hellish and endless torments. Luke 16. 22, 23.

How are men judged at the hour of death?
First, God at that instant pronounceth and conscience apprehendeth, the sentence of blessing or cursing. Heb. 6. 27. Second, the soul of every man accordingly is (by the power of God, and the ministry of Angels) immediately conveyed into that state of happiness or misery, wherein it shall remain till the Resurrection, and from thence forth both body and soul for ever. Luke 16. 22, 23, 26. Eccl. 11. 3.

What gather you of this?
That the doctrine of Purgatory and Prayer for the dead is vain: seeing it appeareth by the word of God, that the souls of those that die in God's favor are presently received into joy. Isa. 57. 2. Joh. 5, 24. Luke 23. 43. Rev. 14. 13. with 1 Thes. 4. 16. and the souls of those that die in their sins, cast into endless torments; no means being left after death to procure remission of sins. Isa. 22. 14. John 8. 24. & 9. 4. Rom. 6, 10.

[51ST HEAD.]

What is the general and final Judgment?
That great day of assize for the whole world (Eccl. 12. 24. 1 Cor. 5. 10.); wherein all men's lives that ever have been, are, or shall be, being duly examined, every one shall receive according to his works. (Acts 17. 31. Eccles. 12. 14. 2 Cor. 5. 10.) In which judgment we are to consider; 1. The preparation to it. 2. The acting of it. 3. The execution of the sentence.

Wherein does the preparation to the last judgment consist?
In five things. First, in the foretokening of the time thereof: which though it be so sealed up in the treasury of God's counsel, that neither man nor Angels, nor yet our Savior himself, as a man in the days of his flesh, had express notice thereof, (that from the uncertainty and suddenness of it we might be taught to be always in readiness for it; Acts 1. 7. Mat. 13. 32.) yet it hath pleased God to acquaint us with some signs whereby we may discern Christ's approaching, as men in the Spring time may discern Summer approaching by the shooting forth of the Fig tree. Mat. 24. 32, 33.

What are the signs foretokening the last judgment?
They are certain notable changes in the World and Church (Mat.24): some further off, some nearer unto the coming of Christ; as,

1. The publishing and receiving the Gospel throughout the world. 2. The Apostasy of most part of professors not loving the truth. 1 Tim 4. 1. 3. The revealing of Antichrist that man of sin and Child of perdition. 2 Thes. 1. 3. 4. Common corruptions in manners joined with security; as in the days of Noah and Lot. 5. Wars and troubles in the world and Church. 6. False Christ's; attended with false Prophets, and armed with false miracles. 7. The calling of the Jews unto the faith of the Gospel. 8. And lastly, signs in Heaven, Earth,

and all the Elements. As the darkening of the Sun, and Moon, &c. Yea, firing of the whole frame of Heaven, and Earth, with the sign of the Son of man; whereby his coming shall then be clearly apprehended by all men. 2 Pet. 3. 7. Mat. 24. 30.

What is the second thing in the preparation?
The coming of Jesus Christ the Judge of the world: who in his human visible body (but yet with unspeakable glory) shall suddenly break forth like lightning through the Heavens, riding on the clouds, environed with a flame of fire, attended with all the host of the elect Angels, and specially with the voice and shout of an Archangel and the Trumpet of God; and so shall sit down in the royal throne of judgment.

What is the third thing?
The summoning and presenting of all both dead and living men, together with Devils, before the glorious throne of Christ the Judge.

How shall all men both dead and living be summoned?
By the voice of Christ, and the ministry of his Angels; and namely by the shut and Trumpet of the Archangel: whereto the Lord joining his divine power (as unto the word preached for the work of the first resurrection (shall in a moment both raise the dead with their own bodies and every part hereof though never so dispersed; and change the living, so that it shall be with them as if they had been a long time dead and were now raised to life again. John 5. 28. Mat. 24. 31. 1 Cor. 15. 52.

Shall there be no difference between the resurrection of the Elect and Reprobate?
Yes. For howsoever they shall both rile by the same mighty voice and power of Christ in the same bodies wherein they lived upon earth, and those so altered in quality, as then they shall be able to abide for ever in that estate whereunto they shall be Judged: yet,

1. The Elect shall be raised, as members of the body of Christ, by virtue derived from his resurrection: the Reprobate, as Malefactors, shall be brought forth of the prison of the grave, by virtue of the judiciary power of Christ and of the curse of the law. 2. The Elect shall come forth to everlasting life, which is called the resurrection of life, the Reprobate to shame and perpetual contempt, called the resurrection of condemnation. 3. The bodies of the Elect shall be spiritual, that is glorious, powerful, nimble, impassible, (1 Cor. 15. 42, 43, 44. Phil. 3. 21.) but the bodies of the Reprobate shall be full of uncomeliness and horror, agreeable to the guiltiness and terror of their conscience, and liable to extreme torment.

How shall all men be presented before the throne of Christ?
First, the Elect being gathered by the Angels, shall with great joy be caught up into the air to meet the Lord. Luk. 21. 28. 1 Thess. 4. 17. Second, the Reprobate, together with the Devil and his Angels, shall with extreme horror and confusion be drawn into his presence. Rev. 6. 15.

What is the fourth thing?
The separation of the Elect from the Reprobate. For Christ, the great Shepherd, shall then place the Elect, as his Sheep that have heard his voice and followed him, on his right hand; and the Reprobates with the Devils, as straying Goats, on the left hand. Mat. 25. 33.

What is the fifth and last thing?
The opening of the book of record, by which the dead shall be judged. Rev. 20. 12. viz.

1. The Several books of men's consciences: which then, by the glorious illumination of Christ, the Sun of righteousness, shining in his full strength, shall be so enlightened, that men shall perfectly remember whatever good or evil they did in the time of the life; the secrets of all hearts being then revealed. 2. The book of life, that is the eternal decree of God to save his Elect by Christ: which decree shall then at length be made known to all.

Thus far of the preparation to judgment: What are we to consider in the second place?
The act of judgment: wherein the Elect shall first be acquitted, that they may after as assistants Join with Christ in the Judgment of the reprobate men and Angels.

How shall the act of judgment be performed?
1. By examination. 2. By pronouncing sentence.

How shall the examination be?
1. According to the law of God, which hath been revealed unto men: whether it be the law of nature only, which is the remainder of the moral Law written in the hearts of our first parents, and conveyed by the power of God unto all men, to leave them without excuse; or that written Word of God, vouchsafed unto the church in the Scriptures, first of the old, and after also of the new Testament as the rule of faith and life. Rom. 2. 12.

2. By the evidence of every mans conscience, bringing all his works, whether good or evil, to light; bearing witness with him or against him: together with the testimony of such, who either by doctrine, company, or example, have approved or condemned him. Mat. 12. 27, 41, 42.

Shall there be no difference in the examination of the Elect & the Reprobate?
Yes. For, 1. The Elect shall not have their sins, for which Christ satisfied, but only their good works, remembered. Ezek. 18. 22. Rev. 14. 17.

2. Being in Christ, they and their works shall not undergo the strict trial of the Law simply in it self; but as the obedience thereof does prove them to be true partakers of the grace of the Gospel.

Shall there be any such reasoning at the last judgment, as seemeth Mat. 7. & 25?
No, but the consciences of men being then enlightened by Christ shall clear all those doubts, and reject those objections and excuses, which they seem now to apprehend.

How shall the sentence be pronounced?
By the Judge himself, our Lord Jesus Christ: who according to the evidence and verdict of conscience touching works, shall adjudge the Elect unto the blessing of the kingdom of God his Father; and the Reprobates, with the Devil and his Angels, unto the curse of everlasting fire.

Shall men then be judged to salvation or damnation for their works sake?
The wicked shall be condemned for the merit of their works; because being perfectly evil, they deserve the wages of damnation. Rom. 6. 23. The godly shall be pronounced Just, because their works, though imperfect, do prove their faith (whereby they lay hold on Christ and his meritorious righteousness) to be a true faith; as working by love in all parts of obedience. James 2. 18. Gal. 5. 7.

[52ND HEAD.]

Hitherto of the act of judgment. What are we to consider in the third and last place?
The execution of his Judgment: Christ, by his almighty power and ministry of his Angels, casting the Devils and Reprobate men into hell; and bringing God's Elect into the possession of his glorious kingdom. Wherein the Reprobates shall first be dispatched, that the righteous may rejoice to see the vengeance; and as it were wash their feet in the blood of the wicked. Mat. 25. 46. Psal. 58. 10.

What shall be the state of the Reprobates in hell?
They shall remain for ever in unspeakable torment of body, and anguish of mind; being cast out from the favorable presence of God, and glorious fellowship of Christ and his Saints (whose happiness they shall see and envy) into that horrible Dungeon figured in Scripture by utter darkness, blackness of darkness, weeping and gnashing of teeth, the Worm that never dieth, the fire that never goeth out, &c. 2 Thess. 2. 9.

What shall be the estate of the Elect in Heaven?
They shall be unspeakably and everlastingly blessed and glorious in body and soul; being freed from all imperfections and infirmities, yea from such Graces as imply imperfection, as Faith, Hope, Repentance, &c. endued with perfect Wisdom and Holiness, possessed with all the pleasures that are at the right hand of God, seated as Princes in Thrones of Majesty, crowned, with Crowns of Glory, possessing the new Heaven and Earth wherein dwelleth Righteousness, beholding and being filled with the fruition of the glorious presence of God, and of the Lamb, Jesus Christ, in the company of innumerable Angels and holy Saints, as the Scripture phrases are.

What shall follow this?
Christ shall deliver up that dispensatory kingdom (which he received for the subduing of his enemies and accomplishing the salvation of his Church) unto God the Father, and God shall be all in all for all eternity.

What use may we make of this doctrine concerning this general end and final judgment?
First, it serveth to confute, not only heathen Philosophers; who, as in other things, so in this concerning the worlds continuance, became vain in their imaginations, and their foolish heart was full of darkness, (Rom. 1. 21) being destitute of the Word of God to guide them: but also to confute many profane Atheists, in the church of God, who do not believe in their hearts those Articles of the resurrection and of the general judgment. It is much indeed, that there should be Athei's in the Church of God, and none in Hell; that any should deny, or doubt of that which the Devils fear and tremble at. But sure the Apostle Peters prophecy is fulfilled, 2 Pet. 3. 3. There shall come in the last days scoffers, walking after their own lusts, and saying? Where is the promise of his coming? for since the fathers died, all things continue alike from the beginning of the creation, and (as they would persuade themselves) so they shall for ever. And answerable their lives are to such conceits: Eccles. 11. 9. But if neither the light of reason; (it being impossible that the truth and goodness and justice of God should take effect, if there were not after this life a doom and recompense, 1 Thes. 1. 6.) Nor secondly, the light of conscience, which doubtless with Felix, Acts 24. 25. makes them tremble in the midst of their obstinate gain-saying; Nor thirdly the light of Scripture can convince and persuade men of this truth: then we must leave them to be confuted and taught by woeful experience, even by the feeling of those flames, which they will not believe to be any other than fancies; and by seeing the Lord Jesus coming in the

clouds when all nations shall weep before him; and these Atheists especially, lament their obstinate infidelity with ever dropping tears, and ever enduring misery.

And this doctrine may be terror to all graceless and wicked livers; to consider that the wrath of God shall be revealed from heaven against all ungodliness and unrighteousness of men: 2. Thes. 1. 6. when all the sweetness of their sinful pleasures shall be turned into gall and bitterness for ever. Wisd. 5. 6, 7, 8.

How may the consideration of this doctrine, touching the end of the world and the day of Judgment, be useful to the Godly?

First, it should teach us: not to seek for happiness in this world, or set our affections on things below: for this world passeth away, and the things thereof.

Secondly, here is a fountain of Christian comfort, and a ground of Christian patience in all troubles, that there shall be an end, and a Saints hope shall not be cut off. If in this life only we had hope, we were of all men most miserable. 1 Cor. 15. 19. But here is the comfort and patience of the Saints: they wait for another world, and they know it is a just thing with God, to give them rest after their labors, 2 Thes. 1. 9. and a Crown after their combat, 2 Tim. 4. 8. and after their long pilgrimage, an everlasting habitation, 2 Cor. 5. 1. Be patient (saith the Apostle) and settle your hearts for the coming of the Lord draweth near. James 5. 7. when they that have sown in tears shall reap in joy. Psal. 126. 5. James. 5. 7. Heb. 10. 36.

Thirdly, from this doctrine, excellent arguments may be drawn to press Christians to a holy life. 2 Pet. 3. 11. Seeing then all these things must be dissolved? what manner of persons ought we to be in all holy conversation, and godliness? And verse 14. Wherefore seeing ye look for such things, give diligence that you may be found of him in peace. We should always live in expectation of the Lord Jesus in the Clouds, with Oil in our Lamps, prepared for his coming. Blessed is that servant whom his master when he cometh shall find so doing: he shall say unto him; Well done good and faithful servant, enter into thy Masters joy. Luke 12. 43. Mat. 25. 21.

FINIS.

THE PRINCIPLES OF CHRISTIAN RELIGION

WITH A BRIEF METHOD OF THE DOCTRINE THEREOF.

Now fully Corrected,
and much enlarged by the Author

JAMES USSHER,

ARCHBISHOP OF ARMAGH.

With his Preface thereunto.

2. Tim. 1. 13.

Hold fast the form of sound words, which thou
hast heard of me, in faith and love
which is in Christ Jesus.

TO THE READER.

When I was about the age of two or three and twenty years, I drew up these two short Summaries of the heads of Christian Religion; the one containing the more necessary and plainer Principles thereof, fit to be known of all: the other, the methodical and more full declaration of some chief points thereof, framed to the capacity of such as had made a further progress in the knowledge of these heavenly truths. I little then Imagined, that such rude draughts as these were, should ever have been presented unto the public view of the world. But seeing, contrary to my mind, they have by many Impressions been divulged, and that in a very faulty manner: I have been persuaded at last, upon some revisal of them, to let them now go abroad in some more tolerable condition than they did before. Hoping, that as at the first I had the favor from God, that none did despise my youth; so now these first fruits of mine will not altogether be condemned, being by me again presented unto thee when my Head is gray, JAMES ARMAGH.

Question. What sure ground have we to build our Religion upon?
Answer. The word of God contained in the Scriptures.

Q. What are those Scriptures?
A Holy writings, indicted by God himself for the perfect instruction of his Church.

Q. What gather you of this, that God is the Author of these Writings?
A That therefore they are of most certain credit, and highest authority.

Q. How serve they for the perfect instruction of the Church?
A. In that they are able to instruct us sufficiently, in all points of Faith that we are bound to believe, and all good duties that we are bound to practice.

Q. What gather you of this?
A. That it is our duty to acquaint ourselves with these holy writings, and not to receive any doctrine that hath not warrant from thence.

Q. What is the first point of Religion, you are to learn out of God's word?
A. The Nature of God.

Q. What is God;
A. God is a Spirit, most perfect, most wise, almighty and most holy.

Q. What mean you by calling God Spirit?
A. That God hath no body at all: and therefore must not be thought to be like unto any thing which may be seen by the eye of man.

Q. Are there any more God's then one?
A. No: there is only one God: though in that one Godhead there be three persons.

Q. Which is the first of these persons?
A. The Father, who begetteth the Son.

Q. Which is the second?
A. The Son begotten of the Father.

Q. Which is the third?
A. The Holy Ghost proceeding from the Father and the Son.

Q. What did God determine concerning his Creatures?
A. He did before all time, by his unchangeable counsel, ordain whatsoever after wards should come to pass.

Q. In what manner had all things their beginning?
A. In the beginning of time, when no creature had any being, God by his Word alone. In the space of six days created all things.

Q. Which are the principal Creatures?
A. Angels and men.

Q. What is the nature of Angels?
A. They are wholly spiritual, having no body at all.

Q. What is the nature of Man?
A. Man consisteth of two diverse parts; a body and a Soul.

Q. What is the body?
A. The outward and earthly part of man; made at the beginning of the dust of the earth.

Q. What is the Soul?
A. The inward and spiritual part of man; which is immortal, and never can die.

Q. How did God make man at the beginning?
A. According to his own likeness and image.

Q. Wherein was the Image of God principally seen?
A. In the perfection of the Understanding; and the freedom and holiness of the Will.

Q. How many of mankind were created at the beginning?
A. Two; Adam the man, and Eve the woman: from both whom, all mankind did afterward proceed.

Q. What does God after the Creation?
A. By his Providence he preserveth and governeth his Creatures, with all things belonging unto them.

Q. What arefell unto the Angels after the creation?
A Some continued in that holy estate wherein they were created, some of them fell, and became Devils.

Q. May the good Angels fall here after?
A. No: but they shall always continue in their holiness and happiness.

Q. Shall the wicked Angels ever recover their first estate?
A. They shall not: but be tormented in Hell world without end.

Q. How did God deal with Man, after he made him?
A He made a Covenant or agreement with Adam, and in him with all mankind.

Q. What was man bound to do by this Covenant.
A. To continue as holy as God at the first made him, to keep all God's Commandments and never to break any of them.

Q. What did God promise unto Man, if he did thus keep his Commandments.
A. The continuance of his favor and everlasting life.

Q. What did God threaten unto Man, if he did sin and break his Commandments?
A. His dreadful curse, and everlasting death.

Q. Did man continue in that obedience which he did owe unto God?
A. No, for Adam and Eve obeying rather the persuasion of the Devil than the Commandment of God did eat of the forbidden fruit, and so fell away from God.

Q. Was this the sin of Adam and Eve alone; or are we also guilty of the same?
A. All we, that are their children, are guilty of the same sin: for we all sinned in them.

Q. What followed upon this sin?
A. The loss of the perfection of the Image of God, and the corruption of nature, in Man called original sin.

Q. Wherein standeth the corruption of Man's nature?
A. In six things principally.

Q. What is the first?
A. The blindness of the Understanding; which is not able to conceive the things of God.

Q. What is the second?
A. The forgetfulness of the memory; unfit to remember good things.

Q. What is the third?
A. The rebellion of the Will; which is wholly bent to sin, and altogether disobedient unto the will of God.

Q. What is the fourth?
A. Disorder of the Affections, of Joy, heaviness, love, anger, fear, and such like.

Q. What is the fifth?
A. Fear and confusion in the Conscience; condemning where it should not, and excusing where it should condemn.

Q. What is the sixth?
A. Every member of the body is become a ready instrument to put sin in execution.

Q. What are the fruits that proceed from this natural corruption?
A. Actual sins: whereby we break the Commandments of God in the whole course of our life.

Q. How do we thus break God's Commandments?
A. In thought, word, and deed: not doing that which we ought to do, and doing that which we ought not to do.

Q. What punishment is mankind subject unto, by reason of original and actual sin?
A. He is subject to all the plagues of God in this life; and endless torments in Hell after this life.

Q. Did God leave man in this woeful estate?
A. No: but of his free and undeserved mercy entered into a New covenant with mankind.

The Principles of Christian Religion

Q. What is offered unto man in this new Covenant?
A. Grace and life everlasting is freely offered by God unto all that shall be made partakers of his Son Jesus Christ; who alone is Mediator betwixt God and Man.

Q. What are you to consider in Christ the Mediator of this Covenant?
A. Two things: his Nature and his office.

Q. How many Natures be there in Christ?
A. Two: the Godhead and the Manhood, joined together in one person; which is no other but the second person of the Trinity.

Q. Why must Christ be God?
A. That his obedience and suffering might be of infinite worth and value, as proceeding from such a person, as was God equal to the Father, that he might be able to overcome the sharpness of death (which himself was to undergo) and to raise us from the death of sin, by sending his holy Spirit into our hearts.

Q. Why must Christ be Man?
A. Because the Godhead could not suffer: and it was further requisite, that the same nature which had offended should suffer for the offence; and that our nature, which was corrupted in the first Adam, should be restored to his integrity in the second Adam, Christ Jesus our Lord.

Q. What is the Office of Christ?
A. To be a Mediator betwixt God and Man.

Q. What was required of Christ for making peace and reconciliation betwixt God and Man.
A. That he should satisfy the first Covenant whereunto man was tied.

Q. Wherein was Christ to make satisfaction to the first Covenant?
A. In performing that righteousness which the Law of God did require of Man: and in bearing the punishment which was due unto Man for breaking of the same Law.

Q. How did Christ perform that righteousness which God's Law requireth of Man?
A. In that he was conceived by the Holy Ghost, without all spot of original corruption; and lived most holy all the days of his life, without all actual sin.

Q. How did he bear the punishment which was due unto Man for breaking God's Law?
A. In that he willingly for mans sake made himself subject to the curse of Law, both in body and soul: and humbling himself even unto the death, offered up unto his Father a perfect sacrifice for the sins of the world.

Q. What is required of Man for obtaining the benefits of the Gospel?
A. That he receive Christ Jesus whom God does freely offer unto him.

Q. By what means are you to receive Christ?
A. By faith, whereby I believe the gracious promises of the Gospel.

Q. How do you receive Christ by faith?
A. By laying hold of him, and applying him with all benefits to the comfort of mine own soul.

Q. What is the first main benefit which we do get by thus receiving Christ?
A. Justification, whereby, in Christ, we receive the forgiveness of our sins, and are accounted righteous: being by that means freed from the guilt of sin and condemnation, and estated in a new interest unto everlasting life.

Q. Whereby then must we look to be justified in the sight of God?
A. Only by the merits of Christ Jesus, received of us by Faith.

Q. What other main benefit do we get by receiving Christ?
A. Sanctification; whereby we are freed from the dominion of sin, and the image of God is renewed in us.

Q. Wherein is this Sanctification seen?
A. In Repentance, and new Obedience springing from thence.

Q. What is Repentance?
A. Repentance is a gift of God whereby a godly sorrow is wrought in the heart of the faithful, for offending God their merciful father by their former transgressions; together with a resolution for the time to come, to forsake their former courses, and to lead a new life.

Q. What call you new Obedience?
A. A careful endeavour which the faithful have to give unfeigned obedience unto all God's Commandments, according to that measure or strength wherewith God does enable them.

Q. What rule have we for the direction of our obedience?
A. The Moral Law of God: the sum whereof is contained in the ten Commandments.

Q. What are the chief parts of this Law?
A. The duties which we owe unto God, set down in the first Table: and that which we owe unto Man in the second.

Q. What is the sum of the first Table?
A. That we love the Lord our God, with all our heart, with all our souls, and with all our minds.

Q. How many Commandments belong to this Table?
A. Four.

Q. Which is the first Commandment?
A. I am the Lord thy God, which have brought thee out of the land of Egypt, out of the house of bondage. Thou shalt have no other gods before me.

Q. What duty is enjoined in this Commandment?
A. That in the inward powers and faculties of our souls, the true eternal God be entertained, and he only.

Q. Which is the second Commandment?
A. Thou shalt not make unto thee any graven image.

Q. What duty is enjoined in this Commandment?
A. That all outward means of religious and solemn worship be given unto the same God alone; and not so much as the least degree thereof (even the bowing of the body)

be communicated to any Image or representation either of God, or of any thing else whatsoever.

Q. Which is the third Commandment?
A. Thou shalt not take the name of the Lord thy God in vain: for the Lord will not hold him guiltless that takes his name in vain.

Q. What is enjoined in this Commandment?
A. That in the ordinary course of our lives, we use the Name of God, (that is, his titles, words, works, judgments, and whatsoever he would have himself known by) with reverence and all holy respect, that in all things he may have his due glory given unto him.

Q. Which is the fourth Commandment?
A. Remember the Sabbath day, to keep it holy, &c.

Q. What does this Commandment require?
A. That we keep holy the Sabbath day; by resting from the ordinary businesses of this life, and bestowing that leisure, upon the exercises of Religion both public and private.

Q. What is the sum of the Second Table?
A. That we love our Neighbors as ourselves.

Q. What Commandments belong to this Table?
A. The six last.

Q. Which is the fifth Commandment?
A. Honor thy father and thy mother, that thy days may be long in the land which the Lord thy God giveth thee.

Q. What kind of duties are prescribed in this Commandment, which is the first of the second Table?
A. Such duties as are to be performed with a special respect of superiors, inferiors, and equals: as namely, reverence to all superiors, obedience to such of them as are in authority; and whatsoever special duties concern the Husband and Wife, Parents and Children, Masters and Servants, Magistrate and People, Pastors and Flock, and such like.

Q. Which is the sixth Commandment?
A. Thou shalt not kill.

Q. What does this Commandment enjoin?
A. The preservation of the safety of men's persons, with all means tending to the same.

Q. Which is the seventh Commandment?
A. Thou shalt not commit adultery.

Q. What is required in this Commandment?
A. The preservation of the chastity of men's persons: for the keeping whereof, Wedlock is commanded unto them that stand in need thereof.

Q. Which is the eight Commandment:
A. Thou shalt not steal.

Q. What things are ordered in this Commandment?
A. Whatsoever concerneth the goods of this life; in regard either of ourselves, or of our neighbors.

Q. How in regard of ourselves;
A. That we labor diligently in an honest and profitable calling; content ourselves with the goods well gotten, and with liberality employ them to good uses.

Q. How in regard of our neighbors?
A. That we use just dealing unto them in this respect, and use all good means that may tend to the furtherance of their estate.

Q. Which is the ninth Commandment?
A. Thou shalt not bear false witness against thy neighbor.

Q. What does this Commandment require?
A. The using of truth in our dealing one with another; especially to the preservation of the good name of our neighbors.

Q. Which is the tenth and last Commandment?
A. Thou shalt not covet thy neighbors house, thou shalt not covet thy neighbors wife, not his man-servant, not his maid-servant, not his or, not his ass, not any thing that is thy neighbors.

Q. What does this Commandment contain?
A. It condemneth all wandering thoughts, that disagree from the love which we owe unto our Neighbors; although we never yield consent thereunto.

Q. What means does God use to offer the benefits of the Gospel unto men, and to work and increase his grace in them?
A. The outward Ministry of the Gospel.

Q. Where is the Ministry executed?
A. In the visible Churches of Christ.

Q. What do you call a visible Church?
A. A company of men that live under the outward means of salvation.

Q. What are the principal parts of this Ministry?
A. The administration of the Word and Sacraments?

Q. What is the Word?
A. That part of the outward Ministry, which consisteth in the delivery of doctrine.

Q. What is a Sacrament?
A. A Sacrament is a visible sign, ordained by God to be a seal for confirmation of the promises of the Gospel unto the due receivers thereof.

Q. Which are the Sacraments ordained by Christ in the new Testament?
A. Baptism and the Lord's Supper.

Q. What is Baptism?
A. The Sacrament of our admission into the Church; sealing unto us our new birth, by the communion which we have with Christ Jesus.

The Principles of Christian Religion

Q. What does the element of water in Baptism represent unto us?
A. The blood and spirit o Jesus Christ our Lord.

Q. What does the cleansing of the body represent?
A. The cleansing of the Soul by the forgiveness of sins and imputation of righteousness.

Q. What does the being under the water, and the freeing from it again, represent?
A. Our dying unto sin by the force of Christ's death; and living again unto righteousness, through his resurrection.

Q. What is the Lord's Supper?
A. The Sacrament of our preservation in the Church; sealing unto us our spiritual nourishment and continual increase in Christ.

Q. What do the elements of Bread and Wine in the Lord's Supper represent unto us?
A. The Body and Blood of Christ.

Q. What does the breaking of the Bread and pouring out of the Wine represent?
A. The sufferings whereby our Savior was broken for our iniquities; the shedding of his precious blood and pouring out of his Soul unto death.

Q. What does the receiving of the bread and wine represent?
A. The receiving of Christ by faith.

Q. What does the nourishment which our body receiveth by virtue of this outward meat and drink seal unto us?
A. The perfect nourishment and continual increase of strength which the inward man enjoyeth by virtue of the communion with Jesus Christ.

Q. After the course of this life is ended; what shall be the estate of man in the world to come?
A. Every one is to be judged, and rewarded according to the life which he hath lead.

Q. How many kinds be there of this Judgment?
A. Two; the one particular, the other general.

Q. What call you the particular Judgment?
A. That which is given up on the Soul of every man, as soon as it is departed from the body.

Q. What is the state of the Soul of man, as soon as he departeth out of this life?
A. The Souls of God's Children be presently received into Heaven, there to enjoy unspeakable comforts: the Souls of the wicked are sent into hell, there to endure endless torments.

Q. What call you the general Judgment?
A. That which Christ shall in a solemn manner give upon all men at once; when he shall come at the last day with the glory of his Father, and all men that ever have been from the beginning of the world until that day shall appear together before him, both in body and soul, whether they be quick or dead.

Q. How shall the dead appear before the Judgment Seat of Christ?
A. The bodies which they had in their life time, shall by the almighty power of God be restored again, and quickened with their Souls: and so there shall be a general resurrection from the dead.

Q. How shall the quick appear?
A. Such as then remain alive, shall be changed in the twinkling of an eye: which shall be to them in stead of death.

Q. What sentence shall Christ pronounce upon the righteous?
A. Come ye blessed of my Father; inherit the kingdom prepared for you from the foundation of the world.

Q. What sentence shall he pronounce upon the wicked?
A. Depart from me ye cursed into everlasting fire; which is prepared for the Devil and his Angels.

Q. What shall follow this.
A. Christ shall deliver up the kingdom of his Father, and God shall be all in all.

FINIS.

A BRIEF METHOD OF THE DOCTRINE OF CHRISTIAN RELIGION.

SHOWING THE CONNECTION OF THE CHIEF POINTS THEREOF, WITH A MORE PARTICULAR DECLARATION OF SOME PRINCIPAL HEADS WHICH WERE BUT SHORTLY TOUCHED IN THE FORMER SUM.

Heb. 6. 1.
Therefore leaving the Doctrine of the beginning of Christ, let us be set forward unto perfection.

THE METHOD OF THE
DOCTRINE OF CHRISTIAN RELIGION.

Question. What certain rule have we left us, for our direction in the knowledge of the true Religion, whereby we must be saved?
Answer. The Holy Scriptures of the Old and New Testament: which God delivered unto us by the Ministry of his Servants the Prophets and Apostles, to inform us perfectly in all things that are needful for us to know in matters of Religion.

Q. What are the general heads of Religion, which in these holy writings are delivered unto us?
A. The knowledge of God's Nature and Kingdom.

Q. What are we to consider in God's Nature?
A. First his essence or being, which is but one, and then the Persons, which are three in number.

Q. What do you consider in God's essence or being?
A. His Perfection and Life.

Q. How are we to conceive of God, in regard of his Perfection?
A. That he is a Spirit, most single and infinite; having his being from himself, and having need of nothing which is without himself.

Q. Why do you call God a Spirit?
A. To declare his being to be such, as hath no body, and is not subject to our outward senses: that we admit not any base conceit of his glorious Majesty, in thinking him to be like unto any thing which can be seen by the eye of man.

Q. What understand you by the singleness or Simplicity of God's Nature?
A. That he hath no parts nor quality in him, but whatsoever is in him, is God, and God's whole essence.

Q. What gather you this, that God hath no parts nor qualities?
A. The he neither can be divided, nor changed; but remaineth always in the same state without any alteration at all.

Q. In What respects do you call Gods essence infinite?
A. In that it is free from all measure both of time and place.

Q. How is God free from all measure of time?
A. In that he is eternal, without beginning and without ending, never elder nor younger, and hath all things present unto him, nothing former or latter, past or to come.

Q. How is God infinite in regard of place?
A. In that he filleth all things and places, both within and without the World, present every where, and contained no where.

Q. How is he present every where? hath he one part of himself here, and another there?
A. No: for he hath no parts at all whereby he might be divided, and therefore must be wholly wherever he is.

Q. What do you call the Life of God?
A. That by which the divine nature is in perpetual action, most simply and infinitely moving it self: in respect whereof the Scripture calleth him the Living God.

Q. What gather you from the comparing of this infiniteness and simplicity (or singleness) of God's nature with his life and motion?
A. That when Strength, Justice, Mercy, and such like are attributed unto God, we must conceive that they are in him without all measure: and further also, that they be not divers virtues whereby his nature is qualified, but that all they and every one of them is nothing else but God himself, and his entire essence.

Q. Wherein does the Life of God show it self?
A. In his All sufficiency and in his holy Will.

Q. Wherein standeth his All sufficiency?
A. In his all knowing, Wisdom, and his almighty Power.

Q. Wherein does his Wisdom consist?
A. In perfect knowledge of all things, that either are or might be.

Q. In what sort does God know all things? does he as we do, see one thing after another?
A. No: but with one sight he continually beholdeth all things distinctly, whether they be past, present, or to come.

Q. How is God said to be Almighty?
A. Because he hath power to bring to pass all things that can be; howsoever to us they may seem impossible

Q. Wherein is the Holiness of his Will seen?
A. In his goodness, and in his Justice.

Q. Wherein does he show his Goodness?
A. In being beneficial unto his creatures, and showing mercy unto them in their miseries.

Q. Wherein showeth he his Justice?
A. Both in his Word and in his Deeds.

Q. How showeth he Justice in his Word?
A. Because the truth thereof is most certain.

Q. How showeth he Justice in his Deeds?
A. By ordering and disposing all things rightly; and rendering to his creatures according to their works.

Q. What do you call Persons in the God-head?
A. Such as having one essence (or being) equally common, are distinguished not divided one from another by some incommunicable property.

Q. How cometh it to pass that there should be this diversity of persons in the Godhead?
A. Though the essence or being of the God-head be the same, and most simple (as hath been declared) yet the manner of having this being is not the same; and hence ariseth the distinction of persons: in that beside the being, which is common to all and

the self-same in all, they have every one some special property which cannot be common to the rest.

Q. Which are these persons and what are their personal properties?
A. The first person in order is the Father, who begetteth the Son. The second is the Son, begotten of the Father. The third is the Holy Ghost, proceeding from the Father and the Son.

Q. Does the God-head of the Father beget the God-head of the Son?
A. No: but the person of the Father begetteth the person of the Son.

Q. Thus much of God's Nature: what are we to consider in his Kingdom?
A. First, the Decree made from all eternity: and then the Execution thereof accomplished in time.

Q. How was the Decree made?
A. All things whatsoever should in time come to pass, with every small circumstance appertaining thereunto was ordained to be so from all eternity, by God's certain and unchangeable counsel.

Q. Did God then before he made man, determine to save some and reject others?
A. Yes surely: before they had done either good or evil, God in his eternal counsel set some apart, upon whom he would in time show the riches of his mercy; and determine to withhold the same from others, upon whom he would show the severity of his Justice.

Q. What should move God to make this difference between Man and Man?
A. Only his own good pleasure: when by having purposed to create man for his own Glory, forasmuch as he was not bound to show mercy unto any, and his Glory should as well appear as well in executing of justice as in showing mercy; it seemed good unto his heavenly Wisdom to choose out a certain number towards whom he would extend his undeserved mercy, leaving the rest to be spectacles of his justice.

Q. Wherein does the Execution of God's decree consist?
A. In the works of the Creation and Providence.

Q. What was the manner of the Creation?
A. In the beginning of time, when no creature had any being, God by his word alone, did in the space of six days create all things, both visible and invisible, making every one of them exceeding good in their kind.

Q. What are the principal creatures which were ordained unto an everlasting condition?
A. Angels, altogether spiritual and void of bodies: and Man consisting of two parts, the body which is earthly, and the soul, which is spiritual, and therefore not subject to mortality.

Q. In what regard is man said to be made according to the Likeness and Image of God?
A. In regard especially of the perfections of the powers of the soul; namely the wisdom of the mind, and the true holiness of his free will.

Q. How are you to consider of God's Providence?
A. Both as it is common unto all the creatures; which are thereby sustained in their being, and ordered according to the Lord's will: and as it properly concerneth the everlasting condition of the Principal Creatures, to wit, Angels and Men.

Q. What is that which concerneth Angels?
A. Some of them remained in that blessed condition wherein they were created, and are by God's grace for ever established therein. Others kept it not, but woefully lost the same; and therefore are condemned to everlasting torment in Hell, without all hope of recovery.

Q. How is the state of Mankind ordered?
A. In this life by the tenor of a twofold Covenant; and in the World to come, by the sentence of a twofold Judgment.

Q. What is the first of these Covenants?
A. The Law, or the covenant of works: whereby God promiseth everlasting life unto man, upon condition that he perform entire and perfect obedience unto his Law, according to that strength wherewith he was endued by virtue of his creation; and in like sort threatneth death unto him, if he do not perform the same.

Q. What seal did God use for the strengthening of this Covenant?
A. The two Trees which he planted in the middle of Paradise: the one of life, the other of knowledge of good and evil.

Q. What did the tree of life signify?
A. That man should have assurance of everlasting life, if he continued in obedience.

Q. What did the Tree of Knowledge of good and evil signify?
A. That if man did fall from obedience, he should be surely punished with everlasting death; and so know by experience in himself, what evil was, as before he knew by experience that only which was good.

Q. What was the event of this Covenant?
A. By one man sin entered into the World, and Death by sin; and so death went over all men, forasmuch as all have sinned.

Q. How did sin enter?
A. Whereas God had threatened unto our first Parents, that whatsoever day they did eat of the forbidden fruit they should certainly die: they, believing rather the word of the Devil that they should not die, and subscribing unto his reproachful blasphemy, whereby he charged God with envy towards their estate, as if he had therefore forbidden the fruit, lest by eating thereof they should become like God himself, entered into rebellion against the Lord who made them, and openly transgressed his Commandment.

Q. What followeth from this?
A. First, the corruption of nature called original sin, derived by continual descent from Father to Son; wherewith all the powers of the soul and body are infected, and that in all men equally: and then actual sin, arising from hence.

Q. Show how the principal powers of the soul are defiled by this corruption of our nature?
A. First, the understanding is blinded with ignorance and infidelity. Secondly, the memory is prone to forget the good things which the understanding hath conceived. Thirdly, the Will is disobedient to the will of God understood and remembered by us; (the freedom of holiness, which it had at the first, being now lost) and is wholly bent to sin. Fourthly, affections are ready to over rule the will, and are subject to all disorder. Lastly, the Conscience it self is distempered and polluted.

Q. In what sort is the Conscience thus distempered?
A. The duties thereof being two especially, to give direction in things to be done, and to give both witness and judgment in things done for the first, it sometimes giveth no direction at all, and thereupon maketh a man to sin in doing of an action otherwise good and lawful, sometimes it giveth a direction, but a wrong one, and so becometh a blind guide, forbidding to do things which God alloweth, and commanding to do things which God forbiddeth. For the second, it sometimes giveth no judgment at all, not checking the offender as it should, but being benumbed and as it was seared with an hot Iron. It sometimes giveth Judgment, but falsely; condemning where it should excuse, and excusing where it should condemn; thereby filling the mind with false fears or feeding it with vain comforts: and sometimes giveth true Judgment, but uncomfortable and fearful, tormenting the guilty soul as it were with the flashes of hell-fire.

Q. What are the kinds of actual sin?
A. Such as are either inward in the thoughts of the mind and lusts of the heart; or outward, in word or deed: whereby those things are done which should be omitted, and those things omitted which should be done.

Q. What is the death which all men are subject unto, by reason of these sins?
A. The curse of God both upon the things that belong unto them (such as are their Wife and Children, honor possessions, use of God's Creatures, &c.) and upon their own persons, in life and death.

Q. What are the curses they are subject to in this life?
A. All temporal calamities both in body (which is subject unto infinite miseries) and in soul, which is plagued sometime with madness, sometime with the terror of a guilty Conscience, sometimes with a benumbed and seared Conscience, sometimes with hardness, of heart, which cannot repent; and finally, a spiritual slavery under the power of the World and the Devil.

Q. What is the death that followeth this miserable life?
A. First, a separation of the soul from the body and then, an everlasting separation of the whole man from the presence of God, with unspeakable torments in hell fire never to be ended.

Q. If all mankind be subject to this damnation; how then shall any man be saved?
A. Surely by this first Covenant of the Law, no flesh can be saved; but every one must receive in himself the sentence of condemnation; yet the Lord, being a god of mercy, hath not left us here; but entered into a second Covenant with Mankind.

Q. What is the second Covenant?
A. The Gospel, or the Covenant of grace; whereby God promiseth everlasting life unto man, upon condition that he be reconciled unto him in Christ: for as the condition of the first, was the continuance of that righteousness which was to be found in mans own person: so the condition of the second is the obtaining of that righteousness which is without himself; even the righteousness of God which is by faith in the Mediator Jesus Christ.

Q. What are we to consider in Christ our Mediator?
A. Two things: his Nature and his Office.

Q. How many natures be there in Christ?
A. Two, the Godhead, and the Manhood: remaining still distinct in their substance, properties and actions.

A Brief Method of the Doctrine of Christian Religion

Q. How many persons hath he?
A. Only one; which is the person of the Son of God: for the second person in the Trinity took upon him, not the person but the nature of man; to wit, a body and a reasonable soul: which do not subsist alone, as (we see in all other men) but are wholly sustained in the person of the Son of God.

Q. What is the use of this wonderful union of the Two Natures in one Person?
A. Our nature being received into the union of the Person of the Son of God; the sufferings and the obedience which it performed became of infinite value, as being the sufferings and the obedience of him who was God, equal with the Father.

Q. What is the office of Christ?
A. To be a Mediator betwixt God and Man?

Q. What part of his office did he exercise in things concerning God?
A. His Priesthood.

Q. What are the parts of his Priestly office;
A. The satisfaction of God's Justice, and Intercession.

Q. What is required of Christ for the satisfaction of God's Justice?
A. The paying of the price which was due for the breach of the Law committed by mankind; and the performance of that righteousness, which man by the Law was bound unto, but is now unable to accomplish.

Q. How was Christ to pay the price which was due for the sin of mankind?
A. By that wonderful humiliation, whereby he that was equal with God, made himself of no reputation, and became obedient unto the death: sustaining both in body and soul, the curse that was due to the transgression of the Law.

Q. What righteousness was there required of Christ in our behalf?
A. Both original, which he had from his conception (being conceived by the Holy Ghost, in all pureness and holiness of nature): and actual; which he performed by yielding perfect obedience in the whole course of his life, unto all the precepts of God's Law.

Q. What is the Intercession of Christ?
A. That part of his priesthood, whereby he maketh request unto his Father for us, and presenteth unto him both our persons, and our imperfect Obedience; making both of them (howsoever in themselves polluted) by the merit of his satisfaction, to be acceptable in God's sight.

Q. Thus much of that part of the office of the Mediator which is exercised in things concerning God: how does be exercise his office in things concerning Man?
A. By communicating unto man that grace and redemption which he hath purchased from his Father.

Q. What parts of this office does he exercise here?
A. His Prophetical and Kingly Office.

Q. What is his Prophetical Office?
A. That whereby he informeth us of the benefits of our redemption, and revealeth the whole will of his Father unto us; both by the outward means which he hath provided for the instruction of his Church, and by the inward enlightening of our mind, by his holy spirit.

Q. What is his Kingly office?
A. That whereby he ruleth his Subjects, and confoundeth all his Enemies.

Q. How does he rule his Subjects?
A. By making the Redemption, which he hath wrought effectual in the Elect: calling those, whom by his prophetical office he hath taught, to embrace the benefits offered unto them; and governing them being called: both by these outward ordinances which he hath instituted in his Church, and by the inward operation of his blessed spirit.

Q. Having thus declared the Natures and Offices of Christ, the Mediator of the new Covenant: What are you to consider in the condition of mankind which hold by him?
A. Two things: the participation of the grace of Christ effectually communicated by the operation of God's spirit unto the Catholic Church, which is the Body and Spouse of Christ, out of which there is no salvation; and the outward means ordained for the offering and effecting of the same vouchsafed unto the visible Churches.

Q. How is the grace of Christ effectually communicated to the Elect, of whom the Catholic Church does consist?
A. By that wonderful Union, whereby Christ and his Church are made one: so that all the Elect, being engrafted into him, grow up together into one mystical body whereof he is the head.

Q. What is the bond of this union?
A. The communion of God's spirit: which being derived from the Man Christ Jesus unto all the Elect, as from the Head unto the Members, giveth unto them spiritual life, and maketh them partakers of Christ with all his benefits.

Q. What are the benefits which arise to God's Children from hence?
A. Reconciliation and Sanctification.

Q. What is Reconciliation?
A. That grace, whereby we are freed from God's curse, and restored unto his favor.

Q. What are the branches of this Reconciliation?
A. Justification and Adoption.

Q. What is Justification?
A. That grace, whereby we are freed from the guilt of sin, and accounted righteous in Christ Jesus our Redeemer.

Q. How then must sinful man look to be Justified in the sight of God?
A. By the mercy of God alone, whereby he freely bestoweth his Son upon him: whereupon the sinner being possessed of Jesus Christ, obtaineth of God remission of sins, and imputation of righteousness.

Q. What is adoption?
A. That grace whereby, we are not only made friends with God, but also his Sons and heirs with Christ.

Q. What is Sanctification?
A. That grace whereby we are freed from the bondage of sin remaining in us, and restored unto the freedom of righteousness.

Q. What are the parts of Sanctification?
A. Mortification whereby our natural corruption is subdued; and Vivification or quicking, whereby inherent holiness is renewed in us.

Q. Is there no distinction to be made among them that thus receive Christ?
A. Yes: for some are not capable of knowledge; as Infants, and such as we term naturals: other some are of discretion. In the former sort, we are not to proceed further then God's election, and the secret operation of the Holy Ghost. In the other there is required a lively faith, bringing forth fruit of true Holiness.

Q. Is it in mans power to attain this Faith and Holiness?
A. No: but God worketh them in his children, according to that measure which he in his wisdom sees fit.

Q. What do you understand by Faith:
A. A gift of God whereby a man being persuaded not only of the truth of God's word in general, but also for the promises of the Gospel in particular applieth Christ, with all his benefits, unto the comfort of his own soul.

Q. How are me said to be justified by faith?
A. Not as though we were just for the worthiness of this virtue, for (in such a respect Christ alone is our righteousness;) but because faith, and faith, only, is the instrument fit to apprehend and receive (not to work or procure) our justification, and so to knit us unto Christ, that we may be made partakers of all his benefits.

Q. What is that Holiness, which accompanieth this justifying faith?
A. A gift of God whereby the heart of the believer is withdrawn from evil, and converted unto newness of life.

Q. Wherein does this Holiness show it self?
A. First, in unfeigned Repentance, and then in sincere Obedience springing from the same.

Q. What are the parts of Repentance?
A. Two. A true grief wrought in the heart of the believer, for offending so gracious a God by his former transgressions. And a conversion unto God again, with full purpose of heart ever after to cleave unto him, and to refrain from that which shall be displeasing in his sight.

Q. What is the direction of that Obedience which God requireth of Man?
A. The moral Law; whereof the ten Commandments are an abridgment.

Q. What is the sum of the Law?
A. Love.

Q. What are the parts thereof?
A. The love which we owe unto God, commanded in the first; and the love which we owe unto our Neighbor, commanded in the second Table.

Q. How do you distinguish the four Commandments which belong unto the first Table?
A. They do either respect the conforming of the inward powers of the soul to the acknowledgment of the true God, as the first Commandment; or the holy use of the outward means of God's worship, as the three following.

A Body of Divinity

Q. What are the duties which concern the outward means of God's worship?
A. They are either such as are to be performed every day, or occasion shall require; or such as are appointed for a certain day.

Q. What Commandments do belong unto the first kind?
A. The Second, concerning the solemn worship of Religion; and the Third, concerning that respect which we are to have of God's honor in the common carriage of our life.

Q. What Commandment belongeth to the second kind?
A. The Fourth; enjoining the special sanctification of the Sabbath day.

Q. How do you distinguish the six Commandments, belonging to the Second Table?
A. The first five do order such actions as are joined with consent of the mind at least: the last respecteth the first motions that arise in the heart, before any consent is given.

Q. What are the duties appertaining to the first kind?
A. They are either due unto certain persons in regard of some special bond; or unto all men in general, by a common right: the first sort is set down in the fifth Commandment; the other in the four next.

Q. What is the outward means whereby the Gospel is offered unto mankind?
A. The Ministry of the Gospel; which is exercised in the visible Church of Christ.

Q. Of whom does the visible Church consist?
A. Of public Officers, ordained to be ministers of Christ and disposers of heavenly things, according to the prescript of the Lord: and the rest of the Saints, who with obedience are to subject themselves unto the Ordinances of God.

Q. What are the parts of the outward Ministry?
A. The administration of the Word, and of the Ordinances annexed thereunto: which are especially Sacraments and Censures.

Q. What is the Word?
A. That part on the outward ministry, which consisteth in the delivery of Doctrine: and this is the ordinary instrument which God useth in begetting Faith.

Q. What order is there used in the delivery of the Word for the begetting of Faith?
A. First, the Covenant of the Law is urged, to make sin and the punishment thereof known: whereupon the sting of conscience pricketh the heart with a sense of God's wrath, and maketh man utterly to despair of any ability in himself to obtain everlasting life. After this preparation, the promises of the Gospel are propounded: whereupon the sinner conceiving hope of pardon, sueth unto God for mercy, and particularly applieth unto his own soul, those comfortable promises; and hath wrought in him, by the spirit of God an earnest desire at the least to believe and repent.

Q. What is a Sacrament?
A. A visible sign ordained by God to be a seal for confirmation of the promises of the Gospel unto those who perform the conditions required in the same.

Q. How is this done by a Sacrament;
A. By a fit similitude between the sign and the thing signified, the benefit of the Gospel is represented unto the eye, and the assurance of enjoying the same confirmed to such as are within the Covenant. Wherefore as the preaching of the Word is the ordinary

means of begetting faith; so both it, and the holy use of the Sacraments, be the instruments of the Holy Ghost to increase and confirm the same.

Q. How many kinds of Sacraments be there?
A. Two: the first of our Admission into the Church: the second of our preservation and nourishment therein; to assure us of our continual increase in Christ. In which respect, the former is once only; the latter often to be administered.

Q. What do you understand by Censures?
A. The order which God hath appointed for the confirmation of the threatenings of the Gospel against the disobedient.

Q. How are these Censures exercised?
A. First, by word alone. in Admonition. Secondly, by inflicting a penalty: either by shutting up the offender in the Lord's prison, till such time as he showeth tokens of repentance; or by cutting off the rotten member from the rest of the body.

Q. Hath this administration of the Gospel been always after the same manner?
A. For substance it hath always been the same: but in regard of the manner proper to certain times, it is distinguished into two kinds; the old and the new.

Q. What call you the old Ministry?
A. That which was delivered unto the Fathers: which was to continue until the fullness of time, wherein by the coming of Christ it was to be reformed.

Q. What were the properties of this Ministry?
A. First. the Commandments of the Law were more largely, and the promises of Christ, more sparingly and darkly propounded: these latter being so much the more generally and obscurely delivered, as the manifesting of them was further oft. Secondly, the promises of things to come were shadowed with a multitude of Types and Figures; which when the truth should be exhibited, were to vanish away.

Q. What were chief States and Periods of this old Ministry?
A. The first from Adam to Abraham, the second from Abraham to Christ.

Q. What were the special Properties of the latter of these two Periods?
A. First, it was more especially restrained into a certain Family and Nation. Secondly it had joined with it a solemn repetition and declaration of the first Covenant of the Law. Thirdly besides the Ceremonies (which were greatly enlarged under Moses) it had Sacraments also added unto it.

Q. What were the ordinary Sacraments of this Ministry?
A. The Sacrament of Admission into the Church was Circumcision, instituted in the days of Abraham: the other of continual Preservation and nourishment was the Paschal Lamb, instituted in the time of Moses.

Q. What is the new administration of the Gospel?
A. That which was delivered unto us by Christ: which is to continue unto the end of the World.

Q. What are the properties thereof?
A. First it is indifferently propounded unto all people, whether they be Jews or Gentiles; and in that respect it is Catholic or Universal. Secondly, it is full of grace and truth, bringing joyful tidings unto mankind that whatsoever was formerly promised of Christ, is

now performed: and so, instead of the ancient types and shadows, exhibiteth the things themselves; with a large and clear declaration of all the benefits of the Gospel.

Q. What are the principal points of the Word of this Ministry?
A. That Christ our Savior (whom God by his Prophets had promised to send into the World) is come in the flesh, and hath accomplished the work of our redemption. That he was conceived by the Holy Ghost, born of the Virgin Mary, suffered under Pontius Pilate, was crucified and died upon the Cross. That the Body and Soul being thus separated, his body was laid in the grave, and remained under the power of Death: and his soul went into the place appointed for the souls of the righteous; namely Paradise, the seat of the Blessed. That the third day, body and soul being joined together again, he rose from the dead, and afterwards ascended up into heaven: where   Page 502 (425) he sitteth at the right hand of his Father, until such time as from thence he shall come unto the last Judgment.

Q. What are the Sacraments of this Ministry;
A. The Sacrament of Admission into the Church is Baptism; which sealeth unto us our spiritual Birth: the other Sacrament of our continual Preservation is the Lords Supper; which sealeth unto us our continual nourishment.

Q. After the end of this life, what is to be looked for in the world to come?
A. A twofold Judgment: the one Particular, upon the soul of every man at the time of his Death; the other General; upon the souls and bodies of all men together at the time of their Resurrection.

[The particulars which concern the two Sacraments of the new Testament, and the twofold Judgment in the World to come, is to be supplied out of the latter end of the former Sum.]

FINIS.

IMMANUEL:
OR, THE MYSTERY OF THE INCARNATION OF THE SON OF GOD.

UNFOLDED BY

JAMES USSHER,

ARCHBISHOP OF ARMAGH.

JOHN 1. 14.

The Word was made Flesh.

THE MYSTERY OF THE INCARNATION OF THE SON OF GOD.

The Holy Prophet, in the Book of the (a) Proverbs, poseth all such as have not learned wisdom, nor known the knowledge of the holy, with this Question. Who hath ascended up into heaven, or descended? who hath gathered she wind in his fists? who hath established all the ends of the earth; what is his name and what is his SONS name, if thou canst tell? To help us herein, the SON Himself did tell us, when he was here upon earth, that (b) None hath ascended up to heaven, but he that descended from heaven, even the Son of man which is in heaven. And that we might not be ignorant of his name, the Prophet Isaiah did long before foretell, that (c) Unto us a Child is born, and unto us a Son is given; whose name shall be called Wonderful, Counselor, The Mighty God, The everlasting Father, The Prince of Peace.

(a) Prov 30. 3. 4. (b) John 3. 13. (c) Isa. 9. 3. (d) Exod. 9. 16. (e) Ibid. chap. 10. 14. & 11. 6.

Where if it be demanded, how these things can stand together? that the Son of man speaking upon earth, should yet at the same instant be in heaven; that the Father of Eternity should be born in time? and that the Mighty God should become a Child; which is the weakest state of man himself? -we must call to mind that the first letter of this great Name, is WONDERFUL. When he appeared of old to Manoah his name was wonderful, and he did wondrously. Judg. 13. 18, 19. But that and all the wonders that ever were, must give place to the great mystery of his incarnation; and in respect thereof cease to be wonderful; for of this work that may be verified, which is spoken of those wonderful judgments, that God brought upon Egypt when he would (d) show his power and have his name declared throughout all the earth (e) Before them were no such neither after them shall be the like.

Neither the creation of all things out of nothing, which was the beginning of the works of God (those six working days putting as it were an end to that long Sabbath that never had beginning t wherein the Father, Son, and holy Ghost did infinitely (f) glorify themselves and (g) rejoice in the fruition one of another, without communicating the notice thereof unto any creature) nor the Resurrection from the dead and the restoration of all things, the last work that shall go before that everlasting Sabbath (which shall have a beginning, but never shall have an end, neither that first, I say, nor the last, though most admirable pieces of work, may be compared with this, wherein the Lord was pleased to show the highest pitch (if any thing may be said to be highest in that which is infinite and exempt from all measure and dimensions) of his Wisdom, Goodness, Power, and Glory.

(f) Joh. 17. 5. (g) Prov. 8. 30.

The Heathen Chaldeans, to a question propounded by the King of Babel, make answer; (h) that it was a rare thing which he required, and that none other would show it, except these Gods, whose dwelling is not with flesh. But the rarity of this lieth in the contrary to that which they imagined to be so plain: that he (i) who is over all, God blessed for ever, should take our flesh and dwell, or* pitch his Tabernacle with us. That as (k) the glory of God filled the Tabernacle (which was a (l) figure of the human nature of our Lord) which was such a kind of fullness, that Moses himself was not able to approach unto it; (therein coming short, (m) as in all things, of the Lord of the house) and filled the Temple of Solomon (a type likewise (n) of the body of our Prince

Immanuel

of Peace) in (o) such sort that the Priests could not enter therein: so (p) in him all the fullness of the Godhead should dwell bodily.

(h) Dan. 2. 11. (i) Rom. 9. 5. * ἐσκήνωσε, John 1. 14. (k) Exod. 40. 34, 25. (l) Heb. 9. 9, 11. (m) Heb. 3. 3, 6. (n) Joh. 2. 19, 21. (o) 2 Chron. 7. 1, 2. (p) Coloss. 2. 9

And therefore, if of that Temple, built with hands: Solomon could say with admiration: (q) But will God in very deed dwell with men on the earth? Behold, heaven and the heaven of heavens cannot contain thee; how much less this house, which I have built? of the true temple, that is not of this building; we may with great wonderment say with the Apostle, (r) Without controversy, great is the mystery of Religion: God was manifested in the flesh; yea was made of a woman, and born of a Virgin; a thing so (s) wonderful, that it was given for a sign unto unbelievers seven hundred and forty years before it was accomplished; even a sign of God's own choosing, among all the wonders in the depth, or in the heights above. Therefore the Lord himself shall give you a sign. Behold a Virgin shall conceive and bear a Son, and shall call his name Immanuel. Isa. 7. 14.

A notable wonder indeed, and great beyond all comparison. That the Son of God should be (t) made of a Woman; even made of that Woman, which was (u) made by himself. That her womb then, and the (x) heavens now, should contain him whom (y) The Heaven of Heavens cannot contain. That he who had both Father and Mother, whose pedigree is upon record even up unto Adam, who in the fullness of time was brought forth in Bethlehem, and when he had finished his course was cut off out of the land of the living at Jerusalem? should yet notwithstanding be in truth, that which his shadow Melchizedek was only in the conceit of the men of his time, (z) without Father, without Mother, without Pedigree, having neither beginning of days nor end of life. That his Father should be (a) greater then he; and yet he his Fathers (b) equal. That he (c) is, before Abraham was, and yet Abraham's birth preceded his, well-nigh the space of 2000 years. And finally, that he who was David's Son, should yet be David's Lord: (d) a case which plunged the greatest Rabbis among the Pharisees; who had not yet learned this wisdom, nor known this knowledge of the holy.

(q) 2 Chron. 6. 18. (r) 1 Tim. 3. 6. (s) Isa. 7. 11. 14. (t) Gal. 4. 4. (u) John 1. 36. Col. 1. 16. (x) Acts 3. 21. (y) 1 Kings 8. 27. (z) Heb. 7. 3. with Isa. 53. 8.

a John 24. 28. b John 5. 18. il. 2. 6. c John 8. 58. d Mat. 22. 42 43. &c.

The untying of this knot dependeth upon the right understanding of the wonderful conjunction of the divine and human Nature in the unity of the Person of our Redeemer. For by reason of the strictness of this personal union, whatsoever may be verified of either of those Natures, the same may be truly spoken of the whole Person, from whithersoever of the Natures it be denominated. For the clearer conceiving whereof, we may call to mind that which the Apostle hath taught us touching our Savior. (e) In him dwelleth all the fullness of the Godhead bodily, that is to say by such a personal and real union, as does inseparably and everlastingly conjoin that infinite Godhead with his infinite Manhood in the unity of the self-same individual Person.

e Col. 2. 9.

He in whom that fullness dwelleth, is the PERSON: that fullness which so does dwell in him, is the NATURE. Now there dwelleth in him not only the fullness of the Godhead but the fullness of the Manhood also. For we believe him to be both perfect God, begotten of the substance of his Father before all worlds; and perfect Man, made of the substance of his Mother in the fullness of time. And therefore we must hold, that there are two distinct Natures in him: and two so distinct, that they do not make one compounded nature: but still remain uncompounded and unconfounded together. But He in whom the fullness of the Manhood dwelleth is not one, and he in whom the fullness of the Godhead, another: but he in whom the fullness of both those natures dwelleth, is one and the same Immanuel, and consequently it must be believed as firmly, that he is but one Person.

And here we must consider, that the divine Nature did not assume an human Person, but the divine Person did assume an human Nature: and that of the three divine Persons, it was neither the first nor the third that did assume this Nature; but it was the middle Person who was to be the middle one, that must undertake this mediation betwixt God and us; which was otherwise also most requisite, as well for the better preservation of the integrity of the blessed Trinity in the Godhead, as for the higher advancement of Mankind by means of that relation which the second Person the Mediator did bear unto his Father: For if the fullness of the Godhead should have thus dwelt in any human Person, there should then a fourth Person necessarily have been added unto the Godhead: and if any of the three Persons, beside the second, had been born of a woman; there should have been two Sons in the Trinity. Whereas now the Son of God and the Son of the blessed Virgin, being but one person, is consequently but one Son; and so no alteration at all made in the relations of the persons of the Trinity.

Again in respect of us, the Apostle showeth, that for this very end (f) God sent his own SON made of a Woman? that WE might receive the adoption of SONS, and thereupon maketh this inference; Wherefore thou art no more a Servant but a SON, and if a SON, then an HEIR of God through Christ; intimating thereby, that what relation Christ hath unto God by Nature, we being found in him have the same by Grace. By nature he is (g) the only begotten Son of the Father: but this is the high grace he hath purchased for us; that (h) as many as received him, to them he gave power or privilege, to become the Sons of God, even to them that believe on his Name. For although he reserve to himself the preeminence, which is due unto him in a * peculiar manner, of being (i) the first born among many brethren: yet in him, and for him, the rest likewise by the grace of adoption are all of them accounted as first borns.

*f Gal. 4. 4, 5, 7. g Joh. 1. 14. & 3. 16. h John 1. 12. * Propter quod unumquodque est tale, illud ipsum est magis tale. i Rom. 8. 29. k Exod. 4. 22, 23.*

So God biddeth Moses to say unto Pharaoh: (k) Israel is my Son, even my first born. And I say unto thee; Let my son go, that he may serve me: and if thou refuse to let him go; behold I will slay thy son even thy first born. And the whole Israel of God, consisting of Jew and Gentile, is in the same sort described by the Apostle to be (l) the general assembly and Church of the first born enrolled in heaven. For the same reason that maketh them to be Sons, to wit, their incorporation into Christ, the self-same also maketh them to be first borns: so as (however it fall out by the grounds of our Common Law) by the rule of the Gospel this consequence will still hold true; (m) if children, then heirs, heirs of God and joint heirs with Christ. And so much for the SON, the Person assuming.

l Heb. 12. 22. m Rom. 8. 17.

The Nature assumed, is the seed of Abraham. Heb. 2 16. the seed of David, Rom. 1 3. the seed of the Woman, Gen. 3. 15. the WORD, (n) the second person of the Trinity, being (o) made FLESH, that is to say, (p) Gods own Son being made of a Woman, and so becoming truly and really (q) the fruit of her womb. Neither did he take the substance of our nature only, but all the properties also and the qualities thereof: so as it might be said of him as it was of (r) Elias and the (s) Apostles; that he was a man subject, to like passions as we are. Yea he subjected himself (t) in the days of his flesh to the same (u) weakness, which we find in our own frail nature, and was compassed with like infirmities; and in a word, in all things was made like unto his brethren, * sin only excepted. Wherein yet we must consider, that as he took upon him, not an human Person, but an human Nature; so it was not requisite he should take upon him any Personal infirmities, such as are, madness, blindness, lameness, and particular kinds of diseases which are incident to some only and not to all men in general; but those alone which do accompany the whole nature of mankind, such as are hungering, thirsting, weariness, grief, pain and mortality.

n 1 John 5. 7. o John 1 14. p Gal. 4. 4. q Luk. 1. 42. Ἠλίας ἄνθρωπος ἦν ὁμοιοπαθής ὑμῖν Jam. 5. 7. Ἡμεῖς ὁμοιοπαθεῖς ἐσμέν ὑμῖν ἄνθρωποι. Acts 14. 15. t Heb. 5. 7. n 1 Cor. 13. 4. Heb. 2. 17, 18. & 4. 15. * Inter Trinitatem, & hominum infirmitatem, & iniquitatem, Mediator factus est homo, non iniquus, sed tamen infirmus ut ex eo quod non iniquus iungeretur Deo; ex eo quod infirmus, propinquaret tibi. Aug. Praef. in ennarrat. 2. Psal. 29.

We are further here to observe in this our (x) Melchizedek, that as he had no Mother in regard of one of his natures, so he was to have no Father in regard of the other; but must be born of a pure immaculate Virgin, without the help of any man.

And this also was most requisite, as for other respects, so for the exemption of the assumed nature from the imputation and pollution of Adam's sin. For (y) sin having by that one man entered into the world; every Father becometh an Adam unto his child, and conveyeth the corruption of his nature unto all those whom he does beget. Therefore our Savior assuming the substance of our nature, but not by the ordinary way of natural generation, is thereby freed from all the touch and taint of the corruption of our flesh; which by that means only is propagated from the first man unto his posterity. Whereupon, he being made of man but not by man, and so becoming the immediate fruit of the womb, and not of the loins must of necessity be acknowledged to be (z) that HOLY THING, which so was born of so blessed a Mother. Who although she were but the passive and material principle of which that precious flesh was made, and the holy Ghost the agent and efficient; yet cannot the Man Christ Jesus thereby be made the Son of his (a) own Spirit; because Fathers do beget their children out of their own substance the Holy Ghost did not so, but framed the flesh of him, from whom himself proceeded, out of the creature of them both, (b) the handmaid of our Lord; whom from thence all generations shall call blessed.

x Heb. 7. 3. y Rom. 5. 12. z Luk. 1. 35. a Gal. 4. 6. Rom. 8. 9. b Luk. 1. 38, 48.

That blessed womb of hers was the Bride-chamber, wherein the holy Ghost did knit that indissoluble knot betwixt our human nature and his Deity: the Son of God assuming into the unity of his person that which before he was not; and yet without change (for so must God still be) remaining that which he was; whereby it came to pass, that (c) this holy thing which was born of her, was indeed and in truth to be called the SON OF GOD. Which Wonderful connection of two so infinitely differing natures in the unity of one person, how it was there effected, is an inquisition fitter for an Angelical intelligence, then for our shallow capacity to look after; to which purpose we may also observe, that in the fabric of the Ark of the Covenant (d) the posture of the faces of the Cherubim toward the Mercy-seat (the type of our Savior) was such as would point unto us, that these are the things which the Angels desire to * stoop and look into?

c Luk. 1. 35. d Exod. 37. 9. * Παρακύψαι, 1 Pet. 1. 12.

And therefore let that satisfaction, which the Angel gave unto the Mother Virgin (whom it did more especially concern to move the question, (e) How may this be?) content us, (f) The power of the Highest shall over shadow thee. For as the former part of that speech may inform us, that (g) with God nothing is possible: so the latter may put us in mind, that the same God having over shadowed this mystery with his own veil, we should not presume with the men of (h) Bethshemesh to look into this Ark of his; lest for our curiosity we be smitten as they were. Only this we may safely say, and most firmly hold: that as the distinction of the Persons in the holy Trinity hindreth not the unity of the Nature of the Godhead, although every Person entirely holdeth his own incommunicable property; so neither does the distinction of the two Natures in our Mediator any way cross the unity of his Person, although each nature remaineth entire in it self, and retaineth the properties agreeing thereunto, * any conversion, composition, commixture, or confusion.

e Luke 1. 34. f Ibid ver. 37. g Ibid ver. 37. h 1 Sam. 6. 19. * Ἰσυγχύτως, ἀτρέπτως, ἀδιαιρέτως, ἀχωρίστως. (Council Chalced. Acts 5. & apud Evag. lib. 2. hist. Eccl. c. 4) inconfuse incommutabiliter indivise, inteperabiliter (Io. Maxemius in catholicoe suae Professionis init. Concil. Rom. Sub Martino I.)

When (i) Moses beheld the bush burning with fire, and yet no whit consumed, he wondered at the sight, and said; I will now turn aside, and see this sight, why the bush is not burnt. But when God thereupon called unto him out of the midst of the bush, and said; Draw not nigh hither, and told him who he was; Moses trembled, hid his face, and durst not behold God Yet although, being thus warned, we dare not draw so nigh; what does. hinder but we may stand aloof off, and wonder at this great sight? (k) Our God is a consuming fire; saith the Apostle: and a question we find propounded in the Prophet, (l) who amongst us shall dwell with the devouring fire? who amongst us shall dwell with the everlasting burning. Moses was not like other Prophets, but (m) God spake unto him face to face, as man speaketh unto his friend: and yet for all that when he besought the Lord that he would show him his glory; he received this answer, (n) Thou canst not see my face: for there shall no man see me and live. Abraham before him though a special (o) friend of God, and the (p) father of the faithful, the children of God: yet held it a great matter that he should take upon him so much as to (q) speak unto God, being but dust and ashes. Yea, the very Angels themselves (r) (which are greater in power and might) are fain to (s) cover their faces, when they stand before him; as not being able to behold the brightness of his glory.

1 Exod. 3. 2, 3, 5, 6. Acts 7. 31, 32. k Heb. 12. 29. l Isa. 33. 14. m Num. 12. 6. 7. 8. Ex. 33. 18, 20. o Isa 4. 1, 8. 2 Chron. 20. Jam. 2. 23. p Rom. 4. 11, 16. Gal. 3. 7. q Gen. [18.] 27. r 2 Pet. 2. 11. s Isa. 6. 2.

With what astonishment then may we behold our dust and ashes assumed into the undivided unity of God's own Person; and admitted to dwell here as an inmate, under the same roof? and yet in the midst of these everlasting burnings, the bush to remain unconsumed, and to continue fresh and green for ever more. Yea, how should not we with Abraham rejoice to see this day, wherein not only our nature in the person of our Lord Jesus is found to dwell for ever in those everlasting burnings; but, in and by him, our own persons also are brought so nigh thereunto, that (t) God does set his Sanctuary and Tabernacles among us, and dwell with us; and which is much more) maketh us ourselves to be the (u) house and the (x) habitation, wherein he is pleased to dwell by his Spirit; according to that of the Apostle: (y) Yee are the temple of the living God, as God hath said; I will dwell in them and walk in them, and I will be

Immanuel

their God, and they shall be my people; and that most admirable prayer, which our Savior himself made unto his Father in our behalf (z) I pray not for them alone, but for them also which shall believe on me through their word: that all may be one, as thou Father art in me, and I in thee, that they also may be one in us; that the world may believe that thou hast sent me. I in them, and thou in me, that they may be made perfect in one; and that the world may know that thou hast sent me, and hast loved them as thou hast loved me.

t Lev. 26. 11, 12. Eze 37 26, 27. Rev. 21 3. u Heb. 3. 6. x Eph. 2. 22. 2 Cor. 6. 16. z John 17. 20, 21, 22, 23.

To compass this conjunction betwixt God and us, he that was to be our (a) JESUS or Savior, must of necessity also be IMMANUEL: which being interpreted is, God with us? and therefore in his Person to be Immanuel, that is, God dwelling with our flesh; because he was by his Office too to be Immanuel, that is, he who must make God to be at one with us. For this being his proper office, to be (b) Mediator between God and man, he must partake with both: and being from all eternity consubstantial with his Father, he must at the appointed time become likewise consubstantial with his children (c) Forasmuch then as the children are partakers of flesh, and blood; he also himself likewise took part of the same, saith the Apostle. We read in the Roman History, that the Sabines and the Romans joining battle together, upon such an occasion as is mentioned in the last Chapter of the book of Judges; of the children of Benjamin, catching every man a wife of the daughters of Shiloh; the women being daughters to the one side, and wives to the other, interposed themselves, and took up the quarrel, so that by the mediation of those, who had a peculiar interest in either side, and by whose means this new alliance was contracted betwixt the two adverse parties; they who before stood upon highest terms of hostility, * did not only entertain peace, but also joined themselves together into one body and one state.

a Mat. 1. 21, 23. Sec. Anselmus. Cur Deus homo. b 1 Tim. 2. 5. c Heb. 2. 14. * Sic pax facta, faedusque per cussum: secutaque res mira dictu, ut relictis sedibus suis novamini Urbem hostes demigrarent, & cum generis suis avitas opes pro dote sociarent L. Flor. histor. Rom. c. 1.

God and we were (d) enemies; before we were reconciled to him by his Son He that is to be (c) our peace, and to reconcile us unto God, and to slay this enmity, must have an interest in both the parties that are at variance, and have such a reference unto either of them, that he may be able to send this comfortable message unto the sons of men, (f) Go to my brethren, and say unto them: I ascend unto my Father, and your Father; and to my God, and your God. For as long as (g) he is not ashamed to call us brethren; (h) God is not ashamed to be called our god; and his entering of our appearance, in his own name and ours, after this manner; (i) Behold, I and the children which God hath given me; is a motive strong enough to appease his Father, and to turn his favorable countenance towards us: as on the other side, when we become unruly and prove rebellious children; no reproof can be more forcible, nor inducement so prevalent (if there remain any spark of grace in us) to make us cast down our weapons and yield, than this. (k) Do ye thus requite the Lord, O foolish people and unwise? Is not he thy Father that hath bought thee; and bought thee (l) not with corruptible things, as silver and gold, but with the precious blood of his own Son.

d Rom. 5. 10. e Eph. 2. 14, 16. f John 20. 17. g Heb. 2. 11. h Heb. 11. 16. i Heb. 2. 13. k Deut. 32. 6. l 1. Pet. 1. 18. 19.

How dangerous a matter it is to be at odds with God, old Eli showeth by this main argument. (m) If one man sin against another, the Judge shall judge him: but if a man sin against the Lord, who shall plead or entreat for him, and Job, before him. (n) He is not a man as I am that I should answer him, and we should come together in judgment: neither is there any Days-man or Umpire betwixt us, that may lay his hand upon us both. If this general should admit no manner of exception, then were we in a woeful case, and had cause to weep much more then S. John did in the Revelation; when (o) none was found in Heaven, nor in earth, nor under the earth, that was able to open the book which he saw in the right hand of him that sat upon the Throne, neither to look thereon. But as S. John was wished there to refrain his weeping because (p) the Lion of the tribe of Judah, the root of David, had prevailed to open the book and to loose the seven seals thereof: so he himself elsewhere giveth the like comfort unto all of us in particular. (q) If any man sin we have an Advocate with the Father, Jesus Christ the righteous: and he is a propitiation for our sins; and not for us only, but also for the sins of the whole world.

m 1. Sam. 2. 25. n Job 9. 32. 33. o. Rev. 5. 3. 4. p Rev. 5. 5. q 1 John 2. 1, 2.

For (r) there is one God, so is there one Mediator between God and men, the man Christ Jesus, who gave himself for a ransom for all and in discharge of this his office of mediation, as only fit umpire to take up this controversy, was to lay his hand as well upon God the party so highly offended, as upon Man the party so basely offending. In things concerning God, the Priesthood of our Mediator is exercised. (s) For every high Priest is taken from among men, and ordained for men in things pertaining to God: The parts of his Priestly function are two; Satisfaction and Intercession: the former whereof giveth contentment to God's justice; the latter solliciteth his mercy, for the application of this benefit to the children of God in particular. Whereby it cometh to pass, that God in (t) showing mercy upon whom he will show mercy, is yet for his justice no loser: being both (u) just, and the justifier of him which believeth in Jesus.

r. 1 Tim. 2. 5, 6. s Heb. 5. 1. & 2. 17. t. Rom. 9. 15, 16. u Rom. 3. 26.

By virtue of his Intercession, Our Mediator (x) appeareth in the presence of God for us, and (y) maketh request for us. To this purpose, the Apostle noteth in the 4. to the Hebrews, 1. That we have a great high Priest that is passed into the heavens, Jesus the Son of God (ver. 14. 2.) That we have not an high Priest which cannot be touched with the feeling of our infirmities, but was in all things tempted as we are, yet without sin. (vers. 15.) Betwixt the having of such, and the not having of such an Intercessor, betwixt the height of him in regard of the one and the lowliness in regard of his other nature, standeth the comfort of the poor sinner. He must be such a suitor as taketh our case to heart: and therefore (z) in all things it behooved him to be made like unto his brethren, that he might be a merciful and faithful high Priest. In which respect as it was needful he should partake with our flesh and blood that he might be tenderly affected unto his brethren: so likewise for the obtaining of so great a suit, it behooved he should be most dear to God the Father, and have so great an interest in him, as he might always be sure to be (a) heard in his requests: who therefore could be no other, but of whom the Father testified from heaven; (b) This is my beloved In whom I am well pleased. It was fit our Intercessor should be Man, like unto ourselves; that we might (c) boldly come to him, and find grace to help in time of need: It was fit he should be God, that he might boldly go to the Father, without any way disparaging him; as being his (d) fellow and (e) equal.

x Heb. 9. 24. y Rom. 8. 34. Heb. 7. 25. z Heb. 2. 17. a John 11. 4. b Matt. 3. 17. c Heb. 4. 16. d Zech. 13. 7. e Phil. 2. 6.

But such was God's love to justice and hatred to sin; that he would not have his Justice swallowed up with mercy, nor sin pardoned without the making of fit reparation. And therefore our Mediator must not look to procure for us a simple pardon without more ado: but must be a (f) propitiation for our sins, and redeem us by fine and (g) ransom: and so not only be the master of our requests, to entreat the Lord for us; but also take upon him the part of an (h) Advocate, to plead full satisfaction made by himself, as our (i) surety, unto all the debt wherewith we any way stood chargeable. Now the satisfaction which our surety bound himself to perform in our behalf, was a double debt: the principal, and the accessory. The principal debt is obedience to God's most holy Law: which man was bound to pay as a perpetual tribute to his Creator, although he had never sinned, but, being now by his own default become bankrupt, is not able to discharge in the least measure. His surety therefore being to satisfy in his stead none will be found fit to undertake such a payment, but he who is both God and man.

f ἱλασμός Rom. 3. 25. 1 John 2. 2. & 4. 10. g λύτρον ἀντίπωλλῶν. Mat. 20. 28. ἀντίλυτρον ὑπέρ πάντων. 1 Tim. 2. 6. See Job 33. 24. h 1 John 2. 1. i Heb. 7. 22.

Man it is fit he should be, because man was the party that by the Articles of the first Covenant was tied to his obedience; and it was requisite that, (k) as by one man's disobedience many were made sinners, so by the obedience of one man likewise many should be made righteous, Again if our Mediator were only God, he could have performed no obedience (the Godhead being free from all manner of subjection:) and if he were a bare man, although he had been as perfect as Adam in his integrity, or the Angels themselves; yet being left unto himself amidst all the temptations of Satan and this wicked world, he should be subject to fall, as they were: or if he should hold out, as (l) the elect Angels did; that must have been ascribed to the grace and favor of another: whereas the giving of strict satisfaction to God's Justice was the thing required in this behalf. But now being God, as well as Man, he by his own (m) eternal Spirit preserved himself without spot: presenting a far more satisfactory obedience unto God, then could have possible been performed by Adam in his integrity.

k Rom. 5. 19. l 1 Tim. 5. 21 m Heb. 9. 14.

For, besides the infinite difference that was betwixt both their Persons, which maketh the actions of the one beyond all comparison to exceed the worth and value of the other: we know that Adam was not able to make himself holy; but what holiness he had, he received from him who created him according to his own image: so that whatsoever obedience Adam had performed, God should have (n) eaten but of the fruit of the vineyard which himself had planted; and (o) of his own would all that have been, which could be given unto him. But Christ did himself sanctify that human nature which he assumed; according to his own saying, Job 17. 19. For their sakes I sanctified my self: and so out of his own peculiar store did he bring forth those precious treasures of holy obedience, which for the satisfaction of our debt he was pleased to tender unto his Father. Again, if Adam had (p) done all things which were commanded him, he must for all that have said: I am an unprofitable servant; I have done that which was my duty to do. Whereas in the voluntary obedience, which Christ subjected himself unto, the case stood far otherwise.

n 1 Cor. 9. 7. o 1 Chro. 29. 14, 16. τα σά ἐκ τῶν σῶν. p Luk. 17. 10.

True it is, that if we respect him in his human nature, (q) his Father is greater then he; and he is his Fathers (r) servant: yet in that he said and most truly said, that God was his Father, (s) the Jews did rightly infer from thence, that he thereby made himself equal with God; and (t) the Lord of Hosts himself hath proclaimed him to be the man that is his fellow. Being such a man therefore, and so highly born, by the privilege of his birth-right, he might have claimed an exemption from the ordinary service whereunto all other men are tied, and by being (u) the Kings Son, have freed himself from the payment of that tribute which was to be exacted at the hands of Strangers. When (x) the Father brought this his first begotten into the world, he said; Let all the Angels of God worship him: and at the very instant wherein the Son advanced our nature into the highest pitch of dignity, by admitting it into the unity of his sacred Person, that nature so assumed was worthy to be crowned with all glory and honor: and he in that nature might then have set himself down (y) at the right hand of the throne of God; tied to no other subjection than now he is, or hereafter shall be, when after the end of this world he shall have delivered up the kingdom to God the Father. For then also, in regard of his assumed nature, he (z) shall be subject unto him that put all other things under him.

q Job. 14. 28. r Isa. 53. 11. Mat. 12. 18. s Joa. 5. 18. t Zech. 13. 7. u Mat. 17. 25. 26. x Heb. 1. 6. y Heb. 12. 21. z 1.Cor. 15. 27.

Thus the Son of God if he had minded only his own things, might at the very first have attained unto the joy that was set before him: but (a) looking on the things of others, he chose rather to come by a tedious way and wearisome journey unto it, not challenging the privilege of a Son, but taking upon him the form of a mean servant. Whereupon in the days of his flesh, he did not serve as an honorable Commander in the Lords host, but as an ordinary soldier, he made himself of no reputation, for the time as it were * emptying his self of his high state and dignity; he humbled himself and became obedient until his death; being contented all his life long to be (b) made under the Law: yea, so far, that as he was sent (c) in the likeness of sinful flesh, so he disdained not to subject himself unto the Law which properly did concern sinful flesh. And therefore howsoever Circumcision was by right applicable only unto such as were (d) dead in their sins, and the circumcision of their flesh; yet he in whom there was no body of the sins of the flesh to be put off, submitted himself notwithstanding thereunto: not only to testify his communion with the Fathers of the old Testament; but also by this means to tender unto his Father a bond, signed with his own blood, whereby he made himself in our behalf a debtor unto the whole Law. For I testify (saith the (e) Apostle) to every man that is circumcised, that he is a debtor to the whole law.

a Phil. 2. ver. 4, 5, 7, 8. Ἑαυτόν ἐκήνωσε. Phil. 2. 7. b Gal. 4. 4. c Ram. 8. 3. d Col. 1. 11. 13. e Gal. 5. 6.

In like manner Baptism appertained properly unto such as were defiled, and had need to have their (f) sins washed away: and therefore when all the land of Judah and they of Jerusalem went out unto John, they (g) were all baptized of him in the river Jordan, confessing their sins. Among the rest came our Savior also: but the Baptist considering that he had need to be baptized by Christ, and Christ no need at all to be baptized by him, refused to give way unto that action; as altogether unbefitting the state of that, immaculate Lamb of God, who was to take away the sins of the world. Yet did our Mediator submit himself to that Ordinance of God also: not only to testify his communion with the Christians of the new Testament; but especially (which is the reason yielded by himself) because (h) it became him thus to fulfill all righteousness. And so having fulfilled all righteousness, whereunto the meanest man was tied, in the days of his pilgrimage (which was more than he needed to have undergone, if he had respected only himself.) the works which he performed were truly works of supererogation, which might be put upon the account of them whose debt he undertook to discharge; and being performed by the person of the Son of God, must in that

Immanuel

respect not only be equivalent, but infinitely over-value the obedience of Adam and all his posterity, although they had remained in their integrity, and continued until this hour, instantly serving God day and night. And thus for our main and principal debt of Obedience, hath our Mediator given satisfaction unto the justice of his Father; with (i) good measure, pressed down, shaken together, and running over.

f Acts 22. 15. g Mat. 3. 6. Mar. 1. 5. b Mat. 3. 15. i Luke 6. 38.

But beside this, we were liable unto another debt; which we have incurred by our default, and drawn upon ourselves by way of forfeiture and nomine poenae. For as (k) Obedience is a due debt, and God's servants in regard thereof are truly debtors: so likewise is sin a (l) debt, and sinners (m) debtors, in regard of the penalty due for the default. And as the payment of the debt which cometh nomine poenae, dischargeth not the tenant afterwards from paying his yearly rent, which of it self would have been due although no default had been committed, so the due payment of the yearly rent after the default hath been made, is no sufficient satisfaction for the penalty already incurred. Therefore our surety, who standeth chargeable with all our debts, as he maketh payment for the one by his Active, so must he make amends for the other by his Passive obedience: he must first (n) suffer, and then enter into his glory (o) For it became him, for whom are all things, and by whom are all things, in bringing many sons unto glory, to make the Captain of their salvation perfect (that is, a perfect accomplisher of the works which he had undertaken) through sufferings.

k Luk. 17. 10. Rom. 1. 12. Gal. 5. 3. l Mat. 6. 12. compared with Luk. 11. 4. m ὀφειλέσαι. Luk. 13. 4. n Luk. 24. 26. o Heb. 2. 10.

he Godhead is of that infinite perfection, that it cannot possibly be subject to any passion. He therefore that had no other nature but the Godhead, could not pay such a debt as this; the discharge whereof consisted, in suffering and dying. It was also fit, that God's justice should have been satisfied in that nature which had transgressed; and that the same nature should suffer the punishment, that had committed the offence. (p) For as much then as the children were partakers of flesh and blood, he also himself took part of the same: that through death he might destroy him that had the power of death, that is, the Devil; and deliver them who through fear of death were all their life time subject to bondage. Such and so great was the love of God the Father towards us, that (g) he spared not his own Son, but delivered him up for us all: and so transcendent was the love of the Son of God towards the sons of men; that he desired not to be spared; but rather then they should lie under the power of death, was of himself most willing to suffer death for them Which seeing in that infinite nature, which by eternal generation he received from his Father, he could not do; he resolved in the appointed time to take unto himself a Mother, and out of her substance to have a body framed unto himself, wherein he might (r) become obedient unto death, even the death of the Cross, for our redemption. And therefore (s) when he cometh into the world, he saith unto his Father: A body hast thou fitted me; Lo, I come to do thy will O God. By the which will, (saith the (t) Apostle) we are sanctified, through the offering of the body of Jesus Christ once for all.

p Heb. [2. 14, 15.] q Rom. 8. 32. r Phil. 2. 8. s Heb. 10. 5, 7. t Ib. ver. 9 10.

Thus we see it was necessary for the satisfaction of this debt, that our Mediator should be Man: but he that had no more in him than a Man, could never be able to go through with so great a work. For if there should be found a Man as righteous as Adam was at his first creation, who would be content to suffer for the offence of others: his suffering could not possibly serve for the redemption of one soul; much less would it be a sufficient ransom for those (u) innumerable multitudes that were to be (x) redeemed to God out of every kindred, and tongue, and people, and Nation. Neither could any Man or Angel be able to hold out, if a punishment equivalent to the endless sufferings of all the sinners in the world should at once be laid upon him. Yea, the very powers of Christ himself, upon whom (y) the spirit of might did rest, were so shaken in this sharp encounter; that he, who was the most accomplished pattern of all fortitude, stood (z) sore amazed, and with (a) strong crying and tears prayed that, (b) if it were possible, the hour might pass from him. (c) This man therefore being to offer one sacrifice for sins for ever; to the burning of that sacrifice he must not only bring the (d) coals of his love as strong as death, and as ardent as the fire which hath a most vehement flame, but he must add thereunto those (e) everlasting burnings also, even the flames of his most glorious Deity: and therefore (f) through the eternal spirit must he offer himself without spot unto God; that hereby he might (g) obtain for us an eternal redemption. The blood whereby the Church is purchased, must be (h) God's own blood: and to that end must (i) the Lord of glory be crucified? (k) the Prince and Author of life be killed; he (l) whose eternal generation no man can declare, be cut off out of the land of the living; and the man that is God's own fellow be thus smitten; according to that which God himself foretold by his Prophet. (m) Awake O sword, against my shepherd, and against the man that is my fellow, saith the Lord of Hosts: smite the shepherd, and the sheep shall be scattered. The people of Israel, we read did so value the life of David their King, that they counted him to be worth (n) ten thousand of themselves: how shall we then value the life of (o) David's Lord; (p) who is the blessed and only Potentate, the King of Kings, and Lord of Lords? It was indeed our nature that suffered; but he that suffered in that nature, (q) is over all, God blessed for ever: and for such a Person to have suffered but one hour, was more than if all other persons had suffered ten thousand millions of years.

u Rev. 7. 9. x Rev. 5. 9. y Isa. 11. 12. z Mar. 14. 33. a Heb. 5. 7. b Mark. 14. 35. 36. c Heb. 10. 12. d Cant. 8. 6. e Isa. 33. 14. f Heb. 9. 14. g Ib. ver. 12. b Acts 20. 28. i 1 Cor. 2. 8. k Acts 3. 15. l Isa. 53. 8. m Zech. 13. 7. with Mat. 25. 31. n 2 Sam 18. 3, o Mat. 22. 43. 44. p 1 Tim. 6. 15. Rev. 19. 16. q Rom. 9. 5.

But put case also, that the life of any other singular man might be equivalent to all the lives of mankind: yet the laying down of that life would not be sufficient to do the deed, unless he that had power to lay it down had power likewise to take it up again. For, to be detained always in that prison, (r) from whence there is no coming out before the payment of the uttermost farthing; is to lie always under execution, and to quit the plea of that full payment of the debt wherein our surety stood engaged for us. And therefore the Apostle upon that ground does rightly conclude; that (s) if Christ be not raised, our faith is vain, we are yet in our sins: and consequently, that as he must be (t) delivered to death for our offences, so he must be raised again for our justification.

r. Mat. 5. 26. s 1 Cor. 15. 17. t. Rom. 4. 25.

Yea our Savior himself, knowing full well what he was to undergo for our sakes, told us before-hand, that the Comforter whom he would send un to us, should (u) convince the world, that is fully satisfy the consciences of the sons of men, concerning that (x) everlasting righteousness, which was to be brought in by him, upon this very ground: Because I go to my Father, and ye see me no more. For if he had broken prison and made an escape, the payment of the debt, which as our surety he took upon himself, being not yet satisfied; he should have been seen here again: Heaven would not have held him, more then Paradise did Adam, after he had fallen into God's debt and danger. But our Savior raising himself from the dead, presenting himself in Heaven before him unto whom the debt was owing, and maintaining his standing there, hath hereby given good proof, that he is now a free man, and hath fully discharged that debt of ours, for which he stood committed. And this is the evidence we have to show of that righteousness, whereby we stand justified in God's sight: according to that of the Apostle. (y) Who shall lay any thing to the charge of God's Elect? It is God that justifieth. Who is he that condemeth? It is Christ that died, yea rather that is risen again; who is even at the right hand of God, who also maketh intercession for us.

u John 16. 10. x Dan. 9. 24. y Rom. 8. 33. 34.

Now although any ordinary man may easily part with his life: yet does it not fall in his power to resume it again at his own will and pleasure. But he that must do the turn for us, must be able to say as our JESUS did. (z) I lay down my life, that I might take it again. No man taketh it from me, but I lay it down of my self: I have power to lay it down, and I have power to take it again. And in another place: (a) Destroy this Temple, and in three days I will raise it up; saith he unto the Jews, speaking of the Temple of his body, An human nature then he must have had, which might be subject to dissolution: but being once dissolved, he could not by his own strength (which was the thing here necessarily required) raise it up again; unless he had (b) declared himself to be the Son of God with power, by the resurrection from the dead. The Manhood could suffer, but not overcome the sharpness of death: the Godhead could suffer nothing, but overcome any thing. He therefore that was to suffer and to overcome for us, must be partaker of both natures: that (c) being put to death in the flesh, he might be able to quicken himself by his own Spirit.

z John 20. 17, 18. a John [2.] 19, 21. b Rom. 1. 4. c 1 Pet. 3. 18.

And now are we come to that part of Christ's mediation, which concerneth the conveyance of (d) the redemption of this purchased possession unto the sons of men. A dear purchase indeed, which was to be redeemed with no less price than the blood of the Son of God: but what should the purchase of a stranger have been to us? or what should we have been the better for all this; if we could, not derive our descent from the purchaser, or raise some good title whereby we might estate ourselves in his purchase? Now this was the manner in former time in Israel, concerning redemptions: that unto him who was the next of kin, belonged the right of being (e) near kinsmen, or the Redeemer. And Job had before that left his glorious profession of his faith unto the perpetual memory of all posterity. (f) I know that my Goel or Redeemer liveth, and at the last shall arise upon the dust (or, stand upon the earth.) And after this my skin is spent; yet in my flesh shall I see God. Whom I shall see for my self, and mine-eyes shall behold, and not another for me. Whereby we may easily understand, that his and our Redeemer was to be the invisible God; and yet in his assumed flesh made visible even to the bodily eyes of those whom he redeemed. For if he had not thus assumed our flesh; how should we have been of his blood, or claimed any kindred to him and unless the Godhead had by a personal union been inseparably conjoined unto that flesh; how could he therein have been accounted our next of kin.

d Eph. 1. 14. e Ruth. 3. 12. & 4. ver. 1, 3, 4, 7. f Job. 19. 25, 26, 27.

For the better clearing of which last reason; we may call to mind that sentence of the Apostle. (g) The first man is of the earth earthly: the second man is the Lord from heaven. Where, notwithstanding there were many millions of men in the world betwixt these two; yet we see our Redeemer reckoned the second man. And why? but because these two were the only men who could be accounted the prime fountains from whence all the rest of mankind did derive their existence and being. For as all men in the world by mean descents do draw their first original from the first man: so in respect of a more immediate influence of efficiency and operation do they own their being unto the second man, as he is the Lord from heaven. This is God's own language unto Jeremiah; (h) Before I formed thee in the belly, I know; and this is David's acknowledgment, for his part; (i) Thy hands have made me and fashioned me (k) thou hast covered me in my mothers womb: (l) thou art he that took me out of my mothers bowels; and Jobs, for his also; (m) Thy hands have made me and fashioned me together round about: thou hast clothed me with skin and flesh, and hath fenced me with bones and sinews; and the (n) Apostle for us all; In him we live, and move, and have our being; who inferreth also thereupon, both that we ore the off-spring or generation of God; and that he is not far from every one of us; this being to be admitted for a most certain truth (notwithstanding the opposition of all gainsayers) that * God does more immediately concur to the generation and all other motions of the creature, then any natural agent does or can do. And therefore, (o) if by one mans offence, death reigned by one; much more they which receive abundance of grace and of the gift of righteousness, shall reign in life by one, Jesus Christ. Considering that this second man is not only as universal a principal of all our beings, as was that first, and so my sustain the common person of us all, as well as he; but is a far more immediate agent in the production thereof: not, as the first, so many generations removed from us, but more near unto us then our very next progenitors; and in that regard justly to be accounted our next of kin, even before them also.

*g 1 Cor. 15. 47. h Jer. 1. 5. i Psal. 119. 73. k Psal. 139. 13. l Psal. 71. 6. m Job 10. 8, 11. n Acts 17. 27, 28, 29. * See Breadwardin decausa Dei, lib. 1 cap. 3. & 4. o Rom. 5. 17.*

Yet is not this sufficient neither: but there is another kind of generation required, for which we must be beholding unto the second man, the Lord from Heaven; before we can have interest in this purchased Redemption. For as the guilt of the first mans transgression is derived unto us by the means of carnal generation: so must the benefit of the second mans obedience be conveyed unto us by spiritual regeneration. And this must be laid down as a most undoubted verity: that, (p) except a man be born again, he cannot see the kingdom of God; and that every such must be (q) born, not of blood, nor of the will of the flesh, nor of the will of man, but of God. Now, as our, Mediator in respect of the Adoption of Sons, which he hath procured for us, (r) is not ashamed to call us Brethren: so in respect of this new birth, whereby he begetteth us to a spiritual and everlasting life, he disdaineth not to own us as his Children. (s) When thou shalt make his seed and offering for sin, be shall see his seed: saith the Prophet Esaias. (t) A seed shall serve him; it shall be accounted to the Lord for a generation: saith his Father David likewise of him. And he himself of himself: (u) Behold I, and the children which God hath given me. Whence the Apostle deduceth this conclusion: (x) For as much then as the children are partakers of flesh and blood, he also himself likewise took part of the same. He himself, that is he who was God equal to the Father: for who else was able to make this (y) new creature, but the same (z) God that is the Creator of all things? (no less power being requisite to the effecting of this, then was at the first to the producing of all things out of nothing:) and these new (a) babes being to be (b) born of the Spirit; who could have power to send the Spirit, thus to beget them, but the Father and the Son from whom he proceeded? the same blessed Spirit, who framed the natural body of our Lord in the womb of the Virgin, being to new mould and fashion every member of his mystical body unto his similitude and likeness.

p John 3. 3. q John 1. 13. r Heb. 2. 11. s Isa. 53. 10. t Psal. 22. 30. u Heb. 2. 13. x Ibid. ver. 14 . y 2 Cor. 5. 17 Eph. 2. 10. Gal. 6. 15. z John 1. 13. James 1. 8. 1 Pet. 1. 3. 1 John 5. 1. a 1 Pet. 2. 2. with 1. 22. b John 3. ver. 5. 6, 8. c Ibid. ver. 4, 9, 10.

For the further opening of which mystery (which went beyond the apprehension of (c) Nicodemus, though a master of Israel) we are to consider; that in every perfect generation, the creature produced receiveth two things from him that does beget it: Life and Likeness. A curious Limner draweth his own sons portraiture to the life (as we say:) yet because there is no true life in it but a likeness only; he cannot be said to be the begetter of his Picture, as he is of his Son. And some creatures there be that are bred out of mud or other putrid matter: which although they have life, yet because they have no correspondence in likeness unto the principle from whence they were derived, are therefore accounted to have but an improper and equivocal generation. Whereas in the right and proper course of generation (others being esteemed but monstrous births that swerve from that rule) every creature begetteth his like:

— *nec imbellem feroces*
Progenerant aquilae columbam.

Now touching our spiritual death and life, these sayings of the Apostle would be thought upon. (d) We thus judge, that if one died for all, then were all dead: and that he died for all, that they which live, should not henceforth live unto themselves, but unto him which died for them and rose again. (e) God who is rich in mercy, for his great love wherewith he loved us, even when we were dead in our sins, hath quickened us together with Christ. (f) And you being dead in your sins, and the uncircumcision of your flesh, hath he quickened together with him having forgiven you all trespasses. (g) I am crucified with Christ. Nevertheless I live, yet not I, but Christ liveth in me: and the life which I now live in the flesh, I live by the Faith on the Son of God, who loved me and gave himself for me. From all which we may easily gather, that if by the obedience and sufferings of a bare man, though never so perfect, the most sovereign medicine that could be thought upon should have been prepared for the curing of our wounds: yet all would be to no purpose, we being found dead, when the medicine did come to be applied.

d 2 Cor. 5. 14 15. e Eph. 2. 4, 5. f Col. 2. 13. g Gal. 2. 20.

Our Physician therefore must not only be able to restore us unto health, but unto life it self: which none can do but the Father, Son, and holy Ghost; one God, blessed for ever. Two which purpose, these passages of our Savior also are to be considered. (h) As the Father hath life in himself: so hath he given to the Son to have life in himself. (i) As the living Father hath sent me, and I live by the Father: so he that eateth me, even he shall live by me. (k) I am the living bread, which come down from heaven; if any man eat of this bread, he shall live for ever: and the bread that I will give, is my flesh, which I will give for the life of the world. The substance whereof is briefly comprehended in this saying of the Apostle: (l) The last Adam was made a quickning spirit, An Adam therefore and perfect Man must he have been; that his flesh, given for us upon the Cross, might be made the conduit to convey life unto the world: and a quickning Spirit he could not have been, unless he were God, able to make that flesh an effectual instrument of life by the operation of his blessed Spirit. For, as himself hath declared, (m) It is the Spirit that quickeneth; without it, the flesh would profit nothing.

h John 5. 26. i John 6. 57. k Ibid ver. 51. l 1.Cor. 15. 45. m John 6. 63.

As for the point of similitude and likeness: we read of Adam after his fall, that he (n) begat a son in his own likeness, after his Image. And generally, as well touching the carnal as the spiritual generation, our Savior hath taught us this lesson, (o) That which is born of the flesh, is flesh; and that which is born of the spirit, is spirit. Whereupon the Apostle maketh this comparison betwixt those who are born of that first man, who is of the earth earthly, and of the second man, who is the Lord from heaven. (p) As is the earthly, such are they that are earthly; and as it is the heavenly, such are they also that are heavenly: and as we have born the image of the earth, we shall also bear the image of the heavenly. We shall indeed hereafter bear it in full perfection: when (q) The Lord Jesus Christ shall change our base body, that it may be fashioned like unto his glorious body; according to the working, whereby he is able even to subdue all things unto himself. Yet in the mean time also, such a conformity is required in us unto that heavenly man, that (r) our conversation must be in heaven, whence we look for this Savior: and that we must (s) put off, concerning the former conversation, that old man which is corrupt according to the deceitful lusts, and be renewed in the spirit of our mind; and put on the new man, which after God is created in righteousness and true holiness. For as in one particular point of domestic authority, (t) the Man is said to be the image and glory of God, and the Women the glory of the Man, so in a more universal manner is Christ said to be (u) the image of God, even (x) the brightness of his glory, and the express image of his person; and we (y) to be conformed to his image, that he might be the first born among those many brethren, who in that respect are accounted (z) the glory of Christ.

n Gen. 5. 3. o John 3. 6. p 1 Cor. 15. 48, 49. q Phil. 3. 21. r Ibid. ver. 20. s Eph. 4. 22, 23, 24. t 1 Cor. 11. 7. u 2 Cor. 4. 4. x Heb. 1. 3. y Rom. 8. 29. z 2 Cor. 8. 23. a Num. 11. 17. 25.

We read in the holy story, that God (a) took of the spirit which was upon Moses, and gave it unto the seventy Elders; that they might bear the burden of the people with him, and that he might not bear it, as before he had done, himself alone. It may be, his burden being thus lightened, the abilities that were left him for government were not altogether so great, as the necessity of his former employment required them to have been: and in that regard, what was given to his assistants, might perhaps be said to be taken from him. But we are sure the case was otherwise in him of whom now we speak: unto whom (b) God did not thus give the Spirit by me sure. And therefore although so many millions of believers do continually receive this (c) supply of the spirit of Jesus Christ; yet neither is that fountain any way exhausted, nor the plenitude of that well-spring of grace any whit impaired or diminished: it being God's pleasure (d) That in him should all fullness dwell; and that (e) of his fullness all we should receive, grace for grace. That as in the natural generation there is such a correspondence in all parts betwixt the begetter and the Infant begotten, that there is no member to be seen in the Father, but there is the like answerable to be found in the child, although in a far less proportion: so it falleth out in the spiritual, that for every grace which in a most eminent manner is found in Christ, a like grace will appear in God's child, although in a far inferior degree; similitudes and likenesses being defined by the Logicians to be comparisons made in quality, and not in quantity.

b John 3. 34. c Phil 1. 19. d Col. 1. 19. e John 1. 16.

We are yet further to take it into our consideration, that by thus enlivening and fashioning us according to his own image, Christ's purpose was not to raise a seed unto himself dispersedly and distractedly, but to (f) gather together in one, the Children of God that were scattered abroad; yea and to (g) bring all unto one head by himself, both them which are in Heaven and them which are on the Earth; that as in the Tabernacle, (h) the veil divided between the Holy place and the most Holy; but the curtains which covered them both were so coupled together with the hooks, that it might still (i) be one Tabernacle: so the Church militant and Triumphant, typified thereby, though distant as far the one from the other as Heaven is from Earth, yet is made but one Tabernacle in Jesus Christ; (k) in whom all the building fitly framed together groweth unto an holy Temple in the Lord, and in whom all of us are built together for an habitation of God through the Spirit.

f *John* 11. 52. g *Eph.* 1. 10. h *Exod.* 26. 33. i *Ib.* V. 5. & 11. k *Eph.* 2. 21, 22.

The bond of this mystical union betwixt Christ and us (as (l) elsewhere hath more fully been declared) is on his part that (m) quickening Spirit, which being in him as the Head, is from thence diffused to the spiritual animation of all his members: and on our part (n) Faith, which is the prime act of life wrought in those who are capable of understanding by that same Spirit. Both whereof must be acknowledged to be of so high a nature, that none could possible by such ligatures knit up so admirable a body, but he that was God Almighty. And therefore although we did suppose such a man might be found who should perform the Law for us, suffer the death that was due to our offence and overcome it; yea and whose obedience and sufferings should be of such value, that it were sufficient for the redemption of the whole world: yet could it not be efficient to make us live by faith, unless that Man had been able to send God's Spirit to apply the same unto us.

l *Sermon to the Commons house of Parliament, anno* 1520. m *John* 6. 63. 1 *Cor.* 6. 17. & 15. 45. *Phil.* 2. 1 *Rom.* 8. 9. 1 *John* 3. 24. & 4. 13. n *Gal.* 2. 20. & 5. 5. & 3. 11. *Eph.* 3. 17.

Which as no bare Man or any other Creature whatsoever can do; so for Faith we are taught by S. (o) Paul, that it is the operation of God, and a work of his power, even of that same power wherewith Christ himself was raised from the dead. Which is the ground of that prayer of his, that the eyes (p) of our understanding being enlightened, we might know what is the exceeding greatness of his mighty power to us ward who believe; according to the working of his mighty power, which he wrought in Christ when he raised him from the dead, and set him at his own right hand in the heavenly places for above all Principality, and Power, and Might, and every Name that is named not only in this world, but also in that to come: and hath put all things under his sect, and gave him to be head over all things to the Church, which is his body, the fullness of him that filleth all in all.

o *Col.* 2. 12. 2 *Thess.* 1. 11. p *Ephes.* 1. 19. 20, &c.

Yet was it fit also, that this Head should be of the same nature with the Body which is knit unto it: and therefore that he should so be God, as that he might partake of our flesh likewise. (q) For we are members of his body, saith the same Apostle, of his flesh, and of his bones. And, (r) except ye eat the flesh of the Son of man, saith our Savior himself, and drink his blood; ye have no life in you. (s) He that eateth my flesh, and drinketh my blood, dwelleth in me, and I in him. Declared thereby, first, that by this mystical and supernatural union, we are as truly conjoined with him, as the meat and drink we take it with us; when by the ordinary work of Nature, it is converted into our own substance. Secondly, that this conjunction is immediately made with his human nature. Thirdly, that the (t) Lamb slain, that is, (u) Christ crucified, hath by that death of his, made his flesh broken, and his blood poured out for us upon the Cross, to be fit food for the spiritual nourishment of our souls; and the very well-spring from whence, by the power of his Godhead, all life and grace is derived unto us.

q *Ephes.* 5. 30. r *Joh.* 6. 53. s *Ibid ver.* 56. t *Rev.* 5. 12. & 13. 8. u 1 *Cor.* 1. 23. &. 2. 2.

Upon this ground it is, that the Apostle telleth us, that we (x) have boldness to enter into the Holiest by the blood of Jesus; by a new and living way which he hath consecrated for us, through the veil, that is to say, his flesh. That as in the Tabernacle, there was no passing from the Holy to the most Holy place, but by the veil: so now there is no passage to be looked for from the Church Militant to the Church Triumphant, but by the flesh of him, who hath said of himself; (y) I am the way, the truth and the life, no man cometh unto the Father but by me. Jacob in his dream beheld (z) a ladder set upon the Earth, the top whereof reached to Heaven, and the Angels of God ascending and descending on it, the Lord himself standing above it. Of which vision none can give a better interpretation then he, who was prefigured therein, gave unto Nathaniel. (a) Hereafter you shall see heaven opened, and the Angels of God ascending and descending upon the Son of man. Whence we may well collect, that the only means whereby God standing above and his Israel lying here below are conjoined together, and the only ladder whereby Heaven may be sealed by us, is the Son of man; the type of whose flesh, the veil, was therefore commanded to be (b) made with Cherubim; to show that we come (c) to an innumerable company of Angels when we come to Jesus, the Mediator of the New Testament: who as the head of the Church hath power to (d) send forth all those ministering spirits, to minister for them who shall be Hers of salvation.

x Heb. 10. 19. 20. y Joh. 14. 6. z Gen. 28. 12. 13. a Joh. 1. 5. 1. b Exod. 26. 31. & 36. 35. c Heb. 12. 22, 24, d Heb. 1. 14.

Lastly, we are to take into our consideration, that as in things concerning God, the main execution of our Saviors Priest-hood does consist; so in things concerning man, he exerciseth both his Prophetical Office; whereby he openeth the will of his Father unto us, and his Kingly, whereby he ruleth and protecteth us. It was indeed a part of (e) the Priests Office in the old Testament to instruct the people in the law of God, and yet were (f) they distinguished from Prophets: like as in the new Testament also, (g) Prophets as well as Apostles, are made a different degree from ordinary Pastors and Teachers, who received not their doctrine by immediate inspiration from Heaven; as those other (h) Holy men of God did, who speak as they were moved by the Holy Ghost. Whence Paul putteth the Hebrews in mind, that God who (i) in sundry parts and in sundry manner's spake in time past unto the Fathers by the prophets, hath in these last days spoken unto us by his Son Christ Jesus: whom therefore he stileth (k) the Apostle, as well as the high Priest of our profession; who was faithful to him that appointed him, even as Moses was in all his house.

e Deut. 33. 10. Hagg. 2. 11. Mal. 2. 7. f Isa. 28. 7. Jer. 6. 13. & 8. 10. & 14. 18. & 23. 11, 13, 34. Lam. 2. 10. g Eph. 4. 11. h 2 Pet. 1. 21. ὁ πολυμερῶς καὶ πολυτρόπως. Heb. 1. 1. k Heb. 3. 12. l Num. 12. 6, 7, 8.

Now Moses, we know, had a singular preeminence above all the rest of the Prophets: according to that ample testimony which God himself giveth of him. (l) If there be a Prophet among you, I the Lord will make my self known unto him in a vision, and I will speak unto him in a dream. My servant Moses is not so, who is faithful in all mine house: with him will I speak mouth to mouth, even apparently, and not in dark speeches; and the similitude of the Lord shall he behold. And therefore we find, that our Mediator, in the execution of his Prophetical office is in a more peculiar manner likened unto Moses: which he himself also did thus foretell. (m) The Lord thy God will raise up unto thee a Prophet from the midst of thee, of thy Brethren, like unto me; and unto him ye shall hearken. According to all that thou desired of the Lord thy God in Horeb, in the day of the assembly, saying, Let me not hear again the voice of the Lord my God; neither let me see this great fire any more, that I die not. And the Lord said unto me, They have well spoken, that which they have spoken. I will raise them up a Prophet from among their brethren, like unto thee, and will put my words in his mouth, and he shall peak unto them all that I shall command him. And it shall come to pass, that whosoever will not hearken unto my words, which he shall speak in my Name, I will require it of him.

m Deut. 18. 25. 16. &c. Acts 3. 22, 23.

Our Prophet therefore must be a Man raised from among his Brethren the Israelites, (n) (of whom, as concerning the flesh, he came) who was to perform unto us, that which the Father requested of Moses: (o) Speak thou to us and we will hear; but let not God speak with us, lest we die. And yet (that in this also we may see, how our Mediator had the preeminence) (p) when Aaron, and all the children of Israel were to receive from the mouth of Moses all that the Lord had spoken with him in Mount Sinai, they were afraid to come nigh him, by reason of the glory of his shining countenance: so that he was fain to put a veil over his face, while he spake unto them that which he was commanded. But that which for a time was thus (q) made glorious, had no glory in respect of the glory that excelleth; and both the glory thereof, and the veil which covered it, are now abolished in Christ: the veil of whose flesh does so over shadow (r) the brightness of his glory, that yet under it we may (s) behold his glory, as the glory of the only begotten of the Father; yea, and (t) we all with open face, beholding as in a glass the glory of the Lord, are changed into the same Image, from glory, to glory, even as by the Spirit of the Lord.

n Rom. 95. o Exod. 20. 19. Deut. 5. 15, 27. p Exod. 34. 30, 32, 33. q 2 Cor. 3. 7, 10, 11, 13. r Heb. 1. 3. s Heb. 1. 14. t 1.Cor. 3. 18.

And this is daily effected by the power of the Ministry of the Gospel, instituted by the authority, and second by the power of this our great Prophet: whose transcendent excellency beyond Moses (unto whom, in the execution of that function he was otherwise likened) is thus set forth by the Apostle. (u) He is counted worthy of more glory then Moses, in as much as he who hath built the house hath more honor then the house. For every house is built by some one: but he that hath built all things is God. And Moses verily was faithful in all his house, as a servant, for a testimony of those things which were to be spoken after: But Christ, as the Son, over his own house (x) This house of God is no other then the Church of the living God: whereof as he is the only Lord, so is he properly the only Builder. Christ therefore being both the Lord and the (y) Builder of his Church, must be God as well as Man: which is the cause, why we find all the several mansions of this (z) great house to carry the title indifferently of the (a) Churches of God, and the (b) Churches of Christ.

u Heb. 3. 3, 4, 5, 6. x 1 Tim. 3. 15. y Mat. 16. 18. z 2 Tim. 1. 20. a 1 Cor. 11. 16. b Rom. 6. 16.

True it is, that there are other ministerial builders, whom Christ employed in that service: this being not the least of those gifts which he bestowed upon men at his triumphant ascension into Heaven, that (c) he gave not only ordinary Pastors and Teachers, but Apostles likewise, and Prophets, and Evangelists; for the perfecting of the Saints, for the work of the ministry, for the edifying of the body of Christ. Which, what great power it requireth, he himself does fully express in passing the grant of his high Commission unto his Apostles. (d) All power is given unto me in Heaven and in Earth. Go ye therefore and teach all Nations baptizing them in the name of the Father, and of the Son and of the Holy Ghost; teaching them to observe all things, whatsoever I have commanded you: and lo, I am with you always, even unto the end of the World. Amen.

c Eph. 4. 11, 12. d Mat. 28. 18, 19, 20.

St. Paul professeth himself that he (e) labored more abundantly then all the rest of the Apostles: yet not I, saith he, but the grace of God which was with me. And therefore although (f) according to the grace of God which was given unto him, he denied not but that, as a wise Master-builder he had laid the foundation; yet he acknowledgeth that they upon whom he had wrought, were Gods building, as well as Gods husbandry. For who, saith (g) he, is Paul, and who is Apollo, but Ministers by whom you believed, even as the Lord gave to every man? I have planted, Apollo watered: but God gave the increase. So then, neither is he that planteth any thing, neither he that watereth: but God that giveth the increase.

e 1 Cor. 15. 10. f 1 Cor. 3. 9, 10. g Ibid. v. 5. 6, 7.

Two things therefore we find in our great Prophet, which do far exceed the ability of any bare Man; and so do difference him from all the (h) Holy Prophets, which have been since the world began. For first, we are taught; that (i) no man knoweth the Father, save the Son, and he to whomsoever the Son will reveal him: and that (k) no man hath seen God at any time; but the only begotten Son, which is in the bosom of the Father, he hath declared him. Being in his bosom, he is become conscious of his secrets, and so out of his own immediate knowledge, enabled to discover the whole will of his Father unto us; whereas all other Prophets and Apostles receive their revelations at the second hand, and according to the grace given unto them by the Spirit of Christ. Witness that place of S. Peter, for the Prophets: (l) Of which salvation the Prophets have inquired, and searched diligently, who prophesied of the grace that should come unto you; searching what or what manner of time. THE SPIRIT OF CHRIST WHICH WAS IN THEM did signify, when it testified before hand the sufferings of Christ, and the glory that should follow. And for the Apostles, those heavenly words which our Savior himself uttered unto them, whilst he was among them: (m) When the Spirit of Truth is come he will guide you into all truth: for he shall not speak of himself, but whatsoever he shall hear, that shall be speak; and he will show you things to come. He shall glorify me: for he shall receive of mine, and show it unto you. All things that the Father hath are mine: therefore said I, that he shall take of mine, and shall show it unto you.

h Luk. 1. 70. i Mat. 11. 27. k Joh. 1. 18. l 1 Pet. 1. 10, 11. m Joh. 6. 1. 13. 14, 15.

Secondly, all other Prophets and Apostles can do more (as hath been said) but plant and water; only God can give the increase: they may teach indeed and baptize; but unless Christ were with them by the powerful presence of his Spirit, they would not be able to save one soul by that Ministry of theirs. We (n) as lively stones, are built upon a spiritual house: but, (o) except the Lord do build this house, they labor in vain that build it. For who is able to breath the spirit of life into those dead stones, but he, of whom it is written; (p) The hour is coming, and now is when the dead shall hear the voice of the Son of God; and they that hear it shall live: and again: (q) Awake thou that sleepest, and arise from the dead; and Christ shall give the light. Who can awake us out of this dead sleep, and give light unto these blind eyes of ours; but the Lord our God, unto whom we pray, that he would (r) lighten our eyes, lest we sleep the sleep of death.

n 1 Pet. 2. 5. o Psal. 127. 1. p Joh. 5. 25. q Eph. 5. 14. r Psal. 13. 3.

And as a blind man is not able to conceive the distinction of colors, although the most skilled man alive should use all the art he had to teach him; because he wanteth the sense whereby that object is discernable: so (s) the natural man perceiveth not the things of the Spirit of God, (for they are foolishness unto him;) neither can he know them, because they are spiritually discerned. Whereupon the Apostle concludeth, concerning himself and all his fellow-laborers, that (t) God who commanded the light to shine out of darkness, hath shined in our hearts; to give the light of the knowledge of the glory of God, in the face of Jesus Christ: but we have this treasure in earthen vessels; that the excellency of the power may be of God, and not of us. Our Mediator therefore (who must (u) be able to save them to the uttermost that come unto God by him) may not want the excellency of the power, whereby he may make us capable of this high knowledge of the things of God, propounded unto us by the ministry of his servants: and consequently, in this respect also, must be God as well as Man.

s 1 Cor. 2. 14. t 2 Cor. 4. 6, 7. u Heb. 7. 25.

There remaineth the Kingdom of our Redeemer: described thus by the Prophet Isaiah, (x) Of the increase of his government and peace there shall be no end, upon the throne of David, and upon his Kingdom; to order it, and to establish it with judgment and with justice, from henceforth even for ever: and by Daniel: (y) Behold, one like the Son of man came with the clouds of Heaven, and came to the Ancient of days; and they brought him near before him. And there was given him Dominion, and Glory, and a Kingdom, that all People, Nations and Languages should serve him, his dominion is an everlasting dominion, which shall not pass away; and his Kingdom that which shall not be destroyed: and by the Angel Gabriel in his Embassage to the blessed Virgin, (z) Behold thou shalt conceive in thy womb, and bring forth a Son, and thou shalt call his name Jesus. He shall be great, and shall be called the Son of the Highest; and the Lord God shall give him the Throne of his Father David. And he shall reign over the house of Jacob for ever; and of his kingdom there shall be no end.

x Isa. 9. 7. y Dan. 7. 13, 14. z Luk. 1. 31, 32, 33.

This is that new (a) David our King, whom God hath raised up unto his (b) own Israel: who was in Truth, that which he was called; the Son of Man, and the Son of the Highest. That in the one respect, (c) we may say unto him, as the Israelites of old did unto their David; (d) Behold, we are thy bone, and thy flesh, and in the other, sing of him as David himself did; (e) The Lord said unto my Lord, Sit thou at my right hand, until I make thine enemies thy footstool. So that the promise made unto our first Parents, that (f) the seed of the woman should bruise the Serpents head, may well stand with that other saying of Saint Paul; that (g) the God of peace shall bruise Satan under our feet. Seeing (h) for this very purpose the Son of God was manifested (i) in the flesh, that he might destroy the works of the Devil. And still that foundation of God will remain unshaken: I (k) even I am the Lord, and beside me there is no Savior. (l) Thou shalt know no God but me; for there is no Savior beside me.

a Jer. 30. 9. Ho. 8. 5. Ezek. 34. 23. & 37. 24. b Gal. 6. 16. c Eph. 5. 30. d 2 Sam. 5. 1. e Psal. 110. 1. Mat. 22. 43, 44. Acts 2. 34, 35. f Gen. 3. 15. g Rom. 16. 20. h 1 Joh. 3. 8. i 1 Tim. 3. 16. k Isa. 43. 11. l Hos. 13. 4.

Two special branches there be of this Kingdom of our Lord and Savior, the one of Grace, whereby that part of the Church is governed which is Militant upon Earth; the other of Glory, belonging to that part which is Triumphant in Heaven. Here upon Earth, as by his Prophetical Office he worketh upon our Mind and Understanding, so by his Kingly, he ruleth our Will and Affections; (m) casting down imaginations and every high thing that exalteth it self against the knowledge of God, and bringing into captivity every thought to the obedience of Christ. Where as, we must needs acknowledge, that (n) it is GOD which worketh in us both to will and to do, and that it is (o) he which sanctifieth us wholly: so are we taught likewise to believe (p) both he who sanctifieth, and they who are sanctified, are all of one, namely of one and the self same nature; that the sanctifier might not be ashamed to call those, who are sanctified by him, his brethren, that as their nature was corrupted, and their blood tainted in the first Adam, so it might be restored again in the second Adam: and that as from the one a corrupt, so from the other a pure and undefiled nature might be transmitted unto the heirs of salvation.

m 2 Cor. 10. 5. n Phil. 2. 13. o 1 Thes. 5. 32. p Heb. 2. 11.

The same (q) God that giveth grace, is he also that giveth glory. yet so, that the streams of both of them must run to us through the golden pipe of our Saviors humanity. (r) For since by man came death; it was fit that by man also should come the resurrection of the dead. Even by that man who hath said: (s) Who so eateth my flesh, and drinketh my blood, hath eternal life; and I will raise him up at the last day. Who then (t) shall come to be glorified in his Saints, and to be made marvelous in all them that believe: and (u) shall change this base body of ours, that it may be fashioned like unto his own glorious body; according to the working, whereby he is able even to subdue all things unto himself. Unto him therefore that hath thus (x) loved us, and washed us from our sins in his own blood, and hath made us Kings and Priests unto God and his Father; to him be glory and dominion for ever, and ever, AMEN.

q Psal. 84. 11. r 1 Cor. 15. 21. s Joh. 6. 54. t 2 Thes. 1. 10. u Phil. 3. 21. x Rev. 1. 5, 6.

PHILIP. 3. 8. I count all things but loss for the Excellency of the Knowledge of Christ Jesus my Lord.

FINIS.

ARCHBISHOP USSHER'S ADVICES TO YOUNG MINISTERS AT THEIR ORDINATION.

That you may see how great a Master he was in the Art of gaining Souls (says Dr. *Parr*, page 87. in the Life of this great Man) it will not be amiss to insert here some of those Directions he used to give those who were newly entered into holy Orders, since they may not be unprofitable to such as mean seriously to undertake this Sacred Calling.

I. READ and Study the Scriptures carefully, wherein is the best Learning, and only infallible Truth; they can furnish you with the best materials for your *Sermons;* the only Rules of Faith and Practice; the most powerful motives to persuade and convince the *Conscience;* and the strongest arguments to confute all *Errors, Heresies,* and *Schisms:* Therefore be sure, let all your *Sermons* be congruous to them; and to this End, it is expedient that you understand them as well in the *Originals,* as in the *Translations.*

II. Take not hastily up other men's *Opinions* without due Trial, nor vent your own Conceits, but compare them first with the Analogy of Faith, and Rules of Holiness, recorded in the *Scriptures,* which are the proper Tests of all *Opinions* and Doctrines.

III. Meddle with *Controversies* and doubtful Points as little as may be in *your popular preaching,* lest you puzzle your hearers, or engage them in wrangling *Disputations,* and so hinder their Conversion, which is the main design of Preaching.

IV. Insist most on those Points that tend to effect sound Belief, sincere Love to God, Repentance for Sin, and that may persuade to *Holiness* of *Life:* Press these things home to the Conscience of your Hearers, as of absolute necessity, leaving no gap for evasions, but bind them as close as may be to their duty; and as you ought to preach *Sound* and *Orthodox Doctrine,* so ought you to deliver God's Message as near as may be in God's Words; that is, in such as are plain and intelligible, that the meanest of your *Auditors* may understand: To which end it is necessary to back all practical *Precepts* and *Doctrines,* with apt Proofs from the holy *Scriptures;* avoiding all *Exotic Phrases, Scholastic Terms,* unnecessary Quotations of *Authors,* and forced Rhetorical *Figures,* since it is not difficult to make easy things appear hard, but to render hard things easy is the hardest part of a good *Orator,* as well as *Preacher.*

V. Get your Hearts sincerely affected with the things you persuade others to embrace, that so you may preach *Experimentally,* and your Hearers perceive that you are in good earnest, and press nothing upon them but what may tend to their advantage, and which your self would venture your own *Salvation* on.

VI. Study and consider well the Subjects you intend to *Preach* on, before you come into the *Pulpit,* and then words will readily offer themselves; yet think what you are about to say, before you speak, avoiding all uncouth, fantastical words, or phrases, or nauseous, indecent, or ridiculous expressions, which will quickly bring *Preaching* into contempt, and make your *Sermons* and *Persons,* the subjects of *Sport* and *Merriment.*

VII. Dissemble not the Truths of God in any case, nor comply with the Lusts of Men, or give any countenance to Sin by word or deed.

VIII. But above all, you must never forget to order your own *Conversation* as becomes the *Gospel,* that so you may teach by *Example* as well as *Precept,* and that you may appear a good *Divine* every where, as well as in the *Pulpit;* for a Minister's *Life* and *Conversation* is more heeded than his *Doctrine.*

A Body of Divinity

IX. Yet after all this, take heed you be not puffed up with *Spiritual Pride* of your own *Virtues;* nor with a vain conceit of your *Parts* or *Abilities;* nor yet be transported with the *Applause* of men, nor dejected, or discouraged with the *Scoffs* or *Frowns* of the wicked and profane.

To which I shall add one Advice more, which I received from a Person of great Worth, and Dignity in the *Church,* who had it from the Mouth of this great Master of Persuasion; it was concerning *Reproof,* where Men were to be dealt with that lay under great *Prejudices* and *Vices,* either by Education, Interest, Passion, or ill Habits, (Cases of much frequency) and therefore to render Admonitions of greater force upon them, his direction was, To avoid giving the Persons intended to be wrought upon, any *Alarm* beforehand, that their *Faults* or *Errors* were designed to be attacked; for then the Persons concerned look upon the *Preacher* as an *Enemy,* and set themselves upon their guard: On such occasions he rather recommended the choosing of a *Text* that stood only upon the borders of the difficult Subject; and if it might be, seemed more to favor it; that so the obnoxious hearers may be rather surprised and undermined, than stormed and fought with: And so the *Preacher,* as St. *Paul* expresses it, being crafty, may take them with guile.

He would also exhort those who were already engaged in this *Holy Function,* and advised them how they might well discharge their duty in the *Church* of God, answerable to their *Calling,* to this Effect: You are engaged in an excellent *Employment* in the *Church,* and entrusted with weighty Matters, as *Stewards* of our great Master, *Christ,* the great *Bishop:* Under him, and by his Commission, you are to endeavor to reconcile Men to God; to convert Sinners, and to build them up in the holy Faith of the *Gospel,* that they may he saved, and that *Repentance and Remission of Sins be preached in his Name.* This is of highest importance, and requires faithfulness, diligence, prudence and watchfulness. The Souls of Men are committed to our care and guidance; and the Eyes of *God, Angels* and *Men* are upon us, and great is the account we must make to our *Lord Jesus Christ,* who is the Supreme *Head* of his *Church,* and will at length reward or punish his Servants in this Ministry of his *Gospel,* as he shall find them faithful or negligent; therefore it behooves us to exercise our best Talents, laboring in the Lord's *Vineyard* with all diligence, that we may bring forth fruit, and that the fruit may remain. This is the Work we are separated for, and ordained unto; we must not think to be idle or careless in this *Office,* but must bend our Minds and Studies, and employ all our Gifts and Abilities in this Service: We must *Preach* the Word of Faith, that Men may believe aright; and the *Doctrine* and *Laws* of *Godliness,* that Men may act as becomes *Christians* indeed: For without *Faith,* no Man can please God; and without *Holiness,* no Man can enter into the Kingdom of Heaven.

I think good (under this Head of Ordination) to insert here a remarkable Story, which I had from an ancient Reverend Divine of the City of *London,* who had it from the Bishop's own Mouth. A Smith with his Leather Apron came to him, Entreating his Grace to Ordain him; the good Bishop looked on him with a smiling, not disdainful, Countenance, and asked him what he was; a Blacksmith, (said he) hast thou any Learning? (said the Bishop) no other but my Mother Tongue, (said the Smith) canst thou answer Gainsayers? (continued the) Bishop) dost thou not know this Kingdom of *Ireland* is filled with Priests and Jesuits? The Smith replied, that if his Grace would examine him he would answer him according to his ability; whereupon the Bishop tried him as to several Points in Divinity, in which the Smith gave him satisfaction to his admiration; the Bishop asked him what Parish he lived in? He told him the place (which I have forgot) and that the Minister of the place was very Sickly, and seldom preached; well (said the Bishop) I see thou has good Natural Parts, I will Write to the Minister to let thee have his Notes, and thou shall Preach them, for I see thou hast a good

Memory; accordingly the Bishop wrote to the Minister to let the Smith have some of his Notes to preach, which as soon as the Smith received, he got a Gown and mounted the Pulpit; the Bishop sent one of his Chaplains to hear him; the Chaplain acquainted his Grace that he delivered all by Memory, with great Affection and *Pathos;* the Bishop thought with himself that this Man may do some good, so sent for him, and not only Ordained him, but gave him a Living of 80 *l. per Annum;* in that Parish there were about 50 Families, whereof 30 of them were Papists, and about 20 Protestants; the Smith by his good Preaching and Living, in a Year or two made strange alterations, so that in so short a time above 30 of the Families were Protestants, and but 20 Popish.

Thus it pleases God many times to effect great Things by unlikely Instruments, therefore we ought not to despise the Day of small Things. We see how this good Bishop respected and preferred this Person, (though a Poor Handicrafts-man) for his good Natural Parts; and what a Spirit of Discerning he had, that he would prove useful in the Church of God.

His Love to the Souls of Men was so great, that he contrived, both by Preaching and otherwise, to do good to the several Sorts of Christians, and particularly did desire Mr. *Baxter* (as Mr. *Baxter* tells us in his Preface to his *Call to the Unconverted*) to write a *Directory* for the several Ranks of Professed Christians, which might distinctly give each one their Portion, beginning with the Unconverted, and then proceeding to the Babes in Christ, and then to the Strong, and mixing some Special Helps against the several Sins that they are addicted to.

Mr. *Baxter* excused himself upon account of his own Weakness; but after the Bishop's Death, he tells us his Words came often into his Mind, and the great Reverence he bore to him, did incline him to think with some Complacency of his Motion; and so we know Mr. *Baxter* has published Books proper for the aforesaid Ranks of Christians.

J. R.

TABLE.

1st HEAD   p. 1
All Men desire Eternal Happiness.
Religion the Means to obtain
Happiness.
No Salvation but by the true Religion.
Divers kinds of false Religions.
What Christian Religion is.
Of Catechizing, what it is.
Where to be used, and by whom.
The necessity of it.
Means to know God.
By his Divine Works, and Holy Word.
Of the Divine works of God.
Plato, Galen, Homer, Virgil Ovid, &c.
The uses of knowing God by his
Works.
Of God's Holy Word, the Scriptures.
How the Scriptures were delivered.
Revelations.
Oracles.
Visions.
What Scripture is.
That the Scriptures are the Word of
God.
Reasons to prove God to be the
Author of the Holy Scriptures.
1. Efficient, Instrumental.
2. Matter.
3. The form and manner of Writing.
4. End.
5. Effects.
6. Adjuncts.
7. The consonant testimony of Men of
all times.
8. Divine Testimonies.
The Testimony of the Spirit in the
Hearts of Men.
That the Authority of the Scriptures
does not depend on the Church.
What are the Books of Holy
Scriptures.
In what Language the Old Testament
was written.
That the Scriptures of the Old
Testament were first written with
Vowels and Pricks.
The Books of Moses.
The Books of the Prophets.
The Historical Books.
The Doctrinal Books.
The Poetical Books.

The Prosaical Books.
The Apocryphal Books.
The Errors of the Apocryphal Books.
Of the Books of the New Testament.
The Properties of the Holy Scriptures,
As,
1. Holy.
2. The highests in Authority.
3. Sufficient in themselves.
That the Scriptures are a perfect Rule,
for Doctrine, Life, and Salvation.
Objections against the sufficiency of
the Holy Scriptures, answered.
Of the perspicuity of the Holy
Scriptures.
The Papists Objections against the
perspicuity of the Scriptures
answered.
Why God hath left some place of
Scripture obscure.
Of the Translation of Holy Scriptures.
An Objection grounded on various
readings, answered.
Why the Scriptures must be
expounded by the Scriptures.
The Uses of Holy Scriptures.
Who must read the Scriptures.
That all must read the Scriptures,
proved.
The Papists Objections against
reading the Scriptures, answered.

2nd HEAD   p. 23
That there is a God.
Of the Nature of God.
Of God's Essence.
Of the Name of God.
Of the Properties or Attributes of God.
A Description of God.
God a Spirit.
The Perfection of God.
The Felicity of God.
Of the Simpleness or Singleness in
God.
God's Infiniteness.
God's Immensity or Greatness.
God's Eternity.
The Life of God.
Of the Knowledge and Wisdom of
God.
Fore-knowledge & Counsel of God.

God's absolute Wisdom and Knowledge.
Of the Omnipotence, or Almighty Power of God.
God's Absolute Power.
God's Actual Power.
God's Power Infinite.
The Uses.
Of God's Will.
Whether God does will evil.

3rd HEAD p. 52
The Holiness of God's Will.
Of God's Goodness.
The Uses of God's Goodness.
The Graciousness of God.
Of the Love of God.
Uses of God's Love.
Of the Mercy of God.
The Uses of God's Mercy.
Of the Justice of God.
The Uses of God's Justice.
Of the Unity of the Godhead.
Of the Trinity.
What a Person in the Trinity is.
Of the Father, the first Person of the Trinity
Of the other Persons of the Trinity in general.
Of the second Person in the Trinity.
Of the third Person in the Trinity.
How to Know that We Have the Spirit.
How to keep the Spirit.
Things common to the three Persons.
In what they all agree.
1. Co-essential
2. Co-equal.
3. Co-eternal.
This proper to each of the Persons.

4th HEAD p. 77
Of the Kingdom of God.
The parts of God's Kingdom.
Of God's Decree.
Of Predestination.
Election.
Reprobation.
Execution of God's Decree.
Creation.
Providence.
Creation in general.
Uses of the Creation.
The Creation of the particular Creatures.
Of the Heavens.
Of the Earth.
Of the Invisible Creatures.
The third Heaven and Angels.
Of Angels.
Of the creation of Visible things.
Of the Chaos or rude Mass.
Of the parts of the rude Mass.
Of the Frame of the World.
Of the Elements
The four Elements.
Of the mixed or compounded Bodies.
The several Works of the six days.
The first day, Heaven, and Earth, and the Light.
The second day, the Firmament. The third day, Grass, Corn, and Trees.
Of the Water and Earth.
The fourth Day. The Creation of the Lights.
The fifth Day. The Creation of Fishes and Birds.

5th HEAD p. 89
The sixth Day. Of the Creation of Man and Woman.
Of the parts of Man: And first of the Body.
Of the Soul of Man.
Of the Immortality of the Soul.
Of the Seat of the Soul
What is the Image of God in Man.
Of the Woman's Creation.
The End of the Creation.

6th HEAD p. 95
Of God's Providence.
Definition of God's Providence.
The Uses of the Doctrine of God's Providence.

7th HEAD p. 102
Of God's special Providence concerning Angels.
Of the Good Angels.
Of the Evil Angels.
Uses of the doctrine concerning evil.

8th HEAD p. 109
Of God's particular Providence over Man.
Of God's particular Providence towards Mankind.

Of the Covenant between God and Man.
1. Covenant of Works.
The State of Man in the time of his Innocence.
Of Man in the State of Corruption; and of his Fall.
That the Breach of all the Commandments concurred in Adam and Eve's sin.
The Effects of the Fall.
Of our first Parents Nakedness.
Of their hiding themselves.

9th HEAD p. 125
Why all Adam's Posterity are Partakers of his sin and misery.
What Sin is.
Imputed sin.
Inherent sin.
Original sin.
The Propagation of Original sin.
The Understanding corrupted.
The corruption of the Memory.
The corruption of the Will.
The corruption of the Affections.
The corruption of the Conscience.
Of the corruption of the Body.
Actual Sin.
Of the divers differences of Actual Sins.
Of the Sin against the Holy Ghost.
Guilt of Sin.

10th HEAD p. 137
Punishment of Sin.

11th HEAD p. 139
Of God's Covenant with Man.
Of the Covenant of Grace.
The Differences between the Covenant of Works, and the Covenant of Grace.
Wherein they agree.

12th HEAD p. 142
Of Jesus the Mediator of this Covenant.
The Natures of Christ. Divine. Human.
Of the Divine Nature of Christ.
Why it was requisite that Christ should be God.
Of the human Nature of Christ.
Why it was requisite that Christ should be Man.
Of the Union of the two Natures of Christ.
Of Christ's Office of Mediatorship.
That there is but one Mediator.
Of his Names Jesus Christ.

13th HEAD p. 150
Of Christ's Priesthood.
The Popish Priesthood overthrown.
Of Christ's Satisfaction.
Of Christ's Sufferings.
Christ's sufferings in his Soul.
Christ's sufferings in his Body.
Uses of Christ's Passion.
Christ's Burial.
His descending into Hell.
Christ's Righteousness in fulfilling the Law.
Christ's Original Righteousness.
Christ's Actual Holiness.
Of the Intercession of Christ.

14th HEAD p. 157
The Prophetical Office of Christ.
Of the Kingly Office of Christ.
Christ's Humiliation.
Christ's Exaltation.
Of the Resurrection of Christ.
Of Christ's Ascension.
Of Christ's sitting at the right hand of God.

15th HEAD p. 166
The state of mankind under the Gospel.
Of the Church of Christ
The Catholic Church.
The Property and Office of the Head of the Church.
The Triumphant Church
The Church Militant.

16th HEAD p. 169
Prerogatives of the Members of the Catholic Church.
Of our Union and Communion with Christ
Communion of Saints.

17th HEAD p. 172
The Benefits of our Communion with Christ.

Of Justification.
Uses arising from the Doctrine of Justification.
Of Faith.
The various exceptions of Faith.
The divers kinds of Faith.
Historical Faith.
Temporary Faith.
Miraculous Faith.
Justifying Faith.
The Popish Implicit Faith confuted.
That the whole Soul is the Seat of Faith.

18th HEAD   p. 179
What Reconciliation is.
What Adoption is.
The benefit of Adoption.

19th HEAD   p. 180
Sanctification.
The Differences between Justification and Sanctification.
The difference between the Law and the Gospel.
The Moral Law the Rule of Sanctification.
Ceremonial Law.
Judicial Law.
The Moral Law.
The end and use of the Law.
Rules to be observed for the interpretation of the Law.
1. Branch of the third Rule.
2. Branch.
3. Branch.
Why the Commandments are propounded in the second Person.
Good Company required.

20th HEAD   p. 185
Why the Commandments are pro pounded Negatively.
The division of the Decalogue.
The Sum of the first Table.
The sum of the second Table.
The division of the first Table.
The Preface of the Commandment.

21st HEAD   p. 191
The first Commandment.
The scope and meaning of this Commandment.
What is forbidden and required in this first Commandment.
The several Branches of the first Commandment.
What it is to have a God.
Of the Knowledge of God.
Opposites to the Knowledge of God.
Ignorance of God.
Affiance in God.
Patience.
Hope.
Love of God.
Thankfulness.
Fear of God.
Reverence.
Humility.
Pride.
Sorrow.
Unity in Religion.
What it is to have other Gods.
Sinful Confidence.
Inordinate Love.
Sinful Fear.
Sinful Joy and Sorrow.
The third branch of the first Commandment; true Religion.
Helps enabling us to obey this Commandment.
Means of the Knowledge of God.
Hindrances.
Means of Ignorance.

22nd HEAD   p. 199
What is enjoined in the 3 following Commandments.
The second Commandment.
What is here forbidden.
What is meant by making Images.
The special branches of the second Commandment.
Prayer.
Fasts.
Vows.
The manner of God's Worship.
Of Preparation.
Of disposition in the Action.
What is required after the Action.
Ecclesiastical Ceremonies.
Bodily Gestures.
Of the abuse of God's Ordinances.
Defects respecting the inward Worship
Defects in outward Worship

Helps in performing God's pure Worship.
The 2d main Branch of the second Commandment.
What forbidden concerning Images.
That it is unlawful to make the Image of God.
That it is unlawful to make the Image of Christ.
What is meant by worshipping Images.
Of countenancing Idolatry.
Reasons to back this Commandment, taken from God's Titles.
Jealous God.
Reasons drawn from the Works of God.
The 1. Reason.
The 2. Reason.

23rd HEAD   p. 212
The third Commandment.
The sum of the third Commandment.
What is meant by the Name of God.
What is meant by the word, in vain.
What is forbidden in the third Commandment.
What is required in the third Commandment.
The particular Duties required in the third Commandment.
The Vices repugnant.
The right use of Oaths.
What Persons may lawfully take an Oath.
The special abuses of an Oath.
How God's Name is taken in vain in regard of his Properties.
How in respect of his Works.
How in respect of his Word.
Of the helps and hindrances.
The reason annexed to the third Commandment.

24th HEAD   p. 218
The fourth Commandment.
The meaning of the fourth Commandment.
What need is there of one day in seven to serve God.
That the Sabbath-day is not Ceremonial.
Of the change of the seventh day to the first and the Reasons of it.
The time of the Sabbath, and when it beginneth.
What is meant by the word, Remember.
Of the Preparation of the Sabbath.
The Parts of the fourth Commandment.
What Works ought to be declined.
What Rest required in the fourth Commandment.
The special breaches opposite to an Holy Rest.
To whom this Commandment is chiefly directed.
The second part of this Commandment, which is the sanctifying of the Rest.
The Exercises and Duties required on the Sabbath.
Prayer with the Congregation.
Hearing the word.
Receiving the Sacrament.
Private Duties of the Sabbath.
Of the Evening preparation.
The first Duties of the Morning.
Of the public Duties of the Sabbath.
What is to be done after the public Ministry.
Sins to be condemned in respect of the second part of this Commandment.
Helps and hindrances to the keeping of this Commandment.
Of the reasons enforcing obedience to this Commandment.
1. Reason
2. Reason.
3. Reason.
4. Reason.

25th HEAD   p. 229
The second Table.
The generals to be observed in this Table.
Division of the second Table.
The fifth Commandment.
The meaning and scope of the fifth Commandment.
The Duty of Equals.
Who are Superiors.
Who are Inferiors.
What it is to Honor.
Duties of Superiors.
The divers sorts of Superiors.

The duties of Aged Persons
Duties of the younger unto them.
Duties of Inferiors to those that are in Authority.
Duties of Superiors in Authority.
Kinds of Superiors in Authority.
Superiors in the Family, and their Duties.
Inferiors in the Family, and their Duties.
Duties of Husbands and Wives.
Duties of the Husband.
Duties of the Wife.
Duties of Parents.
Duties of Children towards their Parents.
Duties of Masters towards their Servants.
Duties of Servants towards their Masters.
Public Superiors, and their Duties.
The sorts of public Superiors.
Superiors in the Church their duties.
The peoples duty to their Ministers.
Superiors in the Commonwealth.
The Magistrates duty in civil affairs.
The duties of Subjects towards their Magistrates
Of the helps and means enabling us to keep this fifth Commandments.
Hindrances to these duties here commanded.
Of the reason annexed to the fifth Commandment.
Of the promise of long life, and how performed.

26th HEAD p. 242
The sixth Commandment.
The sum and meaning of the sixth commandment.
The negative part.
The affirmative part.
The duties respecting out own persons.
Duties respecting our souls.
The contrary vices forbidden.
Duties respecting our bodies.
The contrary vices forbidden.
Duties respecting the time of our departure.
Duties respecting our neighbor while he liveth. Inward duties respecting our affections.
Evil passions opposite to these duties.
Outward duties respecting the souls of our Neighbors.
The contrary vices to the former duties.
Duties respecting the whole person of our neighbors.
Gestures.
Duties required in words.
The opposite vices.
The use.
Duties required in our deeds.
The contrary vices to the former duties.
How we do indirectly endanger our Neighbors life.
How we do directly take away our neighbors life.
Chance-medley, and how proved to be a sin.
Of Manslaughter.
Of Duels.
Duties to be performed to our neighbor after his death.
Of punishments due to the breakers of this Commandment.
Means furthering us in the obedience of this commandment.
Hindrances of our obedience to this Commandment.

27th HEAD p. 249
The seventh Commandment.
The meaning and scope of the seventh Commandment.
All impurity and uncleanness, together with all means and provocations to lust.
Of inward impurity, and the branches of it.
Abuse of apparel.
Of the abuse of meat and drink.
Wanton Gestures.
Chastity in the eyes, &c.
Wanton speeches.
Chastity in the tongue and ears.
Stage-plays.
Breach of the seventh Commandment, in respect of action.
Of Stews, & the unlawful ness of them.
Of Rape.
Incest.
Fornication.

Adultery.
Polygamy.
What is required in the entrance into Marriage.
The contrary abuses.
What is required in the holy use of Marriage.
Unlawful separation.
The punishments of the breach of this Commandment.
Helps and means of keeping this Commandment.
Hindrances of obedience.

28th HEAD p. 257
The eighth Commandment.
The end of the eighth Commandment.
The occasion of this Commandment.
Theft.
The parts of this eighth Commandment.
General duties commanded.
Opposite vices.
Special duties here required.
Arguments dissuading from the love of money and earthly things.
Self-contentedness.
Motives persuading to self contentedness.
Lawful measuring of our appetite.
What in respect of Nature.
Affected poverty.
Covetousness
Ambition
Carking care
Carelessness
Solicitous and distracting cares.
What required to just getting
Lawful calling and labor.
Extraordinary getting.
What is opposite to a lawful Calling
Unjust getting out of contracts
Theft.
Domestic theft.
Theft committed out of the family.
Sacrilege.
Theft of persons.
Rapine.
Oppression.
Accessories to theft.
Acquisition by lawful Contracts
Acquisition by liberal alienation.
Acquisition by liberal alienation.
Merchandise.
Vices and corruptions in selling.
Of buying & what is required unto it.
Of pawning, and what is required unto it.
Of Locations and Letting.
Of conduction and hiring.
Of Usury.
Of Contracts between Magistrates and people.
Of Contracts between Ministers and people.
Of Workmasters and hirelings, and their duties.
Of things deposited and committed to trust.
The duty of Executors.
Of persons committed to trust.
Of just possession of goods, and what is required unto it.
Of Restitution and what is to be considered in it.
Of the right use and fruition of goods.
Of Parsimony and frugality.
Of tenacity and miserliness.
Profusion and Prodigality.
Of Liberality.
Of lending.
Of Free giving.

29th HEAD p. 277
The ninth Commandment.
The scope or end.
The occasion of this Commandment.
The chief sin here forbidden.
The negative part.
The affirmative part.
The sum of the duties here required
Of truth.
Truth must be professed and how.
Opposites to truth.
Lying.
Reasons to dissuade from lying.
Lies.
Three sorts of Lies.
Vices opposite to freedom of speech.
Opposites to simplicity of speaking truth.
Means of preserving truth.
When as it is deserted or opposed.
Profitable speech.
Courtesy and Assability.
Seasonable silence.
Opposites to profitable speech.
1. Unprofitable.

2. Hurtful speech.
3. Rotten speech.
Fame and good name
Public Testimonies.
Rash judgment.
Perverse Judgment
The duties of the Plaintiff, and the vices opposite hereunto.
The vices of the Defendant.
The duties of Lawyers; and the opposite uses.
The duty of witnesses.
False testimony in the public Ministry of the word.
Flattery.
Evil speaking
Whispering
Obtrectation.
Conserving of our own good name.
The means of getting a good name.
A true testimony of ourselves.
The opposites to the profession of truth concerning ourselves.
Arrogance & boasting.
Confession of sin.

30th HEAD p. 291
The 10 Commandment.
The end of this Commandment.
The occasion of this Commandment.
Two sorts of concupiscence
Lawful concupiscence.
Unlawful concupiscence and the kinds thereof.
The growth of sin.
The parts of this Commandment, and first the negative.
Original concupiscence.
That original concupiscence is sin.
Actual Concupiscence.
Evil thoughts.
Evil thoughts injected by Satan.
Evil thoughts arising from natural corruption.
The special kind of concupiscence here forbidden.
What is meant by our neighbors house.
Neighbors Wife.
Our Neighbors servant.
His Ox and Ass.
The affirmative part.
The means enabling us to obey this commandment.
The impossibility of keeping this Commandment.

31st HEAD p. 299
Repentance and new obedience.
Repentance what it is
What Repentance is to be exercised.
A true Trial of unfeigned Repentance may be taken.

32nd HEAD p. 301
Of the spiritual warfare.
Of the spiritual Amour.

33rd HEAD p. 302
Of our first enemy, Satan.

34th HEAD p. 303
2. Enemy, the World.

35th HEAD p. 304
Third enemy, our Flesh.

36th HEAD p. 305
New obedience.
Of good works in general, and of the Properties of them.
That there is no merit in good works.
Wherein our good works fail.
Why God rewardeth our works.
The ends of good works.

37th HEAD p. 309
Of special good works required.
Of Prayer what it is.
What is required that prayer may be holy.
That we must pray to God alone.
That we must pray only in the mediation of Christ.
For whom we must pray.
The parts of Prayer.
Of Petition.
The means of obtaining the gift of prayer.
Motives to Prayer.
Hindrances of Prayer.
The subject of our requests.
Prayer for others.
Of thanksgiving
In what thanksgiving consisteth.
What thanksgiving is required.
The properties of praise.
The means of thanksgiving.

Signs of thankfulness.
Of the Lord's Prayer.
Of the Preface.
Our Father.
Which art in Heaven.

38th HEAD p. 322
The parts of the Lords Prayer.
6. Petitions in the Lord's Prayer.
1. Petition.
What is meant by Name.
What is meant by hallowed.
What we ask in this petition.
What graces we here pray for.
What things we here pray against.
The second Petition.
What is meant by Kingdom.
What is meant by coming.
The particulars here prayed for,
1. respecting the Kingdom of grace.
2. Respecting the kingdom of glory.
The third Petition.

39th HEAD p. 330
The three last Petitions.
The fourth Petition.
What is meant by (bread.)
What is meant by (Give)
Give Us.
This day.
Our.
Daily.
What we beg in this Petition.
The fifth Petition.
What is meant by debts.
What we ask of God in this fifth
Petition.
The reason of the Petition.
The sixth Petition.
The sum of the sixth Petition.
Of temptations and the causes why
we must pray against them.
How God tempteth us.
What is meant by Evil.
What things we pray for in the sixth
Petition.

40th HEAD p. 341
Conclusion of the Lords Prayer.
What is meant By Kingdom.
What is meant by Power.
What is meant by Glory.
What is meant by Thine.
What is meant by or for ever.

What is meant by evil.
Whether lawful to use any other form
of Prayer.
What public Prayer is.
What private Prayer is.
What ordinary prayer is.
What extraordinary prayer is.
Circumstances of prayer
1. Gesture.
2. Place of Prayer.
3. Time of Prayer.

41st HEAD p. 345
Of Fasting.
What an holy Fast is.
Of the Kinds of Fasting.
Of public Fast.
Of private Fast.
Who are to fast.
Of the parts of a Christian fast.
Of a holy feast.
Of the time of feasting.
In what an holy feast consisteth.
Of Vows.
Who are to vow.
What is to be vowed.
The duty of those that have vowed.

42nd HEAD p. 354
Of Alms.
Who are to give Alms.
How much must be given
To whom alms must be given.
What order must be observed in
giving.
With what affection alms must be
given.
The fruits of Alms-deeds.

43rd HEAD p. 356
Of Vocation.
External.
Internal.
Means of Vocation.
Of the Church.
The marks of a true visible Church
Whether the Church may err.
In what cases we may separate from
a corrupt Church.
Of the enemies of the Church.
Of the Word
What things are common to godly and
wicked hearers.
Things proper to godly hearers.

How justifying faith differeth from the faith of Worldlings.

44th HEAD   p. 364
Of the Sacraments.
The Sacraments of great use.
What a Sacrament is.
The use of Sacraments.
The Persons that are actors in Sacraments and their actions.
Of preparation to the Sacraments.
Duties in the action of receiving.
Duties after receiving.

45th HEAD   p. 370
The Old Testament and the Sacraments of it.

46th HEAD   p. 370
The new administration of the Gospel.
The Sacraments of the New Testament only.

47th HEAD   p. 372
Of Baptism and what it is.
Whether diving or dipping be essential to Baptism.
The inward part or thing signified in Baptism.
The similitude between the sign and thing signified.
The benefit of baptism to a common Christian.
To whom baptism is effectual.
How Infants may be capable of the grace of the Sacrament.
What arenefit elect Infants that live to years have by Baptism for the present.
The lawfulness of Infants Baptism.
Baptism not of absolute necessity to salvation.
Baptism to be highly accounted of.
That many have a slight esteem of this Ordinance.
What are the means to reform this slight esteem.

48th HEAD   p. 381
Of the Lords Supper and what it is.
The difference between Baptism and the Lords Supper.
Why is it called the Lord's Supper.
Of the matter of the Lord's Supper.

That the bread and wine are not changed into the body and blood of Christ.
Of the form of the Sacrament of the Lords Supper.
The Sacramental actions of the Minister.
Of the consecration of the Bread and Wine.
The Sacramental actions of the Receivers.
The ends and uses of the Lords Supper.
Who are to receive the Lords Supper.
Of preparation to the Lords Table.
What duties are to be performed after the action.

49th HEAD   p. 390
Of the Censures of the Church.
Of the degrees of Censures.
Of the kinds of Censures.
Private admonitions.
The degrees of private admonitions.
How we must reprove.
The second degree of private Admonition.
Public admonitions.
Of suspension.
Of excommunication.
Anathema Maranatha.
Of the enemies of the Church
Of the general Apostasy.
Of Antichrist: and who he is.
The differences between Christ's miracles and the Popes.
The seat of Antichrist.

50th HEAD   p.403
Of the last Judgment.
Why the righteous die.
Of particular judgment at the hour of death.

51st HEAD   p. 404
The General judgment.
The preparation to the last judgment.
The signs of the last judgment.
The second thing in the preparation.
The third thing.
The fourth thing.
The fifth thing.
The act of judgment, and how performed.

52nd HEAD   **p. 407**
The execution of the last judgment.
The estate of the Reprobates in hell
The estate of the Elect in heaven.
The use of this doctrine concerning
the last judgment.

CLASSIC TRILOGY FOR THE FAMILY
Available Together for the First Time in Over a Century

Solid Ground Christian Books is honored to be able to offer for the first time in more than a century the three volume classic series on the family written by John and Gorham Abbott. John wrote the first two volumes and titled them ***The Mother at Home*** and ***The Child at Home.*** These volumes were so greatly used in both America and Great Britain that John's younger brother Gorham was asked to help compile a larger volume that would serve as a supplement to John's volumes. The result was ***The Family at Home*** which has been the most difficult of all to find, *until now!* These three volumes will serve families for years to come as they set before the reader the first principles that must be learned to lead and guide a family to honor and glorify God. America and Great Britain are facing a severe crisis that can be traced back to the family. We are convinced that these books, under the blessing of our Lord, can be used to turn the tide back and rebuild the walls of our homes.

"Long esteemed as one of the most valued works from the 19th century on the art of mothering and the glory of the work of the mother at home."
Dennis Gundersen, *Grace & Truth Books*

"The Abbotts had a remarkable way of communicating what is most important to parents and children."
Bill Shishko, Pastor, Franklin Square, New York

"In a moving, illustrative way, Abbott's The Child at Home *powerfully cultivates within children's consciences the need to honor God and their parents by promoting the need for heartfelt obedience, religious truth, genuine piety, biblical character traits, a sense of responsibility, and a dread of deception. The dozens of stories included make this book understandable for even very young children, while simultaneously retaining the interest of teenagers. Buy this book for every one of your children and discuss its contents together as a family."*
Joel Beeke, *Reformation Heritage Books*

Call us Toll Free at **1-866-789-7423**
Send us an e-mail at **sgcb@charter.net**
Visit our web site at **solid-ground-books.com**

Burning Issues Series from Solid Ground
Brand New Titles from Living Authors on Red Hot Current Issues

In addition to bringing old classics back into print, Solid Ground is delighted to offer a new series that addresses the **Burning Issues** of our day from authors who have their fingers on the pulse of our world. It is our privilege to offer the following titles at the present time. Keep your eyes open for upcoming titles in this series.

From Toronto to Emmaus
The Empty Tomb and the Journey from Skepticism to Faith
James R. White

"James White has done it again. This timely book handles the infidel ravings of people dedicated to destroy Christianity with care and precision. It is a devastating refutation of an outrageous claim." **- Dr. Jay Adams**

"James White has done a splendid job of answering questions that would have been raised in the minds of thoughtful inquirers by the sensationalistic but dubious documentary *'The Lost Tomb of Jesus'* by James Cameron and Simcha Jacobovici. Readers who think Christians are afraid of hard facts will have to think again after reading this rapidly produced but superbly informed and rigorously reasoned rejoinder." **- Dr. Ligon Duncan**

www.ingramcontent.com/pod-product-compliance
Lightning Source LLC
Chambersburg PA
CBHW080923020526
44114CB00043B/2446